THE
INSIDERS'®
GUIDE
TO
Southwestern
UTAH

THE INSIDERS' GUIDE® TO

Southwestern UTAH

by
Lyman Hafen
and
Linda Sappington

Insiders' Publishing Inc.

Co-published and marketed by:
The Spectrum
275 E. St. George Blvd.
St. George, UT 84770
(801) 674-6200

Co-published and distributed by:
Insiders' Publishing Inc.
105 Budleigh St.
P.O. Box 2057
Manteo, NC 27954
(919) 473-6100

•

FIRST EDITION
1st printing

•

•

Printed in the United States
of America

•

Publications from The Insiders' Guide® series are available at special discounts for bulk purchases for sales promotions, premiums or fundraisings. Special editions, including personalized covers, can be created in large quantities for special needs. For more information, please write to Insiders' Publishing Inc., P.O. Box 2057, Manteo, NC 27954 or call (919) 473-6100 x 233.

ISBN 1-57380-024-4

The Spectrum

Editor and Publisher
Roger Plothow

Sales Management
Jennie Johns
Jody VandenHeuvel

Sales Executives
Joyce Edwards
Rick Evans
Julie Hirst
Michele Nielson
Kass Roe

Photography
Nick Adams
Jud Burkett

Insiders' Publishing Inc.

Publisher/Editor-in-Chief
Beth P. Storie

President/General Manager
Michael McOwen

Affiliate Sales and Training Director
Rosanne Cheeseman

Partner Services Director
Giles MacMillan

Sales and Marketing Director
Jennifer Risko

Online Services Director
David Haynes

Managing Editor
Theresa Shea Chavez

Fulfillment Director
Gina Twiford

Project Editor
Dave McCarter

Project Artist
Stephanie Wills

Preface

Eight gravel-road miles west of the Southwestern Utah town of Parowan is a place called Parowan Gap. It is a classic example of a wind gap, an unusual geological landform that in this case marks where an ancient river cut a 600-foot-deep notch through the red hills.

For the casual visitor, the geology here is captivating. But it is just the beginning. For here, as is the case most any place you stop in Southwestern Utah, there is a story attached to the landscape. And in this instance, the story is literally etched into the surrounding rocks.

That's because Parowan Gap is one of the greatest galleries of petroglyphs — ancient Native American art in the form of drawings and etchings — in the entire southwestern corner of Utah. During a period of 1,000 years, ancient travelers and residents of this region chiseled their stories into the canyon walls, leaving a fascinating bulletin board of geometric designs and images of lizards, snakes, mountain sheep, bear claws and human figures. The art on the rocks at Parowan Gap literally enlivens the landscape with its own story.

In this first *Insiders' Guide® to Southwestern Utah* we share with you both the landscape and the stories we have come to know and love through decades of living here.

It is the landscape of Southwestern Utah that sets this region apart from any other. Within our geographic circle, we have perhaps the greatest concentration and variety of scenic landforms found anywhere. This notion is validated by the fact that Congress has seen fit to establish seven national parks and monuments in southern Utah — the first in 1909; the most recent in 1996 — and the Utah legislature has classified more than a dozen locations as state parks.

We do not have a Disneyland, an Epcot Center or a National Museum of Art in the Southwestern Utah area. But we do have Zion National Park, the North Rim of the Grand Canyon, Bryce Canyon and Cedar Breaks. What we offer is real and tangible, not re-created or high-tech. We invite you to come and view it, hike it, drive it, camp it, climb it, bike it, float it, ride it and photograph it.

Yet, like the living pictures at Parowan Gap, seeing, touching, climbing and photographing are just the beginning. There's something else we want you to do. It has to do with this guide's deeper, more meaningful objective.

We want you to get to know this place.

For this reason, we have shared more than just facts, figures, photos and phone numbers. Just as the ancients left their stories quite literally etched into the landscape at Parowan Gap, we have recorded some of the stories that go with our area in a place less conspicuous than a cliff wall but much more readable. These are stories we hope will make the landscape of Southwestern Utah more than just beautiful to your eyes — we hope it will make it live in your heart. Our goal is not only to help you gain an understanding of what there is to do and see in Southwestern Utah, but also to help you develop what Pulitzer Prize-winning author Wallace Stegner called a "sense of place" for this corner of the state.

As Stegner wrote, "A place is not a place until people have been born in it, have grown up in it, lived in it, known it, died in it — have both experienced and shaped it, as individuals, families, neighborhoods, and communities, over more than one generation." For us, Southwestern Utah is much more than gorgeous canyons, majestic forests and shimmering deserts — it is home.

It is a place where we feel fortunate to live, a place we care about deeply and a place we are very excited to share. We hope the following pages will help you begin to get to know this place the way we do.

About the Authors

Lyman Hafen

Lyman Hafen has lived all but seven of his 41 years in the southwestern corner of Utah. He comes from the fifth generation of a Mormon family that settled along the Virgin and Santa Clara rivers in the early 1860s. Growing up on the edge of St. George, he witnessed firsthand the transformation of his boyhood village into a bustling city. In high school Lyman carried on the family tradition as a cowboy, participating in rodeos as a bull and bronc rider as well as a roper. In 1973 he won the Utah State High School Rodeo All-Around Championship.

At Dixie College, where his grandfather taught humanities for more than 40 years, Lyman discovered a love for scholarship and came to grips with the idea that there was something special about the history and culture of his home region. In 1977 he married his high school sweetheart and began studying communications at Brigham Young University. He published his first article and graduated with a bachelor's degree in 1979. For four years thereafter, he worked his way from staff writer to assistant editor to editor of three trade magazines in Idaho Falls, Idaho.

Like many others of his generation, Lyman could not shake the red sand of Southwestern Utah from his shoes. He returned with his young family to St. George in 1983, where he became founding editor of *St. George Magazine* and began teaching writing classes at Dixie College. He and his wife, Debbie, live in Santa Clara, just west of St. George, with their six children.

During the past 10 years, Lyman's fiction and nonfiction have received seven awards from the Utah Arts Council. He's written for a number of regional and national magazines, among them *Travel-Holiday*, *Nevada Magazine* and *Arizona Highways*, and has published five books, including *Flood Street to Fenway*, a biography of St. George native Bruce Hurst, who pitched the Boston Red Sox to within one game of winning the 1986 World Series; *In The Shade of the Cottonwoods*, a collection of essays about growing up in southern Utah; *Over the Joshua Slope*, a novel for young readers published by Simon and Schuster; *Roping the Wind*, a personal history of cowboying in southern Utah; and most recently, *Mukuntuweap: Landscape and Story in Zion Canyon*.

In his writing Lyman attempts to capture the sense of place he feels so keenly in Southwestern Utah, an understanding connected to deep roots and a lifetime of living among the slickrock, sagebrush and red sand. It is a love and a knowledge he shares openly with others and brings in abundance to the pages of *The Insiders' Guide® to Southwestern Utah*.

Linda Sappington

"What am I doing in the desert?" **Linda Sappington** recalls asking herself in 1978 while unpacking family belongings in a new home in St. George. But Linda fell in love, almost immediately, with Utah's southwestern-most desert community. Affection for the sandy beaches of Southern California turned to passion for the red rocks of Southwestern Utah. After nearly 20 years, she is still intrigued by the geology of clearly visible earthquake fault lines running for miles along Interstate 15. She is awed by the majesty and grandeur of Zion and the abundance of other national and state parks, relaxed by the delicate hues of desert sunsets and clear, starry night skies, inspired by the ever-changing landscape (depending on the time of day) and strengthened through everyday association with good people.

In two decades as a public relations consultant and freelance writer, Linda has enjoyed many interesting and diverse assignments. After five years in public relations at Dixie Regional Medical Center, she left office politics behind to devote herself full-time to freelancing and a growing family of six children. Over the years, the coauthor of this first edition of the *Insiders' Guide® to Southwestern Utah* has appeared frequently in print on the pages of *The Spectrum, Washington County News, St. George Magazine, Dixie Datebook* and the *Senior Sampler*.

Linda was initially introduced to many of Utah's 15 southern counties in her role as area director for the American Cancer Society, alternating between staff member and volunteer for 10 years. Since 1993, she enjoyed the opportunity to rekindle old friendships made during her ACS years and to develop new ones as the Southern Area Director for the Utah Statehood Centennial Commission. Her assignment in those same 15 counties was to coordinate activities during Utah's celebration of a century as the nation's 45th state during 1996.

With a wealth of experience working alongside volunteers, she currently divides her time between 750 RSVP volunteers as the Five County Director for the Retired and Senior Volunteer Program and writing, an activity she incorporates into each work assignment and enjoys in leisure time. Her own volunteer resume includes roles as creator and four-year hairman of the Jubilee of Trees, a hospital holiday fund-raiser; director of the Southern Utah Folklife Festival; and active member in the St. George Rotary Club.

Linda's husband, Ed, recently left a 30-year career in banking to pursue a longtime interest in securities and investments. The six Sappington offspring are mostly grown and, as young adults, are building lives and families in St. George and other communities throughout the intermountain West.

Linda has only positive experiences to relate about years of travel over 300,000 miles on Utah highways and life in the desert. Her roots are planted deep in Southwestern Utah soil. She has red sand in her shoes and can't imagine living anywhere else on earth.

Acknowledgments

Lyman Hafen

When Roger Plothow, editor and publisher of *The Spectrum*, first talked with me about this book, he was very encouraging. He said that because I was born and raised in Southwestern Utah and because I had been writing about the area for more than 15 years, this would be a book I could probably write in my sleep.

I know he meant it as a compliment. And I know he meant it only in a figurative sense. But deep down, as I left his office that day, I wished that it were also true in a literal sense, because I already had a day job — the kind of job that is never finished — and a night job as a husband and a father of five children.

As the reality of the assignment I'd just accepted descended over me, I realized this was indeed a project that would have to be done either in my sleep or in lieu of it. Looking back now, I assure you I was awake during the entire process. I was thoroughly awakened the day Beth Storie, creator, publisher and editor-in-chief of Insiders' Publishing® Inc., visited St. George and shared with Linda and me the wonderful and successful formula that she and her husband have developed for this unique series of books. No, I realized quite finally that day, I would not be writing this book in my sleep — not if it was going to reach the standards and live up to the reputation that *Insiders' Guides*® have set and achieved over the past 19 years.

The next wake-up call came as I got to know Dave McCarter, the editor of this book. If there was ever a moment when I tried to do any of this in my sleep, he snapped me out of it quickly. In addition to being a heck of a nice guy, Dave is the most thorough, competent and effective editor I have ever worked with. We have never met face to face, but we have connected most remarkably over 3,000 miles of fiberoptic line.

My co-author Linda Sappington is another live wire who would never let me doze. She has an amazing capacity to juggle handfuls of bowling pins at the same time, while I do well to keep one in the air. Her ability to press forward and produce so remarkably well has been a true inspiration.

My involvement in this project would not have been possible without the support and understanding of my associates at *St. George Magazine*. Publishers Lyle and Katherine Hurd have been patient and supportive. Office manager T.J. Jones has fielded and screened scores of calls and dragged heaps of faxes back to my office without raising an eyebrow. The folks at *The Spectrum* have been wonderful to work with. It was Roger who grasped the vision for this book and put the mechanism together for it to be assembled. He is the one most responsible for its existence. John Daley aided in a huge way by keeping the e-mail flying between St. George and Manteo. Photographer Nick Adams has made a powerful contribution through his great photos.

Southwestern Utah is a place where people live because they have a passion to be here. This fact came home to me anew as I talked with scores of business people, travel experts, community leaders, teachers, volunteers, rangers, professors, administrators, artists, students, working moms and retirees in compiling information for this book. Their love for this place spilled out through their spirit of cooperation and in their sincere desire to share what they love about Southwestern Utah with the world.

Though I did lose some sleep along the way, the ones who sacrificed most were my wife, Debbie, and my children Tyler, Ryan, Matt, Julie, Joey — and little Joshua, who joined our family midway through the project and brought a degree of love and unity exponentially greater than we could have ever imagined. To each of them: my love, my appreciation and now that this book is finished, my Saturdays, my evenings and my holidays.

Linda Sappington

It has been such fun to co-author this book about Southwestern Utah, the place I call home. But although it is my name on the cover, the completed project is the end result of the work of many Insiders . . . and the loving support of friends and family.

Thanks to Bruce Fullmer and Mary Jane Christy at the Garfield County Travel Council; to Greg Aitkenhead, Steve Puro and Donna Casebolt at the Kane County Travel Council; and to Maria Twitchell and LaRee Garfield at the Iron County Tourism and Convention Bureau, all Insiders themselves who were willing to share their obvious affection for their hometowns in addition to everything I needed to know about people, places, businesses, events and activities.

Thanks, too, to the people of Southwestern Utah. Many are quoted in the text of the book — anonymous Insiders who provided hundreds of tidbits of information about their business, organization or community. And I especially appreciate that most responded quickly to my request for information.

Thanks to Lyman Hafen, with whom I shared this experience. Through it all, he has listened, advised and suggested with his usual good humor, gentle demeanor and professionalism. My appreciation also goes to Roger Plothow, publisher of *The Spectrum* and a fellow Rotarian, who never questions my use of the employee entrance, although, until now, I was not authorized personnel. Roger has been a great friend and supporter.

My gratitude to Beth Storie and David McCarter at the Insiders' Publishing® Inc. offices — Beth for her guidance early on and for never saying, "I told you this was a big project!" and David for his Southern charm, patience, understanding, longsuffering and words of encouragement that pulled me through those difficult deadlines.

My undying love, devotion and gratitude to my four terrific married kids, who have, for most of their lives, shared me with the community; to Michael in the Philippines and to Ed who has, through the years, given me a wealth of affection and support. This is a man who has been a great husband and father, has never missed a paycheck and who has an undisputed reputation for honesty, integrity and devotion to his family, church and community.

And especially to our youngest, Katie (the pick of the litter), I want to say thanks. An atypical teenager, she has carried more than her share of the load while Mom worked into the night to meet IG deadlines. She has helped with Grandma, fixed numerous meals, taken telephone messages, kept the dog and the grandkids quiet and even finishes her homework without being reminded.

And thanks to you both, Katie and Ed, for translating my frantic, "I'm on deadline," to, "You're in charge of everything!"

Dedication

The authors of *The Insiders' Guide®* to Southwestern Utah and the employees of The Spectrum wish to dedicate this book to Laurie Kelley, 1954-1997. Human resources administrator at The Spectrum from 1994 to 1997, Laurie had been attracted to Southwestern Utah by the area's beauty and lifestyle, like so many before and since. In a short three years, she saw more of it than many long time residents and grew to love it.

How to Use This Book

The Insiders' Guide® to Southwestern Utah is a book about discovery. As local Insiders, we authors are presumed to know, if not everything, at least more than most folks about the wondrous natural treasures — both world-renowned and almost anonymous — you shouldn't miss; those out-of-the-way shops, restaurants and attractions you might have to leave the beaten track to find; and the communities and lifestyles that provide the very heartbeat of Southwestern Utah, the North Rim of the Grand Canyon and nearby Mesquite, Nevada.

Often, a treasure map is needed on the road to discovery, and that's what we want this guide to be. Through it, we hope you will learn this arid desert is alive with warm, wonderful and interesting people, exciting places to see and fun things to do. Whatever your reason for being here, you'll find The Insiders' Guide® to Southwestern Utah helpful.

Generally, the chapters of the book are divided into sections that represent the four main geographic areas of the region — St. George/Zion (National Park), Cedar City/Brian Head (Ski Resort), the Bryce Canyon area and the Kanab area. You will find chapters on such topics as restaurants, accommodations, annual events, attractions, kidstuff, area history and other subjects, and you will also find separate chapters detailing the North Rim of the Grand Canyon and Mesquite, St. George's action-packed neighbor across the border in Nevada.

We've focused much of our attention on people, places and events we think you'll enjoy because we do. But we've also discovered some sights, sounds and tastes we may be experiencing for the first time along with you. You are encouraged to read the book from cover to cover, though it is not necessary to do so in any particular order. Each chapter stands as a distinct part of the whole, written to explore and examine the unique as well as the commonplace characteristics of this area.

Even in a casual review of the book, you'll immediately notice how much of the guide is devoted to a study of the landscape and environment. In our high desert region, the vast, scenic beauty of the land and the abundance (or lack) of water have had a profound influence on the past, are factors in our present prosperity and are keys to our bright future.

But even if you don't consider yourself a historian or an environmentalist, reading our History and Environment chapters will help you better understand the area and its culture. The same is true for those other chapters you might be tempted to skip over. We think they all will enhance your visit.

To find information quickly, scan the table of contents or index, then look for boldfaced area, subject or business headers to get you where you want to be. Insiders' tips — those special little details only the locals are likely to know — are scattered throughout each chapter. We hope you will also enjoy the special-interest Close-ups, our series of "Great Views" and the "Legends and Lore" pieces we feel add to the color and flavor of our part of the world.

As of September 21, 1997, a new area code will be introduced in Southwestern Utah to meet the demand on statewide communications resulting from Utah's rapidly expanding population and new technology. The 801 area code will still serve the phone and fax needs of users north on the Wasatch Front. The new 435 area code will serve users in all other parts of the state, including St. George, Cedar City and the rest of Southwestern Utah. To give everyone a chance to get used to the change, until March 22, 1998, your call will get through regardless of which area code you use.

And if you think our street addresses are a bit peculiar, you are not alone. Trust us, they make perfect sense, and once you understand the statewide grid system, it's almost impossible to get lost in Utah. For a quick lesson on how homes and businesses are addressed in Utah, see the "Grid and Bear It: Navigating Utah Streets" section in our Getting Here, Getting Around chapter.

So keep this guide in your car, RV, briefcase, backpack or suitcase. Make notes in the margins. Fold the page corners down to remind you of some special restaurant, park or historic site you want to visit or visit again. Use it but don't lose it, because you'll want to refer to it often.

In our research, one thing we quickly discovered was that even after spending our entire lives here, there is still much to discover about our hometown and surrounding communities. We've tried to make sure all our information is correct. But in an area experiencing unprecedented growth — where neighborhoods and new businesses seem to spring up almost overnight — it's hard to keep tabs on everybody and everything. If you discover omissions; if you disagree with our assessment of the terrain, the people or the amenities of a given place; if we have missed your favorite event, eating establishment or legend; if you have some tips of your own or ideas for future editions, please take a minute to let us know. Tell us about your favorite chapters, Close-ups and tips as well. Write to us at:

The Insiders' Guide® to Southwestern Utah
Insiders' Publishing Inc.
P.O. Box 2057
Manteo, North Carolina 27954

We also encourage you to visit our website: www.insiders.com.

In the meantime, we wish you the joy of discovery!

Southwestern
UTAH

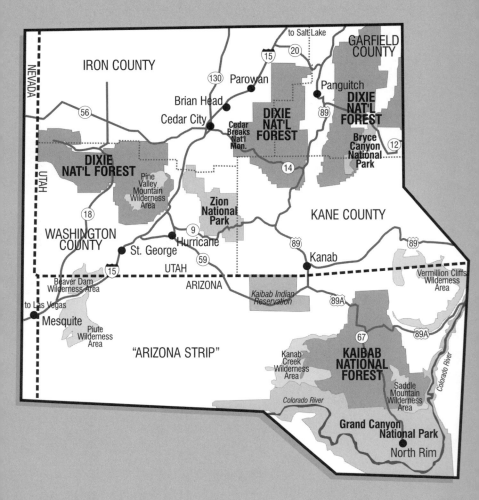

Downtown
St. George

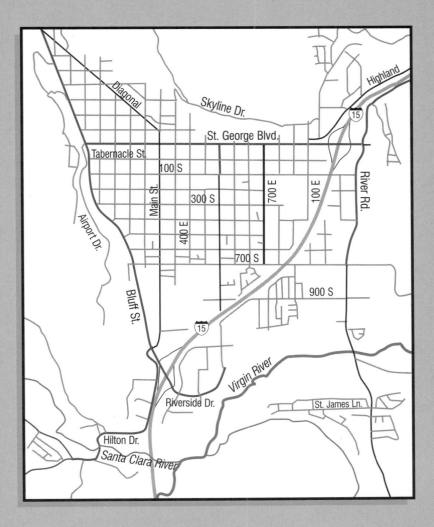

Southwestern Utah
National Parks and other Recreational Areas

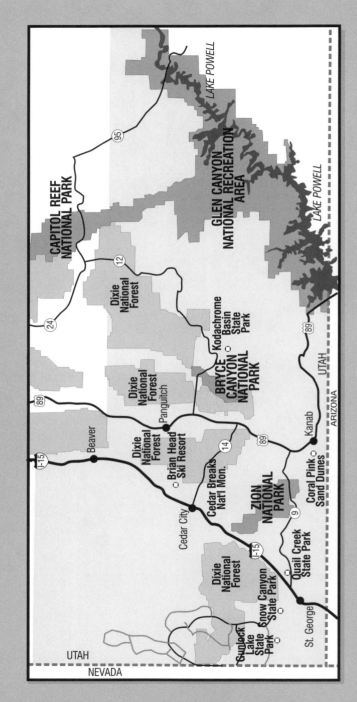

Zion National Park
Park
(excluding Kolob region)

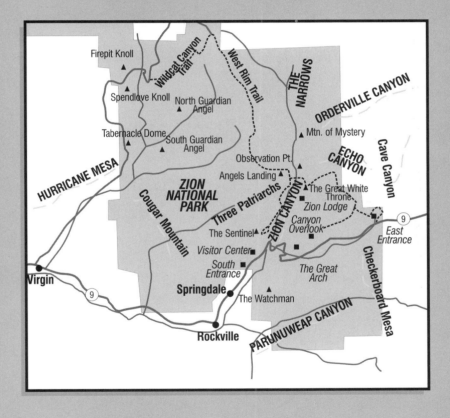

Firepit Knoll

Wildcat Canyon Trail

West Rim Trail

THE NARROWS

ORDERVILLE CANYON

Spendlove Knoll

North Guardian Angel

Tabernacle Dome

South Guardian Angel

Mtn. of Mystery

Cave Canyon

ECHO CANYON

Observation Pt.

Angels Landing

HURRICANE MESA

ZION NATIONAL PARK

Cougar Mountain

Three Patriarchs

ZION CANYON

The Great White Throne

Zion Lodge

Canyon Overlook

9

East Entrance

The Sentinel

Visitor Center

South Entrance

Virgin

9

Springdale

The Watchman

The Great Arch

Checkerboard Mesa

Rockville

PARUNUWEAP CANYON

Bryce Canyon
National Park

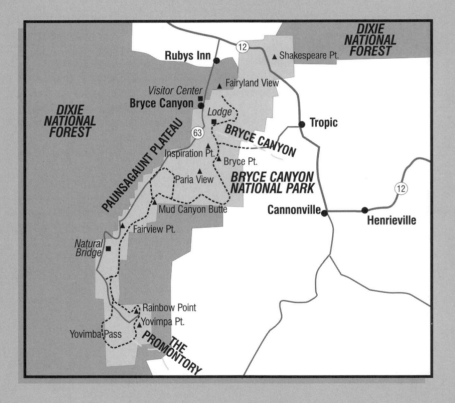

Table Of Contents

Directory of Maps

Welcome To St. George...
Utah's 'Hot' Spot!

SNOW CANYON STATE PARK

ZION NATIONAL PARK

UTAH!
SPECTACULAR
OUTDOOR MUSICAL

St. George is the gateway to the largest concentration of national parks and monuments in America...Zion National Park is just a short 46 mile drive and six others, including Bryce and Grand Canyon National Parks are within just a few hours. The warm, mild climate creates the perfect resort setting for golfing on nine year round courses, experiencing live history tours, enjoying the spectacular outdoor musical "UTAH!", sightseeing in the nearby national parks or just spending a relaxing day shopping.

For more information on planning your vacation in St. George or Utah's Dixie, call or write:

**WASHINGTON COUNTY
TRAVEL BUREAU**
425 South 700 East
St. George, Utah 84770
1-800-869-6635

**ST. GEORGE AREA
CHAMBER OF COMMERCE**
1-801-628-1658
Home Page: www.stgeorgechamber.com
E-Mail: hotspot@infowest.com

Area Overviews

Utah is a state . . . of mind. It is a spirit, a lifestyle, a diverse land with a rich heritage and a bright future. In 1995, Utah was judged "most liveable state in the U.S.," based on an annual survey of state comparisons by Morris Quinto Company of Lawrence, Kansas. Utah was also *Kiplinger's* pick for "top entrepreneurial hot spot" in its January 1996 issue and was designated "best state to locate a business" by *Financial World* magazine, based on property growth, disposable income, low energy costs and high graduation rates. *Financial World* also identified Utah in September 1995 as the state with the healthiest economy.

State residents (we call ourselves Utahns) as a group are among the healthiest Americans, although we consume twice as many marshmallows as the national average. Utah is also the unofficial "green Jell-O capitol of the world," and it is home to Brigham Young University, ranked almost last in a 1996 survey of America's party schools. A fortunate postscript on that note is that at the end of 1996, the national Mothers Against Drunk Driving organization ranked Utah as the state with the lowest percentage of alcohol-related deaths in the nation.

And as the 45th state was celebrating a century of statehood in 1996, the International Olympic Organizing Committee gave Salt Lake City the nod to host the Winter Olympic Games in 2002. In beating out Sion, Switzerland; Osterlund, Sweden; and Quebec, Canada, for the honors, Salt Lake became the first winter games site to be selected on the first ballot.

Here in the southwestern corner of the most liveable state, Cedar City was named in the early '90s as "one of America's most liveable small towns" in Norman Crampton's *The 100 Best Small Towns in America*. St. George was singled out by *Money* magazine as the best place in the West to retire, after appearing on several top-10 lists in national surveys.

Southwestern Utah is a place where prayers are pronounced on community events, at civic club meetings, by school children and public officials. It is diverse communities made up of families with deep roots who work the land on century-old farms and ranches. It is unprecedented population growth, computer software companies with international reputations, Franklin Quest Day Planners to organize days and months, cellular phones, clear air and clean water, unparalleled volunteerism, 100-mile stretches of desert between towns, patriotism and schools with no graffiti or apologies for the respect that teachers and learning still receive.

Southwestern Utah is Dad and Mom taking an afternoon off work to travel 200 miles to see the local team play. It is old and young sharing the neighborhood without fear, frequent and imaginative community events and playing outdoors in the most breathtakingly beautiful scenery on earth. It is 3,600 senior athletes from all 50 states and 15 foreign countries coming together for the Huntsman World Senior Games. It is the St. George Marathon with 4,000 runners and the Dixie Rotary Bowl, America's premier junior college football bowl game. It is pickup trucks and fast cars, Spring Break, "snowbirds," marching teams and dance groups made up of everybody's kids.

In Southwestern Utah, hunting season is considered a sacred obligation, a Constitutional right or a religious experience. Conversely, the world's largest population of healthy desert tortoises are protected under the Endangered Species Act by a Habitat Conservation Plan, created after five years of discussion, threatened litigation, land exchanges and difficult negotiations between landowners, various governmental entities, and a bevy of federal agencies including the Department of the Interior, U.S. Fish and Wildlife Service, the Bureau of Land Management and the Division of Wildlife Resources (see The Environment chapter). Prairie dogs, woundfin minnows, bald eagles, bear claw poppies and other species in this rich desert environment are officially considered endangered, and there are dozens of candidate species waiting to be added to the list.

Southwestern Utah's unofficial official drink is Diet Coke, and golf is the official sport. In any county, the Democratic convention could be held in a telephone booth, and most families don't take or make phone calls on Monday nights between 6 PM and midnight. This is Family Home Evening, a time set aside for play and learning in Mormon households.

Southwestern Utah is not very diverse ethnically, but it isn't because anyone isn't welcome here. Statistics released in 1996 show the region's most populous area — St. George and Washington County — is more than 95 percent white. The other main slivers in the ethnic pie are Hispanics (2 percent) and Native Americans (1.5 percent). Statewide, 11 percent of Utahns belong to non-white ethnic groups.

But during the summer tourism season, other cultures are well represented in Southwestern Utah. According to the Washington County Travel and Convention Bureau, 30 percent of the 2.5 million annual visitors to the area are foreign travelers. Of that number 25 percent are German. Citizens of other European countries visit in considerable numbers along with travelers from the Asian Rim (Japan and Korea). Many of these visitors are anxious to bypass the glitzy side of American culture to get back to nature in Utah's national parks. You'll be surprised after a day of hiking and sightseeing how little English you will recall being spoken.

Issues of concern in today's Southwestern Utah communities are related to tourism, growth and economic development. The growing presence of the federal government and the need to protect school trust lands for future generations are hot topics. The increasing demand for some form of public transportation, at least in high growth areas such as St. George and Cedar City, is beginning to be discussed.

Residents with generations of genealogy in this beautiful corner of the world have learned how to survive in the desert through years of nose-to-nose confrontation with the elements. They are hardworking, generous, loyal to their neighbors and independent to the core. New residents are attracted by clean air, spectacular scenery, low crime rates, value for the dollar in real estate and a solid economy. In the words of the 2002 Olympic Committee: "The world is welcome here!"

St. George/Zion

The St. George area has nearly 70,000 residents, with an 8 percent population increase in 1995 making Washington County Utah's fastest-growing county. The population has doubled approximately every decade since 1950, when census figures reported 4,562 residents in the county. Anchoring the southwestern-most corner of the state, Washington County is bordered on the south by Arizona, on the west by Nevada, on the north by Iron County and on the east by Kane County. It is a region of colorful rocks and spectacular scenery and is unique in the state of Utah in terms of climate, vegetation, animal life and geologic features. It has the lowest elevation and generally the warmest daily temperatures in the state.

Tourism is big business in the St. George area. Gross taxable sales for tourist-related services nearly doubled between 1990 and 1995. According to the Utah State Tax Commission, sales in Washington County jumped from $50 million in 1990 to $93 million in 1995. The Washington County Travel and Convention Bureau reports the local 3 percent transient room tax generated $744,496 in 1993, increased another $100,000 by 1995 and should produce more than $900,000 in 1996.

INSIDERS' TIP

Most families in Southwestern Utah don't take or make phone calls on Monday nights between 6 PM and midnight. This is Family Home Evening, a time set aside for play and learning in Mormon households.

Speech, Southwestern Utah style

Those of us who are longtime residents of Southwestern Utah have our own way of speaking. It has been hypothesized that this strange phenomenon is linked to the potpourri of people who first came to the area — a broad mix of different nationalities and ethnic backgrounds.

Cotton growers settled the town of Washington; many were bona fide Southerners from places such as Georgia, Tennessee, Arkansas, Mississippi and Alabama and had a heavy southern bent. Add the Swiss, Scandinavian, English and other European extractions who settled dozens of rural communities in this desert region and you had a veritable hodgepodge of vocabulary, pronunciation and usage of language. Then came miners to Silver Reef, about 15 miles north of St. George, which went from no population to 1,500 residents in about 60 days. The silver vein brought in Chinese, Irish, Scottish, Cornish and many other linguistic variations into the already stewed-up conglomeration.

As we all melted into one culture, we ended up with a society sounding like it was "barn in a born," that "porks cores in a corepart," and often seems to put the "court before the harse" when it comes to saying things in a conventional manner.

For anyone who finds it difficult to converse with the natives, here are a few dialectic gems, along with their definitions, to help in the process. But remember, the mere act of learning the words and their meanings does not constitute complete comprehension. You must also learn how to place the words in sentences "so's to git the right fill."

You can't always believe your ears in Southwestern Utah.

airpart — A tract of land maintained for the landing and taking off of airplanes.

arange — A pretty color or a globose berry with a reddish-yellow rind and sweet edible pulp.

bard — With many of these you may build a house or what you become when things get monotonous.

barn — Many Christians claim to be "barn" again.

born — A large building for the storage of farm products or the protection of animals.

car — The remaining inedible section of an eaten apple.

carn — A yellow vegetable characterized by kernels that grow on a cob.

carner — A place where two streets intersect.

cart — A place where basketball is played or where a judge performs his duties.

core — An automobile.

court — Do not get this before the "harse."

— continued on next page

Darthy — The little girl played by Judy Garland in the "Wizard of Oz."

dorkroom — A small, light-free room where film is developed.

dorling — Real cute.

dort — A sharp game piece that is thrown for accuracy.

dortbard — The object at which "dorts" are thrown.

Fard — Have you driven one lately?

fark — An eating utensil or split in the road.

farmal — The opposite of casual.

fart — A solidly built edifice used in defending oneself against enemies.

flar — What one walks on.

for — A long, long way.

form — A place with a big red "born" where "carn" is grown.

gargeous — Beautiful.

gorden — A place where vegetables are grown.

harn — That which is honked.

Herrican — A town 18 miles east of St. George.

hord — Difficult.

hort — An organ that pumps blood.

jest — As in "jest fur now." May be used interchangeably with "jist".

jor — A container made of glass.

lorge — Big.

mar — Opposite of less.

morket — A place where you may buy items grown on the "form".

narth — The opposite of south.

Orby's — A popular fast food restaurant.

ore — As in "Where ore you going?" Not to be confused with "are," which is an instrument used to paddle a boat.

ork — Noah's large sailing vessel.

ort — Music, ballet, paintings, literature, etc.

par — The act of transferring liquid from one container to another.

port — One of the indefinite or unequal subdivisions into which something is divided and which together constitute the whole.

repart — To give an account.

sarful — Sad or pitiful.

scar — The outcome of a ball game.

score — The result of a surgical incision or terrible wound.

St. Garge — The largest of Southwestern Utah's communities.

star — See "morket".

stark — A long-legged bird that delivers babies.

store — A bright object that shines in the heavens at night.

tore — Black gooey stuff or a journey for business, pleasure or education.

torist — A person who is on a "tore."

yar — Of or relating to one or oneself: "Yar core," "Yar sargum," "Yar form."

We hope the preceding will aid you in understanding and communicating with the natives. If you have studied carefully you should be able to comprehend and follow directions such as these:

"Ya git in yar core, drive down to where that par kid, in those sarful, arange sharts is standing, then go narth to the next carner, turn and drive until you come to the formyord, and you'll see a deportment star on the other side of the street (where you can get a lorge arder of cormel carn in a dorling cordbard box). "

The scenic beauty of the St. George/Zion area is legendary with brilliant red rocks, clear blue skies and a rich heritage of pioneer history. It is home to Zion National Park, Snow Canyon State Park and Quail Creek Reservoir. The 14 desert communities of Washington County average about 8 inches of rain annually. Summertime high temperatures are usually between 95 and 110 degrees with low humidity. Mild winters and infrequent snowfall attract numerous seasonal residents (known locally as "snowbirds") who winter here, then return home to cooler climates in the North during the hot summer. The elevation in Washington County ranges from 2,800 feet on the streets of downtown St. George to 10,000 feet at the top of Pine Valley Mountain, which still offers a cool respite from blazing temperatures, as it did in the days of the early settlers.

There are no local county or city income taxes anywhere in Utah. State income tax rates start at 2.55 percent and increase to 7.2 percent for all taxable income in excess of $7,500. Individuals older than 65 receive special retirement income deductions of as much as $7,500 per person under certain limits. The state sales tax is 5.875 percent, and each county may levy local sales taxes — most tack on 1 percent.

Washington County's municipalities are each governed by a mayor and a council of elected members. Most also have appointed city managers. The county is governed by a paid commission, elected at large, and St. George is the county seat.

Since 1992, when many state and national corporations began opening branch offices to accommodate the growing population in the St. George area, Washington County's longstanding reputation as a retirement community has given way to a more balanced influx including families with parents working jobs in construction and the service industries. Reflecting that change, the Washington County School District is one of the fastest-growing

districts in Utah with more than 17,500 students. Year-round education has proven to be a successful and money-saving alternative for controlling growth (see our Education chapter). Three of the top-five employers in Washington County are federal, state and local government agencies. The school district, Dixie College and Dixie Regional Medical Center also provide a large share of the paychecks.

Housing costs range from $80,000 for a comfortable starter home to $1.5 million for a high-end, custom address. A variety of locations, sizes, styles and costs are available in the St. George/Zion area. The Washington County Board of Realtors reports an average 1,500-square-foot, three-bedroom, two-bath home sells for about $110,000 (see our Neighborhoods and Real Estate chapter). Annual property taxes on such a home are about $1,100.

In terms of the availability of retail goods, things have changed dramatically since the days 20 years ago when most people commonly traveled more than 300 miles to Salt Lake City or 100-plus miles to Las Vegas to buy school clothes and Christmas gifts. Shopping in Washington County now includes a broad spectrum of choices. More and more Nevada residents from as far away as Las Vegas are adding shopping to their list of things to do in Southwestern Utah. Competitive pricing also brings many Nevadans across the Utah border for healthcare and to purchase cars and recreational vehicles. More than 70 national chains are represented in the Washington County marketplace with new retail outlets opening nearly every week. The Zion Factory Stores attracts residents, tourists and travelers off Interstate 15 and is soon slated to double in size.

The list of area civic organizations is diverse and includes all the regular clubs you would expect as well as a few special-interest organizations. Services for senior citizens and the disabled are plentiful (See our Retirement chapter).

INSIDERS' TIP

Remember, there are 100-mile stretches of road in Utah with virtually no facilities of any kind. When traveling off major thoroughfares, always check for road conditions, keep the gas tank topped off and take along a little food in the car.

CAUTION
YOU ARE IN
DESERT TORTOISE
AREA

OFF-ROAD TRAVEL STRICTLY PROHIBITED
EXCEPT AS AUTHORIZED BY DOE/YMPO

TO PROTECT THE DESERT TORTOISE
OBSERVE ALL ROAD SIGNS
AVOID ALL HARASSMENT OF
THE DESERT TORTOISE
FOC 295-5915

Photo: Courtesy of the Washington County Habitat Conservation Plan

It's no joke! Protection of the Mojave desert tortoise and several threatened and endangered species native to the area is serious business in Southwestern Utah.

Although the Church of Jesus Christ of Latter-day Saints (the Mormon church) is the predominant religion in this and most other areas of Utah, worshippers of any Christian faith will find a varied selection of Protestant and Catholic congregations in most Southwestern Utah neighborhoods (see our Worship chapter). There are still no organized non-Christian houses of worship in the area.

If golf was designated a religion, Washington County would be the church. With more than 10 outstanding courses within 90 miles of downtown St. George, area hotels offer golf packages, but visitors should plan ahead during peak seasons (generally considered the months between the first snow in the northern part of Utah and the temperature hitting 100 in St. George) to avoid the frustration of getting a tee time (see our Golf chapter).

Cedar City/Brian Head

Cedar City and the other nine communities of Iron County are famous for Southern Utah University, the Utah Shakespearean Festival, Iron Mission State Park and Brian Head Ski Resort. Set 3,000 feet higher in altitude than neighboring Washington County, Iron County is a beautiful mountain community with four distinct seasons.

Cedar City, the largest town in Iron County with 20,000 residents, was designated by *Consumer Digest* in 1995 as the city with the best climate and environment in the country. Although the average annual snowfall is nearly 46 inches, the county boasts 310 clear days a year, and a summer afternoon can reach 90 degrees or above.

According to the county's economic profile, 1996 statistics are favorable indicators of continuing prosperity. The county population, currently at more than 32,000, has nearly doubled since 1980, and gross taxable sales have tripled during the same time period. The school district census shows a steady increase in the number of children enrolled. A mid-priced home has doubled in value to about $112,000 since 1990 in a community where the average age has remained constant at about 23.5 years — a reflection of college and school-age residents.

The economy of Cedar City and surrounding communities is based on tourism, education, federal agencies and manufacturing. The largest employer is Southern Utah University, followed by the Iron County School District, TW Recreational Services (concessionaires for the nearby national parks), Wal-Mart, the U.S. Forest Service and Coleman Outdoor Products. Other major employers include Goer Manufacturing (makers of supermarket shelving), the Iron County government, Utah Power and Light, Matrixx Marketing and Western Electric Chemical, a company that produces rocket fuel.

Cedar City, nicknamed "The Festival City," is home of the world-renowned, 36-year-old Utah Shakespearean Festival at SUU. Though the county seat is in nearby Parowan, Cedar City has the largest population of the communities in the county. Amenities in this city include 1,766 hotel and motel rooms and enough good restaurants, movie theaters, museums and art galleries to keep tourists coming back for more. There are also professional theater productions and an 18-hole golf course.

Residents support those activities while recreating in seven municipal parks, three city swimming pools and on a dozen ball fields. There are three rodeo grounds, 16 municipal tennis courts, a bowling center, ATVs to rent and plenty of shopping.

Valley View Medical Center, a 48-bed acute-care facility in Cedar City owned by Intermountain Health Care Inc., is staffed by 40 physicians trained in most medical specialties. The community also has an excellent selection of dentists, optometrists and ophthalmologists (see our Healthcare chapter).

Brian Head Ski Resort is a popular destination for skiers from Las Vegas and parts of Utah. Rising from 9,600 to 11,307 feet above sea level, Brian Head is the highest ski resort in Utah with an excellent snow base and deep powder. Enthusiastic skiers, snowboarders and ice skaters flock to the area during the winter months. In the summertime, Brian Head hosts fun weekend activities and provides extensive mountain bike trail systems offering a thrill-a-minute ride through forests and red rock country (see our Outdoor Recreation chapter).

Religious activity in the county is varied. In addition to dozens of LDS congregations, Iron County has a healthy congregational mix with churches representing Assembly of God, Conservative, Independent and Southern Baptist, Church of Christ, Episcopal, Jehovah's Witness, Lutheran, Catholic and Presbyterian denominations.

Bryce Canyon Area

The communities of the Bryce Canyon area are in Garfield County, 5,217 square miles nestled in the center of some of the nation's most splendid scenic and recreational property, 98 percent of which is owned by state or national government. U.S. 89 and Utah Scenic Byway 12 link the 4,144 county residents in eight communities with I-15 to Salt Lake City, Las Vegas and the west coast. The county seat is Panguitch.

Bordered by Iron, Kane, San Juan, Wayne and Piute counties, Garfield is the home to the largest piece of and provides access into Bryce Canyon National Park. And most of the newly designated Grand Staircase-Escalante National Monument is also within the county boundaries. Other must-sees in the area include Kodachrome Basin State Park, Escalante Petrified Forest, Anasazi Indian Village State Park, Panguitch Lake, Calf Creek Recreation Area and the largest tar sand deposit in the nation (see our Parks and Other Natural Wonders chapter).

In winter, deep snow covers mountain tops 11,000 feet high in 1,576 square miles of Dixie National Forest and in Bryce Canyon. The summers are dry and pleasant with warm days and cool nights. This diversity makes Garfield County the perfect outdoor recreation destination. Wildlife is abundant including deer, elk, pronghorn antelope, an occasional black bear, mountain lions and a wide variety of hawks, eagles and falcons.

The cost of living is comparable to that of the rest of the state. Based on national and state statistics, the cost of groceries, housing and transportation is slightly higher than the national composite index, but the cost of utilities and healthcare in Garfield County are a little lower than average. In other words, new residents will pay about the same to live in the Bryce Canyon area as they would in Salt Lake City or Las Vegas.

Montezuma's Treasure

In the early 1920s, a treasure hunter named Freddie Crystal showed up in Kanab with a map he claimed marked the hiding place of Montezuma's treasure not 30 miles from downtown Kanab. When the blocked-off entrance to a cave was discovered in a place vaguely consistent with the map, the town was swept with treasure fever and virtually shut down for two years while everyone dug in the cave. No treasure ever surfaced, and Kanab's citizens soon reverted to the more stable livelihoods of farming and ranching.

Photo: Nick Adams, Courtesy of The Daily Spectrum

The scenic splendor of Zion National Park peeks over the hillside of the Hurricane Valley.

Major local industries are timber, agriculture (farming and livestock) and tourism. At the peak of the tourist season, Best Western Ruby's Inn and TW Recreational Services are the largest private employers in the area. The county's largest public employers are Garfield County School District with 135 on the payroll and Garfield Memorial Hospital with 65 people providing for the medical needs of the community.

Kanab Area

Kanab, known as "Little Hollywood" for decades of starring roles on the silver screen, is a destination community. The location provided the scenic backdrop for such films as *The Ten Commandments, The Outlaw Josey Wales* and *My Friend Flicka* and has earned a reputation for hospitality by entertaining the great and near-great during the filming of more than 70 movies in and around Kane County. The area is still being used for films. Two re-cent movies with significant shooting near Kanab were *Maverick*, with Mel Gibson, Jodie Foster and James Garner, and *Broken Arrow*, with John Travolta and Christian Slater.

On the Arizona border, Kane County is an ideal vacation spot for families, boating enthusiasts, anglers, golfers, hunters, hikers, bikers and photographers. Such national treasures as the North Rim of the Grand Canyon, Lake Powell, Coral Pink Sand Dunes, Zion National Park and Bryce Canyon are all within the Southwestern Utah area and at most 90 minutes drive-time from downtown Kanab.

In the past two decades, the population of Kane County has doubled to 6,000. Government is the largest employer, but many come here to retire. The attraction to the area is reflected in the county's slogan — "the greatest earth on show" — along with a combination of friendly neighbors and an excellent four-season climate. Summer highs average about 93 degrees, and winter temperatures dip to 22 in January.

INSIDERS' TIP

St. George is just 6 miles from the Arizona border, on the western edge of the Mountain Time Zone. So 15 minutes away (and in all of Nevada, California and other points west), it's an hour earlier. During our warm Dixie summers, it rarely gets completely dark before 10 PM.

Kane County has a fun, Western-movie feel to it. Restaurants, motels, curio shops and movie theaters line center streets. U.S. Highway 89 is the main artery through Kanab and Kane County. Community events take place in the city park, on the rodeo grounds or in the gazebo in the center of town.

The financial future of Kane County, where 95 percent of the land is controlled by the federal or state government, is tied to the scenery, tourism and retirement. Lands held in trust for the state's school children are managed by the state of Utah, while the Bureau of Land Management, U.S. Forest Service and National Park Service oversee the majority of the county's 4,800 square miles. A full 54 percent of the county is now inside the newly created Grand Staircase-Escalante National Monument.

Ranching, mineral claims, hunting and gathering wood for fuel provide income, but the average Kane County resident earns only $19,000 annually. Because wages are disproportionately low, many young people are seeking employment in other parts of Utah or in other states. Tourism provides jobs, but according to the Kane County Economic Development office, employment is "at capacity." Long-range planning calls for small, clean industry to utilize a young, educated and industrious work force and keep more of the kids in their home county.

The landscape started Utah's story eons ago and continues to shape it today.

History

To get to the beginning of Southwestern Utah's story we must plow back through time, beyond the exploits of modern man recorded in books, beyond the messages of prehistoric people etched in rock, all the way back to the most ancient story locked between layers of sandstone, limestone and basalt.

One of the first geologists who seriously studied the complex landscape of Southwestern Utah was C.E. Dutton. In his report written for the federal government in 1880, he often lapsed into near-poetry as he attempted to describe the country's features. "Nature is more easily read here than elsewhere," he wrote. "She seems at times in these solitudes to have lifted from her countenance the veil of mystery which she habitually wears in the haunts of men. The land is stripped of its normal clothing; its cliffs and canyons have dissected and laid open its tissues and framework, and 'he who runs may read,' if his eyes have been duly opened."

With some knowledge of geology it is literally possible to "read" the ancient story written in the landscape of Southwestern Utah. Picture yourself on the corner of St. George Boulevard and Main Street — a billion years ago. It is difficult to know exactly the conditions that might have surrounded you, but geologists believe you'd have been buried several miles deep in a solid mass of mountain range. Five hundred million years go by, and you're still standing on the corner. Now you're submerged in an ominous ocean. Eons pass — a few more hundred million years. The ocean has receded and a great Sahara-like desert has formed all around you.

As the years roll on by the tens of thousands and millions, you're flooded by wide rivers, battered by dust storms, covered again by blue oceans, shaken by earthquakes and threatened by lava flows. Finally, a few million years of relative calm reign, and the serene little valley where you stand is carved in slow motion, forged into its present state between two volcanic ledges by water and wind cascading down the slopes of a giant dome someday to be known as Pine Valley Mountain.

The stretching, pulling, sinking, pushing and eroding of Southwestern Utah over the past 50 million years has resulted in one of the most chaotically beautiful landscapes in the world. The distinct features of this landscape — from the pink and orange cliffs of the Wasatch Formation at Cedar Breaks National Monument and Bryce Canyon National Park, to the towering red, rust and white Navajo Sandstone of Zion National Park — not only form the foundation of Southwestern Utah's history but also have shaped the area to the present day.

The First Inhabitants

All we know about the first Southwestern Utah inhabitants is what we read from the things they left behind. A broken piece of pottery, a bead on a string of yucca, a gleaming worked piece of obsidian, a silkweed net. From such artifacts, anthropologists have painstakingly pieced together a sketch of Utah's earliest residents, but gaps as wide as a desert canyon remain.

Scientists generally believe the ancestors of the first Utahns came from Siberia. They most likely walked here across a land bridge, now flooded by the Bering Strait. About 12,000 years ago a band of those prehistoric migrants probably topped a rise and looked out over a valley that would ages later be part of a place called Utah.

We call them Paleo-Indians. They were not farmers. They lived close to the marshes where food could be hunted in the form of rabbits, ducks, bison, mammoths and giant sloths. The first Utahns hunted with thrusting spears tipped with fluted points.

By around 6,000 B.C. a very different

people had become established in what is now Utah. Known as the Desert Archaic, much of what we know of this people is revealed in caves around the edges of the Great Salt Lake. On the western edge of the lake, Hogup Cave was occupied intermittently from 6,000 B.C. until shortly after the arrival of Columbus, though not exclusively by the Desert Archaic. The layers of artifacts found in such caves — table scraps, worn sandals, broken baskets — are the sketchy clues scientists have used to try to piece together their story.

The Desert Archaic used the atlatl to give them leverage and thrust in throwing a spear. They killed small animals and antelope, using the flesh for meat and the bones, hides and sinews for clothing and tools. But they mostly ate cattail along with salt-tolerant plants like pickleweed, burrowweed and sedge.

Life for the Desert Archaic was not all hunting and gathering. They made beautifully decorated gaming sticks and handsome split-twig animals. There must have been more to their lives than hand-to-mouth existence. The Archaic peoples disappeared after a 6,000-year existence, and the land lay empty for a millennium.

Enter the Fremont. About 500 A.D. a very different culture began to emerge in Utah. In many ways they were like the Archaic. Whether they were descendents is not known, but their advanced ways of life were enough to distinguish them as an entirely different people.

The Fremont Indians had the bow and arrow, which allowed them to take game much more consistently. Rather than live in caves, they built their own shelters, partially underground, with roofs made of poles and dirt. In many cases, several homes and granaries were built close together in small villages.

They picked up the art of growing corn and probably grew beans and squash as well. And the Fremont made pottery. It was a simple, gray-coiled pottery that allowed them to boil food. Though less artistic than that of the neighboring Anasazi, Fremont pottery nonetheless illustrates a high degree of precision, skill and pride in workmanship.

The pictographs — pictures painted on rocks — of the Fremont are among the most distinctive remnants of this people. The style is easily distinguished, characterized by large-size human figures with broad, triangular shoulders and elaborate necklaces. The same style is found in clay figurines discovered at a number of Fremont sites. The figurines are very carefully made of unfired clay and painted in shades of ochre, tan and green. The best place to see samples of Fremont rock art and ceramics is at the Fremont Indian State Park near the junction of Interstate 15 and Interstate 70, 80 miles north of Cedar City.

Living in family groups or clans, the Fremont people apparently borrowed from and shared with other cultures. Yet with all their skills and ability to adapt, it was not enough to sustain them through the incursion of the historic Shoshoneans, who came to the area around 1200 to 1300 A.D. as the Fremont were disappearing. Why the Fremonts left, or died out, is not clear. All they left were the remnants of their homes, the tools and other artifacts of their lives and the vivid pictographs that can still be seen on rocks throughout the central parts of Utah.

Concurrent with the Fremont, a better-known culture of prehistoric Native Americans was living in the canyons and along the streams across all of what is now southern Utah, northern Arizona and the Four Corners region of Colorado and New Mexico. We call them Anasazi, which is a Navajo word meaning "someone's ancestors," "the ancient ones" or "enemy ancestors." Their culture first appeared in the Four Corners area, and by the time of the birth of Christ they were already

To view the entire Cedar Valley, take a morning or evening drive up Utah Highway 14 east out of Cedar City. As you head up the canyon, take the Kolob Reservoir turnoff to the right. Within minutes you'll be climbing the switchbacks and will see several handy spots on the side of the road where you can pull off.

Great Views

proficient weavers and basket makers, existing with an agricultural, hunter-gatherer lifestyle and living in small groups in pit houses. The Anasazi era up to about 700 A.D. is called the Basketmaker Period. It was followed by the Pueblo Period, which lasted until the Anasazi disappeared in about 1300.

Archaeologists divide the Anasazi occupation into three geographic traditions — Kayenta, Chaco and Mesa Verde — all of which lived concurrent with each other and concurrent with the Fremont culture to the north. The Kayenta Anasazi lived in a 10,000-square-mile area of southern Utah and northern Arizona, the Mesa Verde were found in southwestern Colorado and the Chaco were in northwestern New Mexico. Remnants of the Kayenta tradition are found all across the southern strip of Utah, with the most studied, photographed and talked about sites in San Juan County. Yet many important sites are also found in Southwestern Utah in the Kanab-Hildale-St. George areas.

In recent years, the Anasazi have become a kind of symbol for all Native Americans that inhabited the country prior to the arrival of the Spanish, in much the same way the Lakota people symbolize historic Indians. Natural historian Barry Lopez has written of the Anasazi that "much has been made of the 'mystery' of their disappearance. And perhaps because they seem 'primitive,' they are too easily thought of as an uncomplicated people with a comprehensible culture. It is not, and they are not."

As Lopez points out, we do know some things about them. "From the start they were very deft weavers, plaiting even the utensils they cooked with. Later they became expert potters and masons, strongly influencing cultures around them. They were clever floodwater farmers. And astronomers; not as sophisticated as the Maya, but knowledgeable enough to pinpoint the major celestial events, to plant and celebrate accordingly."

The Anasazi were intimate with the landscape and were a successful people. Yet, as Lopez puts it, "Around 1300 A.D. they slipped through a historical crevice to emerge (as best we know) as the people now called Hopi, Zuni, and the pueblo peoples of the Rio Grande Valley — Keres, Tiwa, Tewa."

For more than 100 years now, archaeologists and scientists of many disciplines have concerned themselves with who these people were and why they left their homes after surviving more than 1,000 years as a culture.

About 1300, at the height of their civilization, the identifiable culture of the Anasazi disappeared. When Anglo explorers found the remnants of their villages 100 years ago, it appeared to them as if the people woke up one morning, gathered up what they could carry and left everything else in its place. Hundreds of sites were abandoned, with thousands of pots, tools, sandals and ornaments remaining in their place as if the owner would be back by nightfall.

No one knows for sure why they left. Tree-ring research shows the beginning of a severe drought in 1276, which lasted most of the rest of the century. It's possible the drought starved them out. Others consider the possibility that the arrival of the Navajo and the Apache from the north might have meant a violent end to the basically peaceful Anasazi. The answer may never be known, but the fact remains that the Anasazi, along with their Fremont neighbors to the north, disappeared from Utah around the year 1300 and never returned.

The First Historic Utahns

Most of the indigenous peoples living in Utah at the time of European contact were anything but hostile. In fact, as the Spanish explorer Father Silvestre Velez de Escalante put it, "We found them all very simple, docile, gentle and affectionate."

These were the Shoshoneans, whose cul-

Why "Utah's Dixie"?

As the Mormons arrived in the valley of the Great Salt Lake in the late 1840s, church leader Brigham Young began sending exploring parties throughout the Great Basin in search of the best sites for settlement. His plan was to build a self-sufficient "Kingdom of God" that would allow his people to live in peace and safety.

In 1854, Jacob Hamblin, Ira Hatch, Amos Thornton, A.P. Hardy, Thales Haskell and Samuel Knight were the first Mormon missionaries working among the Native Americans along the Santa Clara River. They started a settlement at Santa Clara, but Hamblin became very ill during winter. Hardy was sent by horseback to the established settlement of Parowan for medicine and food. On his return he also brought a quart of cottonseed tied in a cloth (a gift from Sister Nancy Anderson, a convert from Tennessee) with the suggestion that the missionaries try growing it.

This they did, clearing a small piece of land and planting the seed carefully, one in a hill. The cotton grew and produced beyond belief. When the first pods exploded into a handful of snowy puff, they were sent to Brigham Young in Salt Lake City.

Photo: Nick Adams

The word "Dixie" has been painted on the red bluff north of downtown for as long as anyone can remember.

In the spring of 1857, 28 families led by Robert Dockery Covington settled the town of Washington, just east of what would later become St. George. Covington had been a cotton grower in Mississippi before joining the Mormons and coming west, and most of the rest of the company were from the southern states as well. After a season or two of failure the settlers began to grow excellent cotton, and a mill was built in Washington. With the outbreak of the Civil War in the east and the difficulty of obtaining cotton through traditional sources, the cotton industry thrived in Southwestern Utah.

It was only natural that folks started calling the place "Utah's Dixie." This was the southern region of Mormon colonization. The climate was warmer here. The north was enjoying an ample supply of cotton, grapes and peaches produced here. Southerners from the "real" Dixie had settled here. And, more subtly, because of its isolation from the north and the difficulty of surviving here, residents of the southern part of Utah had developed a distinct sense of pride and even a bit of rebelliousness. The name Dixie fit perfectly and it has stuck for more than 135 years.

Above the Crowd!

Steve A. Vlassek
Broker-Owner

Irma Lookermans, Steve Vlassek, Annette Humphrey,
Linda Johnson, Milli Bowen, Joe Campbell, Bonny Cochrane.
Not Pictured - Jim Wentz.

RE/MAX opened it's Hurricane office in 1992. All agents live in the
Hurricane area and know first hand why it is so great living there.
RE/MAX Realty Resources has five professional agents who average
over ten years of experience.
RE/MAX is an international company with over 45,000 agents in more
than 2800 offices. They have always been ranked among the top Real
Estate Companies in the World. Experienced agents offering professional
service is what RE/MAX is all about.

RE/MAX Realty Resources

535 West State Street
Hurricane, Utah 84737
Office: (801) 635-9414
Fax: (801) 635-9815
Toll Free: 1-800-690-9414

REALTOR **MLS**

Each Office Independently Owned and Operated

ture appeared on the landscape of present-day Utah just as those of the Fremont and Anasazi were disappearing. They most likely came from the southwest and settled into a lifestyle of hunting and gathering similar to the Fremont and Archaic peoples who preceded them. They subsisted on roots, seeds and insects, with a particular affection for pinyon nuts that could be stored and used for winter food. They caught fish and small animals and raised corn, squash and beans.

Though they were perceived as simple by early European observers, the Shoshoneans were adept at surviving in a most inhospitable land. They had the bow and arrow, and they made pottery and baskets. Some lived in pit houses like the Fremont, others built brush shelters called wickiups, and some used caves as they moved along their annual migrations.

Living in small family bands, the Shoshonean people had little tribal organization. It appears they lived peacefully for the most part, striving as best they could to survive in a harsh desert environment.

Today we divide the Shoshonean, or Numic, peoples into four groups that inhabited the Utah area at the time of European contact. They are the Shoshone in the north and northeast, the Gosiutes in the northwest, the Utes in the central and eastern parts of the region and the Southern Paiutes in the southwest. These groups had lived a stable life for more than 300 years before the mounted Spanish Europeans moved north from their bases in Mexico.

Until the arrival of European Americans, the Southern Paiutes were linguistically and culturally very similar to their Ute relatives to the north. That all changed when the Utes embraced the horse, introduced by the Spanish. The Utes mixed a high degree of horsemanship into their culture. As time passed, this would give them the upper hand and allow them to emerge as the dominant culture in Utah when Escalante and Father Francisco Atanasio Dominguez arrived in 1776.

During many years preceding white settlement of Utah, the Utes asserted their dominance over the meeker Gosiutes and Southern Paiutes by raiding their camps and taking slaves.

Arrival of the Spanish

Spanish explorers were the first known Europeans to walk the region that became Utah. Though they left no permanent settlements in Utah, they created an important chapter in our early history and left many names upon the landscape.

Motivated by the hope of finding rich lands and civilized peoples whose wealth they could take, along with a desire to convert the native inhabitants to Christianity, the Spanish moved north from Mexico establishing cities, missions and forts to protect their holdings. Spanish settlements were founded in New Mexico as early as 1593, a few years later than the doomed Lost Colonists of North Carolina's Roanoke Island, but 14 years before the English established Jamestown, Virginia. In fact, the Spanish had explored most of the southwestern part of what is now the United States before any English explorer arrived in America.

It was the penetration of the Spanish into Utah that gave us our first written descriptions of this land, and they are the ones who first began to map it. We still follow many of their trails today as our modern highways snake through the canyons, draws and flats they traversed three centuries ago.

Cabeza de Vaca and a few companions made their way along the coast to Texas in 1527. They passed through part of the Southwest and back to Mexico. Stories began to circulate in Mexico about the "Seven Cities of Cibola." In 1539, one of de Vaca's companions found six villages of Zuni pueblos near present-day Gallup, New Mexico. The next year a major expedition led by Francisco Vasquez Coronado set out to the north but found no riches to compare with those of Mexico and Peru. A small group of explorers dispatched by Coronado and led by Garcia Lopez de Cardenas pushed on to the northwest and, while disappointed to find only more poor Pueblos, this group did work far enough north to discover the Grand Canyon, about 50 miles south of the present-day Utah border.

A 1686 report told of Teguayo, a land west of the Colorado mountains where Native American tribes lived around a lake, most likely referring to Utah Lake in present day Utah County. But it wasn't until 1765 that a party led by Juan Maria Antonio Rivera explored the Colorado River and entered what would one day be known as Utah.

The Spanish need for a new route to deliver supplies and help fortify their interests in California prompted the famous Dominguez and Escalante expedition — a mission that began in the same month and year the Declaration of Independence was signed by British colonists in the East.

Led by the Catholic priests Dominguez and Escalante, who kept the important diary of the expedition, the undertaking did not meet its original goal of establishing a route from Santa Fe to Monterey. It did, however, establish the beginning of the written history of what is now Southwestern Utah and became a monumental reference for future explorers and settlers.

Setting out on July 29, 1776, the expedition entered today's Utah on September 11, passing about a mile south of the dinosaur quarry of the present Dinosaur National Monument. They followed the Duchesne River westward through the Uintah Basin, then crossed over into the Strawberry Valley and through the Wasatch Mountains by way of Spanish Fork Canyon.

They pressed westward toward Monterey but soon cut south as they searched for a western pass. By early October discouragement began to set in. Mountains in all directions were covered with snow, and a sharp north wind blew constantly. With provisions dwindling and the early winter already set upon them, they decided to return to Santa Fe, pushing southward through present-day Southwestern Utah, encountering bands of Southern Paiute along the Virgin River and other places.

They moved quickly southward from what we now call Escalante Valley and passed into present Cedar Valley, then southward through present Kanarraville, Pintura, Toquerville, La Verkin and Hurricane. On October 15 the expedition crossed today's southern boundary of Utah.

They would jut back into Utah again east of present Kanab and once more along the ledges of Glen Canyon where they finally found a place to cross the Colorado River at Padre Creek. From there they returned to Santa Fe, completing a journey of nearly 2,000 miles.

Though their political mission to open a land route to Monterey was a failure, Dominguez and Escalante felt their expedition was well-justified, as noted in their diary, "in having discovered such a great deal of country and people so well disposed to be easily gathered into the Lord's vineyard and to the realms of his majesty."

But it would be another three-quarters of a century before Anglo settlers would come to live permanently among the Utes. They, too, would be interested in teaching Christianity to the Native Americans, but the names they would place upon the land would come from a book called the *Book of Mormon*, and instead of building missions, they would erect buildings called temples.

The Old Spanish Trail

Spain's power in the new world began to fade after Dominguez and Escalante's sojourn

Survival in Panguitch

The original pioneer company that settled Panguitch in 1864 suffered an extremely cold and snowy winter its first year. People were shut in with little to eat and no flour mill

closer than Parowan, 40 miles over the terrible Bear Valley road. Seven men left Panguitch headed to Parowan for flour and food for their starving families. They had two yoke of oxen and a light wagon but had to abandon both at the head of Bear Valley and proceed on foot. The only way they could make progress was to lay a quilt down to pack the snow and ice down, and walk to the end of it, then lay down another, one after another. In this way they finally reached Parowan and secured the foodstuffs that saved their families.

in the wilderness in 1776. Her possessions in North America fell to revolutionaries who created the independent country of Mexico in 1821. Mexico opened its doors to international commerce in North America, and commercial traffic over the Santa Fe Trail between the United States and New Mexico began in 1822. Wool and textiles produced in New Mexico were traded for horses and mules in California.

With this awakening of international trade, another route called the Spanish Trail was opened in 1829. Commercial goods began to flow from New Mexico to California and back across this trail that made a significant sweep through what would later become Utah. It was a horse and mule trail connecting Santa Fe and Los Angeles, and pack trains as much as a mile long made the trip in about two-and-a-half months each way. Herds with as many as 2,000 animals were driven back to New Mexico from California. Along the way traders sometimes took slaves from the Paiute Indians living in Southwestern Utah. Those slaves were sold in New Mexico and California.

For nearly 20 years the trail was used by traders, trappers, Native Americans and settlers. By pushing northward as far as Green River, Utah, those who used the trail avoided the impassable canyons of the Colorado River and the more hostile tribes in Arizona. By 1848, when Mexico lost the region of the Spanish Trail to the United States, overland travel began to take a more direct east-west route, and the old trail faded as a trade route.

Much of the Old Spanish Trail can be followed today on modern highways. The trail came into Utah from Colorado near present day Monticello, crossed the Colorado River at Moab and the Green at Green River. From Castle Dale it curved southwestward through Salina to Parowan, New Castle, Mountain Meadows and down the Santa Clara River, leaving Utah at Castle Cliff, southwest of St.

George. From there it continued across the deserts of Nevada and California.

The trail is a subtle reminder of the Spanish and Mexican influence that was once paramount in Utah, an influence still recalled by names such as Escalante, Virgin and Santa Clara. The names remained, but the Spanish never came back to stay. A century later the map would be covered with new names such as Nephi, Moroni and Brigham.

Mountain Men and Explorers

It could be said that fashion played an important role in Utah's beginnings. One of the quirks of history that helped form the Utah we know today was the popularity in the early part of the 19th century of hats made of beaver fur. The potential of harvesting beaver lured an onslaught of European-American trappers, traders, mountain men and explorers to the western Rockies in the early 1800s. They explored the rivers, streams, valleys, mountain ranges and deserts. They discovered the passes through the mountains, found the Native American trails that would later become roads and highways and established contacts with the Indians, making things easier for later settlers. They drew maps, established posts and generally opened the way for the future.

At the same time Spanish traders were moving east and west along the Old Spanish Trail, fur trappers were working their way into the northern mountains of Utah. They came not only to earn the profits yielded by beaver pelts but to establish a toehold on the land for their respective countries. British and French-Canadian trappers descended from the north, American mountain men pressed in from the east, while French and Spanish traders came out of the south from Santa Fe and Taos.

James Clyman, Jedediah Smith, John H. Weber and Jim Bridger are just a few of the names that formed the roster of the Ashley-Henry fur trapping outfit, names which would live on through the decades in official reports, in stories told around the campfire and, finally, in history books.

Among the best-known and respected of the American mountain men — those men living in the wilderness who were not Native Americans — was Jedediah Strong Smith. In 1826, he attended the mountain man rendezvous held at the southern end of Cache Valley near present-day Hyrum, 400 miles north of what is now St. George. Perhaps it was at this meeting that Smith found the urge to do some exploring of his own, with the particular idea of finding a river to the Pacific.

Leaving the trapping life behind, Smith headed south in 1826 down a route close to today's U.S. Highway 89, then west to the Virgin River. He was probably the first white man to pass through the valley of St. George (Dominguez and Escalante did not make it quite that far west) and the lower reaches of the Santa Clara. The following year, with a group of 18 explorers, Smith passed through Southwestern Utah again.

During the 1840s, emigrant travel to the West increased significantly. Between the time the fur trade ended and the Mormons arrived, the West saw several companies of immigrants pass through to California and Oregon. Much of this activity was made possible by two major explorations of Utah by John C. Fremont. His work helped transform the trader trails into roads, opening travel through the Salt Lake Valley.

The detailed notes of Fremont's two expeditions through Utah in 1843 and 1844 were published in 1845. This widely circulated volume described his adventures in what he named the Great Basin. Perhaps its most lasting impact was the influence it had on a man named Brigham Young and other leaders of a newly organized church who were considering a move west from Nauvoo, Illinois.

The Coming of the Saints

In the spring of 1820, at the same time mountain men were working their way into the wilds of northern Utah, a 14-year-old boy went into a grove of trees near his home in upstate New York to pray. As trappers in search of beaver moved deeper into the mountains of the Wasatch, the boy named Joseph Smith walked into the woods in search of truth. The result of his query led to a series of religious experiences culminating in the publication of the *Book of Mormon* in February of 1830 and the organization of the Church of Jesus Christ of Latter-Day Saints on April 6 of the same year. At the time, no one could have imagined the impact these events would have on the eventual settlement of the American West, and more specifically on the place that would one day become Utah.

From its beginnings, the Church of Jesus Christ of Latter-day Saints was the object of intense persecution. Part of this was no doubt based on the fact that such a young man had claimed that he had seen God and that truths had been revealed to him. The church's members, known then as they are now by the nickname of Mormons, moved west from New York to Kirtland, Ohio, in the spring of 1831, and to Jackson County, Missouri, in the summer of the same year. For seven years, the Ohio and Missouri phases of Mormon settlement proceeded simultaneously.

Even during those early days of the church in Kirtland, Joseph Smith was telling his people their future lay "in the regions westward." Yet the growing body of the church could have scarcely realized at that point how far west they would ultimately be forced to go.

In the mid-1830s, troubles with non-Mormon neighbors escalated in Missouri until the Mormons were pushed out of Jackson County at gunpoint. They moved in state to Clay County, then to Caldwell County. Meanwhile,

INSIDERS' TIP

St. George's best-kept historical secret is the Daughters of Utah Pioneers Museum at 155 N. 100 East. Plan on spending at least an hour there.

This Thing Called Polygamy

Throughout the history of the Church of Jesus Christ of Latter-day Saints the subject of polygamy has been a burning issue. During the early 1840s the church's founder, Joseph Smith, at first privately advocated the practice of plural marriage, calling it a "most holy and important doctrine," and teaching that a "fullness of exaltation" in the hereafter could not be reached without obedience to the principle.

After Smith's martyrdom in Illinois in 1844, a small group of church leaders who had been entrusted with the teaching of polygamy continued to practice it. When the Latter-day Saints came to Utah in 1847, this group formed the nucleus of leadership for the colonization of the Great Basin. Here, they hoped to practice their religion free of persecution. But even in such a far-flung place they could not escape public outcry when the church officially announced its advocacy of polygamy in 1852.

Close-up

Public protest, manifested especially in Eastern newspapers, and government pressure continued for four decades before Mormon president Wilford Woodruff issued a public announcement in 1890 advising church members against new plural marriages. Though the announcement opened the way for Utah to receive statehood in 1896, polygamy continued covertly until 1904 when LDS President Joseph F. Smith authorized the excommunication of all who continued the practice.

Early Southern Utah pioneer Dudley Leavitt with two of his wives. (They were sisters.)

Photo: Courtesy Lynne Clark Collection, donated by Nellie Gubler

Because of its relative isolation, Southwestern Utah became a refuge for polygamous Mormon men who spent much of their time evading federal authorities. Many of the fifth- and sixth-generation Mormons who live here today are descendents of polygamous great-grandparents. They accept the practice as a historical reality but repudiate it in modern times. Polygamy is emphatically not a part of the modern Mormon religion, and those who continue to practice it have no tie to the official church.

But there are those who still have plural marriages. The practice continues among different groups that broke off from the church decades ago, do not use the church name and don't consider themselves Mormons. Communities such as Hildale and Colorado City on the Utah-Arizona state line 50 miles east of St. George openly live the principle of plural marriage. They live in relative peace, with little harassment by government bodies.

problems developed in Ohio, and threats were made forcing Joseph Smith and others to flee to Missouri.

In 1838, conflict again developed in Missouri, and Gov. Lilburn W. Boggs issued an order giving Mormons no option but to leave the state. The prejudice against the Mormons had become rooted in the believers' efforts to monopolize the land in the area in order to build a self-sufficient "Kingdom of God," which was offensive in the eyes of other citizens and churches.

Also, because of their growing numbers, Mormons were becoming a strong political force. Missourians did not want them to control elections in the counties where they resided, and they let this be known. Soon, the Mormons moved east across the Mississippi to Quincy, Illinois. In spring 1839, Joseph Smith began purchasing land along a big bend of the Mississippi River. There the continually growing group of Mormons established Nauvoo, Illinois, as its new headquarters.

At Nauvoo, a new practice introduced among the Mormons called plural marriage, whereby one man could have multiple wives, added fuel to the fires of persecution. An anti-Mormon newspaper, the *Nauvoo Expositor*, took plural marriage to task and its press was ordered destroyed by the Mormon-controlled town council. This brought about the arrest of Joseph Smith and his brother Hyrum, and the two were killed by a vigilante mob while in custody at Carthage Jail near Nauvoo on June 27, 1844. At that point, leadership of the LDS Church fell upon the church's Quorum of the Twelve Apostles, with Brigham Young as its head.

Mob persecution of the Mormons in Nauvoo continued through 1844 and 1845 until, finally, in February of 1846, they fled the city they'd built on an unwanted swamp and crossed the Mississippi River into Iowa. Church leaders had announced plans to leave in the spring, but mob pressures increased, forcing the wagons to depart earlier than planned. Inadequate provisions and freezing weather turned the trek into a journey of suffering for many and death for some.

The advance company led by Brigham Young reached the Missouri River in mid-June of 1846. By April 1847, when the pioneer company was ready to begin the move to Utah, more than 10,000 Mormons were living in temporary dugouts and log cabins in Iowa and Nebraska.

Meanwhile, 238 Mormons living in the eastern states had set sail from New York to San Francisco. Rounding the horn of South America, they arrived safely in California and began an agricultural colony near present-day Modesto. Their leader, Samuel Brannan, rode east to meet Young on his trek west and tried to convince the Mormon leader to bring the main company of Mormons on to California.

Young's decision not to take the Mormons to California was difficult for many followers to understand. From a temporal standpoint, California offered much more potential than the Great Basin. But Young was more interested in the spiritual and social welfare of his people. The Great Basin was a land that no one else wanted. There the Mormons could worship God and establish a unique society that was likely not possible in California. Brannan returned to California, discovered gold at Sutter's Mill, and became wealthy. Meanwhile, the main body of Latter-day Saints stopped at the Valley of the Great Salt Lake, where they would live less than modestly but would finally find relative peace.

Mormon Colonization

The Southwestern Utah we know today is a direct result of Brigham Young's efforts to

Parowan's Evil Waters

The name Parowan is a Paiute Indian word meaning "evil waters." A Paiute legend told to William R. Palmer refers to how the place got its name. One day as the Paiutes were camped along the shores of the Little Salt Lake, a windstorm crossed the lake causing a large monster to rise. The waters from the lake rushed far out onto the shore allowing the monster to grab one of the Paiute maidens and carry her back into the lake. She was never seen again.

Construction of the St. George Temple in the 1870's was a public works project directed by Brigham Young.

establish a Mormon "Kingdom of God" in the West. Within a month of arrival in the Valley of the Great Salt Lake in 1847, "Brother Brigham," as the Mormons called him, sent exploring parties throughout the Great Basin. They were to find every possible spot where water could sustain farms. On each stream in this barren land he intended to establish a mini-Nauvoo, pre-empting the land by virtue of settlement. It was hoped the Mormons would never again be a persecuted minority.

The Mormons got off to a good start with the American Indians of the Great Basin. As exploring parties pushed in every direction, they shared freely of their sustenance with the native inhabitants and cultivated an amiable relationship. Late in 1849, Parley P. Pratt led an expedition to the south looking for potential settlement sites. During the hard winter, they passed over much of the same country crossed by Dominguez and Escalante in 1776 and Jedediah Smith in 1826 and 1827. They

explored the area of Parowan and Cedar City, where they discovered a rich deposit of iron ore, then crossed over the southern rim of the Great Basin into country that would later become known as Utah's Dixie.

During the summer of 1850, plans were laid for colonizing the newly created Iron County, with the seat at Center Creek, later called Parowan. After the harvest in 1850, colonists in the north were "called" by Mormon leaders to settle the region. The group formed in mid-December in Provo under the leadership of George A. Smith and traveled south for nearly a month over a wretched, snow-covered course.

Mormon villages such as the one established at Parowan and thereafter at Cedar City were the result of a conscious plan and not an accident of geography. As historian Douglas Alder states it, "They were the embodiment of a set of convictions the settlers brought with them to the Rocky Mountains. Brigham Young had watched Joseph Smith design his 'City of Zion' at Nauvoo, Illinois. There he witnessed the prophet's concept of community come to fruition. When Young led the Mormons into the Great Basin he had the imprint of Nauvoo with its communal spirit on his mind. He was convinced that living in Zion was as much a group experience as one dependent on individual initiative. . . . This vision of Zion was an inheritance from Joseph Smith, with some influence from the early New England village."

Colonizers were selected from among those already living in the Salt Lake City area or Mormon emigrants just arriving themselves. Those called represented the various trades, skills and talents needed to establish a community — from shoemakers to blacksmiths to musicians. Most church members responded as if their move was a commandment of God.

By 1853, villages of adobe homes and farms had been established at Parowan, Paragonah and Cedar City. Parowan became the "mother town" for most of the subsequent settlements in Southwestern Utah, including Panguitch to the east in the 1860s. In Cedar City the pioneers built a blast furnace to manufacture much-needed iron. Despite its initial success, the Iron Mission faced many difficulties. Troubles with Native Americans, floods, heavy freezes and furnace failure took a toll. In addition, a crop shortage threatened starvation in those early years. The people persevered and eventually prospered, but the iron industry died out in the late 1850s. You can experience the entire story at the Iron Mission State Park in Cedar City (see our Attractions chapter).

Establishment of Utah's Dixie

In the fall of 1851, a party of Mormons pushed south from Salt Lake City under the leadership of John D. Lee with the intention of settling on the Virgin or Santa Clara rivers. Before arriving, however, they got word from Young that they should remain in the Iron County settlements until a period of missionary work among the Southern Paiutes could be completed. In the fall of 1852, Lee and several others settled a place called Harmony, 25 miles south of Cedar City, and a school was established there.

Meanwhile, missionaries had gone south among the Native Americans and began to establish a good relationship with the Southern Paiute Tonaquints and Parusits living along the Santa Clara and Virgin. During the summer of 1854, the Harmony settlers found a better location a few miles upstream on Ash Creek, moved there, built a fort and called it New Harmony.

It was finally determined that a settlement was needed on the Santa Clara where the missionaries could live among the Native Americans. In December 1854, this settlement was started near what is now the town of Santa Clara, and missionaries helped the Native Americans construct substantial dams and ditches for diverting irrigation water.

The Santa Clara area, more connected to the Mojave Desert than the Great Basin, was significantly lower in altitude than other Mormon villages in Utah. The missionaries discovered a longer, warmer growing season, and the idea of producing cotton caught hold. With the first crop planted in 1855 along the Santa Clara, the cotton culture of Southwestern Utah began.

In the spring of 1857, 28 families went to the Virgin River to undertake cotton production on a larger scale. These were mostly converts from the American South who had grown cotton all their lives, hence the quick dubbing of the area as Dixie. They settled the town of Washington.

In May of 1861, Brigham Young made his

first visit to the Dixie settlements. Near the confluence of the Virgin and the Santa Clara, close to the present-day Southgate Golf Course, he stopped his carriage and looked north. His gaze swept the valley bordered on the east and west by lava-capped ridges and the north by red bluffs and the tall blue mound of Pine Valley Mountain. As he stood there he uttered these words: "There will yet be built between those volcanic ridges a city with spires, towers and steeples; with homes containing many inhabitants."

The land he surveyed was nothing but an alkali flat. Today, the scene from where he stood looks almost exactly the way he said it would.

St. George and the Drag-on

Charles L. Walker, an English convert to the Mormon church and early pioneer of St. George, wrote the following song during the 1860s. It was sung at a concert in the St. George Hall during one of Brigham Young's visits, and illustrates the sense of humor it took to survive in such an isolated desert.

Oh, what a desert place was this
When first the Mormons found it;
They said no white men here could live
And Indians prowled around it.
They said the land it was no good,
And the water was no gooder,
And the bare idea of living here,
Was enough to make men shudder.

(Chorus)
Mesquite, soap root, prickly-pears and briars,
St. George ere long will be a place
That everyone admires.

Now green lucerne in verdant spots
Bedecks our thriving city,
Whilst vines and fruit trees grace our lots,
With flowers sweet and pretty.
Where once the grass in single blades
Grew a mile apart in distance,
And it kept the crickets on the go,
To pick up their subsistence.

(Chorus)

The sun it is so scorching hot,
It makes the water siz, Sir.
The reason why it is so hot,
Is just because it is, Sir.
The wind like fury here does blow,
That when we plant or sow, Sir,
We place one foot upon the seed,
And hold it till it grows, Sir.

And Young helped the prophecy along. Under the direction of Mormon apostle Erastus Snow, he sent 309 families to settle the St. George Valley late in 1861. Meanwhile, a company of Swiss converts had settled in Santa Clara, and a cotton mill was built in Washington. Though many years of poverty and struggle lay ahead, Utah's Dixie was on its way to becoming what its adopted poet laureate, Charles Walker, described as a place that "'ere long people will admire."

As the Civil War ignited in the east, the Mormons felt secure in their self-sufficiency, especially now that they could produce their own cotton, grapes and other tropical crops. But as the war ended, cotton became more accessible and affordable from the southern states, and Utah's cotton industry in Dixie faded the same way the iron industry faded in Cedar City.

To help the settlers survive the early years of scarcity, Young devised public works projects to build a tabernacle and a temple in St. George. Church members in better-established areas provided foodstuffs and other necessary commodities to the Dixie pioneers that worked in construction of the buildings. The result was the survival of the communities along the Virgin and Santa Clara rivers and the completion of two marvelous buildings that stand today.

Exceptions to the Village

Not all Southwestern Utahns lived in Mormon villages, though most did. Farming had to be supplemented with ranching, and herds began to be grazed on the vast open ranges. Some stock-raising families kept homes in town as well as at the ranch. Another option was for one polygamous family to split between the ranch and town. They lived at such places as the Canaan Ranch, a church-owned cooperative near Pipe Spring, and at Terry's Ranch near Hebron and present-day Enterprise. Southwestern Utah families also began the rich ranching tradition on the Arizona strip south of Kanab, Hurricane and St. George.

Silver Reef was one of the few exceptions to the pattern of Mormon villages in Southwestern Utah. For a decade in the 1880s it had several saloons, a hospital, a Catholic church, rooming houses, a theater and many mills for processing the abundant silver ore discovered in sandstone there.

More than 1,000 people lived in this rip-roaring mining town. Surprisingly, only about half of them were single men. Still, it was the polar opposite of the nearby Mormon villages of Leeds, Harrisburg and Toquerville. Silver Reef's unbridled lifestyle was repugnant to the Mormons, but the cash flow it generated was not. For more than a decade, Mormon farmers from Southwestern Utah settlements peddled their produce to the miners and finally began to thrive.

On to Kanab

Just as settlement of Iron County had been the stepping stone to settlement of Utah's Dixie, the villages on the Virgin and Santa Clara rivers became stepping stones for opening up Kane County and the Kaibab area of northern Arizona to the LDS Church. As Jacob Hamblin began excursions to the east to do missionary work among the Hopi and the Navajo, the way opened to settle Kanab.

Settlement along Kanab Creek began as early as 1858, yet the town site was not officially laid out under the direction of Brigham Young until 1870. Early on there was conflict between the native Kaibab Paiutes and the first Mormons, but relations improved and the pioneers retained the Paiute name for the place in the anglicized form of the word Kanaw, meaning "willows."

In the winter of 1865, Mormon settlers, together with volunteers from Santa Clara and Washington and a few friendly Paiutes, joined to construct Fort Kanab. Roughly chinked log walls and a willow-mud plastered ceiling prompted one occupant to comment in his journal, "When it rained water outside, it rained mud inside."

Today two plaques are set in a monument at the site of the old fort. One honors pioneer-explorer Jacob Hamblin for his efforts in diplomacy with the Native Americans and colonization of Kanab. The other is a tribute to Kanab's first Mormon bishop, Levi Stewart, who lost his wife and five sons in a tragic explosion that set fire to the fort in 1870.

During the early to mid-1870s, Major John

Wesley Powell used Kanab for his headquarters as he compiled the findings of his historic geographical survey of the area. Powell was also assisted by Hamblin, whose knowledge of the region and rapport with the Indians helped make it possible for the first detailed map of the Grand Canyon area to be created.

Since those historic days in Kanab, both Hamblin and Powell have become larger-than-life figures in the history of the Southwest. Powell is known and revered among canyon enthusiasts as the first to traverse the length of the Grand Canyon by boat in 1869, and Hamblin has been mythicized as the key figure in opening the way for white settlement among the native inhabitants of southern Utah and northern Arizona.

For decades after settlement, Kanab depended chiefly upon ranching and farming for its subsistence. Cattle and sheep ranches thrived on the open ranges to the south and mountain pastures to the north.

In the 1920s and '30s, another natural resource began to be explored in Kanab. It had been staring residents in the face from the beginning, but no one realized it until a few visionaries came up with the idea of promoting the area's scenery as a backdrop for movies.

Kanab's illustrious era as a favorite movie location for Hollywood producers coincided with its transition into a tourist town. Local ranchers became wranglers and stunt riders for the movies, and local entrepreneurs established lodging and catering businesses that continue today. During the heyday of the western, Kanab became Utah's "Little Hollywood" and established a reputation for western hospitality.

A visit to any business along Kanab's main drive will yield a few stories about what movie star ate there, slept there or posed for a picture. Lobby walls are covered with signed black-and-whites of John Wayne, Clint Eastwood, Barbara Stanwyck and Raquel Welch. Most everyone who lived in Kanab during the 1940s, '50s and early 1960s has a story of how they rode as a stunt double, delivered lunches or cleaned rooms for some of the greatest movie legends ever. But as the popularity of westerns waned in Hollywood in the 1970s, so did the movie business windfall in Kanab. Occasionally, producers still use the scenic Kanab area in their films, but it is much less common today.

A Solid Foundation

Each of Southwestern Utah's towns and cities stands on a solid pioneer base. They were settled by faithful adherents to a religion requiring many more life changes than simple attendance at Sunday meetings. They transformed a region no other Anglo settlers were interested in into a place now rated one of the most desirable in America to live in.

For decades they eked out a hardscrabble life. Not until 1896, after polygamy was renounced, was Utah granted statehood. Soon after the turn of the century, a new pioneering effort of reclaiming water with dams and almost-impossible canals — engineering feats that most governments would be unwilling to attempt even today — resulted in such communities as Enterprise and Hurricane. In the 1920s, passable roads began to be built, and the accessibility of the automobile made travel more convenient for many. Gradually, the towering ridges and cavernous canyons of Southwestern Utah became less an obstacle and more an asset to the folks who lived in towns such as Springdale and Tropic.

The magnificent canyon of Zion was declared a national monument in 1909, and brilliant Bryce Canyon to the northeast became a national park in 1928. The north rim of one of the world's greatest wonders, the Grand Canyon, was just 80 miles away. The world began

---

INSIDERS' TIP

The idea of wintering in St. George isn't new. Brigham Young, whose primary residence was in cold Salt Lake City 325 miles north, built a home in St. George where he spent the last several winters of his life. You can visit the beautifully restored home year-round at the corner of 200 North and 100 West.

Photo: Iron Co.

Pioneer wagons and implements are displayed at Iron Mission State Park in Cedar City.

to discover Southwestern Utah, and those who had settled here began to discover the world. Though geography kept the railroad from making it to St. George, Interstate 15 was completed through the Virgin River Gorge in 1973, and a new flowing artery to the world was opened.

Colleges were established in Cedar City and St. George. Bright green golf courses began appearing among the red rocks of Dixie, and a world-class Shakespearean festival emerged in Cedar City. Retirees discovered the relative quiet and beauty of the area. They began to perceive a certain spirit about the place — a spirit founded in the values implanted here by the pioneers and carried on by modern-day Mormons (who still comprise more than 70 percent of the population) and members of more than a dozen other faiths that have established places of worship and strong followings.

The temperate weather and clear air also helped. Seniors began to shun the retirement cities of Florida and Arizona for the peaceful neighborhoods in developments called Bloomington, Green Valley and Kanab Ranchos. Panguitch, where farms and ranches still thrive in a verdant mountain valley, became the jumping-off point for great fishing at Panguitch Lake and touring to the wonders of Bryce Canyon National Park and the wild, backland canyons of the Escalante.

The story that began a billion years ago continues today. It is the landscape — the canyons, rivers, mountains and ridges — that started the story eons ago and continues to shape it.

Wanna Read More?

If you're interested in reading more about the long and colorful history of Southwestern Utah, here are some good titles to help get you started.

I Was Called to Dixie, by Andrew Karl Larson

The Red Hills of November, by Andrew Karl Larson

Golden Nuggets of Pioneer Days: A History of Garfield County, compiled by Daughters of Utah Pioneers

Quicksand and Cactus, by Juanita Brooks

The Giant Joshua (novel), by Maurine Whipple

Land of Living Rock, by C. Gregory Crampton

From Isolation to Destination: A History of Washington County, by Karl Brooks and Douglas Alder

Diary of Charles Lowell Walker, edited by Andrew Karl Larson

The Dominguez-Escalante Journal, edited by Ted J. Warner

Silver, Sinners and Saints: A History of Silver Reef, Utah, by Paul Dean Proctor and Morris A. Shirts

Why the North Star Stands Still (Indian legends), by William R. Palmer

Brigham Young: American Moses, by Leonard J. Arrington

Mormon Country, by Wallace Stegner

St. George is home to the corporate headquarters for SkyWest, the ninth-largest regional airline in the country.

Getting Here, Getting Around

Getting to Southwestern Utah is simple. Just find Interstate 15 or U.S. Highway 89 and follow the parade of cars, RVs, shuttle and tour buses, motor homes and moving vans. You will know you have reached your destination when the vehicles ahead begin to exit into Cedar City — called one of America's 10 most livable communities (see our Area Overviews chapter) — and St. George, 50 miles to the south, named the best place in the West to retire by *Money* magazine.

In the beginning, residents of these remote desert communities came reluctantly. Many of the first pioneers to Southwestern Utah had just begun to settle into their new life at their "Zion" in the valley of the Great Salt Lake when Brigham Young instructed them to pack their meager belongings and head south.

What began in isolation is now a destination.

Getting around in Southwestern Utah is best done by car, but the area is accessible by air and bus line. In fact, St. George is home to the corporate headquarters for SkyWest, a major regional airline. There is no rail service, and there is no public transportation except for a few relatively new taxi services in St. George and Cedar City. Several of the smaller area airports, as well as those in Salt Lake City and Las Vegas, offer rental cars.

By Car

Major Roadways

St. George is about 325 miles south of Salt Lake City on I-15. The interstate also con-nects Southwestern Utah with Las Vegas (125 miles southwest) and Southern California (it's about 400 miles from St. George to Los Angeles). Interstate 70 joins I-15 about 125 miles north of St. George and provides a direct route east to Denver, which is approximately 500 miles from downtown St. George. Running from the southwest corner to the northern border of Utah, a trip on I-15 is a state-long journey filled with spectacular landscapes and friendly communities, all taken in at 75 miles per hour.

On the east side of the Pavant Mountain range, U.S. 89 — a two-lane highway with a varying speed limit that tops out at 55 — runs parallel to I-15 through Southwestern Utah. At the Arizona border north of Flagstaff, U.S. 89 cuts through Kanab and Panguitch (both about 90 miles away from St. George), connects briefly with I-70 then continues north to Salt Lake City and the Idaho border.

For the traveler in no hurry, a trip on U.S. 89, with its slower pace and beautiful scenery along the meandering Sevier River, is a beautiful option for relaxing travel. U.S. 89 is the main thoroughfare through Kanab and Panguitch.

Scenic Byways and Backways

Utah was one of the first states to implement a scenic byway program and make it work. In 10 years, the program has enhanced and improved area roads and signage, created pull-outs to walk the dog or let the kids stretch their legs and provided erosion control along 27 designated byways. A combined effort by several dozen agencies including the Bureau of Land Management, U.S. Forest Service, Utah Travel Council, state parks, counties and towns, the scenic byways program is paid for with federal funding.

Requirements for qualification as a scenic byway are based on safety and beauty from the road. The goal of the program is to get travelers to leave interstates and see the wonder of Utah up close and personally. Following are brief descriptions of the scenic byways that crisscross Southwestern Utah. Many of these roads provide access from the area's two major arteries (I-15 and U.S. 89) to the smaller communities in the region.

FYI

Unless otherwise noted, the area code for all phone numbers listed in this chapter is 801 but will change to 435 in September 1997. Either area code may be used until March 22, 1998.

Scenic Utah Byway 9

This 54-mile byway passes Quail Creek Reservoir, climbs to the crest of Hurricane Cliffs and provides a sweeping view of the Pine Valley Mountains. It is accessed by taking Exit 16 off I-15. On the way to Zion National Park (this route is also known as the Zion Park Scenic Byway), travelers on Utah 9 will catch a glimpse of Grafton, a ghost town where *Butch Cassidy and the Sundance Kid* was filmed (see our Attractions chapter). At the south entrance to Zion, Utah 9 connects with a 6-mile scenic drive through the park then continues eastward, traversing a unique landscape of petrified sandstone mounds to the park's east entrance and the junction of U.S. 89 at Mt. Carmel. Continue another 18 miles, and you will find yourself in Kanab. According to the Utah Department of Transportation, Utah 9 carries 12,000 vehicles a day, making this stretch of highway one of the most heavily traveled in the state.

Scenic Utah Byway 12

Scenic Utah Byway 12 offers a spectacular drive through Red Canyon in the Dixie National Forest, between U.S. 89 and Bryce Canyon National Park 13 miles to the east. Motorists will enjoy stunning views from the canyon rim, accessible by driving south on Utah 63 from Utah 12. East of Bryce Canyon, the balance of this 122-mile highway introduces travelers to such natural wonders as Calf Creek Falls Recreation Area and Anasazi Indian State Park (see our Parks and Other Natural Wonders chapter) before Utah 12 crests at Boulder and drops down into the exquisite beauty of Capitol Reef National Park.

Scenic Utah Byway 14

Markaguant (Paiute for "highland of trees") Scenic Utah Byway 14 climbs east from Cedar City. Take Exit 58 off I-15. From there, Utah 14 connects with Utah 148 some 15 miles east of Cedar City near the Cedar Breaks National Monument (see our Parks and Other Natural Wonders chapter). On its way to the 10,000-foot summit at the top of Cedar Mountain, Utah 14 passes through lava flows and extinct volcanos. Continuing east, travelers on the 41-mile byway will encounter Navajo Lake, Duck Creek and other points of interest. The journey ends at Long Valley Junction on U.S. 89.

Scenic Utah Byway 143

This 55-mile byway connects Brian Head and Panguitch Lake. Take Exit 75 off I-15 and follow Utah 143 as it climbs southeast from Parowan, the Iron County seat, past the pink, perpendicular Vermillion Cliffs to the Brian Head Ski Resort (see our Outdoor Recreation

INSIDERS' TIP

Black ice is a treacherous killer on Utah highways. In high mountain areas where the winter sun rises late in the morning or may never warm the highway at all, black ice is patchy. Slow down to stay in control, especially along highways sheltered by the mountains.

chapter). Utah 143 joins Utah Scenic Byway 148 approximately 5 miles south of Brian Head at Cedar Breaks National Monument, offering a look at spectacular alpine stretches in the Dixie National Forest. Utah 143 ends at Panguitch Lake, a popular year-round fishing and recreation area. Note that even the interstate is subject to closure when the snow gets too deep. In the wintertime, a wise traveler will call for road conditions. Statewide info is available by calling (800) 492-2400.

Kanab Scenic Byway

The 60-mile section of U.S. 89 known as Kanab Scenic Byway will take you past numerous movie locations traveling north from the community of Kanab. Travelers will also see the Vermillion Cliffs, Three Lakes Canyon and Coral Pink Sand Dunes State Park (see our Parks and Other Natural Wonders chapter) and behold a glorious view of the White Cliffs and majestic towers of Zion National Park. Actually, Kanab Scenic Byway connects with Utah 9 at Mt. Carmel Junction. From there it's about 24 miles to Zion. Motorists taking this route can expect a trip of at least 90 minutes, depending on the number of photo opportunities seized.

Grid and Bear It: Navigating Utah Streets

Wherever geography will allow, Utah communities are laid out in a grid pattern. Although intimidating at first, the grid system really does make good sense once you have mastered it. In fact, when visitors understand the method behind the seeming madness, most agree it is one of the simplest and most logical plans ever devised.

In 1847, Brigham Young suggested Salt Lake City be built using a grid system with "blocks of 10 acres and streets 8 rods wide running at right angles with twenty feet on each side given to sidewalks." He fashioned this design after already-established American cities in the East. Following this uniform pattern, the standard layout for Mormon villages throughout the Utah Territory included open land for public buildings, uniform spacing and setback for all buildings and a central square of 10 acres. Major streets of 100-foot widths radiate to the north, south, east and west from the central point in each community.

In Salt Lake City, the center point is the LDS Temple. The streets around Temple Square are called, respectively, North Temple, South Temple, East Temple and West Temple. (An address of 50 E. North Temple refers to a building in the middle of the first block east of Temple Square on the street designated as North Temple.)

From there, streets to the north and south of the main street of each village are called First North Street or First South Street, Second North Street or Second South Street, Third North Street or Third South Street and so on. Numerals coincide with these streets and increase in increments of 100, so that First North Street would be 100 North; Third South Street would be 300 South and so on. North and south streets run parallel to each other.

The same pattern is used for streets to the east and west of the center point — First West Street is 100 West, Second East Street is 200 East, Fifth West Street is 500 West, etc. East and west streets also are parallel to each other. Specific locations within city blocks are then identified using grid coordinates — there will always be a north or south street and an east or west street.

The 29-mile section of I-15 linking St. George to the state of Nevada was carved through the Virgin River Gorge, exposing millions of years of geologic layering in 500-foot cliffs created by the cuts. The cost was in excess of $61 million and the project, finished in 1973, took more than a decade to complete. Drill lines through the cliffs are clearly visible as are native mountain sheep and other wildlife.

Great Views

Sky's the Limit for This Airline

The first words that spring to mind when describing Jerry Atkin, president of SkyWest Airlines are not likely to be "tycoon," "mogul" or "power broker." If asked, the adjectives his friends and co-workers might choose to portray the man who has successfully taken his company to the brink of the 21st century might be "family man," "soft-spoken" or "a really nice guy."

Close-up

Atkin, 48, is an executive who believes in family first. He finds pleasure in riding motorcycles with his teenage, identical twin sons. He takes tremendous pride in the accomplishments of his oldest child and only daughter and will tell you, without apology, of the bright future in store for his youngest boy. But, putting aside his clean-cut good looks, boyish charm and pleasant demeanor, no one, except perhaps Jerry, will deny he is the moving force in this company's success story.

SkyWest's meteoric rise to its current ranking as the nation's ninth-largest regional airline was not always smooth. Atkin has experienced his share of white knuckles while at the controls of the company.

In the decade of the '60s, with Bruce Stucki at the helm, Dixie Airlines began to carve a niche in the marketplace by offering round-trip flights from St. George to Las Vegas, Phoenix and Salt Lake City. Six-passenger, twin-engine planes left St. George each Monday, Wednesday and Friday morning, dropping business travelers at their destination then transporting them home again at the end of the day.

The fledgling company was sold to a group of investors in 1969, but when profits failed to materialize, they sold it back in 1972. Stucki, again the owner, sought out local attorney Ralph Atkin and offered the airline to him and his extended family — a collection of Atkin uncles, brothers and cousins. Ralph Atkin was excited about the prospect of success in a rapidly expanding marketplace, but realized the first order of business would be to find a qualified CPA who could help run the company. This slot was filled by his nephew, Jerry Atkin.

By that time, the company had grown to include 20 employees and three nine-passenger, twin-engine planes. Too proud to admit defeat, the Atkinses dug deep into family resources, begging and borrowing from friends, neighbors and anyone with a few dollars and faith in their future. Clayton Atkin, anxious to keep his son nearby, was willing to pump some financial life into the company, but only on the condition Jerry be named president. Looking back, Jerry Atkin admits he was "too broke and too stupid to know I couldn't succeed. The

Photo: The Spectrum

Jerry Atkin has led SkyWest Airlines rise to the nation's ninth-largest regional airline.

— continued on next page

books were a mess. No one wanted the company. We couldn't give it away . . . even for free."

That was then! Today, SkyWest Airlines has 1,100 stockholders and a dynamic board of directors. Two thousand employees serve the needs of travelers in 48 cities in 12 western states. The company is in great financial shape, and the future looks bright, even though fluctuations in the market continue to dictate change to maintain a competitive edge.

The airline currently boasts an impressive 550 flights each day, but growing competition from other airlines, flooding in northern California (which caused the cancellation of hundreds of flights) and fare wars have impacted the company's bottom line. SkyWest recently signed an agreement to be the Continental Airlines connection in Los Angeles, although it will be some time before they can reap the rewards of the move.

The company is systematically reducing the number of metroliners in its fleet, replacing each outdated aircraft with 30-passenger Brasilias and 50-passenger jets in order to vie for the California market, where passengers have alternative flight options that offer stand-up head room. The need to stay competitive resulted last year in a one-time, operating restructuring expense amounting to $6.2 million, or 38¢ per 1996 share. The multimillion dollar price tag on SkyWest's new fleet means net income dropped from $13.7 million in 1995 to $4.3 million in 1996.

As SkyWest adjusts for the future, the company continues to expand their horizons by seeking ways to offer consumers a complete transportation package. Scenic Airlines, a subsidiary, offers tours of the Grand Canyon. Because Scenic Airlines depends on seasonal traffic in a saturated market, SkyWest hasn't seen much profit from this venture. SkyWest is also the holding company for National Parks Transportation Inc., an Avis franchise in five locations (including St. George and Cedar City).

According to the president, the company's goals have not changed since the first SkyWest flight lifted off the runway 24 years ago. "Our objectives are simple . . . we want to be a better company, a better employer and a better investment."

So a typical Utah street address might be 250 W. 2000 South. That would be a home in the middle of the second block west of center and 20 blocks south of center. If you're looking for 500 E. 1150 North, you would be five blocks east of center and between the 11th and 12th blocks north.

This system is used in most Utah communities except where geography is prohibitive. In those towns, city planners are forced to resort to the use of more complicated, confusing street names such as Elm Street, Maple Avenue and Broadway.

Note that the layout in St. George deviates a bit from the norm, as the city's major thoroughfares form a triangle, not a square. The northbound exit off I-15 funnels traffic onto the state highway known as St. George Boulevard, and the southbound exchange delivers travelers to Bluff Street. Red Cliffs Drive, which runs parallel to the interstate, takes shoppers toward bargains at the Zion Factory Stores, Red Cliffs Mall, other retail outlets and restaurants and adjoining neighborhoods in north St. George and Washington. (See our Shopping chapter and our Neighborhoods and Real Estate chapter for more information.) River Road connects downtown St. George to the golf course communities and residential neighborhoods of Bloomington Hills and Bloomington.

By Air

While there are several airport options in Southwestern Utah to accommodate smaller craft, visitors flying by the large commercial carriers will arrive in Southwestern Utah by way of Salt Lake International Airport, 575-2400, or McCarran International Airport in Las Vegas, (702) 261-5743. Salt Lake International is a whole lot of hustle and bustle and everything else a traveler would expect at a facility servicing the "crossroads of the West."

In addition to the big boys (United, Southwest, Delta, America West, Continental, Frontier, Northwest and TWA), SL International has runways specifically designated for all types and styles of smaller aircraft. Several rental car agencies have outlets at the terminal, including Alamo, 575-2211; Avis, 575-2847; Budget, 575-2830; Dollar, 575-2580; Hertz, 575-2683; and National, 575-2277. Thrifty Rent-A-Car, 595-6677, is about 1½ miles off airport property — within a short cab ride or a brisk walk. At SL International you are in close proximity to world-class snow skiing and lots of history, art and culture (see our Daytrips and Weekend Getaways chapter). But you are also 250 to 300 miles away from Southwestern Utah.

McCarran International Airport is 120 miles from the Utah-Arizona border, but the glitz and glitter of downtown Las Vegas — a sharp contrast to the natural beauty of the national and state parks of Southwestern Utah — is a place everyone should experience at least once. Shuttle and taxi services at the airport will transport visitors the 5 miles to and from the Las Vegas Strip, and, more importantly for our purposes, the St. George Shuttle (628-8320) and the Autobus (628-2287) make scheduled trips from Las Vegas to Southwestern Utah. Note that due to crossing from the Pacific to the Mountain time zone, the trip takes three hours from Vegas; one hour to Vegas.

Like the city it serves, McCarran is a pretty flashy airport with neon lights and pop music featuring voiceovers of Las Vegas personalities inviting you to this or that casino. It's all designed to get you into a party mood. Thirty-eight carriers are serviced by two terminals

FYI

Unless otherwise noted, the area code for all phone numbers listed in this chapter is 801 but will change to 435 in September 1997. Either area code may be used until March 22, 1998.

(with additions always under construction) at the ninth-busiest airport in the country. Only the major carriers fly into McCarran. Private planes use nearby Signature Flight Support (formerly Hughes) or Executive Air Terminals, a few blocks away. Private pilots also fly into Sky Harbor Airport at nearby Henderson.

Rental cars are available on-site from Airport Rent-A-Car, (800) 631-8909; Allstate, (702) 736-6147; Budget, (702) 736-1212; Avis, (702) 261-5595; Dollar, (702) 739-8408); Hertz, (702) 736-4900; National, (800) 227-7368; and Sav Mor Rent-A-Car, (702) 736-1234.

St. George/Zion

St. George Municipal Airport
Airport Rd., St. George • 634-3830

On a mesa at an elevation of 2,038 feet, St. George Municipal Airport — about a half-mile from downtown — is headquarters for SkyWest, the nation's ninth-largest regional airline. SkyWest has hubs in Salt Lake City and Los Angeles (see Close-up in this chapter).

The airport accommodates SkyWest's 60 jet and turbo-prop aircraft, including 30-passenger Brasilias, 50-passenger jets and a variety of private and corporate aircraft. The runway is 6,600 feet long. The airport accommodates helicopter activity and air freight companies including FedEx, Airborne Express and Pony Express. Life Flight and Air Ambulance Service also fly into and out of St. George Municipal Airport.

Rental car agents for Avis, 634-3940, and National, 673-5098, are at the airport. In town, there are additional options with ABC Auto Sales and Rent-A-Car, 628-7355; Budget, 673-

Photo: St. George Magazine

Horses are still a viable means of transport in some Southwestern Utah areas.

6825; Dollar, 628-6549; Leasemark, 674-3102; Quality, 634-0090; and Thrifty, 674-2234.

Hurricane Municipal Airport
2300 S. 800 West, Hurricane • 632-4502, 674-1469

Hurricane Municipal Airport is approximately 3 miles south of Utah 9 on 700 West in the city of Hurricane. With a runway length of 3,410 feet, this airport serves light twins, private single-engine aircraft and helicopters flying in on business or for a scenic tour of Zion National Park. Occasional parachute activities

attract enthusiasts, and soaring is available by reservation. Is fuel available? Not yet, but Hurricane Airport can provide minor aircraft maintenance and car rentals with 12 hours advance notice.

Cedar City/Brian Head

Cedar City Municipal Airport
2281 Kittyhawk Dr., Cedar City • 586-3033

Cedar City Municipal Airport is 2 miles west of downtown Cedar City. At an elevation of

INSIDERS' TIP

Visitors from the city may be delighted, but are generally unprepared for the hazards associated with critters grazing along the highway. In areas where open grazing is permitted, frequent accidents occur involving cattle. Large herds of deer cross highways, byways and interstates to forage for food. Bear, mountain lions and other four-legged Utahns can create traffic hazards. Slow down! Enjoy the scenery and the wildlife.

5,623 feet, this mile-high flight center provides air access to the Utah Shakespearean Festival at Southern Utah University in Cedar City and the natural sites in and around Iron County. There is a 7,802-foot runway, and services available include tiedowns and hangars, and 24-hour self-serve fueling. Rental car agencies at Cedar City Airport include Alamo, (800) 327-9633, Avis, (800) 831-2847, and National, 586-7059. Cedar City Cab Company offers cab service at 559-TAXI.

Parowan Airport
Parowan Airport Rd. • 477-8911

The city-owned Parowan Airport can adequately accommodate most turbo-prop and light jet aircraft. North of Parowan at the base of Cedar Mountain, this public airport is a favorite for those flying in for a ski vacation at Brian Head or a summer evening at the Utah Shakespearean Festival.

Parowan Airport is the scene of lots of soaring activity during summer. There are no shuttle services or taxis, but according to the airport manager, he can help you get at least to Brian Head. Parowan Airport offers jet fuel, gas and light engine and aircraft maintenance.

Bryce Canyon Area

Bryce Canyon Airport
450 N. Airport Rd., Bryce • 834-5239, 679-8684

Bryce Canyon Airport is 3 miles north of the national park of the same name. At an elevation of 7,586 feet, the airport's 7,400-foot runway welcomes small business and corporate jets and some 19-passenger commuter planes. Tiedowns, hangars and fuel are available.

Panguitch Municipal Airport
off Riverlake Rd., Panguitch • 676-8585

The Panguitch Municipal Airport is just outside the community of the same name. There are no rental cars, no shuttles, no fuel

and no services, but unscheduled charters, twin-engine and small corporate jets frequent the facility a short distance from Bryce Canyon National Park.

Kanab Area

Kanab Municipal Airport
2370 S. U.S. Hwy. 89A, Kanab • 644-2299

Kanab Municipal Airport gives visitors a bird's-eye view of the "greatest earth on show." On the way to Kanab, most passengers will be treated to a flyover of the Grand Canyon, the Vermillion Cliffs, White Cliffs or Zion National Park. Two miles south of Kanab, the airport is 4,864 feet above sea level and offers a 6,044-foot runway that accommodates twin-engine jets and most turbo-prop aircraft with passenger loads of up to 30. Fuel available to private planes is 100LL, and there is jet fuel from an on-site truck. The airport is equipped for major repairs. Hunt's Rental Car, 644-2370, provides the only rental services in the area, but a courtesy car is available at the airport to transport passengers to Kanab.

Bus Service/ Taxi Service

Greyhound Bus Lines
1235 S. Bluff St., St. George • 673-2933, (800) 231-2222
1355 S. Main St., Cedar City • 586-9465

Greyhound provides ticketed transportation for the communities of St. George, Cedar City and Parowan with reservations available through any travel agent. Greyhound's national reservation service can be reached at (800) 231-2222.

Taxis, Shuttles

Taxi service is relatively new in Southwestern Utah. Dixie Taxi (673-4068), Pete's Taxi (673-5467), or St. George City Cab and Shuttle

INSIDERS' TIP

In 1997, Salt Lake International Airport was listed as one of the 10 best in the nation by *Condé Nast Traveler*.

Service (628-8320) will answer the call. In Cedar City, the Cedar City Cab Company, 559-TAXI, will fetch you. Shuttles from the Holiday Inn, Hilton Inn, Ramada Inn and most larger motels in downtown St. George can meet passengers at the airport.

Except for an occasional good-hearted neighbor with an extra seat in the car, no other taxi services are available in the small rural communities of Southwestern Utah.

As the gateway to several national parks and recreation areas, Southwestern Utah is home to a burgeoning hospitality industry.

Accommodations

Since the early 1920s, when roads began to connect Southwestern Utah with the rest of the world, we've been seriously pursuing the business of hospitality. In fact, the small towns and cities of this region owe much of their economic health to the millions of travelers and visitors passing this way each year.

The large number of lodging places per capita in Southwestern Utah is due to the fact that we are centrally located between Los Angeles, Phoenix, Salt Lake City and Denver. And, of course, we are literally the gateway to the greatest concentration of national parks in America. As a result, a burgeoning hospitality industry has emerged here — one that has evolved to fit the needs of growing numbers of visitors.

In the listings that follow we present many of the brightest and best motels, bed and breakfast inns, rental properties and RV parks throughout the region. These are properties we feel confident in recommending either as a result of our own experience or by reference of people we trust.

Most lodging places in Southwestern Utah accept major credit cards and have smoking and nonsmoking rooms, cable television and facilities to accommodate the handicapped. We've also found that many properties allow small pets with certain stipulations. If there are certain amenities we do not discuss that are particularly important to you, be sure to ask for details when you call for reservations.

Many area accommodations offer senior, group or corporate discounts. Be sure to ask about these when you call. Because golf is such a popular activity here, we've mentioned those properties that will offer a golf package with your stay.

Relatively speaking, there is not a large spread in lodging rates in Southwestern Utah. There are some acceptable rooms for less than $40, but most come in at about $60. Rates can go as high as $80 or $90 but rarely are more than that. Prices do fluctuate during the year.

Price Key

We've listed accommodations by categories that include hotels and motels, bed and breakfast inns, RV parks and weekly rental companies. Each location will have a price guide of from one to four dollar signs based on the price for a one-night, double-occupancy stay in the high season, which varies throughout Southwestern Utah (see the next section on Reservations). Rates do not include tax.

$	Less than $40
$$	$41 to $60
$$$	$61 to $90
$$$$	$91 and higher

Reservations

It is a good idea to make reservations as early as possible for any accommodation in Southwestern Utah. It is possible to find vacancies on short notice just about any time of year, but it's a risk we don't recommend you take. Busy seasons fluctuate by area — St. George is especially busy in the spring and fall; Springdale and Hurricane peak during the summer months; Cedar City is booked solid during the Utah Shakespearean Festival (June through August) and Brian Head Ski Resort is very tight in the wintertime.

St. George is normally booked a full year in advance for the Easter and President's Day weekends. These weekends host the city's version of Spring Break, and northern Utahns — mostly young people — tend to flock south. The first weekend of October, which marks the running of the St. George Marathon, is also jam-packed. On those nights when you can't find a room in Southwestern Utah, it is sometimes possible to book one in Mesquite,

Nevada, about 35 miles southwest of St. George (see our Mesquite chapter).

The listings of accommodations that follow are extensive, but if you have additional questions, contact the local travel bureaus — they are good clearinghouses for information on lodging in each of the four geographical regions of Southwestern Utah. These agencies include the Washington County Travel and Convention Bureau, 634-5747 or (800) 869-6635; Iron County Tourism and Convention Bureau, 586-5124 or (800) 354-4849; Kane County Travel Council, 644-5033; and Garfield County Travel Council, 676-8421.

Hotels/Motels

St. George/Zion

Most of St. George's lodging properties are clustered either at the south interchange of Interstate 15 (Exit 6), the north interchange (Exit 8) or along St. George Boulevard. Northbound or southbound traffic headed to St. George can exit at either interchange.

Best Western Abbey Inn
$$$ • 1129 S. Bluff St., St. George • 652-1234, (888) 222-3946

One of the newest properties in town, this 130-unit hotel built in 1996 has a refrigerator, microwave and wet bar in each room and offers a daily, full, free continental breakfast. There's a large indoor spa and outdoor pool, an exercise room and a video game room. Rooms are elegantly appointed in a Victorian style. There are mini-suites available as well as larger suites with spas. It's near the largest cinema complex in St. George and excellent shopping at the St. George Commercial Center. There are six restaurants within walking distance. Golf packages are available.

Best Western Coral Hills
$$ • 125 E. St. George Blvd., St. George • 673-4844, (800) 542-7733

The Wittwer family, with three generations of St. George hospitality experience, owns and manages this popular downtown motel. The

98-unit property is within easy walking distance of several excellent restaurants and is right on the edge of the downtown historic district. Kids younger than 12 stay free, and there's a daily continental breakfast, indoor and outdoor pools, two spas and an exercise-game room. All rooms have king or queen beds, refrigerators, cable and HBO. There are also some elegant suites with in-room spas.

Best Western Travel Inn
$$ • 316 E. St. George Blvd., St. George • 673-3541, (800) 528-1234

With two restaurants next door, this 30-room motel has been newly remodeled and has a heated indoor pool and spa. The motel has a courtyard setting right in the middle of downtown. There are family rooms with king and queen beds, cable TV and The Movie Channel. There are larger units for five or six people, and all rooms are on the ground floor.

The Bluffs Motel
$$ • 1140 S. Bluff St., St. George • 628-6699

Just off the southbound St. George interchange at I-15 Exit 6, this is a beautifully decorated 33-room motel offering a free continental breakfast. There are two king-bed suites with a private Jacuzzi in each, and some rooms have microwaves and refrigerators. There's a heated pool and a large Jacuzzi for use by all guests.

Budget 8 Motel
$$ • 1221 S. Main, St. George • 628-5234, (800) 275-3494

Near the south St. George interchange of I-15 at Exit 6, this is an easily accessible, clean, comfortable place to stay. With 53 units, there's a heated pool and Jacuzzi, cable TV and Showtime. Budget 8 is near a cinema complex, plenty of shopping and several restaurants. Golf packages are available.

Budget Inn
$$ • 1221 S. Main, St. George • 673-6661, (800) 929-0790

Here's one of the newer motels in St.

FYI

Unless otherwise noted, the area code for all phone numbers listed in this chapter is 801 but will change to 435 in September 1997. Either area code may be used until March 22, 1998.

George. It opened in 1995 and is near restaurants, a cinema complex and a shopping center. There's free continental breakfast, indoor and outdoor pools and a wading pool and huge playroom for children. Rooms are decorated in deep, warm colors with a Southwestern style. The property's landscaping is styled after a tropical garden. There are 79 rooms with either one king or two queen beds, cable TV and HBO.

Claridge Inn
$$ • 1187 S. Bluff St., St. George
• 673-7222, (800) 367-3790

This is a 50-unit motel, and all rooms are for nonsmokers. There's a pool, Jacuzzi and free continental breakfast. The location is excellent, just off the south interchange of I-15 (Exit 6) with several restaurants and shopping options within walking distance. All rooms have queen beds, cable TV and Showtime. The Claridge is a clean and affordable place to stay.

Comfort Inn
$$ • 999 E. Skyline Dr., St. George
• 628-4271, (800) 221-2222

With 49 rooms, this property is near several restaurants and a three-screen cinema. It is about two blocks off St. George Boulevard, away from the hustle and bustle of the city's busiest street. If you are a jogger, you can trot right out the door onto Skyline Drive and run across the red sandstone bluff north of St. George. There's a free continental breakfast, cable TV with HBO and an outdoor heated pool.

Comfort Suites
$$$ • 1239 S. Main, St. George • 673-7000, (800) 245-8602

This is the first hotel on your right after leaving I-15 at Exit 6, the busy south St. George interchange. With 123 mini-suites featuring microwaves and refrigerators, cable TV, HBO and whirlpool baths in select rooms with king beds, this is a popular place to stay in St. George. There's an outdoor heated pool and Jacuzzi, free continental breakfast and two restaurants next door. Golf packages are available, and the hotel even offers a putting green. There are conference rooms, and there's ample parking for large rigs.

Days Inn Thunderbird
$$ • 150 N. 1000 East, St. George
• 673-6123, (800) 527-6543

This 99-unit motel is just off the north St. George interchange of I-15 (Exit 8) with several restaurants and a three-screen cinema next door. Children younger than 18 stay free, and there's a pool and a Jacuzzi. Continental breakfast is served daily, and adjacent to the lobby is a gift shop with a remarkable little art gallery featuring Southwestern paintings and sculptures (see "Art Galleries" in our Arts and Culture chapter). Rooms have king or queen beds. There's cable TV with the Disney Channel and HBO, and golf packages are available.

Hampton Inn
$$$ • 53 N. River Rd., St. George
• 652-1200, (800) HAMPTON

This 130-unit motel opened in 1995 just off Exit 8 of I-15 north, the north St. George interchange. It offers one of the more elaborate continental breakfasts in St. George. There is a pool and two Jacuzzis, and the motel is just across the street from the Zion Factory Stores and several of St. George's best restaurants. All double-occupancy rooms have two queen beds, and golf packages are available.

Hilton Inn of St. George
$$$ • 1450 S. Hilton Dr., St. George
• 628-0463, (800) HILTONS

With 100 units, this hotel is designed in a

Great Views

The St. George motel with the greatest view is Sullivan's Rococo Inn at 511 Airport Road on the west ridge of St. George. From most rooms you can see a panorama stretching from Pine Valley Mountain to the north, to Kolob and the West Temple of Zion to the east.

Southwest courtyard setting with plenty of water and greenery contrasting with the surrounding desert. It's just off the south St. George interchange of I-15 (Exit 6). There's a sauna, spa, lighted tennis courts and a complete health club adjacent. Tony Roma's, a popular St. George restaurant, is under the same roof. Rooms open onto a courtyard or have views of the surrounding landscape. Double-occupancy rooms have two queen beds or one king. Southgate Golf Course is three minutes away, and golf packages are available.

Holiday Inn Resort Hotel & Convention Center
$$$ • 850 S. Bluff St., St. George • 628-4235, (800) HOLIDAY

With 164 rooms, eight of which are suites, this is one of the best and most popular places to stay in St. George. Children as old as 18 stay free. The Holidome recreation area includes a putting green, indoor/outdoor pool, spa, exercise room, children's playground, tennis court and game room. The hotel is right across the street from one of St. George's best shopping areas, the St. George Commercial Center. The Palms restaurant is part of the hotel and offers fine dining. With 5,000 feet of convention space, the hotel can handle meetings of up to 500 people. Rooms have queen and king bed options, and there are some luxury suites with individual whirlpools. Golf packages are available.

Howard Johnson's Four Seasons Convention Center
$$ • 747 E. St. George Blvd., St. George • 673-6111, (800) 635-4441

This was the first convention center in St. George, built in the early '70s. It has been remodeled during the past two years and offers 96 rooms, indoor and outdoor pools, Jacuzzis and tennis courts. Luigi's Restaurant is part of the facility, which still hosts conventions and meetings. There's a complimentary continental breakfast, and rooms have cable

TV, HBO and king or queen beds. Some rooms offer microwaves and refrigerators. Golf packages are available.

Quality Inn
$$ • 1165 S. Bluff St., St. George • 628-4481, (800) 231-4488

There are 96 rooms at this property among the cluster of hotels and motels on South Bluff Street, near the south St. George interchange of I-15 (Exit 6). Children younger than 12 stay free, and there's a complimentary continental breakfast, an indoor/outdoor Jacuzzi, heated pool, sauna, bridal suite and satellite TV. Golf packages are available.

Ramada Inn
$$$ • 1440 E. St. George Blvd., St. George • 628-2828, (800) 228-2828

Insiders consider this one of St. George's finest places to stay. There are 136 rooms, with several suites included. Just off I-15 Exit 8, the hotel is actually on the far east end of St. George Boulevard at the foot of the east lava ridge. There's a pool, Jacuzzi and hot tub, and the property is conveniently set at the south end of the long Zion Factory Stores complex. All those name brands are just waiting next door. Room options include two queen beds or one king bed, and there are three meeting rooms with a total capacity of 250 people. Complimentary breakfast is included. Golf packages are available.

Ranch Inn
$$ • 1040 S. Main, St. George • 628-8000, (800) 332-0400

This is the place if you're planning on spending more than a few days in St. George. There are 33 kitchenette suites, 18 double-queen suites and one master suite in this motel just off Exit 6 at the southern end of St. George. Kitchenette suites include a microwave, refrigerator, sink and counter space. If you're not cooking in your room, there's free continental breakfast plus a heated pool, in-

---

INSIDERS' TIP

Try Zion National Park in winter. Sure it's cold, but the scenery is magnificent in white, it's easy to get a room in Springdale and there are actually parking places inside the park.

door Jacuzzi, sauna and laundry facilities. The Ranch Inn offers daily, weekly and monthly rates. Golf packages are available.

Shoney's Inn

$$ • 245 N. Red Cliffs Dr., St. George • 652-3030, (800) 222-2222

Built in 1996, this property sits just across the street from the Shoney's Restaurant, the factory stores complex and a cluster of other excellent restaurants just off Exit 8 of I-15. Its 52 rooms include some whirlpool suites with microwave and refrigerator. There is in-room coffee and a guest laundry. Four suites are available along with a heated pool and a Jacuzzi. Free continental breakfast at the Shoney's across the street comes with your stay.

Singletree Inn

$$ • 260 E. St. George Blvd., St. George • 673-6161, (800) 528-8890

This 48-room property has long been one of St. George's most popular motels due to its prime location in the middle of downtown. It's adjacent to Andelin's Restaurant (see our Restaurants chapter) and features a swimming pool and Jacuzzi. There's free continental breakfast, and you're just five walking minutes from the downtown historic district. Rooms have queen or king beds, and some have microwaves and refrigerators. Some family suites are available as are golf packages.

Sleep Inn

$$ • 1481 S. Sunland Dr., St. George • 673-7900, (800) SLEEPINN

On the south side of I-15, off Exit 6, this 68-room motel has one queen bed in all rooms and "super-size" showers. There's a pool, Jacuzzi and cable TV. Golf packages are available.

Southside Inn

$$ • 750 E. St. George Blvd., St. George • 628-9000

This is the closest motel to Dixie College and the Dixie Center. It has 40 large rooms, most with king or queen beds, a heated pool, Jacuzzi, cable TV with Showtime and several fast-food and fine dining restaurants within five minutes walking distance. Children younger than 12 stay free.

Sullivan's Rococo Inn

$ • 511 Airport Rd., St. George • 628-3671

Don't let the price fool you. This is a good little motel (27 units) in a spot like no other in St. George. It's just a quarter-mile down the road from the St. George Airport terminal on the edge of the lava bluff overlooking St. George. Many of the rooms have an incredible eastward view over the city to the far-off towers of Zion National Park on the horizon. There's a solar-heated pool and a Jacuzzi. Each room has a refrigerator and wet bar. Adjacent is the famous Rococo Steak House (see our Restaurants chapter), one of the best places for steaks in Southwestern Utah.

Sun Time Inn

$ • 420 E. St. George Blvd., St. George • 673-6181, (800) 237-6253

Right in the heart of downtown St. George, this is a good place to stay at very affordable rates. About 40 of the motel's 46 rooms are nonsmoking. There are 27 double-queen rooms, some with kitchenettes, and two rooms with king beds and Jacuzzi. There's a swimming pool and free HBO and Disney Channel. Weekly and monthly rates are available.

St. George Travelodge

$$ • 175 N. 1000 East, St. George • 673-4621, (800) 578-7878

Just off Exit 8 of I-15, this motel has 40 units, surplus parking for large rigs, a swimming pool and several restaurants nearby. There are double-queen and single-king rooms as well as some suites. In-room cable TV offers 35 channels, and some rooms have microwaves and refrigerators. A three-plex cinema is just next door.

Weston's Econolodge

$$ • 460 E. St. George Blvd., St. George • 673-4861, (800) 424-4777

Here's a great downtown lodging place just around the corner from the discount cinema complex, Flood Street Theaters. Weston's is within a 10-minute walk of most downtown shopping. With 54 rooms, this motel has a swimming pool and a therapy pool. The Fairway Grill (see our Restaurants chapter) is adjacent.

Pine Valley

The small, summer-home community of Pine Valley is 32 miles north of St. George off Utah Highway 18. This historic community was settled by Mormon pioneers in the 1850s, and it is now a favorite summer retreat for Southwestern Utahns.

Pine Valley Lodge

$$ • 960 E. Main, Pine Valley • 574-2544

For a little more rustic stay in the St. George area, drive 32 miles north on Utah 18 to the small historic town of Pine Valley along the northern flank of Pine Valley Mountain. There are four rooms and six cabins with a convenience store next door, a mini-zoo where the kids can pet sheep and goats, and there's horseback riding.

Hurricane

The peak season for Hurricane lodging is summertime, when the world is flocking to Zion National Park 25 miles to the east. Hurricane is 18 miles east of St. George on Utah Highway 9. Most of the motels are along, or just off, State Street, which is Utah 9 running through town.

Best Western Weston's Lamplighter

$$ • 280 W. State St., Hurricane
• 635-4647, (800) 528-1234

Smack in the center of Hurricane, this is a 63-room motel with an excellent reputation. All rooms are recently renovated, and this Best Western offers queen beds, free continental breakfast, a swimming pool and Jacuzzi. Weston's Lamplighter is near the Hurricane Valley Heritage Park (see our Attractions chapter).

Comfort Inn

$$ • 43 N. Sky Mountain Blvd., Hurricane
• 635-3500, (800) 228-5150

At the turnoff from Utah 9 to Sky Mountain Golf Course, this new 53-room motel has great views of the open landscape on the west edge of Hurricane. It has queen beds, an outdoor heated pool, Jacuzzi, laundry facilities and free continental breakfast. Golf packages are available.

Park Villa Motel

$$ • 650 W. State St., Hurricane
• 635-4010, (800) 682-6336

This 45-room motel is in the heart of Hurricane, within walking distance of stores and the Hurricane Valley Heritage Park. The Park Villa has a distinctly Mediterranean look on the outside and is surrounded by beautiful landscaping and huge trees. The fine touch of decor extends into the rooms, all of which have either one or two queen beds. Some rooms offer full kitchens. There is a heated pool, spa and laundry facilities. Weekly rates and golf packages are available.

Super 8 Motel

$$ • 65 S. 700 West, Hurricane • 635-0808, (800) 800-8000

There are 52 rooms, including four deluxe suites, in this motel in the middle of Hurricane. Most rooms have two queen beds. Suites have two bedrooms with a Jacuzzi in each bathroom as well as a refrigerator, microwave and cable TV with HBO. There's a conference room that accommodates as many as 30 people, and several fast-food restaurants are nearby. Golf packages are available.

Springdale

Most of Springdale's lodging properties are found along Zion Park Boulevard, which is Utah 9. It winds through town to the entrance of Zion National Park on the north edge of Springdale.

Best Western Driftwood Lodge

$$$ • 1515 Zion Park Blvd., Springdale
• 772-3262, (800) 528-1234

This has been a perennially popular lodging place in Springdale. It was recently remodeled and several new rooms have been added to bring the total to 48. Rooms have large picture windows with views of Zion Canyon from either a patio or balcony. The lodge is surrounded by tree-shaded lawns, and there's a free continental breakfast. There's also a gift shop and art gallery.

Bumbleberry Inn

$$ • 897-A Zion Park Blvd., Springdale
• 772-3224, (800) 828-1534

Large rooms with private patios or balco-

Photo: St. George Magazine

RVs, like this one on Utah 9 above Hurricane, fill up travel parks throughout the area.

nies characterize this Springdale landmark. It has 32 rooms, all nonsmoking, a heated pool and great scenic views from private balconies. The Bumbleberry Restaurant (see our Restaurants chapter) is adjacent as well as a gift shop and a live theater that features a nightly play Memorial Day through September (see our Nightlife chapter).

Canyon Ranch Motel
$$ • 668 Zion Park Blvd., Springdale • 772-3357

In the heart of Springdale, this 21-unit motel has new and remodeled rooms, some with kitchens, all set around a quiet, shady lawn with a panoramic view of Zion. The motel is made up of a cluster of separate buildings, each with two or four rooms. You can choose from rooms with one or two queen beds, with or without a kitchen. There's also a new pool and Jacuzzi.

Cliff Rose Lodge & Gardens
$$$ • 281 Zion Park Blvd., Springdale • 772-3234, (800) 243-UTAH

Each of the 32 new units in this motel have a nice view of the Zion Canyon ledges. The property has frontage along the Virgin River, with 5 acres of lawns, trees and flower gardens for guests to walk through. Rooms are

beautifully appointed with queen or king beds, but this is a place that beckons you out onto its spacious grounds. There's also a large pool.

El Rio Lodge
$$ • 995 Zion Park Blvd., Springdale • 772-3205

This small, 10-room, family-owned and operated motel is a quiet stop near the entrance to Zion National Park. Clean, quiet and friendly, there's a shady lawn with a sun deck and excellent views of the canyon.

Flanigan's Inn
$$$ • 428 Zion Park Blvd., Springdale • 772-3244, (800) 765-7787

At the north end of Springdale, near the entrance to Zion National Park, this 37-room motel is a traditional favorite. Flanigan's Restaurant (see our Restaurants chapter) is adjacent, and guests get a free continental breakfast buffet. Rooms, cheerful and fresh with large windows, open onto decks and garden patios. There's a pool and spacious grounds.

Pioneer Lodge
$$$ • 838 Zion Park Blvd., Springdale • 772-3233

Each of the 41 rooms in this Springdale lodge has been newly refurbished. Rooms have cable TV, and a rustic stone building next door houses the Pioneer Restaurant (see our Restaurants chapter) and a gift shop. The lodge has a heated outdoor pool and indoor spa. There's also a one-bedroom suite and a three-bedroom apartment, each with a kitchen.

Terrace Brook Lodge
$$ • 990 Zion Park Blvd., Springdale • 772-3932, (800) 342-6779

There are great views at this 26-room lodge. You can choose from accommodations with one queen bed up to a three-queen-bed suite with a kitchen. There's cable TV with HBO, and Terrace Brook Lodge features a heated pool as well as a barbecue and picnic area. The rustic grounds are surrounded by a split-rail fence and wagon wheels.

Zion Park Inn
$$$ • 1215 Zion Park Blvd., Springdale • 772-3200, (800) 934-7275

Just opened in 1996, this is a beautiful, full-service convention hotel with 82 units. There's a great outdoor pool. Designed with VIP and corporate retreats in mind, it is also a wonderful place for more traditional travelers to stay. Choose from rooms with two queens or one king bed, or take your pick of a variety of suite options. Rooms have excellent views of the canyon walls, and the Switchback Grille (see our Restaurants chapter) is just next door.

Zion Park Motel
$$ • 855 Zion Park Blvd., Springdale • 772-3251

Newly remodeled with some new units, this family-owned and oriented motel offers kitchenettes, cable TV, laundry facilities, a playground, picnic area and a heated pool. Next door is a market and restaurant.

In Zion National Park

Zion Lodge
$$$ • Zion National Park • (303) 29-PARKS

Deep within the canyon walls, this is the only lodging place inside the Zion National Park boundaries. There are 40 cabins and 80 new motel units. All lodge rooms have either one or two queen beds. Cabins have two double beds, a gas fireplace and a porch beneath the towers of Zion. There are some suites in the lodge with one king and one queen bed, a beautiful balcony and a refrigerator. Note there are no TVs at Zion Lodge. There's a restaurant (see our Restaurants chapter), gift shop, post office, tram service through the park and park trails leading in every direction.

An Old Wives Tale?

The Seven Wives Inn, which became St. George's first bed and breakfast when Jay and Donna Curtis restored the home in the early 1980s, is reputed to have been a haven for polygamous Mormon men trying to elude federal authorities. With passage of federal laws cracking down on the practice of polygamy in the 1880s and '90s, some Mormon men became fugitives. The relative isolation of Southwestern Utah made it an ideal place to hide. Some homes in the area, such as the one Edwin G. Wooley built on the corner of 200 North and 100 West in 1873, were equipped with secret passageways and hidden rooms where polygamous men could retire when authorities came knocking at the door. Today, guests at the Seven Wives Inn are shown the secret door leading to the attic. Donna Curtis has named the seven bedrooms in the home for the seven wives of her Great Grandfather B.F. Johnson, who spent much of his life in the St. George area, and was likely one of the polygamists who hid in the attic.

Cedar City/Brian Head

Abbey Inn
$$$ • 940 W. 200 North, Cedar City
• 586-9966, (800) 325-5411

Next to Shoney's Restaurant, this 81-room inn offers king and queen beds. Each room has its own refrigerator, microwave and cable TV with HBO. There's an indoor pool and spa, guest laundry, one kitchenette, a Jacuzzi, honeymoon suites and free continental breakfast. The Abbey is easily accessible off I-15 at Exit 59, and there are six restaurants within two blocks.

Best Western El Rey Inn
$$$ • 80 S. Main, Cedar City • 586-6518, (800) 688-6518

These are the closest accommodations to the Utah Shakespearean Festival. There's a heated pool, sauna, whirlpool and game room. Some family suites that sleep up to six are available with microwaves and refrigerators. All 73 of the rooms (some poolside) have cable TV with HBO. An elevator is available to get you to the second floor. A complimentary continental breakfast is served, and there's a restaurant next door.

Best Western Town & Country Inn
$$$ • 189 N. Main, Cedar City • 586-9900, (800) 528-1230

Smack in the center of town, within walking distance of the Shakespearean Festival, shopping and several restaurants, this 157-room motel has two heated pools — one indoor and one outdoor — a spa and several family units and suites. There's free continental breakfast, a game room and coin laundry. Next door there's a convenience store and gas station, a Sizzler restaurant and a Godfather's Pizza.

Comfort Inn
$$$ • 250 N. 1100 West, Cedar City
• 586-2082, (800) 627-0374

Just off I-15 Exit 59, this is one of the newest inns in town, and it sits right between Denny's and McDonald's. There's an indoor pool, spa, exercise room and free continental breakfast. This Comfort Inn has 93 rooms.

There are two- and three-bedroom suites with king beds and kitchenettes, laundry facilities and private whirlpool baths.

Holiday Inn/Convention Center
$$$ • 1575 W. 200 North, Cedar City
• 586-8888, (800) 432-8828

There's a heated pool, exercise room, whirlpool and sauna in this excellent facility just off Exit 59 of I-15. With large rooms and an interior corridor, the Holiday Inn has satellite TV and suites with a microwave and refrigerator. Treat yourself to either one king bed or two queens. There's also valet laundry service, video and Nintendo rental, a gift shop and a restaurant.

Quality Inn
$$$ • 18 S. Main, Cedar City • 586-2433, (800) 228-5151

This is a completely renovated inn, conveniently located downtown. The 50 new rooms have microwaves, refrigerators and king or queen beds. There's a complimentary continental breakfast and a heated pool. The Utah Shakespearean Festival and several restaurants are within a five-minute walk.

Brian Head

Brian Head Hotel
$$$ • 223 Hunter Ridge Dr., Brian Head
• 677-3000, (800) 272-7426

With 183 rooms, this is the largest lodging property at Brian Head Ski Resort. It features a full-service hotel, private club and Southwestern cuisine in its dining room. Here you can also make reservations for (depending on the season) horseback riding, Jeep tours, mountain biking and cross-country skiing. There's a pool and spa. Some rooms have refrigerators. Note that summer rates are significantly lower than winter rates.

The Lodge at Brian Head
$$$ • 314 W. Hunter Ridge Dr., Brian Head
• 677-3222, (800) 386-5634

The lodge at Brian Head is a rustic, homey option to the hotel. Most rooms have two queen beds. There are also some studios with king beds, in-room Jacuzzis and wet bars. There are 93 rooms total, some with kitchenettes. For all guests, there's an indoor pool, sauna and Jacuzzi for leg-weary skiers and mountain bikers. The property has its own restaurant, The Steakhouse, plus a lounge featuring live music from time to time (see our Nightlife section).

Parowan

Twenty miles north of Cedar City, just 12 miles from Brian Head Ski Resort, Parowan is a small community adjacent to I-15.

Best Western Swiss Village
$$$ • 580 N. Main, Parowan • 477-3391, (800) 793-7401

Just a dozen miles from Brian Head Ski Resort, this 28-unit motel has a seasonal pool and year-round hot tub. From the pool area, there's a great view of the awesome red ledges above Parowan. Take Exit 78 off I-15, then go a quarter-mile south on Parowan's Main Street. There's a restaurant and gift shop adjacent.

Days Inn
$$$ • 625 W. 200 South, Parowan • 477-3326, (800) 329-7466

Off Exit 75 in Parowan, this inn, with king and queen beds, is an excellent staging point for a skiing expedition to Brian Head, which is just 12 miles up the canyon. There are 44 rooms with either two double beds or one king.

Duck Creek Village

The Inn at Cedar Mountain
$$$ • 116 Color Country Rd., Duck Creek Village • 682-2378, (800) 897-4995

Located on the alpine heights of Cedar Mountain, 30 miles east of Cedar City, this inn is open year round and has eight condominium units with sitting rooms and kitchens. Amenities include a game room and hot tub. Summertime outdoor activities include horseshoes, volleyball, and, of course, hiking.

Bryce Canyon Area

Best Western New Western Motel
$$ • 200 E. Center, Panguitch • 676-8876, (800) 528-1234

Open year round, this motel has 37 rooms

— some recently renovated; some brand-new with king or queen beds. There's a heated pool and coin laundry. This Best Western is about 25 miles from Bryce Canyon and is close to many Panguitch restaurants.

Bryce Canyon Pines
$$$ • Utah Hwy. 12, Bryce Canyon • 834-5441

There are 50 rooms in this motel, which is in the pines just off Utah 12, 6 miles from Bryce Canyon National Park. Open year round, rooms have two queen beds and some have kitchenettes and fireplaces. There's an enclosed heated pool. You can browse in the gift shop and eat at the Bryce Canyon Pines Restaurant, which is adjacent. Horseback rides into Red Canyon ($15 for one hour; $35 for a half-day) are offered during the summer season.

Color Country Motel
$$ • 526 N. Main, Panguitch • 676-2386, (800) 225-6518

Located near restaurants and shopping, this motel has 26 newly refurbished rooms. It has king and queen beds, cable TV and a swimming pool. A recent remodeling project has given the Color Country a very homey feel.

Pink Cliffs Village
$$$ • Jct. of Utah Hwy. 12 and Utah Hwy. 63, Bryce Canyon • 834-5351, (800) 834-0043

At the gateway to Bryce Canyon National Park, where Utah 12 and Utah 63 meet, this is a 52-unit motel with 14 cabins (original cabins built in Bryce Canyon National Park in the 1930s), a 14-bed hostel, restaurant, service station, 32-site RV park (see listing in this chapter), campground, heated indoor pool and laundry facilities. There are rooms with king or queen beds. Stay in one of the original cabins for an authentic Old West experience. The 156-acre complex is open year round.

Ruby's Inn
$$$ • Utah Hwy. 63, Bryce Canyon • 834-5341, (800) 528-1234

Just outside the entrance to Bryce Canyon National Park, this is one of Southwestern Utah's

legendary lodging places. Sadly, the original historic lodge was destroyed by fire several years ago, but the new inn has 216 rooms, making it one of the largest motels in the state. There are units with two bedrooms and kitchenettes, and the inn has an indoor swimming pool, restaurant, general store and laundry. Open year round, Ruby's Inn is the ideal headquarters for such outdoor activities as horseback trail rides, van tours, mountain biking and helicopter tours (see our Outdoor Recreation chapter). There's Ruby's General Store, Ruby's Western Arts Gallery, Cowboy's Buffet and Steak Room and the Canyon Diner. Ruby's also has an RV park (see listing below).

Tropic

Tropic is a small town 7 miles southeast of Bryce Canyon on Utah 12.

Bryce Pioneer Village
$$ • 80 S. Main, Tropic • 679-8546, (800) 222-0381

Three miles east of Bryce Canyon on Utah 12, this inn has 48 motel rooms and cabins and is open April through October. You can choose from rooms with single, double or queen beds, and some units offer kitchenettes. This is a rustic, Old West setting and atmosphere. It is the home of the Ebenezer Bryce Cabin. Bryce was the Mormon pioneer and cowman for whom the canyon was named (see our chapter on Parks and Other Natural

Wonders). With advance reservations you can join in an old-fashioned, Dutch-oven cookout and a genuine cowboy breakfast.

Bryce Valley Inn
$$$ • 200 N. Main St. (Utah Hwy. 12), Tropic • 679-8811, (800) 442-1890

Open March through October, this inn is in the heart of the small town of Tropic. It has 65 rooms with double or queen beds, a gift shop, restaurant and laundry. This is a clean, quiet place where you can relax and rejuvenate for another romp through the canyons tomorrow.

Bryce Canyon National Park

Bryce Canyon Lodge
$$ • Utah Hwy. 63, Bryce Canyon National Park • (303) 297-2757

Two miles inside the national park border just off Utah 63, these are the only accommodations inside Bryce Canyon National Park. The historic lodge on the canyon rim is extremely popular, and you need to make reservations up to a year in advance. Open April through October, the lodge evokes the rustic elegance of the 1920s and '30s. All the furniture is made of hickory in the style used originally at the lodge years ago. There are 114 units, including 70 rooms, 40 historic cabins with fireplaces that have been remodeled with gas logs and four suites in the upstairs area of the lodge. Built in the 1920s by the Utah Parks Company, the lodge is on the National Register of Historic Places. The dining room (see our Restaurants chapter) is almost as legendary as the lodge itself.

Kanab Area

Kanab has been hosting visitors since Tom Mix appeared in movies filmed there in the 1920s. Most accommodations are right along U.S. Highway 89, which runs through town.

Best Western Red Hills
$$$ • 124 W. Center, Kanab • 644-2675, (800) 528-1234

This is an excellent motel in the middle of downtown Kanab with 72 rooms, a heated pool and whirlpool. There's cable TV with HBO, and most rooms have a refrigerator. This Best Western has laundry facilities, and several restaurants are within easy walking distance.

Four Seasons Inn
$$ • 36 N. 300 West, Kanab • 644-2635

Smack in the middle of Kanab, this inn has 41 newly remodeled rooms with double, queen or king beds. There's cable TV, an outdoor heated pool, a Native American gift shop and an adjacent restaurant. The Four Seasons puts you in easy walking distance of Kanab's downtown shops and historic sites.

Holiday Inn Express
$$$ • 815 E. U.S. Hwy. 89, Kanab • 644-8888, (800) 574-4061

Next to the majestic Coral Cliffs Golf Course, this inn is on the east side of town on the highway leading to Lake Powell. The Express has 67 nicely decorated, well-kept rooms with queen or king beds, cable TV and HBO. There's a heated pool and Jacuzzi, a bridal suite, complimentary breakfast bar and a Western gift shop.

Parry Lodge
$$$ • 89 East Center, Kanab • 644-2601, (800) 748-4104

Built in 1929, this picturesque lodge in the middle of Kanab has reached legendary sta-

FYI

Unless otherwise noted, the area code for all phone numbers listed in this chapter is 801 but will change to 435 in September 1997. Either area code may be used until March 22, 1998.

tus. The lodge, which has played host to many of Hollywood's greatest stars, has been expanded from its original 15 rooms to 89. It has a beautiful outdoor pool and adjoining restaurant (see our Restaurants chapter). There's cable TV, and you can choose from tastefully decorated rooms with single, double, queen or king beds. During the heyday of the Hollywood western, from the 1930s to the early '60s, Kanab hosted dozens of production companies on location in the area. Parry Lodge made an art of providing hospitality to the stars. Among those who stayed at the lodge are John Wayne, Ronald Reagan, Frank Sinatra, Dean Martin, Sammy Davis Jr., James Garner and numerous others. You'll see their pictures on the walls and their names above the doors of the rooms where they stayed. It all contributes to a homey atmosphere in a terrific, picturesque setting.

Shilo Inn
$$$ • 296 W. 100 North, Kanab • 644-2562, (800) 222-2244

This is an excellent place to stay in Kanab. It has 119 rooms, a heated pool, whirlpool and laundry. It offers free continental breakfast, and there are mini-suites. Room options include one queen or king bed or two queens, and each room has a microwave, refrigerator, satellite TV and a VCR. There are fine restaurants adjacent to the Shilo and ample parking for big rigs.

Mt. Carmel

This is a small community at the junction of Utah 9 and U.S. 89, 14 miles east of Zion National Park.

Thunderbird Resort
$$ • U.S. Hwy. 89 and Utah Hwy. 9, Mt. Carmel • 648-2203

Seventeen miles north of Kanab and 14 miles east of the east entrance to Zion National Park, this motel sits at the junction of U.S. 89 and Utah 9, in the little community of Mt. Carmel. It has 66 large rooms with king or queen beds and balcony views. This is a quiet

Photo: Nick Adams

During Utah's early history, a secret room in the upper floor of the Seven Wives Inn was used to hide polygamous husbands from Federal agents.

spot midway between Zion and Bryce Canyon parks. There is a heated pool and an adjacent restaurant. Next door is the delightful little Thunderbird Golf Course, a nine-hole track (see our Golf chapter).

Bed and Breakfast Inns

Most of the bed and breakfast properties in Southwestern Utah are restored historic homes now owned by people who are intrigued by the history of the area and love to share it.

St. George/Zion

An Olde Penny Farthing Inn Bed and Breakfast
$$$ • 278 N. 100 West, St. George • 673-7755

Each room in this five-unit home has its own individual theme, appealing to a variety of tastes. The Sego Lily Room is decorated pioneer-style with a fourth-generation, iron-and-brass bed. It has a private bathroom with a claw-foot tub and shower and a country flagstone floor. The Betsy Ross Room has stenciled red, white and blue walls and a four-poster queen bed. This is an 1870 pioneer home that has been completely restored. It's just a block north of the historic Brigham Young Winter Home (see our Attractions chapter),

right in the heart of the downtown historic district. All rooms have private baths, a full English breakfast with fresh fruits is included and golf packages are available.

Greene Gate Village Bed & Breakfast Inn
$$$ • 76 W. Tabernacle, St. George • 628-6999, (800) 350-6999

Right in the heart of the downtown historic district, this complex of restored pioneer homes is one of St. George's treasures — a kind of mini-Williamsburg for Southwestern Utah. Within the beautifully landscaped cluster of buildings, built by Mormon settlers in the 1870s, are 18 rooms, including the Greene House for groups of up to 20 people. These rooms have been carefully restored and decorated by Dr. Mark and Barbara Greene. They are decorated with pioneer furniture and historic photos that capture the essence of early Mormon St. George. In spite of the pioneer ambiance, this is an elegant place. The pioneers, after all, were often fond of fine detail such as intricately crocheted curtains. A stay here is more than a relaxing experience, it's a history lesson. A hearty country breakfast is served in the Bentley House. There's a swimming pool, whirlpool and tennis court, and the old Judd's Store, where the settlers bought their dry goods, is adjacent. There is also easy access to all the amenities of downtown. Golf packages are available.

Horseman Inn Bed and Breakfast
$$$ • 164 W. 100 South, St. George
• 634-9494, (800) 640-9498

This newly restored 1886 pioneer home is full of antiques, has private baths and is conveniently located near restaurants, shopping, and the downtown historic district. The 1886 Greek Revival home was built by legendary Mormon pioneer cowman and horseman James Andrus for his wife Manomas. Each guest room, full of pioneer antiques, has a private bath, cable TV and a view of St. George. A full breakfast, including fresh baked goods and fruits, is served.

Morris Mulberry Inn Bed and Breakfast
$$$ • 194 S. 600 East, St. George
• 673-7383, (800) 915-7070

If you want to get a taste of residential St. George, here's a restored historic home with five units smack in the middle of a traditional St. George neighborhood. It has French country decor and offers a gourmet breakfast. There's a honeymoon suite, and long-term rates are available. It's just a five-minute walk from the Dixie College campus and the Dixie Center. Golf packages are available.

Quicksand and Cactus Bed and Breakfast
$$$ • 346 N. Main, St. George • 674-1739

This is the historic pioneer home where the renowned author and historian, Juanita Brooks, lived and did her writing. Located on the hill on North Main Street, there are great views of the city from here, and the entire downtown historic district is within walking distance. The original two rooms of this house were built by George Brooks, with chips and irregular stones from the cleanup of the temple and tabernacle construction sites. Rooms have queen beds, private baths and shaded porches. A full, pioneer-style breakfast is served.

Seven Wives Inn
$$$ • 217 N. 100 West, St. George
• 628-3737, (800) 600-3737

Holding the distinction as Southwestern Utah's first bed and breakfast inn, this 12-unit duo of restored pioneer homes has developed an avid following over the years. Each room is handsomely decorated with pioneer antiques and beds with hand-sewn quilts. Owners Jay and Donna Curtis are pioneers in their own right, introducing the bed and breakfast concept to St. George in the early 1980s when they restored the Edwin G. Wooley home (c. 1873) and named each of its seven bedrooms for Donna's great-grandfather's seven polygamous wives. Guests enjoy a gourmet breakfast each morning in the historic dining room.

Hurricane

Pah Tempe Mineral Hot Springs
$$ • 825 N. 800 East, Hurricane • 635-2879

Just off Utah 9 at the east end of Hurricane, in the majestic canyon where the Virgin River breaks out of the Hurricane Fault, Pah Tempe is a resort built around historic grotto pools that have rejuvenated visitors for centuries. These enchanted waters were sacred to the Anasazi and Southern Paiute tribes. Early Spanish explorers noted the place in their journals, and Mormon pioneers renewed their aching bodies in the pools during the building of canals in Hurricane and LaVerkin. Today, visitors from all over the world come to soak at Pah Tempe. Waters from the spring here flow into several pools at various depths and temperatures, then cascade into the Virgin River at a rate of 12,000 gallons per minute.

The resort includes six rooms, and no smoking or alcohol are allowed. The least expensive option is for a room with one double bed and a shared bath. Other rooms have two double beds and private baths, and one room has a fireplace and a shared bathroom. A full

Great Views

Brian Head Hotel offers some of the best alpine winter and summer views in Southwestern Utah. From many rooms, you take in pine-studded mountain ridges, dark green in summer and powdery white in winter.

Photo: St. George Magazine

The restored Brigham Young winter home was originally built in St. George in the 1870s.

breakfast is served in the central dining room. Use of the hot springs is included in the lodging rate.

If you aren't a guest, day passes to the hot springs are $10 for adults and $5 for children 2 to 12. A 10-day pass is $50. The resort also offers body treatments such as massages, facials, mud wraps and herbal wraps, with prices from $35 to $60.

Rockville

The Blue House Bed and Breakfast
$$$ • 125 E. Main, Rockville • 772-3912, (800) 869-3912

This is Rockville's first bed and breakfast inn. The Wine and Wicker Room has a king bed, private bath and high, vaulted ceiling. Set well back from the road, this home has a quiet, country feeling. Just 5 miles from the entrance to Zion National Park, the Blue House has a total of four guest units and serves a huge breakfast including Belgian waffles, ham, eggs and fresh fruit.

Handcart House Bed and Breakfast
$$$ • 244 W. Main, Rockville • 772-3867

Antique brass beds covered with handmade quilts characterize this home with three guest units, each with a private bath. The pioneer decor will take you back 100 years. Just 5 miles from the entrance to Zion National Park, this is a quiet, convenient place to stay.

Hummingbird Inn Bed and Breakfast
$$$ • 37 W. Main, Rockville • 772-3632, (800) 964-BIRD

This is a new home with each room decorated to fit a historical time period. Sara Elizabeth is a pioneer room with a wrought-iron bed and marble tabletops. Sinawava has Anasazi-based decor with a lodge pole pine queen bed. Emeline is decorated in 1920s style, and Isabella is a Spanish-style room with a queen bed. A large country breakfast is served, and there's an upstairs deck and a library/game room loft. Outside there's horseshoes, croquet and badminton. Zion National Park is just 5 miles away.

Springdale

Harvest House Bed and Breakfast
$$$ • 29 Canyon View Dr., Springdale • 772-3880

There's a private bath and a queen bed in each of the four guest rooms here. Children older than 6 are welcome, and hot and cold beverages are available any time at the wet bar in the dining room. There's a year-round outdoor hot tub. Two rooms have private decks with awesome views of two Zion landmarks — The Watchman and Bridge Mountain. Harvest House offers an elegant breakfast with homemade muffins and pastries.

Morning Glory Bed and Breakfast
$$$ • 26 Big Springs Rd., Springdale • 772-3301

There's a large family room in this home with a library, lawn, garden area and a balcony offering a great view of the canyon. The home has three guest rooms and offers a full gourmet breakfast. Morning Glory is off the main highway in a quiet, secluded area with gardens, grape arbors and water fountains.

O'Toole's Under the Eaves Guest House
$$$ • 980 Zion Park Blvd., Springdale • 772-3457

The original home here was built in 1929 of sandstone blocks cut from the canyon cliffs. Today, O'Toole's is furnished with antiques and Southwestern accents. Two rooms on the first floor share a bath, while each room has its own sink. Upstairs, there's a large honeymoon suite with a claw-foot tub in its private bath. A full breakfast is served, and golf packages are available.

Red Rock Inn Bed & Breakfast
$$$ • 998 Zion Park Blvd., Springdale • 772-3139

Your breakfast basket is delivered to your room at this Zion Canyon inn. The guest units are new cottages, and each is individually decorated — one country, one modern, one antique. Rooms have private baths, whirlpool tubs, queen beds and a porch with a great view of Zion. Inn rooms have vaulted ceilings and are intimate. There's also a shaded lawn area. Breakfast includes a hot dish, muffins, fruit and juice.

Zion House Bed and Breakfast
$$$ • 801 Zion Park Blvd., Springdale • 772-3281

With four spacious guest rooms, this is a highly touted bed and breakfast inn just minutes from the entrance to Zion National Park. Three rooms' names come from the views they afford — Canyon View, Garden Suite and West Temple — and the Master Suite looks out on The Watchman, a mighty Zion Canyon landmark. Zion House, a 13-year-old contemporary brick home, was the first bed and breakfast inn in Springdale. It has been recom-mended by Jerry Hulse in his *Los Angeles Times* column, "Travel Tips," and it has been mentioned in *Outside* magazine. Each unit has a great view of the canyon cliffs.

Toquerville

Toquerville, named for Chief Toquer of a band of the Southern Paiutes, is a small town about 5 miles north of LaVerkin on Utah Highway 17 or 3 miles off Exit 27 of I-15.

Your Inn Toquerville
$$ • 650 Springs Dr., Toquerville • 635-9964

In the heart of the little town of Toquerville, about 20 minutes from Zion National Park, this inn offers four large guest rooms with a king bed in each and private baths. The home has a long porch in front for evening relaxation and conversation. There's one suite that can handle Mom, Dad and the kids. Guests are welcome to bring their own beer or liquor here. Your Inn Toquerville is located off the busy path to Zion in a 10-acre orchard along a stream.

Virgin

The town of Virgin is on Utah Highway 9 midway between Hurricane and Springdale.

Snow Family Guest Ranch Bed and Breakfast
$$$ • 633 E. Utah Hwy. 9, Virgin • 635-2500

Set along the highway between Virgin and Rockville, this picturesque ranch with its white fences and green fields at the foot of red sandstone cliffs looks as if it jumped right off a postcard. Rooms are ranch-style with log headboards on queen beds. Each room has a window seat and private bath. The bridal suite has an antique water closet with a claw-foot tub. Each of the nine units has a great view of the surrounding cliffs. Breakfast is hearty, with bacon, sausage, French toast and scrambled eggs. There is a swimming pool, and, yes, the horses in the fields are real. And they're not just to look at — you can ride them on special trail excursions offered by this popular lodging place.

Zion Blue Star Bed and Breakfast
$$$ • 28 W. Utah Hwy. 9, Virgin • 635-3830

The three units in this Spanish-style home have beautiful views of the surrounding can-

What many consider "the barren desert" is actually a rich ecosystem alive with a wide variety of plants and animals — some found no where else in the world.

yon landscape. The spacious house has a red-tiled roof, and the rooms have queen beds and shared baths. A separate cottage sleeps seven and offers a private bath and kitchen. A hearty country breakfast is included. Set on a hill just off the highway at the mouth of Kolob Canyon, this is a quiet location offering an excellent starting point for exploring Zion.

Cedar City/Brian Head

Bard's Inn
$$$ • 150 S. 100 West, Cedar City • 586-6612

Just two blocks from Festival Square, this inn has the charm of olden days with the comforts of modern times. There are seven rooms, each with a queen bed and a private bath. A glass-enclosed porch has a sink and refrigerator for use by all guests, and homemade pastries are part of the breakfast. The house was built in 1908 as a two-story bungalow, and it is furnished with antiques.

The Paxman House
$$$ • 170 N. 400 West, Cedar City • 586-3755

This turn-of-the-century farmhouse has three porches and has been carefully restored and furnished with antiques. The Paxman is a Queen Anne-style home with the original, white gingerbread woodwork on the porch. The original parlor is full of antiques including a Victrola. Just two blocks from the Utah Shakespearean Festival, it has four rooms with queen beds and private baths. Breakfast includes fruit, cereals and fresh-baked breads, and no one leaves here hungry.

Parowan

Adams Historic Home
$$$ • 94 N. 100 East, Parowan • 477-8295, (800) 994-1414

Built in about 1870, this is a recently restored pioneer home with a rich history. Here you'll relax in the quiet town of Parowan and learn about the influence the Adams family had on local theater. Each of the three rooms has a private bath. One room sleeps two, another four and the restored granary (a separate building on the property) accommodates up to six. There's a wraparound porch on the house and a porch swing, and in Parowan, the stars shine brightly at night.

Janet Lynn House Bed and Breakfast
$$$ • 390 E. 200 South, Parowan
• 477-1133, (800) 891-1132

At the mouth of beautiful Parowan Canyon, this is a new Tudor-style log home, just 18 miles north of Cedar City. There are four rooms — two share a bath, two have private baths. The Parowan Trails Room has two aspen log beds. The Hundred Acre Wood Room has a lodge pole pine bed and Winnie the Pooh decor. In the Mary Catherine Room, you'll find a Victorian brass bed and maple furnishings, and the Diamond Run Room is decorated in a skiing motif with a black, wrought-iron queen bed, plus a double and a twin for the kids. There's a gift shop, recreation room, spa, pool table, volleyball court, croquet lawn and horseshoe pit. Brian Head Ski Resort is just 12 miles up the canyon.

Bryce Canyon Area

Bryce Point Bed and Breakfast
$$$ • 61 N. 400 West, Tropic • 679-8629

Each of the six rooms in this delightful home

has a private bath, TV, VCR and extensive video library. All rooms have queen beds. The proprietors, LaMar and Ethyl LeFevre, became the first owners of a bed and breakfast inn in the little town of Tropic when they opened this business in 1990. Separate from the house is a honeymoon cabin that was one of the early cabins in Bryce Canyon National Park. The LeFevres know the Bryce area intimately and can help you see and experience the region to the fullest.

MaeMae's Bed and Breakfast
$$ • 501 E. Center St., Panguitch
• 676-2388

In 1993, NidaMae Jensen and her husband, Douglas, turned this 1890s red brick home into a bed and breakfast inn. The house was originally owned by the Henrys, a founding family of Panguitch, and is open May through October. There are three rooms with queen beds and a shared bath, but plans are in the works to add private baths for each room. There's a continental breakfast of homemade cinnamon rolls, fruit, cereal and juice.

Kanab Area

Judd House Bed and Breakfast
$$ • 116 S. 100 East, Kanab • 644-2936

This century-old home on the original property of Mormon pioneer Zadoc Judd has four bedrooms, two with private baths, and offers a great Western breakfast. The home sits right on U.S. 89 in the heart of town, and the proprietors offer custom tours of the Kanab area.

The Last Green Gate

According to local legend, in 1877 Mormon Church President Brigham Young ordered green paint for the fences and gates surrounding the St. George Temple. With the provision that they paint their own gates and fences, Young supplied gallons of excess paint to St. George citizens who were still building homes and shaping up their lots. For many years the yards of Utah's Dixie were accented in bright green, but a century later, only one of those green gates remained. Today the gate is on display at Greene Gate Village, named both for its owners, Dr. Mark and Barbara Greene, as well as for the green gate itself.

Miss Sophie's Bed and Breakfast
$$ • 30 N. 200 West, Kanab • 644-5952

Each of the four rooms in this historic home has a queen-size bed and private bath. Built in the 1890s by Frederick Lundquist, it is open May through October and is furnished with turn-of-the-century antiques.

Nine Gables Inn Bed & Breakfast
$$$ • 106 W. 100 North, Kanab • 644-5079

In Kanab's early days when there were no hotels, this historic house accommodated visitors while it was still a private home. It was built in 1872 by Levi Stewart, the first Mormon bishop of Kanab, and was later the home of Mary Woolley Chamberlain, the first woman mayor of Kanab and one of the first female mayors in America. Zane Grey and Buffalo Bill Cody stayed here. Today, room options include single, double and queen beds. Each room is furnished with antiques of the Mormon pioneer era, and an excellent breakfast is served.

RV Parks

More and more visitors to Southwestern Utah are bringing their bedrooms with them.

A number of excellent RV parks have opened in the area in the last 10 years. They host overnighters as well as a growing number of "snowbirds," who spend the winter months in the region. Many of these parks are like small communities with recreation facili-ties, entertainment options, convenience stores and planned activities provided.

Here we share a sampling of the many RV parks in the area. Be sure to call ahead to check on space availability. St. George parks fill up in the wintertime, while the Cedar City/Brian Head, Bryce Canyon and Kanab areas are all very busy in the summer.

Rates quoted are daily rates for two people and a full hookup. Some parks offer cable TV and other options at an additional charge. Most also offer weekly and monthly rates at a significant discount off the daily rate.

St. George/Zion

Brentwood RV Resort
150 N. 3700 West, Hurricane • 635-2320

Five miles off I-15 Exit 16 for Hurricane, this park is on Utah 9, just west of the little town. There are 187 full hookups, tent sites, a small golf course, showers, laundry, dump station, clubhouse, indoor pool, tennis courts, a water slide park, bowling alley and a miniature golf course. Small pets are allowed. The nightly rate is $17.44.

Harrisburg Lakeside RV Resort
P.O. Box 2146, St. George • 879-2312

This is technically a private membership park, but they will be happy to host you for a night to show the place off to you. Next to

Quail Lake, 2 miles south of Leeds, this park has 200 full-hookup sites. It's a combination resort and campground with a convenience store, soda fountain, deli, clubhouse, pool, laundry, Jacuzzi, showers and dump station. Northbound travelers take Exit 22, and southbounders take Exit 23. Then it's a 2-mile drive on the frontage road that runs parallel to I-15. The nightly rate is $17.

McArthur's Temple View RV Resort
975 S. Main St., St. George • 673-6400, (800) 776-6410

This park has established a great reputation as a result of the efforts by its owners to keep guests occupied via tours of the area, arts and crafts classes, exercise classes and other activities. There are 266 sites with full hookups. The list of amenities includes a clubhouse, phones for all sites, swimming pool, Jacuzzi, cable TV, dump station, laundry, showers, putting green, shuffleboard, horseshoes and billiards. Shopping at the St. George Commercial Center is a block away. The nightly rate is $20.95, weekly rates run $125 and monthly rates are a big savings at $269. Pets are welcome.

The Palms RV Resort
150 N. 3050 East, St. George • 628-2371

An all-adult park with 106 full hookups, The Palms is 2 miles southeast of St. George off Washington Exit 10 of I-15. Located on a ridge above the Virgin River, this park is set among beautiful walking areas. There's a year-round pool, hot tub, sauna, pay phones, phone sites, laundry and showers. Pets are accepted. The nightly rate is $16.75.

Quail Lake Resort
4400 W. State St., Hurricane • 635-9960

Set on the Virgin River near Quail Lake, this resort offers 55 sites with full hookups. There are showers, a laundry and a dump station, and small pets are allowed. The park

is 3 miles off I-15 Exit 16, near Hurricane. The nightly rate is $15.24.

Redlands RV Park
650 W. Telegraph St., St. George • 673-9700, (800) 553-8269

Just off I-15 at Washington Exit 10, this park is characterized by its many mature shade trees and large lawns. There are 200 full hookups. Pets are OK. There's a swimming pool and a store. Other amenities include cable TV, laundry facilities, Jacuzzi, showers and a dump station. The nightly rate is $19.75.

Settlers RV Park
1333 E. 100 South, St. George • 628-1624

Near the Zion Factory Stores and several excellent restaurants, this park is on the east edge of the St. George Valley beneath the east lava ridge. There are 155 full hookups with cable TV and phone sites. There's a swimming pool, Jacuzzi, showers, laundry, shuffleboard, horseshoes, recreation hall and a dump station. Leashed pets are welcome. Nightly rates are $16.90.

Silver Springs RV Resort
44 W. 500 North, LaVerkin • 635-7700

Located on the corner where Utah 9 turns east out of LaVerkin, this park has a nicely landscaped picnic area with a waterfall. With 55 full hookups, Silver Springs has a swimming pool, convenience store, laundry, showers and dump station. Small pets are allowed. Nightly rate is $18.

Willow Wind RV Park
1150 W. 80 South, Hurricane • 635-4154

This is a refurbished park on Utah 9 along the way to Zion National Park. It has plenty of shade trees and grassy sites. There are 85 full hookups, and the park offers a new hot tub, restrooms, laundry facilities, showers and dump station. There's a supermarket right across the street. The nightly rate is $18.

INSIDERS' TIP

If you're staying in St. George, ask the desk clerk for a free copy of the Historic Downtown Walking Tour. You can make the walk in as little as an hour.

Tourism provides employment for a large share of SW Utah's residents. Motels, restaurants, and services are busy year round.

Zion Canyon Campground
479 Zion Park Blvd., Springdale
• 772-3237

Just a half-mile from the south entrance to Zion National Park, this park has 75 full hookups with many sites along the Virgin River. There's a recreation hall, an outdoor pavilion, restaurant, laundry facilities, showers and dump station. Small pets are accepted. Nightly rate is $19.

Cedar City/Brian Head

Cedar City KOA Kampground
1121 N. Main, Cedar City • 586-9872

There are 68 full hookups along with 55 pull-throughs in this park. There are restrooms, showers and laundry facilities plus a heated pool, game room, playground and barbecue area. Nightly rate is $20.

Country Aire RV Park
1700 N. Main, Cedar City • 586-2550

This is a Good Sampark at the north end of Cedar City. It has 48 full hookups. There's a pool, convenience store and playground with a swing set and slide. There are also restrooms, showers and laundry facilities. The nightly rate is $19.

Red Ledge Campground
15 N. Main, Kanarraville • 586-9150

In Kanarraville, a little town just south of Cedar City off I-15 Exits 42 or 51, this is a small park with 24 full hookups in a quiet, peaceful setting with many hiking options nearby. It has restrooms, showers, a patio, a gas barbecue pit and full laundry facilities. Nightly rate is $15.

Bryce Canyon Area

Bryce Canyon Pines RV Park
Utah Hwy. 12, Bryce Canyon • 834-5441

There are 45 campsites, 25 of which have full hookups, in this park just 6 miles from the entrance to Bryce Canyon National Park off Utah 12. There are restrooms, showers, laundry facilities, a small selection of groceries and snacks, a playground, game room and indoor pool. The nightly rate is $18.

Red Canyon RV Park
Utah Hwy. 12, Bryce Canyon • 676-2690

Just three-quarters of a mile east of U.S. 89 on Utah 12, the Red Canyon RV Park also has a campground and convenience store. Open mid-March through mid-November, this is a Good Sampark with convenient pull-throughs, full-hookup sites, tables and canopies, a pavilion, restrooms with hot showers, shaded sites, grassy tent areas and campground cabins. Red Canyon Indian Store has one of the largest selections of Native American arts and crafts in Southwestern Utah. The nightly rate is $16.

Ruby's Inn RV Campground
Utah Hwy. 63, Bryce Canyon • 834-5301
This is the closest RV park to Bryce Canyon. It has 80 large, shaded, pull-through sites, showers, restrooms and laundry facilities. There's an indoor heated swimming pool, recreation hall and arcade. All of Ruby's Inn's famous amenities are close at hand including chuckwagon dinners, hoedowns, horseback rides, bike rentals and other activities. Nightly rate is $23.40.

Kanab Area

Bryce-Zion KOA
U.S. Hwy. 89, Glendale • 648-2490, (800) KOA-8635
There are 60 spaces with hookups and 25 tent sites at this park on U.S. 89, midway between Zion and Bryce Canyon national parks. Open May through mid-October and located 5 miles north of Glendale, this is an ideal staging point for forays into Zion, Bryce and the North Rim of the Grand Canyon. There are restrooms, showers, a heated pool, game room and playground, and you're near some great trout fishing. Horseback riding is also available.

Crazy Horse Campground
625 E. 300 South, Kanab • 644-2782, (800) 382-4908
Just east of Kanab, off U.S. 89, this park has 74 RV sites with full hookups and pull-

through locations. There are also camping sites for tenters. Open year round, it has clean restrooms, showers, a swimming pool, game room, arcade, playground and picnic tables with plenty of great shade trees. There's also a camp store with a variety of RV supplies. The park is adjacent to the Coral Hills Golf Course (see our Golf chapter).

Rentals

If you're coming to Southwestern Utah for an extended stay, or if the idea of a standard motel room doesn't interest you, here are some other short-term lodging options including condominiums, townhomes and apartments.

St. George/Zion

Bloomington Townhomes
$$$$ • 141-A Brigham Rd., St. George • 673-6172
Adjacent to the Bloomington Country Club Golf Course south of downtown St. George, these 18 townhomes are fully furnished. They are complete one- to four-bedroom units with adjacent swimming pool, tennis courts, and, of course, golf (see our Golf chapter for more on the Bloomington course). They're decorated in Southwestern style, and many open onto patios bordering on the golf course with views of the surrounding sandstone ridges of Bloomington.

Coronada Vacation Condominiums
$$ • 559 E. St. George. Blvd., St. George • 628-4436
A less expensive rental option, this converted motel in the heart of St. George has 60 suites with living room, kitchen, bath, two queen beds and a hideaway bed in some

---

INSIDERS' TIP

On Easter weekend, thousands of high school and college-age students flock to St. George for fun in the sun during their annual spring break from studies. As a result, motel rooms are at a premium, and restaurants, movie theaters and street corners are overflowing with exuberant teenagers and young adults. Traffic on St. George Boulevard comes to an almost complete standstill for two or three days and nights.

rooms. There's a heated indoor pool and Jacuzzi and laundry facilities. Weekly and monthly rates are available.

Green Valley Resort Condominium Rental
$$$$ • 1871 W. Canyon View Dr., St. George • 628-8060, (800) 237-1068

Green Valley is the resort that put St. George on the map. There are 70 one- to four-bedroom condominiums in the complex, and they come with one of the best amenities packages in the St. George area including indoor and outdoor pools, a separate diving pool, indoor and outdoor tennis, racquetball courts, volleyball, Jacuzzis and basketball courts. There's also a complete spa.

Green Valley Sports Village
$$$$ • 860 S. Village Rd., St. George • 673-1392

Just west of the Green Valley Resort, these 15 condominiums are fully furnished with their own common swimming pools and tennis courts. The Sports Village is set on a hill with spectacular views to the north encompassing the red Kayenta Cliffs to the west, the mouth of Snow Canyon to the north and Pine Valley Mountain to the northeast. There's racquetball, basketball, a clubhouse with billiards and an exercise room.

Cedar City/Brian Head

Aspen Condominiums
$$$$ • 424 N. Utah Hwy. 143, Brian Head • 677-2806

The Aspens Rental Agency can set you up in any of a number of privately owned condominiums within the Brian Head Ski Resort. This complex is a small set of condos set in a grove of spruce and aspen trees near Brian Head chairlifts 2, 3, 5 and 7. There are also condos available for rent at Chalet Village (across from the Giant Steps lift area), Snowshoe Village and Pine Tree (among the aspens and pines close to chairlifts 4 and 6), Brianwood (also within walking distance of chairlifts) and Giant Steps (with ski-in ski-out to the Giant Steps lift area.) These units come in a variety of configurations from one to four bedrooms, some with lofts and up to three bathrooms. Most are cozy, comfortable condos with spacious living areas, fireplaces, cable TV, full kitchens and great views, and many have an accompanying indoor pool, sauna, Jacuzzi and covered parking.

Dalton Apartments
$ • 135 S. 300 West, Cedar City • 586-6077

These are two- and three-bedroom apartments in four different locations within walking distance of the Utah Shakespearean Festival. Many have bathrooms off each bedroom. Some have a washer and dryer, and linens are provided. Weekly rates begin at $210 and up, depending on occupancy.

Timberbrook Village Condominiums
$$$$ • 424 N. Utah Hwy. 143, Brian Head • 677-2806

The 90 condo units in this complex have full kitchens and fireplaces. There's an indoor pool, exercise room and covered parking. The complex, set in the middle of the Brian Head Ski Resort, has two three-story buildings with underground parking. Studios with bunks, one-bedroom units with queen beds and loft units that sleep up to eight people are also available.

The world is beating a path to Southwestern Utah, and everyone who comes seems to be hungry.

Restaurants

Restaurant dining is a relatively new concept for Southwestern Utahns. For generations, eating out meant Dutch-oven potatoes cooked over an open campfire in some remote corner of the Arizona Strip. It was a Sunday afternoon barbecue in the backyard or beef jerky at the end of a steep climb to the summit of a red rock cliff.

A few area restaurants have been around for 30 or 40 years. One or two even have histories that span generations, but they are the great exception. Most restaurants in our small rural communities existed to meet the needs of a few tourists who passed through the area on their way to somewhere else. The locals prepared their own meals and ate at their own dinner tables.

With the discovery of Southwestern Utah as a place to live and work, retire or vacation, the world is beating a path to our door . . . and everyone who comes here is hungry! There aren't many four-star restaurants here yet, but in most communities there are really good, varied choices for breakfast, lunch and dinner. A wait for a table is still rare, but it does happen more often as the community — and the demand for service — continues to grow.

This chapter is written in an effort to guide you to the best and brightest — and in some cases, the only — restaurants in each of our represented geographical areas of interest. Listed alphabetically by area, you'll find a respectable mix of fine dining, faster foods and some out-of-the-way surprises.

Not every restaurant can sell you an alcoholic beverage. But while Utah liquor laws are considered peculiar by some, most restaurateurs can easily guide you successfully through the maze of legislative jargon (see "Nay, Bartender?" in our Nightlife chapter for more on area laws regarding alcohol).

Note the price code assigned to each restaurant listing. The little dollar signs are a hint at the bottom line for your evening's repast — an indicator of the usual amount you can expect to pay for dinner for two, not including dessert, drinks or gratuity.

$	Less than $20
$$	$21 to $40
$$$	$41 to $60
$$$$	More than $60

Most establishments will accept major credit cards, cash or travelers checks. Some might even accept your personal check (we here in Southwestern Utah have a reputation for sometimes being a little too trusting). Your credit card is good at all the restaurants we list, unless otherwise noted.

St. George/Zion

Perhaps just because it is the largest population center in Southwestern Utah, the St. George area has a good number of respectable restaurants — even one boasting a four-star rating. As in any community on a major thoroughfare like Interstate 15, there is at least one (maybe more) of most all of the fast-food and national chain restaurants. You'll find a McDozen golden arches and about that many Pizza Huts, Little Caesars, Denny's and Dairy Queens.

Restaurants have a strange history in Southwestern Utah. Some open to rave reviews, stay a while then disappear. Others move around until they find the ideal location and success. A few seem to have all the right ingredients from the start — location, visibility, an interesting menu — but after a while, they move or disappear. Still, as you'll see, there are dozens of terrific options. We hope you'll venture past the places you're familiar with and try a few of these popular favorites in the St. George area.

Andelin's Gable House
$-$$ • 290 E. St. George Blvd., St. George • 673-6796

Andelin's Gable House is where the locals go for a delicious à la carte meal, a five-course feast or a delectable dessert. Tour buses, too, find Andelin's a great place to stop for lunch or dinner on the way to Zion or our other national parks. In an English country garden setting, Andelin's is very well-known in Southwestern Utah and just may be St. George's signature restaurant. Over the years, Mike and Doris Andelin have garnered lots of stars from newspaper food editors, and the restaurant has been featured in numerous magazines and guide books, not only for fine dining, but also for excellent service from friendly waiters and waitresses in old English attire. The most popular menu items include the house speciality of prime rib, roast brisket of beef, shrimp salad or the Monte Cristo sandwich. In the Captain's Room, the five-course dinner with soup, salad, appetizer, entree and dessert is a wonderful way to celebrate a promotion, a birthday or an anniversary, though you may waddle a bit when you're finished. The three-course dinner comes with a choice of soup or salad, appetizer and entree, or you can pick your favorite flavors from the à la carte menu.

The homemade soups, rolls, breads and desserts at Andelin's are legendary. Ask your waitress to give you a dessert list, then try to decide between pot-au-creme, German chocolate pie, deep-dish apple pie with a light rum sauce, pralines-and-cream pie, raspberry cream cake or one of a half-dozen cheesecakes. You'll just have to come back to try them all. Andelin's Gable House is open Monday through Saturday for lunch and dinner, but closed on Sunday. Reservations are not required, but it's a good idea to call ahead.

Bentley House Restaurant
$$ • 76 W. Tabernacle St., St. George • 656-3333

To see the Bentley House today, it's hard to imagine it is the same house shown in the photo gallery in the entrance hallway. After 30 years of disuse, the Bentley House has risen phoenix-like from the ashes of decay. The restored pioneer home, filled with beautiful antique furnishings, is the centerpiece of Greene Gate Village Bed and Breakfast Inn, a cluster of nine dwellings in a garden setting.

Open for dinner Thursday, Friday and Saturday only or by reservation for special parties, the Bentley House Restaurant is a fine-dining experience with five-course meals and delectable "from scratch" baked goods and desserts. The most popular entrees are filet mignon, salmon and pork tenderloin with all the trimmings. Kids are welcome, but may be a little out of place among couples who enjoy the private dining rooms or groups in the main room.

You'll enjoy dinner even more if you've arranged an overnight stay in one of the dozen rooms at Greene Gate Village (see our Accommodations chapter). Or come early and ask for a tour of Greene Gate Village. You'll love the stories associated with each home. Don't miss the chance to study the photos and pioneer artifacts in the main hallway of the Bentley House. During the evening, dinner music is played on an antique piano. Parking is plentiful, either along Tabernacle Street or in the Greene Gate Village parking lot.

Bit and Spur Restaurant and Saloon
$ • 1212 Zion Park Blvd., Springdale • 772-3498

Southwestern cuisine such as stuffed jalapeños, deep-dish-style chicken enchiladas, chile-crusted tenderloin, fresh wild mushroom tamales, white chocolate cheesecake with blueberries, hazelnut lace cookies and Cadillac Margaritas are on the menu at the Bit and Spur Restaurant and Saloon, making it well worth the drive to Zion Canyon. Besides good food, the garden patio with its rustic saloon, billiards and TV attracts tourists, sports fans and families to this stylishly casual eatery. The restaurant opened in 1981 and serves dinner

---

FYI

Unless otherwise noted, the area code for all phone numbers listed in this chapter is 801 but will change to 435 in September 1997. Either area code may be used until March 22, 1998.

every night of the week beginning at 5 PM. Reservations are not necessary but are suggested, particularly during the spring and summer tourist season. The Bit and Spur is liquor-licensed (see our Nightlife chapter).

Cafe Basila's
$$ • 2 W. St. George Blvd., Ancestor Square, St. George • 673-7671

Perhaps Southwestern Utah's only four-star restaurant (as proclaimed by Salt Lake City's *Deseret News* and *Utah Holiday Magazine*), Basila's (pronounced bay-sil-ah) is authentic European dining with a hint of California cuisine. Basila herself is the chef, combining a rich culinary heritage from her Baghdad homeland with her life as an immigrant in Detroit. You'll want to return because it's all so good, but first-timers are guaranteed to rave about any pasta dish, salad or the spinach pie. Treat yourself at least once to the saganaki — a flaming fried cheese served with french bread. Oppa! And leave room for dessert. Her baklava and spumoni pie are to die for!

Cafe Basila's is open for lunch or dinner Monday through Saturday in the downtown historic district near the Pioneer Center for the Arts (see our Arts and Culture chapter). Reservations are a good idea, but not necessary. If you have to wait a few minutes, spend the time browsing through Basila's European gift items. Parking is adequate except at noon, when everyone in town heads for Ancestor Square.

Catfish Charlie's
$ • 545 N. Main St., Leeds • 879-2267

It stands to reason SOUTHwestern Utah should have a southern-style restaurant. Catfish Charlie's is one-of-a-kind between the Wasatch Front and Las Vegas — uniquely southern, right down to the most popular menu items of catfish and frog legs. Open since 1994 in Leeds (the town known as the "historic portal to Southern Utah"), Catfish Charlie's specialty is farm-raised catfish from Mississippi, deep-fried in a seasoned, Louisiana fish-fry batter. Top off the evening with a slice of pie or homemade peach cobbler. The place is small, with seating for only 40 at a time, but Catfish Charlie's is open for dinner only Tuesday through Saturday.

Charlie's Supreme Malts and Ice Cream
$ • 287 W. St. George Blvd., St. George • 628-6304 • No credit cards

If your waistline is not an issue (maybe even if it is), Charlie's Supreme Malts and Ice Cream is the people's choice for extra-thick malts and shakes, according to *The Spectrum's* 1995 and 1996 Annual Readers Poll. In a fun, relaxed atmosphere amid '50s and '60s decor, families, business people and students come back again and again for great food, big portions and reasonable prices. There are three choices of soup — homemade daily — along with deli sandwiches and fresh salads. Charlie's uses fresh meats, cheeses and breads to make every meal an enjoyable experience.

Ice cream treats are the specialty, but bring a big appetite. Treat yourself to a super-sized banana split or any of several rich, thick, gooey delicacies made with real ice cream and yogurt. The popularity of Charlie's has not been built with flashy advertising, but by word of mouth and referrals by satisfied customers. Charlie's is open Monday through Saturday for lunch and dinner.

Claimjumper Restaurant
$$ • 1110 S. Bluff St., St. George
• 674-7800

The Claimjumper doesn't take reservations so you might have to wait, especially on weekends. We think you'll agree it's well worth it. There are some pretty impressive things about the Claimjumper. For starters, check out the bar, inlaid with thousands of silver dollars (estimates run as high as $10,000 worth of coins). Then there's the prime rib and steaks, aged a full 21 days to guarantee the most tender cut you've ever tasted. Choose from the delicate "ladies" cut — 12 to 16 ounces of meat — or the regular cut, weighing in at 16 to 20 ounces. For the really big appetite, the double cut tips the scale at 32 ounces. The Baseball Steak is one huge chunk of meat — the center cut of a top sirloin — as big as a baseball. If there's any room left, linger over a generous slice of cheesecake, mud pie or carrot cake, plain or à la mode.

The St. George Claimjumper, one of four in Utah, is decorated in an early cowboy motif with antiques. The walls are covered with memorabilia of the old West — wagon wheels, barbed wire, chaps, ropes and authentic brands from modern or historic ranches in the area. Cowboys from the Arizona Strip or Cedar Mountain are likely to find their brand among those burned onto the wall. Lunch is served Monday through Friday, and dinner is served daily. Reservations are suggested for parties of eight or more but must be guaranteed with a credit card.

Cosmopolitan Steakhouse
$$ • 1915 Wells Fargo Dr., Silver Reef
• 879-2978

The Cosmopolitan Restaurant is in Silver Reef, a 20-minute drive north of downtown St. George (about 30 minutes from Cedar City), and is worth the drive. Popular for its charming boom-town atmosphere, the Cosmopolitan specializes in steaks, chicken, seafood and fajitas (either beef or vegetarian). Wrap your tasty entree with a Tumbleweed — an appetizing onion cut to bloom when batter-dipped and deep-fried. For dessert, try the restaurant's own creation called the Silver Reef Delight — a delicately baked meringue topped with fresh whipped cream and raspberries.

The Cosmopolitan is open Thursday through Saturday for dinner only. If you've never been to Silver Reef, you may want to get to town during the daylight hours and have a look around. High-end, custom homes are scattered throughout the desert community, but the real attraction is the still-standing structures left when the mining town was abandoned. Bring your appetite and a camera, there's lots to see. Reservations are not necessary but are suggested, especially for groups of 20 or more.

Dick's Cafe
$ • 114 E. St. George Blvd., St. George
• 673-3841

The sign in the well-worn parking lot of this near-legendary eatery says, "If you think our parking lot has character, wait til you meet the guys inside." The guys inside are as much a part of the place as the Western decor. Just about every morning since 1935, when Dick Hammer first opened on the Boulevard, a gang of local farmers, ranchers and business people have gathered for coffee and conversation before starting the day. Families, tourists and Hollywood stars on location have also frequented Dick's for four decades, enjoying the friendly exchange of stories and jokes as much as the great-tasting homemade breakfasts, lunches and dinners served seven days a week (Dick's closes early on Sunday afternoon).

Diners will tell you they especially love the homemade soups, oven-roasted turkey or beef and the Navajo tacos. And where, in this age of instant everything, can you find real whipped potatoes and homemade gravy? You guessed it! But you'd better hurry to experience Dick's Cafe at this location. By the end of this year, Dick's will be in a new building across the street. The food will be the same, but the character of the place? We'll see!

Ernesto's Mexican Restaurant
$ • 929 W. Sunset Blvd., No. 18, St. George
• 674-2767

Ernesto's in Phoenix Plaza is a tasty Mexican restaurant, specializing in chile rellenos, chimichangas and salsa so good you'll want to slurp it through a straw. Chicken and crab enchiladas (Enchilada Acapulco is on the menu), Tacos de Carnitas and tamales are local choices for most popular menu items. Ernesto's dessert menu features fried ice cream and New York-style piña colada cheesecake. The atmosphere is a mix of American Southwest and Mexican. Ernesto's is open for lunch and dinner Monday through Saturday.

Fairway Grill
$ • 430 E. St. George Blvd., St. George
• 656-4448

OK, we admit it. We thought the location was jinxed, since the past few years have seen a number of restaurants at this address. But judging from the full parking lot and the smiles on the faces of diners, the Fairway Grill, open less than a year, looks like it may have staying power. The menu is basic American served amid a golf course motif. Tourists, families and

business people are enthusiastically spreading the word about the baked halibut supreme, marinated ribeye steak, bread pudding and deli sandwiches served on homemade white and wheat twist rolls. They're telling their friends and co-workers about the breads and rolls baked fresh daily and the soups, dressings and sauces made from scratch.

Fairway Grill has a liquor license. Open seven days a week, the restaurant serves breakfast and has daily lunch and dinner specials. Reservations are suggested on weekends and holidays, but not usually necessary.

Flanigan's Restaurant
$-$$ • 428 Zion Park Blvd., Springdale
• 772-3244, (800) 765-7787

Flanigan's is an oasis in your travels — a cozy cafe featuring fine dining at reasonable prices. In the magnificent splendor of Zion Canyon, Flanigan's specializes in fresh fish including salmon and Utah trout, pastas, light specials and desserts. A liquor license allows the sale of beer, wine and other spirits as well as Utah micro-brewed beers on tap.

Open since 1984, Flanigan's serves a light lunch and regular dinner menu seven days a week. No reservations are needed during the off-season (mid-October to mid-April), but during the peak tourist months, when millions visit the park, it's a good idea to call ahead.

Harley's Diner and Sports Grille
$ • 790 S. Bluff St., St. George • 656-9018
$ • 550 S. Main St., Cedar City • 867-8202

You won't see poodle skirts or letterman sweaters, but Harley's is certainly reminiscent of Arnold's from the popular TV sitcom *Happy Days*. The food is a mix of American and Mexican. Choose from sizzling fajitas, finger-licking-good ribs or gourmet burgers. Wash it all down with a tall, cold Coke or a thick shake in your favorite flavor. The place is bright, fun and decorated in '50s memorabilia including a Harley-Davidson (known as "Fatboy") suspended from the ceiling. And don't worry about missing any big games, races, matches, meets or tournaments. Harley's has 8 TVs, always on and tuned to the most popular sports channels. Harley's is open daily for lunch and dinner.

JJ's Frostop

$ • 138 W. State St., Hurricane • 635-4047 • No credit cards

The local family that owns this business is proud of JJ's reputation for good food, good service and cleanliness. Take your choice between inside seating, the convenience of a drive-up window or the old-fashioned fun of curb service for hamburgers, shakes and fries. Call-in orders are welcome. JJ's is open for lunch and dinner Monday through Saturday.

J.J. Hunan Chinese Restaurant

$-$$ • 2 W. St. George Blvd., St. George • 628-7219

If you like Chinese food, J.J. Hunan is likely to be your restaurant of choice in the St. George area. Perched in the tower at Ancestor Square, J.J. Hunan has been a repeat favorite for families and tourists since 1988. Open seven days a week for lunch and dinner, the most popular menu items are sesame beef or chicken, lemon chicken, chow mein, kung pao chicken, shrimp or a combination including beef. Cooked-to-order options for most menu items include no oil or no MSG. The atmosphere is casual, and youngsters are welcome. J.J. Hunan has received *The Spectrum's* people's choice award for Chinese food among area restaurants for two successive years. Unless you're taking a large group, you don't need a reservation.

Libby Lorraine's

$-$$ • 567 S. Valley View Dr., St. George • 673-7190

The country decor, plenty of parking and delicious choices on the menu add up to a fine dining experience at Libby Lorraine's. The clientele ranges from families with kids to couples on vacation to locals out for a romantic evening on the town. Libby's offers great fare with an Italian flair. Marinated chicken breasts, lasagna, halibut, snapper and sauces made from scratch satisfy the most discriminating tastebuds and keep customers coming back. Libby's serves lunch and dinner Monday through Saturday, and a classical guitarist entertains on weekend nights. The restaurant is licensed to serve liquor.

Log House Restaurant at Majestic View Lodge

$$ • 2400 Zion Park Blvd., Springdale • 772-3000

The Log House Restaurant in Zion Canyon is one-of-a-kind. The massive logs that form the building were "fire-killed" in the infamous Yellowstone National Park fire in 1988. With a majestic view from every table, the Log House has a reputation for great food, a relaxed atmosphere and a unique setting outside the park. The house specialties are a variety of chicken dishes — including the popular chicken fried steak — and gourmet hamburgers.

Following lunch or dinner, take a tour of the wildlife museum, home to a splendid collection that includes displays of polar and grizzly bears, Rocky Mountain sheep, mountain goats, great white shark, elk, piranha, wild turkey and a one-in-a-million find of two bucks with their horns interlocked. Next, visit the Log House Gift Shop for a little something to take home to the kids. The 72-room Majestic Lodge is in the planning stages, scheduled for completion in the spring of '98.

Silver Reef Lives

The Cosmopolitan Restaurant in Silver Reef is a replica of its predecessor, built at the same location in 1875. The Cosmopolitan was one of five restaurants built to meet the needs of 1,500 miners who arrived almost overnight following the discovery of a rich vein of silver. The vein ran out some 15 years later, and miners abandoned the town as quickly as they had come. They took their dreams of prosperity, but left behind a rich historic site that still attracts tourists today.

Flanigan's INN

Mark Twain Restaurant

$$$ • 1185 W. Utah Ave. on Utah Hwy. 59, Hildale • 874-1030

The Mark Twain Restaurant is a bit of a surprise. Midway between St. George and Kanab on Utah Highway 59, the Mark Twain is an upscale restaurant in the community of Hildale — in other words, in the middle of a vast expanse of Southwestern Utah desert. Fine-dining menu choices include steak and seafood, prime rib and crab legs. Delicious appetizers, drinks (Mark Twain's is liquor-licensed) and desserts also make the 45-minute drive from St. George worth the trip.

For holiday parties, office retreats or other occasions involving large gatherings, the Mark Twain has a banquet room that can accommodate up to 150 people. The Mark Twain Restaurant operated in Salt Lake City for 10 years before relocating to this Utah-Arizona border community in 1992. Open Monday through Saturday for breakfast, lunch and dinner, reservations are suggested but not required. An adjacent motel is under construction and scheduled for completion by late summer of 1997.

McGuire's

$$ • 531 N. Bluff St., St. George • 628-4066

It doesn't look like much from the outside, but the combination of fine dining, a liquor license, the ambiance of a golf and jazz motif and live entertainment not only draws a happy combination of tourists, couples, singles and sports fans to McGuire's but keeps them coming back. Management is proud of the number of repeat tourists and seasonal snowbirds who return each year — like swallows to Capistrano — because they like the consistent quality of McGuire's filet mignon, veal picata, chicken marsala and pasta linguine with clam sauce as well as other tasty menu items. McGuire's is open for dinner only Monday through Saturday. Live entertainment on Wednesday, Thursday and Friday nights include guitarists, pianists and vocalists (see our Nightlife chapter). If there are more than six in your party, its a good idea to make reservations.

Pancho and Lefty's

$ • 1050 S. Bluff St., St. George • 628-4772

Pancho and Lefty's, in St. George and Cedar City, is famous for hefty portions of hot and tasty Mexican food. Recent additions to the menu are chile verde and asada platters, biste ranchero, asada and chile verde burritos, Burrito Bendito and pork, chicken or vegetable tamales. Still, the most popular menu item remains sizzling, hot fajitas.

Pancho and Lefty's is open daily for lunch and dinner. Families, tourists and singles will all enjoy the Spanish-style atmosphere, and the eatery is liquor-licensed. Reservations are only required for parties of 20 or more.

Panda Garden Chinese Restaurant

$ • 212 N. 900 East, St. George • 674-1538

Local families like this Chinese restaurant. Specializing in Mandarin, Szechuan and Cantonese menu items, the Panda Garden was chosen in 1994 by *Spectrum* readers as the best Chinese restaurant in Southern Utah. The restaurant offers hefty servings of house pan-fried noodles, honey-garlic chicken, teriyaki chicken and pot stickers — a type of dumpling filled with pork. Open every day for lunch and dinner, the Panda Garden can seat up to 150 people. Parking is adequate, and reservations are only necessary for large groups.

Pasta Factory

$-$$ • 2 West St. George Blvd., St. George • 674-3753

It hasn't been around as long as the Pizza Factory, but it's the same owner and success formula that has already made the Pasta Factory a popular eatery for custom-built pasta dishes. Whether you select fettucine with Alfredo sauce and chicken, Shrimp Ronaldo or ravioli with pesto sauce, your lunch or dinner will be consistently good. The breadsticks are a nice touch, and the desserts are decadent.

In this desert region where summertime temperatures soar above the century mark and winter temps can get down into the teens, many still prefer outdoor patio dining at the Pasta Factory. If you want to eat outside, you'll be comfortably warmed by heaters in the winter; comfortably cooled by mist systems during summer. The Pasta Factory is open for lunch and dinner Monday through Saturday.

Photo: Jud Burkett

Southwestern Utah offers a wide variety of dining options.

Paula's Cazuela
$ • 745 Ridgeview Dr., St. George
• 673-6568

This place is always crowded on Friday and Saturday nights. The food is abundant Tex-Mex, the atmosphere is friendly and the service is fast and efficient. It all equals a pleasant combination when coupled with a location high above busy Bluff Street. You'll enjoy a beautiful view, any time of day, of the area's red rock cliffs from your table. The restaurant is clean and appropriately adorned in south-of-the-border decor.

The most popular menu items include taco salads, a variety of enchilada and burrito dinners and everyone's favorite: Paula's Chimichanga. A liquor license means you can get a cold beer with your dinner, and parking is on the hillside next to the restaurant. Paula's is open Monday through Saturday for lunch and dinner. Paula's Too, which opened in 1996, is a smaller version of the original, which has been around since 1972, and offers many of the same menu items. Reservations are suggested, especially on weekends when everyone thinks of Paula's for dinner.

Pier 49 — San Francisco Sourdough Pizza
$ • 1930 W. Sunset Blvd., St. George
• 628-7774

If you're burned out on pizza, Pier 49 invites you to "fall in love with pizza again." Made-from-scratch sourdough crust and six specialty sauces create such gourmet delights as the Alcatraz (a combination pizza) or Lombard Street (a barbecued chicken version). Open Monday through Saturday for lunch and dinner, Pier 49 is a place the whole family will enjoy. Decked out with benches and booths, the eatery is reminiscent of a Pacific coast waterfront cafe — there's an abundance of Frisco photos on the walls. Parking is ample, and there's seating for up to 75.

Pioneer Restaurant
$$ • 828 Zion Park Blvd., Springdale
• 772-3009

The homestyle speciality at the Pioneer Restaurant is chicken-fried steak, but families and tourists alike also line up for veggie specials, exceptional baked goods and melt-in-your-mouth prime rib served Friday, Saturday and Sunday nights. The eatery is decorated in antiques and cowboy stuff to give it a real western feel. The Pioneer is liquor-licensed, so you can enjoy a cold beer or cocktail on a hot summer day in Zion Canyon. Breakfast, lunch and dinner are served seven days a week, and reservations are not needed.

Pizza Factory
$ • 2 W. St. George Blvd., St. George • 628-1234

If big crowds and frequent remodeling are any indication, this place must be one of the most successful restaurants in town. The secret? The Pizza Factory simply has really good food, consistently. With a three-floor store at Ancestor Square, the Pizza Factory has been a favorite of local families and tourists since 1979. The menu is limited to terrific custom-built pizza, pasta, sandwiches, calzones, homemade soups and chili, spaghetti, desserts (including homemade cookies) and a great salad bar.

The Pizza Factory uses quality cheeses, tomato products and meats. If it's supposed to be crispy, it is. If it's supposed to be hot, it is. Open Monday through Saturday for lunch and dinner, you may have to wait for a few of the 160 seats to vacate — it's a good bet they'll all be full when you get there, and the Factory doesn't take reservations. If you'd prefer to eat at home, you can order from the same menu (but a different phone number) for delivery by the Pizza Factory Express. Call 634-1234.

San Franciscan Bakery Cafe
$ • 968 E. St. George Blvd., St. George • 674-2800

Original San Francisco sourdough bread is the central ingredient on this cafe's menu of sandwiches, soups, pizza and pastries. Favorite menu choices for hungry professionals and tourists include turkey on sourdough, clam chowder or sourdough pizza, all enjoyed in the canopy-shaded, sidewalk cafe setting. The San Franciscan is the trendy spot in St. George for a full line of gourmet coffees, brewed fresh all day. Open for breakfast, lunch or dinner Monday through Saturday, the San Franciscan is proud of their reputation for quality and quick, efficient, friendly service.

Scaldoni's Gourmet Grocer and Grill
$$ • 929 W. Sunset Blvd. (Phoenix Plaza), St. Gorge • 674-1300

We try to avoid labeling any restaurant "the best" or "THE place to eat," but we considered bending the rule for Scaldoni's. Named for owner John DeVivo's Italian immigrant grandparents, Scaldoni's Gourmet Grocer and Grill opened in January 1995 to meet Southwestern Utah's needs for a great meatball sandwich and hard-to-find gourmet foods. Its Old World charm makes it the ideal place for fine dining on prom night or an anniversary, but it also attracts business people and families. The DeVivos, St. George Area Chamber of Commerce's 1996 Entrepreneurs of the Year, blend Giovanni and Giavanna Scaldoni's traditional family recipes with delectable '90s flavors and cooking methods. The supreme black Angus steaks and prime rib are flavorful and melt-in-your-mouth tender. Popular menu items for diners in the restaurant or outside on the patio include vegetable lasagna, penne pasta with sausage and peppers, shrimp scampi or the daily lunch and dinner specials. And save room for dessert. Whatever you choose, it will be worth an extra few minutes of aerobics. Open Monday through Saturday, Scaldoni's has a liquor license and suggests, but does not require, reservations.

Shonesburg Restaurant
$$ • 897 Zion Park Blvd., Springdale • 772-3522

Visiting in Zion Canyon? Don't you dare miss Shonesburg's bumbleberry pie, a delectable concoction of burpleberries and binkleberries, which are similar to black or boysenberries. But don't look for them in *Webster's*. Burpleberries and binkleberries were named by area youngsters 50 years ago as a way to identify the yummy nuggets in grandma's pies. Shonesburg is a newly remodeled, fine-dining restaurant specializing in a delicious choice of chicken, beef or fish entrees including Chicken à la Shonesburg, Trout Almondine or Whiskey Steak. All should be followed with pie, of course, and the jams and jellies are excellent. Shonesburg's is liquor-licensed.

The vaulted, pine-ceilinged dining room is

filled with antiques. A summer-stock theater presents nightly musicals in a community with few other choices for nightlife (see our Nightlife chapter for more information). Shonesburg Restaurant is open for breakfast, lunch and dinner seven days a week. Reservations are not required but are suggested, at least for the dinner crowd.

Sullivan's Rococo Steakhouse
$$ • 511 S. Airport Rd., St. George • 673-3305, (888) 628-3671

Sullivan's Rococo Steakhouse has enjoyed a long run as one of the best steakhouses in Southwestern Utah. For a fine dining experience, Rococo's does an exceptional job with steaks, seafood, prime rib and fresh salmon. You'll also appreciate homemade bread and pies baked fresh daily.

Rococo's is within walking distance of the airport terminal, so it is a logical choice for hungry tourists flying in for a tour of nearby national parks. What attracts the locals besides the good food? Rococo's has a liquor license for those who want a drink with dinner, but the real drawing card is a breathtaking view of St. George. Wraparound windows provide a panorama, day or night, of red hills, freeway lights and historic downtown buildings. For many, the view itself is worth the cost of dinner. Rococo's is open daily for lunch and dinner. Reservations are not necessary.

Switchback Grille and Trading Company
$$ • 1149 S. Zion Park Blvd., Springdale • 772-3777

Subaru executives toured Zion National Park then dined at the Switchback Grille and gave both the park and the restaurant their highest rating! Spit-fired chicken, steak, brick-oven pizza, full liquor services, good parking and the pleasant, outdoorsy decor and atmosphere of Zion National Park combine for a unanimous thumbs-up experience. Add in the view of the natural splendor of Zion Canyon, and you've got something really special. The Switchback is open seven days a week for breakfast, lunch and dinner. Reservations for dinner are suggested but not required. The Switchback may just be one of the top-10 restaurants in Utah. We'll let you decide.

2 Lazy 2 Ranch Steakhouse
$$ • 358 W. Buena Vista Blvd., Washington • 674-2022

In 1994, Kim and Marcie Andrus sold their Idaho holdings and headed south to St. George where they constructed — from massive Canadian cedar logs — a 14,000-square-foot log cabin. Now they're working hard to manage the herd of families, couples, tourists and snowbirds who come for lunch and dinner to enjoy the succulent crab, tender and flavorful prime rib and finger-licking goodness of barbecue baby-back ribs. 2 Lazy 2 Ranch Steakhouse cuts and ages its own beef . An old, family recipe is the secret to the hot homemade bread.

2 Lazy 2 Ranch Steakhouse is versatile too. In decidedly country-western decor, they have served numerous black-tie banquets. Live entertainment and dancing Monday through Saturday attracts teens through seniors (see our Nightlife chapter). 2 Lazy 2 Ranch Steakhouse has a large parking lot to accommodate cars off the freeway, buses or semis. Reservations are suggested.

Zion Lodge Dining Room
$$ • Utah Hwy. 9, Zion National Park, Springdale • 772-3213, ext. 160

In the rustic lodge where kings, presidents and movie stars have dined since 1939, you'll enjoy the food almost as much as the surroundings. Zion Lodge Dining Room offers a full menu (liquor is served) of steak, seafood, pasta and vegetarian entrees. The most popu-

---

INSIDERS' TIP

Leeds, the home of Catfish Charlie's Restaurant, was once home to Robert LeRoy Parker (a.k.a. Butch Cassidy), Harry Longabaugh (a.k.a. Hyrum Beebee, a.k.a. "Sundance Kid") and Ann Bassett Willis, known as Queen of the Rustlers of Brown's Park.

lar choices are prime rib or Utah red trout — one of several regional offerings with a Southwestern flair. The dining room is on the second floor of the historic park lodge, with panoramic views of world famous Zion Canyon. The dining room is open every day for breakfast, lunch and dinner, and reservations for dinner are required. Parking is easily accessible and plentiful.

Zion Pizza and Noodle Company
$ • 868 Zion Park Blvd., Springdale
• 772-3815

Zion Pizza and Noodle Company, in the old church in Springdale, knows how to create a great gourmet pizza and pasta dishes. Chef Bruce Vander Werff, with a degree from LaVarene in Paris, offers 11 authentic pizzas baked in a slate stone oven. But assisted by his sons, Jakob and Joshua, Bruce has also forged a reputation for really good calzones and salads. And this is one of those rare places in Utah where you can get a cold beer with your lunch or dinner. This restaurant is popular with the townies, but it is particularly appealing to hungry tourists. Who could mistake the smell of pizza wafting on a summer breeze? Reservations are not needed, and there is plenty of parking adjacent to the building.

Cedar City/Brian Head

The business of restaurants in the Cedar City/Brian Head area has grown as the tourists have come in growing numbers. Skiers and bikers needed somewhere to eat after a day on the slopes or in the mountains . . . Visitors to the Utah Shakespearean Festival wanted places where they could discuss the works of the Bard over a good steak, pizza or a delectable dessert. Plan around this interesting phenomenon in these communities: Several restaurants are open only seasonally.

Boomer's Pasta Garden
$ • 5 N. Main St. (upstairs), Cedar City
• 586-5152

The flavors hint of old Italy, but the location is upstairs in the Main Street Plaza, just two blocks from the world-famous Utah Shakespearean Festival. In its first year, Boomer's Pasta Garden has gained a reputation and a loyal following of locals and festival visitors who enjoy the creativity of build-your-own pasta dishes. The restaurant was honored as 1996 Small Business of the Year in Cedar City. Popular menu items include lasagna, shrimp capellini, chicken parmigiana, manicotti or shrimp scampi prepared by Chef Mike Damavandi.

Couples, business people and tourists all enjoy Boomer's. Parking is plentiful. Boomer's Pasta Garden is open for lunch and dinner Monday through Saturday. Reservations are not necessary.

FYI

Unless otherwise noted, the area code for all phone numbers listed in this chapter is 801 but will change to 435 in September 1997. Either area code may be used until March 22, 1998.

Boomer's Restaurant
$ • 5 N. Main St., Cedar City
• 865-9665

In the Main Street Plaza, two blocks from the home of the Utah Shakespearean Festival, Boomer's Restaurant boasts one of the largest menus in Southwestern Utah. This Boomer's is a sister eatery to Boomer's Pasta Garden (listing above), Grandma Boomer's Ice Cream Factory and Grandma Boomer's Candy Factory. The half-pound Boomer Burger is the most popular menu item here, but diners may also choose steaks and fries, Mexican flavors such as chimichangas, fish dishes and specialty sandwiches. If dessert is your thing, Boomer's is the place for deep-fried ice cream — a gooey concoction of vanilla ice cream, corn flakes and cinnamon in a tortilla shell smothered with chocolate syrup and whipped cream. Boomer's also serves up homemade bread pudding, hot fudge brownies with ice cream and thick sauce, and deep-dish mud pie with ice cream and a graham cracker crust. The building has recently been remodeled to include a large waterfall and several fun shops. Boomer's is open for lunch and dinner Monday through Saturday.

Brickhouse Cafe
$ • 227 S. Main St., Cedar City • 865-1770
In the quaint charm of a Victorian cottage

setting, the upbeat Brickhouse Cafe offers a varied menu of American and Italian fare. At the Brickhouse Cafe, you can choose from quiches, croissant or bagel sandwiches, omelets, pastas, vegetarian dishes, shrimp, prime rib, elaborate desserts and specialty coffees for breakfast, lunch or dinner seven days a week. A gazebo garden and front patio are options for dining outside. A newly paved lot in the rear provides plenty of parking. Reservations are generally only needed during the Utah Shakespearean Festival, June through early September.

Bristlecone Restaurant
$$ • 1575 W. 200 North, Cedar City • 586-8888

At the Holiday Inn in Cedar City (see our Accommodations chapter), the Bristlecone Restaurant is named for one of nature's oldest living things. At Cedar Breaks National Monument, high above the town of Cedar City, you'll find the restaurant's namesake in the form of a twisted, gnarly bristlecone pine tree believed to be 1,600 years old. Open since 1986, fine dining at the Bristlecone Restaurant combines a longstanding reputation for excellent food with the stunning beauty of the Cedar City area. Lunch or dinner fare includes a full buffet as well as delicious choices of seafood — lobster, halibut and crab — and prime rib, the popular favorite. Famous for "scratch cooking," the Bristlecone Restaurant also features a tasty breakfast menu for a really good morning whether you're in town for business or vacation or live right in the neighborhood. Bristlecone Restaurant is open daily. Reservations are only necessary for large parties.

Bump and Grind
$ • 259 S. Utah Hwy. 143, Brian Head • 677-3111

After a day of downhill skiing or mountain biking, warm up or cool down at the Bump and Grind. In addition to a great cup of coffee, espresso, cappuccino or specialties such as mochas, Irish cream and other lattes, try something from the deli or grill. Bump and Grind's most popular menu item is the Double Diamond Burger (it's a skiing thing . . . The Black Diamond is supposedly the ultimate ski run, but the managers here say the Double Dia-

mond is even better than the ultimate!). Pasta Caliente and other pasta dishes, a variety of other tasty burgers and healthy sandwiches also please the palate. The restaurant is decorated in a pleasant combination of maroon, green and black with a generous showing of posters advertising Southwestern Utah's favorite ski resort. The restaurant is open seven days a week year round for breakfast and lunch only.

China Garden Restaurant
$ • 64 N. Main St., Cedar City • 586-6042

This is Cedar City's choice for Chinese. Since 1965, the China Garden Restaurant has specialized in oriental Cantonese-style cooking. The China Garden is famous for its fried shrimp, sweet-and-sour pork tenderloin, homemade soups and a daily luncheon special that pleases the tastebuds and the pocketbook. Parking is available in the rear of the building. The China Garden is open every day for lunch and dinner. Reservations are not necessary.

Club Edge and Restaurant
$$ • 406 S. Utah Hwy. 143, Brian Head • 677-3343

You'll find lots to relish in this restaurant and private club at the base of the Brian Head resort lifts. You don't need to be a member to dine at Club Edge, the local choice for seeing and being seen. From the fresh, 20-item salad bar to the prime rib or Chicken Angelo made to order by experienced chefs, you'll learn that this Brian Head restaurant specializes in everything. Particularly popular with skiers, ski boarders, other slope hounds and their families, Club Edge draws them in with good food, a ski-town atmosphere, a cozy dining room with a roaring fire to take off the chill and a 50-inch big-screen TV.

Reservations are only necessary for parties of six or more. The restaurant is open for dinner every day except during the "mud months" of May and October, when they close down to allow parking lots to dry out or freeze over. The Club Edge bar is open until midnight or later through the end of the ski season on April 30 (see our Nightlife chapter). Lunch is served between Memorial Day and September 30 to accommodate the growing number of bikers who enjoy the area. During the summer season, reservations are suggested.

The Dog and Duck
$ • 50 W. Center St., Cedar City • 586-0355

The Dog and Duck is a coffeehouse with a deli, entertainment and good food, but limited hours of operation. Only open May through the last performance of the Utah Shakespearean Festival around Labor Day, the Dog and Duck has spaghetti and a barbecue on the patio each night. The Dog and Duck specializes in large and tasty deli sandwiches and vegetarian meals with zippy coffee drinks and milk shakes to top it all off.

With loyal customers returning year after year, the Dog and Duck is also popular for nightly entertainment, featuring music, plays and poetry readings in a relaxed and friendly, pub-type atmosphere (see our Nightlife chapter). Patrons can park in the city lot behind the restaurant, which is open Monday through Saturday for continental breakfast, lunch and dinner.

Golden Hills Restaurant
$ • Jct. of U.S. Hwy. 89 and Utah Hwy. 9, Mt. Carmel • 648-2602

If you're looking for very good homestyle cooking while traveling through the grand circle of state and national parks, try Golden Hills Restaurant in Mt. Carmel. It's casual dining for the whole family, with popular favorites including homemade soups, fresh, hot scones with honey and a well-stocked salad bar. Golden Hills specialties are combinations of steak, chicken and halibut, and the baked goods — breads and sweet rolls — top the list. For dessert, save room for a slice of apple, cherry or coconut-cream pie. The restaurant is divided into two rooms — a bright and airy dining area in the front with large booths to accommodate many diners, and a cozier room with a fireplace in the back. Golden Hills is licensed to sell beer. Parking is adjacent to the restaurant.

Hermie's Drive Inn
$ • 294 N. Main St., Cedar City • 865-0612 • No credit cards

Hermie's Drive Inn has been serving up the best burgers and fries in Southwestern

Utah since 1973. Now, *Spectrum* readers in three counties have made what was pretty obvious official — Hermie's was the area's favorite fast-food choice in 1996.

Specializing in batter-dipped fish and chips and cooked-to-order burgers, Hermie's is next to the city park in downtown Cedar City, convenient for local families, business people and tourists. Hermie's management is proud of the restaurant's reputation for high-quality, freshly prepared lunches and dinners served seven days a week. It's not an ordinary fast-food place, and the difference is clear in the products they serve. Hermie's has changed to a '50s theme for 1997. The new Hermie's is decorated in a crisp, clean black, white and red motif. A jukebox has been added, but the menu includes the same good food, so eat in or just drive up for service.

Milt's Stage Stop
$$ • Utah Hwy. 14, 5 miles east of Cedar City • 586-9344

If you had to name the most popular restaurant in Cedar City, it would have to be Milt's. In a rustic lodge 5 miles into Cedar Canyon, Milt's has been the place to take a date, talk over a business deal or celebrate a special occasion since 1956. Voted Cedar City's favorite steak and seafood restaurant in *Spectrum* polls for '95 and '96, Milt's longstanding reputation for excellence makes it easy to find — just ask anyone in Cedar City for directions.

After a leisurely drive through the colorful canyon, you'll enjoy a choice of steaks or seafood. The salad bar is popular with most diners, but the best things about Milt's — and the reasons loyal customers willingly make the drive several times a year — are the mountain-lodge atmosphere, friendly staff and cooked-to-perfection prime rib and beer-battered shrimp. Reservations are not required, but because of the restaurant's popularity, particularly during summer, a call ahead on holidays and weekends is a good idea.

Papa Murphy's
$ • 70 E. 200 North, Ste. 1, Cedar City • 586-7100

We like our pizza in Southwestern Utah. This "make-and-take" franchise is included because it's different. In its first year, Papa Murphy's in Cedar City and St. George has already gained a following, especially among impoverished college students and harried moms or weary dads hurrying home after a day at the office. Papa Murphy's unique claim to fame is they don't cook anything. You can watch your pizza, calzone or lasagna being made, but you get to take it home and pop it into your own oven. In about the time it takes to set the table, you'll have a tasty lunch or dinner at about one-third the cost of restaurant fare. For extra bargains, check out the in-store specials in this fast-growing western franchise.

Pinewoods
$$ • 121 Duck Creek Ridge Rd., Cedar Mountain Village • 682-2512, (800) 848-2525

When the desert heat becomes unbearable or you want to get away for a quiet, romantic dinner, there's no place like Pinewoods. At an altitude of 8600 feet, you'll find deer in the front yard during summertime and snow in the trees in the winter. This fine-dining restaurant is decorated with antiques and specializes in steaks, seafood and chicken. Popular favorites? Try steak with sautéed shrimp or chicken marsala. Beer can be ordered with your meal.

It's a 30-mile trip each way from Cedar City to Pinewoods; 80 miles from St. George. The restaurant is open five days a week (closed Tuesday and Wednesday) year round for dinner only. It's most popular in the wintertime, as Pinewoods also offers snowmobile rentals, tours and night rides. Reservations are not necessary, but because you'll have to invest some travel time, a phone call will guarantee your meal.

Rusty's Ranch House
$$ • Utah Hwy. 14, 2 miles east of Cedar City • 586-3839

In an Old West setting just 2 miles east of Cedar City in Cedar Canyon, Rusty's Ranch House is famous for steaks, barbecued ribs and pasta dishes. The most popular vittles on the menu, according to most families, tourists, couples and groups, are coconut shrimp, fresh salmon and barbecue chicken. If you're looking for a great place to impress your date, close a business deal or celebrate a successful lifetime, marriage or promotion, try Rusty's Ranch House. The atmosphere is rustic, with lots of wood, saddles, Indian blankets and an adobe brick fireplace. Rusty's Ranch House serves dinner only Monday through Saturday and is licensed to sell liquor. Reservations are not required but are suggested during the sum-

Photo: The Daily Spectrum

The Bentley House Restaurant at Greene Gate Village Bed and Breakfast Inn is famous for excellent fine dining.

mer months, weekends and on holidays. Parking is plentiful.

Sullivan's Cafe and Sulli's Steakhouse
$-$$ • 301 S. Main St., Cedar City • 586-6761

You'll find Sullivan's Cafe at the south entrance of 301 S. Main Street and Sulli's on the north side of the building. The cafe serves homestyle American cuisine for breakfast, lunch and dinner; the steakhouse serves dinner only using the same homestyle menu and adding some tasty Italian entrees.

Sullivan's Cafe opened for business in 1946. A recent remodeling has resulted in a bigger and better Sullivan's. Sulli's is all new. A fireplace is now the central feature of the dining room, which is decorated in colors of soft burgundy, mauve and green. Note the mural depicting the Iron Mines of Cedar City — the mines were the reason many early settlers came to this part of the state.

Popular with families and tourists, Sullivan's and Sulli's are famous for homemade soups, desserts and breads, fresh-cut french fries and hash browns, cut-to-order steaks, pot roast, chicken-fried steak and succulent prime rib. Approximately 100 parking spaces are provided adjacent to the building. Both the cafe and the steakhouse are open seven days a week and are liquor-licensed. Reservations are suggested for Sulli's, but Sullivan's invites you to come on in.

Top Spot
$ • 650 S. Main St., Cedar City • 586-9661

If you've ever passed through Cedar City, you've probably seen the cow on the roof of the Top Spot. The cow — and the restaurant — have been around since 1963, specializing in American and Mexican fast food, sandwiches and ice cream treats. Not only can you use your regular plastic, you can even use your gas credit card at Top Spot. Construction workers like the portions, kids enjoy the video arcade and tourists appreciate the one-stop convenience of filling their gas tank, then having breakfast, lunch or dinner.

So what's up with the cow? After 35 years, no one even remembers its original purpose. It might have been a reference to a menu rich in dairy products, a restaurant mascot or simply a way to attract hungry travelers — something it still does today.

Bryce Canyon Area

For generations the Bryce Canyon area was off the beaten track, and the choice of where to eat was relatively simple. But with the dedication of the Grand Staircase-Escalante National Monument in September 1996, the world has taken serious notice of this pristine desert wilderness. New restaurants will doubtless begin to appear. In the meantime, there are some darn good options already ready for your visit.

Bryce-Zion-Midway Resort
$ • 244 S. U.S. Hwy. 89, Hatch • 735-4199

There's something for everyone at the Bryce-Zion-Midway Resort. Open daily for breakfast, lunch and dinner during the summer tourist season (closed Sundays during the winter), the menu includes 18 breakfast choices, quick lunches, burgers, pizza, steak and seafood. New in 1996, the resort now specializes in such delectable breakfasts as Midway pan-fry, egg dishes and corned beef hash with melted cheese. For a quick lunch, order a bacon-cheeseburger or a super-sized piece of pizza at the walk-up window.

Midway between the splendor of Bryce Canyon and Zion national parks (hence the name), the resort is a great place to stretch your legs and satisfy your hunger. Deer and elk mounts, softened with daisies and yellow pine, decorate the interior. Rooms for overnight accommodations at the resort are being added a few at a time. The first four rooms became available in May 1997. No reservations are required.

Buffalo Java Cafe
$ • 47 N. Main St., Panguitch • 676-8900

In the middle of historic downtown Panguitch, you'll find Buffalo Java Cafe, recipient in 1996 of a Utah Heritage Foundation award for restoration of a building built in 1906. Since 1994, Buffalo Java has been the subject of numerous articles in national and international travel guides. This Panguitch enterprise is listed in a Brazilian guide and a European guide, and the *Hollywood Chef's Guide* raved about the outstanding espresso, fresh-squeezed juices, bagels and the atmosphere at Buffalo Java.

The cafe shares space with Wild Horses Mercantile (see our Shopping chapter) in the old Southern Utah Equitable building, built in 1906 and now carefully and lovingly restored. As one of only three buildings in the state with a cast-iron front, the restoration, reminiscent of a turn-of-the-century general store, was recognized in 1996 by the Utah Heritage Foundation.

Open daily May through October, Buffalo Java serves breakfast, lunch and dinner. Visitors tell their friends about the fantastic sandwiches, soups, salads, gourmet coffees, muffins and bagels, so the word is getting around. Whether you are on a bicycle or in an RV, there's plenty of parking on Main Street or behind the building. No reservations are needed.

Doggie Delight
$ • 75 W. Utah Hwy. 143, Panguitch Lake • 676-2445 • No credit cards

The decor? Fresh air and sunshine! The menu includes all the things kids of any age love — burgers and fries, hot dogs and ice cream — but you'll have to eat outside in the splendid surroundings of Utah's red rock country. Tough duty, but someone has to do it, right? Families and sportsmen enjoy this mom-and-pop operation, where everything is prepared on-site daily. Doggie Delight has picnic tables and benches, but no restrooms. The eatery is open for lunch and dinner every day from mid-May until October, then Doggie Delight is shut down for the winter. There's plenty of parking for campers, boats and RVs.

Escobar's Mexican Restaurant
$ • 445 E. Center St., Panguitch • 676-8222

Escobar's is the place for Mexican food in the Bryce Canyon area. The decor is country, but the menu is filled with chimichangas, burritos, tacos and chile verde. Open since 1990, Escobar's serves the gastronomical needs of customers Sunday through Friday. The restaurant is decorated in bright blue accented with flowers and piñatas. No reservations are necessary.

Flying M Restaurant
$ • 614 N. Main St., Panguitch • 676-8008

The Flying M Restaurant boasts "the biggest darn rolls you've ever seen!" They also get raves for their turkey pot-pies, hotcakes and fruit pies. In business in the Bryce Canyon area since 1939, the Flying M management encourages tourists and residents to tell their friends and neighbors "if the food and service is good . . . If it's bad, tell the waitress and she will shoot the cook." Breakfast, lunch and dinner are served daily. The restaurant has a Southwestern ambience. An addition is in the works with plans for a curio shop, additional banquet rooms and possibly a bar. A large parking lot on the side of the building can accommodate most large rigs. Families, tourists and buses are welcome.

Prospector Restaurant
$-$$ • 380 W. Main St., Escalante • 826-4658

If you like real food — not prepackaged or precooked and kept hot under a lamp — the Prospector Restaurant is your choice in the Bryce Canyon area for American homestyle cooking, steaks and fish. Drop in for filet, trout and fresh veggies. The Prospector Restaurant is open daily for breakfast, lunch and dinner.

Ruby's Inn Lodge
$$ • Utah Hwy. 63, Bryce Canyon • 834-5265

The scenery is spectacular and the food is filling at Ruby's Inn Lodge on the periphery of Bryce Canyon National Park. Ruby opened for business in 1924. Today, his children and grandchildren serve breakfast, lunch and dinner to hungry tourists and travelers, carrying on the tradition of good service and good food. Up to a dozen bus tours at a time can be

INSIDERS' TIP

The final scene of *The Electric Horseman*, starring Robert Redford and Jane Fonda, was shot at the counter of Dick's Cafe in downtown St. George.

served in Ruby's dining room. Choose from a tasty buffet, sandwiches such as patty melts and BLTs, succulent steaks or tasty trout. Ruby's is also known for their fresh, hot baked goods and delicate desserts.

The third and fourth generations of Ruby's family rebuilt the lodge after a devastating fire in 1984. Since then, they have continued to expand to keep up with the world's growing interest in Garfield County. There are now nearly 375 rooms at the lodge (see our Accommodations chapter), an art gallery (see our Arts and Culture chapter) and parking for up to 20 buses. A full-service garage and car wash (for buses, too) were completed in the spring of 1997. Tourists who are vacationing at Ruby's Inn or staying for a business convention will enjoy rim-trail rides, a Dutch-oven cookout and country hoedown, cowboy poets, roping and trick horses.

Rustic Lodge
$$ • 186 S. Westshore Rd., Panguitch • 676-2627, (800) 427-8345

The Rustic Lodge serves "innovative American fare" during the tourist season in Bryce Canyon. The most popular menu items are Rustic-style New York steaks, homemade pies and taste-tempting desserts. Special dietary needs can be met or vegetarian meals prepared with advance notice. Ask about Rustic's daily specials. Open summertime only for breakfast, lunch and dinner. Closed every Tuesday. No reservations needed.

Kanab Area

Restaurants in the Kanab area are often coffee shops next door to motels. Many of the listings included are the only option in the community. But Parry's Lodge and several others have an impressive history serving tourists and locals. We think you'll find several places to like among the restaurants in Kanab and the surrounding communities.

Chef's Palace Restaurant
$ • 176 W. Center St., Kanab • 644-5052

Country-fried steak and prime rib are the Chef's Palace's claim to fame. Since 1986, this Kanab eatery has been taking good care of hungry tourists and residents looking for a

satisfying repast at a reasonable price. Chef's Palace is a quaint, country restaurant with a counter where coffee drinkers gather for conversation. There's plenty of variety, with good stuff like grilled steaks, tasty pastrami or Reuben sandwiches or burgers — served for adult or kid-sized appetites. Desserts are an assortment of cream or fruit pies served with or without ice cream. Breakfast, lunch and dinner are served daily. Reservations are not needed and there is plenty of parking.

Junction Drive Inn
$ • 185 E. 300 South, Kanab • 644-8170 • No credit cards

Since 1988 the Junction Drive Inn has fed just about everyone in Kanab. Local families and tourists passing through on their tour of the grand circle of parks have enjoyed lunch and dinner Monday through Saturday. This fast-food favorite specializes in burgers, fries, shakes, chicken and fish dishes. Junction Drive Inn has a reputation for some of the best shakes in Utah. It isn't official, mind you, but according to the kids behind the counter, everyone says so! Junction is home of the Big Red — a burger with everything, including ham, bacon and cheese. And for a touch of nostalgia, Junction Drive Inn still uses car-hops to provide curb service.

JV's Cafe
$ • 110 E. State St., Orderville • 648-2475

This is good ol' American homestyle cooking at its best. JV's Cafe has been in business in Orderville for 23 years, feeding hungry families and tourists on their way to or from the area's national parks. Country cooking in a country atmosphere is what JV's is all about. The most popular menu item? Your choice of sandwich fixings on homemade bread or rolls. For dinner, try steak cooked to order, Yankee pot roast, chicken-fried steak . . . even liver! No kidding, it's a big favorite with the locals, and it's good for you to boot. Don't pass up the homemade soups and pies. Open Monday through Friday for breakfast, lunch and dinner, and serves breakfast and lunch only on Saturday. JV's has game and pool tables, lots of pretty plants and a drive-up window for those in a hurry.

Nedra's Too
$ • 310 S. 100 East, Kanab • 644-2030

Nedra's Too, situated at the only stop light in Kanab, has been serving authentic Mexican and American food to tourists and residents since 1990. The current ownership is the fourth generation of restaurateurs in this family-owned business. Nedra's Too serves the breakfasts, lunches and dinners that have been 40-year favorites of those living on the Arizona Strip. Specialties include carnitas, hearty country breakfasts and charbroiled steaks. Planning a party? Nedra's Too can handle lots of guests and is licensed to sell beer. Enjoy a balmy evening on their outdoor patio (in season, of course) and bring the family. Nedra's Too is open daily.

Parry Lodge
$$ • 89 E. Center St., Kanab • 644-2605

This is the place the stars have hung out during 65 years of filmmaking history here in the greatest earth on show. John Wayne, William Powell, Jodie Foster, Christian Slater, Ronald Reagan, James Garner, Frank Sinatra, Dean Martin, Arlene Dahl, Sammy Davis Jr., Don Knotts, Omar Sharif, Robert Preston, Barbara Stanwyck, Gregory Peck . . . They've all enjoyed the same hospitality and food at Parry Lodge that you will find as a overnight guest (see our Accommodations chapter) or a dinner patron.

Showbiz greats on location in Kanab have appreciated hearty helpings of Parry Lodge's world-famous chicken and dumplings after a long day of filming. Other favorites on the menu include prime rib, steaks, several kinds of fish, homemade bread in mini-loaves and delightful desserts such as cheesecake, apple crisp and rice pudding. Give yourself some extra time to enjoy the hundreds of autographed photos lining the walls of Parry Lodge. Outside of Hollywood, this may be one of the richest photographic histories of the industry around. It's safe to say that if they filmed in Southwestern Utah, they stayed at Parry Lodge. The restaurant is open daily for breakfast, lunch and dinner only during the warm months of the year — April to mid-October — and reservations are suggested.

Wok Inn
$ • 86 S. 200 West, Kanab • 644-5400

The Wok Inn is a favorite with families, tourists and bus tours. The tasty Chinese fare cooked up on the namesake wok include sweet-and-sour dishes, house-special chicken and sizzling Chinese platters . . . a dish for every appetite. Under Oriental lanterns, top off your lunch or dinner with banana fritters or almond cookies and ice cream. The Wok Inn, is open daily, is liquor-licensed and features an extensive wine and beer menu. Reservations are not needed . . . unless you're bringing a tour bus.

Despite the fact a lot of people will tell you it's impossible to get a drink in Utah, there are actually several ways to purchase your favorite alcoholic beverages.

Nightlife

Nightlife, in the traditional sense of the word, is a fairly sparse commodity in Southwestern Utah. This is a place where the most exciting activities generally occur during the daytime. Hiking, biking, sightseeing, skiing, climbing, swimming, golfing, tennis, fishing, horseback riding. . . . When the sun goes down, the most common activities are a low-key dinner, maybe a little shopping, a movie or a concert. Most folks just don't stay up too late around here because they know tomorrow's recreation is going to be just as full-bore as today's was.

For the more common type of nightlife, we'll first refer you to our friendly neighbor two state lines and 35 miles away. Mesquite, Nevada, is a great little border town offering dining, dancing, drinking, legal gaming and exciting live entertainment every night of the week. (See our Mesquite chapter for complete details.)

Along with this reference we post a strong warning. The stretch of Interstate 15 between Southwestern Utah and Mesquite, cutting across the tip of the northwestern corner of Arizona, is one of the most unforgiving stretches of highway in the entire Interstate system. Remember that if you're going to Mesquite and returning to Southwestern Utah the same night, you or someone with you will be negotiating an asphalt ribbon through the Virgin River Gorge. The highway winds and bends through very narrow places in the canyon where there's almost no median between the northbound and southbound lanes. Highway shoulders are narrow in many places, and the dropoffs are severe. No one who is sleepy or who has been drinking, however moderately, should drive this stretch of road any time of day, let alone at night.

Sorry to continue the wet blanket treatment, but this is also a good spot to remind you that the legal drinking age in Utah is 21, and anyone pulled over with a blood-alcohol content of .08 or higher will have a DUI on his or her record and will be spending the night in jail. Utahns are proud of the fact that Mothers Against Drunk Driving, Advocates for Highway and Auto Safety and Nationwide Insurance released a report card in November 1996 ranking Utah as the state with the lowest percentage of alcohol-related deaths in the nation. Drunk-driving laws in Utah are strict and are strictly enforced. The state also has a "zero tolerance" law for convicted drunk drivers who are under the legal drinking age.

Nay, Bartender?

While those are laws few people haggle with, many do take issue with Utah's laws governing the way liquor is distributed and obtained. In fact, many think they are downright wacky. Despite the fact a lot of people will tell you it's impossible to get a drink in Utah, there are actually several ways to purchase your favorite alcoholic beverages.

There are four state-owned liquor stores in Southwestern Utah: one in St. George in the Phoenix Plaza at 929 W. Sunset Boulevard, 673-9495, one in Cedar City at 356 S. Main, 586-1644, another in Kanab at 120 E. 100 South, 644-2383, and one in Panguitch at 33 N. Main St., 676-8550. These stores offer most major brands of spirits in various sizes. They're open every day but Sunday, with varying hours. The liquor stores are freestanding agencies of the state government; package agencies are generally privately operated.

Beer with a 3.2 percent alcoholic content is a little less strong in Utah but just as available as anywhere else — you can get it seven days a week in most every grocery and convenience store. Stronger brews such as "ice" beers are sold in the state liquor stores, some restaurants and private clubs. Wine is available only in liquor stores. Package liquor agencies are in most resort centers, lodges and major hotels.

Many of the restaurants in Southwestern Utah have liquor licenses. Our Restaurants chapter listings indicate those that do. You may purchase mixed drinks, wines and beer at licensed restaurants, and you may bring cork-finished wine into restaurants. A wine or liquor menu will not be provided nor will alcoholic beverages be offered unless you request them. If in doubt, just ask your server about the availability of wine or liquor.

Utah's non-exclusive private clubs offer "over the bar" drinks, which are the standard cocktails you are used to ordering. Visitors may purchase a two-week membership to most private clubs for $5. Visitors with a two-week membership may host up to five guests. Lounges and taverns sell "3.2 beer" only, and do not offer wine service or mixed drink setups. No liquor, wine or beer may be brought into such establishments.

With that out of the way, here are some area-by-area ideas on how to spend an evening Southwestern Utah style. Again, for Nevada-type nightlife with a little more octane, check our Mesquite chapter — you'll find all the options available less than an hour away.

St. George/Zion

Let's face it, most of the best things to do in the area around St. George, Hurricane and Springdale require sunlight. Except for the popular moonlight hike of Zion's West Rim Trail (a daring option that's only for the truly adventurous three or four nights a month during the summer season), the scenic wonders of Southwestern Utah are best experienced pre-dusk.

In fact, if you're out doing all that experiencing all day, you'll be looking forward to Southwestern Utah's top-rated nightlife activity — dinner at a quiet restaurant near the hotel, 20 minutes in the Jacuzzi and the movie of your choice on whatever cable or pay-per-view option your hotel offers.

But if you still feel like sprucing up and going out after a day of mountain biking, horseback riding or rock climbing, St. George does offer a few options. Check our Restaurants

FYI

Unless otherwise noted, the area code for all phone numbers listed in this chapter is 801 but will change to 435 in September 1997. Either area code may be used until March 22, 1998.

chapter for some of the excellent possibilities that are within walking distance of many hotels. Yes, you can safely walk the streets of St. George at night, on sidewalks that aren't officially rolled up at dark. However, if you're here during Spring Break or on a three-day winter or spring weekend such as President's Day, you'll find yourself among a sea of high school students, many of whom are away from home and Mom and Dad for the first time.

St. George Movie Theaters

They make 'em here, and we watch 'em here. After dinner you can take in a movie at one of several theaters. One phone number, 673-1994, will get you a recording of what's playing at what time at every theater in town. The standard St. George movie ticket is $5.50.

A couple of notes for the frugal-minded: At the Dixie Theater at 35 N. Main, all seats for first-run movies are $3.50, and at the Flood Street Theater, 170 N. 400 East, tickets are $1.50 for movies making their second round. Some theaters occasionally offer reduced-price matinees. The same number will provide that information as well.

Concerts Aplenty

Chances are that on one of the nights you're here in the St. George area, there will be some kind of concert going on. Check out the schedules for the following by calling the accompanying phone number, and read more about all the organizations and productions listed by checking out our Arts and Culture chapter.

The **Southwest Symphony**, 656-0434, offers a concert about every six weeks during a season that runs September through June at the Dixie Center's Cox Auditorium stage. The **Celebrity Concert Series**, 652-7992, brings in nationally and internationally touring musicians and dancers, and **St. George Musical Theater Company** stages locally written and produced plays as well as classic musicals at the St. George Opera House, 634-5859.

Other Nightlife Options

2 Lazy 2 Ranch
358 W. Buena Vista Blvd., Washington • 674-2022

If you're of a mind to get out and do a little boot-scootin', 2 Lazy 2 Ranch in Washington not only offers up some of the juiciest steaks in town (see our Restaurants chapter) but also opens the dance floor to western line and swing dancing at 9:30 PM every night but Sunday. There's a $5 charge to dance unless you have dinner, in which case the dancing's free. On Wednesday night from 7:30 to 10:30 PM, couples waltz, swing, two-step and round dance. Line dancing is the attraction Thursday night, beginning at 7:30 PM. Local radio disc jockey John Carter teaches the latest steps. It's great exercise and a fun way to socialize. If you're not eating, lessons are $3 per person.

Acoustic Concert Series
Ancestor Square, corner of Main and St. George Blvd., St. George • 673-1437

This popular series brings about 20 acts a year to St. George for a night of folk, blues, bluegrass, New Age and other types of music played on acoustic instruments. The concerts are usually held on Thursdays, and summer concerts are outdoors at Ancestor Square (bring a lawn chair or blanket). Cold weather concerts are held just up the street inside the St. George Opera House on Main and 200 North. Among the nationally touring acoustic artists who have performed in this series are guitarist Bill Mize and the duet Small Potatoes.

Bit and Spur Restaurant and Saloon
1212 Zion Park Blvd., Springdale • 772-3498

The Bit and Spur has developed a great reputation as a night spot in Springdale. The evening atmosphere is casual both inside, where the rustic saloon has billiards and TV, and outdoors on the garden patio, where you'll enjoy conversation beneath the majestic ridges of Zion Canyon (see our Restaurants chapter).

Blarney Stone Pub
800 E. St. George Blvd., St. George • 673-9191

This is a favorite local spot for socializing over a beer. The pub has five pool tables and a jukebox and is open Monday through Saturday from 11 AM to 1 AM. Wednesday is karaoke night, there's live entertainment on Friday and a deejay spins tunes on Saturday. The Blarney Stone does not serve food, and there is no cover charge to get in.

Grandma Ruby's Playhouse at Bumbleberry Village
897 Zion Park Blvd., Springdale • 772-3522

Grandma Ruby's offers a fun night for the whole family five nights a week (closed Sunday

Willie and the Boys

The night Willie Nelson jammed at Merlin's 101 Rancho in Virgin (ask around for directions . . . it's not even listed in the phone book), the joint actually stayed open a few extra hours. It was one of those once-in-a-lifetime evenings. Willie was on the road again

circa 1980, in town with the cast of *The Electric Horseman*, starring Robert Redford and Jane Fonda. They'd been filming in the St. George-Zion Canyon area, and when the day's work was done, Willie and some of his buddies headed up to Merlin's. "We were just getting ready to leave," remembers one of Merlin's lucky patrons. "Then someone said, 'You don't want to leave yet,' and pointed toward the door . . . Willie Nelson was walking in." Willie and the boys played well into the morning for those fortunate few who happened to be at Merlin's.

and Monday) from Memorial Day through Labor Day. At the east end of the Bumbleberry Inn in Springdale, this is an intimate, 200-seat theater where a cast of local residents and college students put on a full-blown musical each summer. Past seasons have included *Joseph and the Amazing Technicolor Dream Coat* and *Seven Brides for Seven Brothers*. The productions always offer plenty of singing and dancing. Tickets are $10 for adults, $9 for seniors and $8 for children. Ask about family ticket specials.

McGuire's Restaurant
351 N. Bluff St., St. George • 624-4066

McGuire's Restaurant has live entertainment while you dine on Wednesday, Thursday and Friday nights. They feature some of the area's finest singers, piano players and guitarists.

UTAH!
Tuacahn Amphitheater, 1100 N. Tuacahn Dr., Ivins • 674-4949, (800) 746-9882

From mid-June through early September, required viewing in Southwestern Utah includes the spectacular outdoor musical, *UTAH!* Staged nightly except Sunday at the Tuacahn Amphitheater in Ivins, this is a two-hour extravaganza staged beneath towering sandstone ledges. Galloping horses, thundering wagons, simulated lightning bolts, magnificent music and delightful dancing, singing and acting by a cast of 80 fill the night air. The amphi-

theater has 2,000 seats. The best ones go for $24.50 for adults and $16 for children younger than 12. "Area 2" seats are $19.50 and $14; "Area 3" seating is $14.50 and $9 (see our Attractions chapter for more on *UTAH!*). There's a pre-show on the plaza as well as a Dutch-oven dinner ($9 for adults, $7 for children 12 and younger) if you want to spend the early as well as late evening there.

Red Cliffs Mall
1750 E. Red Cliffs Dr., St. George • 673-0099
Zion Factory Stores
250 N. Red Cliffs Dr., St. George • 674-9800

For folks who just can't get enough shopping in during the daytime, we suggest you walk the two-block-long outdoor gallery of the Zion Factory Stores, open until 9 PM. Or make an indoor jaunt through the Red Cliffs Mall, 1750 E. Red Cliff Dr., 673-0099, also open until 9 PM. The factory stores have a number of name-brand clothing outlets, discount book places and gift stores. The mall is anchored at one end by the ZCMI department store and Wal-Mart at the other. (See our Shopping chapter for more on these options.)

Cedar City/Brian Head

One of the centers of Cedar City's nightlife is Southern Utah University, with main admin-

---

Dancing By The Light Of The Moon

During the '30s, '40s and '50s, outdoor dances with live orchestras were the staple of nightlife in Southwestern Utah. The water tank on the red bluff north of downtown St. George (look directly north from 500 East) used to have a railing around it, and dances were staged on its flat, round, concrete roof on Friday and Saturday nights. In Santa Clara, there was an outdoor dance pavilion called Santa Rosa. It's gone now and there are homes where it once stood. A beautiful remnant of this era has been restored in the little town of Kanarraville, 7 miles south of Cedar City. Cobble Crest, as it's been known for six decades, is a quaint pavilion with a half-dome over the stage where the orchestra played. At the corner of 100 South and 200 West, dances and other activities are still held there from time to time. It was built by volunteers in 1934 and has been the site of countless memorable Southwestern Utah nights.

Photo: Jud Burkett

The Pioneer Opera House in St. George sponsors a series of acoustic concerts.

istrative offices at 351 W. Center Street, 586-7700. Whether it's the nightly (except Sunday) performances of the world-renowned Utah Shakespearean Festival, 586-7878, that runs from late June through early September (see our Annual Events and Arts and Culture chapters), or any of the SUU productions staged during the school year, chances are you'll be able to take in a great performance while you're in town.

Cedar City Movie Theaters

As in St. George, there is a 24-hour phone line to find out what's playing where and when in the Cedar City area. Call 586-7469 for movie information. Tickets for first-run movies at the couple of venues in Cedar City are $5 for adults and $3 for children and senior citizens. Matinee prices are $3 for adults and $2 for children. In Parowan, the Parowan Theater, 27 N. Main, 477-8732, shows first-run movies as well.

Other Nightlife Options

Ashcroft Observatory
Off West View Dr., 3.5 miles west of Cedar City • 586-7707

An unusual Monday night activity in the Cedar City area is the opportunity to do some stargazing at SUU's Ashcroft Observatory. The observatory is open to the public on Monday nights only, from just a little past dusk (about 7 PM in the wintertime and about 9 PM during summer) for two to three hours. Get there early. A guide (could be a professor or a student) is on hand to aim the telescope at star clusters, galaxies, planets or the moon if it's up. You might get to see Saturn up close and personal like you've never seen it before, or particular craters of the moon like Copernicus or Tycho. It's free of charge and just 3.5 miles from Cedar City. Drive west on 200 North, which becomes Utah Highway 56 as you leave town.

Go about 2 miles west to West View Drive, turn left (south) and continue 1¼ miles. The last one-eighth of a mile is on the dirt road up the hill to the observatory.

The Dog and Duck
50 W. Center St., Cedar City • 586-0355

This coffeehouse, deli and restaurant is one of Cedar City's favorite night spots. It's only open May through the end of the Shakespearean festival season in early September. Offering a variety of coffees, the Dog and Duck wags and quacks with nightly entertainment in a pub-like atmosphere. You'll enjoy live music and play and poetry readings.

Sportsman's Lounge
900 S. Main, Cedar City • 586-6552

A favorite nightspot in Cedar City, the Sportsman's Lounge is open from 1 PM to 1 AM seven days a week. They serve beer and wine coolers and have three pool tables and two Foosball tables. Pool tournaments often are held on Wednesday, when a live deejay is on hand playing dance music. There's usually a live band on Thursday, Friday and Saturday, and, depending on who's playing, there might be a cover charge. Sportsman's does not serve food.

Partners Getaway Restaurant
215 S. 600 West, Parowan • 477-8646

Open for lunch and dinner every day, Partners has a liquor license open to the general public and a private club. Right next door, the private club is open until 1 AM nightly. There are two pool tables, and you can purchase a visitor membership for the standard $5.

Club Edge and Restaurant
406 S. Utah Hwy. 143, Brian Head • 677-3343

It's a restaurant and private club, but you don't have to be a member to dine here. There's a warm, cozy atmosphere with a roaring fire and a big-screen TV. After a winter day on the ski slopes or a summer day on a mountain bike at Brian Head, this is a great place to unwind.

Bryce Canyon Area

Other than a quiet dinner at a nice restaurant, you're simply not going to find much to do at night in the Panguitch area. And that's the way the folks here like it. But just like your mother always told you, some of the best things in life are free, and it won't cost you a penny to take a starlit walk along the edge of Bryce Canyon. Why not just park your car near the shore of Panguitch Lake, 15 miles south of Panguitch, and watch the moon rise over the lake?

OK, here's one other suggestion that will allow you to actually do some evening whooping and cheering in a very traditional atmosphere.

A Western Bryce Evening
Ruby's Inn, Utah Hwy. 63 • 834-5341, (800) 468-8660

You have a couple of options here. Either take in the Bryce Rodeo right across from Ruby's Inn, or sign up for a chuckwagon dinner ride and Western hoedown. The rodeo takes place at 7:20 PM every night but Sunday from Memorial Day through Labor Day, and it's a full-fledged event. Riders from southern Utah and surrounding states compete in roping, steer wrestling, bull riding and bronc riding. Admission is $7 for adults and $4 for children. The chuckwagon ride is also offered every night but Sunday. For about $28 (call for current season's prices), you get a short ride in a covered wagon, during which you'll be attacked by hostile bad guys and saved by

---

INSIDERS' TIP

Check with the chamber of commerce or travel bureau in the town where you're staying for current schedules of concerts, performances or sports events. There are interesting evening events year-round. Check out the Restaurants chapter for those establishments that have a liquor license and offer entertainment.

mountain men. After the excitement, there's a Dutch-oven dinner with barbecue chicken, corn on the cob, hot rolls and cherry cobbler. The event is capped off with a Western hoe-down complete with singing, dancing and skits.

Kanab Area

Nightlife in Kanab is very Western in a tra-ditional sort of way, which is understandable, considering the town's history. The place to catch a flick in the town where so many have been made is Kanab Theater, 29 W. Center St., 644-2334.

Frontier Movie Town
297 W. Center St., Kanab • 644-5337, (800) 551-1714

A good way to get a taste of the Old West and this area's movie legacy is to make reser-vations at Frontier Movie Town for a Dutch-oven dinner and Western show. They put on a rip-roaring program complete with a shootout, and they've got a liquor license to help keep spirits high. You can refresh yourself at the Robber's Roost Saloon or have a sandwich at the Hole-in-the-Wall Snack Bar. They're both open from 7:30 AM to 11 PM daily. Call for dinner and show reservations. (For more on Frontier Movie Town, see our Attractions chap-ter.)

Buckskin Tavern
2321 N. U.S. Hwy. 89A, Fredonia, Ariz.
• (520) 643-7094

Just across the state line, 5 miles south of Kanab in Arizona, the Buckskin Tavern is geo-graphically situated to be a little more accom-modating if you're looking for nightlife that in-cludes a wider choice of drinks. Open 10 AM to 1 AM weekdays and 11 AM to 1 AM Satur-day and Sunday, the Buckskin has live music every other weekend for a $1 cover charge. There are three pool tables and a bar stocked with spirits, but the tavern's claim to fame is what is allegedly the longest bar in Arizona. Take your yardstick and belly up, then be care-ful getting back to Kanab.

Southwestern Utah's most defining characteristic is its environment.

The Environment

About 1850, Parley P. Pratt, a Mormon church leader and early explorer to Southwestern Utah, noted the terrain "showed no sign of water or fertility . . . a wide expanse of chaotic matter presented itself, huge hills, sandy deserts, cheerless, grassless plains, perpendicular rocks, loose barren clay, dissolving beds of sandstone . . . lying in inconceivable confusion — in short a country in ruins, dissolved by the pelting of the storm of ages, or turned inside out, upside down by terrible convulsions in some former age."

The desert terrain that makes up Southwestern Utah is varied. The most dominant features are the striking rock formations. Some are exquisite, others intriguing, challenging or awe inspiring. All attract attention for their grandeur and color and as a reminder of the tremendous forces of nature that created this region. At the same time, there are seemingly endless stretches of barren desert, with acres of nothing but scraggly sagebrush. Small, unobtrusive hillsides give way to dramatic mountain ranges that run north-south, dividing the state into two almost equal portions, with Interstate 15 on one side and U.S. Highway 89 on the other, converging in Salt Lake City.

To be sure, Southwestern Utah's most defining characteristic is its environment. Nicknames like "color country" and "red-rock country" and area mottos such as the Bryce Canyon area's "aged to perfection," the St. George Chamber of Commerce's "where the summer sun spends the winter," and Kanab's "the greatest earth on show" are indicative of the local connection with the earth and its gifts.

Some of the same features attracting new residents and thousands of visitors each year also explain the wide variety of animal and plant life in Southwestern Utah. Few places in the world offer such a diversity of life or provide opportunities to see — up close — an assortment of the earth's most fascinating and rare living things.

When Worlds Collide: The Land

While the varying climate is generally referred to as the key factor in the diversity of flora and fauna in Southwestern Utah, it is only one of the variables involved. A more complex, lesser-known determinant is the convergence of three major, distinct geographic areas — each with its own unique biological personality — in Utah's southwestern corner.

If you drew a line and cut the state in half from top to bottom, the Great Basin Desert would be on the west side of the line, the Colorado Plateau on the east. In the southwestern corner of Utah, a tip of the Mojave Desert meets the other two areas to create one of the most richly diverse ecosystems in the nation.

The Great Basin Desert is a cold desert, dominated by sagebrush, grasslands, pinion-juniper woodlands and other low-to-the-ground shrubbery that, individually, may dominate the landscape over many square miles. The largest U.S. desert lies between the Sierra Nevada-Cascade mountain ranges and the Rockies, covering most of Utah and parts of the surrounding states of California, Oregon, New Mexico, Arizona and Colorado. Elevations range from 3,000 to 6,500 feet above sea level. Seven to 12 inches of precipitation is usually evenly distributed throughout the year, falling as snow in the winter months.

The Colorado Plateau — sometimes considered a desert of its own, sometimes viewed as a part of the Great Basin Desert — includes large areas of barren desert, spectacular geological formations, and several species of plant life found nowhere else on earth. The endangered bear-claw poppy, for instance, grows only in the St. George area and is now protected against extinction by the Washington County Habitat Conservation Plan.

In stark contrast, the Mojave Desert has vast

areas of creosote bush, yucca, shadscale and in years of good rainfall — there's usually less than 6 inches, falling mostly in the winter months — a spectacular array of annual grasses and wildflowers. Located midway between the cooler Great Basin Desert and the hotter Sonoran, the Mojave is home to about 200 plant species peculiar to this desert and not existing in the other two. Cactus thrive in the coarse, sandy soil, but trees are few in number and diversity. The exception is the tree-like Joshua, which occurs only at higher elevations. In the Mojave, winter temperatures drop to freezing, while summer days are hot, dry and often windy.

Climate

Weather in the southwestern tip of the state is as diverse as the landscape. St. George holds the state's record high temperature. On June 28, 1892, the thermometer hit 116 degrees. Although temperatures that high are rare, 100-degree days are not unusual in mid-May, and days stay hot until well into October. It makes for a long growing season for local farmers and home gardeners. The average annual rainfall in the St. George area is less than 8 inches.

Fifty miles to the north in Cedar City, the altitude has climbed by 3,000 feet and annual precipitation is measured in a range of 12 to 16 inches a year — alternating between rain and snow. The average temperature in January is about 30 degrees. In July, Cedar City sees daytime temperatures of 75 to 85. Brian Head's altitude of more than 11,000 feet means cool summer nights and excellent skiing conditions in the wintertime. Snow levels at Brian Head vary yearly but are generally some of the most impressive of all the state's resorts.

The Bryce Canyon area, at an elevation of about 6,670 feet enjoys pleasant summer days averaging about 70 degrees; snow and cold, with temperatures of 25 degrees or lower in the winter months. Rain and snowfall totals about 12 to 16 inches annually, falling mostly in winter. There are long dry periods through the spring and summer.

Speaking of Soil

On the subject of soil, one of Southwestern Utah's pressing environmental issues is how to deal with moisture-sensitive soils. "Blue" clay, named for its obvious color (though not all clay here is blue), is a layman's term for an expansive soil. When this type of soil is saturated with water, volume changes can result in cracks, separation and other alterations in foundations, sidewalks and concrete slabs. The swell of the clay and movement of the ground "rocks and rolls" the foundation's surface much like a snowshoe rides on top of newly fallen snow.

Construction problems associated with blue clay can be resolved through soil testing, appropriately designed foundations and proper moisture control in landscape planning. Blue clay, the powdery residue of volcanic ash, is generally found above ground in a rainbow of colors. But while it is clearly visible in some areas, blue clay may also be camouflaged in the soil, requiring complicated geologic tests to determine its presence prior to construction.

Area builders have been relatively successful in offsetting the damaging effects in identified areas of blue clay by building on caissons. Such foundations involve drilling holes 18 to 24 inches in diameter to a depth of 3 to 6 feet in the clay. A generous amount of steel rebar enforces the strength of cement columns to prevent the powerful force of the expanding clay from snapping them in two, similar to a carrot being pulled from the ground. The costs for the security of this sort of helical steel pier foundation (imagine a coiled mattress spring) is about the same as for a slab-on-grade. However, there are other add-on costs associated with the structural flooring. All in all, the additional costs associated with the security of a caisson foundation are offset when construction related distress is greatly reduced or avoided all together.

There are large pockets of blue clay throughout Washington County. Known areas include much of Santa Clara Heights (see our Neighborhoods and Real Estate chapter) — especially on the rim of the ravine, residential neighborhoods around the Sunbrook Golf Course and on the hillside above Southgate. Local homeowners can be assured of the structural integrity of their home by insisting their builder follows soils engineering reports and, when indicated, builds on a foundation designed for expansive soils. Lots should be properly prepared to prevent movement and breakage of sidewalls, driveways and side-walks. In many areas, xeriscape landscaping, which requires a minimal amount of water, will also help.

Up Came A-Bubblin' Crude?

Washington County had a brief history of oil production when "black gold" was discovered in the small town of Virgin just outside Zion National Park. About 1930, drillers struck oil at 480 feet. Pumps brought only about 15 barrels a day to the surface, but the small success — especially during the Great Depression years — encouraged local businessmen to try another well. At 739 feet, they struck oil again — and hot sulphur water. Although an attempt was made to cap the well, it continued to produce a steady flow — equal parts oil and hot sulphur water — until the early 1960s.

Although Virgin's oil business experienced only limited success, the town did produce a high-quality stove oil used throughout the territory. And Virgin oil was used on area dirt roads to control dust, since water, then as now, was at a premium in the desert. Estimates of wells dug in the area number in the thousands, though Virgin's venture into the petroleum market generated only the poor quality product residents nicknamed "stinkoline."

Water, Water Anywhere?

In Southwestern Utah's desert environment of extremes, where there is always either too much or not enough, water is the lifeblood. The diversion of water for irrigation preceded then paralleled the settlement of most all the communities along the banks of the Virgin River. It is generally understood the future growth of the area is dependent on the continued development and conservation of water.

Municipal and privately owned wells, springs, creeks and rivers supply water to developing communities throughout the region. Underground water is owned by the State of Utah, and individual municipalities and subdividers have negotiated rights to use the water. With population growth expected to continue into the 21st century, supplying adequate water is a concern and a limiting factor. The Washington County Water Conservancy District is currently developing plans for bringing water from Lake Powell. Use of the Virgin River as a resource for culinary water is also being explored.

Examining the effect of water on local communities, historians Dr. Douglas Alder and Dr. Karl Brooks, authors of *From Isolation to Destination: A History of Washington County*, note

Stop-gap Measures

Keeping the Virgin River between its banks has been a difficult task since the first pioneers arrived. In his journal, pioneer farmer Brigham Jarvis Sr. related an experience in which a friendly native Paiute named Buck Hairlip helped avert a disaster. Jarvis and

his father had discovered a break in their earthen dam caused by a "gopher's foul prank," and they were trying desperately to shovel dirt and gravel into the breach when Buck Hairlip happened by. Noting their combined efforts were doomed to failure, Buck shouted across the field for his wife to help. At Hairlip's insistence his ponderous helpmate placed herself in the gap where the water was fast melting away the ditch bank, and with her ample bulk she held the water back while the men shoveled the dirt against her back until the ditch was mended.

"the Great Basin is a vast region whose streamflows do not reach the ocean . . . The Virgin and its tributaries, along with groundwater from wells and a few fresh water springs are the main sources of water in this piece of the second driest state in the nation. . . ."

The Virgin River runs through Zion National Park, then cuts west through the Hurricane Valley and into St. George. Depending on rainfall, snow melt or the absence thereof, the Virgin River rises sharply during thunderstorms and seasons of runoff, then slows to a trickle by summer's end. Runoff season, brought on by melted snow, is usually in mid- to late spring.

The area's early history is punctuated with stories, both of flooding and of praying for rain. Excerpts from "The Old Virgin Ditch," a poem by Mabel Jarvis, chronicle the early settlers' efforts to control this element of nature:

"My grandfather told me some stories one day, 'bout the Old Virgin Ditch;

How the pioneers first led the water that way, through the Old Virgin Ditch.

How they sweated and toiled, while the summer sun boiled,

And the ditch banks went slipping out like they were oiled.

No doubt your grandparents have told tales to you,

As full of excitement and equally true;

For every old settler has something to say,

About irrigating the pioneer way

On that Old Virgin Ditch.

One time when Grandfather was called to patrol, on the Old Virgin Ditch,

For two days and nights with his shovel and pole,

On the Old Virgin Ditch,

He tramped down and back, mending each break and crack,

That the burned thirsty acres no water should lack,

And only one dish of bran porridge he'd eaten,

Without any milk on, or sugar to sweeten,

Though weary and famished, he kept the patrol,

Up and down, back and forth, with his shovel and pole,

On that Old Virgin Ditch."

Though it sometimes appears to be a chaotic one, the relationship between water and land in Southwestern Utah is, ultimately, symbiotic. There is give and take. As Alder and Brooks add, "Rivers such as the Virgin are the creations of the topography which reflect the underlying geologic structures. Some rocks are more resistant than others to destructive weathering and erosion. Movement of crystal can cause fractures which become lines of weakness to be exploited by the streams at Bryce, Grand and Zion Canyons."

Elevated land — whether the result of uplift or the piling up of masses of igneous rocks — guides air movement around it. Rising air is cooled and precipitates its moisture as rain or snow. Hence, the principal sources of water, both on the surface and in the underground aquifers, are these same plateaus and mountains. The Navajo sandstone forming the colorful cliffs of Zion and snow canyons also contains great quantities of good water."

In modern times, too, water has been the central player in environmental dramas such as the Quail Creek Dam break on New Year's Eve in 1989. Construction on the dam, located about midway between St. George and Hurricane off Interstate 15 on Utah Highway 9, began in 1982. By 1987, the 40,000-acre-foot project was complete, but the process was plagued by problems throughout. Lake soils were porous and before long, water began to seep under the dike. Truck loads of cement were used in a futile attempt to stop the leaks, but at 11:45 PM on December 31, the dike broke.

A massive wall of water scarred the landscape and threatened the downriver communities around St. George (see our Neighborhoods and Real Estate chapter). Officials tried to keep the problem under wraps so the community at large didn't know how serious things really were until minutes before the dam broke. Warning signals sounded, but in the midst of New Year's Eve festivities, they mostly went unheeded. Luckily, the water took longer to reach populated areas than had been predicted. It was nearly morning before the wall of water reached the Bloomington bridge. However, water scoured the desert floor and rushed into the area known as Washington Fields. It swept away livestock and destroyed fields and barns.

Photo: Nick Adams

The first explorers of Zion Canyon were awed by its splendor, just like the three million visitors that visit each year.

The loss of the dike amounted to $12 million in damages. Bridges to Washington Fields and Bloomington Hills were destroyed. Sections of the highway to Bloomington Hills were washed away. Several homes in Bloomington were flooded as the water reached the 100-year floodplain mark — a height the area should see only once in 100 years. Miraculously, no lives were lost in the nation's first national disaster in 1990.

There is a need to educate the public about water conservation. Periodic public awareness campaigns have resulted in short-term fixes during times of drought. After months of long, hot, dry summer days, municipal governments and the media have been moderately effective in encouraging homeowners to water in the cool part of the day, take shorter showers and flush less frequently. But there are no ongoing public awareness efforts. Historically, there have been some enforced restrictions resulting in fines for those who water during the hot, daytime hours, but it is not yet routine in Southwestern Utah to conserve this precious resource.

Animal Life

The strange yet harmonious mixture of earth, water and air leads to habitat conditions unique in the world. For this reason, many animals find a habitat in this region perfectly suited to their needs. Like plants, animal life varies, with common sightings of mule deer, mountain lion, peregrine falcon and the rare Mexican spotted owl. A few are indigenous to certain areas, but there is certainly an overlap. Mule deer, mountain lions and a few bears live in the higher elevations of our region. Throughout the area, you'll see elk, moose, ducks, geese, pheasants, falcons, bald eagles and quail.

Because man, too, has found Southwestern Utah desirable for habitation, a rapidly increasing population threatens the existence of these plants and animals.

Taking Care of What We've Got

While some may question the need for preservation, Congress created the Endangered Species Act of 1973, and Southwestern Utah has become intimately familiar with its message in the past decade. The area around St. George has the distinction of being home to the largest, and thought to be the only, healthy population of Mojave desert tortoise in the world.

The desert tortoise, with a high, domed shell, reaches maturity at about 15 years and lives to be 50 to 60. Their stumpy hind legs are reminiscent of an elephant foot — quite different than the flippers and webbed feet of their aquatic cousins. They hibernate in the winter as temperatures drop below 50 degrees and take shelter from the summer heat in burrows. The largest populations of desert tortoise are found in the Southwestern United States. There are other groups in the dry areas of the Southeast and in parts of Texas, but most of those are infected with a fatal, contagious respiratory disease. The tortoises in and around Washington County show no evidence of the disease.

As a result of the mixed blessing of providing a home to so many unusual and endangered species like the desert tortoise, the community's continued prosperity has been dependent on a plan to achieve a delicate balance between man and nature. It's a plan that allows protection and development to peacefully coexist in the state's fastest growing county.

HCP Spells Protection

The creation of a federally approved Habitat Conservation Plan to preserve 61,000 acres (about 90 square miles of Southwestern Utah real estate) and guarantee the tortoises' continued existence has taken six years of complicated negotiations with numerous government agencies. There have been land exchanges and threatened litigation in this sometimes contentious process. Land uses acceptable under the federal government's "take" permit issued in February 1996 are still being negotiated, but are expected to include hiking, hunting, horseback riding, biking and research and educational activities within designated areas. The Cedar City area is midway through the same HCP process for the protection of the endangered Utah prairie dog.

An HCP, once considered a rare piece of legislation, provides for the protection of plants, animals (including fish and insects) within a designated area. From 1970, when the Endangered Species Act became law, until 1990, there were only a handful of HCPs in the nation. Today they are more commonplace but still difficult to obtain.

So the tenuous issues of development versus protection — lightning rods for public debate all over the state — are being addressed. Until a resolution in the form of an HCP is approved by the U.S. Fish and Wildlife Service, the Endangered Species Act provides penalties for persons who knowingly disrupt a threatened animal's habitat, destroy animals or both. The Fish and Wildlife Service is prepared to levy fines up to a maximum of $50,000 and one year imprisonment per animal taken.

The act defines "take" as "any act by an individual or group of individuals with intent to harm, harass, pursue, hunt, shoot, wound, kill, trap, capture or collect, or attempt to engage in any such conduct. "Harm" is further defined as an act that kills or injures such species. Such an act may include altering habitat, impairing essential breeding patterns, breeding, feeding or shelter. Federal courts also have the authority to stop all development, grazing and outdoor recreational activities.

Arrests are not common but have occurred. Take is serious business in these parts. An example of the type of problem folks can run up against came during the construction at

The steep ledge on the east side of Interstate 15 between Cedar City and Hurricane is the result of the uplift of a section of the earth's crust along a spectacular break known as the Hurricane Fault. The fault and the resulting cliffs may be seen to the southeast past Laverkin and Hurricane for 100 miles, continuing beyond the Colorado River. The Hurricane Fault is about 170 miles long. As you leave the town of Hurricane heading east, either on Utah Highway 9 to Zion National Park or Utah Highway 59 to Kanab, you ascend the face of the Hurricane Fault and gain a beautiful vista of the landscape to the west.

Great Views

Tuacahn Center for the Arts. The developers of the center built a tortoise fence to run on both sides of the full length of the mile-long entry road. The project was held up for some time because of the HCP, and the road was left unpaved, even after the school and the amphitheater were completed and in use.

In Southwestern Utah, the Endangered Species Act protects not only the desert tortoise and Utah prairie dog, but also nearly 30 other species of plants and animals in the region. In the St. George/Zion area, these include the desert tortoise, peregrine falcon, dwarf bear-claw poppy, bald eagle, Southwestern willow flycatcher, Siler pincushion cactus, Mexican spotted owl, Virgin River chub and woundfin minnow. In the Cedar City/Brian Head region, threatened or endangered species are the Utah prairie dog, peregrine falcon, bald eagle and Mexican spotted owl.

Near Bryce Canyon, there are several species that are threatened, including the autumn buttercup, bald eagle, black-footed ferret, bonytail chub, Colorado squawfish, humpback chub, Jones cycladenia, Mexican spotted owl, peregrine falcon, razorback sucker, Southwestern willow flycatcher, Utah prairie dog and the Utah ladies-tresses. In the Kanab area, watch for these threatened critters: tiger beetle, bald eagle, Jones cycladenia, Kanab ambersnail, Kodachrome bladderpod, Mexican spotted owl, peregrine falcon, Siler pincushion cactus, Southwestern willow flycatcher and Welsh's milkweed.

The Bureaucracy of Land Management

The management of millions of acres of Southwestern Utah's natural areas involves a phalanx of agencies and bureaucratic players. It's not so surprising when you realize just how much land is involved.

A whopping 98 percent of the land in the Bryce Canyon area's Garfield County and 93 percent of the acreage in the Kanab area's Kane County is owned by the federal, state or local government. Preservation of land, plants and animals is both a team effort and a layered bureaucracy. Included are many of the agencies of the U.S. Department of the Interior (the National Park Service is one) and the U.S. Department of Agriculture (these include the U.S. Forest Service). With differing responsibilities, the Bureau of Land Management (the BLM, custodians of the federal acreage) and the U.S. Fish and Wildlife Service (guardians of the species) oversee the federal interest in protecting the region's natural resources.

In a national park, the most restrictive land use policies apply. The list of no-no's includes no picking flowers or gathering firewood, no hunting or spotlighting, no dogs or open fires (except in designated campgrounds in the front country) and no picking up rocks or other natural souvenirs. Additional restrictions in the backcountry include backpacking by permit only and limiting group size to fewer than 12. National parks follow the "leave no trace" rule: Take nothing but pictures, leave nothing but footprints. In addition, any and all cultural and natural resources including archeological and historical sites, and the flora and fauna found within a national park are protected. National parks in the Southwestern Utah area are Zion, Bryce Canyon and Capitol Reef (see our Parks and Other Natural Wonders chapter).

The BLM-governed areas have fewer restrictions, particularly on recreational land use. Though BLM lands are carefully watched, uses such as mining, grazing, camping, hiking, driving for pleasure, gravel extraction or tree cutting are permissible activities, generally by permit.

The U.S. Forest Service exists to provide the "highest and best" land use for the enjoyment of the public, while preserving the nation's forests for the production of future generations of woodlands and products. This multiple-use agency produces wood, water, wildlife, recreation, wilderness and range. On Forest Service land, mining, grazing and rights-of-way for power and water lines are by permit, and timber is harvested and sold. Cultural preservation and recreation such as hunting, fishing, camping, bird watching and riding ATVs are allowable activities. Dixie National Forest is the only Forest Service-managed area in our coverage area. It includes such scenic gems as Navajo Lake, Panguitch Lake, Pine Valley Reservoir, Yankee Meadow and Duck Creek (see our Outdoor Recreation chapter).

On a state level, the Department of Natural Resources oversees state parks and lands,

The protection of the endangered Mojave Desert Tortoise has been the subject of intensive and delicate negotiations for a half-dozen years.

managing their natural wealth. State parks in our corner of the state include Snow Canyon and Quail Creek in the St. George area, Kodachrome Basin and Anasazi Indian Village near Bryce Canyon and Coral Pink Sand Dunes in the Kanab area (see our Parks and Other Natural Wonders chapter). The Division of Wildlife Resources, also known as the Fish and Game Department, protects the wildlife within the state, working closely with the BLM and the U.S. Forest Service. The office of Utah State Trust Lands administers properties set aside at the time of Utah's statehood in 1896 to create generations of funds for the state's school children. Trust lands, dotted throughout federal holdings, are incredibly valuable, providing tax revenues from land-use leases including mining and other permitted land uses. The interdisciplinary bureaucratic team at times also includes interested private parties, special interest groups, Native American tribes and the governor's office.

At The Local Level

Intimately connected with the environment, many Southwestern Utah communities are tak-

ing steps to protect the geology and aesthetics of the area. In particular, St. George has an ambitious program in place to ensure future generations will be able to enjoy the natural attractions that today attract new residents and visitors to the area in ever-growing numbers. City fathers have designed the plan to include a generally low-profile form of development while assuring an uncrowded feeling with ample open space, particularly along the Virgin and Santa Clara rivers.

In its broadest sense, open space is land not used for buildings or structures. As a respite from development, open space might be farmland, mountains, river bottoms and mesa-top vistas. It could be parks, cemeteries, golf courses or tree-lined streets. Open space within the community is important to the citizens' quality of life, and in Southwestern Utah it is planned for, not just viewed as land left over after development.

Also, by controlling development on hillsides with slopes of 25 percent or more, the city hopes to protect against rock fall, scarring, slope failure, erosion, storm water control and to prevent difficult traffic access. Ordinances assure hillsides will retain their character and remain mostly undeveloped. Where developed, regulations mandate homes are located on the lower slopes in such a way to be certain hillside cuts are covered by the dwelling units and for the most part unnoticeable. Homebuilders are encouraged to use colors and materials that blend with the surroundings. All roofs, visible building fronts, retaining walls and other features should be constructed of materials with earth-toned colors and texture to match or blend unobtrusively with the immediate adjacent natural setting.

Zoning plays a part in this. Restrictive covenants, put in place by the city and/or the builder or developer are agreed upon by individual homeowners. Some have put the covenants to the test, and the city hesitates to get in the middle of it. But certain restrictions (on farm animals, garish exterior colors, odd landscaping or gardens in peculiar locations on the property) are enforced by the city.

St. George has also been progressive in creating neighborhood parks and hiking and biking trails. The municipal government has also worked to line major streets and thoroughfares with shade trees and create beautifully landscaped freeway entrances to the downtown commercial centers. Neighborhood parks are usually within walking distance from the population served and include an interior trail that connects to the neighborhood served, a playground with an open play area, pavilion and minimal parking. There are 17 such parks in existence now, and two more are under construction. In an effort to meet future needs, the city sets aside land in each new neighborhood to be used for parks at some future date.

In Iron County, impact fees have been assessed on new construction to provide future funds for additional parks. At the moment, Cedar City has two parks — Cedar City Municipal Park in the center of town and Cedar Canyon Park on Utah Highway 14 on the outskirts. At the moment, there doesn't seem to be immediate concern over open lands, but the city is beginning to look to the future.

Alder and Brooks, local authors and historians, sum up the relationship between man and nature in this corner of Utah: "This is an arid place. The land, weather, water and sunshine are always dominant features. These elements attract visitors and newcomers and make every day stimulating, but the desert is a jealous mistress as the Anasazis found out centuries ago.

"So the future most likely will still be a contest between human ingenuity and nature's limitations."

The newest national monument shares the desert with a number of state parks, recreation areas and four beautiful national parks.

Parks and Other Natural Wonders

In September 1996, President Clinton signed into existence the Grand Staircase-Escalante National Monument, preserving 1.7 million acres in the heartland of Southwestern Utah wilderness for future generations.

With a single pen stroke, the president used Theodore Roosevelt's 1906 Antiquities Act to create not only the newest, but also the largest national monument in history. Only slightly changed during the 150 years since Mormon pioneers first arrived to colonize the area, the red rock cliffs and canyons are considered some of the nation's most strikingly beautiful and scientifically important landscapes.

The Grand Staircase-Escalante National Monument is on the Kaiparowits Plateau straddling the Garfield and Kane county line. Don't be thrown by the term "monument," which may have you thinking of a smaller statue or obelisk. According to the Department of the Interior, a national monument is "the smallest possible land designation compatible to the protection of objects of historic or scientific interest situated upon lands owned or controlled by the government of the United States." In this case, the monument just happens to be one-and-a-half times the size of the Grand Canyon National Park.

The Grand Staircase-Escalante monument is bordered on the south by the Utah-Arizona border, on the west by the Dixie National Forest, on the east by Lake Powell and to the north by Capitol Reef National Park. From Bryce Canyon National Park, the land known as the Grand Staircase descends in a series of gigantic "stairs" beginning with the pink cliffs of the Aquarius Plateau. The gray, white, ver-

million and chocolate cliffs step down to the south beyond the Kaibab Plateau of the Grand Canyon's North Rim to the Colorado River at the bottom of the famous gorge.

The Grand Staircase area chronicles eons of history in the form of exposed layers dating from the first upheavals of the earth's crust to modern geological times. Rich in minerals, the area also contains uranium and untapped coal deposits. Because the newly designated monument is undeveloped, wildlife is abundant. Studies of timber cutting and ranching and their long-term effects on the region and its resources are producing a wealth of information for future land use in this and other areas of the country.

Highway access is limited, so perhaps only hikers and biking enthusiasts fully understand why this monumental area is worthy of its new designation. Great descents such as The Gap, Barney Top and Powell Point for years have called mountain bikers from the cities. Names like Hell's Backbone hint at the thrill in store on a climb into the rugged backcountry. Only experienced bikers should try this route, so named because the precipitous road skims along a mountain ridge with sheer dropoffs on both sides.

The newest national monument shares the desert with a number of state parks, recreation areas and four beautiful national parks: Zion, Bryce Canyon, Capitol Reef and the Grand Canyon (see our North Rim of the Grand Canyon chapter). And here in Southwestern Utah, natural beauty helps oil a crucial cog in the state's economic wheel.

Travel is a $3.55 billion industry in Utah, ranking it among the most important economic activities in the state. It is also one of the fastest-growing industries, outpacing the overall growth of the state's economy in most years of the past two decades. Travel-related employment jumped 7.6 percent in 1996, providing 91,000 Utahns with jobs both directly and indirectly supported by tourism. Strictly speaking, it is not a single industry but a combination of parts of several major sectors including wholesale and retail trade and financial, transportation and other miscellaneous services.

Utah's overall economy, and, more specifically, the tourism sector, was exceptionally strong in 1996. The impact of direct tourism-related taxes to state and local governments reached $262 million in 1995 and is expected to have exceeded that figure in '96.

Statistics for 1990-95 provided by the Utah Travel Council help show how inextricably the southwestern section of the state is economically tethered to its natural wonders.

In the St. George/Zion National Park area, transient room tax, gross taxable room rents and taxable retail sales continue to mirror the area's healthy tourism industry, and non-agricultural employment is also reflecting a marked increase. However, the most dramatic statistic — 29.3 percent — indicates a sharp increase in visits, not to Zion, but to Snow Canyon State Park. Between 1990 and 1995, the number of visitors to seven Utah state parks rose more than 100 percent.

The Cedar City/Brian Head area of Southwestern Utah has seen steady but consistent growth as well, although the numbers are not as dramatic as in neighboring counties. Gross taxable retail sales in the past five years have shown the largest growth at 12.1 percent, followed by 8.4 percent jumps in both gross taxable room rents and transient room tax.

The Bryce Canyon area has experienced limited population growth but steady increases in travel and recreation-related employment, spending by tourists and travelers and transient room tax. Visits to Garfield County's two national parks have remained constant during the past five years of the state study, but the numbers of visitors discovering Escalante State Park jumped by 21 percent and tourists to Kodachrome Basin State Park increased 14 percent.

The percentage of population growth in the Kanab area has remained constant for most of the past five years, but economic and travel numbers are up by double-digits. Spending by tourists and travelers, for instance, has increased 10.1 percent, while taxable room rent and transient room tax figures have grown by 16.1 percent.

Land preservation decisions in all parts of Utah, but particularly the protection and management of the Grand Staircase Escalante National Monument, must take into consideration the relationship between the land and the economy, since most rural jobs are tied to mining, agriculture and tourism on public lands. In the coming years, the state intends to focus on the needs of rural counties, particularly Kane and Garfield, that were most seriously impacted by the monument designation. It is hoped that real, meaningful and sustainable employment opportunities can be created in these areas.

But there is more to Southwestern Utah than five national parks. Long considered the crown jewels of the state's tourism economy, the national parks may soon be overshadowed by increasing numbers of visitors in popular state parks, according to recent tourism reports.

Although the geologic raw materials and creative forces that formed these scenic wonders are essentially the same, each of Southwestern Utah's parks is uniquely magnificent.

> ## FYI
>
> Unless otherwise noted, the area code for all phone numbers listed in this chapter is 801 but will change to 435 in September 1997. Either area code may be used until March 22, 1998.

INSIDERS' TIP

Never underestimate the power of nature in our beautiful region. In the deserts of Southwestern Utah, flash floods are deadly, so always be aware of changing weather conditions.

St. George/Zion

The landscape in and around St. George, including Zion National Park, is some of the most diverse on earth. The red rocks invite not only admiration but exploration. From 2,000 feet above sea level at the bottom of the Virgin River Gorge (see our Getting Here/Getting Around chapter) to the 10,000-foot peak of Pine Valley Mountain, national and state parks, ghost towns, canyons, coves and cliffs, the desert in bloom, streams, mineral pools, waterfalls and pioneer structures offer endless possibilities for hikers, bikers, photographers and other curious visitors.

Zion National Park
Utah Hwy. 9, north of Springdale • 772-3256

No matter how often you visit Zion, in a way it's always the first time. It's the first time every time you watch the summer sun slip behind a rocky-top 1,000 feet in the sky. And when adults splash and play like children in the "whoop-de-doo" (see our Kidstuff chapter) on the Virgin River or stretch out with a double-decker ice cream cone on the lawn in front of Zion Park Lodge. Whether you've been here once or 100 times, your vision of Zion's massive, multicolored vertical cliffs and deep canyons changes with the season, time of day, weather or your mood.

Nearly three million visitors a year from all over the world seem to agree with geologist Clarence Dutton's appraisal of Zion National Park. In 1880 the scientist declared, "Nothing can exceed the wondrous beauty of Zion. In its proportions it is about equal to Yosemite, but in the nobility and beauty of the sculptures there is no comparison. There is an eloquence in their forms which stirs the imagination with

a singular power and kindles in the mind a glowing response." Through eons of time, rain, wind, changing temperatures and the shallow, generally peaceful Virgin River have chipped and chiseled massive stone formations to create the splendor of such monoliths as the Great White Throne and The Watchman.

Zion was added to the national park system in 1909. Open all year, each season is distinctly spectacular. Surprise springtime showers create waterfalls that cascade over 1,000-foot cliffs and swell the Virgin River. In the sizzling hot summer — the park's busiest season — the canyon is vermillion, magenta, cyan, azure and emerald. Visitors cool off in 100-plus temperatures by splashing in the meandering Virgin River or its tributaries, wading in pools of freestanding water collected in rock formations or in the mist of Weeping Rock. Fall and winter in Zion find brilliant red and gold foliage accented with an occasional dusting of snow as temperatures sometimes descend into the nippy teens.

Hiking trails are abundant, but Zion is well-designed to accommodate visitors who prefer to tour the park on red-tinted paved roads. A 6-mile scenic drive starts at the south entrance on the outskirts of Springdale and includes views of Angels Landing, the Great White Throne and the West Temple.

Angels Landing rises 1,500 feet from the floor of Zion Canyon. Although it is only about three-fourths as high as its nearby neighbor the Great White Throne, Angels Landing has the appearance of great height because it stands free of the canyon wall. The name stuck when an early visitor to the park noted the peak was so high "only an angel could land there."

For those with nerve, a strong body and no fear of heights, the view from the top of Angels Landing in Zion National Park is 360 degrees of spectacular. The 5-mile round trip to the summit is perilous with steep dropoffs exceeding 1,500 feet on both sides. Park rangers advise against making the trek in icy conditions, when thunderstorms threaten or when strong winds are blowing. The hike will take three hours, but the reward for perseverance is an unequalled view of deep canyons, perpendicular sandstone cliffs and the Virgin River.

Great Views

Photo: Nick Adams

Kodachrome Basin State Park was appropriately named by a team of National Geographic photographers.

The Great White Throne (actually, only half the top is white) is 2,000 feet from base to pinnacle. Paintings of this Zion Canyon landmark have graced the walls of museums, railroad depots and fine homes across the nation, and in 1934, a postage stamp of the Great White Throne was issued.

The West Temple is near the southwest corner of the park and is the highest point on the canyon wall. In 1903, Frederick S. Dellenbaugh described it as "a titanic mountain of bare rock" that "lifts its opalescent shoulders alluringly against the eastern sky." Viewed from the Zion Canyon Visitor Center, the West Temple and several other peaks form one of the world's great skylines.

Souvenirs and printed materials on these and other natural wonders in the Grand Circle of national parks are on sale at the historic Zion Canyon Lodge. At the park's south entrance, Zion Canyon Visitor Center, open year round except Christmas Day, also provides information, slide programs, exhibits, books and a museum.

The Zion-Mt. Carmel Highway, with two narrow tunnels chiseled through solid rock, connects lower Zion with its high plateaus and Checkerboard Mesa to the east. The landscape of this 8-mile section of the park is slickrock, resembling, except for the green trees and shrubs, a vast sand dune. That's exactly what it was 140 million years ago. The term "slickrock" is of local origin and is a misnomer since these rocks aren't actually slick. As a matter of fact, the sandstone that bears the name is quite rough to the touch. There is, however, a limit to the angle on which a shoe will adhere. Zion has no exclusive claim to the term or the phenomenon, as this geology is common throughout the Colorado Plateau.

Except for those susceptible to motion sickness, all visitors to the area will want to see the multimedia presentation, *Treasure of the Gods,* at Zion Canyon Cinemax theater and the Grand Circle multimedia presentation at O.C. Tanner Amphitheater in adjacent Springdale. Shown on the odd hours throughout the day and evening at Zion Canyon Cinemax, *Treasure of the Gods* explores the history and spectacular inner canyons hidden from the casual Zion explorer. On the even hours, *Great American West* depicts the emotionally moving story of the western migration and the settling of the area on the 60-by-80 foot Cinemax screen. The theater is privately owned and features a delicatessen and two gift shops.

Off Interstate 15, about 18 miles south of

Cedar City, the Kolob Fingers Scenic Byway leads through switchbacks to the spectacular Kolob Fingers Canyons. Several hiking trails, including the 14-mile hike to Kolob Arch, the world's largest freestanding arch, begin just off the main road at Lee's Pass. Kolob Canyon Visitor Center offers information and limited souvenir items year round.

Zion National Park is 42 miles east of St. George, off I-15 on Utah Highway 9. The Mt. Carmel entrance is accessed from U.S. Highway 89. The Kolob entrance, which offers one of Southwestern Utah's greatest little-known views, is off I-15 midway between the communities of St. George and Cedar City. Park entrance fee is $10 per vehicle or $5 per person. Annual individual passes are $20. It is common knowledge in Southwestern Utah we are loving the park to death. Due to Zion's increasing popularity and limited roadways, there are restrictions limiting oversized vehicles at the east and south entrances to 7 feet 11 inches wide and 11 feet 4 inches. Also, there is a $10 escort fee for oversized vehicles through the narrow, 1.06-mile Zion-Mt. Carmel Tunnel.

For detailed information and maps of the park, call 772-3256 or write Zion National Park, Springdale, Utah 84767.

Snow Canyon State Park
Utah Hwy. 8, Ivins • 628-2255

More than 686,000 visitors enjoyed the spectacular scenic beauty of Snow Canyon State Park in 1995. Movie buffs will likely recognize the landscape of the park, which is a popular Hollywood backdrop featured in the film *Butch Cassidy and the Sundance Kid*.

At 6,000 acres, Snow Canyon is small compared to other parks and natural wonders in the area. While it is only 5 miles from beginning to end, there are many things to do. Also featured in *The Electric Horseman* and many commercials, the park is popular with the TV and film industries because of its dramatic geologic features and easy accessibility 9 miles north of downtown St. George on Utah Highway 18.

The park features volcanic cones, sand dunes, deep red sandstone cliffs and twisted rock formations that can be enjoyed through a camera lens, during a comfortable drive or over several days of hiking on dozens of trails.

Visits during spring, fall or southern Utah's moderate winter months (when even a gentle dusting of snow is rare) are usually preferable to the area's summertime sizzle. Although there is a bolting ban that prevents adventurous rock climbers from creating new trails on the park's 500-foot cliff faces, established routes attract more and more climbers every year (see our Outdoor Recreation chapter). Snow Canyon is also a favorite destination among cyclists who often enjoy the beauty of the canyon after making the 1,000-foot climb from Bluff Street in downtown St. George.

Snow Canyon facilities include 36 year-round campsites with modern restrooms, hot showers, electric hookups, sewage disposal and a covered pavilion for groups. A day use fee for the park of $4 per vehicle was instituted in 1996. For more on camping options, see our Outdoor Recreation chapter. For general information write Snow Canyon State Park, P.O. Box 140, Santa Clara, Utah 84765.

Gunlock State Park
Utah Hwy. 91, 1 mi. south of Gunlock
• 628-2255

Just 15 miles northwest of St. George on Utah 91, Gunlock is one of two state parks

Smith Mesa Overlook is breathtaking, unique and relatively accessible by car by traveling on Utah 9 about 7 miles out of the communities of Hurricane and LaVerkin on the way to Zion. Just be very careful along the cliff edges — there are no guardrails, and it's a bit of a drop to the desert floor. Seven miles out of LaVerkin on the highway to Zion is a road leading up to Hurricane Mesa. At the top of a steep incline, adventurers will find themselves on Smith Mesa. The well-graded, dirt road climbs about 300 more feet to a parking area and the overlook with beautiful views of Zion and Kolob.

Great Views

that offer a quick getaway for folks visiting Southwestern Utah's largest city. Gunlock is perfect for fishing, camping, boating, watersports or cooling off on hot summer days. There are no fees or facilities at this undeveloped 600-acre park, so don't expect to wake up to a hot shower or flushable toilet while camping. On the route of the Old Spanish Trail, the 240-acre Gunlock Reservoir provides ample opportunity for year-round watersports. A ramp and dock provide boating access, and anglers vie for bass, crappie, bluegill and catfish.

For more information, call 628-2255 or write Gunlock State Park, P.O. Box 140, Santa Clara, Utah 84765.

Quail Creek State Park
Utah Hwy. 18 off Utah Hwy. 9, St. George
• 879-2378

One of the nation's first natural disasters of 1990 occurred at Quail Creek State Park on New Year's Day. Throughout the afternoon of December 31, news of the failing Quail Creek Dam spread through down-river communities such as Hurricane and the St. George suburb of Bloomington, altering party plans and forcing evacuations. The dam break in the early morning hours of January 1 caused no loss of life but did result in a raging wall of water that destroyed a historic bridge — one of the first that crossed the Virgin to make it possible to develop communities on both sides of the river — and flooded basements in a few homes along the Virgin River.

The park, 3 miles east of Exit 16 off I-15, provides excellent year-round camping, picnicking, boating and fishing for rainbow trout, bass, bluegill and crappie. There is a $5 day

fee. Facilities include a clean beach with good boat launch access, but there are no equipment rentals for watersports in the area — bring your own toys. There is an $8 fee for overnight camping at the 23 campsites at Quail Creek, and the park offers modern restrooms.

For more information, call 879-2378 or write Quail Creek State Park, P.O. Box 1943, St. George, Utah 84771.

Red Cliffs Recreation Area
Old U.S. Hwy. 91, 4.5 miles south of Leeds
• 628-4491

We can't leave this one out! The Bureau of Land Management (BLM), a division of the U.S. Department of the Interior, maintains Red Cliffs Recreation Area, another of Southwestern Utah's spectacular, out of the way, scenic treasures. Red Cliffs is off Exit 22, 4.5 miles south of the community of Leeds.

The campground is tucked into a narrow canyon on the edge of the Dixie National Forest. You can wake to the sun on the majestic red cliffs at the base of Pine Valley Mountain and spend the day exploring the landscape. In all but the hot summer months when water is diverted for irrigation, Quail Creek wends its way through desert shrubbery.

Enjoy a leisurely afternoon with a picnic lunch or a weekend spent hiking and "rock hounding" to start that new rock collection. Small stones are free for the taking, but remember that permits are necessary for lava and flagstone collecting. At Red Cliffs you can also camp or explore the remnants of pioneer communities in nearby Harrisburg and Silver Reef. In these old towns there are skeletal remains of stone houses, cemeteries and a restoration of the Wells Fargo station that now

The scenic dirt road that opens to a view of Smithsonian Butte is accessed from Utah Highway 59, 8 miles west of Hilldale (between Hurricane and Kanab). The road runs north to the Rockville Bridge before joining Utah 9 in Rockville. The two-lane dirt road is 9 miles each way, and drivers can expect the trip to take at least an hour. The road is maintained and can be safely driven when dry in a passenger car. In wet weather, it is impassable. Along the drive you'll see Canaan Mountain and Smithsonian Butte, which Clarence Dutton called "a scene never to be forgotten." Travelers along this stretch will get an outside-the-park panorama of Zion National Park as well.

Great Views

The Western World of Ranger Bart

Bart Anderson is Southwestern Utah's pied piper of natural history.

Every Saturday, regardless of the season, the self-styled naturalist can be found leading groups of locals or tourists, seniors and families free-of-charge on "Bart's Hikes." At 10 AM, rain or shine, you'll find Bart waiting for you in the parking lot of Outdoor Outlet at 1062 E. Tabernacle in St. George.

Along with the exercise, hikers learn about nature and pioneer heritage as they discover the hidden geologic and historic treasures of the region.

Many nights, Bart can be found lecturing to standing-room-only crowds in the Old Pioneer Courthouse in St. George or to "snowbirds" at local RV parks. On warm summer evenings, Bart and his wife, Delorice, travel 35 miles from their home in St. George to Pine Valley Mountain, where the naturalist's talks get rave reviews from guests in U.S. Forest Service campgrounds. Bart is also a frequent speaker to civic clubs, church groups and conventions in the area. His spellbinding

Photo: The Spectrum

stories, often augmented with historic pictures from local photographer Lynne Clark's collection, carry titles such as "Outlaws of Dixie," "Saints Without Halos," "How Dixie Towns Got Their Names," "Building the Zion Tunnel" and "Romancing the Cotton."

It's all added up to a community service resume that in 1993 earned Bart the Award of Merit for Service to Utah History and recognition from First Lady Hillary Rodham Clinton as one of the nation's top-10 amateur historians.

Since moving to Utah's Dixie nearly three decades ago, Ranger Bart has brought history alive for thousands. The Idaho native was enticed to Southwestern Utah because of the area's reputation for hiking and out of a personal interest in the Mountain Meadows Mas-

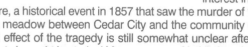

If Ranger Bart is leading a tour while you're in town, don't miss it.

sacre, a historical event in 1857 that saw the murder of 120 men, women and children in a meadow between Cedar City and the community of Enterprise. While the cause and effect of the tragedy is still somewhat unclear after 140 years, a combination of events brought hysterical Mormons, area Native Americans and Arkansas travelers on their way to California together in a deadly ambush. Ranger Bart's curiosity about the facts, fiction and lore surrounding the event was the beginning of a lifelong fascination with local history.

What he discovered was a wealth of fascinating stories gleaned from interviews with oldtimers and his own insatiable curiosity about local legends and events. What he conveys to his audiences, totaling more than 20,000 in 1996, is a contagious enthusiasm for the drama, humor, tragedy and triumph of Southwestern Utah's early settlers.

Other than an obvious personal enjoyment for his avocation, Bart receives no

— continued on next page

compensation for untold hours spent researching, planning, preparing and scheduling for his unique brand of volunteer service. He still maintains his day job overseeing the lab at a local doctors' office. His den wall, however, is filled with awards and plaques recognizing his contribution. Along with the award bestowed by the First Lady, in 1989 Bart was the first recipient of the Quiet Pioneer Award, sponsored by KSL-TV in Salt Lake City and the "Days of '47" committee in charge of the annual celebration of the arrival of the Utah pioneers in July 1847.

---

offers a museum, gift shop and restaurant (see our Restaurants chapter).

The on-your-honor campground fee for one of 10 sites is $6 per vehicle, payable in a metal box at the campground gate. Water and picnic tables are available. A campground host locks the gate each night at 10 PM.

Cedar City/Brian Head

Iron County, with Cedar City as its central and largest community, is renowned for its recreation and relaxation opportunities. The beauty of the area and the added benefit of a slower pace provide the perfect escape from the pressures of the workplace and society. Conveniently located at the center of the Grand Circle of national parks, Cedar City is within 100 miles of some of the most spectacular real estate in the world.

Cedar Breaks National Monument
Utah Hwy. 148, 24 miles east of Cedar City • 586-9451

From the 10,000-foot peak of Cedar Breaks National Monument, the panoramic view of the "circle of painted cliffs" from Rim Drive (Utah Scenic Byway 148) spreads out before you. The area was designated a national monument by federal proclamation in August 1933 "for the preservation of the spectacular cliffs, canyons, and features of scenic, scientific and educational interests contained therein."

There is a basin of graceful limestone formations and seemingly endless stretches of juniper and ancient bristlecone pines, trees that early settlers mistakenly thought to be cedars. Hikers along the rim can revel in numerous other spectacular vistas. A rare, 360-degree view is found atop Brian Head Peak, but at an elevation of 11,300 feet, the altitude may be uncomfortable for some. In fact, some people may find the 10,000-foot elevation at the monument peak will cause quicker fatigue, shortness of breath, headache and other symptoms of altitude sickness.

Spring and summer transform the meadows of Cedar Breaks National Monument into a thick carpet of brightly colored wildflowers. In the winter months, the great open spaces become a snowmobiler's paradise. With Brian Head Ski Resort on the park's northern boundary, excellent downhill and cross-country skiing make the area a favorite for outdoor enthusiasts. The first snows fly as early as October. Midwinter daytime temperatures are normally in the teens but can plummet to zero or below at night. Wind-chill factors are some-

---

INSIDERS' TIP

There are options to make visits to national parks and recreation areas more economical for frequent travelers. Zion and most other national parks have annual passes good for the calendar year of purchase. The cost is $20. A year-long Golden Eagle Passport offers unlimited access to all federal fee areas for $50 per family. The free Golden Access Pass provides free entrance for any U.S. citizen or resident with disabilities and the Golden Age Passport provides unlimited lifetime access for seniors older than 62 for a one-time fee of $10. Passes are available at all park entrance stations.

times dangerously cold. The flipside is that during summer, visitors will find the monument pleasant and mild, rarely topping 75 degrees on the warmest days.

The monument is open from late May to mid-October, although the campground has a slightly shorter season. Don't miss the unique Cedar Breaks Visitor Center, built in 1938 as a Civilian Conservation Corps public works project. Listed on the National Register of Historic Sites, the center is an excellent example of the rustic, log architecture that was typical in early western parks.

Cedar Breaks is on Utah Highway 148, 24 miles east of Cedar City and 4 miles north of the junction with Utah Highway 14. The park entry fee is $4 per vehicle or $2 per person. For more information, call 586-9451 or write Cedar Breaks National Monument, P.O. Box 749, Cedar City, Utah 84720.

Bryce Canyon Area

The Bryce Canyon area is known primarily for its colorful, picturesque landscape. The current focus of media attention with the designation of the Grand Staircase-Escalante National Monument, Garfield County is almost entirely owned and managed by the federal government. An astounding 98 percent of the land area in the county is controlled from Washington.

For generations, the area's small population has lived at one with the land. Over the years, ranching, agricultural interests and timber-cut-

ting have given way to tourism and related cottage industries as local ways to earn a living.

Bryce Canyon National Park
Utah Hwy. 63, Bryce Canyon • 834-5322

It kind of takes your breath away, and not just because of the altitude. Unlike Zion, where awestruck visitors look up at towering cliffs, the view at Bryce Canyon National Park is across a bowl-shaped canyon the Paiute's described as "red rocks standing like men." Not really a canyon, Bryce is actually a 56-square-mile amphitheater alive with deep green ponderosa and bristlecone pines, spruce and fir trees peeking through delicately eroded red, pink and orange limestone "hoodoos" — those funny-looking, elfin-featured rocks left over after Mother Nature has had her fun. From scenic overlooks on 21 miles of paved road in the park, you may not be able to see forever, but you can sure get a clear shot to a distance of 200 miles.

The park is named for Ebenezer and Mary Bryce, who helped settle Southwestern Utah (see Legends and Lore in this chapter). In 1875 Ebenezer built a home at the mouth of what his neighbors dubbed "Bryce's Canyon." Ebenezer earned his livelihood harvesting timber, until he got discouraged trying to make a living in this geographically isolated community and moved on to Arizona. In 1923 the canyon was designated a national monument, in 1924 it became Utah National Park and in 1928 Bryce Canyon National Park was officially created.

A Moo-ving Experience

Anyone who has ever hiked in Bryce Canyon National Park will appreciate Ebenezer Bryce's appraisal of his canyon. During a period of colonization between 1850 and 1880, the LDS Church sent tradesmen to settle in outlying areas in an effort to build a "Kingdom of God" in the mountains. Bryce, a carpenter, accompanied by his wife Mary, cut timber, farmed and chased his few head of cattle through the badlands below the canyon's Sunset Point. He eventually became discouraged in his efforts to irrigate his land and emigrated to Arizona. But he left behind his oft-repeated, wryfully amusing description of the national park that bears his name: "It's a hell of a place to lose a cow!"

Summer is the busiest of the four seasons at the park. Rangers conduct walks, talks and campfire programs, and visitors hike more than 50 miles of trails in the 50-square-mile park. Sightseeing, horseback riding and photography are also popular. A total of 218 campsites are available (see our Outdoor Recreation chapter), but the only water available in the park is from the Paria River at the bottom of the canyon, a 2,000-foot drop in elevation from the rim. Regardless of the season, bring plenty of your own water.

Winter at the park's 8,500-foot elevation is the most colorful season, when snow provides a striking white contrast to dramatic red rocks and dazzling blue sky. Cross-country skiing, snowshoeing and snowmobiling are popular winter activities in the area.

About 126 miles northeast of St. George and 24 miles east of Panguitch, the park is accessible on Utah Highway 12 (consistently rated one of America's most scenic byways) a short distance from its junction with U.S. Highway 89. Park entry fees are $5 per vehicle or $2 per person for buses. For frequent visitors, a $15 annual pass is available. For additional information, call 834-5322 or write Bryce Canyon National Park, Bryce Canyon, Utah 84717.

Capitol Reef National Park
52 Scenic Dr. on Utah Hwy. 24, Torrey • 425-3791

Capitol Reef, a popular gemstone in the national park system's crown, is on the Garfield and Wayne county line approximately 130 miles northeast of Bryce Canyon National Park. This park was named Capitol Reef because of its domed, white formations the pioneers thought resembled the government buildings in the nation's capitol.

The craggy rock formations were a perfect hideout for Butch Cassidy and the Wild Bunch during their riotous heyday more than a century ago. Evidence of pioneer families in what is now Capitol Reef can also be found in century-old orchards, the old Fruita school and other pioneer structures. In season, visitors can pick peaches, pears, apricots, cherries and apples by the pound or bushel. The restored, one-room Fruita schoolhouse is staffed seasonally by costumed interpreters or park ranger guides. The historic Gifford farmhouse is also open to tourists in the summertime and features a representative display of period furnishings.

The park's colorfully stripped cliffs, natural bridges, domes and stone arches inspired early Native American inhabitants to call the area "land of the sleeping rainbow." The Waterpocket Fold stretches 100 miles through the park, reminding visitors of the tremendous force of nature that caused the earth to buckle 50 to 70 million years ago. A long wrinkle in the earth's crust, the Waterpocket Fold is a classic monocline — a regional fold with one very steep side in an area of otherwise horizontal layers. The fold, studied by scientists from all over the world, has lifted the rock layers on its west side more than 7,000 feet higher than the layers on the east. The ridge runs north and south and is visible from the Nottom Road on the park's east boundary, but it is best viewed from the air. Unfortunately, your nearest option for a flyover tour would depart from Moab, 145 miles east, or at Glen Canyon Recreation Area, 327 miles south.

FYI

Unless otherwise noted, the area code for all phone numbers listed in this chapter is 801 but will change to 435 in September 1997. Either area code may be used until March 22, 1998.

Great Views

Grosvenor Arch is worth the additional 10-mile drive south beyond Kodachrome Basin State Park. The intricate double arch is especially dramatic against a clear blue sky. Grosvenor Arch is accessible along a dry-weather, well-signed road on the Cottonwood Canyon Scenic Backway that continues into the canyon and follows the Paria River. Skip this trip if storm clouds are threatening.

Photo: Nick Adams

Cedar Breaks National Monument, a mix of dizzying heights and meadows carpeted with wildflowers, is another of Southwestern Utah's world-famous scenic attractions.

Several fairly easy hiking trails and a 25-mile drive lead from the Capitol Reef National Park Visitor Center to scenic overlooks, remote canyons, natural arches and slickrock wilderness among the park's 378 square miles of area.

Capitol Reef National Park is 11 miles east of the community of Torrey and 37 miles west of Hanksville on Utah Highway 24. Fruita Campground has 71 sites, flush toilets and picnic tables, but no hookups. A group site is available by reservation only, and two primitive overnight sites are open all year (see our Outdoor Recreation chapter). Backcountry camping is allowed through much of the park, but a free permit is required. Other accommodations are available in nearby Torrey or Bicknell.

Entrance into the park is $3 per vehicle or $1 per person. Annual passes are available for $10 per person. For more information, call 425-3791 or write Capitol Reef National Park, HC 70/Box 15, Torrey, Utah 84775.

Escalante Petrified Forest State Park
710 N. Reservoir Rd., Escalante
• 826-4466

Vast deposits of colorful petrified wood and dinosaur bones attract visitors to Escalante Pet-

rified Forest State Park, 1 mile west of the Garfield County community of Escalante. Open year round, this state park boasts a variety of leisure activities including hiking, wildlife observation, picnicking, swimming, boating and fishing for rainbow trout and bluegill on 30-acre Wide Hollow Reservoir. In the winter months, ice fishing is a popular added attraction.

A well-marked, self-guided tour makes it easy to identify the superb specimens in the petrified forest. Over millions of years, the once-living trees were transformed cell by cell into brightly colored stone. Annual growth rings are countable on some trees; knotholes are visible on others, making these tombstones of living matter some of the finest petrified specimens in the nation.

A 22-site campground has modern restrooms with showers. Campsites can be reserved by calling (800) 322-3770 or 826-4466 during regular business hours or by writing Escalante State Park, P. O. Box 350, Escalante, UT 84726-0350.

Kodachrome Basin State Park
Utah Hwy. 12, 9 miles south of Cannonville
• 679-8562

As the eagle flies, Kodachrome Basin State

Park is not far from Bryce Canyon National Park. Some 80 miles east of Cedar City, this photographer's paradise was appropriately named by a National Geographic expedition in 1949. Kodachrome's surrealistic setting is a spectacular mix of ever-changing color accenting unique spires and chimneys created by sand pipe intrusions jutting up from the valley floor, the rock-hard remnants of thermal activity similar to that in Yellowstone National Park. These chemical formations are believed to be the leftovers when geysers forced their way through hollow sandstone. According to park rangers, the complex process can be simply explained: "It looks like a Roadrunner and Wile E. Coyote cartoon."

In this semi-desert terrain, the climate is most comfortable in the spring and fall when cacti and wildflowers are abundant in the 2,200-acre park. However, winter months add the striking contrast of snow on the red rocks. Hiking and mountain biking trails throughout the park allow nature lovers and photographers to explore slickrocks, coves and arches. Horseback and stagecoach rides, available seasonally through Trail Head Station on Utah 12 near the center of the park, add to the experience of the Old West setting

Overnight accommodations are available in the nearby Bryce Canyon area or in the communities of Tropic, Escalante, Hatch or Panguitch (see our Accommodations chapter). Kodachrome has a 24-site campground set into a circle of cliffs with picnic tables, cement slabs, barbecue pits, hot showers and restrooms. The cost is $10 per vehicle or $43 for a day use pass. Trail Head Station has supplies for campers and travelers. For more information, call 679-8562 or write Kodachrome Basin State Park, P.O. Box 238, Cannonville, Utah 84718.

Panguitch Lake Recreation Area (Dixie National Forest)

18 miles southwest of Panguitch on Utah Hwy. 143 • 676-8826, (800) 444-6689

Dixie National Forest is Utah's largest. Nearly two million acres of pristine land divided into four individual parcels, Dixie stretches for 170 miles from the Utah-Nevada border on the west to Capitol Reef National Park on the east. This spectacular timberland straddles the divide between the Great Basin and the Colorado River.

Red Canyon is at the center, but Brian Head Ski Resort and Panguitch Lake on Utah 143, Pine Valley Mountain north of St. George off Utah 18 and Navajo Lake on Utah 14 east of Cedar City are all within the boundaries of the forest.

Panguitch Lake is no secret to serious anglers. The natural, alpine lake, 9 miles around its shoreline and 75 feet deep in summer, is 17 miles southwest of the Garfield County community of Panguitch on Scenic Utah Byway 143, in the heart of the Dixie National Forest. The city and the lake are named for the Paiute word for "big fish." Fed by fresh mountain streams, the lake is heaven for anyone who likes to fish and a prolific nursery for the next generation of rainbow, brook, cutthroat and brown trout.

Panguitch Lake Recreation Area also offers a plethora of hiking and mountain bike trails through scenic wilderness that connects to Brian Head Ski Resort about 13 miles west of the lake. In winter, those same trails become a playground for snowmobilers. Cross-country skiing and ice fishing are also popular. Augering services are free, but a gratuity is always welcome.

Campgrounds for both RV and tent campers, a general store with gas and a gift shop,

The LaVerkin Overlook Trail is a favorite of Ranger Bart. Take Utah 9, which connects Hurricane and LaVerkin to Springdale and Zion, and head south. About a mile past the Toquerville-LaVerkin junction, at the top of the hill, turn right onto a well-graded dirt road. Take this road about one-half mile to a parking area with a beautiful view of the Virgin River and communities of Hurricane and LaVerkin. Ranger Bart also recommends the scenic 2-mile hike down into LaVerkin.

Great Views

Snow Canyon State Park, in the St. George area, hosts more than 600,000 visitors annually.

five restaurants and one fast-food outlet (two are open in winter), six lodges, two public boat ramps, a fish-cleaning station and dump sites round out the list of amenities available at the lake. Fees for overnight camping are generally in the neighborhood of $10 to $15 a night but will vary depending on the campground used and type of hookups (see our Outdoor Recreation chapter).

For more information, call (800) 444-6689 or 676-8826 or write Garfield County Travel Council, P.O. Box 200, Panguitch, Utah 84759.

Red Canyon (Dixie National Forest)
7 miles south of Panguitch on U.S. Hwy. 89 • 676-2676

Red Canyon is one of many happy surprises along Utah Scenic Byway 12 off U.S. Highway 89, but don't expect any glossy brochures or slide shows. It's a quiet place where streams and kids run free; where climbing to an interesting rock formation, reading a good book or taking a nap are top priorities. The canyon itself is 4 miles long and part of the larger, 15-acre Red Canyon area.

Though the visitor center and modern campground are closed during the winter months, Red Canyon provides a spectacular year-round scenic drive over well-paved roads. Depending on the weather, the visitor center operates from mid-May to mid-October. The campground includes 37 sites, plus picnic tables, fire pits, flush toilets and showers (see our Outdoor Recreation chapter).

In Red Canyon, you will discover giant pines and look up into impressive red rock formations sculpted by thousands of years of wind and rain. Hiking trails and rental horses are available for side trips into the hidden areas of the canyon. For those with real endurance, an all-day horseback ride will take you to the hideout of infamous outlaw Butch Cassidy. Ride back immediately or throw your saddle blanket down and sleep out under the stars.

For more information, call (800) 444-6689 or 676-8826 or write Garfield County Travel Council, P.O. Box 200, Panguitch, Utah 84759.

Anasazi Indian Village State Park
460 N. Hwy. 12, Boulder • 335-7308

In approximately 1050, a community of some 200 Kayenta Anasazi Indians occupied the site now known as Anasazi Indian Village State Park. Scientists believe there is also sufficient evidence that representatives of the Fremont Indian culture lived in the area for a time, making this one of the largest known communities of "ancient ones" west of the Colorado River. Year-round self-guided tours begin at an excellent museum filled with ancient artifacts of this early civilization (see our History chapter for more information) and end at the site of the partially excavated village. The museum was renovated in 1996 and expanded to include an auditorium, increased display space and a BLM forest service information center. A picnic area is also part of the 6-acre park.

Anasazi Indian Village State Park is on Utah 12, 28 miles northeast of Escalante. For more information, call 335-7308 or write Anasazi Indian Village State Park, P.O. Box 1429, Boulder, Utah 84716.

Calf Creek Falls
Utah Hwy. 12, 16 mi. east of Escalante
• 826-5499

Calf Creek Falls is one of the many spectacular natural wonders within the boundaries of the newly designated Grand Staircase-Escalante National Monument. Managed by the Bureau of Land Management, Calf Creek Falls is a favorite with families and nature lovers. Though summertime temperatures typically reach 100 to 105, it is a great place for a family reunion or multi-generational outing. Things to do include picnicking, exploring Calf Creek Canyon and hiking to the falls.

Along 2.75 miles of sandy trail (5.5 miles round trip, as you have to back-track to the trailhead), you'll notice evidence of the canyon's earliest inhabitants. Self-guided with the help of a printed interpretive brochure, you'll observe (from a distance) two rock art panels and a couple of granaries carved into the canyon wall, attesting to the presence of the Anasazis many years ago. The spectacular waterfall known as Lower Calf Creek Falls cascades 126 feet into a shallow pool before continuing on its way to the Escalante River.

Mother Nature has provided this beautiful natural basin as a perfect place to cool off before the hike back — be sure to bring a swimsuit and a camera.

Five miles east on Utah 12 is the trailhead to Upper Calf Creek Falls. Serious hikers will enjoy the splendor of the falls, but be warned: It's a strenuous climb over slickrock. BLM staffers won't stop you if you are sure you want to attempt it, but every year they are called upon to rescue nonbelievers overcome by the heat. Whichever hike you choose, the rule of thumb is a gallon of water per person per day.

Calf Creek Falls, approximately 15 miles east of Escalante, has a campground and picnic area. Other accommodations are available in Escalante or the town of Boulder, 13 miles to the north. For more information, call 826-5499 or write Escalante Interagency Visitor Center, P.O. Box 246, Escalante, Utah 84726.

Kanab Area

Kanab, an anglicized version of "kanaw," the Paiute word for "willows," has earned its nickname, "Little Hollywood." The site of more than 100 motion picture and television productions during the past 60 years, Kanab has made a name for itself on the silver screen worthy of the local motto — "the greatest earth on show."

Kane County has nearly doubled in population during the past two decades, but it depends heavily on tourism for revenue. More than 4 million people a year pass through the Kanab area on vacations to the North Rim of the Grand Canyon to the south, Lake Powell to the east, Pipe Spring National Monument and Zion National Park to the west and Coral Pink Sand Dunes and Bryce Canyon National Park on the north.

INSIDERS' TIP

Southwestern Utah's changes in altitude are dramatic and can sometimes cause discomfort. In some areas the elevation differs by thousands of feet within a few short miles, and that can significantly decrease oxygen levels. Be alert for symptoms of altitude, or mountain sickness, which include shortness of breath, headache, nausea, difficulty seeing or hearing, dizziness and sometimes vomiting.

Photo: Nick Adams

Quaking aspens dressed for autumn stand as sentinels along the shoreline of Panguitch Lake.

Coral Pink Sand Dunes State Park
12 mi. west of U.S. Hwy. 89 • 648-2800, (800) 322-3770

Kane County's Coral Pink Sand Dunes State Park, 11 miles off U.S. 89 near Kanab, is an exceptional find for off-road vehicle enthusiasts, hikers and families. The unusual sand, made pink by the iron oxide in the region's abundant sandstone, offers more than 3,000 acres of play area and miles and miles of trails. There are several developed four-wheeling roads on BLM land adjacent to the park's borders. ATVs and dune buggies are free to roam the park.

Photographers and kids will have a field day in the sand of this colorful state park. In addition to the dunes, Coral Pink offers picturesque pinion forests, stands of pine trees, a ranger station and a 22-site, pull-through campground designed so campers don't have to back up to get out. Amenities in the campground include restrooms with hot showers, picnic tables and fire pits with grills. Overnight fees are $11 per site (see our Outdoor Recreation chapter for more information). Reservations are not necessary, but due to growing popularity, it is advisable to call ahead, (800) 322-3770, or write Coral Pink Sand Dunes, P.O. Box 95, Kanab, Utah 84741.

The North Rim, remote and removed from most commercial concerns, is considered by many to offer the canyon's most overwhelming vistas.

Grand Canyon's North Rim

The Southern Paiutes called it Tuweap — "The Earth." For them, it may have marked the edge of the world since it represented such a formidable barrier. When the Spaniards discovered it from the south in the 1540s, they were overwhelmed but also disappointed because what they were really looking for was gold in the Seven Cities of Cibola.

Four centuries later, the Grand Canyon of the Colorado River has become a treasure more precious than the gold the Spaniards sought. The canyon hosts millions of visitors a year, most of whom speak of their love for the Grand Canyon from the perspective of its South Rim.

While the South Rim is where more of the trappings of modern tourist culture are found, the North Rim, remote and removed from most commercial concerns, is considered by many to offer the canyon's most overwhelming vistas. Yet only one of every 10 Grand Canyon visitors gets to the North Rim. Our approach to the mighty canyon will be limited strictly to the North Rim and the adjacent Arizona Strip country to the north. Though technically and politically part of Arizona, this 14,000-square-mile stretch of country is more easily comprehended geographically as a southern extension of Utah. Though roughly 1½ times the size of the state of New Hampshire, only a little more than 3,200 people live here.

The great chasm of the Grand Canyon isolates the North Rim and the Arizona Strip (the area of land between the canyon and the Utah state line) from its mother state in all ways except political. There are places where you can stand at the North Rim and view the South Rim less than a dozen miles across the canyon, yet it's a 225-mile drive from the national park's visitors center on the North Rim to the South Rim visitors center. The realities of geography, economics, culture, history, highways and distances connect this vast stretch of Arizona with Utah in very intimate ways. So when we talk about Southwestern Utah — St. George, Hurricane, Kanab — we're also talking about the landscape extending south across the state line all the way to the Colorado River which, with but one bridge in 250 miles, has cut a much more significant boundary than the arrow-straight state line.

Overview

The Grand Canyon gouges and serpentines 277 miles across the northwestern corner of Arizona. It is a mile deep and in some places more than 10 miles wide. The Arizona Strip north of the Grand Canyon is one of the most remote regions remaining in the continental United States. This is due to two major reasons. First, there are very few roads, and most all of those that exist are dirt roads. Secondly, there is very little live water (as in springs, wells or running streams) on the Strip. The shortage of water accounts for the small amount of development in the region, which, in turn, means there is little need for highways. Residents of Moccasin, near Pipe Spring National Monument on the Arizona Strip, have a 357-mile drive to their county seat in Kingman. To get there, they will travel through corners of Utah and Nevada before they re-enter Arizona at Hoover Dam.

Getting Around the Rim

If you don't have a horse or mule, the only way to get around in North Rim country is by car or on foot. You can access St. George by commercial airline (see our Getting Here/Getting Around chapter), but once you're on the ground you'll either need your own car or a rental. There's plenty to see in this country from a car or within a short walk of your vehicle, but if you're up to hiking, you'll get to see much more and experience it more intimately. We also offer information in this chapter on horse and mule rides along the North Rim, but for the most part you will want to depend on your own set of wheels or your own two feet.

Services are scarce in this region. You need to plan your trip to take advantage of the sparsely placed filling stations, water holes and food outlets between St. George and Marble Canyon, Arizona. If you plan to take some of the dirt roads we mention, you should have a high-clearance vehicle, preferably with four-wheel drive, extra gasoline on board, extra water and an extra spare tire.

While most of the Strip is accessible only by dirt road, we will tell you about some spectacular overlooks of the Grand Canyon from the North Rim accessible on paved roads, with a short walk after parking. Most of these are found in the Kaibab National Forest and within the North Rim of Grand Canyon National Park.

From St. George, you can reach the North Rim by taking Interstate 15 north out of town, then exiting onto Utah Highway 9 at exit 16. Continue to Hurricane, where you turn south at the city's main intersection (State Street and Main Street) and get onto Utah Highway 59. This will take you over the Hurricane Fault and into Arizona. Once you pass Hildale on the Utah side and its sister community, Colorado City, on the Arizona side, the road becomes Arizona Highway 389 and takes you across the northern reaches of the Strip past Pipe Spring National Monument to Fredonia, Arizona.

From Fredonia, about 80 miles from St. George, you can either turn north to Kanab (this will take you back into Utah) or south on Alt. U.S. 89, which begins the climb to the top of the Kaibab Plateau. The change in altitude and weather in the 40 miles from Fredonia to Jacob Lake at the top of the Kaibab is immense. Note that this part of the highway is susceptible to snowstorms and poor driving conditions from November to early May.

From Jacob Lake, you can either drive south on Ariz. 67 to the North Rim or east on Alt. U.S. 89 to Marble Canyon, Arizona, where the Navajo Bridge crosses the Colorado River. The bridge is the only access to the South Rim between Glen Canyon Dam at Page, Arizona, and Hoover Dam at Boulder City, Nevada — a distance of 250 miles. This outlined route from St. George to Jacob Lake, the North Rim or Marble Canyon is the Strip's only major paved artery other than the section of I-15 south of St. George through the Virgin River Gorge. Most other travel in this region will require a vehicle that handily negotiates dirt roads.

Destination: Desolation — The Land

The Arizona Strip truly is a land apart. Remote and awesome, it rises from the low reaches of the Grand Wash Cliffs near Nevada (about 2,000 feet above sea level) to the 8,000-foot heights of the Kaibab Plateau on the east. Perhaps the best way to gain a picture of this rising landscape is to envision a wide staircase beginning with the Shivwits and climbing eastward to the Kaibab Plateau.

Shivwits Plateau

Beginning at the Grand Wash Fault about 60 miles southwest of St. George, this plateau marks the lower end of the Grand Canyon. The Shivwits stretches eastward 25 miles to the Hurricane Fault, much of which can be seen along its 200-mile, north-south demarcation from Cedar City to Peach Springs, Arizona, south of the Grand Canyon. The fault is a gray ridge that lifts some 500 feet upward and can be viewed easily from the road between St. George and Hurricane. The fault is the ridge that shoots up directly east of the town of Hurricane.

The 250-million-year-old Kaibab limestone layer caps this plateau, as it does most of the North Rim country. This accounts for the dearth

Be thankful for railings! Some North Rim views rise above deep, plunging gorges.

of springs and live water, as precipitation sinks through the limestone and spouts out of springs deeper in the canyon to the south. Lava-capped formations more recent in origin dot the landscape.

This is pinyon-juniper country with sagebrush and cacti. At the south edge of the Shivwits, as the plateau nears the Grand Canyon, the country rises into ponderosa pine, with elevations reaching as high as 7,000 feet at Mt. Dellenbaugh. This area is actually part of the Lake Mead National Recreation Area. There are some wonderful overlooks of the Grand Canyon from the remote, southern edge of the Shivwits Plateau, but they are only accessible by long hikes or four-wheel drive vehicle and require someone with local knowledge as a guide.

The Shivwits Plateau was the summering ground of the Shivwits band of Southern Paiute Indians. Here they gathered pine nuts and enjoyed the cooler air before returning to the St. George area for winter. Since the late 1800s,

this has been prime grazing land for ranchers, mostly Mormon cattlemen living in Southwestern Utah communities. Many of the grazing rights (whereby ranchers pay a fee to the Bureau of Land Management for the right to graze their herds on certain allotments at certain times) have been cut in recent years, but some ranchers remain.

The lack of live water necessitated the building of ponds across the region. Cattle farmers have always depended on the unpredictable rains of the Arizona Strip to fill their ponds. Hence, their livelihood is tenuously tied to the elusive clouds in the sky and the whims of federal bureaucrats controlling the land laws.

Uinkaret Plateau

Between the Hurricane Fault on the west and the Toroweap Fault on the east sits the Uinkaret (you-IN-ka-ret) Plateau. This is a wedge-shaped plateau that narrows like a funnel as it draws closer to the Grand Canyon. On the Uinkaret sit numerous volcanic formations such as Vulcan's Throne near Toroweap, Mt. Trumball and Mt. Logan high on the horizon. There was volcanic activity here as recently as a million years ago. Due to movement along the faults, molten rock emerged, much of it pouring into the Grand Canyon at such places as Whitmore Wash and Toroweap Point.

One of the great landmarks of the Uinkaret Plateau and perhaps one of the most spectacular views on earth is at Toroweap Overlook. To get to this incredible place requires a 65-mile drive on a one-way dirt road (only try it with a high-clearance, four-wheel drive vehicle), which is virtually impassable after storms — they don't come that often but can hit at any time of the year. There's a National Park Service ranger station near the end of the drive.

When you arrive at Toroweap, your heart will be in your throat as you inch your way (if you're like some, it will be on your stomach) to the edge of the sandstone and look down a sheer 3,000-foot drop-off to the whispering ribbon of river below. This is a place that makes parents with small children cringe. Note: There are no guard rails. There's a primitive campground close by. It is not a campground for sleepwalkers.

The Uinkaret country is covered with desert species such as blackbrush and shadscale.

Higher up the flanks of Mt. Trumball you'll find old-growth ponderosa pines and Gambel oaks. Mule deer abound here.

Remember, this is extremely remote country. The nearest services are the ones you left behind in St. George, Hurricane, Hildale, Colorado City or Fredonia. At times you will be more than 100 dirt-road miles from gas, food or water.

Kanab Plateau

The nearly flat Kanab Plateau is a 30 to 40-mile treeless plain stretching from the Toroweap Fault on the west to the foot of the Kaibab Plateau on the east. Midway across the plateau, as explorers Francisco Atanasio Dominguez and Silvestre Velez de Escalante learned in 1776, the earth suddenly falls away into a deep chasm — Kanab Creek — with hardly any warning at all.

Gently flowing Kanab Creek, originating in the drainages above the community of Kanab to the north, has whittled itself deep into the Kaibab and Toroweap limestones on its persistent push to the Colorado River. Once it reaches the bottom of the Grand Canyon, Kanab Creek has worked its way 5,000 feet into the earth. Along the gorge of Kanab Creek peregrine falcon hunt as they sail the updrafts

Thanks, But No Thanks

One day in November 1892, Buffalo Bill and a party of English noblemen, American army officers, sportsmen and a collection of businessmen stepped off the train at Flagstaff, Arizona. They were outfitted with an arsenal of weapons and were on their way to the North Rim of the Grand Canyon to hunt deer and bear on the Kaibab. The 150-mile wagon ride from Flagstaff to the V.T. Ranch on the eastern flank of the Kaibab was probably the roughest ride most of them had ever experienced. It nearly did them in.

John. W. Young, a son of Brigham Young and a canyon country entrepreneur, had

met Buffalo Bill and the group of English aristocrats while in England. He attempted to interest them in investing in the Kaibab as a sporting area and hunting ground. They accepted his invitation to visit and found the hunting and the scenery to be spectacular, but the English lords declined the invitation to invest in the North Rim as a center for tourism, sporting and sightseeing. It was simply too far away and too hard to get to. Rather than take the long, rough road back to Flagstaff, the party went out through Kanab and the Utah settlements to the north where the roads were better.

from the canyon. This is one of the least accessible parts of the Arizona Strip by road. But it offers some of the most coveted areas for backpackers, rock climbers and other serious outdoor types.

As you cross the Kanab Plateau on Ariz. 389, be sure and stop at Pipe Spring National Monument for a look at the historic Mormon fort and cattle ranch established in the 1870s. It's just off the highway, 40 miles east of Hurricane.

Kaibab Plateau

The Southern Paiutes called this area Kaibab (pronounced KY-bab), or "Mountain Lying Down." As you approach the Kaibab Plateau from Kanab or Fredonia it's a bit of an illusion. You're still in shirt-sleeves as you drive southeast on Alt. U.S. 89 and look out across a blue-green hump on the horizon that gradually rises like the back of a buffalo. Within 20 minutes, you begin to climb out of the desert into the pinyon-juniper forest, and you keep climbing until you reach the cold air swishing though the ponderosa pines on top of the plateau.

By the time you get to Jacob Lake Lodge and stop for gas and goodies, you've ascended into a new world — one that might motivate you to pull out a jacket. This is what most people know as the Grand Canyon's North Rim. Here, surrounded by greenery and engulfed in pine-scented air, you've reached the highest level of the Arizona Strip. At between 7,000 and 9,000 feet above sea level, you're positioned to take in stunning vistas in every direction. But the main one you have come to see — the Grand Canyon — is still 45 miles south.

On top of the Kaibab you're in dense forest that opens up occasionally to lush green mountain meadows surrounded by blue spruce, white and Douglas fir, quaking aspen and ponderosa pine. In summer, the trees are filled with the songs of yellow-bellied sapsuckers, black-headed grosbeak and hermit thrush. Mule deer come into the meadows in the evening. You can imagine the desert depths below and realize that, as the crow flies, you are only moments from the bottom of one of earth's greatest chasms. That short, 45-mile distance separates two worlds as distinct as Canada and Mexico.

Precipitation here is double or triple that of the surrounding plateaus. The North Rim is about 1,000 feet higher than the South Rim. Snow can reach depths of 6 to 10 feet. Summers are cool and fresh, with temperatures running in the 60s and 70s. Yet, as we've pointed out, those temperatures rise markedly as you descend the canyon. Don't be fooled — in recent years there have been a half-dozen deaths in the lower canyon due to overexposure to the heat and lack of adequate water.

North Rim Recreation Areas

We've given you a general overview of the vast and mostly undeveloped Arizona Strip area. From a visitor's perspective, the largest portion of the Arizona Strip is inaccessible unless you're in a high-clearance vehicle with plenty of supplies, detailed maps, and the preparations for adventure. Now we set our focus exclusively on the Kaibab Plateau, which is easily accessed by paved highway and offers a great deal of recreational opportunities developed by the National Forest Service in Kaibab National Forest and the National Park Service in the North Rim portion of Grand Canyon National Park.

Kaibab National Forest

Kaibab Plateau Visitor Center
Junction of Alt. U.S. Hwy. 89 and Ariz. Hwy. 67, Jacob Lake, Ariz. • (520) 643-7298

Just north of the North Rim boundary of Grand Canyon National Park is the North Kaibab District of Kaibab National Forest. The district covers more than 645,000 acres, with 68,340 acres set aside in the Kanab Creek Wilderness Area and 40,610 acres in the Saddle Mountain Wilderness Area.

The forest is managed for multiple-use and sustained-yield, with the objective of balancing the many, often conflicting uses of forest lands. Traditional uses of the North Kaibab have included logging, grazing, hunting, mining, sightseeing, hiking, camping and cross-country skiing. Woodcutting for personal use and Christmas tree cutting is allowed in certain parts of the forest, but only with a Forest Service permit. For more information on district policies and regulations, call (520) 643-7395.

The visitor center is just south of Jacob Lake Inn. It's an attractive pine building with an information desk staffed by a forest ranger. Open 8 AM to 5:30 PM daily, it has a small bookstore with dozens of titles relating to the natural and human history of the area. A number of interpretive displays describe the flora and fauna of the forest as well as its human history of pioneering, hunting and cowboying. In the middle of the building is a relief model of the entire Kaibab Plateau that puts this fascinating landscape into perspective. As you walk around the table, you get an excellent look at the way the plateau rises above the surrounding country and ends abruptly at the edge of the Grand Canyon.

Lodging

Lodging in the Kaibab National Forest is available at Jacob Lake Inn and Kaibab Lodge. Information on these are included in the "Lodging, Fuel and Food on the North Rim" section later in this chapter. It is a good idea to make your reservations to stay in the Kaibab National Forest as far in advance as possible since the number of rooms is limited, and the demand is high.

Picnicking and Camping

From May through October (unless winter comes early), the Kaibab National Forest is a great place for picnicking and camping. You'll find groceries and supplies available at locations listed below.

A Note On Jacob Lake

One of the most commonly heard geographical names on the Kaibab Plateau is Jacob Lake. It is also one of the most misunderstood names, since there is not a body of water on the Kaibab that even comes close to most folks' definition of the word "lake." Jacob Lake is ac-

tually nothing more than a small pond just a couple of miles from the Jacob Lake Inn.

Named for the early Mormon pioneer explorer Jacob Hamblin, this is one of the few year-round water holes on a mountain you would expect to be covered with lakes. In fact, the Kaibab probably would be covered with lakes if its crust were not made up of the very porous Kaibab limestone layer that forms the cap of the North Rim of the Grand Canyon. The Kaibab receives several feet of snow every winter, but when it melts, the water seeps into the porous ground rather than running into streams and lakes. Most of the water used at the North Rim and across the Kaibab Plateau is pumped from springs beneath the rim of the canyon. At places such as Roaring Springs below the Grand Canyon Lodge, water from the plateau bursts out from beneath the Kaibab Limestone.

What it comes down to is the fact that Jacob Lake is nothing more than a pond or sinkhole where winter runoff accumulates and percolates into the ground. It's a beautiful sight to see, but don't expect to fish, boat or swim at Jacob Lake.

Jacob Lake Campground
Junction of Alt. U.S. Hwy. 89 and Ariz. Hwy. 67 • (520) 643-7232, (800) 283-CAMP

This is a developed campground 30 miles southeast of Fredonia at the intersection of Alt. U.S. 89 and Ariz. Highway 67. The elevation here is 7,920 feet, and the season of use runs from May 15 to approximately November 1, depending on snowfall. There are 53 single units with tables and fire grills, drinking water, toilets and nature trails. The fee is $10 per vehicle per night, and the facility is handicapped-accessible.

Jacob Lake accepts tents, trailers, and motor homes shorter than 26 feet long, but there are no utility hookups (RVers see Kaibab Camper Village listing below). In addition to camping, the area is ideal for picnicking and hiking and as a base for sightseeing, wildlife viewing and forest service interpretive programs. Again, Jacob Lake is somewhat of a misnomer

---

INSIDERS' TIP

Remember, take only photos, leave only footprints.

Photo: St. George Magazine

Cattlemen work their herds on the Arizona Strip beneath the Hurricane Fault.

(see "A Note on Jacob Lake" above). About 2 miles from the campground, it is actually little more than a pond, and there's no fishing or swimming in it. This campground offers good access to the North Rim, and there are guided tours, horseback riding concessions and chuckwagon meals. Call for reservations up to three months in advance of your trip.

Jacob Lake Group Campground
Adjacent to Jacob Lake Campground
• **(520) 643-7232, (800) 283-CAMP**

Near the Jacob Lake Campground (see previous listing), this facility is designed to accommodate two large groups at a time. Facilities, uses and reservation number are the same as Jacob Lake Campground, listed above. There's a $15 non-refundable fee applied to the first day fee, plus $1 per person per day, plus $25 per day per group.

DeMotte Campground
7 mi. north of Grand Canyon National Park boundary on Ariz. Hwy. 67
• **(520) 643-7298**

About 26 miles south of Jacob Lake on Ariz. 67 and 7 miles north of the boundary to the North Rim-Grand Canyon National Park, this developed campground sits at an elevation higher than 8,700 feet. Depending on snowfall, the season runs from May 15 to November 1.

Facilities include 22 tent sites with tables, grills, toilets and drinking water. The fee is $7 per vehicle per night. DeMotte places you close to the North Rim, and there are gasoline, supplies, telephones and a restaurant nearby.

Indian Hollow Campground
Forest Rd. 232, 50 mi. south of Fredonia, Ariz. • **(520) 643-7298**

This is a semi-developed campground 50 miles south of Fredonia on gravelled Forest Roads 422 and 425. The last 4½ miles on Forest Road 232 requires a pickup truck or other high-clearance vehicle. Elevation here is 6,300 feet. The season, depending on weather, is May 1 to late November.

There's primitive camping and hiking, including access to the Kanab Creek Wilderness Area and the Thunder River Trail in Grand Canyon National Park. There's no fee for use

INSIDERS' TIP

For road conditions in northern Arizona, call the Arizona Highway Department at (520) 643-7249.

of one of the three single-unit sites. There are cooking grills and pit toilets. Remember, for overnight trips into Grand Canyon National Park, a park service permit is required.

Kaibab Camper Village
1 mi. south of junction of Alt. U.S. 89 and Ariz. Hwy. 67 • (520) 643-7804, (800) 525-0924

The village, formerly Jacob Lake RV Park, is set among the tall ponderosas. There are 80 motor home and trailer sites with full hook-ups and 50 tent sites on a forested ridge over-looking Jacob Lake and the beautifully restored North Kaibab forest ranger's cabin, which dates back to 1910. Guests have use of 70 picnic tables and a number of firepits. Spring opening and fall closing dates depend on weather and temperatures, but you can count on the village being open by May 15 through mid-October. Full hookup RV sites are $22 per night. Tent sites are $12 to $15.

Exploring
the Backcountry

Camping

Since camping is not limited to camp-grounds on national forest lands, those who prefer solitude and have the necessary skills and equipment can camp anywhere within Kaibab, unless posted otherwise. The Forest Service suggests you camp at least a quarter-mile away from paved roads. Be sure to use common sense when camping. In this arid region, camping is generally prohibited within a quarter-mile of water sources, allowing wild-life undisturbed access. You should also camp at the fringes of meadows rather than in the middle to keep from tramping vegetation.

The logging industry has opened a number of roads throughout the Kaibab Forest, making backcountry campsites with incredible views quite accessible. At the visitor center, you can get information on a number of backcountry sites where you can camp with a view. Among the best are Crazy Jug Point, Buck Farm Over-look, Jumpup Point, Marble Viewpoint, Quaking Aspen Spring, North Timp Point, Sowats Point and East Rim Viewpoint. Here's a closer look at a couple of our favorites.

Crazy Jug Point

This backcountry camping spot with an awesome overlook is about 32 miles southwest of Jacob Lake on the rim of the Grand Canyon. To get here, go about a quarter-mile south of the Kaibab Plateau Visitor Center on Ariz. 67 and turn west on Forest Road 461. You drive 9 miles on Forest Roads 461 and 462 to 422 (all relatively well-maintained gravel roads). Take 422 south for 11½ miles to Forest Road 425, then turn right (west) on 425 and go 10 miles to Big Saddle Point. From there you go south on 292 and 292 B for about 1½ miles to the end of the road at Crazy Jug Point.

The beauty of the drive through tall pon-derosa pine to Crazy Jug Point is as reward-ing as the destination. At the point, you're sur-rounded by pinyon, juniper, oak and cliffrose. The view from the edge is stunning as you look out across Grand Canyon National Park into Tapeats Amphitheater, Fishtail Mesa and Steamboat Mountain.

If you've got a high-clearance vehicle that you don't mind getting dirty and risking a dent or two with, you must drive to Toroweap Overlook. It is perhaps the most overwhelming view of the Grand Canyon, and you can drive right to it in the right kind of vehicle. From Ariz. Highway 389, 9 miles west of Fredonia, turn south at the sign signifying that Mt. Trumball is 53 miles away. From there, it is a 60-mile, one-lane dirt road to Toroweap. About 6 miles before the overlook, you'll pass the remote Tuweep Ranger Station on the left. Looking south and to your right, you'll see the volcanic dome called Vulcan's Throne, then within minutes you will literally be standing at the edge of the earth.

Great Views

Buck Farm Overlook

This is a backcountry camping spot that gives you an excellent experience on the east side of the Kaibab Plateau in House Rock Valley. It's about 50 miles east and south of Jacob Lake and can be accessed by going east on Alt. U.S. 89 about 20 miles to Forest Road 445, which is the Buffalo Ranch headquarters turnoff. You go south on the relatively well-maintained gravel road for 23½ miles to where it forks. Take the left fork 2 miles to Forest Road 445 H, continuing 3 miles to the end of the road. It's about 100 yards to where the earth drops out from under you, and you're looking into Marble Canyon. This scenic drive takes you off the east rim of the plateau into House Rock Valley. Here you camp in the massive shadow of the Kaibab Plateau with the Vermillion Cliffs to the North and Navajo Mountain on the eastern horizon.

Hiking and Mountain Biking

You can also obtain detailed information at the visitors center regarding great hiking trails in the Kaibab Forest. Some of the most popular backcountry trails are Snake Gulch-Kanab Creek Trail, Kaibab Plateau Trail, Crystal Spring Trail, Nankoweap Trail and Navajo Trail. Rangers can also provide detailed directions on mountain bike routes. Ask about Buckridge Point, Horse Spring Point, Jensen Point, Willow Point and the Slide Point Loop.

Backcountry hiking and biking affords the opportunity to see some of the Kaibab's variety of wildlife. The Kaibab squirrel is a subspecies found nowhere else in the world. It is a tassel-eared squirrel with a charcoal-black body, tufts of fur standing up on its ears and a bright, white tail. There are also mule deer, mountain lion, bobcat, coyote, porcupine, turkey, Stellar's jay, raven, raptors and the very occasional bison or black bear.

Winter Sports

If you think the Kaibab Plateau is Arizona's best-kept secret in summertime, try it in winter. Once the snowy season sets in, few tourists wend their way across the lonely stretches of the Arizona Strip, but Alt. U.S. 89 is plowed and open all winter. You usually can't, however, drive south beyond Jacob Lake on snowpacked Ariz. 67.

If you're into cross-country skiing, snowshoeing or snowmobiling, the staff at the visitors center will point the way to some of the best snow trails you'll find anywhere. Be prepared for sub-zero temperatures at night and nothing higher than the 40s during the day.

South of Jacob Lake and east of Ariz. 67, the entire forest east of the road is closed to snowmobiles and other motorized access. West of Ariz. 67, the snowpacked forest roads are well-suited for snowmobiling and other winter uses. In fact, access to the North Rim of Grand Canyon National Park during winter can be gained only by cross-country skiing or on snowshoes. If you want to enter the park from the Kaibab Forest, you must obtain a winter-use permit from the park's backcountry reservation office. Call (520) 638-2474 for more information. Following is another wintertime option.

North Rim Nordic Center at Kaibab Lodge
26 miles south of Jacob Lake off Ariz. Hwy. 67. • (520) 526-0924, (800) 525-0924

The Kaibab Lodge (see listing in "Lodging, Food and Fuel on the North Rim" below) has turned the North Rim into a winter vacation spot by offering two-, three- and four-day winter packages including lodging, track and backcountry skiing, snowshoeing, photo workshops, guided snow van trips, cross-country skiing lessons, hot tubs, fine dining and a number of other activities. Access to the lodge is by snow van only, since Ariz. 67 is generally closed all winter from Jacob Lake south. The winter vacation packages are offered in January, February and March, and range in price from $370 per person (double occupancy for two nights) to $590 per person (double occupancy for four nights). The price includes all meals (served at the Kaibab Lodge dining room), lodging, snow van, ski lessons, guided trips and other special events.

Grand Canyon National Park — North Rim

The southern tip of the Kaibab Plateau is within the boundaries of Grand Canyon National Park. You cross the park boundary 30 miles south of Jacob Lake on Ariz. 67, after a beautiful drive on a winding road lined with majestic ponderosa pines that open periodically into wide, green meadows where deer are often grazing. From the park boundary, it's another 7 miles to the rim where Ariz. 67 abruptly ends at "the edge of the earth."

At the park entry station, there's a $20 per vehicle or $10 per individual fee. You'll get a colorful Grand Canyon brochure and a handy trip planner printed on newsprint. It contains information on current ranger programs and other activities in the park.

The North Rim of Grand Canyon National Park is open from May 15 to October 16,

weather permitting. The Grand Canyon Association operates a beautiful new visitor center next to the Grand Canyon Lodge at Bright Angel Point. The log building just opened in the summer of 1997 and houses an excellent bookstore, as well as a large relief model of the Grand Canyon area to help you get your bearings. Association personnel and park service staff are on hand to answer your questions and help you on your way.

If you have children 14 or younger, ask for a Junior Ranger brochure. Following a five-step program, including a nature walk and other activities, the kids can qualify for a Junior Ranger patch that costs $1.50 upon completion of the program.

Whether you're staying at the lodge (see "Lodging, Food and Fuel on the North Rim" below) or not, you should stroll through the historic building built in the late 1920s at the edge of Bright Angel Point. The Grand Canyon Lodge is a great attraction in and of itself, and the views from its patios and lobby are stunning.

Lodging

The Grand Canyon Lodge and the Phantom Ranch are the two lodging options available within the North Rim boundaries of Grand Canyon National Park. Information on these are included in the "Lodging, Food and Fuel on the North Rim" section later in this chapter. It is very wise to make your reservations to stay inside the Grand Canyon National Park as far in advance as possible — lodging is scarce and demand is extremely high.

Camping

North Rim Campground
Ariz. Hwy. 67, 1 mi. north of Grand Canyon Lodge • (800) 365-2267

There are no hookups at North Rim Campground, but it does put you within the boundaries of the national park just a mile from the North Rim. There are 82 tent sites, showers, a laundry and an excellent grocery store. Stays are limited to seven days in season. Reservations are strongly recommended and can be made up to five months in advance.

Bus Tours

A narrated bus tour will take you past some of the North Rim's grandest sites — Cape Royal, Point Imperial and others. The tours are conducted by park concessionaires, and you can make reservations at the mule rides desk in the Grand Canyon Lodge lobby. A three-hour tour is $20 for adults and teens and $10 for children 4 through 12.

Mule Rides

Mule rides are a classic symbol of the Grand Canyon. South Rim mule rides go all the way to the Colorado River, but the North Rim is much farther away (14 miles from the Colorado on the North Kaibab Trail). Thus, rides are limited to the canyon rim and lesser distances into the canyon.

Grand Canyon Trail Rides
Grand Canyon Lodge • In season,
(520) 638-2292; Winter, (801) 679-8665

This is the only mule riding option on the North Rim. One-hour rim rides cost $15 per person. Half-day trips down the North Kaibab Trail or along the rim, with no riders younger than 8, are $35. Full-day rides to Roaring Springs, with a minimum age of 12, are $85 a person, and the price includes lunch. A daily schedule of rides is available in the Grand Canyon Lodge lobby. Reservations are a good idea.

Whitewater Trips

Most North Rim overlooks of the Grand Canyon do not offer a view of the Colorado River. The winding river that formed this incredible chasm is mostly hidden far down in a network of tributary canyons. You can see the river at a great distance from Cape Royal (see subsequent listing), hike to it from the North Rim via the 14-mile North Kaibab Trail (see listing below), or you can cross it by driving 40 miles east from Jacob Lake on Alt. U.S. 89 through House Rock Valley to Navajo Bridge at Marble Canyon. Six miles upstream from Marble Canyon is the historic site of Lee's Ferry. This is also Mile 0, where all boats are launched for Grand Canyon river trips.

Whitewater rafting on the Colorado River is a completely separate experience from visiting the North Rim. It requires reservations at least six months in advance — a year for some companies. There are 18 river-running concessions licensed to make commercial river trips in Grand Canyon National Park. The season runs from April through October. A list of the companies can be obtained from Grand Canyon National Park, P.O. Box 129, Grand Canyon, Arizona 86023. Call (520) 638-7888 for more information.

Trips vary from three days to three weeks on motorized or oar-driven boats. Costs vary from $150 to $250 per day. All boats put in at Lee's Ferry, but some companies offer partial trips ending at or starting from Phantom Ranch (see subsequent listing). Food, portable sanitation facilities, some or all necessary camping gear and guide services are provided by the river companies. Most companies also offer private charter trips in addition to their regularly scheduled trips.

If you'd like a rather tame introduction to the Colorado River, we suggest the following company.

Aramark Wilderness River Adventures
P.O. Box 717, Page, Ariz. 86040
• (520) 645-3296, (800) 992-8022

Aramark offers a half-day or full-day

The most accessible overlook on the North Rim is Bright Angel Point. You can drive directly to a parking lot near the overlook by heading south from Fredonia on Alt. U.S. 89, then turning south on Ariz. 67 at Jacob Lake. From there, continue south about 45 miles through the Kaibab National Forest and into Grand Canyon National Park. Bright Angel Point offers a stunning view across the upper reaches and inner gorges of the Grand Canyon.

Great Views

smooth-water raft trip on the Colorado River just north of Grand Canyon National Park beginning at Glen Canyon Dam, right outside Page, Arizona (see our Daytrips and Weekend Getaways chapter). This is an ideal way to get a taste of river rafting without having to plan well ahead, take two weeks out of your schedule or spend a fortune. Page is 121 miles from the North Rim via Alt. U.S. 89, or 160 miles from St. George via U.S. 89.

Trips depart from the Wilderness Outfitters Store at 50 S. Lake Powell Boulevard in Page, or from Wahweap Marina, 5 miles from Page on the shore of Lake Powell. You descend to the canyon bottom through the 2-mile tunnel used to construct Glen Canyon Dam and emerge on the banks of the Colorado River, just below the dam. From there you float 15 miles in pontoon boats on placid waters through Glen Canyon to Lee's Ferry, then return to Page via a 45-minute bus ride. The cost for half-day trips (including shuttle) is $44 for adults and $37 for children. All-day trips are $65 for adults and $57 for children.

Backcountry Permits

Day hikes or stays at Phantom Ranch near the end of the North Kaibab Trail do not require park service permits. But any overnight camping trips require a $24 permit, obtainable at the backcountry office at the North Rim Ranger Station. Located a mile north of the lodge, just off Ariz. 67, this is where you can pick up a backcountry trip planner that has a map, explains the regulations of backcountry use and has a reservation form. The number of campers allowed in each section of the park at a given time is limited, so try to make reservations as early as possible, especially for holidays. The backcountry office is open daily during the season from 8 AM to noon. For more information, call (520) 638-7888.

Reserved permits must be picked up by 9 AM on the day prior to the trip or the reservation is cancelled. If you're going to be camping in an area some distance from the backcountry office, it's possible to arrange to have your permit mailed.

Rim Shots: The Best North Rim Views

While only one in 10 Grand Canyon National Park visitors comes to the North Rim, those who do seem to feel that the North Rim offers the greatest views. The North Rim is also an equal-opportunity view provider — offering just as spectacular views to those who drive right to them as to those who hike a distance. The following world-class views are all accessible by automobile, although each one is also the beginning for a hike on improved trails that will take you to a variety of other vantage points.

Put That in Your Pipe

At Pipe Spring National Monument, 67 miles southeast of St. George, Mormon pioneers built a fort and headquarters for their cooperative cattle operation. The spring got its name from an incident involving Jacob Hamblin's brother, Will. Apparently Will

was an excellent marksman, and one day, as he and others were camped at the spring, one of the men challenged Will by asserting he could not shoot a hole in a handkerchief hanging from a tree limb. Hamblin took the challenge and shot at the cloth. The bullet was said to be on target, but the force of air in front of it apparently blew the cloth aside before the bullet could puncture it. So Will Hamblin, bent on regaining his honor, set the bowl of a pipe on a stump several yards away and with one shot blew the bottom out of the pipe. The bullet did not so much as scratch the sides of the small pipe bowl.

The mighty Grand Canyon makes the North Rim and Arizona Strip easily identified with Utah.

Photo: St. George Magazine

Bright Angel Point

When you get out of your car at the Grand Canyon Lodge parking lot you're only a few steps from a view off Bright Angel Point. There's a quarter-mile walk from the parking lot around to vantage points from the tip of this promontory. The view opens onto a number of tributary canyons plunging deeper and deeper into the inner gorge. If you've never seen the Grand Canyon before, this is an ideal place to orient yourself. Below and to the east lies North Kaibab Trail, a 14-mile hike to Phantom Ranch and the river. Grand Canyon Lodge is set at the end of the point and is designed to afford a number of views of the canyon.

Cape Royal Scenic Drive

About 23 miles from Grand Canyon Lodge, Cape Royal is the southernmost view point from the Kaibab Plateau. To get there you first go north from the lodge about 3 miles on Ariz. 67 to the paved park road that takes off to the right (east). Drive about 5 miles to the three-way intersection, where you can either go left to Point Imperial or right to Cape Royal. From there it's another 15 miles to Cape Royal, with several overlooks of the canyon to the east along the way.

Cape Royal juts out into the big bend of the canyon allowing awesome views to the east and south, including the Colorado River itself. Angel's Window protrudes in front of you. It's a gigantic wall of Kaibab limestone with a huge opening in the rock through which you can view the Colorado River deep down in the canyon. A short nature walk, with interpretive signs identifying the vegetation and animal life along the way, leads out to the point above Angel's Window. In other words, you can actually walk out over this natural arch.

Point Imperial

Here, at 8,800 feet above sea level, you get your northernmost roadside view of the canyon. Point Imperial overlooks the beginning of the Grand Canyon, where the Colorado River emerges from the narrow Marble Gorge. Proceed as if you were going to Cape Royal (see previous listing), and turn left at the three-way intersection 8 miles from the lodge. From there it's 3 miles to Point Imperial. While here, we suggest you take a full day to enjoy the 58-mile round trip to Point Imperial and Cape Royal. Be sure to take lunch and plenty of water.

Trail Blazin' — Our Favorite Hikes

North Kaibab Trail

This is one of the classics of all national park trails in the entire park system. It is not for the novice or the faint of heart, but beginners can descend it a short way and have a wonderful experience. The problem is that once you start you want to keep going to see what's around the next bend. You can get into trouble if you don't take into account the fact that however deep you descend, you must also climb back out.

The trailhead is at the lower end of the parking lot, 2 miles north of Grand Canyon Lodge. You start in the cool forest of the North Rim, descend through woods to Roaring Springs Canyon, then follow Bright Angel Creek all the way to the Colorado River. It's 14 miles one-way. Don't plan on going all the way unless you are a very experienced hiker and you have a permit or made reservations to camp at Phantom Ranch at the bottom.

The picnic ground near Roaring Springs is a good destination for a day hike. It's about a 9½-mile round trip from the North Rim, with an elevation change of 3,160 feet. In places, the trail is cut along ledges with incredible drop-offs. This trek tests you physically as well as psychologically — it is dangerous, and it is arduous. Don't try it if you're not up to it. And remember, even if it's cold in the morning when you leave, it will heat up considerably during the day. Carry plenty of water, wear a hat and use sunscreen.

Widforss Trail

For most folks, this is a much more practical hike than trying the North Kaibab Trail. The Widforss has gently rolling terrain and great canyon views. It's a 10-mile round trip, and you should allow at least five hours to complete it. The trail, named in honor of the Swedish artist Gunnar Widforss (painter of beautiful watercolors of the canyon after the turn of the century), will take you through ponderosa pine and meadows to an overlook near Widforss Point. Many people enjoy cutting the trip short and going only partway and back. To access the trailhead drive 2.7 miles north from Grand Canyon Lodge, turn left and drive 1 mile on the dirt road. The turnoff is about one-third mile south of the Cape Royal turnoff.

Ken Patrick Trail

From Point Imperial, the Ken Patrick Trail winds about 3 miles along the rim to Cape Royal Road. From there it continues 7 miles through the pines to the head of the North Kaibab Trail. That makes it a trail of nearly 10 miles, with views across the headwaters of Nankoweap Creek. The trail has a lot of up and down terrain, but it is not nearly as arduous as descending into the canyon. You need to allow six hours for the entire one-way hike, or you can access the trail from several different points and hike parts of it.

Uncle Jim Trail

This is a three-hour, 5-mile hike beginning on the Ken Patrick Trail from the North Kaibab Trailhead. After a mile on the Ken Patrick, turn southeast toward Uncle Jim Point. From the point there are views of Roaring Springs Canyon and the North Kaibab Trail. This trail is well-marked and not difficult.

Lodging, Food and Fuel on the North Rim

There's a very small amount of commercial activity on the North Rim. At times this can prove uncomfortable for visitors, but it's part of what sets the North Rim experience apart from the more "touristy" South Rim. The nearest traditional accommodations are 80 to 100 miles away at Fredonia, Arizona and Kanab, to the northwest, or Marble Canyon and Page, Arizona, to the east.

Yet there are a few places inside the national park and national forest to get gas and goodies, a sit-down meal and a good night's sleep, albeit they may all be a little rustic. Here are some of the most popular stops.

Grand Canyon Lodge

South terminus of Ariz. Hwy. 67, 43 miles south of junction at Alt. U.S. Hwy. 89
• (520) 638-2611, (303) 297-2757

At the edge of Bright Angel Point, this historic lodge is operated within the park boundaries by the licensed concessionaire AmFac. Reservations are made through AmFac's Colorado office at the 303 area code number listed above. Unless you plan to camp, this is as close to the edge of the canyon as you can stay. The lodge, built of native limestone, is an attraction itself. It was built in the late 1920s by architect Gilbert Stanley Underwood, who also designed the Ahwahnee Hotel in Yosemite and the lodges at Bryce Canyon and Zion national parks. Now a national historic landmark, the lodge is an informal and spacious hotel constructed of massive stone walls and high-timbered ceilings and offers incredible views of the canyon. Its rustic style complements the canyon rim environment.

The giant lobby sits right at the edge of the canyon. You can sit in comfortable chairs and gaze out the large windows at the gorge that seems to change by the hour as the sun and clouds move across the sky. In one corner of the lodge is a fitting memorial to the famous burro named Brighty. There's a bronze statue of the animal and photos on the wall telling the story of this dependable little animal that inspired the book and movie *Brighty of the Grand Canyon*.

With more than 400 units, there are several accommodation options at the lodge. But you should make your reservations months in advance. There are only a handful of rim-view rooms, which are generally booked two years in advance. They have double beds and full baths and are $103 per night. The best-furnished of the cabins are the western cabins, with double beds and private baths. They are $93 a night. Next are the pioneer cabins, with different combinations of double and twin beds at $87 a night. There are about 50 motel units, each with private bath and combinations of double and twin beds, for $76 a night. The most rustic cabins are the frontier cabins, with private baths and combinations of double and twin beds for $67 a night.

All of these units are set among the pines of Bright Angel Point within a short walking distance of the lodge with its post office, curio and gift shop, saloon, snack shop, dining room and auditorium where ranger talks are held.

The lodge dining room serves breakfast, lunch and dinner in a large, timber-beamed dining hall with tall windows overlooking the canyon. For lunch you can feast on smoked trout and spinach salad for $5.75, or chicken mandarin salad for $7. The lunch menu includes a number of meat, pasta and vegetable specialties under $7. Dinners run $10 to $20 with the menu

---

INSIDERS' TIP

It is tempting, when leaving from high country in the cool morning, to assume you won't need much water. But in the North Rim area, you're often descending into hotter, drier country. Carry all the water you can.

featuring pasta, seafood, beef, pork, trout and chicken. The hickory smoked prime rib is $17.45.

Just outside the main entry to the lodge, the snack shop offers a number of fast-food options. You can get a burger for $3.10 and a soft drink for $1.25.

North Rim Campground
Grocery Store
1 mile north of Grand Canyon Lodge off Ariz. Hwy. 67 • (800) 365-2267

Back in the pines, just off Ariz. 67, you'll find the best little grocery store on the plateau. Located at the entrance to the campground (see previous listing), this store has a wide variety of food items, including fresh bread, fresh vegetables and all kinds of drinks. It also has a snack bar and gift shop. There's a gas station nearby, laundry facilities and showers.

Phantom Ranch
N. Kaibab Tr. • 638-2401, 638-2631

All you take to this lodging facility is what you're willing to carry on your back for 14 steep, downhill miles. Dormitory beds, cabins and meals are available at Phantom Ranch near the bottom of the North Kaibab Trail on Bright Angel Creek. These facilities are always booked well in advance. Dorm-type accommodations are approximately $21 per night, and cabins are approximately $55 ($10 for each extra person). Meals range from $5 boxed lunches to $28 steak dinners. Reservations are made through Grand Canyon Lodge.

Kaibab Lodge
26 miles south of Jacob Lake off Ariz. Hwy. 67 • (520) 638-2389, (800) 525-0924

This rustic lodge is just off Ariz. 67, 18 miles north of the Grand Canyon Lodge. Lying in the heart of the Kaibab National Forest, the lodge was built in the mid-1920s and was originally part of a working cattle ranch. At 8,770 feet above sea level, it has become a wonderful summer refuge for travelers. (It's also a great winter resort — see our listing under "Winter Sports" above.)

This is the nearest lodging facility to the North Rim outside the national park. Its summer season is mid-May through October. Inside the lodge you can relax around an old stone fireplace, enjoy a glass of wine or browse around the little souvenir shop. Because water is scarce on the plateau — drinking water is hauled in from 60 miles away — the lodge has no swimming pool. But that's OK, because if you take in all the wonderful sights, you're not going to have time for such trivial pursuits as swimming anyway.

Rooms at the Kaibab Lodge are rustic duplex buildings a short walk from the main lodge. They are basic sleeping accommodations with private shower, sink and toilet. There are no phones or televisions in the rooms. However, pay phones and satellite TV are available in the main lodge. Rates range from $68 for one bed to $95 for three beds.

Open for breakfast, lunch and dinner, the Kaibab Lodge is a favorite place to eat among regular plateau visitors — whether they're staying at the lodge or not. There's a breakfast buffet, traditional western lunches and dinners featuring a variety of entrees in the $10 to $20 range.

Operated by the same folks who run the Kaibab Lodge, the North Rim Country Store is an adjacent gas station and mini market with basic food items, including some fresh fruits.

Jacob Lake Inn
Junction of Alt. U.S. Hwy. 89 and Ariz. Hwy. 67 • (520) 643-7232

Known as the gateway to the North Rim of the Grand Canyon, Jacob Lake Inn sits at the junction in the pines where Ariz. 67 breaks off from Alt. U.S. 89, 45 miles north of the Grand Canyon Lodge. Alt. U.S. 89 is kept open through the winter even though Ariz. 67 closes once it's snowpacked. Jacob Lake Inn and restaurant remain open year round.

INSIDERS' TIP

When traveling the backroads of the Arizona Strip and North Rim country, top off your gas tank at every opportunity. It's not a bad idea to carry an extra spare tire as well — that means two.

The inn has a long tradition dating back to the early part of the century. It's a rustic mountain lodging and dining place whose owners and staff are very knowledgeable about the history of the Kaibab Plateau and its lore of cowboys, hunters, prospectors and trappers. Historic pictures on the wall of the lobby attest to the heritage of the place, and the friendly waitresses will be happy to tell you the story of how Jacob Lake got its name. The gift shop in the lodge is full of authentic arts and crafts as well as all kinds of souvenirs.

The inn has about 50 units, including basic motel rooms and cabins. Each room has a private bath, and there are different combinations of queen beds. Rates range from $71 to $97 per night.

Inside Jacob Lake Inn, you'll find a western-style restaurant with a counter where you can sit and sip coffee. And right through the door is a beautiful dining room decorated with Native American arts and crafts. They serve breakfast, lunch and dinner. Sandwiches and burgers are in the $5 to $7 range. The dinner menu features New York steak, mountain trout, grilled Salisbury steak and fried chicken, ranging from $9.50 to $15. There's also a children's menu with several choices under $4.

Fuel Stops

There are three places to fill your gas tank on the Kaibab Plateau. The first is **Jacob Lake Inn** at the junction of Alt. U.S. 89 and Ariz. 67.

The next is the **North Rim Country Store**, 26 miles south on Ariz. 67. And the closest to the rim is at **North Rim Campground**, 45 miles south of the junction on Ariz. 67. See the listings for more on each of these stops.

The next fuel stops are at Fredonia, Arizona, 30 miles northwest of Jacob Lake, and Marble Canyon, Arizona, about 40 miles east of Jacob Lake. Both are on Alt. U.S. 89.

More North Rim Information

Following are addresses for some clearinghouses for information on the North Rim and Arizona Strip region.

Arizona Strip Interpretive Association Visitor Center and Bookstore, 345 East Riverside Drive, St. George, Utah 84790. Call 673-3545. Off the south St. George interchange of I-15 at exit 6, this is an excellent place to stop for maps, books and first-hand information from the staff of the Interpretive Association. There are a number of terrific interpretive exhibits of the region.

North Kaibab Ranger District, U.S. Forest Service Office, P.O. Box 248, Fredonia, Arizona 86022. Call (520) 643-7395

Southwest Natural and Cultural Heritage Association, Drawer E, Albuquerque, New Mexico 87103.

Grand Canyon Field Institute, P.O. Box 399, Grand Canyon, Arizona 86023. Call 638-2485.

Even though there aren't billboards and marquees shouting out for the world's attention, there's an abundance of exciting attractions in Southwestern Utah.

Attractions

Most of the attractions in this part of the world are either natural or historical, and many are touched on in our chapters on The Environment and Parks and Other Natural Wonders. In this chapter, we share some of the dazzling manmade attractions available in Southwestern Utah — among them an amusement park, a giant-screen motion picture theater and several museums filled with fascinating exhibits. Still, you will find these sights are usually tied to the landscape — its history, its uniqueness and the people who have learned to love it and live with it.

In each of our four geographic areas, we've shared attractions we feel most visitors should experience. They include walking and driving tours, historic buildings, movie sets, monuments, caves, museums and ghost towns.

As you visit these attractions you'll learn of others that link to them in different ways. Follow the leads as they reveal themselves, and you'll discover that even though there aren't billboards and marquees shouting out for the world's attention, there's an abundance of exciting attractions in Southwestern Utah.

St. George/Zion

Zion Canyon Cinemax
145 Zion Park Blvd. (Utah Hwy. 9), Springdale • 772-2400

Since April 1994, the Zion Canyon Cinemax, at the south entrance to Zion National Park, has featured the giant-screen feature film, *Treasure of the Gods*. The film lasts slightly less than an hour and includes heart-stopping footage of the canyons of Southwestern Utah, much of it shot from the air. Warning: You'll come out of this movie feeling like you've been on a great roller coaster, but it's worth it. The music is marvelous, and the photography is stunning.

The theater has added a second film, *The Great American West*, that will be shown through most of 1997. Call to find out if it is showing during your visit. The new film chronicles the major events of the settling of the frontier from the early to late 1800s. It runs alternately with *Treasure of the Gods* on one of the largest screens in the world (60 feet high and 82 feet wide). The perf/70mm projection system includes a CD-ROM digital audio system employing 20 amplifiers pushing in excess of 25,000 watts.

The Great American West relates the story of settlement of the West in human terms. Using stories and words from diaries and letters of actual historic figures, the film evokes not only the astonishingly beautiful landscape, but also the true, often heart-wrenching stories of those who risked everything to explore and settle it. Narrated by Academy Award-winning actor Jason Robards, the film is much more than just another shoot-'em-up western.

The Great American West runs four times daily (noon, 2, 4 and 6 PM), while *Treasure of the Gods* shows at 11 AM and 1, 3, 5 and 7 PM. November through the end of February, Cinemax hours are 11 AM to 7 PM, seven days a week. From March to the end of October, hours are 9 AM to 9 PM. Cost for each show is $7 for adults and $4.50 for children 3 to 11. A special double-feature allows you to see both films at a discount rate of $12 for adults and $7 for children. Group rates are available.

O.C. Tanner Amphitheater
West off Zion Park Blvd. (Utah Hwy. 9), near entrance to Zion National Park, Springdale • 652-7994

Set at the foot of the 2,000-foot towers of Zion Canyon's West Rim, this is one of the most spectacular outdoor theaters in the world. Summer concerts under the stars are staged every Saturday from Memorial Day to Labor Day at the amphitheater, which is owned and operated by Dixie College. And every night, either at dusk or after the concert, the multimedia production called *The Grand Circle — A National Park Odyssey* is shown. The show includes multiple slide projectors, video and five-channel sound. The film is projected onto a 24-by-40-foot screen and offers a matchless look into Zion National Park and many of the other fabulous wonders within the area known as the Grand Circle (including Arches, Canyonlands and Mesa Verde parks to the east; the Grand Canyon to the south; Bryce Canyon, Cedar Breaks and Capitol Reef to the north; and Zion on the west). Tickets, available at the gate, are $4 for adults and $3 for anyone 18 or younger. A family ticket is $10.

Fiesta Family Fun Center
171 E. 1160 South, St. George • 628-1818

This is Southwestern Utah's only amusement park. Just off I-15, the park is open seven days a week all year from 10 AM to 10 PM. It is a clean and attractive park with a pizza stand and seven attractions that you pay to play individually. There is no admission to get into the center.

For $4 per round or ride, the kids can play on a wonderfully designed, well-maintained miniature golf course or splash about in bumper boats that can carry one or two passengers. The youngsters can crash their boats into each other and pilot them under a refreshing waterfall.

There are two go-cart tracks, also $4 a ride, with over- and underpasses and carts that really can get out and move. A soft play area for children 10 and younger allows the kids to crawl, climb, run and slide through a jungle of soft obstacles, and it includes a special area reserved just for toddlers. It's $2 for unlimited use of this area.

A series of batting cages with five different pitching speeds for baseball and softball offers adults or kids a chance to learn to bat or work on their swing. A $1 token gets you 15 pitches. The video arcade is chock full of the latest video games. It takes 25¢ tokens, and you can play for fun or collect winning tickets and redeem them for goodies at the prize center.

Upstairs at Perky's Pizza, you can buy a slice of delicious pizza and a cool, tasty Fiesta Freeze milk shake. The park offers $8, $10.40 and $32 value packs that give you a reduced rate to enjoy multiple attractions. (See our Kidstuff chapter for more on Fiesta Family Fun Center.)

FYI
Unless otherwise noted, the area code for all phone numbers listed in this chapter is 801 but will change to 435 in September 1997. Either area code may be used until March 22, 1998.

Historic St. George Downtown Walking Tour
97 E. St. George Blvd., St. George • 628-1658

Allow yourself about two hours to make this delightful stroll through the mulberry trees and historic pioneer buildings of downtown St. George. It begins at the St. George Chamber of Commerce offices, housed in the handsome red-brick restored pioneer courthouse at St. George Boulevard and 100 East. There you can pick up a free brochure that will guide you along an 11-block walk that includes the Daughters of the Utah Pioneers Museum, the restored St. George Opera House (see our Arts and Culture chapter), several beautifully restored pioneer homes, the old Woodward School, Greene Gate Village and Judd's Store (see our Accommodations chapter), the Mormon Tabernacle, the original Dixie Academy that became Dixie College and the old *County News* building, which was originally a saloon in the mining town of Silver Reef in the 1880s. Most of the buildings pointed out in the brochure have plaques at the gate with a short interpretive message about the place.

INSIDERS' TIP

While visiting the historical attractions of Southwestern Utah, seek out local residents who might be passing by. Generally they're very willing to share a story or point out another related attraction.

Daughters of the Utah Pioneers Museum
145 N. 100 East, St. George • 628-7274

Allow yourself at least an hour to browse through this museum, where you'll see original pioneer furniture, kitchen implements, musical instruments, clothing, photos and a variety of other articles from the early pioneer period in St. George. Time spent here will help you gain a deeper understanding of the pioneer culture of Southwestern Utah. Admission is free.

Brigham Young's Winter Home
50 W. 200 North, St. George • 673-2517

A free tour of Brigham Young's Winter Home is offered by missionaries of the LDS Church. They're on hand daily from 9 AM to dusk. It takes about 45 minutes and is an excellent introduction to the pioneer history of the area. Inside the home you'll see the actual furniture, dishes, trunks, clothing and other items which Brigham Young and his wives (he is said to have had more than 20) used. Interestingly, it was Young who started the "snowbird" tradition in St. George. During the last several winters of his life, he came to the city to escape the winter snows of Salt Lake City.

St. George Tabernacle
Main and Tabernacle Sts., St. George • 628-4072

Step inside the magnificent St. George Tabernacle at Main and Tabernacle Street. Here as well, LDS missionaries are on hand from 9 AM to dusk to tell you the story of how this stunning building (considered one of the most architecturally beautiful buildings in the state) was constructed of red sandstone quarried from the red bluffs north of town. The building is designed like an old New England church, reflecting the northeastern roots of many of the original Mormon pioneers.

Historic St. George Live Tour
Southwest corner, Main St. and St. George Blvd., St. George • 628-1658

If you're fortunate enough to be in St. George between Memorial Day and Labor Day don't miss this delightful opportunity to acquaint yourself with the history and culture of the area. It's a two-hour tour beginning in the historic plaza adjacent to Zions Bank on the southwest corner of Main and St. George Boulevard. Call the St. George Chamber of Commerce at the number above to make sure tours are running the day you are here. If they are, you'll be greeted by a reasonable facsimile of Erastus Snow, leader of the Dixie Cotton Mission in the 1860s when the Mormons first came to St. George. He'll tell you about his home which was once on the corner where you are standing. Then you'll get on a mini-bus and travel to six other historic sites where volunteer actors in authentic costumes relate the history of the buildings you are looking at. Among the historic figures you'll meet and visit with are Orson Pratt, Jacob Hamblin, and Judge John Menzies Macfarlane. Part of the tour is a stop at the restored St. George Opera House, 210 N. Main Street, 634-5800 (see "Pioneer Center for the

The Weeping Fireplace

There are several versions relaying the story of silver's discovery in the sandstone of Silver Reef 17 miles northwest of St. George. One is the story of the weeping fireplace. In this tale, a traveler supposedly took winter refuge with a pioneer family in the town of Leeds, just a couple of miles from where Silver Reef would later be established. As the stranger warmed himself beside a roaring fire, he noticed large droplets of pure silver "weeping" from the sandstone making up the fireplace. Legend says the traveler located the quarry where the rock came from, staked a mining claim to it and made a fortune.

Arts" in our Arts and Culture chapter for more on the St. George Opera House).

There is a $1 tour charge for persons 12 and older. Children are welcome. Because the tour is organized and run strictly by volunteers, there are occasional changes in the format and schedule. The plan for 1997 is to start tours at 9, 10 and 11 AM Tuesday through Saturday. Tours begin and end at the plaza, and require two or three blocks of walking.

St. George Temple Visitor Center
300 E. 500 South, St. George • 673-5181

There is no manmade landmark in all of Southwestern Utah more imposing than the giant white building standing like an iceberg in the desert in the center of St. George. The St. George LDS Temple was built in the 1870s by the newly arrived Mormon pioneers. The Mormons had built a temple in Kirtland, Ohio, and one in Nauvoo, Illinois, before being forced out of both places. Once they arrived in Utah, one of their first priorities was to build a temple where sacred ordinances reserved for a place more holy than the chapels where they met weekly could be performed. Work began on the temple in Salt Lake City, but aging church president Brigham Young could see that if a temple was going to be completed in his lifetime, it would need to be built in the southern part of the territory, where the threat of intervention by the federal government due to the church's teachings was less likely and where weather allowed work to continue year round.

Young chose St. George and selected a plot of ground well south of the emerging little town. When people questioned his location so far out in the brush from the existing town, and in a marshy spot as well, Young told them the temple would one day stand in the center of the city. The temple was completed in 1877, just months before Brigham Young's death, and today it stands on a solid foundation almost exactly in the center of St. George.

Only those members of the LDS Church who have been recommended by their bishop may enter the temple building itself, but visitors are welcome on the temple grounds. We suggest you stop by the visitor center on the southeast corner of the temple block. There you'll see a number of displays interpreting the building. Guides will tell you about the history of the church, Mormon beliefs, and answer any questions.

Jacob Hamblin Home
Santa Clara Dr. and Hamblin Dr., Santa Clara • 673-2167

Jacob Hamblin was the Leatherstocking of Southwestern Utah. (For the uninitiated,

Gold in Them There Hills

There was a short gold rush in the Kanab area in the 1890s. In 1896, a fellow named Dake Train is said to have found a rich gold placer in a hidden box canyon just off Paria Creek, several miles east of Kanab. Some of the folks in Kanab witnessed a copper kettle full of coarse gold nuggets that Train carried in his pack saddle on a donkey. For a month, Train camped in his secret gold gulch and mined gold until his supplies ran out. It's said he then made his way to California, cashed in his gold for more than

$100,000 and bought a small farm near San Bernardino. He married a widow with several children and settled down for many years, until the itch to go back to the mine overtook him. In 1911 he came back to the Kanab area and for a month searched for the hidden canyon where he'd found his fortune, but he never found it. He returned again in 1916. By then, no one in Kanab remembered him, and everyone took pity on this now-poor man who appeared to them as just another crazy prospector looking for gold that did not exist.

Photo: Lyman Hafen

Get on your high horse for *Utah!* at the Tuacahn Amphitheater.

that's a reference to a trailblazing James Fenimore Cooper character.) He was the Mormon missionary who opened the way for settlement of the region by establishing a fort at Santa Clara and developing a friendly and productive relationship with the Southern Paiute Indians living in the area.

His home, now restored and open to visitors on the west edge of the town of Santa Clara (about 6 miles from downtown St. George) was built in 1862. It is a roughly constructed rock home standing behind a grape orchard and green lawns. Its simple beauty is a reminder of the importance of aesthetics in the lives of the pioneers, in spite of the crude tools and sparse resources they had to work with. A variety of pioneer artifacts are on display. LDS missionary guides will show you through the house and answer all your questions. There's no charge for the tour.

Tuacahn Amphitheater
1100 Tuacahn Dr., Ivins • 674-4949

June through September, one of America's greatest pioneering stories comes to life in the spectacular outdoor setting of the Tuacahn Amphitheater near the mouth of Snow Canyon in Ivins. *UTAH! America's Most Spectacular Outdoor Musical*, runs nightly, except Sundays, in the amphitheater that seats nearly 2,000 people. The two-hour production features live galloping horses, covered wagons, lightning bolts, fireworks and even a real flash flood that gushes across the stage. A cast of 80 singers, dancers and actors recreate the drama of the settling of Southwestern Utah. There's also pre-show entertainment, Western-style Dutch Oven dinners, backstage tours, a gift shop — enough to see and do to fill an afternoon before the show.

Set beneath majestic red sandstone cliffs,

deep in a canyon near Snow Canyon State Park, the view from the open air stage is, in itself, an incredible experience. The special effects here are first rate, the music stunning and the choreography puts one in mind of a Broadway musical. This is a must-see for anyone visiting the St. George area. Tickets range in price from $9 to $16 for children younger than 12; $14.50 to $24.50 for adults. The amphitheater is 12 miles from downtown St. George. Take U.S. Highway 91 west through Santa Clara to Ivins, then follow the Tuacahn signs. (For more on Tuacahn Center for the Arts, site of the Tuacahn Amphitheater, see our Arts and Culture chapter.)

Historic Cotton Mill
375 W. Telegraph Rd., Washington
• 634-1880

The city of Washington was established in 1857, four years before St. George, and Mormon pioneers with expertise in growing and manufacturing cotton were sent there by Brigham Young. Many were LDS converts from the Southern U.S. who had descended from generations of cotton growers. As tensions between North and South increased in the eastern United States in the late 1850s, Brigham Young, in his quest for Mormon self-sufficiency, encouraged the production of cotton in Southwestern Utah. Washington became the center for that industry, and in 1866, construction of the cotton mill began.

The one-of-a-kind building has been beautifully restored, but is privately owned and can be viewed only from the exterior. That is, unless you arrange with the owners (use the above number) to visit or hold a party, meeting, family reunion or other activity there. The mill is a three-story structure set near a grove of cottonwood trees along Washington's Mill Creek. As is, you can park nearby, walk around the grounds and marvel at the ingenuity of the indomitable pioneers who settled this desert country.

Pine Valley/Pine Valley LDS Chapel
32 miles north of St. George, off
Utah Hwy. 18

Take Utah 18 north out of St. George, proceed 25 miles, turn right at the town of Central (clear signs will guide you) and drive another 7 or so miles to the beautiful mountain town of Pine Valley.

The drive itself is spectacular. As you head north out of St. George, you will begin to gain altitude. You'll pass through sedimentary layers of red and white sandstone, then skirt the edge of Snow Canyon before you come to a volcano field about 10 miles north of St. George. On your right, you'll see two black cinder cones, now extinct, that are responsible for much of the black lava rock you see strewn throughout the St. George area. North of the volcanoes you'll pass through Diamond Valley, Dammeron Valley and the town of Veyo, then you'll arrive at the turnoff at Central.

By the time you get to Pine Valley you will have left the Mojave Desert behind and will have climbed about 4,000 feet into the Great Basin. In St. George, you are at an elevation of about 2,500 feet. In Pine Valley, you've climbed to about 7,000 feet. And the peaks above you at the top of Pine Valley Mountain reach 10,500 feet.

As you drive into Pine Valley, your eyes will be drawn to what is possibly the most photogenic chapel in all of Utah. The Mormon chapel in Pine Valley is a two-story, white-frame building constructed in 1868. It is the oldest Mormon chapel still in continuous use. It was designed and built by Ebenezer Bryce, the same man Bryce Canyon National Park was named for, using the techniques he had learned as a shipbuilder in Australia. The wood frame walls were assembled on the ground, then raised into position and joined with wooden pegs and rawhide. A red-brick tithing office sits just east of the chapel. Free tours are given at the chapel during summer from 9 AM to dusk.

Mountain Meadows Massacre Site
28 miles north of St. George, off
Utah Hwy. 18

A monument recalling the darkest tragedy in Southwestern Utah history sits on a knoll covered with scrub oak overlooking the site of the Mountain Meadows Massacre. Drive north out of St. George on Utah 18 until you see the sign for the site. Turn left (west) into a parking lot just off the highway and make the five-minute walk up a wheelchair-accessible asphalt trail to the monument.

Juanita Brooks: Shining Light on a Dark Time

Juanita Leavitt Brooks was born in 1898 in the Mormon village of Bunkerville, Nevada, which was linked culturally, commercially and spiritually to Utah's Dixie. As a girl she found herself growing up in a society in transition from the former isolated, anti-federal, polygamous society.

An early marriage suggested her future would follow a predictable course, but the death of her husband, the need to raise a young son and a passion for knowledge led to many turns in her life. Juanita worked her way through St. George's Dixie College, where she would later join the faculty, went on to Brigham Young University and ultimately left her sheltered world in Utah to earn a master's degree at Columbia University.

Returning to St. George in the early 1930s, she married the widowed county sheriff, Will Brooks, and inherited four more sons. Along with her teaching at Dixie College, she embarked on a career of research and writing under the Works Progress Administration of the Depression era. As more children came along (eight in all) she continued to write. In 1934 her "Close-Up of Polygamy" appeared in *Harper's Monthly* magazine, the first of more than 40 articles and 16 books published during her career.

Photo: Juanita Brooks Collection

Juanita Brooks and her son, Ernie, in about 1928, before Juanita earned her reputation as one of the west's most-respected historians.

At mid-life, Brooks gained national notoriety and respect with the 1950 publication of *The Mountain Meadows Massacre*. This study exposed the fact that the 1857 killing of more than 100 California-bound emigrants in Southwestern Utah had not been carried out solely by Native Americans, but in concert with a Mormon militia activated under the threat of war as Johnston's federal army approached Utah. The book put the entire affair into the context of the times, helping modern-day readers understand how such a lamentable thing could happen. It also exposed the fact that John D. Lee, the only person tried and convicted in connection with the incident, did not bear full responsibility and was probably acting under orders of superiors.

Brooks was a faithful and active member of the Church of Jesus Christ of Latter-day Saints, but her courageous stand in telling the truth about this dark moment in Mormon history established her as an outstanding historian. Her dogged insistence that church authorities change their stand on the incidents at Mountain Meadows was motivated by the same determination she used to see that all her children received a good education and that the diaries of Southwestern Utah pioneers were carefully collected and preserved.

The desire to tell the truth as she saw it became her hallmark. Faithful to her church to the end, Juanita Brooks died in St. George in 1989 at the age of 91.

The Mountain Meadows Massacre was a complex tragedy that occurred in September 1857, when 120 California-bound immigrants were killed by southern Utah Mormon militiamen and their Native American allies. The 18 small children whose lives were spared lived with local Mormon families until federal officials returned them to their relatives in Arkansas and Missouri.

It is believed the incident grew out of the legacy of persecution the Mormons experienced in Missouri and Illinois before their exodus to Utah, and hysteria regarding a potential war between Mormons and federal troops at the time. In the summer of 1857, a large force of federal troops was marching to Utah to put down an alleged Mormon rebellion. The ill-fated party of immigrants from Arkansas and Missouri happened to pass through Utah late that summer during the height of the hysteria.

Local Southern Paiutes believed the immigrants poisoned a water hole after they left it. Hence, these Native Americans sided with the Mormons against the threats of the "Mericats," as they called non-Mormon Americans.

When the immigrants stopped at Mountain Meadows for a few days of restoration for themselves and their livestock before dropping into the Mojave Desert, a complex chain of events occurred. After an initial encounter, the conflict escalated and several men acting under military orders killed 120 Americans.

John D. Lee, a respected Mormon pioneer in Southwestern Utah, was the only man convicted for participating in the massacre. He was executed at Mountain Meadows in 1877 by federal authorities. In 1950, a St. George teacher and housewife, Juanita Brooks, published *The Mountain Meadows Massacre*, which is still in print and regarded as the definitive study of the tragedy. Written by a devout Mormon, the book is nonetheless an objective linking of the chain of events leading to this lamentable incident. The monument is of white marble, set into a hillside above the valley. Many of the names of the victims are inscribed in the stone. It was erected jointly by representatives of the LDS Church and descendants of the victims.

Hurricane Valley Pioneer Heritage Park
35 W. State St., Hurricane • 635-3245

On the southwest corner of the intersection of State Street and Main Street in Hurricane (18 miles from St. George) is the Hurricane Valley Pioneer Heritage Park. Also on the grounds is the Hurricane Valley Pioneer and Indian Museum, and just across Main Street is the restored Bradshaw House, which is now the Hurricane Valley Chamber of Commerce. On this historic square you'll see statues, implements and artifacts of pioneer life, and you'll sense the struggle and the sacrifice that settlers of this valley went through to bring water to the land and create a sustainable community.

Around the park's central statue of a pioneer man, woman and children, are interpretive plaques telling the story of how the town of Hurricane was founded after the 13-year ordeal of building the Hurricane Canal. Spreading out from the statue like spokes in a wagon wheel, several walkways take you to large artifacts from the early days of Hurricane — buggies, plows and threshers. The Pioneer and Indian Museum, housed in the restored library on the square, displays several collections of pioneer antiques as well as Paiute and Anasazi artifacts. Across the street at the Bradshaw house you'll find more information on Hurricane at the chamber of commerce as well as a display of an intriguing collection of early medical equipment. There is no charge to visit any of these sites.

Silver Reef Museum
Exit 22 off I-15, 17 miles north of St. George • 879-2254

What was a ghost town at Silver Reef has in recent years become a neighborhood of beautiful modern homes, yet much of the old townsite remains, including the restored Wells Fargo Building (see "Leeds, Silver Reef" in

---

INSIDERS' TIP

Utah's only commercial winery is Arches Vineyard, which includes a tasting room, just 3 miles south of Moab.

our Neighborhoods and Real Estate chapter). The square, rock building with tall, iron doors has been converted into a museum and art gallery that are certainly worth the effort to stop and see.

Take the Leeds exit as you drive north on I-15, 17 miles from St. George. Drive through the quiet little town of Leeds on the remnant of old U.S. Highway 91. As you exit the north end of town, rather than taking the ramp back onto I-15, proceed north toward Pine Valley Mountain on the horizon. Two miles from I-15 you will arrive at the old town site of Silver Reef, and signs will guide you to the museum. On display are authentic mining tools and other pioneer artifacts as well as old newspapers reporting on shootings, lootings and the rise and fall of this once rip-roaring mining town. The adjacent Jerry Anderson Studio and Art Gallery is filled with bronze sculptures by Anderson and paintings by some of the West's finest artists (see our Arts and Culture chapter).

There's no admission charge, but you're likely to spend some money while you're there. Just north of the museum is the Cosmopolitan Steak House, a restaurant built on the original site of Silver Reef's Cosmopolitan Saloon (see our Restaurants chapter).

Grafton Ghost Town
3.5 miles west of Rockville

While visitors are not prohibited from this picturesque ghost town along the Virgin River, it is on private property and is not an official visitor's site. You can drive to the town by crossing the old truss bridge across the Virgin River in Rockville (which is 3 miles west of Springdale on Utah 9), making an immediate turn west and following the dirt road 3.5 miles. Make sure there's film in your camera, because the old adobe church and few remaining homes in this long-deserted town are beautifully situated beneath the red ridges leading into Zion Canyon.

If some of these buildings look familiar, it's probably because you saw them in *Butch Cassidy and the Sundance Kid*. Remember the scene where Paul Newman takes Katherine Ross on a bike ride? With the song, "Raindrops Keep Falling On My Head"? This is where it was filmed.

Cedar City/Brian Head

Iron Mission State Park
585 N. Main, Cedar City • 586-9290

You'll find this park and museum, established to preserve the history of the Mormon Iron Mission, in the heart of today's Cedar City. Displays include horse-drawn wagons, surreys, sleighs, buggies and coaches used from 1870 to 1930. There's a milk wagon, a white hearse that was used for children, a replica of a Wells Fargo stagecoach and the actual stagecoach used between the city of Price and San Juan County around the turn of the century — complete with an authentic bullet hole. You'll see hundreds of pieces of horse-drawn farm machinery and wagons used in the early development of Southwestern Utah agriculture. There are items on display manufactured during the days of the pioneer iron industry in Cedar City, including a bell cast in 1854. The oldest remaining residence in Southwestern Utah is on display. It is the log cabin built by George Wood in 1851. Originally built in Parowan, it was later moved to Cedar City. A fascinating collection of more than 200 Native American artifacts including tools, clothing and hunting weapons is also on display.

Admission to the indoor and outdoor museum at the state park is $1 per person if you walk in or $3 per car. The park is open year round — daily from 9 AM to 5 PM September through May; 9 AM to 7 PM June through August. There's a picnic area but no camping.

Rock Church
Center and 100 East, Cedar City
• 586-4484

This is one of Cedar City's most fascinating buildings. Still in use as a Mormon chapel, it was built in the 1930s during the Great Depression. Because the Mormon First Ward in Cedar City had no permanent place of worship at the time and the cost of a new building was prohibitive, church members decided to use local materials to construct a meeting place they could all be proud of. The result was a church built of multicolored rock gathered from nearby creek beds, with interior walls and pews made of native red cedar and carpets woven from the wool of local sheep. There is a rock baptismal font in the basement. The building was crowned with a steeple containing the old town clock that had been saved from the tabernacle that had been torn down. Tours are conducted every day except Sunday from mid-June through Labor Day from 11 AM to 5 PM. There's no admission charge.

Iron County Centennial Circle Driving Tour
286 N. Main, Cedar City • 586-5124

Stop by the Iron County Travel and Convention Bureau Office at the 286 N. Main and pick up a free brochure outlining this one-day or multi-day excursion that will give you the full picture of Iron County's history. There's a map that pinpoints the location of 16 sites and gives a historical snippet on each one. Among the sites you'll visit is a marker 39 miles from Cedar City on the route of the historic Old Spanish Trail. You'll see Paragonah's town square, Parowan's Heritage Park, Vermillion Castle (a geological feature, not a building with turrets) and Yankee Meadow up Parowan Canyon, the Brian Head Ski Resort (see our Outdoor Recreation chapter), Cedar Breaks National Monument (see our Parks and Other Natural Wonders chapter), the old rock church in Cedar City, Iron Mission State Park, Cedar City's old Union Pacific Depot, a monument marking the south rim of the Great Basin and the old Cobble Crest Dance Pavilion in Kanarraville (see "Dancing by the Light of the Moon" in our Nightlife chapter). Also along this driving tour are a portion of the Dominguez-Escalante Trail, Page's Ranch, Old Iron Town, a monument to Jefferson Hunt at the crucial turning point in the trail taken by members of the Death Valley 49ers, the historic railroad towns of Lund and Modena, Parowan Gap and the site of Johnson's Fort along the Old Spanish Trail, where all that remains is a grove of cottonwood trees.

It's possible to make the entire circle in one day, but to truly take in each of the sites and enjoy the scenery and history that go with them, we suggest you divide the tour into a minimum of two days. Plan to spend the night in either Cedar City, Parowan or Brian Head (see our Accommodations chapter).

Adams Memorial Theater
Center St. 300 West, Southern Utah University, Cedar City • 586-7878

Situated among the greenery of Southern Utah University's campus, you'll find the outdoor Adams Memorial Theater — a faithful replica of the Tiring House Theater of William Shakespeare's era. The nationally acclaimed Utah Shakespearean Festival (see our Annual Events and Arts and Culture chapters) has been staged here for more than three decades. The theater is patterned after drawings and extensive research of 16th-century Tudor stages. Experts say it is one of a few theaters in the world that comes close the design of the Globe Theatre, where Shakespeare's plays were originally performed. Free tours of the theater are given during the festival season, which begins in late June and runs through the end of August.

Parowan Gap
10½ miles west of Parowan • 477-8340

Turn west on 400 North in Parowan, drive 10½ miles to Parowan Gap Canyon and you'll find two distinct features — one natural and one manmade. The pass is a classic example of a wind gap, an unusual geological landform where, in this instance, an ancient river has cut a 600-foot deep notch through the red hills. The gap also includes an incredible gallery of Native American rock art that was etched into the stones here over a period of 1,000 years. Geometric designs, images of lizards, snakes, mountain sheep, bear claws and human figures cover the canyon walls. It's one of those rare, out-of-the-way places we highly recommend. There's no admission charge.

Bryce Canyon Area

Panguitch's Historic Buildings
55 E. Center St., Panguitch • 676-8421

Within a couple of blocks of the historic Garfield County Courthouse, which is at the listed address and home to the offices of the Garfield County Travel Council, are several buildings of historic interest. The courthouse is one of Panguitch's most storied buildings. It was built of native brick in 1907. The weather vane at the top was carved by pioneer John F. Sevy. The Panguitch Social Hall, just across Center Street, was built in 1908, but a fire soon after completion required the building to be reconstructed. This was the social center of the community, mostly used for public dances. Today the building is still used for musical programs, basketball, dancing and gymnastics.

Just down Center Street at the northeast corner of Center and 100 East, is the Daughters of Utah Pioneers Museum. The museum is housed in what was originally the Panguitch Tithing Office or Bishop's Storehouse. Built in 1907 of the same attractive red brick so prevalent in Panguitch, this was the place where the tithes of the people were stored and distributed to the needy. In the early days the Mormons often paid their tithing "in kind" with produce, livestock or other commodities. The bishop stored items in the tithing office, and livestock was kept on the surrounding lot.

Those pioneers' descendents pay their tithes in cash, so the old tithing office has become a museum full of pioneer artifacts such as tools, clothing, housewares and other antiques. The museum is open Monday through Saturday, Memorial Day through Labor Day,

from 1 to 5 PM. If you visit at a time when the museum is not open, there may be a note on the door with a phone number. Make the call, and someone will probably come and let you in. There is no admission charge.

Paunsagaunt Wildlife Museum
250 E. Center St., Panguitch • 676-2500

The newest attraction in Panguitch is in the middle of the small, mountain town's downtown business district. Named for the Paunsagaunt Mountains in the Panguitch area, this museum exhibits more than 200 well-preserved animals native to North America. Through the art of taxidermy, the museum gives you a close-up view of animals that live in the nearby wilderness. Cougars, black bears, beavers, coyotes, elk, mule deer and foxes are all displayed as well as 50 exotic game animals from Africa, India and Europe. There is also an excellent fossil collection, a gallery of rare birds of prey and exhibits of Native American artifacts including pottery, tools and weapons.

The museum is 24 miles from Bryce Canyon National Park, on Utah Highway 89 in Panguitch. It is open from 9 AM to 10 PM daily

Photo: Nick Adams

The Old Rock Church was built in Cedar City during the Great Depression.

from May 1 to November 1. Admission is $4 for adults and $2.50 for children ages 6 to 12. Kids younger than 6 are free.

Kanab Area

Moqui Cave
5½ miles north of Kanab on U.S. Hwy. 89 • 644-2987

Kids and adults alike love this literal hole in the wall, where Lex Chamberlain carries on the legacy his father began 45 years ago. In 1951, Garth Chamberlain, who had played football in the NFL during the '40s, bought a cave right alongside the highway, 5.5 miles north of Kanab. The huge opening in the sandstone, which extended naturally 80 feet back into the bluff, had been expanded to 200 feet deep by a silica sand mining operation, so there was plenty of room to build a tavern and set up a dance hall.

Today, Garth's son, Lex, and Lex's wife, Lee Anne, have taken over the business and turned it into a museum with displays of artifacts, fossils and minerals. They've redone the exterior of the cave to give it an Anasazi cliff-dwelling look and reflect the prehistory of the area. Inside you'll find what the Chamberlains call the largest display of fluorescent minerals in the country as well as an extensive exhibit of Native American artifacts, fossilized dinosaur tracks and a gift shop with Native American turquoise jewelry, rugs, arts and crafts.

The cave is open mid-February through mid-November, Monday through Saturday, from 8:30 AM to 7:30 PM. The cave remains cool during summer, but it's not so cold that you would need a jacket. Admission is $3.50 for adults, $3 for seniors, $2.50 for youngsters 13 through 17 and $1.50 for kids between 6 and 12. Kids younger than 6 get in free.

Frontier Movie Town
297 West Center St., Kanab • 644-5337, (800) 551-1714

In the heart of Kanab, this attraction captures and shares the essence of the town's filmmaking legacy. Movie sets from many of the filming locations around Kanab have been brought to Lopeman's Frontier Movie Town for public viewing. During the summer sea-

son, mock gunfights involving character actor-movie wrangler Ray Lopeman are performed nightly. Movie Town offers a Dutch-oven dinner show, costume rental for pictures snapped on a movie set, a museum with movie memorabilia, and a trading post and gift shop. You can refresh yourself at the Robber's Roost Saloon or have a sandwich at the Hole-in-the-Wall Snack Bar. They're both open from 7:30 AM to 11 PM daily. Call for dinner and show reservations.

Beginning with the filming of *Deadwood Coach* in 1924, Kanab began to build a reputation as "Little Hollywood." That reputation grew as the town became a key location in films such as *The Lone Ranger*, 1938; *My Friend Flicka*, 1943; *Buffalo Bill*, 1944; *The Rainmaker*, 1956; *Sergeants Three*, 1962; *The Greatest Story Ever Told*, 1965; *Brighty of the Grand Canyon*, 1967; *Planet of the Apes*, 1968; *The Man Who Loved Cat Dancing*, 1973; *The Outlaw Josey Wales*, 1976; *How the West Was Won*, 1976; *Maverick*, 1995; and a host of TV series such as *F Troop*, *Lassie*, *Have Gun Will Travel*, *Gunsmoke*, *Grizzly Adams* and *Six Million Dollar Man*. And this is just a sampling. (See more on Frontier Movie Town in our Kidstuff chapter.)

Johnson Canyon
9 miles east of Kanab off U.S. Hwy. 89

A drive through Johnson Canyon is a scenic joy in and of itself. But this is one of those drives that can take on many dimensions. Drive east out of Kanab 9 miles on U.S. 89, where you'll see a sign indicating the turnoff to Johnson Canyon to the left (north). Proceed on the road, which is paved for about 15 miles before it turns to dirt. Enjoy the scenic cliffs and bluffs that have been the backdrops for many of the movies and TV shows you've seen.

About 5 miles up the road you'll come upon what looks like an old ghost town on the right (east). Depending on how old you are, you may very well recognize it as Dodge City, for this is the place where many of the episodes of the classic TV series *Gunsmoke* were filmed. This is private property belonging to the Bertolla family of northern Utah. Max Bertolla is a history buff and writer who purchased the place a few years ago and is in the process of establishing it as a visitor attraction. Some visitors are even fortunate enough to visit when Max's teenage children are there — they spend much of the summer on the property in a mobile home. Knock on the door, and for $3 you may just get a delightfully narrated tour of the town.

You'll see the saloon doors that Marshall Dillon tossed ne'er-do-wells through into the street — the same street where many a gunfight unfolded. What we recognized most vividly was the stairway up the side of one wood-slatted building to Doc's office on the second floor. We could almost hear the voice of Festus still floating in the air.

Drive on, find a place to park along the road to the canyon and hike a while. You might want to spend some time looking for Montezuma's Treasure. They say it's buried somewhere around here. In the 1920s, Kanab residents searched for the treasure in this very canyon after a man named Freddy Crystal showed up with a map he'd uncovered in Mexico. It's not likely you'll find the treasure, but you'll hoard a trove of precious memories hiking on the slickrock of these vermillion cliffs and stumbling onto Native American petroglyphs and all sorts of geological features.

Here, the idea is to do more than see the country — this is a place where the country beckons to be experienced.

Outdoor Recreation

Nobody comes to Southwestern Utah to sit. And nobody comes here to stay inside. This is a place where you get up and get out. Those red bluffs aren't just to look at, those mountain ridges aren't just to marvel over, and those snow-covered plateaus aren't just to talk about.

Here, the idea is to do more than see the country; this is a place where the country beckons to be experienced. That means hiking it, driving it, camping it, climbing it, biking it, floating it, riding it and photographing it. In this chapter we have compiled an overview of the kinds of outdoor recreation available in Southwestern Utah with suggestions on how to experience it to the fullest.

Since the changing of seasons brings vastly different activities to our four different geographic areas and so many of our outdoor pursuits overlap in their timing, we have arranged the sections in this chapter in what may seem to be an arbitrary way. But there is a method to our modus operandi. Since priority number one will be where you lay your head, we start with camping options. Next are traditionally warmer-weather activities including hiking and backpacking, rock climbing, bicycling and horseback riding. Four-season standards — fishing, hunting and off-road, four-wheelin' fun — come next. And we finish off the chapter with winter sports such as downhill and cross-country skiing and snowmobiling.

Of course, there's almost no end to the options in Southwestern Utah. Your own creativity will ultimately style the adventures best suited to your lifestyle, but here are some great places to start.

Camping

While Southwestern Utah has plenty of comfortable accommodations with king and queen beds, soft sheets and hot tubs, there's just nothing quite like roughing it if you really want to get intimate with the place we call home. Camping is big stuff in Southwestern Utah — camping the old-fashioned way with a tent, a cook stove and a sleeping bag. For those who believe the best way to experience a place is to take it as primitive as possible, we share the following suggestions of campgrounds.

We have limited this section to great places to pitch a tent or pull in with a camp trailer. Some of them also have hookups for RVs, but the listings of full-service RV parks are in our Accommodations chapter. The campgrounds listed here are all on public lands — either in state parks, national parks, national forests or on land administered by the Bureau of Land Management. Camping in these areas is generally on a first-come, first-served basis, although reservations are sometimes required for large group sites in national parks, forests and BLM-monitored locations. For more general information about the parks or recreation areas where these campsites are located, see our Parks and Other Natural Wonders chapter.

For all state parks, you need to make advance reservations by calling the number provided in the listing. If you want to pay by credit card, instant confirmation of the campsite reservation can be given. Overnight and/or day-use fees are charged at most of the public campgrounds based on the facilities provided.

These listings include the address and phone number of the public agency administering the campground, which in some cases may be 50 miles from the campground itself. Within each listing is a description of where the campground is located.

St. George/Zion

In Zion National Park

More information for the following campgrounds in Zion National Park may be obtained by writing P.O. Box 1099, Springdale 84767, or calling the numbers listed.

Zion National Park South Campground

Off Zion Park Blvd., 0.5 mile north of Springdale • 772-3256

Just inside the south entrance to Zion National Park, about a half-mile north of Springdale, this campground is open April 14 through September 15 and has a 14-day limit. It sits at 4,000 feet above sea level amidst the towering ledges of Zion Canyon. There are 140 sites, and there are picnic tables, flush toilets, dump sites and facilities for the handicapped. This campground hugs the Virgin River and is ideally located for hiking and biking excursions into the upper canyon. If you arrive before noon you can generally get a campsite (available only on a first-come, first-served basis). Fee: $10 per night.

Zion National Park Watchman Campground

Off Zion Park Blvd., 1 mile north of Springdale • 772-3256

Just a few hundred yards up the river from the South Campground near the south entrance to the park, the Watchman Campground has 229 tent sites and is open year round. Also sitting at 4,000 feet, this campground gives you handy access to the upper canyon either by car, bike or on foot. Bikers and hikers can step right onto the Pa'Rus Trail and head up canyon. There's a 14-day limit in this campground, which includes picnic tables,

dump sites and facilities for the handicapped. Available on a first-come, first-served basis, arrival before noon usually ensures a campsite. Fee: $10 per night.

Zion National Park Lava Point Campground

Off Utah Hwy. 9, 26 miles north of Virgin • 772-3256

This is a high-altitude campground in the Kolob section of Zion National Park, 26 miles north of the town of Virgin off Utah Highway 9. At 7,900 feet, the Lava Point Campground is open from June 1 through October 15. There are just six tent sites here and there's a 14-day limit. There are picnic tables and primitive toilets. This is an ideal place from which to explore the upper reaches of Zion. From here, you can hike the entire West Rim Trail, an outstanding 14-mile trek (see the Hiking and Backpacking section of this chapter.) There is no fee at this campground.

Other Area Campgrounds

Baker Reservoir Campground

Off Utah Hwy. 18, 25 miles north of St. George • 628-4491

The Bureau of Land Management administers this campground north of St. George off Utah 18. Open year-round, the campground sits at 5,000 feet above sea level and has 10 sites with picnic tables. Camping limit is 14 days, and you need to supply your own drinking water. The main reason for choosing this spot at the northwestern flank of Pine Valley Mountain is to fish in Baker Reservoir just a stone's throw away (see Fishing later in this chapter). For more information, write 345 E. Riverside Drive, St. George 84790. There is no fee to use this campground.

Honeycomb Rocks Campground (Dixie National Forest)

Off Utah Hwy. 120, 11 miles west of Enterprise • 634-4654, (800) 280-2267

This is a Dixie National Forest campground west of Enterprise off Utah 120. Adjacent to

---

FYI

Unless otherwise noted, the area code for all phone numbers listed in this chapter is 801 but will change to 435 in September 1997. Either area code may be used until March 22, 1998.

Photo: Jud Burkett

Rock climbing is popular here in Snow Canyon and at other area red rock cliffs.

---

excellent fishing at Enterprise Reservoir (see Fishing in this chapter), the campground has 20 sites open from May 15 to October 31 with a 14-day camping limit. At an altitude of 5,700 feet, this is pinyon-juniper country, where summer nights are cool and days can get pretty warm. You'll find picnic tables, drinking water and toilets here, and you'll enjoy the fishing, boating, and swimming in this pristine setting. More information on Honeycomb Rocks may be obtained by writing to 345 E. Riverside Drive, St. George 84790. Fee: $7 per day.

Oak Grove Campground
Off I-15 Exit 22, 10 miles north of Leeds
• 634-4654, (800) 280-2267

Take Exit 22 for Leeds off Interstate 15, 12 miles north of St. George, then proceed 10 more miles on the dirt road leading north from Silver Reef. The road is quite well maintained — it does not require a four-wheel drive vehicle but can get rough in places and is treacherous when wet. Though the road is relatively narrow, you can pull a small camp trailer over it. Oak Grove is a beautiful, secluded place at the foot of the south slope of Pine Valley Mountain. Here, among the thick wild oak and towering pine trees you place a large buffer between yourself and civilization. Quiet hiking and wildlife viewing (deer and a variety of bird life) are the key activities here. At 6,800 feet above sea level, this campground has 10 sites with picnic tables, drinking water and toilets. There's not much else, but that's what makes this secluded setting so special. Write to 345 E. Riverside Drive, St. George 84790 for more information. The fee is $5 per day.

Pine Valley Recreation Area (Dixie National Forest)
Off Utah Hwy. 18, 3 miles east of Pine Valley • 634-4654, (800) 280-2267

The Pine Valley Recreation Area of Dixie National Forest is 3 miles east of the town of

Pine Valley, which is 32 miles north of St. George off Utah 18. Within the area are the Blue Springs (19 sites), Ponderosa (nine sites), Pines (13 sites) and Juniper Park (12 sites) campgrounds, and a short way off is an equestrian area where privately owned horses can be corralled and fed for the night. This area sits at 6,800 feet above sea level at the foot of the alpine peaks of Pine Valley Mountain, which reach to over 10,300 feet. The campgrounds are open from May 20 to October 31 and have a 14-day camping limit. You'll find picnic tables, drinking water and toilets here. There's fishing just a short walk away at the Pine Valley Reservoir (see Fishing in this chapter). For more information, write to 345 E. Riverside Drive, St. George 84790. Fees: $10, singles; $30-$40 for group sites.

Quail Creek State Park Campground
Utah Hwy. 9, 3 miles east of I-15, Hurricane • 879-2378, (800) 322-3770

There's great year-round camping, picnicking, boating and trout and bass fishing (see Fishing section of this chapter) at this beautiful manmade lake 3 miles east of I-15 off the Hurricane exit on Utah 9. Facilities include 23 campsites, modern restrooms, a fish-cleaning station and two covered, group-use pavilions. Set at 3,300 feet above sea level, this is an ideal location for seeing the St. George, Hurricane and Zion areas. For more information on Quail Creek, write to P.O. Box 1943, St. George 84770. Day-use fee is $5. Camping fee is $8.

Red Cliffs Campground
Off I-15 Exit 22, 4½ miles southwest of Leeds • 628-4491

This is a beautiful Bureau of Land Management campground 4½ miles southwest of Leeds (I-15 Exit 22, 12 miles northeast of St. George). At 3,600 feet above sea level, this is a desert campground with a 14-day camping limit, set amidst the red Navajo sandstone through which Quail Creek has cut a beautiful canyon. Open year-round, the facility has 10 sites with picnic tables and drinking water. The order of the day here is hiking and photography among the swirls, waves and rounded gullies in the slickrock. More information may be obtained by writing 345 E. Riverside Drive, St. George 84790. Fee: $6 per night.

Snow Canyon State Park Campground
Off Utah Hwy. 18, 11 miles northwest of St. George • 628-2255, (800) 322-3770

Eleven miles northwest of St. George off Utah Highway 18, Snow Canyon State Park is like a miniature Zion Canyon. At 3,400 feet, this year-round campground has 21 tent sites with a 14-day limit. There are excellent restrooms, hot showers, a disposal station and a covered, group-use pavilion. Early spring and fall use of the park is especially appealing because of the temperate weather and lighter use. Hiking, biking and photography are the main activities here among the mounds and ledges of white and red Navajo sandstone. For more information, write to P.O. Box 140,

How the Canyons Were Made

An ancient Paiute myth explains the formation of Southwestern Utah's canyon country this way: Once the earth was smooth and plain. Then one day Shinob told Kusav (they were gods, of course) to place his quiver at a short distance from where they stood so that it might be a mark for him to shoot. Then Shinob sent an arrow from his bow. The arrow struck the quiver, but glanced off and plowed its way about the face of the earth in every direction. The arrow dug deep gorges and canyons, making valleys, plowing up mountains, hills and rocks. In this manner the river courses, the hills and the mountains were made, and the big broken rocks were scattered about the country.

Santa Clara 84765. Park day use is $4 per person. Fee: $9 to $13.

Cedar City/Brian Head

Cedar Breaks National Monument Point Supreme Campground
Utah Hwy. 143 • 586-9451

Two miles north of the south entrance to Cedar Breaks National Monument on Utah Highway 143, this beautiful alpine campground sits at nearly 10,000 feet above sea level and is open from June 15 to September 15. There are 30 sites here with picnic tables and flush toilets, and there's a 14-day limit. This is a wonderful mountain setting surrounded by open meadows with wild flowers and thick pine, spruce, fir and aspen forests. The summer nights can get quite chilly, and most folks don't spend more than a night or two here. For that reason, the campground generally has vacancies, although it usually fills up tight on holidays. From here you can hike or drive to several awesome overlooks of Cedar Breaks. Fee: $9.

Cedar Canyon Campground
Off Utah Hwy. 14, 13 miles east of Cedar City • 865-3200, (800) 280-2267

This is a Dixie National Forest campground 13 miles up the canyon from Cedar City off Utah Highway 14. At 8,100 feet above sea level, this facility is open from May 15 through October 31. It has 19 tent sites with a maximum stay of 14 days. There are picnic tables, dump sites and flush toilets. This campground, which is the nearest forest campground to Cedar City, opens a month earlier and stays open about six weeks longer than the other forest campgrounds on Cedar Mountain. Fee: $6.43.

Deer Haven Campground
Webster Flat Rd., off Utah Hwy. 14 • 865-3200, (800) 280-2267

Administered by Dixie National Forest, this campground is 16 miles east of Cedar City, up the canyon off Utah 14, then 3 miles on Webster Flat Road, a dirt road. At 8,900 feet above sea level, this campground has 20 tent sites designed for groups, and there's a limit of 14 days camping. There are picnic tables,

limited drinking water and flush toilets. There are also handicapped-accessible facilities and group sites. The facility is open from June 15 to September 1. Set among the tall pines and aspen groves of the west slope of Cedar Mountain, this is an idyllic alpine getaway. Group fee is $50.

Duck Creek Campground
Off Utah Hwy. 14, 30 miles east of Cedar City, Duck Creek • 865-3200, (800) 280-2267

East of Cedar City off Utah 14, the Duck Creek Campground is a Dixie National Forest facility with 79 tent sites and a limit of 14 days camping. At an altitude of 8,600 feet, this campground is open June 15 through September 15 and has drinking water, picnic tables and flush toilets. There are dump sites, handicapped-accessible facilities and group sites. Just 5 miles away at Navajo Lake, there's great fishing (see Fishing, later in this chapter). Fee: $9.

Navajo Lake Campground
Off Utah Hwy. 14, 28 miles east of Cedar City • 865-3200, (800) 280-2267

Set along the shores of Navajo Lake, this campground is east of Cedar City off Utah 14. At an altitude of 9,200 feet, this is an awesome setting next to one of the most beautiful mountain lakes in Utah. Even at the height of summer, it can get very cold here, so pack light sweaters, flannel shirts and thermals. The campground has 28 sites and is open from June 15 to September 15 with a limit of 14 days camping. There are flush toilets, picnic tables and drinking water. There are handicapped-accessible facilities, dump sites and group sites. And you can fish in Navajo Lake (see Fishing below). Fee: $7.

Spruces Campground
Off Utah Hwy. 14, 28 miles east of Cedar City • 865-3200, (800) 280-2267

Next door to Navajo Lake, this is another Dixie National Forest campground east of Cedar City off Utah 14. There are 28 sites at this facility, which sits at 9,200 feet above sea level and is open from June 15 to September 15. There's a 14-day limit on camping here, where you'll find picnic tables, group sites, drinking water, flush toilets and facilities for the handicap. Great fishing at Navajo Lake is just a stone's throw away (see Fishing below).

Vermillion Castle Campground
Forest Road 049, off Utah Hwy. 143
• 865-3200, (800) 280-2267

Just 5 miles up the canyon from Parowan (4 miles on Utah 143, then 1 mile on Forest Road 049), this Dixie National Forest campground is sits at 7,000 feet above sea level. The campground is open May 15 through October 15 and has 16 sites with a 14-day camping limit. Here you'll find picnic tables, drinking water, flush toilets and group sites. There are a number of terrific hiking options beginning at this majestic mountain setting. Fee: $6.43.

Bryce Canyon Area

Bryce Canyon National Park North Campground
Off Utah Hwy. 63, Bryce Canyon
• 834-5322

Just inside the park boundaries off Utah Highway 63, this campground sits immediately east of park headquarters. At an elevation of 8,000 feet, this facility is open year-round, although during the winter months it is generally covered in snow. There are 55 tent sites as well as picnic tables, flush toilets and showers. Fee: $10.

Bryce Canyon National Park Sunset Campground
Utah Hwy. 63, Bryce Canyon • 834-5322

Two miles south of the park entrance on Utah 63, the Sunset Campground sits at 8,000 feet above sea level and is open May 15 through October 1. There are 50 tent sites here, and there are picnic tables, flush toilets and dump sites. This campground is connected to some

beautiful rim trails from which you can hike to several great Bryce overlooks. Fee: $10.

King Creek Campground
Off Utah Hwy. 12, 26 miles southeast of Panguitch • 676-8815, (800) 280-2267

Southeast of Panguitch off Utah 12 (from Utah 12 take East Fork Road 7 miles to Tropic Reservoir), this is a Dixie National Forest campground. At 8,000 feet above sea level, this facility is open from June 1 through September 15 and has a 14-day camping limit. There are 36 sites with picnic tables and drinking water. You'll enjoy the fresh mountain air, the peaceful breeze through the pines and the great fishing at Tropic Reservoir (see Fishing, below). For more information on this site, write 225 E. Center Street, Panguitch 84759. Fee: $6.

Red Canyon Campground
Utah Hwy. 12, 9 miles southeast of Panguitch • 676-2676, (800) 280-2267

Open April 15 to November 15, this is a Dixie National Forest campground with 36 sites 9 miles southeast of Panguitch on Utah 12. There's drinking water and flush toilets. Camping limit is 14 days. This great campground is a staging point for a number of excellent hiking trails in the Red Canyon area (see Hiking and Backpacking in this chapter). More information on Red Canyon Campground may be obtained by writing 225 E. Center Street, Panguitch 84759. Fee: $7.20.

Kanab Area

Coral Pink Sand Dunes State Park Campground
Off U.S. Hwy. 89, 35 miles northwest of Kanab • 648-2800, (800) 322-3770

This is an off-road vehicle paradise northwest of Kanab, 12 miles off U.S. Highway 89.

INSIDERS' TIP

While hiking in Southwestern Utah you'll encounter little water. If you refill water containers in streams, pools or springs along the way, be sure to boil, treat or filter the water before drinking. Surface waters may be contaminated with giardia, which can cause significant gastrointestinal distress.

The wide, sweeping expanse of Coral Pink Sand Dunes State Park is a wonderful place for riding off-highway vehicles, taking photos or just playing in the sand. The park has a resident ranger, a 22-unit pull-through campground, modern restrooms, showers, disposal station and paved roads. Set at 6,000 feet, the park is open year round. Write P.O. Box 95, Kanab 84791 for more information. Day-use rate is $3, and camping, limited to 14 days, is $11 per night.

Paria Movie Set Campground
BLM Paria Contact Station, Off U.S. Hwy. 89, 35 miles east of Kanab • 644-2672

This is a primitive campground 35 miles east of Kanab off U.S. 89, administered by the Bureau of Land Management. Drive east from Kanab 30 miles on U.S. 89, then turn at the sign for the campground and drive 5 miles on the dirt road (impassable when wet). At 4,000 feet above sea level, the campground has just three tent sites and is open May 1 through November 1. Other than a pristine desert setting near the remains of the Paria movie set, the campground offers little more than picnic tables and plenty of peace and quiet. Bring your own water. There is no fee.

Hiking and Backpacking

Among the myriad outdoor activities available in Southwestern Utah, the most basic, the most fulfilling and the most popular is hiking. This is a region crying out to be hiked. Nearly 80 percent of the landscape is public land, and much of it is accessible by trails, dirt roads or wide-open country. We don't think anyone who is capable of walking should pass through this area without stopping at least once, getting out of the car and heading up a trail, down a canyon, across a plateau or through a forest.

Here we share some of our favorite hikes and backpacking excursions, with a little something for everyone — from softies to hard-core mountaineers. For the uninformed, hiking is generally defined by walks lasting from an hour to a full day. Backpacking is defined by walks that include at least one night of camping, away from improved campgrounds and ser-

vices. For additional detailed information on hiking in Southwestern Utah, consult the travel bureaus for any of the county's in our geographical area: Washington (St. George/Zion), Iron (Cedar City/Brian Head), Garfield (Bryce Canyon) or Kane (Kanab area).

St. George/Zion

If you're lucky enough to be here on a Saturday when Bart Anderson (see the Close-up on Ranger Bart in our Parks and Other Natural Wonders chapter) is conducting a hike in the greater St. George area, don't miss it. There's no better way to be introduced to Southwestern Utah than on one of his weekly guided excursions.

Otherwise, we suggest you drive to Snow Canyon State Park, Pine Valley Mountain Recreation Area or Zion National Park (again, see our Parks and Other Natural Wonders chapter for more details), where there are a number of trailheads from which you can embark on a short or long hike.

Pine Valley Recreation Area

North of St. George, 32 miles off Utah 18, the Pine Valley Recreation Area of Dixie National Forest has several trailheads where you can begin a trek up a canyon leading to the green meadows at the 10,000-foot reaches of Pine Valley Mountain. For day hikers we suggest either the **Whipple Trail** at the east end of the recreation area, or the **Forsyth Trail,** which begins right in the little town of Pine Valley. Hike as far as you're comfortable going — you'll reach some incredible vistas of the valley — then turn back.

Backpackers can take in the entire mountain trail system, beginning at either of the trailheads, camping on the mountain (much of which is inside the Pine Valley Wilderness Area) and making a full circle by descending the mountain on the other trail. For more detailed information on hiking or backpacking in the Pine Valley area, contact the Interagency Visitor Center, 345 E. Riverside Drive, St. George, 628-4491.

Snow Canyon State Park

Just 11 miles northwest of St. George off Utah 18, this is a slickrock wonderland. Stop in at the ranger station midway through the canyon and pay the $4 day-use fee, then you're on your own to simply scurry up, over and around the slickrock formations or to hike along several marked trails in the canyon. We suggest the **Three Ponds Trail**, which will take you into a side canyon where the towering walls draw closer together as you proceed. It's about a 3-mile walk each way, but you can turn around at any point and still have a great experience.

It gets awfully hot in Snow Canyon in the summertime. Morning and evening hiking is best, especially if you're taking photographs. Carry plenty of water, and don't let the ledges tempt you. It seems like every year at least one hiker tries to climb where he or she should have known better and ends up having to be rescued off a cliff. You can contact Snow Canyon State Park by calling 628-2255.

Zion National Park

To drive through Zion National Park without getting out and walking is a cardinal sin. It doesn't matter what kind of shape you're in — as long as you are capable of walking even 50 yards, you must let your feet touch the ground at some point while you're here.

A variety of hiking trails enhance the Zion experience. Many of them were built in the 1930s by the Civilian Conservation Corps. Admittedly, many of the trails are steep and require a strong heart and lungs, but several others are relatively easy, at least for the first part of the way. As you drive up the 6-mile stretch of the main canyon you will see signs indicating most of the trails. One of the best places to start is the **Weeping Rock Trail**. This is an easy, self-guided trail that begins at the Weeping Rock parking lot and ends at a spectacular rock alcove with hanging gardens. It's a half-mile round trip and takes about 30 minutes.

Lower Emerald Pool is an easy hike starting at the Zion Canyon Scenic Drive opposite the Zion Lodge and ending at Lower Pool. This is a 1.2-mile, handicapped-accessible trail that takes about an hour, round trip. The walk gives you an awesome perspective of the canyon and a look at slickrock bowls that hold water year-round. Swimming and wading in the pools is prohibited.

Another easy trail is the **Riverside Walk**, which starts at the Temple of Sinawava parking lot where the road ends at the head of Zion Canyon. It's a mile up and a mile back and requires about 90 minutes. This hike gives you a feel for how the quiet little Virgin River has cut this deep sandstone canyon and a taste of how the canyon narrows as you work your way upstream. **Canyon Overlook** is an easy to moderate hike that starts at the Zion-Mt. Carmel Highway, just east of the mile-long tunnel, and ends with a spectacular view of lower Zion Canyon. It's about a 1-mile, one-hour round trip. For a moderately strenuous hike, take the **Watchman Trail**, which begins at the Watchman Campground (see Camping in this chapter) and climbs to a viewpoint of the lower Zion Canyon. This is a 2-mile, two-hour round trip and is not recommended for midday hiking during the summer.

Perhaps the signature hike in Zion National Park — one we highly recommend if you are up to it — is the **Angels Landing Trail**. This is a strenuous hike beginning at the Grotto Picnic Area in the main canyon. It's a 5-mile, four-hour round trip that begins easily, then becomes steeper and steeper as you go. Along this trail you'll come to Walter's Wiggles, a unique set of switchbacks built in the 1930s that give this trail its wonderful character. When you reach Scout Lookout at the summit you get an incredible view of the canyon — a true payoff for the effort you've made.

Then, if you have the stomach for it, you can continue the last half-mile out to the edge of Angels Landing. This is a steep, narrow ridge with a drop-off of 1,500 feet. There's a railing in some of the worst places to assist you, but it's awfully scary going even for the stout of heart. Don't try it if you have a greater than normal fear of heights. If you do try it, again, the reward will be unbelievable. There can't be many views on earth more heart-stirring than the one from the edge of Angels Landing.

Observation Point is another outstanding destination that requires a truly strenuous effort to accomplish. The hike begins at the Weeping Rock parking lot and climbs 4 miles to the upper reaches of the canyon. It's an 8-mile, six-hour round trip.

In the Kolob section of Zion National Park,

we recommend the **Taylor Creek** hike, accessible off I-15, 25 miles north of St. George and 2 miles up the canyon from the Kolob visitor center just off Exit 40. This is a moderately strenuous hike that follows the middle fork of Taylor Creek to Double Arch Alcove. Your feet will get wet as you cross the creek several times. This is a 5-mile, four-hour round trip. It takes you into the Kolob Fingers, a formation of towering red and pink ledges that characterize the northwest section of Zion National Park.

For backpackers we suggest the world-famous **Narrows** hike beginning in the upper reaches of the Virgin River drainage and ending at the Temple of Sinawava parking lot in the main Zion Canyon. The Narrows is an 18-mile stretch of the upper canyon where the towering walls in some places are little more than an arm-span apart. This hike requires a backcountry permit (available at the park visitors center 2 miles north of Springdale for $5 per person per night) and is closed during times of potential flash-flooding.

The **West Rim Trail** is another excellent backpacking route usually started at the top in the Kolob section of the park at Lava Point, about 20 miles north of the town of Virgin on the Kolob Terrace Road. This is a 14-mile hike, with a 3,000-foot drop in elevation. It is often done in one day but is best experienced as an overnight backpacking trip (again, a $5 per person per day backcountry permit is required). The trail ends by connecting with the Angels Landing Trail, which leads you to the bottom of the canyon and ultimately to the Grotto Picnic area.

The **Kolob Arch Trail** is in the Kolob Canyons area off I-15 at Exit 40, 25 miles north of St. George. Usually done as an overnight backpacking trip (again, requiring a backcountry permit — pick one up for this trail at the Kolob

Visitors Center at I-15 Exit 40 for $5 per person per night), this is a 14-mile, 10-hour round trip. It's a strenuous hike beginning at Lee Pass, following Timber and LaVerkin creeks and ending at Kolob Arch — one of the world's widest freestanding arches.

For guided hiking in Zion National Park, contact Zion Adventure Company, 36 Lion Boulevard, Springdale, 772-1001.

Cedar City/Brian Head

Hiking in the Cedar City/Brian Head area is generally a summertime proposition. Most of the great trails are on Cedar Mountain, which most years is covered by snow from November through April or May. June, July and August offer perfect weather for getting out into the forests and enjoying the seclusion of alpine groves of tall spruce, fir, ponderosa pine and aspen. There's great mountain hiking all across Cedar Mountain, from Duck Creek and Navajo Lake to Cedar Breaks National Monument and Brian Head Ski Resort.

Cedar Breaks

On Utah 148, 23 miles east of Cedar City and 19 miles southwest of Parowan, Cedar Breaks is a 9½-square-mile national monument at an elevation of 10,350 feet above sea level. Consisting mostly of a giant amphiteater breaking out of the west slope of Cedar Mountain, the main activity here is driving, parking, getting out of the car, looking off the edge and taking photos. But there are a couple of short hikes that will allow you to become a little more intimate with this beautiful country.

Spectra Point Trail and **Alpine Pond Trail** are two fairly easy, although somewhat rugged, hikes requiring sturdy footwear. Remember, you're at 10,000 feet here so don't be surprised if you get a little short of breath with

St. George's Foremaster Ridge affords an incredible view from the Kolob and Zion cliffs to the northeast, all the way to the Virgin Mountains to the southwest. Drive to 700 South in St. George, then head east until you cross River Road. Continue east about a half-mile and the road will take you to the top of the lava-capped ridge. It's a 10-minute drive from downtown.

Great Views

Photo: Jud Burkett

The St. George area is gaining a reputation as a haven for mountain bikers.

some extra strain on your heart and lungs. Hike slowly and rest often — easy advice to follow since in this dreamy setting the hustle and bustle of daily life will quickly fade. The 1-mile Spectra Point Trail begins at the visitor center on the rim midway along the 5-mile rim drive. It follows the rim out to a stand of ancient bristlecone pines. From there the trail continues another mile along the ramparts of the breaks and through a lovely forested area, ending at another dramatic view point.

Just beyond Chessmen Ridge Overlook is the Alpine Pond Trail, a 2-mile round-trip trail that winds through the evergreen forest and passes a mystical, spring-fed pond.

To actually enter the gorge, you should first consult a ranger. There is a steep, 10-mile hike along a forest service trail, descending 3,400 feet along the Rattlesnake Creek through the Ashdown Gorge Wilderness Area. In places, this trail can be very difficult and is especially dangerous during summer storms when flash floods occur. The trailhead is off Utah 143, between Brian Head Resort and the north entrance to Cedar Breaks National Monument.

Dominguez-Escalante Trail

While most of the best hiking in the Cedar City/Brian Head area is in the mountains to the east, here's a fascinating option down in the Great Basin to the west. The Bureau of Land Management has designated a hiking trail along part of the historic route used by the Catholic fathers Dominguez and Escalante, who passed through this area in October 1776 (see our History chapter). The marked portion of the trail begins 30 miles northwest of Cedar City. Drive about 1 mile out of Cedar City on Utah Highway 56, turn right onto Utah Highway 19 and drive about 30 miles to Lund. Turn right at the railroad tracks at Lund and follow the sign that says **Thermo Hot Springs**.

The hike begins at Thermo Hot Springs and a mile later you arrive at the site of the **Casting of the Lots**. This is the historic camping place where the expedition cast lots to decide whether to push on to Monterey in California or turn back to Santa Fe. The decision was to turn back, which they did by heading south on the same route you will follow if you continue the remaining 24 marked miles to the intersection with Utah 56, about 2 miles west of Cedar City. This hike can be greatly enhanced by taking along a copy of the Dominguez and Escalante journal. It is available in paperback from the University of Utah Press under the title, *The Dominguez-Escalante Journal: Their Expedition Through Colorado, Utah, Arizona, and New Mexico in 1776*. It is edited by Ted J. Warner and translated by Fray Angelico Chavez.

Spring Creek Canyon

From Cedar City take I-15 south to Exit 51, then follow the road on the east side of the interstate for 5 miles south to Kanarraville and another half-mile south to Spring Creek Canyon. Here you can pull off at the trailhead leading into an awesome, narrow, red rock canyon that is part of an area now under study by the Bureau of Land Management for possible wilderness designation. This area is right at the northern boundary of Zion National Park, and it is a very secluded, pristine place. You can head up the trail as far as you like, then backtrack to your vehicle. If you are coming north on I-15 from St. George, take Exit 42 and follow the frontage road north to Kanarraville.

Bryce Canyon Area

Dixie National Forest and Bryce Canyon National Park offer some of the best hiking you'll find anywhere. Between May and September you'll encounter an endless array of possibilities from the forest trails of Red Canyon to the mystical little jaunts through the hoodoos, pinnacles and spires of Bryce's amphitheater.

Bryce Canyon National Park

Bryce is a place where, in just a couple of hours on the trail, you can see some truly spectacular scenery and come away feeling fulfilled. But you need to keep in mind that at Bryce you generally start out downhill, and every step you take down means a corresponding step coming back up. It is easy to get caught up in the beauty of the moment going down, and then find yourself in trouble as heat, altitude and steepness conspire against you on the way out. Know your limits, and be especially careful if you have heart disease or respiratory ailments.

Once inside the park, pull into one of the overlook parking lots (Sunset Point, Bryce Point, Sunrise Point and Rainbow Point, to name a few), and from there you can take your pick of a number of short, intermediate and long hikes. The **Rim Trail** is the easiest walking trail. It winds along the rim but is not a loop. There are several access points from Utah Highway 63. To do the entire rim is 11 miles and takes five to six hours round trip. The **Queen's Garden Trail** is the least strenuous trail beneath the rim. It begins at Sunrise Point and descends 320 feet. This is a 1½-mile trail that takes about 90 minutes to make, round trip.

The **Bristlecone Loop Trail** is a moderate hike along the top of the 9,000-foot plateau that begins at Rainbow Point. There are dramatic views of the canyon and cliffs through the spruce-fir forest with ancient bristlecone pines along the cliff edges. This is a 1-mile walk, and you should allow about two hours for the round trip. **Navajo Loop Trail** is a fairly strenuous hike past the Bryce formation called the Silent City. It begins at Sunset Point and descends 521 feet. You should carry water on all Bryce hikes, but definitely make sure you carry plenty for this one. It's 1½ miles and takes about an-hour-and-a-half to make round trip — unless you connect to the Queen's Garden Loop, which will double the distance.

The **Fairyland Loop** is a strenuous trail

that drops more than 900 feet. It begins at Fairyland Point and winds through spires, columns and temple formations of red rock past the Chinese Wall, Tower Bridge and Fairyland. This trail joins the Rim Trail at the North Campground Amphitheater and at Fairyland Viewpoint. Carry water. It's 8 miles and takes four to five hours round trip. The **Peekaboo Loop Trail** is another strenuous hike that winds past the Alligator, Fairy Castle, Cathedral and Wall of Windows. It is accessed either from Sunset Point or Bryce Point and descends 827 feet. Definitely carry water. You share this trail with horses and mules, and you need to remember that they have the right of way. It's about 5½ miles and requires three to four hours round trip. The **Riggs Springs Loop Trail** is about 9 miles and takes four to five hours to complete round trip. It's a very strenuous hike that starts at Yovimpa Point and drops 1,625 feet. For those who are up to it, the steepness down and back is a small price to pay for the incredible views of the pink cliffs.

Backpackers can spend two to three days on the **Under-the-Rim Trail**. It is a strenuous backcountry hike connecting Bryce Point with Rainbow Point to the south. This trail offers you everything great about Bryce in one package. It's 22 miles one-way. Backcountry camping requires a free permit. Stop at the visitor center at the park entrance for detailed information.

The Cassidy Trail

There are a dozen great hiking trails beginning at the Red Canyon Campground (see Camping above), which is 9 miles southeast of Panguitch on Utah 12 on the way to Bryce Canyon. The longest hike is the **Cassidy Trail** (named after the famed outlaw Butch Cassidy, who rode this area). It leaves Utah 12 about a half-mile from the Red Canyon Campground and heads north through the beautiful red rock formations of the area.

After about 8 miles, the trail meets another trail coming up Casto Canyon from the west.

From here you can either retrace your route back to Utah 12 or take the **Casto Canyon Trail** for about 5½ miles to the mouth of the canyon, where the trail meets with a gravel road that comes off U.S. 89 just south of Panguitch. The trail goes through the bottom of the canyon through some of the most majestic scenery in the area. You can make a vigorous day hike out of this, or pack a backpack and make it an overnighter. There is no water along the route; you'll have to carry all you need. Contact the U.S. Forest Service in Panguitch at 57 N. Main St., 676-8815, for more details and maps of this hike and others branching off from the Cassidy Trail.

Kanab Area

The Kanab area is the kind of place where you can pretty much stop anywhere, get out and just start walking. In fact, you will probably find yourself doing just that as you drive along the foot of the Vermillion Cliffs and gaze in awe at the rolling, multicolored sands, the twisted and modeled sandstone pinnacles and the canyons that break out of the long line of cliffs. Watch for scenic pullouts. Stop and read the plaques; head off on a little jaunt. There's nothing quite like fashioning your own adventure in this slickrock wonderland.

Paria Canyon

This is a narrow, majestic and historic canyon 45 miles east of Kanab off U.S. 89. Pronounced "Pah-REE-ah," the word is Paiute for "muddy water." Depending on the time of year (we suggest late spring, summer and early fall), you'll be walking through either a little bit or a lot of that muddy water as you work your way into this enthralling canyon. You can make of this hike what you want. It can be a half-day mini-adventure (in as far as you like and back out) or a three-day backpack expedition covering the entire 35-mile length of the canyon — all the way from the BLM's Paria Canyon

---

INSIDERS' TIP

While hiking in the canyon country of Southwestern Utah, stay a safe distance back from cliff ledges. They can be unstable and slippery. More accidents occur on these cliffs each year than you would imagine.

Wilderness station to Lee's Ferry, Arizona, where the Paria River empties into the Colorado River. This, of course, will require that you arrange a shuttle. No local companies we know of currently offer this service.

This is a wilderness area administered by the BLM, and hiking permits are required. They are free and used mainly to help monitor the foot traffic through the narrow canyon during the summer, when flash floods are a possibility. The ranger station is at the trailhead, just off U.S. 89. There you can get complete, detailed information on this hike including information on an optional route through Buckskin Canyon where the canyon width at the bottom averages 15 feet for a 12-mile stretch. The 35-mile, narrow canyon can take from three to six days to negotiate and requires proper gear and preparation.

As you descend into this gash in the earth you come to places where the canyon is but 12 feet from wall to wall and 1,500 feet to the top. You pass ancient Native American ruins, natural arches, rock slides, springs and seeps and experience a unique kind of seclusion. Be sure to check in advance with the BLM, 318 N. 100 East, Kanab, 644-2672, for specific guidelines, since this hike is becoming more widely known all the time.

Squaw Trail

Stop by the Kane County Travel Council office at 78 S. 100 East, 644-5033, for a trail guide to this great little hike that starts right in the heart of Kanab. It's a 3-mile trek, perfect for an early summer morning. The well-graded trail begins near the city park at the north end of 100 East. From there it ascends 800 feet into the Vermillion Cliffs north of Kanab. It's a strenuous climb that offers a wonderful reward as you reach the top of the mesa. From there you can see the beautiful community of Kanab below and take in the entire expanse of the Kaibab Plateau to the south. Turning to the north, you'll get a spectacular perspective of the Grand Staircase as you gaze across the geological steps of the White, Gray and Pink cliffs in the distance.

Rock Climbing

Because so much of Southwestern Utah's landscape is at a right angle to the horizon, the sport of rock climbing is growing every year. The sheer cliffs of Zion National Park, the sandstone ledges of Snow Canyon State Park and several locations in the Cedar City and Kanab areas are popular among local climbers.

Because of the specialized nature of this activity, we assume that most who participate in it will have some knowledge of where they're going and what they're going to do before coming. If not, we suggest you stop by **Outdoor Outlet**, 1062 East Tabernacle in St. George, 628-3611, and begin to infiltrate the climbing network that has formed in Southwestern Utah. The folks at Outdoor Outlet like to talk climbing and sell specialized climbing gear. Some of them are experienced climbers who can answer questions, give suggestions and help you get acquainted with the climbing scene. They also have a couple of locally published climbing guide booklets to get you started.

At the Veyo Pool Resort, 20 miles north of St. George off Utah 18 in Veyo, 574-2300, the owners have established **Crawdad Canyon Rock Climbing Park** in a lava rock canyon. Touted as the second-largest privately owned rock climbing park in the U.S., they have established more than 120 routes for beginners to advanced climbers. For a mere $2.25, a climber can spend the day on the cliffs.

Bicycling

With the exception of I-15, which runs through the heart of Southwestern Utah, every highway, road and trail in this corner of the state is a potential option for cyclists. State highways between towns, old logging roads in forests and designated scenic byways and backways all offer great opportunities for road cyclists as well as mountain bikers. While some of these roads have very narrow shoulders and require a great deal of caution, the options are absolutely endless, presenting themselves around every bend.

We have chosen to share some of the favorite bike routes in each of the four geographical areas of Southwestern Utah. Remember that this is just the tip of the iceberg for cyclists in an area that is fast gaining a reputation as one of the most scenically stimulating bicycling areas in the world. For more information on cycling in Southwestern Utah, call or write **Bicycle Utah**, P.O. Box 738, Park City, Utah 84060, (801) 649-5806.

St. George/Zion

Between St. George and Zion Canyon you'll find a number of loops, short or long, that take you through splendid scenery. There's Snow Canyon State Park (where you must stay on the roads — don't let those slickrock mounds tempt you), the Virgin River Walkway and Bikeway along the river between Bloomington Hills and Bloomington in St. George, the roads and trails of Pine Valley Mountain in Dixie National Forest, Utah Highway 9 between Hurricane and Springdale, the Kolob Terrace Road from Virgin to Kolob Reservoir and, of course, the 6-mile ride through Zion Canyon. For more information on cycling in the St. George/Zion area, as well as rentals and bike service, we suggest you stop in St. George at **Red Rock Bicycle Company**, 146 N. 300 East, 674-3185, or **Bicycles Unlimited**, 90 S. 100 East, 673-4492.

Grafton Ghost Town

Give yourself at least 90 minutes for this out-and-back, 6-mile mountain bike ride. It begins at the old bridge on Bridge Road, which crosses the Virgin River at the east end of the little town of Rockville, about 3 miles west of Springdale. It's a year-round ride, weather permitting, with little elevation change.

Follow the pavement as the road turns to dirt. You'll go over a gradual hill for about a half-mile, then you turn right at the intersection and continue down river with fields on your right and sandstone mesas on your left for 2 miles. Just before you get to the ghost town, the Grafton Cemetery appears on your left. Here you will find markers of pioneer graves from more than a century ago when Grafton was a fledgling settlement daunted by the whims of the Virgin River. The old church and houses in Grafton might well look familiar

since they were part of one of the most memorable scenes in the Paul Newman-Robert Redford film, *Butch Cassidy and the Sundance Kid*. Does the image of Newman and Katherine Ross on a bicycle ring a bell? Return the same way you came. For bike rentals, repairs and tours in Springdale, contact **Bike Zion** at (800) 4-SLIK ROK.

Snow Canyon Loop

This is a 24-mile loop that will take you about three hours to complete and is appropriate for either road or mountain bikes. You can make the ride year round, though if you're doing it in summer, we suggest you start early in the morning and carry lots of water. Winter temperatures will be in the 50s, while summer temperatures will hover above 100. Start the ride at the intersection of Bluff Street and St. George Boulevard in downtown St. George. Head north on Utah 18 to the intersection with U.S. Highway 91, which is identified as Sunset Boulevard. Turn left (west) and continue to the town of Santa Clara. There will be steady traffic along this part of the route.

In Santa Clara you can stop at the historic Jacob Hamblin Home (see our Attractions chapter) before heading on to the Ivins turnoff, where you turn right (north) and head toward the massive Red Mountain directly ahead. From here it's 6 miles to Snow Canyon, where you can refill your water bottle in the park and take in the majestic sandstone beauty of the canyon. You may recognize some of the backdrops here since they have appeared in several movies, including *Butch Cassidy and the Sundance Kid*, and John Wayne's *The Conqueror*. As you make the steep pull to the north end of the park, you'll come to the junction with Utah 18, about 13 miles into your ride. From here the highway takes you directly back to St. George on a welcome downhill ride most of the way.

Cedar City/Brian Head

The Brian Head area has become a mountain biker's mecca in recent years. Come sum-

---

FYI

Unless otherwise noted, the area code for all phone numbers listed in this chapter is 801 but will change to 435 in September 1997. Either area code may be used until March 22, 1998.

mer, when the snow melts off the ski slopes and the dirt mountain roads dry out, there's no end to the options peddlers can find in the pine-studded reaches of Cedar Mountain. The area offers literally hundreds of miles of single-track and double-track trails as well as forest service roads reaching up the canyons and crossing over the tops of ridges.

You can start high above timberline and ride through alpine meadows covered with wildflowers or get swallowed by the thick, pine forests that seem to hold you prisoner until you break out onto splendid overlooks of red rock canyons. For more information on mountain biking in the Cedar Mountain area as well as bike rentals, we suggest you stop by **Brian Head Cross Country Ski and Mountain Bike Center**, 223 West Hunter Ridge Drive, 677-2012.

Cedar Canyon

This is a one-way road ride for experts only. It begins in Cedar City and ends at Cedar Breaks, 21 miles and 4,500 vertical feet later. Allow at least four hours for this April through November ride. The road has narrow shoulders and there are some steep switchbacks. The payoffs here are the incredible overlooks you'll get of the upper reaches of Zion Na-

tional Park and the amazing red rock amphitheater of Cedar Breaks National Monument.

From Cedar City, set out east on Utah 14 and simply follow the signs to Cedar Breaks National Monument. You'll climb through Cedar Canyon, following the course of Coal Creek, and enter Dixie National Forest. At the Cedar Canyon Campground (see Camping in this chapter), you'll begin a series of switchbacks before you reach the Zion overlook, which is about 3 miles from the turnoff to Cedar Breaks at the Utah 143 junction. By now you've covered 15 miles and climbed 4,000 feet. Turn left on Utah 143 and continue the remaining 6 miles to Cedar Breaks National Monument, where overlooks are always open and the visitor center operates June 1 to October 15. If you wish, you can return by the same route, but it's a steep route and the switchbacks are very difficult to negotiate downhill.

Twisted Forest

Beginning at Brian Head, this is an out-and-back, 12-mile mountain bike ride for intermediate riders. Give yourself about four hours to make this scenic mountain trip. You can begin at the Brian Head Hotel parking lot, where you turn left on Utah 143 and go one-

Lurking in the Shadows

In the fall of 1858, Nephi Johnson was the first known Anglo to follow the Virgin River into Zion Canyon. He was a Mormon missionary looking for suitable places for settlement in the upper Virgin area. A native Paiute led him to Oak Creek, just above where the visitor center of Zion National Park is today. There the Indian stopped and refused to go any further.

Apparently the guide did not wish to enter the narrow canyon where the unpredictable spirit called Wainopits might be waiting in the shadows. According to Paiute

mythology recorded by Angus Woodbury, Wainopits was a spirit always at cross purposes — the one who caused no end of trouble. He would hide in the shadows, intent upon evil. It was Wainopits who visited camps and brought sickness and caused all sorts of dire calamities. The Paiutes always tried to avoid him, and because the narrow canyons of Zion cast so much shadow, it seemed to be a favorite dwelling place for Wainopits. When Johnson rode back out of the canyon late in the day, his Paiute guide was still waiting.

third of a mile to Aspen Drive. Turn left and ascend the graded road over Navajo Ridge. From there you descend to Third House Flat and Dry Lakes Road and ride across the meadow into the aspens. After 2½ miles, you'll come to a junction marked Twisted Forest Trail Head (the sign will be on your left). If you wish to take this option, turn left and ride to the Twisted Forest Trail Head marked with a large Ashdown Gorge Wilderness Area sign. From here you can walk on the trail to the Twisted Forest, which is an area of ancient bristlecone pines and pink cliffs.

A short way to the south you'll come to a cliff edge dropping 500 feet into Cedar Breaks. After you've returned to your bike, ride the same route back to Dry Lakes Road, then continue west on the road until you come to a junction to your left marked Trail 052. Continue straight ahead uphill on the main road, and at the top of the hill turn onto the first road past the 052 sign. Now you're riding uphill through aspen and the High Mountain Meadow. Continue to the summit of High Mountain (which is your turnaround point), and you will take in awesome views of Cedar Breaks, Black Mountain, Brian Head Peak and the Ashdown Gorge Wilderness Area.

Bryce Canyon Area

Bryce Canyon country has a little bit of everything for cyclists. You can ride from 11,000-foot forests in the west to slickrock in the east. Fat- and thin-tire cyclists discover an abundance of routes for every season and every ability. Road riders especially enjoy the scenic byways connecting Bryce Canyon, Red Canyon and Dixie National Forest. Utah 143 from Panguitch to Cedar Breaks is a special favorite as well as U.S. 89 and Utah 12 between Panguitch and Bryce Canyon.

Mountain bikers will find spectacular mountain roads throughout Dixie National Forest. Ruby's Inn, 834-5341, on Utah 63 (see our Accommodations chapter), near the entrance to Bryce Canyon National Park, offers bike rentals and shuttle service to bikers in the Bryce area. The folks at Ruby's have a mountain of information and maps on trails in the area. Road biking is not recommended in Bryce Canyon National Park because the roads are narrow and very congested in summer months. In keeping with policies in all national parks, no off-pavement biking is permitted in Bryce.

Dave's Hollow

This mountain bike ride begins about 1 mile south of Ruby's Inn at the northern boundary of Bryce Canyon National Park. It's an 8-mile, out-and-back ride through pine forests and meadows along a double-track road. Take the dirt road heading west from Utah 63 just before you enter the park. You'll ride about three-quarters of a mile and then turn right onto Dave's Hollow Trail. Follow the trail for approximately 3 miles to its junction with Forest Road 087 near Dave's Hollow Forest Service Station. You can either return the way you came or continue north along Forest Road 087 to its junction with Utah 12. There you turn right (east) and ride along the highway to the junction with the Bryce Canyon Road (Utah 63), then return to Ruby's Inn. This option adds about 4 miles to the ride, making it a total of 12 miles.

Horse Valley/Caddy Creek

Beginning at the northeast corner of Panguitch Lake on North Shore Road, this is a 17-mile mountain bike loop that takes you through a variety of pristine high country on Forest Service roads. Take Forest Service Road 076, which leaves the North Shore Road at the northeastern corner of the lake. Continue on the road 6 miles to the Horse Valley-Myers Valley junction. From there, go north through the grassy meadows of Horse Valley for about 5 miles until the road crosses a small pass and drops for a mile to the Caddy Creek Jeep Road — Forest Road 396. Ride east for about 4 miles to Forest Road 082 and follow it

---

INSIDERS' TIP

Don't roll or throw rocks from ledges. You never know who or what might be below you, and it accelerates erosion as well as destroys vegetation.

Photo: St. George Magazine

Hikers hang out on the slickrock in Snow Canyon State Park.

back to the beginning point. There are a lot of ups and downs — you climb from about 8,800 feet to about 9,300 feet — and there's a chance you'll see some deer, antelope or elk along the way.

Kanab Area

Kanab is an ideal staging point for cyclists of the road, trail or slickrock. In addition to the highways connecting Kanab with such scenic wonders as Zion Canyon, Coral Pink Sand Dunes and the Paria Wilderness Area, there are more than 600 miles of dirt roads winding through the county's vast expanse, giving mountain bikers to access to ghost towns, canyons, high plateaus and ancient Native American rock art panels. We suggest you stop by the Kane County Travel Council office in Kanab at 78 S. 100 East, 644-5033, for additional detailed information on cycling in the Kanab area.

Coral Pink Sand Dunes

An excellent road bike route begins at the turnoff from U.S. 89 (3 miles south of Mt. Carmel Junction) to Coral Pink Sand Dunes State Park. This is an 11-mile, paved access road offering a 22-mile round trip with relatively little traffic. The road swings along the northwest edge of the sand dunes and allows you a unique perspective — perhaps the only place in Utah where the view is dominated by sprawling, windblown waves of sand.

Kanab-Johnson Canyon

For scenery, history and all-around enjoyment, here's a great road ride of about 40 miles that will take the intermediate rider about four hours to complete. This is an April through October ride that begins in the city of Kanab and heads east on U.S. 89. You'll ride past the Coral Cliffs Golf Course on your left and continue east below those same cliffs for about 9 miles. The turnoff (north, left) to Johnson Canyon is marked by road signs.

The road up the canyon generally has little traffic and is an excellent route for handicapped riders. The paved road continues for 2 miles to the mouth of Johnson Canyon. Now you're surrounded by pastures and old ranches. About 6 miles into the canyon, you'll see the old *Gunsmoke* film set to the right (see our Attractions chapter). You'll continue to ride through white and pink cliffs to the end of the pavement, which is about 8 miles from the highway turnoff. This is the turnaround point. Along the route, you'll be tempted to explore side canyons and take a closer look at Native American rock art that beckons from the surrounding walls.

Horseback Riding

Most of the early explorers and pioneers of Southwestern Utah arrived by foot or on horseback. In spite of all the other options that have appeared in the years since, those two modes of transportation are still very popular here. In fact, next to hiking, going horseback is probably the best way to experience this country.

If you ask a horse purist in these parts, he or she will tell you that Southwestern Utah is the main reason God created horses in the first place. If you have a hankering to mount up and ride, there are plenty of opportunities throughout Southwestern Utah. If you prefer spectating as opposed to participating, we suggest you attend the nightly Bryce Canyon Rodeo at Ruby's Inn (see our Attractions chapter). Watching the cowboys ride those high-kicking broncs will either cure you of any further thought of riding, or it will whet your desire to get a true hands-on taste of the West. Don't worry, though: The horses at Southwestern Utah's riding stables are gentle and understanding, and the guides who will take you into the canyons or through the forests have a reputation for being gentle and understanding themselves.

For those with their own horses in tow, the backroads and trails of Dixie National Forest and the wide stretches of BLM-managed land offer a myriad of independent riding options.

St. George/Zion

Pine Valley Lodge
960 E. Main St., Pine Valley • 574-2544

In the picturesque mountain town of Pine Valley, 32 miles north of St. George off Utah 18, Pine Valley Lodge offers horse-packing and trail rides on the forest trails of Pine Valley Mountain. Guided rides on the lodge's 18 horses take in the same trails listed in the Hiking section of this chapter. The season begins April 1 and runs through October, with rates ranging from $20 for an hour ride to $125 for a full day.

The Pine Valley trails are also excellent for riders with their own horses. The Forest Service maintains an equestrian campground just east of the town of Pine Valley. For more information on this neat camping option, contact the Interagency Visitor Center at 345 E. Riverside Drive in St. George, 628-4491.

Snow Family Guest Ranch
633 E. Utah Hwy. 9, Virgin• 635-2500

Between the little communities of Virgin and Rockville, on the way to Zion Canyon, you'll see this picturesque ranch on the north side of Utah 9. It's one of Southwestern Utah's nicest bed and breakfast inns (see our Accommodations chapter), and it also offers horseback rides, not only to its guests, but also to folks who just stop by. You can simply ride around the beautiful pasture in front of the ranch at a minimal charge, or arrange for a two-hour guided ride up the canyon for $40.

Snow Canyon Stables
11 miles northwest of St. George, off U.S. Hwy. 91 • 628-6677

At the south entrance to Snow Canyon State Park, the Snow Canyon Stables offers hourly horseback riding over trails that wind through the sandy wash bottoms and across the red slickrock of Snow Canyon. During summer they're open from 8 AM to noon and from 6 to 9:30 PM. The rest of the year they're open from sunup to sundown. In addition to hourly

For one of the most stupefying views in all of Southwestern Utah, take Utah 14 out of Cedar City and continue up the canyon toward Cedar Breaks. Just before you reach the summit, you'll pass the Webster Flat turnoff. Continue a little farther on Utah 14 and you'll come to a scenic view area where you can park and look southward across the wide-open mountain drainage feeding into the head of Zion Canyon, visible far to the south.

Great Views

rides, they offer riding lessons, overnight rides, breakfast rides and steak dinner rides. This is the best opportunity close to St. George to get on a horse and ride through some great country. Rates for adults are $20 for one hour and $35 for two hours. For kids younger than 16, it's $17 for one hour and $30 for two.

Zion National Park Trail Rides
Zion Lodge • (303) 29-PARKS

Horseback tours within Zion National Park can be arranged at Zion Lodge, midway up the main Zion Canyon, about 3 miles from the visitor center at the south entrance. Seven days a week between early March and November 1, you can take one-hour or half-day rides through the canyon splendor of Zion. To schedule a horseback tour before arriving at the park, contact Canyon Trail Rides, Box 58, Tropic, Utah 84776, or call 772-3810 during the summer season (Memorial Day to Labor Day) or 679-8665 during the off-season. One-hour rides are $12, and the half-day ride is $35.

Cedar City/Brian Head

Cougar Country Outfitters
Off I-15 Exit 42, New Harmony • 586-3823

Off Exit 42 of I-15, 18 miles south of Cedar City, this is a well-equipped outfitter based in the little town of New Harmony. Cougar Country offers horse and mule rides as well as cattle drives in Southwestern Utah. You can write for more information at P.O. Box 55, New Harmony, Utah 84757.

Navajo Trails and Outfitters
30 miles east of Cedar City off Utah Hwy. 14, Duck Creek Village • 635-7071

Between Memorial Day and Labor Day, Navajo Trails and Outfitters offers horseback rides on the Cedar Mountain trails around Duck Creek Village. They have short, one- or two-hour rides, day rides, overnight trips, covered wagon rides and Dutch-oven dinners. During the fall and spring they also offer rides in lower country. Call for more details.

Bryce Canyon Area

Bryce Canyon National Park Trail Rides
Bryce Canyon Lodge, Utah Hwy. 63
• (303) 29-PARKS

You can take either a two-hour or half-day horseback tour in Bryce Canyon National Park seven days a week between April 1 and November 1. The park's horse trails are spectacular, and with all the steep up and down grades it's nice to let a gentle, 1,200-pound animal do the walking for you. To schedule a horseback tour of Bryce before arriving at the park, contact Canyon Trail Rides, Box 128, Tropic, Utah 84776, or call 679-8816 between Memorial Day and Labor Day or 679-8665 in the off-season. The two-hour trip is $25; the half-day ride is $35.

Bryce Canyon Pines
Utah Hwy. 12, Bryce Canyon • 834-5441

The Rich family has a long tradition in rodeo and horsemanship in the Bryce Canyon area. During the summer months, they offer horseback rides into Red Canyon beginning at their Bryce Canyon Pines Motel (see our Accommodations chapter) 6 miles from Bryce Canyon National Park. You can ride for an hour ($15), two hours ($20) or a half-day ($35).

Outlaw Trail Rides
Scenic Rim Trail Rides
Best Western Ruby's Inn, Utah Hwy. 63, Bryce Canyon • 834-5341 (800) 468-8660

Want to see the country Butch Cassidy and the Hole-in-the-Rock Gang called home? You won't forget the splendor of Bryce Canyon where real outlaws found themselves a perfect hiding place. Half-day trips (approximately three hours) with Outlaw will take you through the wild, untamed, spectacularly beautiful red rocks and among Bryce's trademark hoodoos. Bring your camera. You'll find plenty to shoot. The cost per person is $38. A shuttle departs from Ruby's Inn to start the fun at 8:30 AM and 1 PM. An all-day adventure on the Outlaw Trail is $75, and it includes a box lunch and a beautiful ride through Butch Cassidy country on the Casto/Losee Canyon Loop.

For $18, Scenic Rim takes you on a one-hour horseback ride over a 3-mile loop through the Dixie National Forest to the beautiful rim of Bryce Canyon National Park. Rides depart from Ruby's Inn at 9 or 10:30 AM and 1, 2:30, 4, 5:30 and 7 PM. For the more adventuresome, Scenic Rim's two-hour tour takes in the forest and the rim, then leads to a higher ridge covered with 1,600-year-old Bristlecone pine trees — some of the oldest living things in North America. From high atop this ridge, you will have a bird's-eye view of Boat Mesa and Sinking Ship Peak, some of the most spectacular sights in Fairyland Amphitheater. Departing from Ruby's Inn at 9:30 AM and 12:30 and 5 PM, the entire two-hour trip covers 5½ miles.

Hunting

The Utah Division of Wildlife Resources administers a variety of hunting opportunities in Southwestern Utah. By far, deer hunting is the most popular big game sport in this corner of the state. In fact, it is so popular, it's almost impossible to get a license anymore, unless you are willing to stand in line for several hours on a specified day in April to buy a tag for that year's October hunt. In 1997, the limited number of deer tags made available in the Southwestern region of Utah sold out in five-and-a-half hours.

Those who are fortunate enough to get a tag can hunt in specified areas of Dixie National Forest and BLM lands. The Pine Valley and Cedar Mountain areas are popular deer hunting grounds.

The very specialized sport of quail hunting is popular in the desert washes on BLM land west of St. George. There's some fall duck and geese hunting around the lakes and reservoirs listed in the fishing section of this chapter.

Conditions for all types of hunting vary greatly from year to year. For this reason, and because of the specialized nature of each type

of hunting, we suggest you stop by **Hurst Sports Center** at 160 N. 500 West in St. George, 673-6141, or at 165 S. Main Street in Cedar City, 865-9335. They have knowledgeable people who like to talk hunting, the latest hunting proclamations issued by the Division of Wildlife Resources and current information on hunting opportunities in the area. Other good resources are **Dixie Gun and Fish** at 1062 E. Tabernacle in St. George, 674-4008, and **Ron's Sporting Goods** at 138 South Main in Cedar City, 586-9901.

Fishing

Though the fishing choices in Southwestern Utah are not nearly as plentiful as the hiking, biking and camping options, you'll find a lot to like about the trout and bass angling in this corner of the state. From mountain lakes to desert reservoirs, you'll be able to catch your limit of rainbow, brook, cutthroat and German brown trout as well as largemouth, smallmouth and striped bass, walleye, bluegill and crappie. Many of our fishing holes have been stocked by the Utah Division of Fish and Wildlife.

Fishing licenses can be purchased at sporting goods stores and lodging facilities in St. George, Hurricane, Kanab, Cedar City and Panguitch. License fees for Utah residents ages 14 through 64 are $18 per year (the season runs January 1 through December 31, 24 hours a day). A one-day fishing permit for a state resident 14 or older is $4; a seven-day permit is $9. An annual license for residents 65 and older is $9. For non-residents, the annual license is $40. A non-resident one-day license is $5; a seven-day license is $15.

Anyone 13 years old or younger wanting to take a full bag and possession limit can purchase a license at the above rates. Be sure to pick up a current free Utah Fishing Proclamation when you purchase your license. In it you'll find specific information about fishing

---

INSIDERS' TIP

Depending on the temperature, March, April or May will find the desert blooming as a rose! Bring a camera for intimate close-ups of cactus flowers and to capture critters (on film, of course).

limits, regulations and guidelines pertaining to the particular fishery you're interested in.

St. George/Zion

Baker Reservoir

This little lake on the northwest flank of Pine Valley Mountain is about 22 miles north of St. George on Utah 18, between the towns of Veyo and Central. It's a small waterhole along the Santa Clara River where you can catch rainbow and German brown trout (they're a little browner than traditional brown trout). You can almost throw a rock across the reservoir, but boats are still allowed. There's a nice campground here as well (see Camping earlier in this chapter).

Enterprise Reservoir

The town of Enterprise is 35 miles north of St. George on Utah 18. Enterprise Reservoir is a secluded, manmade body of water 10 miles west of town off Shoal Creek Road leading out the west end of town. The reservoir has a boat launch, and the excellent Honeycomb Rocks Campground (see Camping in this chapter) is nearby. Enterprise is stocked with rainbow, German brown and brook trout. Locals also enjoy fishing for bass here. Check the Utah Fishing Proclamation — the reservoir is generally closed to fishing from January 1 through late May. June is an excellent month to fish here.

Gunlock Reservoir

Built in 1970, this state park captures the water of the Santa Clara River for irrigation and flood-control purposes. A wonderful by-product is the excellent fishing that has resulted. The reservoir is about 25 miles from St. George off U.S. 91, about 1 mile south of the historic community of Gunlock. The lake is 2 miles long, about a half-mile wide and reaches a depth of 115 feet. There's a boat ramp, and the lake is stocked with largemouth bass, black crappie, threadfin shad and channel catfish. The lake has a great reputation among bass anglers, but they say it can be temperamental at times.

Kolob Reservoir

Just outside the boundaries of Zion National Park, 23 miles north of the town of Virgin on the Kolob Terrace Road, Kolob Reservoir is a majestic body of water, set among aspen and pine trees, stocked with rainbow, German brown, brook and cutthroat trout.

Pine Valley Reservoir

For pure mountain serenity, this is a favorite fishing hole sitting among the towering ponderosa pines at the foot of Pine Valley Mountain. It's 36 miles north of St. George off Utah 18. The brook and rainbow trout are not large here, but chances are good you'll fill your frying pan. While fishing from the shore (you may not fish from a boat or float tube here), look over your shoulder once in a while and you'll probably see a mule deer grazing behind you. The Pine Valley Recreation Area campgrounds are just a couple hundred yards down the road (see Camping, above).

Quail Lake

Built in 1985, this is a 40,000-acre-foot reservoir 14 miles northeast of St. George off Utah 9. It is in a state park (see our Parks and Other Natural Wonders chapter) and has an excellent campground (see Camping in this chapter). The facility is well-equipped with modern restrooms, drinking water and picnic facilities, and it is wheelchair-accessible. There are two boat ramps.

This reservoir is known as one of Utah's best fisheries for largemouth bass. There's also rainbow trout, bluegill and crappie. According to some in the know, trout hit best in late spring

---

INSIDERS' TIP

Note that in Utah a new state law allows minors 12 to 17 years of age to operate personal watercraft (PWC) on their own only if they have successfully completed a PWC class offered by Utah State Parks and Recreation.

at Quail Lake, then go deep until October. You can entice the bass here until early summer. Trout limit is six, same as the bass limit.

Zion View Ostrich Ranch Trout Ponds

Okay, we know it sounds a bit non sequitur — ostrich ranching and fishing. So for now, just forget the ostrich ranch part and think about the trout. These are private ponds near Hurricane which just happen to be next to an ostrich ranch.

Take Utah Highway 59 out of Hurricane (this is the road to Kanab and Lake Powell), and drive 3 miles to the turnoff to Zion View. Three ponds with varying sizes of trout grace this pristine setting. With advance reservations you can fish for a half-day or full-day at rates ranging from $15 for kids to $40 for adults. There's bait as well as fly fishing, and it's catch and release unless you wish to purchase the fish you land for an additional $4 per pound. The average rainbow trout taken here is three pounds, but trophies of up to eight pounds are sometimes caught. In an area where fishing can be feast or famine, this is a great place to guarantee yourself or your kids a bountiful angling experience. Contact Hurst Sports Center in St. George, 160 N. 500 West, 673-6141, for more details.

Cedar City/Brian Head

Navajo Lake

In its awesome setting in the 9,000-foot reaches of Cedar Mountain, this is one of the few natural lakes in Southwestern Utah. It is just off Utah 14, about 28 miles east of Cedar City. Here you can fish for rainbow, German brown, brook and cutthroat trout in a setting not much different from what it would have

been a century or two ago. There's plenty of great camping around the lake (see Camping in this chapter).

Contrary to what you might think, Navajo Indians never inhabited the Cedar Mountain area. The name of the lake resulted from a skirmish fought near there in pioneer times — Navajos came from the southeast and encountered early Mormon pioneers in the area. The indigenous Paiutes called the lake "Pah-cu-ay," meaning Cloud Lake.

Newcastle Reservoir

Off Utah Highway 56, about 30 miles west of Cedar City, you'll find the very popular Newcastle Reservoir. Smallmouth bass abound here as well as stocked rainbow trout. Fed by the waters of Pinto Creek, the lake has a good reputation for both those fish types in a setting that is right on the borderline between desert and mountain.

Parowan Creek

Fishing on Parowan Creek begins about 5 miles south of Parowan on Utah 143 at the road to Yankee Meadows. You can fish the narrow, rapid stream most of the way up the 8-mile canyon to Brian Head Resort. It's a great place to test your fly-fishing skills in a crystal-clear stream stocked with rainbow, brook, cutthroat and German brown trout.

Bryce Canyon Area

Panguitch Lake

This beautiful mountain lake has got to be the fishing heart of Southwestern Utah. On Utah 143, about 42 miles from Bryce Canyon and 18 miles southwest of Panguitch, the lake sits at 8,250 feet above sea level. It has two public boat ramps and a fish-cleaning station.

INSIDERS' TIP

The desert is a wonderful place, but extreme variation in temperature and altitude as well as many unmarked or unpaved wilderness roads are potential problems for unwary travelers. When exploring in the desert, always use a map and tell someone where you are going. Be sure you have food, water and a full gas tank.

The lake's 10-mile shoreline offers some good fishing, but it's better from boats that can be rented at several businesses along the shore.

Rainbow trout here average 11 inches, and there are larger cutthroat and brook trout. Trout limit is six. Panguitch Lake also has the best (and just about the only) ice fishing in Southwestern Utah, and the frozen lake provides a popular surface for cross-country skiers (see Cross-Country Skiing, above). Check with the Garfield travel office in Panguitch, (800) 444-6689, for current information on what roads are open leading to Panguitch Lake. Conditions will vary according to snowpack and snow removal.

Panguitch Creek

Much of this creek is accessible along the 18-mile route of Utah 143 between Panguitch and Panguitch Lake. Just pull off the highway and try your luck. The creek is stocked with rainbow and brown trout.

Tropic Reservoir

A very popular mountain reservoir, Tropic is about 7 miles south of Utah 12. Take U.S. 89 south from Panguitch to Utah 12, then about 3 miles west of the Bryce Canyon junction of Utah 12 and Utah 83 turn south onto the King Creek Campground gravel road — it is accessible by two-wheel drive vehicles. At an elevation of 7,831 feet, this is a large lake surrounded by ponderosa pines. You'll catch rainbow, brook and cutthroat trout here. There's a boat ramp, but fishing is best in the streams above the lake and below the dam — just fair to good in the lake itself. King Creek Campground (see Camping in this chapter) is next to the lake.

Watersports

Watersports facilities are one of Southwestern Utah's weaknesses, unless, of course, we fudge and include one of the largest and most popular manmade lakes in America — Lake Powell. While Powell is outside the geographic parameters of our book, it is just 150 miles away — a three-hour drive from St. George — and definitely should be considered as part of your Southwestern Utah itinerary if you're passionate about houseboating, waterskiing, windsurfing or using your personal watercraft. (See the Glen Canyon Recreation Area entry

in our Daytrips and Weekend Getaways chapter for more on Lake Powell.)

Closer to home, the two bodies of water in Southwestern Utah best-suited for the above activities (excluding houseboating) are Gunlock State Park and Quail Creek State Park. The other lakes in this area are dedicated mainly to fishing — most of the boats you see on them will have fishing lines dangling over the side as opposed to ski ropes trailing off the back.

The use of Jet Skis and other personal watercraft is growing here. Note that in Utah a new state law allows minors 12 to 17 years of age to operate personal watercraft (PWC) on their own only if they have successfully completed a PWC class offered by Utah State Parks and Recreation. Upon completion, a brightly colored tag is issued that must be attached to the operator's life jacket while riding. Besides the education requirement, operators 12 to 15 years of age must be under direct supervision of someone 18 or older. Anyone younger than 18 who has not met these requirements may not operate a PWC unless accompanied onboard by a person who is at least 18. For PWC class information, contact the state's PWC education hotline at (800) RIDE-PWC.

Gunlock Reservoir
Gunlock State Park, Off U.S. Hwy. 91, 15 miles northwest of St. George, Santa Clara • 628-2255

This 240-acre reservoir captures water from the Santa Clara River in a majestic red rock and black lava rock setting 15 miles northwest of St. George off U.S. 91. Boating, windsurfing, waterskiing and personal watercrafting are favorite activities here. It's also a great fishing spot (see Fishing). Because the boating options are few in Southwestern Utah, Gunlock is a very busy place. We suggest early- and late-season use — March, April and September are good months to find less traffic. Also, if you can avoid weekends and holidays you'll have a much better experience. There's an excellent boat ramp and toilets but not much more.

Quail Lake
Quail Creek State Park, Off Utah Hwy. 9, 14 miles east of St. George • 879-2378

The scenic splendor of Quail Lake gives you the feeling you've come to a smaller Lake

Powell The 590-acre lake is 3 miles east of I-15 Exit 16 (Hurricane), a total of 14 miles from St. George. This is the largest boating lake in Southwestern Utah (barring Lake Powell, of course) and is ideal for waterskiing, windsurfing and riding personal watercraft. Open year round, you can enjoy trout and bass fishing here when you're not boating (see Fishing). There is a paved boat ramp and docks, a nice campground (see Camping, above), modern restrooms, a fish-cleaning station and two covered, group-use pavilions. Day-use fee is $5, and the camping fee is $8 per night.)

Off-Road Outings

Due to the millions of acres of public lands and thousands of miles of dirt roads in Southwestern Utah, off-highway vehicle (OHV) enthusiasts love the place. There are few areas dedicated exclusively to OHV use, but there are plenty of places available to drive your four-wheel-drive vehicle, all-terrain vehicle, dune buggy or dirt bike.

Registered OHVs may be operated on public lands or roads that are signed or designated as open to OHV use. The U.S. Forest Service and BLM offices in each area have maps indicating areas where OHV use is permitted. No one under 8 years old may operate an OHV on public roads, trails or lands. Drivers 8 to 15 must have an OHV education certificate issued by the Utah Division of Parks and Recreation. The certificate is obtainable by completing an education course offered by the Parks and Recreation folks or passing an OHV knowledge and skills test. Drivers 16 years and older must have a valid driver's license or an OHV certificate. If you're under 18, the law requires you wear a helmet. If you're older than 18, you should be wise enough to wear one even though you're not required to.

Coral Pink Sand Dunes

This is the ultimate off-highway vehicle venue in Southwestern Utah, 12 miles off U.S. 89 and 22 miles northwest of Kanab. The park is administered by the Utah State Parks and

Recreation office. The wide-sweeping expanse of the sand dunes makes this one of the most popular places to four-wheel, dune buggy or ride an ATV in all the West. There's a resident ranger on duty year round, reachable at 648-2800. Plan to pay a $3 day-use fee. There's also a great campground (see Camping in this chapter).

Downhill Skiing

Since the 1930s, Utah has been building a reputation as the home of some of the greatest downhill skiing in the world. That reputation was officially cast in stone in 1995, when Salt Lake City was selected by the International Olympic Committee as the site of the 2002 Winter Olympic Games. Ski resorts such as Alta, Brighton, Snowbird, Park City, Deer Valley, Sundance and others have hosted skiers from all over the world for decades. Those resorts are clustered 300 miles north of Southwestern Utah in the high reaches of the Wasatch Mountains near the metropolitan areas of Salt Lake City, Ogden and Provo.

While the southern portion of Utah is best known for its national parks and desert-style recreation such as hiking, camping, rock climbing and biking, a quirk of nature and geography has placed one of the state's best ski resorts smack in the middle of our area, within a 90-minute drive of St. George. Every year, more and more people prove the claim that it's possible to get in a comfortable morning round of golf on a St. George course and a great afternoon on the ski slopes of Brian Head Resort on the same winter's day.

Brian Head Resort
Utah Hwy. 143, Brian Head • 677-2035, (800) 27-BRIAN

Twelve miles up the canyon from Parowan on Utah 143, Brian Head Resort is not only Utah's southernmost ski facility, it is also the highest-altitude ski resort in the state. Elevations range from 9,600 to 11,307 feet above sea level, assuring great snow conditions through most of the winter.

Ample state-of-the-art snowmaking equipment helps take up the slack for Mother Nature when necessary. Lifts are nearly always open by Thanksgiving; often much earlier. The season continues into April. Average snowfall at Brian Head is 450 inches. Lifts normally open at 9 AM and close at 4:30 PM. There's night skiing until 10 PM on weekends and holidays. Set at the top of Cedar Mountain at the southern end of the Wasatch range, Brian Head is a year-round community nestled within a lush forest of pine, fir and aspen trees.

The contrast between this alpine setting and the Mojave Desert, just 60 miles to the south, is phenomenal. As you enter Brian Head after the 12-mile climb on a two-lane, multi-switchback highway from Parowan, you see the Brian Head Hotel complex on the right. Next you come to the turnoff to **Navajo Lodge**, visible from the highway, where you can purchase lift tickets and rent skis. There's also a snack bar and ski shop, but no overnight lodging. (See our Accommodations chapter for information on places to stay in Brian Head.) Utah 143 continues to wind up the mountain another mile past condominium complexes, shops and restaurants (see our Restaurants and Shopping chapters for more information), to the **Giant Steps Lodge** on the left. There's a huge parking lot at the base of Giant Steps. Here you can also purchase lift passes, rent skis and enjoy the snack bar and socialize.

With six lifts that can accommodate more than 10,000 skiers per hour, Brian Head has 53 runs, trails, chutes and bowls offering terrain for every level of skier and snowboarder. For beginners, there's a great "bunny hill" on the double-chair Pioneer lift at Navajo Lodge. A number of other great runs termed "easy" are accessible from Navajo Lodge on the triple-chair Navajo lift. Named after Las Vegas streets and landmarks, there's The Strip, Maryland Parkway, Fremont and Paradise. These are very friendly runs that allow beginner and intermediate skiers a chance to really get their legs under them before venturing on to Brian Head's greater challenges.

The Giant Steps Lodge is where the more experienced, thrillseeking skiers of Brian Head congregate. From Giant Steps there are four more triple-chair lifts, including Giant Steps, Blackfoot, Roulette and The Dunes. There are a few easier runs at Giant Steps, among them Hunter's Run, Bear Paw and Heavenly Daze, but most of the runs here are termed "more difficult" or "most difficult." Among the many difficult runs are Last Chance, The Plunge, Giant Steps, Bear Paw Pitch, Wild Ride and Straight Up. The skiing from Giant Steps Lodge is considered by many as some of the best in Utah, which, in turn, makes it some of the best in the world.

Snowboarding

The relatively new phenomenon of snowboarding has caught on big at Brian Head. In fact, on any given day you're liable to see as many snowboarders on the slopes as skiers. Obviously, snowboarders are welcome at Brian Head. They have access to the same runs skiers do, but there's also an exclusive snowboarding area with tree runs and free-riding through the glades. It's an ideal place for bonking, big air and half-pipe antics.

All the Way to the Top

For those up to the challenge, Brian Head offers daily snowcat service (weather permitting) to the top of Brian Head Peak at 11,307 feet above sea level. The shuttle leaves on the hour and takes you to extreme heights, where black lava-capped ridges jut out of snow piled at unbelievable depths. From here, once you've swallowed the incredible views, you plunge into narrow chutes, deep powder and big bowls. Check in at Giant Steps Lodge for details.

Ski and Snowboard Rates

Adult skiers and snowboarders can purchase an all-day lift ticket at Brian Head for $32. Again, lifts open at 9 AM and close at 4:30 PM, except weekends and holidays, where there is night skiing. Children ages 6 to 12 and seniors 62 to 69 are $16. Young adults (13 to 18; ID required) are $28. Seniors 70 and older, as well as children 5 and younger who are accompanied by a ticketed adult, are free.

College students with a current student ID can buy an all-day lift ticket for $28. Half-day lift tickets (12:30 to 4:30 PM) are $24 for adults and young adults; children and seniors are $12. Adults and young adults can buy multiple-day lift tickets by paying full price for the

Photo: Lyman Hafen

This waterskier kicks up a wake at Gunlock Reservoir.

first day, $28 for the second day and $26 for each additional day. Children and seniors pay $12 for each additional day. Note that all rates listed are from the 1996-97 ski season and are subject to change in subsequent years.

Ski and Snowboard Rentals

Ski and snowboard rentals are available at both Navajo and Giant Steps lodges. Ski equipment packages (including skis, boots and poles) are $17 per day. Child packages (12 and younger) are $11 per day. Snowboard packages (including board and boots) are $25 per day. Child snowboard packages (12 and younger) are $20 per day. There are multiple-day discounts on all regular rental packages. Ask for details at either lodge.

Instruction/Day Care

Brian Head is a very family-oriented resort. It's popular Kids' Camp at Navajo Lodge is the center of children's programming including day care, lessons, supervision, lift tickets and equipment packages for kids up to 13 years old. Day care for infants and toddlers, open 8:30 AM to 4:30 PM, is $6.50 an hour or $40 for a full day. Kids 2½ years and older are $5 an hour and $27 for a full day.

The "Tiny Tracks," "Kid Cruisers" and "Kid Shredders" programs for children ages 3 to 12 include lift passes, lessons, equipment rentals, lunch and other activities from 8:30 AM to 4 PM. A full day is $65, and a half day is $50. For teenagers there's the "Mt. Explorers," "Mt. Shredders," "Teen Cruisers" and "Teen Shredders" programs — two-hour lessons offered at 10:30 AM and 1:30 PM for $23 (lift and rentals not included).

For frequent family guests, there's the Kids' Camp Mini Pass, providing everything for 10 full days of instruction and skiing for $550. Private, 90-minute lessons are offered at Brian Head for $69. You can add a friend for another $21.

Words of Caution

Obviously, there is an inherent risk in the sports of snow skiing and snowboarding. Under Utah law, that risk is assumed by the skier. Before starting to ski, you should become familiar with the skier's responsibility code, available at both Brian Head ski lodges. Skiers who need to be rescued outside designated area boundaries are responsible for the cost of their own rescue.

Cross-Country Skiing

The mountains and high plateaus of Southwestern Utah offer a variety of possibilities for cross-country skiers. On a bright winter's day there's no better way to experience these pristine mountain settings than by gliding through the forests on a pair of Nordic skis.

Mornings are the best time to experience optimum snow conditions. The quiet and solitude will astound you, and you'll be surprised at how much wildlife activity you'll see. Among the animals you might encounter are foxes, coyotes, mule deer, weasels, porcupines, eagles, ravens, wild turkeys, jays and a variety of other birds.

St. George/Zion

Pine Valley

It's hard to believe you can step off the golf course in a sweater at noon on a sunny winter's day in St. George and within an hour be pushing through powder or gliding across hard-pack on cross-country skis in Pine Valley, just 32 miles away. In the past five years, the Pine Valley Ranger District of Dixie National Forest has begun to groom trails and set track for cross-country skiers in the Pine Valley Recreation Area.

Along the north base of Pine Valley Mountain you can ski to your heart's content among towering ponderosa pines and groves of aspen trees. Trails begin at the reservoir parking lot. There are usually about 5 miles of set track trail and 6 miles of other marked but ungroomed trails. Although you are not restricted to the trails, it's a good idea to stay on them for safety reasons. With the variations in snow conditions, we suggest you call the Pine Valley Ranger District office, 628-0461, ahead of time for current conditions and information on what trails are groomed and open. Cross-country trail maps are available at the Interagency Information Center at 345 E. Riverside Drive in St. George, 628-4491. Ski rentals are available at the **Pine Valley Lodge**, 960 E. Main Street, Pine Valley, 574-2544.

Cedar City/Brian Head

Brian Head-Cedar Breaks

Perhaps the most phenomenal cross-country skiing in Southwestern Utah can be found in the Brian Head/Cedar Breaks area. A number of groomed trails are maintained out of Brian Head, some of which connect with the Cedar Breaks National Monument area. Along the rim of Cedar Breaks, you can follow groomed as well as ungroomed trails that allow you to emerge from the forest from time to time and look out across the vast and ragged red breaks below.

A number of cross-country ski services are offered in Brian Head, including rentals, instruction, maps and guide services at **Brian Head Cross Country Center**, 677-2012, in the Brian Head Hotel at 233 Hunter Ridge Drive; **Brian Head Sports Inc.**, 677-2014, 269 S. Brian Head Boulevard; and **Georg's Ski Shop**, 677-2013, 612 S. Utah 143.

Cedar Mountain

Up the canyon east of Cedar City, you'll find a variety of cross-country skiing options. The best place to start is at **Duck Creek Village**, 682-2495, 30 miles from Cedar City on

---

INSIDERS' TIP

Off-road vehicle drivers who are 8 to 15 must have an OHV education certificate issued by the Utah Division of Parks and Recreation.

Utah 14. At Duck Creek you can rent skis, receive instruction and embark on a number of groomed cross-country trails that take you through heavily forested areas, open meadows and to a number of scenic overlooks. Cross-country ski rentals are also available in Cedar City at **Cedar Mountain Sports**, 921 S. Main Street, 586-4949, in the Albertsons shopping center.

Bryce Canyon Area

Bryce Canyon National Park

Cross-country skiing, in our humble opinion, is the ultimate way to see Bryce Canyon National Park. You basically have the place to yourself, and the white trim of winter snow on the delicate pink spires and pinnacles of the canyon give this already unbelievable place an added degree of magic.

Cross-country skiing is encouraged within the park on a number of marked ski trails. The Fairyland and Paria roads are unplowed during the winter and make excellent skiing routes. The park strongly discourages skiing on the hiking trails leading into the canyon. They are narrow and steep and extremely unsafe for cross-country skiers. Since snow conditions vary throughout the winter and from year to year, you should inquire ahead of time at the park visitors center, 834-5322, for current conditions and to see what trails are opened and groomed.

Panguitch Lake

Just 17 miles southwest of Panguitch, the Panguitch Lake area is crisscrossed by a number of forest roads that make for excellent cross-country skiing adventures. You can make your headquarters anywhere along the lake shore and head out from there. The lake itself offers a great skiing surface, where you're sure to encounter a number of ice fishermen (see Fishing in this chapter) as you glide across the 2-to-3-mile stretch from shore to shore.

You won't find many groomed trails in the Panguitch Lake area, but the forest roads open the way to a number of mountain vistas. Bring your skis with you — no rentals nearby.

Ruby's Inn

Just outside Bryce Canyon National Park on Utah 63, **Ruby's Inn Nordic Center**, 834-5341, maintains about 18 miles of groomed trails and set track for cross-country skiing. In addition, there are many miles of backcountry roads and trails in the Ruby's Inn area. Some of the trails connect with the ungroomed ski trails inside Bryce Canyon National Park.

Snowmobiling

Snowmobiling is a sport that requires either a great deal of expertise and investment in equipment or the services of a local rental and guide agency. Veteran snowmobilers have a variety of options throughout the Southwestern Utah region on unplowed, backcountry roads within Dixie National Forest as well as BLM and state-owned lands.

On the other hand, snowmobiling novices and those who dabble in the sport occasionally can rent machines and take guided or self-guided rides from several business establishments in the Cedar Mountain and Bryce Canyon areas (note that no snowmobiling is allowed within the boundaries of Bryce Canyon National Park). Utah State Parks and Recreation Off-Highway Vehicle (OHV) program managers offer an OHV hotline with updated snowmobile conditions, potential avalanche dangers and trail-grooming schedules. Riders can access the hotline 24 hours a day by calling (800) OHV-RIDE. The hotline also provides information on snowmobiling laws and rules, survival tips and maps.

Cedar Mountain

We suggest you base your snowmobiling adventure at either Brian Head, Duck Creek or Ruby's Inn. Each of these staging points of-

---

INSIDERS' TIP

It's rust — iron oxide — that gives our sandstone formations their beautiful red color.

fers snowmobile rentals, fuel and mechanical service, trail maps and guide service. In between each point are hundreds of miles of marked trails, both groomed and ungroomed depending on current conditions. At 9,000, 10,000 and pushing 11,000 feet above sea level, you can ride through wooded areas, wide open valleys and deep bowls. But the element that makes this region one of the most talked about snowmobiling locales in the world is the incredible number of scenic view points you can ride to. In many places you will break out of the trees and just like that find yourself at the edge of the earth — looking off into such awe-inspiring expanses as Cedar Breaks, Bryce Canyon and the upper reaches of Zion National Park.

Brian Head

Though skiing is the staple activity here, a number of snowmobiling opportunities present themselves at Brian Head. Several unplowed roads as well as groomed trails take you into the surrounding mountain passes and meadows. The most popular route is to exit the town along a trail following Utah 143 eastward to the Cedar Mountain summit, then explore the roads across the top of the mountain, taking in several views of Cedar Breaks looming nearby. Snowmobile rentals and guide service are available at **Crystal Mountain Recreation** in Brian Head, 539 N. Utah Hwy. 143, 677-2386, and in Cedar City at **Cedar Ridge Sports**, 1014 S. Main Street, 586-8272.

Duck Creek

About 30 miles up the canyon east of Cedar City on Utah 14 is Duck Creek Village. You can rent snowmobiles and take daily guided tours on several different groomed trails. One trail is a 45-mile loop extending north into Cedar Breaks National Monument, where you'll experience breathtaking views of the red and pink breaks dusted in white. Another trail takes you southward to Strawberry Point where you can see 100 miles or more to the south, across the drainage that forms Zion Canyon and all the way into Arizona. From Duck Creek you can also ride to Panguitch Lake. Contact **Majestic Mountain Tours**, 61 Movie Ranch Road, Duck Village, 682-2564, for rentals and tour information.

Ruby's Inn

At the entrance to Bryce Canyon National Park on Utah 63, Ruby's Inn, 834-5341, is an ideal staging point for excellent snowmobiling. Bring your snowmobile, and you can enjoy more than 20 miles of groomed trails that begin at Ruby's Inn and extend to the East Fork/Tropic Reservoir area. The trails wind through Dixie National Forest and take you to wonderful open play areas and overviews of Bryce Canyon. Trail maps and guide service are available at Ruby's Inn.

Red Cliffs Mall was the first between Las Vegas and the big cities of the Wasatch Front, and it is still the most recognized mall in Southwestern Utah.

Shopping

Until the Red Cliffs Mall opened in St. George in 1990, the only way a Southwestern Utahn could shop 'til they dropped was by driving to Las Vegas (125 miles south of St. George) or Salt Lake City (275 miles north of Cedar City) for a weekend. Through the years, most of the area's rural communities had been successful in meeting the basic needs of family members for household goods, clothing and shoes. But because most of us made our purchases at the same stores, it was not uncommon to see yourself coming and going — not a lot of variety, in other words. So while the necessities were met at home, the more special items — dresses, furniture, baby clothes, Christmas or back-to-school clothes, even vehicles — required a shopping trip to the big city.

Today, many residents in the outlying communities of Southwestern Utah make regular treks to the Red Cliffs Mall, the rapidly expanding and popular factory outlet stores or to pop in at one of many fun specialty shops in St. George or Cedar City. On any given weekend, Wal-Mart or Kmart in either community look like it might be December 24. And the corner grocery store in most communities still provides both commodities and social opportunity, as friends bump into each other in front of the dairy case.

The suggestions for shopping in this chapter are listed by type of items — antiques, bookstores, family clothes, souvenirs, etc. — and then by geographic area. We can't list every option, but this chapter will give you a good cross-section of stores and shopping in our communities. Those of us who appreciate a good sale agree the choices of merchandise are getting better and better. Trips to Las Vegas and Salt Lake City are less frequent and not much of a necessity anymore, though an occasional jaunt (see our Daytrips and Weekend Getaways chapter) is still a nice break from the routine.

Malls

Along with his work in the Mormon church, Brigham Young is said to have organized America's first department store in 1868 (*Famous First Facts*, by Joseph Kane). Zion's Co-operative Mercantile Institution, an organization of merchants with various wares to sell, opened in Salt Lake City with separate department managers, central control of credit, record keeping and store maintenance. ZCMI (still open, see Red Cliffs Mall listing) started out as "a large building or complex of buildings containing various shops, businesses and restaurants accessible by common passageways." But while the concept of malls may not be new in Utah, their existence in most communities is still pretty uncommon.

We provide a rundown here of the three major mall complexes in Southwestern Utah. As mentioned, Red Cliffs got the mall ball rolling in the area back in 1990, the Zion Factory Stores offers appreciable discounts on your favorite name brands and Promenade at Red Cliff is a brand-new option for shopaholics. All three are in St. George.

Promenade at Red Cliff
250 N. Red Cliff Dr., St. George • 674-9800

The beautiful new Promenade at Red Cliff has been designed to be a gathering place — a place to meet your friends . . . where a leisurely walk might qualify as a social event. An elegant fountain and waterscape murals hanging throughout the facility create an atmosphere of opulence. Opened in June 1997, it's so new the paint is still wet.

Promenade at Red Cliff is off St. George's north exchange of Interstate 15, immediately across from Zion Factory Stores. Southwestern Utah's newest mall has 20 stores. **Big Five** is a sporting goods store headquartered in Las Vegas. **Staples** is a branch of the nationwide chain marketing office supplies and equipment. **Little Professor** is the newest of Southwestern Utah's bookstores, featuring a wide assortment of reading choices for the whole family. You can get your hair cut or styled at **Cost Cutters,** while **Sally's Beauty Supply** carries a full line of merchandise to add sparkle and color to your do.

Gold Standard Jewelers is a fine jewelry store, and **Franklin Quest** helps you manage your time with pocket-size, purse-size and notebook-size planners and accessories. **Bread Basket**, with whole-wheat and other healthy breads and sandwiches; **Juice Crew**, with a variety of fresh-squeezed juices; **Cold Stone Creamery**, makers of fresh ice cream; and **RJ's Nut House** will satisfy your craving for lunch, dinner or a sweet treat. **Vitamin World** aims to keep you healthy.

Music Oasis is moving across the street from Zion Factory Stores to offer a large selection of cassettes and CDs. **Rags** is a department store outlet with six stores in Utah. This newest addition will feature discount pricing on overruns of department store merchandise including clothing for everyone in the family, cosmetics, furniture, shoes and other goodies. There are still a few empty spaces available for tenants, but Promenade at Red Cliff will open August 1 with the usual fanfare.

Red Cliffs Mall
1770 E. Red Cliff Dr., St. George
• 673-0099

"Where do you get off looking for good shopping?" queries a billboard near Exit 10 on I-15. The answer for most of us in Southwestern Utah (and many folks in eastern Nevada) is Red Cliffs Mall.

Though Red Cliffs Mall is no longer, by the dictionary's definition, the only mall in the area, it was the first between Las Vegas and the big cities of the Wasatch Front, and it is still the most recognized in Southwestern Utah. This large building contains various shops, businesses and restaurants accessible by common passageways opened with a great deal of hoopla and fanfare in 1990. A jubilant community of shoppers saw the mall's opening as

a step in the right direction in our area's commercial progress.

Red Cliffs Mall boasts 50 stores catering to just about any shopping need. **Debs** and **Vanity** fill the fashion bill for teens and young women, while **Adrian's** dresses the guys for business, prom night or leisure time. A nice assortment of footwear for the athlete and the wannabes sells at **Foot Locker**, while shoes for the whole family can be found at **Payless**, part of the national chain.

Still looking for shoes and more? Try **ZCMI** (Zion's Co-operative Mercantile Institution) — America's first department store (see above) and one of the mall's three anchor stores. **JCPenney**, a perennial favorite for just about anything, and **Wal-Mart** are the other two anchors.

The mall sports two eyewear options. **Lee Optical** provides eyeglasses and exams, while **Sun Stop** can fit any face with fashionable sunglasses. There's a jewelry store on three corners of the mall's center court. **McArthur Jewelers** is the second of two successful homegrown, family-owned stores (the other is on Main Street in downtown St. George); **Fred Meyer Jewelers** is a division of the national department store chain by the same name; and on the third corner, **Adams Fine Jewelry** is the new kid on the block. Corner number four houses **Software Inc.**, a computer software retailer.

For cosmetics or beauty services, Red Cliffs Mall has three options: **Regis Hairstylist** offers hair care for walk-ins or by appointment; **Robyn Todd** can give you a new do or help you stock up on your favorite hair care and beauty products; and **Uncommon Scents** sells bath and beauty products and candles. Then when your hair and face look just right, accessories — earrings, ribbons, bows, baubles, bangles and beads — can be found at **Claire's Boutique**, another national chain store.

Specialty apparel is on sale in a variety of locations up and down the mall's common passageways. For denims and school attire, **County Seat** attracts the teen crowd. **Maurice's** snares the young and young-at-

FYI

Unless otherwise noted, the area code for all phone numbers listed in this chapter is 801 but will change to 435 in September 1997. Either area code may be used until March 22, 1998.

heart drawn in by attractive window displays and the look for the '90s. **Pro Image** has clothing lines for the sports fan(atic) who believes in putting his money where his team loyalty is. Hats, T-shirts, jackets, even kids' clothes monogrammed with your team-of-choice can be found at Pro Image. If frills and lace are your thing, **Lee's** is certain to have something tempting. Dresses for girls of any age are Lee's specialty.

Helping to round out Red Cliffs Mall's tenant list are **Keith Jorgensen Music**, a piano store and more; **Radio Shack**, with lots of electronics including telephones, answering machines, toys, games and other amazing gadgets for the technologically inclined; **Sam Goody Records and Tapes**; and **Tilt**, a razzle-dazzle game heaven where a few quarters will keep the kids occupied for hours.

Wait! There's more. **Alert Medical** is a retailer of medical supplies, **Nilsson Hearing Center** offers hearing aid sales and services, **STIX** sells golfing merchandise, **B. Dalton Bookseller** is part of the national chain for books and magazines and **Coach House** and **Spirit of the West** have gifts that run the gamut from elegant to just plain fun. **Home Sweet Home** is perfect for kitchen gadgetry and cooking utensils of every size, shape and purpose, and **GNP** is the local outlet in the national health-food store chain.

OK, you've checked everything off your shopping list. You're tired, hungry and just want to do a little people watching. Try any of the nine restaurants and eateries in the Red Cliffs Food Court. Kids of any age will enjoy a slice of tasty pizza from **Pizza Cutter**, a burrito supreme from **Taco Time** or a burger from **Broilerworks**. For the more mature palate, **Jazzy Java** offers espresso and other coffee favorites, and **Orange Julius** is the place for whipped fruit drink specialties and gourmet hot dogs. Try **Blimpies** for a hoagie sandwich made your way. Then for dessert, **Dixie Frozen Yogurt** has a variety of flavors with your choice of fruit or candy toppings, or you can sample some hand-dipped chocolates at **Kara Chocolates**.

Red Cliffs Mall prides itself on its creative events as well as its fashion statements. Throughout the year, mall managers keep coming up with new and different displays, activities and entertainment. Trick-or-treat in the mall is a safe way to celebrate Halloween. The mall's Santa Village for the Christmas season gets bigger and better every season. A gigantic sand sculpture that occupies the center court for a month or more at a time is an imaginative method for showing off the best features of the area. "Be True to Your School" is a creative fund-raiser where the mall donates a percentage of profits to the school of your choice based on your sales receipts.

There are also live dance and musical performances and art exhibits at Red Cliffs. The mall serves as the starting point for the annual Southern Utah Homebuilders Association Parade of Homes and participates in a number of health fairs, symphony performances and fashion shows during any calendar year. Red Cliffs Mall is open Monday through Saturday from 10 AM to 9 PM and Sunday from noon to 5 PM. The mall is off I-15 at Exit 8 if you're traveling northbound or Exit 10 heading south.

Zion Factory Stores

250 N. Red Cliff Dr., St. George • 674-9800, (800) ANY TOUR

Bus tours love this place! So do travelers who pull off the freeway to check it out, families with tight budgets and teens with an affinity for recognizable brand names. Every day prices are advertised at 20 to 70 percent off regular retail prices for merchandise by heavy-hitters like **Van Heusen**, **ENUF**, **Carole Little**, **Polo-Ralph Lauren**, **Corning Revere**, **Bugle Boy** and **Carter's Childrens Wear**.

Zion Factory Stores currently has 39 vendors. Designer fashion and apparel outlets also include **Clothestime**, **J. Crew**, **Fashion Gear**, **Full Size Fashions**, **Nautica**, **SBX**, **Westport LTD** and **Westport Woman**. Shoes and accessories are sold at **Banister**, **Bass Shoes**, **Coach Factory Stores**, **Etienne Aigner**, **Leather Loft**, **L'Eggs/Hanes/Bali**, **Nine West** and **Socks Galore**. The locally owned **Rebel Sports** also markets famous-brand sportswear. Corning Revere and **Kitchen Collection** offer housewares, cooking utensils and gadgets for the family chef.

Gifts and specialty items are available through **Book Warehouse**, **Canyon Land Gifts**, **Keepsake Korner**, **Prestige Fragrance and Cosmetics**, **Welcome Home** and **Music**

Oasis. And while you have your photos processed in an hour at **Camera Country**, you'll enjoy sampling the wares at **Rocky Mountain Chocolate Factory** and **Red Rock Bagels**. Zion Factory Stores is open Monday through Saturday from 10 AM to 8 PM and Sunday from 11 AM to 5 PM.

Antiques

Collectors will like Southwestern Utah. In 150-year-old communities, history and heritage are a part of our everyday lives. Antique shops — or at least shelves with a few treasures for sale — can be found just about anywhere you go.

St. George/Zion

Antique Showcase
9 N. 100 West, St. George • 652-9956, (888) 652-9956

Antique Showcase specializes in delectable collectibles and antiques. They have sold such rare and interesting pieces as a 2-foot-wide roll top desk, the brass bell from a locomotive (c. 1890), a Remington pistol (c. 1880) with dice in the handle and a brass lamp from a ship sunk off the California Coast in the late 1800s. Antique Showcase is also home to a lamp doctor with hard-to-find replacement parts for antique lamps. You'll find reflector bowls, UNO sockets (for the old-fashioned, brass pull-chain sockets), other sockets in antique brass and bronze, rayon cord sets and glass shades for hurricane lamps.

The staff at Antique Showcase also makes custom lampshades. Other merchandise includes Victorian and vintage lighting, clocks, glasswares, unique cookie jars, railroad and mining memorabilia, paper and labels and depression glass. Antique Showcase is open in winter Monday through Friday from noon to 6 PM and on Saturday from 10 AM to 6 PM.

During summer, the shop is open Monday through Saturday from 10 AM to 6 PM.

Dixie Trading Post
111 W. St. George Blvd., St. George • 628-7333

Cowboy collectors take note! The shelves of Dixie Trading Post are lined with beautiful depression glass, old bottles, collectible pottery and crocks and decorative, rustic Western collectibles. You'll find old silverplate pieces, cast-iron apple peelers, coffee grinders, ceramic water pitchers and unusual memorabilia from seasoned spurs and jewelry to well-used tools.

Dixie Trading Post also has some wonderful framed treasures in Victorian-era prints, old movie posters and prints of Charles Russell paintings. They will help you decorate your new home or condominium in much the same way they've helped decorate a lot of area businesses and restaurants. Dixie Trading Post, on the Boulevard, is open Monday through Saturday from 10:30 AM to 6 PM.

General Store Antiques
640 E. St. George Blvd. St. George • 628-8858

There's only so much you can buy for yourself, says Aggie Barnum of her enthusiasm for antiques and collectibles. Fourteen years ago, the same enthusiasm that drew her to garage sales and swap meets from central Utah to Las Vegas turned into a business. Scrounging for merchandise eventually gave way to an eclectic inventory supplied by people in the community who want to peddle their treasures for others to enjoy.

General Store Antiques specializes in both antiques (those rare finds more than 100 years old) and collectibles (the special items people are crazy about, but that aren't yet old enough to be considered antiques). General Store Antiques is open Monday through Saturday from 11 AM to 5 PM.

INSIDERS' TIP

Red Cliffs Mall opens every morning, Monday through Saturday, at 6 AM to allow walkers the opportunity to get in a few laps up and down the corridors when it is raining, too cold or too hot outside.

Holland House
70 N. 500 East, St. George • 628-0176

This little antiques-and-more shop is in a quaint, historic home just off St. George Boulevard at 500 East. Although they sell beautiful old things, the place is as much a Victorian-era boutique as a traditional antique store. Holland House carries a wonderful assortment of decorator accessories, delicate dried floral arrangements, aromatic fragrances and pot-pourri, bath oils, kitchen decor, oil lamps, Boyd's Bears and Battenburg lace. Holland House customers come back again and again to check out new products. The store is open Monday through Saturday from 10 AM to 5 PM.

Kanab Area

Antiques 'N' Wanna-Bees
1739 S. 175 East, Kanab • 644-5955

A "wanna-bee" is an antique that hasn't quite made it. It could be just a little too young (100 years makes it official) or a copy rather than an original. But for those who enjoy unique and fun merchandise, this shop has lots of goodies to choose from. Collectors will want to browse through the foundry patterns — everything from chocolate molds to crap table designs, kerosene lamps, flat irons and spittoons. Primitives include Native American dolls, jewelry and art work. There's "carnival" glass in iridescent beige or blue and an authentic Rockola jukebox (c. 1925). Antique furniture on display includes an armoire, wardrobes, a wash stand (*sans* the marble top) and a fainting couch. There's a wood-burning stove plucked from the caboose of a fast-moving train and waterfall furniture designs. Antiques 'N' Wanna-Bees is open Monday, Thursday and Friday from 10:30 AM to 5 PM (closed during lunch hour).

Past Tymes Antiques and Crafts
4 E. Center St., Kanab • 644-8855

In the open, friendly atmosphere of Past Tymes Antiques and Crafts, you'll find a delightful collection of antiques, collectibles, country items and local crafts for sale at reasonable prices. This is one of those places you'll want to check out every time you pass through Kanab, since their merchandise changes regularly. They do, however, maintain a good selection of Fenton glass, Boyd's Bears and antique glassware. Past Tymes in Kanab is open Monday through Saturday from 9 AM to 6 PM.

Bookstores

Bookstores abound in Southwestern Utah, where reading is a combination of leisure time activity, educational pursuit and a way to stay in touch with the world around us. After a pleasant day on the ski slopes of Brian Head, relaxing in front of a roaring fire with a good book is the stuff true vacations are made of! When it's too hot to hike, golf or play tennis, the backyard hammock, a shade tree, a tall cool drink and a book . . . ahhh, it doesn't get any better than that!

The area offers lots to choose from. Children's books, hardback studies of religion and politics, popular fiction and paperback romance novels can be found through a variety of outlets. Most campgrounds in and around our spectacular state and national parks have a place to buy, sell or trade your paperback novels.

St. George/Zion

Art In Nature Emporium
868 Zion Park Blvd., Springdale
• 772-3877

Art In Nature is in the Old Church in the center of Springdale. Built in the early 1930s, this renovated brick building now houses Zion Pizza and Noodle Company, Michael Fatali Gallery (see our Arts and Culture chapter) and this popular bookstore specializing in unique books and gifts. Interested in the natural history of the area? The old West? Art In Nature has a large assortment of regional, hiking, natural history, general information, Western fiction, psychology and spirituality books. Gifts include ceramics, glass art, posters and prints, jewelry, T-shirts and children's educational toys. Art In Nature Emporium is open daily year round from 9 AM to 10 PM.

Inventor Finds A Niche For His Chums

"I wish I'd thought of that!"

Is there anyone alive who hasn't said it about some simple invention that has made it big in the worldwide marketplace?

Mike Taggett, from Hurricane, is living proof that with a good idea and a little luck, the great American dream of running your own multi-million-dollar company can still become a reality.

Chums, an eyewear retainer company, has thrived in Hurricane since 1983. The company goal from the beginning has been to strengthen the local economy while building an international reputation for practical, well-made products. Now employing more than 65  residents from surrounding Southwestern Utah communities, Chums manufactured and shipped its 10-millionth eyewear retainer in 1996. A variety of 16 products bearing the Chums label are sold throughout the United States and to foreign markets in 30 countries.

The good idea part of this story came to Taggett in the early '80s while he worked as a guide on the Colorado River. All summer long he watched the roaring whitewater rapids claim its fair share of glasses from thrill-seeking river runners. With a $60 sewing machine, some fabric, elastic and an adjustable bead, Taggett created Chums (named for a friend's loyal Labrador retriever) — a solution to keeping glasses and their wearers together.

Photo: David Stoecklein Photography

Mike Taggett has seen his Chums become must-have eyewear accessories.

The luck came in 1984. After a few improvements and revisions to the original design, Taggett struck it big when a U.S. Swatch licenser purchased 10,000 Chums as part of a "gift with purchase" program. Impressed with the positive reaction from the giveaway promotion, Swatch placed an order for 280,000 more Chums.

With a down payment from Swatch, Taggett set up shop in Hurricane using contracted seamstresses and assembly workers to help complete the enormous order. Even as the order was being shipped, Taggett was at work extending the Chums line.

An inventor at heart, Taggett in 1987 introduced Little Chums, a shorter, smaller version for kids, and a key fob called the Chumthing. At the same time, he began designing and manufacturing a clothing line that the company markets as "the ultimate in relaxation wear."

HelloWear is heavy-duty, all-cotton sportswear, perfect for slipping on after a hard day on the river, the slopes or at the workplace. Chums Research was formed in 1988. With a focus on designing new machinery for Chums production, engineers also began looking for alternative energy systems and automation for use by other companies.

— continued on next page

Japanese consumers have embraced HelloWear in a big way. Retailers in that country and worldwide are placing enormous orders that have required Chums to step up production to meet the demand. George Seifert, former head coach of the NFL's San Francisco 49ers, has officially endorsed Chums as his eyewear retainer of choice. Chums has now become a necessary part of the standard outdoor and sports uniform. The retainer is important as a way to enforce the use of safety glasses and goggles by keeping the protective devices within easy reach.

Taggett, not content with the status quo, is always on the lookout for new ideas, new markets and ways to improve on existing products and manufacturing techniques. The future looks bright for Taggett and his Chums.

Beehive Book

1330 W. Sunset Blvd., St. George
• 652-1011, (888) 652-1011

Looking for a bargain on a nice gift? Buzz on over to Beehive Book. They carry lots of LDS-related books, tapes and CDs, pictures, children's books, classics, some computer software and more. Beehive Book also has copy, laminating and fax services, and they carry a large assortment of scrapbook supplies. This new entry in the bookstore marketplace opened in 1996. Hours of business are Monday through Friday from 9 AM to 6 PM and Saturday from 10 AM to 6 PM.

Deseret Book

779 S. Bluff Street St. George • 628-4495, (800) 300-0242

Deseret Book opened in St. George in 1984 but is part of a nationwide chain of bookstores known for its large selection of Mormon publications. Committed to selling quality merchandise, some of which is secular, Deseret Book has hundreds of titles in fiction, nonfiction, gospel study, scriptures, videos, music tapes and CDs, children's books and gift items. Deseret Book is open Monday through Friday from 10 AM to 9 PM and Saturday from 10 AM to 7 PM.

Doc's Book Loft

295 S. Main Street, St. George • 634-1039

The Doc has always enjoyed a good book — from childhood all the way through medical school. It wasn't enough just to read one, he had to own it. His collection grew and grew until the only thing left to do was open his own bookstore. In an old pioneer home on St. George's Main Street, he opened Doc's Book Loft in 1995, specializing in old, rare and used books. He'll trade or sell. Browse through the main selection area at Doc's, where books are arranged by categories and alphabetized, or immerse yourself in your favorite topic in any of several theme rooms. There are rooms specializing in Westerns, romance, collectibles, mystery and adventure, science fiction and fantasy, and new and popular titles. Doc's Book Loft is open Monday through Saturday from 10 AM to 6 PM.

Purple Crayon Bookstore

344 E. Sunland Drive, No. 6, St. George
• 674-7707

The Purple Crayon Bookstore appeals to the child in all of us. Remember those gentle stories that shaped your perspective of the world even as they sent you nodding off to dream land? Books for babies, picture books and storybooks for children from infants to early teens are the speciality at the Purple Crayon. The staff is very knowledgeable about books in stock, can make recommendations for all age ranges and can order any children's book still in print. The Purple Crayon Bookstore also holds book fairs at local elementary schools and has a story hour at the store every Thursday from 10:30 to 11:15 AM for little ones ages 3 through 7. The Purple Crayon Bookstore is open Monday through Friday from 10 AM to 6 PM and Saturday from 10 AM to 5 PM.

Water, Wind and Time Bookstore

145 Zion Park Blvd., Springdale
• 772-2445

Get in touch with nature at Water, Wind and Time Bookstore in Springdale, outside the gates of majestic Zion National Park. Water, Wind and Time specializes in books on natural history and the cultures of Utah and the American Southwest. This store, in the Zion Canyon Cinemax complex (see our Attractions chapter), also offers a unique mix of gift items including Native American flute music, scenic videos, T-shirts and posters. The bookstore is open from 8:30 AM to 10 PM daily from March through October; 10:30 AM to 7 PM November through February.

Cedar City/Brian Head

A&B's Bookstore
987 N. Main St., Cedar City • 865-1253

The folks at A&B's Bookstore try to treat every customer like they're the only one. In Cedar City, home of Southern Utah University and the famous Utah Shakespearean Festival, A&B's Bookstore carries a varied selection of books including college textbooks and LDS materials. The store is open Monday through Saturday from 8 AM to 6 PM.

Mountain West Books
77 N. Main St., Cedar City • 586-3828, (800) 336-3828

You'd think a selection of 20,000 books in stock would be sufficient to meet the needs of local residents — but if you don't find the book you're looking for, Mountain West Books will special order it and have it in your hands in a day or two. Mountain West offers a complete selection of best sellers and nationally published books along with LDS titles. Don't miss the chance to visit the Sticker Patch, a terrific scrapbook store downstairs at Mountain West Books. This is the place for the hobbyist to find everything for creating heirloom-quality scrapbooks. Mountain West Books has been open Monday through Saturday from 9 AM to 6 PM since 1979.

Kanab Area

Willow Creek Books, Coffee and Outdoor Gear
263 S. 100 East, Kanab • 644-8884

Willow Creek Books, Coffee and Outdoor Gear is certainly eclectic. There's a little bit of bookstore and a hint of coffee shop mingled with the only outdoor gear store within 80 miles of Kanab. The bookstore and coffee shop portions complement each other nicely. Over a hot steamy cup of java, you can leisurely peruse hardbacks, paperbacks, brochures and maps, all designed to provide you with more than a little information about the splendor of Southwestern Utah. (For more on the outdoor product lines, see our listing under Outfitters below.) Willow Creek Books, Coffee and Outdoor Gear is open daily from 8:30 AM to 8:30 PM from mid-April to mid-October.

Crafts/Handmades

Handmade items make wonderful gifts and holiday and home decorations. Besides that, they're just plain fun. Crafters in Southwestern Utah have found their niche in numerous outlets such as these listed.

St. George/Zion

Forget-Me-Nots
431 W. Tabernacle St., St. George • 656-2930, (888) 656-2930

Forget-Me-Nots is new to the area. Opened in December 1996, the store offers a variety of wonderful items, mostly handcrafted by Utah artists and crafters. Forget-Me-Nots has miniatures, dolls, bears, floral displays, home decorator accessories, baby gifts, toys, cards, hemp and bead jewelry — memorable gifts and handmade treasures. Their most popular items are Beanie Babies and Tender Heart Treasures. These merchants pride themselves in the quality of their work and that of the crafters whose work they accept to sell in their shop. They charge no space rental fees for artisans whose work they display, and this allows each crafter to keep prices down. Forget-Me-Nots, across from Smith's Food King on Tabernacle Street, is open Monday through Saturday from 10 AM to 7 PM.

Heindselman's Too
50 E. Tabernacle St., St. George • 652-4694, (888) 414-4694

Heindselman's is a household word in the northern Utah community of Provo. In business since 1904, they have specialized for nearly a

century in helping crafters create products that look "handmade, not homemade." Too is newer to Southwestern Utah, opening in 1994 with the same top-quality supplies for knitting, crocheting, cross-stitchery, needlepoint, crewel, rug making, tatting, lace making, spinning and weaving. Heindselman's Too also provides expert instruction and guidance from selecting the right materials to finishing and framing each item. Too also carries an extensive inventory of gift items including soaps and home products, Madame Alexander collectible dolls, Precious Moments figurines and Nao porcelain figurines from Lladro. Heindselman's Too is open Monday, Tuesday, Thursday, Friday and Saturday from 10 AM to 6 PM.

Cedar City/Brian Head

Country and More
925 S. Main St., Cedar City • 586-3116

Country and More should really be called Country and Lots More. This is really a small mall that displays the handiwork of many crafters in Cedar City and the surrounding communities. For those who enjoy the creative process but have run out of wall space or friends and family to give the stuff to, Country and More is the perfect solution. Crafters are invited to rent 4-by-4-by-8-foot cubicles, then fill them from floor to ceiling with their wares. Open floor space is also available to

antique collectors or larger craft concerns. It's a veritable supermarket of unique gifts for others or treasures to keep for yourself. On display, you'll find home decorating items, dry and silk floral arrangements, gifts, holiday decorations, antiques and country furniture. Country and More is open Monday through Saturday from 10 AM to 6 PM.

Bryce Canyon Area

Favorite Pastimes
415 E. Center St., Panguitch • 676-2689

If handmade craft items are on your list of things to purchase while visiting the Bryce Canyon area, don't miss Favorite Pastimes — a most unique boutique. Open since 1988 in downtown Panguitch, Favorite Pastimes has custom-made bears, dolls, yard-watering figures and other interesting crafts made locally. Business hours are a little out of the ordinary as well. Favorite Pastimes is open 9 AM to 6 PM, Wednesday through Monday during the summer months and Wednesday through Sunday in the winter. Remember it this way: Open Sunday, closed Tuesday.

Family Fashions

Clothing the family for school, church or outdoor activities in Southwestern Utah has never been easier. Department stores in some version or another exist in most small communities, where families can buy coats, shoes and Levis. JCPenney has a presence in St. George and Cedar City. Christensen's is a locally owned department store (see subsequent listing) with outlets in a half-dozen communities. Sears is here, there and everywhere too, most often in the form of catalog stores. Specialty shops, appealing to the fashion sense and style of men, women and children are also popular.

St. George/Zion

Christensen's
761 S. Bluff St., St. George • 628-4213
929 S. Main St., Cedar City • 586-9851

This is one of those really nice stores where the clerks are pleasant and well-dressed, the merchandise is beautifully displayed and you are free to browse to your heart's desire. Christensen's in St. George opened for business in 1983 and is one of several outlets in a family-owned business. Recognizable brand names for ladies, men, juniors and boys and girls include Liz Claiborne, Pendleton, Jones New York, Calvin Klein, Karen Kane, Levis/Dockers, Carol Anderson, Esprit, Lucky, Nautica, Gant, Mossimo and Hart Shafner/Marx. Shoes and accessories are Nine West, Rockport and the current popular favorite Dr. Martens. The merchandise is stylish, prices are competitive and sales are frequent. Unless you're just looking for an excuse to drive to Las Vegas, Christensen's can provide the answer for most of your family clothing needs. They're open Monday through Saturday from 10 AM to 8 PM.

Danco Family Fashions
80 N. Central St., Colorado City, Ariz.
• (520) 875-2715

Colorado City is on the Utah-Arizona border about midway between the Southwestern Utah communities of Hurricane and Kanab. Danco is a popular retailer for men's, women's and children's attire. At this beautiful, outlying location, you'll be pleasantly surprised at the variety of elegant and casual styles available for every member of the family. Danco Family Fashions is open Monday through Saturday from 10 AM to 7 PM.

Evelyn's
23 N. 100 East, St. George • 673-3951

You'll find the nicest things at Evelyn's. The women who shop there are stylish and fashion-conscious, and they come back again and again because owner Kathleen Gubler orders with them in mind. Evelyn's fashions include traditional and updated dresses, sportswear and delicate lingerie with names like Howard Wolf, City Girl, Joseph Ribkoff and Spencer Alexis. At the same location since 1965, the staff at Evelyn's takes great pride in making sure their clientele is also well cared for through special orders, alterations, gift-wrapping and free delivery. Evelyn's is always willing to preview their new merchandise in fashion shows around town. The store is open Monday through Saturday from 10 AM to 6 PM.

FreiDaze
435 N. 1680 East, St. George • 628-8654

Sandra Frei of FreiDaze learned her marketing skills through the years by working with local retailers. She worked hard and paid close attention, picking up the ins and outs of good service, buying, displaying and selling top-quality merchandise. She was such a good student, the time came when she decided to venture out into the world and create her own shop filled with distinctive women's fashions for sizes 3 through 16. FreiDaze specializes in dressy sportswear, contemporary apparel, classic denim and personalized customer service in a shop with plenty of charm and friendly personnel. FreiDaze is open Monday through Saturday from 10 AM to 6 PM.

Cedar City/Brian Head

Enjoy Wear
574 S. Main St., Cedar City • 586-9750

Shoppers enjoy the prices and the clothes at Enjoy Wear, which specializes in the same kind of popular merchandise junior girls and women normally would go to the mall to find. Wardrobe staples including casual wear, knee-length shorts, pants and comfortable denim or knit dresses are offered at low prices. In Renaissance Square for more than 23 years, Enjoy Wear also does a brisk business in T-shirt imprinting. There are hundreds of designs

In an area of the country that draws visitors from all over the world, Zion Factory Stores is a tourist attraction in and of itself.

to choose from, or you can create your own. Enjoy Wear is open Monday through Saturday from 10 AM to 6 PM.

Impressions
45 N. Main St., Cedar City • 586-2261

Impressions has been in the Cedar City area since 1988, offering varied merchandise ranging from sportswear and casual items to dressy dress, formal wear, jewelry, lingerie and other accessories. For junior girls and women, Impressions carries Alfred Dunner, Plaza South, Focus, Z Cavaricci and Lawman. Impressions is open Monday through Saturday from 10 AM to 6 PM.

Mr. R. Menswear
24 N. Main St., Cedar City • 586-2494

Mr. R. has a longstanding reputation for excellent service and quality merchandise including men's suits, sport coats, blazers, dress slacks and shirts, ties, tuxedos and casual clothing. If looking your best is important to you, Mr. R. Menswear is worth checking out. Famous brand names at Mr. R. include Haggar, Arrow, Biltwell suits, Wembley, Wrangler, Rugged Wear, Tabasco shirts and ties and Florsheim shoes. Mr. R. Menswear is open Monday through Saturday from 9:30 AM to 6 PM.

Kanab Area

Duke's Clothing
39 W. Center St., Kanab • 644-2318

For many of us in Southwestern Utah, the official uniform is denim! We like our Levi's and Duke's has a great selection — no, a huge selection . . . in lots of comfortable and popular styles. In addition, you'll find shirts, shorts, jackets and Nike, Reebok and Hi-Tech shoes for running, cross-training and outdoor recreation. Duke's Clothing has a variety of choices for men, women and the kids at reasonable, affordable prices. Need a gift? Duke's ships their Levi's anywhere in the world. This Kanab clothier is open Monday through Saturday from 8 AM to 10 PM during the summer months and from 10 AM to 5 PM from mid-October to mid-May.

Food

St. George/Zion

The Prime Minister
29 W. 200 North, St. George • 652-4682

This little shop gives a whole new perspective on unique. The Prime Minister specializes in British and European specialty foods. You'll find bangers (a breakfast sausage), pastries, crumpets, shepherd's pies, steak and kidney pies, Danish bacon, pork pies, haggis and black pudding. If you want something they don't carry, they'll try to get it for you. The Prime Minister also carries collectibles such as tea services and David Winter cottages and castles. The shop has designated special weeks for English and European gatherings — meet your countrymen during English Week, Irish Week, Scottish Week or Netherlands Week, sign the guest book and enjoy the company. The Prime Minister is open Monday through Saturday from 10 AM to 6 PM.

Rocky Mountain Chocolate Factory
250 N. Red Cliff Dr., No. 20, St. George • 652-4327

If you are one of millions of Americans who consider chocolate a food group or the cocoa bean a vegetable, you will not want to pass through St. George without visiting the Rocky Mountain Chocolate Factory in the Zion Factory Stores. At least a couple of senses will go into overdrive when you enter the door. Rocky Mountain Chocolate Factory sells handmade gourmet chocolates, caramel apples and a large supply of sugar-free candies — all made right in the store. There are also chocolate-themed aprons, T-shirts, mugs and recipe books. By the way, don't miss the bear by the

front door. He's stuffed, and you will be too, unless you have an iron will. Rocky Mountain Chocolate Factory is open Monday through Saturday from 10 AM to 8 PM and on Sunday from 11 AM to 5 PM.

Furniture/Housewares

Choices for furniture and housewares were limited until the past decade, when business people began to realize Southwestern Utahns no longer wanted to drive to Las Vegas or Salt Lake for quality home furnishings. There are a few longstanding furniture stores — Boulevard Home Furnishings in St. George and Antone's Interiors in Cedar City, to name two — but for the most part, retail outlets, furniture rental companies, designers and custom builders are relatively new to this marketplace.

St. George/Zion

2 Design
25 N. Main St., St. George • 673-9796

2 Design is new to the area but not to the business. Talented designers provide complete residential interior design services. Merchandise is versatile — from traditional to the most unique. 2 Design can add a few new touches for a fresh look or completely redo any home from the floor to the ceiling. Upholstery and accessories, custom-built furniture and metal accoutrements, window treatments and floor coverings? They have it all. 2 Design will put together an interior that will sing to your soul. The shop is open Monday through Friday from 10 AM to 6 PM and Saturday from 10 AM to 3 PM.

Boulevard Home Furnishings
176 E. St. George Blvd., St. George • 673-9657, (800) 677-2029

It's three levels of furniture, appliances, electronics, carpet and accessories on Southwestern Utah's busiest and most famous main street. Boulevard Home Furnishings has everything you'll need to build or redecorate. Floor to ceiling, wall-to-wall, Boulevard has window treatments, draperies, wallcoverings, hardwood floors, laminates, carpet, tile, pictures, lamps, statuary and greenery. In the center of downtown St. George, Boulevard has been serving building contractors, new home owners and do-it-yourselfers in the tri-state area since 1974. The store also carries dishwashers, refrigerators, ranges, microwaves, freezers, vacuums, stereos, camcorders, TVs, VCRs and furniture for any room in the house or condo. The sales staff is pleasant, and the merchandise is diverse enough to appeal to just about any sense of style or taste. Hours are extended to accommodate busy schedules — Boulevard is open Monday through Friday from 10 AM to 9 PM and Saturday from 10 AM to 6 PM.

Designer Furniture Gallery
170 N. 400 East, St. George • 673-2323, (888) 673-2323

Designer Furniture Gallery is a total home furnishings store. Including what they tout as the largest selection of home accessories in all of Southwestern Utah, Designer Furniture Gallery also has floor and window coverings, a floral shop and interior design services. They can create custom blinds, shutters and draperies and carry such name-brand merchan-

dise as Action, Universal, Bassett, Sealy, Benchcraft and Pro Flooring along with a variety of choices in fabrics and styles. Plant shelf packages and custom florals to match any kind of room decor are affordable and made on the premises. Designer Furniture Gallery is open Monday through Friday from 10 AM to 7 PM. They close at 6 PM on Saturday and are closed Sunday. Can't find a sitter? Bring the kids along. They'll enjoy the play room (fresh cookies baked daily!) while Mom and Dad shop.

Impressions Interior Design and Gifts
929 W. Sunset Blvd., Ste. 8, St. George • 674-2806

This place has pretty and unique merchandise. There are so many nose prints on the windows of this store, it's obvious we're not the only one who thinks so. (We're joking about the nose prints, of course.) Impressions offers high-end furnishings, wallcoverings, carpet, lighting and accessories, but the main emphasis is interior design, customized to the client's budget and style. Brand names include Sherrill

Hidden Treasures at Judd's Store

When you enter the Thomas Judd Store at Greene Gate Village it is truly a "step back in time." The soda fountain, a display of dozens of kinds of candy, the wood floor that has been polished to a rich patina by thousands of busy feet belonging to children from nearby Woodward Elementary School, the smell of Greene Gate's famous breadsticks baking, the tin ceiling and shelves lined with 19th-century merchandise — everything points to past generations and another time. After years of restoring the nine pioneer structures at Greene Gate Village Bed and Breakfast Inn, Mark and Barbara Greene once again in 1988 rolled up their sleeves and began the arduous task of transforming another hidden treasure. This time their project involved cleaning out the adobe brick building behind the store. The Thomas Judd Store had served the merchandising

needs of pioneers, and for years the building out back was used for storage. For several weeks, the Greene's worked to clear and haul away almost a century of accumulated odds and ends. Truckloads of refuse were transported to the city dump, but the Greene's also found some exciting treasures. One obvious find — today on display on the top shelf of Thomas Judd Store — was 50 pairs of new shoes. High-button shoes, manufactured in the 1890s, were stacked neatly in a corner — all still in their original boxes though very much outdated.

Furniture, Frederick Cooper and Tyndale, Thayer Coggin, Hart accessories and Shaw Industries carpeting. If you're looking for some custom treatment, Impressions Interior Design also offers faux finishes and custom furnishings. Impressions has been providing specialized design services to Southwestern Utah homeowners since 1994. The showroom is open Monday through Friday from 10 AM to 6 PM and Saturday from 10 AM to 3 PM.

Rooster Hollow
193 S. Bluff St., St. George • 656-5454

This place is new. Just opened the doors in the spring of 1997, in fact. How do we know it will be a success? The owner/decorator is Mike Andelin, in cahoots with his lifelong partner, Doris (along with Andre and Vanessa Andelin Shields). They created Andelin's Gable House, one of the best-known restaurants in Southwestern Utah (see our Restaurants chapter). OK, you say. So he's a restaurateur. He's also one of the most recognized interior designers in the state. Rooster Hollow, the Andelin family's newest venture, features American country classic antiques and reproductions as well as collectible gift ideas. If you know the Andelin's, you won't be surprised by the eclectic array of furnishings and accessories. If you don't, you'll love the introduction to out-of-the-ordinary treasures for the home, including a great "outdoor living" garden area. And best of all, Mike Andelin's talent is available for design services. Rooster Hollow is open Monday through Saturday from 10 AM to 6 PM.

Zola's Interiors
91 W. 1470 South, St. George • 628-1500

Zola's lifelong passion for fabrics, color and design began in childhood when her grandmother sat her down with a shoe box filled with quilt pieces. After studying for a degree in interior design, Zola worked for others until 1989, when she established her own business specializing in home accessories, beautiful fabrics and interior design services. Zola now has

her own shop, in partnership with her equally talented daughter. Zola's Interiors has everything for the home including exquisite choices in custom drapery, bedspreads, upholstery fabrics, wallcoverings, sofas, chairs, lamps and mirrors. Zola's Interiors is open Monday through Friday from 10 AM to 6 PM and Saturday from 10 AM to 1 PM, or by appointment.

Cedar City/Brian Head

Antone's Interiors
145 N. Main St., Cedar City • 586-4464, (800) 220-4464

FYI

Unless otherwise noted, the area code for all phone numbers listed in this chapter is 801 but will change to 435 in September 1997. Either area code may be used until March 22, 1998.

Antone Hunter, a professional member of the American Society of Interior Designers for more than 30 years, has been offering quality home furnishings to residents of Cedar City and surrounding communities since 1967. Antone's Interiors also provides professional design service, floor and window coverings, wallpaper and accessories for the home. Middle to high-end product lines include Karastan Carpets and Rugs and Pennsylvania House furniture. Antone's Interiors has gained such a following of happy customers through the years, it has been necessary to expand the business. The interior design business has incorporated rooms from the old Lunt Hotel, built in 1929, for their gallery of display rooms. Antone's is open Monday through Saturday from 9 AM to 6 PM.

Brian Head Interiors and Gift Boutique
468 N. Utah Hwy. 143, Brian Head • 677-3330

No job is too small for Brian Head Interiors, where they specialize in making your condominium, mountain cabin or second home a cozy retreat. Open since 1992, Brian Head Interiors has a complete line of home furnishings and accessories in the showroom, and they also handle special orders. The designer/artist also does unique graphic wall art in your choice of style, design, faux finish and color. She admits to "making it up as I go," but the

final product is created with a combination of opaque and transparent paint, pulling from the colors of the room and drawing on the individual taste of each customer. She has done a "leather" wall embellished with local cattle brands, "suede" designs and has worked in marble and knotty pine. Brian Head Interiors is open from 10 AM to 5 PM Thursday through Tuesday. It's closed Wednesday.

Gift Shops/Souvenirs

In an area that sees millions of tourists each year, we have an abundance of terrific gift and souvenir shops. Collectibles, T-shirts, Native American jewelry and crafts, handmade items and postcards can be found in most every town and along the way to the national parks.

St. George/Zion

Bumbleberry Gifts
897 Zion Park Blvd., Springdale • 772-3522

After you've experienced the world-famous bumbleberry pie at Shoneburg's (see our Restaurants chapter), take home some bumbleberry jam or syrup as a souvenir of your trip to Zion National Park. Bumbleberry Gifts, adjacent to Shoneburg's, sells the jam that has been a tourist and local favorite for 50 years. They also carry syrup and Shoneburg's poppy seed salad dressing, Southwestern-style baskets, Native American crafts, rugs, kachina dolls, curios and souvenir T-shirts. Bumbleberry Gifts is open daily from 7 AM to 10 PM, though hours may vary slightly in the winter months.

Christensen's Homeworks
769 S. Bluff St., St. George • 673-2512

Shopping for gifts, housewares and collectibles? Christensen's Homeworks carries a wonderful selection for the bride and groom, holiday giving or to give your own home a lift. The shelves are stacked to the ceiling, filled with decorator pillows, unique cookie jars, bowls and Department 56 miniature holiday houses. There's tableware here that you won't see in every kitchen in your neighborhood. Christensen's also carries glassware, crystal stemware, potpourri, candles, picture frames in a variety of colors and textures, lush rugs for the bathroom, an assortment of Fieldcrest towels and designer doodads of all shapes and sizes. The bridal registry offers the convenience of phone-in service. Call Homeworks to put the amount of your choice toward the bride and groom's shopping list or drop by the store to make a personal selection for the happy couple. Christensen's Homeworks is open Monday through Saturday from 10 AM to 8 PM.

Christmas Cottage
900 S. Bluff St., St. George • 628-3771

Nothing smells, sounds or feels like Christmas. Here at the cottage, the toy train sounds its whistle as it passes around the base of a year-round tree where lights twinkle merrily summer or winter. Whether it's April, July or October, it is yuletide when you enter the doors of this Bluff Street store. Actually, the Christmas Cottage has wondrous displays of decorations for all the holidays. For collectors, they are Department 56 Gold Key Dealers for Heritage and Snow Village, Snowbabies, Yankee Candles and have a large assortment of decorations. The Christmas Cottage is open Monday through Saturday from 10 AM to 6 PM. Beginning October 1 and throughout the holiday season, hours are 9 AM to 8 PM.

Country Charmer
37 E. St. George Blvd., St. George • 674-1534

Nervous energy motivated owner Babs Jorgensen to establish another new business after retiring from a long career in retailing. She had successfully managed a dress shop for a number of years, then tried her hand at catering weddings for a while. It is mostly family and a few hired crafters who fill the shelves of this store in the old Snow's Market in downtown St. George. Specializing in handcrafted and commercial gifts, Country Charmer is particularly well known for beautiful, customized floral arrangements and Christmas yard displays that are cut from plywood and colorfully handpainted for outdoor use during the holiday season. Country Charmer is open Monday through Saturday from 10 AM to 6 PM.

Eagle's Nest
2331 Zion Park Blvd., Springdale • 772-3275

Believed to be the oldest gift shop in Springdale, Eagle's Nest is an authentic trading post that opened in 1950 and was bought by the present owners in 1975. Eagle's Nest has a little bit of everything. You'll find fishing and hunting licenses, picnic supplies and camping equipment, souvenirs, cold soft drinks and candy, top quality Native American jewelry and one of the area's largest and most beautiful beadwork collections. If you just want to stop in for a chat or to view the peaks of Zion National Park from a different vantage point, you'll be welcome — take your time to browse and shop. Eagle's Nest is open daily from 9 AM to 7 PM.

Gentle Giraffe Gifts
1450 S. Hilton Dr., St. George • 674-GIFT

First you'll have to find the Hilton Inn (see our Accommodations chapter) just off the south exchange of I-15. Once you are settled into a plush, comfortable room or arrive as a visitor ready to explore the surroundings, you'll find Gentle Giraffe Gifts — so named because they say their gifts are above the rest. This little store, tucked away between the hotel lobby and Tony Roma's Restaurant, is filled to the rafters with Native American jewelry and offers tremendous savings on handpainted sandstone pictures, Southwestern accessories, gifts and souvenirs, T-shirts and Tee-Pee Creeper Slippers — genuine sheepskin to keep feet warm in the winter, cool in the summer. Gentle Giraffe also caries a nice line of kids clothes and original Nancy Lund watercolors. The store is open Sunday through Thursday from 8 AM to 9 PM, and Friday and Saturday from 8 AM to 10 PM. They also offer free gift-wrapping.

Gifts Limited
145 Zion Park Blvd., Springdale • 772-3555

The natural setting is breathtaking, the merchandise is impressive and you are welcome to browse before or after showings of

---

INSIDERS' TIP

During the hunting season in October, many merchants host Midnight Madness or Deer Hunter Widows' sales. Advertised "for the ladies," these late-night forays frequently have entertainment and refreshments as an added incentive.

Treasure of the Gods or *The Great American West* in the Zion Canyon Cinemax Theater next door (see our Attractions chapter). Gifts Limited is a one-stop souvenir shop featuring Zion National Park souvenirs and T-shirts, Native American jewelry, pottery and wall hangings. Gifts Limited is open daily in the winter months from 10 AM to 7 PM. During summer, hours are extended to 8 AM to 10 PM.

Silver Reef Gallery and Gifts
1901 Silver Reef Dr., Silver Reef
• 879-2750

When the rich vein of silver ran out in the mid-1870s, the population of Silver Reef disappeared as quickly as it had arrived. But they left behind some wonderful buildings. Silver Reef Gallery and Gifts has a rich array of silver jewelry, pottery, antiques, unusual gifts, T-shirts, art prints and leather goods, all on display in the mining town's restored Rice Bank Building. Somewhere along the way, the building was partially destroyed by fire, but the result of the careful restoration is a delightful retail outlet for gifts and souvenirs. Silver Reef Gallery and Gifts is open Tuesday through Saturday from 10 AM to 5 PM.

Toaquim's Village
145 Zion Park Blvd., Springdale
• 772-2420, (800) 903-2420

Toaquim's Village is another gift shop in the Zion Canyon Cinemax Theater complex outside the gates of Zion National Park. Catering to the visitor who appreciates the beauty of fine, handcrafted jewelry and other Native American crafts, Toaquim's Village also carries decorative candles, pottery and Minnetonka Moccasins. Toaquim's Village has been open daily from 9 AM to 9 PM since 1994.

Virgin Workshop
16 W. Utah Hwy. 9, Virgin • 635-7730,
(888) 635-7730

You could miss this place if you're not watching for it. On the way to Zion National Park, the Virgin Workshop is an outlet for unusual handmade items of wood, metal and clay. Local and other artists are represented, along with an eclectic array of home furnishings, gifts, jewelry, pottery, glassware, weavings and rocks. Virgin Workshop also crafts lifetime-guaranteed Dutch ovens and carries a unique line of clothing made of antique silk. In other words, it is crammed with unusual, top-quality merchandise at good prices. Hours are 9 AM to 6 PM Wednesday through Monday for most of the year. During the weeks from mid-January to March, the owner is often traveling to shows, and regular hours are catch-as-catch-can. Call ahead to make sure Virgin Workshop is open.

Wilkinson's House of Lighting
245 W. Tabernacle St., St. George
• 673-9641

Wilkinson's truly is a unique place to shop. This family-owned business began in 1946 as a lighting store where they sold electronics, lamps, fixtures and bulbs. Then they branched out into appliances, selling dishwashers, refrigerators and stoves. When they grew some more, the second generation began bidding to provide electrical installation on large commercial projects. All along the way, they added gift items and collectibles until today they have a well-established reputation for beautiful merchandise, glassware, delightful rubber stamps and housewares. Wilkinson's convenient wedding registry allows you to choose a gift within a certain price range. The staff will select from the choices made by the bride and groom, wrap and deliver the piece for you. Wilkinson's has a frequent turnover of rare items. Many employees have been on Wilkinson's payroll for a decade or more, and second- and third-generation members of the Wilkinson family are part of this strong, local business. Wilkinson's House of Lighting is open Monday through Friday from 8 AM to 6 PM and on Saturday from 10 AM to 5 PM.

Cedar City/Brian Head

Bulloch's Drug Store
91 N. Main St., Cedar City • 586-9651

Bulloch's is a modern drug store in an old-fashioned setting. Shoppers will enjoy the experience as much as their purchases, especially if the buying is followed by a tasty ice cream treat from Bulloch's soda fountain (c. 1942). The soda jerk behind the counter will create a mouth-watering, taste-tempting malt, shake, sundae, soda or cone. Bulloch's Drug Store is also a great place to buy greeting cards, gifts, candy and stuffed animal toys. Special brand names are Russ Berrie, Ty Animals, Jelly Belly and Fernwood, and Coca-Cola memorabilia is also offered. Bulloch's is open Monday through Saturday from 9 AM to 9 PM.

Cedar Post Gifts
117 N. Main St., Cedar City • 586-1224

Cedar Post Gifts, next door to its sister shop, Cedar Post Pawn, has a splendid assortment of gifts, Utah souvenirs, Native American jewelry, rugs and kachina dolls. They also have a nice collection of antique reproductions including those wonderful little wicker doll buggies and locally made pie safes. Cedar Post Gifts is open Monday through Friday from 9:30 AM to 6 PM.

Her Majesty's Shoppe
15 S. 300 West, Cedar City • 586-2227

Next door to the Randall L. Jones Theater, where the works of Shakespeare and other noteworthy playwrights are performed at the Utah Shakespearean Festival (see our Annual Events chapter), Her Majesty's Shoppe offers gifts of distinction including William Shakespeare throws, pewter mugs and accessories, crystal, English teapots and other British imports, books, James Christensen prints, Winnie the Pooh collectibles, cards, puzzles and Catskill Candles. The shop is only open during theater season (June 1 through August 30), during the Thanksgiving and Christmas seasons or by appointment. During the festival, Her Majesty's doors open from 10 AM to 9 PM.

Hunter Cowan
79 N. Main St., Cedar City • 586-6549

In the midst of the Great Depression, when Utah's unemployment rate stood at 63 percent, a Hunter's daughter married a Cowan's son and they created Hunter Cowan, then a hardware and furniture store. Since the store opened 66 years ago, the address has remained the same, but the merchandise has changed. Today, Hunter Cowan handles all kinds of gifts, wind chimes, candles, tarts (scented potpourri that can be steamed or set out in dishes), Lenox, Mikasa, Noritake and Pfaltzgraf china, crystal, pewter and stemware. Special orders are their specialty. If they don't have it, they'll find it for you. Hunter Cowan is open Monday through Saturday from 9 AM to 6 PM.

Victorian Charm
30 W. Harding Ave., Cedar City • 586-1414

Victorian Charm is one of Southwestern Utah's best-kept secrets. Hidden away behind Mountain West Books on Cedar City's Main Street, Victorian Charm is a treasure trove of elegant furnishings and interior accessories as well as delightful, hard-to-find gift items for sentimental buyers. At Victorian Charm, you'll find furnishings, dry floral arrangements, toiletries — such as the popular Crabtree and Evelyn product lines — lace, candles, fine art prints and collectibles. You can step back in time Monday through Saturday from 9:30 AM to 6 PM.

Wood-n-Lace Place
97 N. Main St., Cedar City • 586-8151

The Wood-n-Lace Place opened for business in 1986, but they have moved to the Main Street Mall and changed the look of the interior and exterior of their store. Wood-n-Lace Place has wonderful gifts for all occasions, and you will also find delightful decorator items from Ganz, Enesco and Kim Anderson. The Wood-n-Lace Place carries handcrafted accessories, country furniture and dried or silk florals. You'll find the doors open Monday through Saturday from 10 AM to 6 PM.

INSIDERS' TIP

Staying overnight in a rural Southwestern Utah community? A leisurely stroll down any Main Street is certain to take you to any of many unique shopping adventures. We found an all-time favorite sweater in a tack shop, amid the saddles and bridles.

Bryce Canyon Area

Ruby's Inn General Store and Old Bryce Town Shops
Utah Hwy. 63, Bryce Canyon • 834-5341

During its 80-year history, a whole lot of travelers have purchased souvenirs, sustenance and supplies from Ruby's Inn General Store. Just 1½ miles from the entrance to Bryce Canyon National Park, Ruby's Inn is an attraction all its own with a huge selection of Native American jewelry, weavings, sand paintings and art. Open year round, Ruby's Inn General Store also carries Western wear, casual clothing, collectibles and gifts, groceries, auto and RV supplies, film, paperback books and just about anything else vacationers might need. Wrangler, Justin, Kodak, Stetson, Resistol, Bradford Exchange, Millcreek, Legends, Breyer and Enesco are nationally known brands on sale at Ruby's Inn (more on Ruby's Inn can be found in our Accommodations, Restaurants and Outdoor Recreation chapters). The general store is open 365 days a year from 7 AM to 11 PM.

Old Bryce Town Shops, across from Ruby's Inn, is also a unique attraction. Individual shops, open seasonally from mid-May to early September, feature Christmas decorations, Western wear, rocks and lapidary supplies, kitchenware and specialty foods.

Wild Horses Mercantile
47 N. Main St., Panguitch • 676-8900

The locals know it as the old SUE building (for Southern Utah Equitable), but the Utah Heritage Foundation knows it as one of only three buildings in the state with a cast storefront. The ornate exterior of Wild Horses Mercantile was brought across the plains in pieces by covered wagon. For its careful and loving restoration of the storefront and the building, Wild Horses Mercantile was officially recognized in 1996 by the Heritage Foundation.

The interior of the store displays an eclectic array of merchandise. The ladders used to gain access to items placed on high shelves are store originals that date back to 1906. Wild Horses Mercantile shows and sells the work of tribal artists from the Four Corners region, Native American music on tapes and CDs, and hiking guides, history and kids books. They also have kitchen linens and accessories, jewelry and a bath section with interesting smells from natural pinion and sage soaps and food-based creams. Wild Horses Mercantile is open from mid-May to mid-October from 7:30 AM to 10 PM daily.

Kanab Area

Denny's Wigwam and Curio
78 E. Center St., Kanab • 644-2452, (888) 954-9544

Denny of Denny's Wigwam is a fifth-generation native of Kanab. His gift shop — stocked with everything from Western hats and Kachina dolls to spurs and ropes — opened in 1970. Tourists on their way to one national park or another love his great selection of boots and cowboy wear, along with the handmade Native American crafts from the Navajo, Hopi and Zuni tribes (pottery, rugs, silver jewelry and the like). But here in "Little Hollywood," where more than 100 Western flicks were filmed over the years, Denny's also has a reputation as a magic place where the Old West comes alive. Denny, in his role as director, has shot more than 5,000 episodes of "How the West Was Lost" starring . . . YOU! The plots are always similar. There's the ingenue, the leading man in a white hat, the bad guy in a black hat, Indians with feather head dresses, a pioneer couple, a mountain man in buckskin and the U.S. cavalry. A wagon master sits in the covered wagon, shakes the reins over a wooden horse cutout and yells, "Circle the wagons." Everyone gets into the act. Denny's serves lunch for $8.50 and dinner for $18.50, and the moviemaking entertainment is included in the price. The menu usually includes roast beef, barbecue chicken and other frontier fare. Denny's Wigwam is open daily from 8 AM to 9 PM in the summer and 9 AM to 5 PM in winter.

TJ's Trail West Gifts
157 W. Center St., Kanab • 644-2420

TJ's has tried hard to become Trail West Gifts, but the sign says TJ's and everyone in town knows the shop as TJ's, so for the time being it's still TJ's Trail West Gifts. The store is open from mid-March to mid-November, depending on how soon it gets cold . . . or hot. Trail West Gifts carries a large inventory of Native American jewelry; Navajo, Hopi and Zuni sand paintings; a nice line of pottery; Southwestern gifts and souvenirs; and T-shirts. It's all sold by friendly sales people. You will also find an assortment of books and videos about Southwestern Utah. TJ's has four rooms to rent in the adjacent, clean Trail West Motel. The gift shop is open daily from 8 AM to (at least) 10 PM.

Music

Music is as much a part of Southwestern Utah's culture as the red rocks. From our humble beginnings, most every small community has had a choir. Local legends tell of broken violins, pianos or organs brought across the plains in pieces then reassembled, and the popularity of brass bands for community events. Music made life in the desert a little more bearable, added a touch of culture and provided a lot more fun.

Today music stores are popular retailers. Most residents play for fun, but some are serious in their pursuits. Band is a required class for Southwestern Utah sixth-graders and orchestras, choral groups and children's performing companies are easy to find (see our Arts and Culture chapter). Tuacahn Center for the Arts, Dixie College and Southern Utah University are all proud of their music departments.

St. George/Zion

Daynes Music
445 E. St. George Blvd., No. 101, St. George • 674-2869, (888) 4DAYNES

Daynes Music is the West's oldest music store and the second oldest in the United States, according to statistics compiled by the National Association of Music Merchants. Opened by great-grandpa Daynes in Salt Lake City in 1862, the St. George affiliate store opened in 1996. The family attributes its staying power to taking good care of their customers. Daynes is best known as a Steinway dealer — top of the piano line — but also sells Boston, a midrange ($10,000 to $18,000) grand, and Weber, an excellent, less expensive option. Daynes carries quality digital pianos and sheet music. The St. George store is open Monday through Saturday from 10 AM to 6 PM.

Gentry Music
243 N. Bluff St., St. George • 673-0373, (800) 672-0373

The Gentry twins grew up loving music and performing together around the community. As an adult, Garry has remained close to his roots. Gentry Music is a local outlet for Roland, K. Kawai and Kurzweil pianos. Garry Gentry sells grands, uprights, organs, keyboards, digital pianos, sheet music, band and orchestral instruments, accessories and interactive software. Garry tries to keep prices low on the best products available and offers affordable lessons for different skill levels. Gentry Music is open Monday through Friday from 9 AM to 7 PM and on Saturday from 10 AM to 2 PM.

Music Music
188 E. 300 South, St. George • 673-5552

Music Music has moved around over the years, settling at 188 E. 300 South. You will find everything you need to pursue a casual interest, school studies or a career in music. Music Music specializes in all things musical including guitars, amplifiers, sheet music, band instruments, karaoke hardware and tapes, CDs and music lessons. They will buy, sell, trade or rent instruments. Music Music is the local dealer for such brands as Peavey, Fender, Ibanez, Takamine,

---

INSIDERS' TIP

The center court at Red Cliffs Mall is always filled with interesting displays. In the summer of 1997, the display du jour was a sand sculpture depicting the children's nursery rhyme "The Old Lady Who Lived in a Shoe." The shoe in this instance was two stories high. Unusual merchandise such as Native American jewelry and pottery, home decorating items, do-it-yourself projects . . . you name it, it's been on sale in a center-court kiosk.

Photo: Jud Burkett

You can shop 'til you drop at the Red Cliffs Mall.

Trace Elliot, Jasmine, Ovation, Dod and Digitech. The store has an in-house instrument repair shop and knowledgeable musicians behind the counter to answer any and all questions. Music Music is open Monday through Friday from 9 AM to 6 PM and Saturday from 9 AM to 5 PM.

Cedar City/Brian Head

Munson's Music
602 S. Main St., Cedar City • 586-8742

Munson's Music, opened in 1983, may have the largest selection of guitars and the most complete library of sheet music and music books in all of Southwestern Utah. Select from popular brand names such as Fender, Ovation and Ibanez guitars. Tucked away in just about every nook and cranny of the store, Munson's Music has amps, drum kits, karaoke machines, Casio keyboards, lesson books and accessories. Munson's is open Monday through Saturday from 10 AM to 6 PM.

Outfitters

Willow Creek Books, Coffee and Outdoor Gear
263 S. 100 East, Kanab • 644-8884

The three components of this unique re-tailer include a bookstore, a coffee shop of sorts and a well-stocked outfitter of hiking and backpacking gear. Those in-the-know will recognize such names as Sierra Designs, Camelbak, Gregory Packs, Mountain Safety Research Stoves, Eagle Creek, Royal Robin and Sequel. Willow Creek carries a variety of technical clothing designed for survival under adverse outdoor conditions. Stop by. Have a hot cup of coffee, browse through an assortment of books, maps and other materials to familiarize yourself with the terrain. Add to or build your outdoor gear and apparel inventory, then get out and enjoy the "greatest earth on show." Willow Creek Books, Coffee and Outdoor Gear is open daily from 8:30 AM to 8:30 PM from mid-April to mid-October.

Plants and Flowers

Trees and flowers have played an important and functional role in the history of Southwestern Utah. Many of the early settlers arrived from the green, rolling hills of the South, well-established Atlantic Coast communities, Great Britain or the emerald isle. Life in this barren desert was improved one tree at a time.

Trees, such as the mulberry, served several purposes. They provided food for silk worms, fueling a short-lived industry created to produce silk for fashion. Also, because they grew to great heights quickly, mulberry trees planted adjacent to newly constructed adobe homes provided shade and protection from the hot sun.

The desert has, indeed, blossomed, and today independent nurseries are plentiful. Kmart and Wal-Mart in St. George and Cedar City both have entire departments set aside for the purpose of selling seedlings, starts and fertilizers. Sod farms are generating a good income because of the booming construction and housing industry — plenty of the stuff is needed to landscape around new homes, parks and condos. Working in the yard is a popular leisure activity here. Getting back to nature is what life in Southwestern Utah is all about.

St. George/Zion

Ballard's Nursery
691 N. State St., Hurricane • 635-4274

Among Southwestern Utah's rapidly expanding communities, the Hurricane Valley is seeing its share of new construction which, in turn, requires green and growing things. For the do-it-yourself landscaper, Ballard's Nursery has a complete line of nursery stock, fertilizers, tools and bedding plants — more than 200 varieties — grown in their own special plant material (a combination of composted soil, peat moss and cinders). Ballard's has been serving the nursery needs of the community since 1969, and it is open Monday through Saturday from 9 AM to 5 PM.

Cactus Connection
2691 W. Santa Clara Dr., Santa Clara • 674-2424

For years, Rose Garden Nursery was a popular choice for bedding plants, trees, shrubs and gardening supplies. But with stiff competition from discount stores, the owners made a smart decision to change the name and the merchandise. The same friendly faces are at Cactus Connection offering the same fine service. But now, instead of annuals and perennials, ground cover and fruitless shade trees, you'll find a wide variety of cactus, succulents and drought-tolerant plants. With more and more homeowners giving in to Mother Nature and moving toward xeriscape designs for the front

yard, plants indigenous to Southwestern Utah seem like a good, easy choice for landscaping. Cactus Connection is open year round Monday through Friday from 8 AM to 6 PM.

Little Valley Trees
3646 S. Little Valley Rd., St. George • 674-7769

When the pioneers first arrived in St. George there weren't many trees. It took patience and many years before trees shaded the little adobe homes that sprung up. Today Little Valley Trees says, "Why wait for shade?" On their tree farm near the old airport, they grow their own! Little Valley currently has 3,000 ball-and-burlap, grade-A stock shade trees for your yard. They specialize in the big variety — the ones that look like trees, not twigs. Little Valley Trees is open Monday through Saturday from 8 AM to 6 PM, or by appointment.

Thrift Stores

Even in the state with the healthiest economy, everyone loves a bargain! Thrift stores are popular in Southwestern Utah as a way to stretch budgets in large families and a source for economical purchases for seniors on fixed incomes. Thrift stores attract people from every walk of life, tax bracket and job description. Donations of housewares and clothing are tax deductible — and let's face it, sometimes the item we thought looked so great on the store hanger just doesn't measure up to our measurements. Why not pass it along to someone who will love it as much as you thought you would?

St. George/Zion

Deseret Industries
2480 E. Red Cliff Dr., St. George • 652-8232
535 S. 110 West, Cedar City • 586-3337

Deseret Industries, with stores in St. George and Cedar City, is a first class thrift store and training center. Deseret Industries first opened in Salt Lake City in 1938. Other stores soon opened around the state and throughout the West. The DI has been in Cedar City since the early '70s and opened its newest store in St.

George in 1996. As a federally certified, sheltered workshop for the training and employment of individuals with special needs, the DI gives a new life to goods and a better life to people. Deseret specializes in one-of-a-kind items, reclaiming donated goods for sale at great prices to the general public. Deseret Industries is open in St. George Monday through Friday from 10 AM to 8 PM and Saturday from 10 AM to 6 PM. In Cedar City, DI is open Monday through Saturday from 9 AM to 8 PM "helping people help themselves."

Family Thrift Store
596 E. Tabernacle St., No. C, St. George • 628-6660

The Family Thrift Store exists to recycle good, clean reusables from one family to another. Proceeds from this nonprofit organization support underprivileged children in the St. George and Cedar City communities. The Family Thrift Shop welcomes your housewares, clothing, toys, books and other items no longer of use to you or your family. Shoppers in this clean, organized store will find great bargains Monday through Friday from 10 AM to 5 PM and on Saturday from 10 AM to 2 PM. Often, they will open early or stay late if you want to make special arrangements to accommodate your schedule. The 25¢ rack is always filled with great deals and is popular with shoppers. Any item that has not sold within two months is offered at half price. Every Tuesday is Senior Citizen Day, with a 25 percent discount on all merchandise for shoppers 65 and older. Family Thrift Shop is supported by donations from the local community.

Repeat Performance Economy Store
74 E. Tabernacle St., St. George • 674-7522

One person's discards are another one's treasure. Repeat Performance Economy Store is a not-for-profit community thrift shop serving the needs of working families and individuals trying to stretch their budgets. Repeat Performance has treasures galore in the way of clean, pressed, repaired and ready-to-wear secondhand clothing — some of it nearly-new, designer brand stuff. The store also has a large assortment of accessories, housewares, books and children's items (including refurbished toys) as well as limited pieces of furniture and equipment.

Proceeds, after expenses, are donated to Dixie Regional Medical Center to enhance patient care services (see our Healthcare chapter). In 1996, DRMC's charity care added up to more than $1.3 million in 3,223 cases. Repeat Performance Economy Store, staffed by volunteers, is open Monday through Friday from 10 AM to 5 PM and on Saturday from 10 AM to 4 PM.

Kanab Area

Kane County Hospital Auxiliary Thrift Shop
41 S. 100 East, Kanab • 644-8175

A small group of volunteers, determined to raise funds to benefit Kane County Hospital (see our Healthcare chapter), opened a thrift shop in 1989. From its humble beginnings, the Kane County Hospital Auxiliary Thrift Shop has moved five times. With the help of the Kane County Commission, the State of Utah and the Arizona Job Training Program, the hospital auxiliary is now in a 2,500-square-foot, permanent location in downtown Kanab, where they raise funds through the sale of used clothing, household goods and books. The organization is not-for-profit, and the store is open Monday through Friday from 10 AM to 4 PM and on Saturday from 10 AM to 2 PM.

Community calendars throughout the region are filled on any given night with recitals and concerts, plays or other cultural events.

Arts and Culture

Almost as soon as the settlers arrived at their destination in places such as Panguitch, Parowan, Cedar City, St. George, Orderville and Kanab, they began to plant crops and plan concerts. The pioneers enjoyed dances and stage performances of works by the great playwrights and poets.

At first, during the colonization days between 1850 and 1865, these cultural offerings took place under trees or from the bed of a wagon. After a hard day dealing with the desert elements, plowing and planting or building a cabin, the settlers wanted to sing, listen to a literary review or brass band concert, or enjoy an evening at the community social hall, where traveling thespians staged melodramas or the latest play from the East. Nearly every small community had this sort of hall that might have doubled as a schoolhouse or a town hall or courtroom.

In the 1990s, as in the 1890s, the people of Southwestern Utah love the arts. Community calendars throughout the region are filled on any given night with recitals and concerts, plays or other cultural events. High school and college theater performances attract full-house audiences. Interstate 15 brings big-name talent traveling between shows in Las Vegas or Salt Lake City. Jazz festivals, country-western stars and top artists from the concert stage have found their way to Southwestern Utah. The list of recent visitors includes the Judds, the Beach Boys, Travis Tritt, Sawyer Brown, the Harlem Globetrotters, Mel Torme and jazz piano legend McCoy Tyner. On some weekends, residents and visitors are forced to choose from several events, but there is never a shortage of cultural enrichment.

This chapter includes what we believe to be some of the obvious cultural choices in our area, but we hope that — mixed with the lesser-known options — they will be the beginning of a wonderful adventure in discovery. Ask any 10 people in a given Southwestern Utah town about the arts, and chances are they will mention a few of the organizations listed here.

Music and Dance Organizations

St. George/Zion

Southwest Symphony
P.O. Box 423, St. George 84771 • 656-0434

The cornerstone of cultural arts in the St. George area is the Southwest Symphony, under the baton of Maestro Gary Caldwell. This 16-year-old full orchestra is made up of about 65 talented volunteers who practice their professions managing corporations, classrooms, households and the like by day, then pick up their instruments for rehearsals and performances at the Dixie Center's Cox Auditorium at night. The Southwest Symphony has an ambitious annual performance schedule that always includes sellout performances of the popular holiday tradition of Handel's *Messiah*.

Always on the lookout for future musicians to fill the orchestra chairs, the Southwest Symphony auditions and selects the area's best and brightest young musicians to perform in the annual "Salute to Youth" concert in mid-April. In addition to five or six concerts a year spread out between October and June, the orchestra also hosts a special afternoon during which they invite most of the area's 3rd-, 4th- and 5th-grade students, encouraging them to following music as a career.

Organized in 1982 by Dr. Norman Fawson, a local physician and violist, and governed by a broad-based board of trustees, the orchestra continues to develop, regularly receiving kudos from a grateful community. Season tickets are available through the address above and are generally less than $50 for adults and about $35 for seniors. There are special student and family rates as well. Tickets to individual performances are available at the Dixie Center box office. Prices top out at about $8 but vary according to age and performance night. Call the box office for more details.

Southwest Symphonic Chorale
425 S. 700 East, St. George • 628-7944

The Southwest Symphonic Chorale is the Southwest Symphony's sister organization, formed to provide vocal interaction with the community orchestra. A year younger than its instrumental counterpart, the chorale is under the direction of J. H. Kim. Created from a small core of vocalists who first performed around a living room piano, the Southwest Symphonic Chorale is now 60 members strong and growing, not only in skill and repertoire, but also in reputation as an outstanding choir.

Southern Utah Heritage Choir
2982 Bloomington Dr. W., St. George • 652-9709

In two years, the Southern Utah Heritage Choir has gained both a reputation as a remarkable singing group and a following that extends far beyond the borders of the St. George area. It all began when organizers Mary Stewart and Floyd Rigby took 200 volunteer vocalists from the community and united them for a single event during the holiday season of 1994. In a word, it was wonderful! The audience and the musicians were delighted . . . so delighted, in fact, choir members asked for another chance to perform together.

The result was an organized choir where everyone pays annual dues of $25 to participate, with funds used to purchase music. Today the choir is at home in the St. George Tabernacle where they prepare and perform numerous programs throughout the year. The Southern Utah Heritage Choir toured the Czech republic in April 1997, and, under the direction of Rigby, performed with the Czech national orchestra at the end of a nine-day itinerary. Because not every musician could afford the cost of travel and accommodations, the choir undertook a vigorous fund-raising campaign, complete with car washes and benefit concerts.

Southern Utah Heritage Choir concerts are well-attended. The talents of its members are appreciated. As ambassadors of Southwestern Utah, the choir is professional in every sense of the word — except for paychecks.

Celebrity Concert Series
425 S. 700 East, St. George • 652-7994

According to its mission statement, the Celebrity Concert Series exists to "provide culturally uplifting art experiences for the community." Every year since its inception in 1972, the Celebrity Concert Series has brought in a variety of artists from near and far, who generally perform at the lowest possible ticket price to ensure everyone has the opportunity to enjoy this quality, multi-disciplinary series. Shows are usually held on the stage of the M.K. Cox Auditorium at the Dixie Center. Five recitals — part of the concert season — are also scheduled in the Browning Auditorium.

Board members for the Celebrity Concert Series admit taking an occasional risk on new artists, but art forms, as much as the artists themselves, are considered for this prestigious and well-respected community program. Variety in programming includes everything from Dixieland jazz, string quartets, ballet and ballroom dance companies and choir performances to guitar, clarinet, harp and percussion soloists. New Age musicians Montreaux, concert pianist Christopher O'Riley and prima ballerina Galina Mezentseva of the St. Petersburg Ballet Company have performed in the series. No two years are alike, but the cost of season tickets has remained remarkably constant at $85 for an adult ticket to a dozen or more performances. Season tickets for children are $25. Individual show tickets are $12 for adults and $9 for children older than 5.

FYI

Unless otherwise noted, the area code for all phone numbers listed in this chapter is 801 but will change to 435 in September 1997. Either area code may be used until March 22, 1998.

Photo: Lyman Hafen

The Southwest Symphony poses on the red rocks north of St. George.

Cedar City/Brian Head

American Folk Ballet
351 W. Center St., Cedar City • 586-0622

Founded more than three decades ago by renowned choreographer Burch Mann, the American Folk Ballet exhibits the spirit of this nation and its people. One of the more unique dance companies in the world, the American Folk Ballet uses America's heritage, roots and folk history for the company's theme, substance and style. Although the ballet is undeniably American, the company, based at Southern Utah University, has universal appeal. Audiences from Muncie, Indiana, and Athens, Greece, to Copenhagen, Denmark, and Haaretz, Israel, have responded with delight to the company's concerts.

The dance company has performed in gyms in rural hamlets; at the Kennedy Center in Washington, D.C., for President Jimmy Carter's inaugural celebration; at kibbutzims in Israel and at the great outdoor amphitheater at Caesaria. One of the first American dance companies to be invited to Russia after the fall of the Iron Curtain, the tour resulted in *Distance Dance*, a special widely featured on public television stations across the nation.

The dance company Mann created has continued since the death of its founder in 1996 and exists as a tribute to one of America's most distinctive and innovative choreographers. More than 30 years later, The American Folk Ballet continues to educate and entertain, sustained by the late choreographer's genius.

Orchestra of Southern Utah
75 N. 300 West, Cedar City • 586-8414

Since the mid-1850s, when the first pioneers settled the area, there has always been an orchestra in Cedar City. In the same way a plant sends out new shoots and branches, the musical organization has evolved through the years. The result of a century and a half of striving toward perfection is an impressive organization called the Orchestra of Southern Utah.

The orchestra, under the direction of Hal Campbell, is a tradition in the Cedar City area and its future remains bright. The number of musicians varies from concert to concert but averages about 60, all of whom are volunteers. Some are middle and high school students, with a sprinkling of musicians who are attending SUU, but others are from the community — chiropractors, inventors, teachers, business people, retailers and homemakers. Four concerts are performed each year, including a spring program featuring up-and-coming young talent. Concerts are a pleasant mix of works by classical composers interspersed with the fun of lighthearted musical selections.

The American Folk Ballet from SUU has performed with the orchestra, as have an impressive and growing list of guest soloists and conductors. Audience attendance is increasing, and the orchestra has a new home: Orchestra Hall has been renovated through a community effort. Money, work and equipment were donated to clean and fix up an auditorium that sat unused for more than 20 years above the offices of the Iron County School District. (Yes, you were reading that correctly . . . The orchestra's home is in a second-floor auditorium.) It will be used primarily for rehearsals and performances of the Orchestra of Southern Utah, but also as a community resource for use by middle and high school musical groups.

Right now, you can get a good seat at a performance for whatever you want to pay. There is no charge, though donations at the door are always accepted. Someday that will likely change, if stipends for orchestra members are to become a reality. But for now, the hall is in good shape, and the musicians themselves are working hard to strengthen their musical skills. There is little doubt the Orchestra of Southern Utah will continue as a Cedar City tradition.

Kanab Area

Kanab Civic Orchestra
797 W. Willow Dr., Kanab • 644-8149

The nearly 70 members of the Kanab Civic Orchestra come from five counties and two states — some from as far away as 80 miles — for weekly rehearsals and regular performances. The Kanab Civic Orchestra was created in 1985 when a community theater production needed an orchestra to provide music. Admittedly, the results were pretty weak. But afterward, a request to the Utah Arts Council produced some start-up funds, and a community campaign generated more financial support through donations used to purchase music. Musicians from near and far were invited to dust off the instruments from their high school days and join the orchestra.

Members range in age from 10 to retired, and those old enough to work make a living in diverse occupations such as teachers, meat cutters, real estate agents and postal workers. A couple of members are professional musicians. Under the direction of local pharmacist Kortney Stirland, the orchestra has done a terrific job reaching the goals of its mission statement, which "seeks to find members of the community with current or latent musical abilities and provide a venue for musical development and performance."

With members from the Utah towns of Kanab, Hurricane and Panguitch and the Arizona towns of Page and Fredonia playing together, the orchestra has been invited to participate in a variety of events both in the area and as far away as Salt Lake City. Programs have included an annual performance of Handel's *Messiah,* Halloween and Christmas holiday benefits and patriotic shows around the Fourth of July. A fall 1996 concert saluting America's armed services 50 years after the end of World War II was broadcast live on local radio.

Theater

St. George/Zion

Graff Theater
175 S. 700 East, St. George • 652-7800

Performances in the 500-seat Graff Theater at Dixie College are a longstanding tradition in the St. George community. Although the Graff Theater, housed in the campus fine arts center, primarily serves as a hands-on laboratory for developing acting and technical skills for Dixie College theater students, open auditions generate a fair amount of community involvement each year on stage and backstage.

An ambitious season of five plays during the school year includes a combination of theater styles with musicals, comedy and drama. Recent productions have included *Shadowlands*, the C.S. Lewis love story; *Joseph and the Amazing Technicolor Dreamcoat*, a musical version of the Old Testament story of Joseph; and *See How They Run*, *Dames at Sea*, *Antigone* and *Sleeping Beauty*. Practical experience aside, sellouts are common — the Graff Theater season is eagerly anticipated and well-supported by the community. Tickets range from $3 for children to $7.50 for adults. Season tickets are available.

St. George Musical Theater Company
510 E. 900 South, St. George • 673-8183

The St. George Musical Theater was the brainchild of the late Mark Ogden. From its organization in 1990 to perform *So This is Dixie* in celebration of the 130th anniversary of the founding of St. George, the company has gone on to produce a number of very successful shows — most written and directed by Ogden. At the same time, the group has struggled with its own homelessness, public apathy and poverty, any one of which might have been the undoing of a lesser body of thespians. Since Ogden's untimely death in 1994, St. George Musical Theater Company has been guided with energy, determination and vision by director Dawna Kenworthy and producer Kristine Bennion.

Now on solid footing with a season of three performances, the company has found a temporary home in the St. George Opera House. Receptive audiences are showing up to enjoy

a performance then often return with friends and family. The cost of tickets varies from show to show but average between $5 and $8.

Cedar City/Brian Head

Mainstage Theater
351 W. Center St., Cedar City • 586-7880

Residents of Cedar City and students in the Southern Utah University theater department look forward each year to the opportunity to participate, on stage or in the audience, in eight productions during the school year. Programming is a well-rounded mix of musicals, drama, comedy, dance showcase and the performance of an original student script. Some of the performances are directed by students, others by faculty.

Would-be actors from the community respond to open auditions. One show is prepared with children in mind, and the audience is made up of local students from the elementary and middle school grades. Tickets for most productions are $9 for adults and $7 for anyone younger than 18 or older than 62. SUU students with current activity cards are admitted for $2. The annual subscription rate is $42 per season.

Utah Shakespearean Festival
351 W. Center St., Cedar City • 586-7878, (800) PLAYTIX

The Utah Shakespearean Festival (see the June listings in our Annual Events chapter) has a rich and well-established history. Now in its 36th season, Shakespeare and Cedar City are nearly synonymous in theater circles.

The USF performs nightly except Sunday from mid-June to early September on the stage of the Fred C. Adams Theater (see our Close-up on Adams in this chapter). You'll get a real feel for life in Elizabethan England by attending

INSIDERS' TIP

Take a minute to see the underpinnings of the stage at the St. George Opera House. Brigham Young loved stage plays as much as he loved to dance. The floor was designed to raise and lower to accommodate both activities. It's the only known floor of its type in the nation!

Much Ado About Shakespeare

In 1961, few people in Southwestern Utah knew much about Shakespeare except that it was hard to decipher his old English. Enter a man named Fred C. Adams.

Adams' plot was to make the famous playwright as large an icon in Southwestern Utah as its sandstone monoliths. More than three decades later, he has done it. Today, the Utah Shakespearean Festival in Cedar City draws nearly 130,000 visitors who roll

in from every corner of the United States and around the globe. The festival works on a $3.2 million annual budget and has developed a reputation as one of the most prestigious summer theater festivals in America.

When Adams first suggested his idea to the residents of Cedar City and the administration of what is now Southern Utah University, they must have taken him for a court jester. But Fred Adams was not kidding. A fledgling theater instructor at the university, he began to piece together the elements of his dream. In 1961, the festival was born with a budget of $1,000. Little more than 3,000 people came to see the local actors and simple props and to listen to the difficult-to-decipher words of William Shakespeare.

But year to year the festival grew, revenues increased and the ability to entice better actors, directors, costumers and set designers improved. By 1971, the festival was able to build a beautiful replica of the kind of outdoor theater where Shakespeare's plays were originally produced. The theater complex, appraised today at more than $7 million, was built 26 years ago at a cost of $180,000. Fred Adams, who served from the beginning as the festival's executive director, had gone from court jester to the hero of the story.

Today, Adams still gives insightful and entertaining pre-show orientations during the festival's 10-week summer run. He is generally available among the

Fred C. Adams is founder and executive producer of the Utah Shakespearean Festival.

crowd before and after the shows and is very gracious and accessible to the public. Recently he's been a featured personality in such magazines as *Condé Nast Traveler*, *Mature Outlook*, *American Heritage*, and *MidWest Living*. He has been praised by theater greats around the world and has received honors including Geneva Steel's 1992 Modern Day Pioneer Award, the National Parks and Recreation 1991 award for Outstanding Contribution by a Citizen and the 1984 Governor's Honors in the Arts award. He is a member of the Salt Lake City Chamber of Commerce Hall of Fame.

Yet Fred Adams stays close to his roots in Southwestern Utah, a region that had a tradition for embracing the arts but was a little skeptical at first about the idea of Shakespeare among the slickrock. Fred Adams is one of the few who has successfully proved the phrase, "If you build it, they will come." (For more on the festival, see the June listings in our Annual Events chapter.)

the free Greenshow outside the theater — a fast-moving, high-stepping rush filled with puppetry, food vendors, jugglers, dancers and acrobats; the pre-show, an entertaining lecture to fill you in on all the details of the play of the day; or the Royal Feaste, a playful meal fit for a king.

The economic impact of the Bard on this and surrounding communities is immense. In 1996, total direct and indirect expenditures by the festival and its patrons were estimated at nearly $21 million. Projections into 2001 increase to $48 million. The festival currently employs 25 people year round, with approximately 300 in the summertime production company. More than 200 community members donate time in support of festival activities volunteering as ushers, data processors, "ambassadors" and information desk staffers.

In 1996 the festival produced Shakespeare's *The Comedy of Errors*, *Macbeth*, *The Winter's Tale* and *Henry IV, Part 1*. Alexander Dumas' *The Three Musketeers* and Gilbert and Sullivan's *The Mikado* also took to the boards. Ticket prices for each play range from $10 to $27.

Cedar Drama Club
262 S. 200 West, Cedar City • 586-4346

The Cedar Drama Club has never sold a ticket in more than 60 years of performing, but this group of 30 women — originally a book club — continue to gather each summer to read and enjoy a variety of plays. On a rotating basis and divided into three groups of 10, one cluster hosts the club, the second provides the food and the third bunch reads one of a variety of plays, from classical works to modern comedies. In the past three years, the Cedar Drama Club has performed *The Devil and Daniel Webster*, *No Exit*, *Dracula* and *The Valiant*. Although there are only 30 slots, there are occasional openings for new members.

Parowan Community Theater
27 N. Main St., Parowan • 477-3778, 477-8732

The Parowan Community Theater relies on the talents of local actors, directors and musicians as well as plumbers, carpenters and electricians to carry on the theatrical tradition of pioneer settlers. Always lovers of the theater, the area's first settlers would be proud of the musical productions of this community theater group including *Man of La Mancha*, *The King and I* and *South Pacific*.

Carol and Gordon Farnsworth provided a permanent home for the artists and musicians in 1989 through a contribution of the old Parowan movie theater. The building has since been renovated through the volunteer efforts of local residents to include refurbished theater seats and a fresh coat of paint. The company acquired additional land directly behind the theater in 1996, providing an expanded backstage area, and plans are under way for the addition of dressing rooms and a costume shop.

The Parowan Community Theater performs one major musical a year, participates in the traditional holiday program *Christmas in the Country*, and offers an eclectic mix of dance reviews, recitals and other events. Costs vary depending on the performance but are in the economical range of $3 to $7.

Bryce Canyon Area

Panguitch Community Theater
69 W. Center St., Panguitch • 676-8513

The Panguitch Community Theater offers an opportunity for neighbors, friends and high school students to give the residents of Bryce Canyon a taste of Broadway through performances of such classics as *Oklahoma* and *Guys and Dolls*. Roque Willard, a sometimes-director sometimes-actor, says "to describe our theater as loosely organized is kind." Everyone gets a part, a role, an assignment. Springing from the drama program at Panguitch High School — eliminated in 1996 due to budget constraints — the group is led by music teacher Paul Hathcock, Willard and others, who are considering ways and means to guarantee a future for the little theater. Tickets for the one or two productions a year are $25 for the family, $5 for adults and $3 for students.

Art Galleries

Artists are flocking to Southwestern Utah in ever-increasing numbers, drawn by a love of the area's history, environment and energy. A growing awareness of art and culture has

resulted in the formation of cooperatives, guilds and support organizations for artists. Galleries are popping up as well so these same artists will have a place to show and sell their work. Call ahead for hours of operation — as in most places, our artists are free spirits who are wont to follow their creative whims.

St. George/Zion

Artists' Gallery
5 W. St. George Blvd. (Ancestor Square), St. George • 628-9293

Artists' Gallery, an artist-owned cooperative with 24 members, displays paintings from traditional Southwestern to the abstract, along with sculpture, pottery and jewelry. Established in 1989, the large, two-story gallery spotlights one artist a month in oil, watercolor, graphic art or another medium, and there is still sufficient space left over to showcase a half-dozen pieces from each of the other 23 co-op members! On the second Friday of each month, the artists' co-op and other gallery tenants in Ancestor Square participate in a gallery walk that the public is invited to attend.

Fatali Gallery
868 Zion Park Blvd., Springdale • 772-2422, (520) 645-3553

Michael Fatali, an artist with a camera, dis-

plays his work in this Springdale gallery, which is open March through November. The Page, Arizona, resident and award-winning photographer captures the Southwestern Utah landscape through the lens of his camera.

Gallery Ten
10 S. Main St., Leeds • 879-2394

Gallery Ten joins Jerry Anderson's Bronze Studio and Gallery as the second artists' showcase in the Leeds area. Gallery Ten is housed in a pioneer home built in 1881 by Willard McMullin, an accomplished stone mason, for his son, BY. "It's not your average gallery," says proprietor Joanne Thornton, granddaughter of BY and Ada McMullin, but it is the perfect setting for showing the terrific art works. There are watercolors, acrylics, oils and other mixed media produced by local artists.

Jerry Anderson Bronze Studio and Gallery
1903 Wells Fargo Rd., Silver Reef in Leeds • 879-2254

Southwestern Utah's history and heritage is captured in the bronze and oils of Jerry Anderson. This gallery, in the authentic restored Wells Fargo station in Silver Reef, features two- and three-dimensional art with an emphasis on landscape and Native American subjects. The gallery showcases the works of Jerald Bishop, Norma Jean Cope, Randy

Fullbright, Denis Milhomme and other noted artists.

Main Street Gallery
55 N. Main St., St. George • 652-8101
Main Street Gallery is the newest in the St. George area. Centrally located in the downtown historic district, the gallery specializes in affordable fine art and features displays of local and regional artists every other month.

Prince Gallery
2 W. St. George Blvd. (Ancestor Square), St. George • 656-3377
The Prince Gallery operators claim "it's not just a gallery — it's an adventure." The gallery showcases fine art and world-class framing. Featured limited editions on display are by such renowned artists as Arnold Frieberg, Al Rounds, Lindsay Scott, Hal Sutherland, Greg Alexander, Dawna Barton and many others. Prince Gallery is Southwestern Utah's only authorized dealer for Greenwich Workshop and Millpond Press, perhaps the nation's finest publishers of fine art prints.

River Art and Mud
720 S. River Rd., St. George • 674-1444
One of the area's newest galleries is River Art and Mud, which features the work of gallery owner Boni McCowan, along with a rich mix of works from Southwest scenes to fantasy art by Wallace Brazzeal, George Kehew, Suzanne Conine, Glen Blakely and L'Deane Trueblood. The gallery shares space with River Realty and Development Company and furnishes artwork for the Southern Utah Homebuilders Association Parade of Homes and model homes in the area.

Roland Lee Art Gallery
2 W. St. George Blvd., Ste. 1N
(Ancestor Square), St. George • 673-1988
Roland Lee is a name most local art lovers associate with exquisite watercolor paintings. The gallery that bears his name also features works by Jerry Anderson, Randy Fullbright, Patrick Farneman, Donna Jensen, Thomas Kinkade, Frank Riggs, Marilee Campbell, Wallace Lee and other regional and national artists. The landscape and historic buildings of Southwestern Utah are captured in watercolor, oils and bronze, but the gallery also includes custom jewelry, raku pottery, art gift items, art books and custom framing.

Thunderbird Art Gallery
150 N. 1000 East at Days Inn, St. George • 673-6123
The Thunderbird Art Gallery is one of the largest galleries in Southwestern Utah, specializing in classic and Southwest-style art. The gallery is in the Days Inn (see our Accommodations chapter) and is open round the clock.

Originals in oil, acrylic, watercolor and photography are featured as well as prints and reproductions. Areas of the facility are dedicated to bronzes, handpainted gourds, leather works and Native American art such as turquoise jewelry. Highly acclaimed pieces of Southwestern pottery and ceramics by Glen Blakely and Andy Watson are on display along with the work of featured artists including Joni Haws, Tom Finley, Shirley Robinson, Wallace Lee, Melanie Scott, Mark Willard and others.

Worthington Gallery
789 Zion Park Blvd., Springdale
• 772-3446

Pottery, sculpture, watercolors and jewelry by more than 20 artists from Utah and other Western states are displayed in the Worthington Gallery. In a pioneer home built in 1871, Greg Worthington also designs and creates the Cliff Dweller Series, a tribute to the artistry, craftsmanship and ceremonial character of the ancient art of the Anasazi Indians, the first great potters of the Southwest.

Cedar City/Brian Head

Braithwaite Fine Arts Gallery
351 W. Center St., Cedar City • 586-5432

The Braithwaite Fine Arts Gallery, on the campus of Southern Utah University, was named for Dr. Royden C. Braithwaite, who presided over the university and was instrumental in establishing the gallery in 1976. The gallery hosts monthly exhibits, alternating annually scheduled shows that feature the works of faculty, student and local artists with various traveling exhibits throughout the year. The gallery is only closed during exhibit changes and university holidays. It is supported by institutional funds, federal, state and local grants and local donors.

Bryce Canyon Area

Ruby's Western Arts Gallery
Utah Hwy. 63, Bryce Canyon • 834-5341

Tourists from all over the world have taken home a piece of Southwestern Utah with purchases of pottery, Navajo rugs, jewelry, framed fine art, drums and collectibles from Ruby's Western Arts Gallery. Pottery from all major pueblos is represented. Collectors can choose from Santa Clara, San Juan, San Idelfonso, Jemez, Acoma and Cochiti pueblos. Rare pieces from Maria Martinez' black-on-black collection and the tiny works of Joseph Lonewolf, Lucy Lewis, and the Lewis and Tafoya families are also represented.

A spectacular variety of Navajo rug designs include Storm and Tree of Life, and Navajo sand paintings in all price ranges are on display. Silver; turquoise; Navajo, Zuni and Hopi jewelry; Taos drums; a good selection of Kachinas along with Zuni and Navajo fetishes (animal spirits carved from rock) have given this gallery its reputation as one of the finest in the Southwest. Ruby's Western Art Gallery also includes an excellent selection of framed fine art prints from such notable Western artists as Jack Terry, Remington and Russell, J. D. Challenger and wildlife artist Nancy Glass. Utah artists, including Eric Dawdle, Brent Todd and Robert Duncan, are also represented. The gallery is in the world-famous Ruby's Inn (see our Accommodations chapter). It opens early and stays open late to accommodate early-risers and night owls.

Serenidad Gallery
360 W. Main St., Escalante • 826-4810

The Serenidad Gallery features Western paintings and color and black-and-white photographs of the area in and around the Grand Staircase-Escalante National Monument. The gallery's principle artist is Lynn Griffin, a real-

---

ist whose medium of choice is acrylics. The works of Rachel Bentley, Carolyn Bowmar, Greg Holiday and Harriet Priska are also on display along with a collection of antiques including primitive glass, sterling silver, china and Navajo jewelry.

Kanab Area

Center Street Gallery
10 E. Center St., Kanab • 644-5230

The Center Street Gallery in downtown Kanab represents Glen Edwards, Barbara Edwards, John Haley, Michael Gentle, Denise Meyers and Donald Carter, local and regional artists who have each captured the scenic beauty of Southwestern Utah in their own way. The Center Street Gallery offers an exciting combination of Cibachrome limited-edition photographs, original oils, watercolors, acrylics, intaglio and lino cuts, sculpture, ceramics and painted gourds. Although they may not be on display, there are also limited-edition reproductions available from some artists.

Johnson Canyon Rock Art Gallery
5424 N. Johnson Canyon Rd., Kanab • 644-3110

Johnson Canyon contains some spectacular examples of Virgin Kayenta Anasazi cliff dwellings in excellent condition. The civilization, which existed between 200 B.C. and 1050, left a record of their habitation on the cliff walls. The Johnson Canyon Rock Art Gallery has found a method for casting the rock images of the Virgin Kayenta Anasazi using a silicon-based poly-resin material that allows reproduction without damage to the original work of art. The gallery markets the 1½-inch-thick slabs as a new form of old art — architectural design elements suitable for incorporating into structures or hanging on existing walls. The idea seems to be catching on in Southwestern Utah office buildings and custom homes.

Crafts

Kanab Area

Kanab Quilt Guild
99 E. 100 South, Kanab • 644-2477

The quilt was a utilitarian item during the days of the pioneers. Its purpose was simply to help make comfortable those whose lives were anything but. The humble quilt has since become an art form combining elaborate new designs, complicated patterns and dynamic colors and textures. The Kanab Quilt Guild, formed in 1983, brings together quilters from around Kane County for the purpose of socializing and creating. The organization meets monthly, rotating its meeting place depending on who needs help finishing a project.

Around Mother's Day, the guild proudly displays its handiwork for the pleasure of the community, inviting participants from neighboring counties. The 20 current members also create other handmade items to sell — all merchandise based on quilt designs. These include a fun and varied assortment of table runners, wall hangings, placemats, appliance covers and clothing items such as vests and jackets. All proceeds go to support local groups and needs — one current focus is on getting a new library started in town. The Kanab Quilt Guild meets every month on the second Tuesday at 1 PM, but you'll need to call to find out where.

Support Organizations

Funding for the arts is generally scarce no matter where you live. Music and dance add much to civilized society, yet orchestras, dance companies and music schools are frequently limited by budgets. The same organizations that add charm and grace to our lives must beg, borrow and plead for nearly every dollar of their support.

Though the arts in Southwestern Utah may vary from community to community, most support organizations have found creative ways to promote the cause of beauty and culture. If you are new to your community and have an interest in the arts, ask around: You can be sure there is some way you can get involved.

St. George/Zion

Southwest Guild
P.O. Box 994, St. George • 652-7994

The Southwest Guild was formed in 1973 to encourage local support for the arts. To that end, the guild conducts annual fund-raising for donations to the Celebrity Concert Series, Southwest Symphony, Southwest Symphonic Chorale and for fine arts scholarships at Dixie College. In 1988, the guild accomplished one of its primary goals — purchase of a concert grand piano for the Dixie Center, where many local performances are staged. To provide for the long-term care of the new instrument, the Southwest Guild has gone one step further to create a fund for maintenance and repair.

Over the years, this organization has become as well-known as the arts and cultural events it supports, the result of such activities as the Spring Fashion Show and Luncheon, chocolate sales during intermission at Celebrity Concert Series performances and the yuletide "Homes for the Holidays" event that showcases imaginatively decorated area homes. An annual membership campaign, perhaps

Happily Ever After, Or Else

The early settlers of Southwestern Utah loved the theater. Many had crossed the ocean to follow their religious convictions but did not want to sacrifice the arts and culture of their European homelands. A stage performance brought everyone in from the fields, with the cost of admission paid with squashes, eggs, poultry, flour or corn.

Shakespeare and other notable English writers were performed often with quilts and wagon covers as curtains. Melodramas such as *The Rose of Etterick Vale*, *Two Blind Orphans* and *The Miller and His Men* were played on Monday and Tuesday evenings every other week, giving two performances of each play and farce. But while church leaders encouraged drama, they wanted it to mirror the ideals of the people. If a script did not have a proper ending, the final scenes were rewritten so justice might be realized, even if the hero had to bring a villain back and hang him.

the most significant of the organization's fund-raising activities, resulted in 166 individuals paying for the privilege of membership in 1996. Members of the guild pay an annual fee of $25, but often contribute more as a gift to the local arts community. Members are also listed on concert series programs and are invited backstage following each performance.

Tuacahn Center for the Arts
1100 N. Tuacahn Dr., Ivins • 674-9909, (800) 746-9882

Tuacahn Center for the Arts has functioned as a community arts school since 1992 and was recognized almost immediately for membership in the National Guild of Community Schools of the Performing Arts. Instruction is offered in musical instruments, drama, dance and voice. In 1996, Tuacahn added visual arts to its curriculum as well. In early 1997, the institution was honored with a major national grant awarded to appoint Phillip Bimstein, a composer from Springdale, as the first composer-in-residence.

The school moved into its present 42,000-square-foot facility in January 1995. Since that time, the school has experienced severe growing pains. The new facility was financed primarily by incurring a debt of nearly $13 million. Tuition and proceeds from events was insufficient to carry either the operating deficit or the burden of debt service. In 1996, necessary changes were made in management and operating procedures. Funds from anonymous donors have gone a long way toward clearing up the construction debts.

The amphitheater — home of *UTAH! America's Most Spectacular Outdoor Musical* (see the Tuacahn Amphitheater listing in our Attractions chapter) — and center for the arts are now in a good position to develop a positive cash flow from a successful show season and an expansion of the tuition base from an enlarged student body of dedicated young artists.

Washington County Historical Society
356 N. Main St., St. George • 673-5614

The society oversees the historical interests of St. George and coordinates activities in other communities such as Hurricane, Wash-ington City, Leeds and Santa Clara. In a dozen years, the Washington County Historical Society, with more than 100 members, has been instrumental in breathing new life into the Old Pioneer Courthouse (home of the St. George Area Chamber of Commerce) on the corner of 100 East and St. George Boulevard. Through society efforts, the large upstairs courtroom has been renewed and revitalized, the judge's bench and jury box have been restructured, and the room is now a popular setting for art shows and lectures by Ranger Bart Anderson (see the Close-up on Ranger Bart in our Parks and Other Natural Wonders chapter).

The society is now heavily involved in the restoration of the building's basement, including jail cells used in bygone days to house horse thieves and cattle rustlers. Looking ahead, the members of the Washington County Historical Society are hoping to restore the Temple Trail, a pathway used for transporting quarried rock in the days of the construction of the St. George LDS Temple. The society holds luncheon meetings on the last Thursday of the month at the old courthouse building on the corner of 100 East and St. George Boulevard, hosting speakers on topics of historical interest.

Cedar City/Brian Head

Cedar City Arts Council
110 N. Main St., Cedar City • 865-1919

The Cedar City Arts Council, established in 1988 by the Cedar City Council, consists of 11 volunteer members who collectively serve as advocates for local arts including theater, dance, visual arts, literature, Native American arts and music. In addition to its advocacy role, the council sponsors several annual events such as Mayfest, a celebration of the arts held each spring. Mayfest provides a venue for performances by community groups, amateur talent, poets and showings of Hollywood classics filmed in the area.

The Cedar City Arts Council also supports concerts, gallery openings, theatrical presentations, craft shows, square dancing, one-day festivals and other activities ranging from performances by the Color Country Cloggers to the Utah Shakespearean Festival. The council publicizes details of their events free in a quarterly community arts calendar. Information on current events is available on the Arts Hotline at the previously listed number.

Bryce Canyon Area

Southwest Arts Guild
395 W. 500 South, Panguitch • 676-2224

In the Bryce Canyon area, arts and culture probably won't involve opera or ballet. Cowboy poetry, a string band performance or a community theater production are more likely. The charge to oversee the local activities associated with the arts falls on the Southwest Arts Guild. Not to be confused with the Southwest Guild in St. George, this organization meets sporadically but manages to pull off its share of top-quality programs and activities every year. Appreciative audiences come from as far away as Kanab and Fredonia to the south and the small farming towns of Piute County to the north.

Popular local cultural events include cowboy poetry readings and festivals, folklore and history lectures, a fair share of literary readings and theater. The Southwest Arts Guild also supports the active Panguitch Community Theater (see listing in this chapter), which combines neighbors and friends under the direction of the disbanded local high school drama department and has recently given the Bryce Canyon area a taste of Broadway. The arts guild also chose to throw its efforts and support to celebrating Utah's Statehood Centennial in 1996, but plans are in the works to bring artists and performers to the area in 1997.

During the Christmas season, the Southwest Arts Guild sponsors a holiday performance of Handel's *Messiah* in which the Kanab Civic Orchestra (see listing in this chapter) and a half-dozen or so Panguitch residents join forces. Rehearsals are held in Kanab — a distance of 67 miles one-way — and most Bryce

area musicians carpool together to make the trip as many as three times a month. Throughout the year, the association between musicians in both communities continues through the guild's ambitious program schedule.

The Southwest Arts Guild receives great support from two statewide organizations — the Utah Arts Council and the Utah Heritage Foundation — that help provide regular choices of programming. The guild also works with the English, music and drama departments at Dixie College and Southern Utah University in Cedar City. String quartets, dance groups, and well-known entertainers have stopped over in Panguitch, and many have been accommodated in private homes. Popular shows have included the Brough Wolf Duo, Douglas Spotted Eagle, the Sundance Children's Dance Theater and the Utah Ballet; photographer Don Marshall and his wife, Jean, a doll collector; and the visual talents of artists Pancho Sanchez, Lynn Griffin and Wallace G. Lee. "We do anything and everything to defray costs," says guild chairman Steve Marshall, whose cost-cutting efforts have at times been creative. One visiting entertainer was paid with a cut of wrapped venison!

Kanab Area

Canyon Arts
4250 N. Kanab Canyon Dr., Kanab • 644-5070

"Went out to the open desert land
Empty as the sky.
Stood on top of sacred mountain there
And watched an eagle fly
Over ghosts of ancient ocean
And on her wings I heard the sound
Of the voice that I'd forgotten
Said I'm standing on Holy Ground"

These are the words of Cyrus Mejia, who paints visionary landscapes with the soft shapes and colors of Southwestern Utah as

---

INSIDERS' TIP

Many restored historic buildings are open for view in communities all over Southwestern Utah. Ask around. Insiders will know what you should see!

his inspiration. His work is an expression of his dreams. On canvas they take on their own identity and provide those who view his work a window into another world.

In 1967, while still a student, he dreamed of finding a spiritual place — a place of healing. The dream had such an impact he spent the next 20 years searching for the place. Mejia's travels took him to Kanab. When he saw Angel Canyon, he recognized it at once as the healing location in his dream! As an artist he had come full circle. The bright landscapes would forever be the source of his inspiration.

During brief periods outside his studio, Mejia has helped create Canyon Arts, a loose-knit group of artists in the Kanab area. Sculp-

tors, potters and other artists in a variety of mediums have found each other in the community. Together they share ideas, create and display the products of their imagination. Although there is no formal organization, Canyon Arts members planned to exhibit for the first time as a group during the community's 1997 Fourth of July Festival.

Variety Arts Council
37 E. 200 North, Kanab • 644-5013

With at least two decades of guaranteed funding put in place in June 1984 by city leaders, the Variety Arts Council of Kanab has been designing top-notch community events that feature both homegrown talent and entertainers from far and wide. Variety Arts entices per-

Photo: Lyman Hafen

The O.C. Tanner Amphitheater in Springdale is a popular area arts venue.

formers to this splendid corner of the world with promises of appreciative audiences, and it delivers the goods.

Seven arts council members put their creative heads together on a regular basis to consider what has been done, what is currently planned and what are the options for quality activities. At the moment, the Young Ambassadors, a polished singing and dancing company from Brigham Young University, are on the calendar. In the summer of 1996, a traveling Smithsonian exhibit of World War II memorabilia spent two weeks in Kanab and provided the backdrop for a community salute to America's armed forces. The Kanab Civic Orchestra performed, and the community was invited to add personal souvenirs of life in the war years.

The Wednesday Night in the Gazebo program (see our Kidstuff chapter) was started by Variety Arts Council as a way to entertain busloads of tourists who converged on Kanab between jaunts to Zion National Park and the Glen Canyon Recreation Area in Nevada. Free performances by cloggers, western bands and singers delight an audience made up of a growing number of regulars from the community and visitors from all over the globe.

The makeup of the Variety Arts Council changes from year to year as board members come and go on to other community assignments. What remains constant is a love of the arts and a desire to build on what has been accomplished.

Venues

St. George/Zion

Dixie Center
425 S. 700 East, St. George • 628-7003

The Dixie Center is a multiuse community complex designed to promote economic growth through conventions, meetings and events and to provide cultural, educational and recreational opportunities for the area known as Utah's Dixie. Opened in 1987, the Dixie Center is designed for flexibility with an overall area of 145,000 square feet. There is seating for 5,000 in the Burns Sports Arena, 1,200 in the M.K. Cox Performing Arts Center and 13,000 square feet of space in Smith Convention Center. Eccles Fitness Center (see our Community Recreation chapter) has a pool and workout rooms.

The Dixie Center has played host to such major events as Utah Jazz basketball and the Harlem Globetrotters, and entertainers including Alabama, the Oak Ridge Boys, the Beach Boys, the Mormon Tabernacle Choir, the Utah Symphony, the Western Opera Theater, the St. Petersburg Ballet, Ballet West and others. Convention gatherings ranging in size from 100 to 8,000 have been attracted to Utah's hot spot for statewide and national conventions. Inviting scenery, climate, recreation activities and the facilities available at the Dixie Center have helped make the St. George area an ideal setting for many groups.

Pioneer Center for the Arts
212 N. Main St., St. George • 634-5850

For years the St. George Opera House, built about 1875, sat vacant and decaying. Today the beautifully restored structure is the centerpiece for the dazzling Pioneer Center for the Arts, a complex that includes the opera building Brigham Young saw constructed to encourage the performing arts. The center also features a 10,000-square-foot, two-story museum that houses St. George's permanent art collection, the Statehood Centennial Legacy Collection; provides exhibit space for rotating art shows; and includes a gift shop.

A deck with tables and chairs will soon be added to the east wall of the Opera House, encouraging visitors to enjoy the afternoon shade while taking advantage of the view of

---

INSIDERS' TIP

Don't miss the opportunity to tour Tuacahn Amphitheater and Center for the Arts in Ivins. Descriptive adjectives pale compared to the actual grandeur of both the facility and its setting.

downtown St. George and the desert beyond. Plans for a tea room, additional display areas, restrooms and storage are planned for the finished restoration of a third building. Tying it all together, a garden area will be crisscrossed with walkways, trees, a peace garden and benches. A water feature and a restored adobe schoolhouse should provide a spectacular future to a corner that for years residents argued should be used for a parking lot.

St. George Art Museum
47 E. 200 North, St. George • 634-5942

On the same plaza as the St. George Opera House, this impressive museum just opened in January 1997. An old sugar beet seed storage building has been transformed into a handsome two-story museum that houses St. George city's permanent art collection. Included are 12 inspiring paintings of historic scenes commissioned for Utah's Centennial celebration in 1996; traveling exhibits by noted artists rotate at the museum throughout the year.

There is no admission charge, but note the widely varied hours of operation. The museum is open from 6 to 8 PM Monday; noon to 5 PM on Tuesday, Wednesday and Thursday; noon to 8 PM Friday; and 10 AM to 5 PM Saturday. The museum is closed on Sunday.

Cedar City/Brian Head

Centrum
150 S. 800 West, Cedar City • 586-7872 (tickets), 586-1937 (scheduling)

Its 5,500 chair-back seats makes the Centrum the center for large events and activities in the Iron County area. The basketball arena is a popular setting for a variety of sporting events, concerts by the local symphony orchestra or big-name country stars, school programs, a regional history fair competition, gymnastics and other competitions during the Utah Summer Games (see our Annual Events chapter). On the campus of Southern Utah University, the Centrum is also the home of the university's history, arts and letters, communications and art departments. Classrooms are spread around the interior perimeter of the building.

The Utah Shakespearean Festival has become the most recognized and respected annual event in Southwestern Utah.

Annual Events

Community events add life to the land-scape in Southwestern Utah.

This chapter offers a sampling of the kinds of events and festivals you'll find all over this red rock country. The events listed are annual affairs. Some occur on a specific date, others during a particular time of a specific month. We've listed prices where possible, and there's a phone number with each listing that will allow you to get specific information on this year's event.

Many of the events we share are quite folksy and homey but nonetheless exciting and endearing to visitors and newcomers. Others, as you will see, are widely famous and draw people from all over the world. They range from the tradition-rich Old-Time Fiddlers and Bear Festival in Cannonville to one of the most respected Shakespearean festivals in the world in Cedar City.

January

St. George Heritage Week
Various locations, St. George • 634-5850

Heritage Week commemorates the birth of the city of St. George in January of 1862. The mid-month celebration includes musical performances, a heritage fair, historic exhibits, programs on local history, plays and special activities for youth. Events are held at various places throughout St. George, including the Dixie Center, the Pioneer Opera House and the St. George Tabernacle. Events in this week-long celebration, sponsored by the City of St. George, vary from year to year and are generally free. Bring along some money for the food vendors. Call for details on any specific events planned for this year's Heritage Week.

Parowan's Birthday Celebration
Various sites, Parowan • 477-3331

The City of Parowan was the first Mormon pioneer settlement in Southwestern Utah,

founded on January 13, 1851. Each year on that day the community celebrates its birthday with a town meeting, a luncheon and a birthday ball. The activities are geared toward the local residents, but the past two years have drawn more visitors than ever, probably due to the keynote speakers: Utah Gov. Michael Leavitt and LDS Church President Gordon B. Hinckley.

February

Bryce Canyon Winter Festival
Various locations, Bryce Canyon
• (800) 444-6689

At elevations of more than 10,000 feet, the Bryce Canyon area gets a great deal of snow in the wintertime. To celebrate, a winter festival is held for three days over President's Day weekend. There are cross-country ski races, snow sculpting contests, ski archery competitions, evening entertainment and photography clinics. All events are free except for ski lessons ($5 per person) and the ski archery competition, which has a $10 entry fee.

Dixie College Invitational Art Show
Graff Fine Arts Center, Dixie College, 225 S. 700 East, St. George • 652-7500

During the past 10 years, the Dixie Invitational has become one of the most respected annual art shows in the West. Only the best artists in the western states are invited to show work in this six-week exhibit that begins on President's Day weekend at the Graff Fine Arts Center on the Dixie College campus. Paintings of Southwestern landscapes, people and historic places as well as an exciting selection of modern art and some sculptures are selected each year. There is no admission, but patrons are invited to purchase paintings (ranging in price from $200 to about $5,000), with a percentage of the proceeds going to fund a new art museum on the college campus. Whether you're interested in buying or not, this is a delightful place to spend an hour or two in early spring.

Southern Utah Parade of Homes
Greater St. George area • 674-1400

At a cost of $5 per person you can tour approximately 20 new homes in the St. George area built by members of the Southern Utah Homebuilders Association. As you register at the Red Cliffs Mall, 1770 E. Red Cliff Drive in St. George, you get a complete magazine detailing the features of each home and a map to guide you. Homes usually are spread as far west as Kayenta, beneath the Red Mountain 7 miles west of the city, and as far east as Washington, about 20 miles away. In between, you'll have a chance to walk through a variety of different homes built especially for the show. Prices range wildly — from about $120,000 to $1 million. It's wonderful entertainment, and if you're serious about building or remodeling, there's no better way to gather ideas.

FYI

Unless otherwise noted, the area code for all phone numbers listed in this chapter is 801 but will change to 435 in September 1997. Either area code may be used until March 22, 1998.

March

St. Patrick's Day in Springdale
Various locations, Springdale • 772-3434

The town of Springdale, at the southern entrance to Zion National Park, is the only community in Southwestern Utah with a full-fledged St. Patrick's Day celebration. The day's events vary each March 17 but are anchored every year by a parade in the morning. There is usually a dance and a green (remember, it's St. Paddy's Day!) Jell-O molding contest, and many restaurants serve green beer.

Women's Conference in Dixie
Dixie Center, 425 S. 700 East, St. George • 628-7003

This one-day conference, held on a Saturday in mid-March, features a new theme of vital importance to women each year. Sponsored by Dixie College, Dixie Regional Medical Center and Washington County Extension Service, recent topics have included careers, health, home and family and social issues. Registra-

tion is $15 in advance or $20 at the door, which allows you to hear some of the nation's most respected speakers on women's issues and concerns. Workshops are also designed to help women meet the challenges of today.

St. George Art Festival
Main Street, St. George • 634-5850

There's no admission charge for the regionally famous St. George Art Festival, but be prepared to pull out your wallet anyway. This exciting, two-day street show (held Friday and Saturday of Easter weekend) features so many varieties, styles and tastes in art, it's nearly impossible to walk down Main Street between Tabernacle and First South without buying something.

More than 100 artists are accepted into this juried show, and the artists themselves are behind the counter showing and talking about their watercolors, oils, ceramics, jewelry, sculptures, clothing designs, metal work, woodwork and other types of art. How much do you want to spend? You can find earrings for $5 and paintings for $5,000. In the meantime, there are food booths, continuous entertainment on a stage just off the street (clogging and country-western bands are featured) and all kinds of activities for the kids, including face painting. Plan on spending several hours to take it all in.

Hurricane Easter Car Show
Various locations, Hurricane • 635-2471

This show includes all types, makes and years of cars, trucks and motorcycles. There are 40 classes and more than 350 cars on display on the Hurricane High School campus throughout the Easter weekend. The show is sponsored by a local coalition of car buffs and regularly draws about 7,000 visitors a year. The Zion Park Rod Run, a relaxed poker run through the canyons of Zion, is held on Sunday morning. Poker run participants receive a card at each of five stops, and the best hand at the end of the ride receives a prize. Admission to view the cars is $5 for adults; children accompanied by a grownup are free.

More than 4,000 runners participated in the 1996 St. George Marathon.

Z-Arts Workshops
Various locations, Springdale • 772-3748

What better place to brush up on your photography skills, writing or watercolor and oil painting than within the towering walls of Zion Canyon. From March through May each spring, Z-Arts, a community arts foundation in Springdale, offers a series of Saturday art workshops that generally include photography, painting, writing and more rare arts such as papermaking. Many instructors are Southwestern Utah artists; others are brought in from surrounding Western states. The series usually runs for four weekends, with a different workshop taking center stage each week. Workshop fees are about $50, with some requiring an additional materials fee.

April

Buck-a-thon
Dixie Center, 425 S. 700 East, St. George • 628-7003

Diamond "G" Rodeo Company puts on an annual rodeo in the indoor Dixie Center arena each spring. Ticket prices are in the $10 range for this heart-stopping night of bronc and bull riding. Whether you're a die-hard rodeo fan or just looking for a thrilling evening, the Buck-a-thon is something you'll long remember. Many of the top professional cowboys in the country participate in the two-night show, and more than $40,000 in prize money is up for grabs. Steve and Cyndi Gilbert of Diamond "G" Ranch in nearby Toquerville (about 25 miles east of St. George off I-15) own some of the meanest bucking bulls and highest-kicking broncs in America. You'll see their animals and the hard-riding cowboys up close in the Dixie Center.

Dixie Downs Horse Races
Washington County Fair Park, 15 miles east of St. George on Utah Hwy. 9 • 628-7003

For more than 25 years, the St. George Lions Club has sponsored two April weekends of horse racing at Dixie Downs. The original Dixie Downs track in northwest St. George was torn down in 1997, and a new track opened at the Washington County Fair Park, east of St. George. The April horse racing tradition will continue at the new facility, where 400 racing stalls will accommodate winter training. The April meet will give the horses an opportunity to race before they leave to run at larger tracks in the summer.

Races are held on the second and fourth Saturdays beginning at 1 PM. Both quarter horses and thoroughbreds compete in some 12 races each day. The race meet is sanctioned by the Utah Racing Commission. Admission is usually $5 or less.

May

Southern Utah Poetry and Western Art Gathering
Parowan High School, 168 N. Main St., Parowan • 477-3512

During the past eight years the City of Parowan has developed a great tradition with its poetry and Western art gathering. The three-day event over Memorial Day weekend begins with a free show on Friday at 7:30 PM with Western bands, cloggers and cowboy poetry readings. On Saturday morning the festivities begin at 9 AM. There's no charge to stroll through the booths of Western exhibits and vendors featuring all kinds of cowboy art, from paintings to jewelry to leather work. Concurrent with the exhibits are open-mike performances from 9 AM to 5:30 PM for anyone who wants to share cowboy poetry or perform Western music.

From 5 to 7 PM, a Dutch-oven dinner is served featuring ribs or chicken, cowboy beans and Dutch-oven spuds. The dinner is $8. At 7 PM, the main program gets under way. It only costs $5 to see some of the West's best musicians and cowboy poets. Past performers have included poet Don Kennington and banjo picker Bob Fletcher. On Sunday there are free banjo, guitar and fiddle workshops from 4 to 6 PM, and from 6 to 8 PM there's an informal jam session where everyone, pro and novice alike, is invited to join in.

Cedar City Mayfest Artwalk
Orchestra Hall, 74 N. 300 West • 865-1919

Now in its seventh year, the annual Mayfest and Artwalk provide an excellent opportunity to become familiar with the great art community in Cedar City. Held on a Saturday in early May, the free event includes performances and exhibits by Cedar City's many fine performing, literary and visual artists. Past events have included Utah's poet laureate David Lee, the Southern Utah University Ballroom Dance Company, pianist Charity Whittaker and violinist LuAnne Brown. Among the city's nationally recognized visual artists who exhibit during the event are Jeff Wolf, Steve Taylor, Perry Stuart, Brian Hoover and Arlene Braithwaite. Displays open at 6 PM, and performances begin at 7 PM.

Washington Cotton Festival
Various locations, Washington • 634-9850

Plan on a cotton-pickin' good time at the annual Cotton Festival in early May in Washington. Except for food concessions, there's no cost for the various public activities. During this three-day event there are beauty pageants, Dutch-oven dinners, a 5K fun run/walk as well as arts and crafts booths, children's races, mountain bike races, firefighter competitions and even a golf tournament at the city's highly rated Green Spring Golf Course. Take your swings for $25 per golfer. If you're in a conundrum over cotton, it all links back to the days when Washington was settled by Mormon converts from the Southern states (see our Close-up, "Why Utah's Dixie?" in our History chapter).

High Country Drag Races
High Country Raceway, 10 miles south of St. George off River Rd. • 652-9560

For more than 30 years, Southwestern Utah speed buffs have gathered each Memorial Day weekend at High Country Raceway, south of St. George (take River Road south across the Virgin River and follow the signs) on a secluded bluff, where an abandoned airport has been converted into a drag strip. On the quarter-mile track more than 50 cars owned by locals and racers from surrounding states run head-to-head in different divisions ranging from street cars to roadsters to dragsters. The races, sponsored by the High Country Raceway Association, begin at 1 PM, and there's a $5 admission charge. The traditional races kick

off a season that usually includes one Saturday of racing each month from June through November. The June, July and August races are held in the evening under the lights.

June

Utah Summer Games
Various locations, Cedar City • 586-7228

The world will soon begin to focus on Utah as we prepare to host the Winter Olympic Games in 2002, but Southwestern Utah is already accustomed to an annual athletic spectacle on a much smaller scale. Each June, Cedar City hosts the Utah Summer Games at venues throughout the area. Only those amateur athletes in the state who have qualified in regional competitions are invited. It is the state's most popular showcase for amateur athletes, who compete in nearly 40 events from archery to water polo. In 1996 the two-week games drew 6,899 participants from every corner of the state. There are uplifting, Olympic-style opening and closing ceremonies, and

the events are open to the public and televised by regional TV stations. More than 3,000 local volunteers help make it all happen.

Paiute Restoration Gathering
Various locations, Cedar City • 586-1112

This Native American celebration includes a powwow, a parade, a queen and princess contest, a dinner, a talent night and a softball tournament. The Paiutes were the native culture of Southwestern Utah when white settlers arrived in the mid-1850s. In the eyes of the federal government, they lost their status as a tribe in the 1950s but were reinstated as a recognized tribal organization in June 1980. The annual gathering, held the second weekend in June in Cedar City, commemorates this restoration. Visitors are welcome.

Utah Shakespearean Festival
Southern Utah University, Cedar City • 586-7878

With more than three decades of success behind it, the Utah Shakespearean Festival has become the most recognized and respected annual event in Southwestern Utah. Each year the festival produces six plays between late June and early September that run in matinee and evening performances every day but Sunday. Four of the plays are always Shakespearean; two are by other internationally known playwrights. Ticket prices for each play range from $10 to $27. Package deals are available that can save you up to $3 per ticket.

In 1996 the festival produced Shakespeare's *The Comedy of Errors*, *Macbeth*, *The Winter's Tale* and *Henry IV, Part 1*. Alexander Dumas' *The Three Musketeers* and Gilbert and Sullivan's *The Mikado* were also done. The festival is run by a full-time, year-round staff and brings in some of the most respected directors and stage actors in America. Plays are staged at the outdoor Adams Memorial Theater on the Southern Utah University campus and inside the subtly ornate Randall Theater, just across 300 West. The festival is given added character by the stunning outdoor theater structure, cited by the British Broadcasting Company as one of the most faithful reproductions of a Shakespearean stage in the world.

The surrounding landscape of the SUU campus, with its tall pines and sprawling lawns, is a joyful respite from the sage-covered Great Basin surrounding Cedar City, and before each evening performance you'll swear you've walked right out of the Southwestern Utah desert into merry old England. The festival spirit is enhanced by jugglers, dancers, musicians, Punch and Judy shows and Renaissance games. Strolling, costumed maidens speaking in authentic dialects bear baskets full of tarts, horehound and humbug candies. Plan on spending several days in order to see all the plays, participate in daily seminars, take a

backstage tour for $7 and eat at the rowdy and robust Renaissance Feaste. The Feaste, $29 per person, indulges all your senses as you dine and play with the lords and ladies of medieval England. It's a seven-course spread eaten in the style of the day — with your hands — amid the continual hubbub of song, dance and merriment.

The festival also offers child care for children up to age 8 during all plays, but not during the Royal Feaste and other festival activities. The clean, safe, child-care facility is professionally staffed and adjacent to the festival complex. The festival urges parents to take advantage of this service as no one younger than 5 is admitted to performances.

Note that it is best to make ticket reservations for the festival at least six months in advance. Also, be sure to make time to attend the morning lectures by experts on the Bard as you sit among the trees in outdoor classrooms.

July

Midsummer Renaissance Faire
Cedar City Park, 200 N. Main St., Cedar City • 586-1124

During the peak of the Utah Shakespearean Festival on the campus of SUU, this delightful fair takes place for four days in mid-July just a few blocks away in the Cedar City Park. There's a full city block of booths, performers, displays and vendors. You are surrounded by Renaissance period music, folks in full costume, dancing, games, displays and crafts. There's no admission charge, but you can plan on spending about $5 per person for food, choosing from a smorgasbord including Asian, Mexican or traditional

---

As you're driving south from Enterprise or Veyo toward St. George, pull off Utah Highway 18 a mile south of the Diamond Valley turnoff, just after you've passed the two black cinder cones of extinct volcanoes. From here, look to the southwest across the rising ledges of Snow Canyon State Park. If you're there in the morning, you'll see what runners in the St. George Marathon see — red rock towers that seem to be lit by some magical fire inside the stone.

Great Views

American eats. The event is put on by volunteers, who bring in belly dancers, cloggers and all sorts of other interesting forms of entertainment. Kids can stop by the petting zoo and even milk a goat if they want. Items for sale range from medieval costumes to jewelry and handcrafted items.

American Folk Ballet Festival
Southern Utah University, Cedar City
• 586-0622

Now in its fourth decade, the American Folk Ballet is headquartered at Southern Utah University in Cedar City. The traveling troop hosts a week-long festival each July on the campus of SUU during the Utah Shakespearean Festival. The ballet presents matinee and evening performances throughout the week.

Old-Time Fiddle and Bear Festival
Cannonville City Park • 676-8826,
(800) 444-6686

Come midsummer, the 160 or so residents of Cannonville, just east of Bryce Canyon National Park, get mighty serious about the topics of fiddles and black bears. For nearly 20 years they've held an old-time fiddlers' concert in the open air of the city park at 7:30 PM on a July Saturday night. The tradition took on an added dimension in 1987, when the town added a "bear barbecue" to the evening's events. That year, meat from a marauding black bear that had been dining on residents' chickens and apricots made up the main course of the evening's feast. Government officials determined the bear had become a little too gregarious when he tried to enter the home of a Cannonville couple. Authorities subsequently shot and killed the bear, whose meat was donated to the town starting a new tradition of bear burgers as part of the annual festivities. Now each year, the town combines the old-time fiddle concert with a bear festival including demonstrations, art displays, community booths and some of the West's best fiddling. There's a modest charge for dinner — bear burgers, or traditional hamburgers and homemade root beer — beginning at 5:30 PM. Then you can settle in for a free evening of fiddle music under the stars.

Photo: St. George Magazine

A face-painter puts on a happy face at the St. George Art Festival on Easter weekend.

Utah Shakespearean Festival
Cedar City • 586-7878

The Utah Shakespearean Festival has become the most recognized and respected annual event in Southwestern Utah. Each year the festival produces six plays between late June and early September that run in matinee and evening performances every day but Sunday. For more information, see the previous listing in this chapter under June events.

Pioneer Day
Towns throughout Southwestern Utah

Pioneer Day marks the day Mormon pioneers entered the Valley of the Great Salt Lake in 1847. For the past century-and-a-half, the cities and towns of Utah have commemorated that day on July 24 with parades, programs, banquets, rodeos and fireworks. Each community has its own style of celebrating. Check with the city office, chamber of commerce or travel bureau in the town where you plan to visit.

August

Washington County Fair
Washington County Fair Park, 3 miles east of I-15 off Utah Hwy. 9 • 634-5706

The Washington County Fair is an early August tradition dating back more than 100 years. Traditionally held at various venues in the community of Hurricane, the fair moved in 1997 to its new home at the county fair park about 15 miles east of St. George. During the three-day celebration there are parades, a 5-kilometer walk/run, rodeo events, boxing, a baby contest, baseball and basketball tournaments and food booths. Also scheduled each year are a horse show, poetry competition, car show, home and fine arts displays, 4-H projects and exhibits, seed displays and even a petting zoo. There's no charge to the exhibits, but you will be charged a nominal fee (always less than $10) for certain programs or events such as boxing and the rodeo.

Enterprise Corn Festival
Town Square, Enterprise • 878-2221

It's the coolest spot, literally, in Washington County in late August, and the corn is delicious. These are just two good reasons to drive the 35 miles north from St. George to the town of Enterprise for the annual Corn Festival that has been held now for more than a decade. The Enterprise area is noted for its productive farms and its tidy homes and gardens. Excellent corn is grown both commercially and privately in this area, and the people take pride in their crop. When it's time to harvest, they celebrate with a weekend day of selling fresh, bright yellow corn on the cob, playing games and staffing food and concession booths. There are also a craft boutique, quilt exhibits, roping at the rodeo arena and other sports activities. There's no admission fee.

Utah Shakespearean Festival
Cedar City • 586-7878

The Utah Shakespearean Festival has become the most recognized and respected annual event in Southwestern Utah. Each year the festival produces six plays between late June and early September that run in matinee and evening performances every day but Sunday. For more information, see the previous listing in this chapter under June events.

September

Iron County Fair
Iron County Fairgrounds, Parowan
• 477-8380

The Iron County Fair is one of the biggest annual celebrations in Southwestern Utah. Festivities begin on the Wednesday before Labor Day weekend with a horse show in the afternoon and a Little Buckaroo Rodeo in the evening (adult admission, $5; children younger than 12, $3). A complete carnival amusement park opens on Thursday, and there's a free dance that evening. The exhibit hall opens at 3 PM on Friday with traditional fair exhibits of baked goods, candy, crops and flowers. There's also free continuous entertainment by local singers and dancers concurrent with the exhibits.

On Friday night the main rodeo starts at 7 PM at the fairgrounds. Admission is $8 for adults and $4 for children younger than 12. The rodeo continues on Saturday and Monday nights as well. On Saturday, in addition to the ongoing exhibits, carnival and other entertainment, the fair hosts a 5K and 10K run in Cedar City, a 4-H fun day in Parowan, a Firemen's Olympics at the Parowan City Park, Utah Horse Racing Association sanctioned races at the fairgrounds at 1 PM, softball and basketball tournaments, chili and pie bake-offs and a horseshoe tournament.

On Labor Day Monday there's a parade through downtown Parowan at 10 AM, a car show at the Parowan City Park from 10 AM to 4 PM and a Daredevil Auto Show at 7 PM (admission is $10 for adults and $5 for children younger than 12).

Southern Utah Folklife Festival
Various locations, Springdale • 772-3434

Each year as fall begins to descend upon Zion Canyon, the town of Springdale (about 45 miles east of St. George) becomes the setting for hundreds of performers, artists, craftspeople and others dedicated to preserving the folk traditions of Southwestern Utah. Entrance to the three-day Folklife Festival in early September is free, though there are many

The Cost of Admission

During the early days of Southwestern Utah, the Mormon people were highly supportive of the arts. Even their leader, Brigham Young, placed the diversion of plays, dances and festivals high on the list of priorities. Admission to plays was usually 50¢, but actual money was as scarce as rain in this desert. A typical play brought in 40 or 50 dollars, yet only $1 or $2 of the total could be accounted for in hard cash. The rest was paid in molasses, vegetables, fruit, grain, flour or labor. A pair of shoes, always in short supply in these parts, would provide tickets for a whole family. If someone brought, say, a very large squash, he might receive a smaller squash or a bunch of grapes for change.

ways to spend money: You may find yourself buying an authentic piece of Indian jewelry or a pair of handmade silver spurs. The festival, which draws hundreds of people from throughout the region, is characterized by the variety of folk artists who participate each year. Saddle makers, cowboy poets, fiddlers, storytellers, dancers and many other preservers of folk expression are represented at the three-day event in early September. We say it is one of Southwestern Utah's best-kept secrets. Don't miss it.

Lions Dixie Roundup
150 S. 400 East, Sun Bowl, St. George • 628-1658

One of the great traditional events in St. George each fall is the three-day celebration of the Dixie Roundup. There are three mid-September nights of rip-roaring rodeo in the legendary Sun Bowl, sanctioned by the Professional Rodeo Cowboys Association. There are parades in downtown at 5 PM each day. Admission to the rodeo usually runs about $6 per day for adults and $3 for children. The weather is almost always perfect in September (shorts in the daytime, long sleeves at night), and the roundup has become a tradition for many residents. In fact, the Lions Club of St. George has been sponsoring the event for more than 60 years. Rodeo on the green grass of the Sun Bowl is a novelty, and the event consistently draws the best ropers and riders in the country.

Santa Clara Swiss Days
Various locations, Santa Clara • 673-6712

On the last Friday and Saturday in September, the small town of Santa Clara celebrates its Swiss heritage with an array of events including historical displays, a fun run, craft and food booths, games, a parade, and a tour of historical homes. There is no charge for any of the events, but you may want to buy some of the beautiful crafts and tasty food. Many descendents of the original Swiss pioneers (Mormon converts who emigrated to Southwestern Utah in 1861) still live in this growing community along the Santa Clara River. For them, Swiss Days is a way to share their heritage with the rest of the Southwestern Utah community as well as with visitors, all of whom are welcome.

October

St. George Marathon
86 S. Main St., St. George • 634-5850

The St. George Marathon has grown dur-

Taken in by the Show

One of the most popular plays produced at the St. George Opera House before the turn of the century was *Jeannie Brown*, or *The Relief of the Lucknow*. It was the tale of a cold husband and a wife seduced by a scoundrel, then abandoned. In the last act, the woman is suffering from a terrible disease, and she crawls through the snow toward her home. Prostrate upon her husband's doorstep she pleads to see her children one more time. The audience wept as the husband proclaimed, "No! No! A thousand times, No!"

At this point, a miner from Silver Reef seated in the audience is said to have jumped to his feet, pulled his pistol and aimed it at the actor playing the husband. Apparently the miner had stopped for a few drinks on his way to St. George. With a hardy shout, he ordered the man to let the wife see her children or he would blow his brains out. A man seated next to the miner arose, grabbed the miner's arm and pulled it up just as a shot rang out. When actors and spectators got up from the floor, they realized the drunken miner had shot a hole in the Opera House ceiling.

Photo: St. George Magazine

Thespians in period garb emote during Greenshow activities at
The Utah Shakespearean Festival.

ing the past 20 years into one of the most popular marathons in the West. The course begins in the pines north of the town of Veyo and runs more than 26 miles, mostly downhill, beneath extinct volcanoes and along the rim of majestic Snow Canyon to the finish line at Vernon Worthen Park in central St. George.

The weather in Utah's Dixie the first weekend in October is usually ideal for running (temps in the mid-60s and dry) and the St. George Leisure Services Department takes great pains to treat the runners with respect and appreciation. City residents and visitors from all over the country line the course and cheer the runners on. More than 1,300 volunteers help staff the aid stations and take care of numerous other race responsibilities.

In 1996, more than 4,000 runners — from 49 states and 11 foreign countries — crossed the finish line in St.George. For visitors and residents the marathon is an inspiring event. Everyone is invited to either sit at the finish line or find spots along the course to watch. There's no charge to watch, and participating is a pretty good deal as well. For the $26 entry fee (one dollar per mile), you'll get a T-shirt, medallion, poster, certificate, a shuttle to the starting line and drinks and fruit after the race is finished.

Michael Martin Murphey's WestFest at Tuacahn

1100 N. Tuacahn Dr., Ivins • 652-3718, (800) 746-9882

Dreamcatcher Promotions of St. George has secured a three-year contract with Michael Martin Murphey's production company to produce the singer's famous WestFest at the Tuacahn Amphitheater, 11 miles northwest of St. George. In 1997, the event will be staged

INSIDERS' TIP

If you're planning to visit St. George for reasons other than to attend an event or festival, we suggest you avoid Easter weekend (St. George Art Festival) and the first weekend of October (St. George Marathon). Accommodations are full to overflowing on those dates and generally require reservations at least a year in advance.

October 9-11. Known as America's greatest singing cowboy since Gene Autry, Murphey has staged WestFests in more than 35 locations throughout the West over the past 12 years. The event is designed to perpetuate the art, music and lifestyle of the West, with concerts by top names in Western music; booths displaying Western arts, crafts, jewelry and clothing; a mountain man encampment; a Native American village; exhibitions of horse training and trick roping; and a cowboy and Native American poetry gathering.

Murphey has distinguished himself as a songwriter and performer with more than 20 top-10 country hits during the past 25 years. His song "What's Forever For" hit number one in 1982, and his 1975 smash "Wildfire" is a country classic. Murphey's agreement to bring WestFest to Southwestern Utah affords residents and visitors a unique opportunity to get a taste of a culture that was once a dominant part of the area but is now quickly fading. A daily ticket price of $22.50 includes all activities as well as admission to that day's concerts. Major country artists are expected to perform.

Huntsman World Senior Games
Various locations, St. George
• (800) 562-1268

Held at venues throughout the St. George area, the Huntsman World Senior Games is a two-week, mid-October extravaganza attracting hundreds of athletes age 50 and older. These seniors compete in events that include basketball, bowling, cycling, golf, horseshoes, racquetball, road racing, soccer, softball, swimming, table tennis, track and field, triathlon and volleyball.

More than 3,500 participants competed in the games in 1996, representing nearly every state in the Union and several foreign countries. The public is invited to all events, which are free of charge, including the opening ceremonies at Hansen Stadium on the Dixie College campus. In past years, the opening ceremonies have included appearances by such sports stars as Jackie Joyner-Kersee, Florence Griffith-Joyner and baseball Hall of Famer Harmon Killibrew.

November

Celebrity Golf and Tennis Classic
Various locations, St. George • 628-1658

Usually held on the first Friday and Saturday of November, this two-day tournament was initiated about 10 years ago by Bruce Hurst, a St. George native who pitched for the Boston Red Sox (remember the 1986 World Series?). The golf tournament is held at Sunbrook Golf Course; the tennis tournament and exhibition take place at the Green Valley Tennis Center. There's no charge to watch the tournament, but for a $10 ticket you can attend an awards dinner and sports auction on Saturday night, during which a number of sports items autographed by legendary players are sold. Neat stuff from stars such as Steve Young, Roger Clemens and Danny Ainge have been featured. All proceeds go to charity. The event brings to St. George several past and present sports stars each year.

Jubilee of Trees
Dixie Center, St. George • 673-5235

This DRMC fundraiser launches the Christmas season in Utah's Dixie. The five-day jubilee, held the week before Thanksgiving, is a showcase for some of the most beautiful Christmas trees you will ever see. Trees are sponsored by local businesses, organizations and individuals, and are custom-decorated according to any imaginable theme. The designs and ornaments sometimes stagger the

While at the Utah Shakespearean Festival in Cedar City, take some time before your next play to walk the campus of Southern Utah University. The views of the landscape and some of the old buildings there might trick you into thinking you've stepped out of the desert and into New England.

Great Views

mind. There's something for everyone at the Jubilee, which charges a nominal entrance fee. Booths, fashion shows, gift ideas, live entertainment (Christmas music, of course), activities for children and the auctioning of the trees to interested buyers are traditional elements of this holiday celebration.

December

Dixie Rotary Bowl Football Game
Hansen Stadium, St. George • 652-7546

This is one of the top-rated junior college football bowl games in America. The St. George Rotary Club sponsors the event and invites the two best junior college football teams available to play head-to-head in Hansen Stadium on the first Saturday in December. During the past 10 years, St. George's own Dixie College Rebels have appeared several times in the game. Consistently ranked in the national Top 10, the Rebels have won all but one of their Rotary Bowl appearances against schools from as far away as Nassau College in New York. The bowl is sanctioned by the National Junior College Athletic Association. Tickets are approximately $10. Bowl festivities include a parade, marching band competition, tailgate party, golf tournament and a banquet featuring a keynote speaker from the sporting world.

St. George Leisure
Services offers a wide
variety of classes and
sports programs to keep
the youngsters busy.

Kidstuff

The kids are bored stiff. There's nothing to do. Whether it's a long, hot summer day, a free afternoon or a Saturday, every parent knows a child's attention span is always half the length of Mom and Dad's creativity. Here are some suggestions for activities guaranteed to keep the little people interested while receiving the stamp of approval from parents.

Just like teens in bigger cities, something to do for the adolescent set in Southwestern Utah might include meeting friends at the mall, but since the Red Cliffs Mall in St. George is the only such site in the region, it narrows the options for those in outlying communities. Dragging Main Street — or in the case of downtown St. George, the "'Vard" (short for Boulevard) — is a popular pastime, especially for newly licensed drivers.

Most rural communities in Southwestern Utah have at least one movie theater, and some have a dozen or more. For some kids, the only thing better than being one of the first to see the newest Hollywood blockbuster on the big screen is to see it over and over again at the dollar theater. The bonus, of course, is found in a cushioned seat, with an overpriced big drink and a super-size bag of movie theater popcorn (see our Nightlife chapter).

Of course, it's easy for us to take the natural beauty of Southwestern Utah for granted, but the great outdoors offer kids healthy, wholesome, often educational fun. From hiking, swimming, mountain biking, in-line skating, skateboarding and team sports to combing the very landscape the dinosaurs roamed ages ago, make it part of your kid's nature to enjoy nature.

Following are some of our favorite places to go with our own kids. There are some indoor and outdoor suggestions — from classic to Jurassic — for each of our four main geographical areas.

St. George/Zion

Art Attack
86 S. Main St., St. George • 634-5850

Art Attack is an ongoing program administered by St. George City Youth and Children's Community Education that provides imaginative, fun ways for kids to express their creativity and build self-confidence in an environment where everyone can succeed. Students ages 8 to 18 can participate in programs such as "Monthly Masterpieces on Monday" (an art program that one month will have kids working with ribbon, then dabbling with finger paint or crayons the next), "Spectacular Sculptures" or "Christmas Crafts." These classes cost $15 to $20 per child (materials included) and get kids of all ages together at the St. George Arts Center every Monday for four weeks. Other courses include "I Love to Draw or Paint," an experience with various mediums and techniques; "Art Start for Little Kids," with lots of fun projects for the little hands of kids ages 4 to 7; and "Creative Kids," which offers budding thespians an introduction to theater vocabulary, movement, mime and characterization. "Artful Acting" creates an imagined environment through appearance, voice, movement and theatrical technique.

Bloomington Country Club Tennis Center
3174 Bloomington Dr. E., St. George • 628-4350

Bloomington Country Club Tennis Center offers a world-class tennis school with a growing reputation for producing top-notch young players, several of whom have been ranked nationally. Tennis pro Clark Hancock and his assistants provide group and individual instruction for anyone from pee-wee (4 years old) to 18 regardless of ability. Membership in the Bloomington Country Club is not a necessary criteria to enroll, but club members do get a discount. For non-BCC members, the cost is $7 for a group lesson, $14 for a half-hour private lesson, $21 for a 45-minute private lesson or $28 for a full hour of individual instruction. Lessons are free every Wednesday night for youngsters 4 to 6 years old, regardless of their parents membership status.

Fiesta Family Fun Center
171 E. 1160 South, St. George • 628-1818

Fiesta Family Fun Center is a play-time paradise for kids from age 4 to 104. The complex's 9 acres include an arcade, batting cages, an 18-hole minigolf course and a lighted driving range. For toddlers to age 10, a soft play area has ball pits, slides and tunnels. Bumper boats are great fun for little people taller than 48 inches. Two go-cart tracks provide a driving experience for those at least 4 years old and 60 inches tall. Perky's is the on-site pizza provider. Birthday or other group parties includes use of center facilities, balloons and a visit from the park's mascot. Costs vary depending on the number of guests and the party package selected, but plan to spend anywhere from $5.07 to $8 per child, with an extra charge for pizza and cake. There are no day-care or babysitting facilities on site, so children younger than 10 must be accompanied by a paying adult. Fiesta Fun is open Monday through Thursday from 10 AM to 10 PM. On Friday and Saturday, the park stays open until 11 PM.

Lava Cave
Off Utah Hwy. 18, Snow Canyon State Park, Santa Clara • 628-2255

Claustrophobes beware! Some parents may find it a little uncomfortable squeezing into a dark hole in the ground, but kids will love the adventure of spelunking during a visit to Snow Canyon's Lava Cave. Tucked inside this state park 15 miles northwest of St. George, the popular Lava Cave is about a half-mile walk from Utah Highway 8, which runs through the center of the park. The pull-off for the cave site is well-marked. According to area

rangers, the cave — which is actually an air pocket in ancient molten lava — is 150 feet deep, so bring a flashlight. It is safe for any age, but remember that the hardened lava has some sharp edges. Be careful in your descent. For more detailed information on Snow Canyon State Park, see our Parks and Other Natural Wonders chapter.

Nature's Window at Morgan Pest Control
76 E. Tabernacle, St. George • 673-9172

It's no joke, and no "pest" puns intended! Nature's Window at Morgan Pest Control is a dazzling collection of exotic butterflies and insects from around the world. Displayed on hand-painted "jungle" walls in the front office of Morgan Pest Control are thousands of moths, scorpions, tarantulas, cockroaches and other creatures. Some are living, but the majority of the critters are mounted. Jungle background sounds add ambiance. An observation beehive is alive with thousands of bees coming and going through a tiny opening in Morgan's outside advertising billboard. The "hive" is actually a see-through glass display attached to an inside wall, so you can spend a few fascinating minutes watching the activity of thousands of bees. There isn't much wall space for printed information about the species on display, but there is always someone close by who can serve as a tour guide. Visitors are welcome to browse through the collection free of charge during business hours. This is one for real Insiders — many of the area's longtime residents don't know about this hidden treasure in downtown St. George.

Outer Limits Skate Center
1301 W. Sunset Blvd., St. George • 628-2054

Outer Limits Skate Center is a great way for kids to have fun and escape the summer heat or winter chill any day of the week except Sunday. Outer Limits offers skating and roller hockey as well as racing and games such as tag and dodge ball. Birthday, church or school parties and all-night skates bring youngsters

FYI

Unless otherwise noted, the area code for all phone numbers listed in this chapter is 801 but will change to 435 in September 1997. Either area code may be used until March 22, 1998.

Photo: The Spectrum

In-line skaters and skateboarders have transformed a street game into a challenging, artistic, athletic ballet.

back again and again. Outer Limits is closed Mondays and Tuesdays. On Wednesday and Thursday, skating takes place in two sessions: 6:30 to 9 PM and 9 to 11:30 PM (for those who don't have to get up early the next morning). The cost, including skates, is $3.75 per person. On Friday and Saturday, hours are extended, and the price goes up to $4.50 per person. The kids will also enjoy a Saturday afternoon skate, either from noon to 2:30 PM or 3 to 5:30 PM. Discounts are offered to church or youth groups of 15 or more. Fifteen area schools have one day a month when they can bring all their students to skate for free. Outer Limits also provides roller hockey instruction.

St. George Leisure Services
86 S. Main St., St. George • 634-5850

The community education arm of St. George Leisure Services offers a wide variety of classes and sports programs to keep young-

sters of all ages busy. There are instructional classes in guitar, lapidary, Native American drumming and singing, lapidary and leatherwork, silversmithing and jewelry making and wood bow-and-arrow making. Sports activities for kids include gymnastics, basketball, tennis, wrestling, flag football, soccer, baseball, T-ball and girls' fast-pitch softball. Classes for kids change often to keep them fresh and interesting. Class schedules vary and may run from a few weeks to a few months. Summertime has fewer options than winter, but there are some year-round opportunities. As part of this comprehensive community education program, costs are kept low to be affordable for families.

St. George Recreation Center
285 S. 400 East • 634-5860

The city recreation center in St. George is growing in popularity as kids tell their friends about the fun to be had for just $1.50 a day. The facility itself is the recently renovated National Guard Armory, built in 1950-something. The recreation center opened for business in July 1995 and is already making plans for an expansion in early 1998. From early morning until after 9 PM, any night but Sunday throughout the year, youngsters can come and go (with a stamped hand) as often as they like and enjoy any combination of center activities including basketball, board games, billiards, shuffleboard and table tennis. It is all first-come, first-served, and the center, which is directly across the street from a city park, has a clean, well-maintained TV room and video game area.

The REC Mobile (short for Recreation, Education and Cultural Arts) makes a regular weekly circuit to area elementary schools, where kids may not be able to participate because of time or lack of transportation. Sponsored by the city of St. George and United Way of Washington County, REC Mobile is a truck full of recreational activities. Provided free of charge on a rotating schedule, the REC Mobile shows up in each community and waits for the bell to end the school day. Then, until 6 PM, leaders provide reading and tutoring, and youngsters can take part in arts and crafts projects, learn puppetry and play any of dozens of board games.

St. George Skate Park
995 E. Tabernacle St., St. George
• 673-2654

In-line skaters and skateboarders at the St. George Skate Park have turned a street sport into a graceful and daring athletic ballet. Drive by any afternoon after school or on Saturday, and you'll be mesmerized by the skill these kids show flying through the air, executing amazing feats and landing skateboards or in-line skates precisely on target. Helmets are required (rentals are available for $1), pads are optional, but bring your own skates for use on a variety of different courses. These include the U-shaped vertical ramp, the mini-ramp (a smaller version of the larger "vert" with an added spine, box and bump) or the street course, which provides another level of interest. Kids ages 7 to 18 will need a signed parental consent form to skate or bike at this drug- and alcohol-free amusement park. Bikers and skaters will also enjoy four or five video games on-site and a small concession stand that specializes in candy and cold soft drinks. For spectators, St. George Skate Park provides a covered section with benches and picnic tables. The park is open 6 to 9 PM Tuesday and Thursday, 2:30 to 10 PM on Friday and 11 AM to 10 PM on Saturday. The cost during the week is $3 per skater. On Friday the rate is $5, and on Saturday the one-time fee is $6 to come and go as often as you like.

Washington Fields
Off Warner Valley Rd., Washington City

Dinosaur tracks in the area around Washington Fields are tangible evidence of great beasts that roamed the desert millennia ago. Little feet and hands will be dwarfed next to these giant footprints. The tracks are those of the Coelurosaur, a carnivorous raptor similar to those ultra-scary ones featured in *Jurassic Park*. The most easily accessible dinosaur tracks are near Washington City. Take Exit 10 off Interstate 15 and drive east on Telegraph Road to the center of town. At Nisson's Foodtown, turn north on Main Street. You'll pass back under I-15 and follow the dirt road up the hill about a mile. Any car can make it, but you can expect some dust. A gate prohibits driving directly to the tracks, which are on private property. Park at the pink water tank, proceed on foot about 500 yards (a bit of a climb but not too difficult — especially with excited kids tugging on your sleeve) until you come to the wash. It's dry now, but at some point, a rush of water carried away the topsoil

---

INSIDERS' TIP

Keep your shoes on! In the hot Southwestern Utah desert, the summer sun can make sidewalks, parking lots and streets hot enough to literally fry an egg. Barefoot children can experience burns on their feet.

and left the tracks exposed. Follow the wash downstream, but let the kids be the first to see the dinosaur tracks on a flat slab rock. They aren't marked, but they are easily visible — especially to those who are already so close to the ground!

Other clearly visible tracks are found off Warner Valley Road in the Washington Fields area. This is a Bureau of Land Management site, so it is well marked and interpreted. Stop by their offices at 345 S. Riverside Drive and pick up a map and information about this and other BLM geologic or historic sites in Southwestern Utah or along the Arizona Strip. There are two different types of dinosaur tracks preserved in Washington Fields. The larger prints belong to a Prosauropod, an early duckbill dinosaur. The smaller ones are other examples of the aforementioned Coelurosaur. The area was a wetland 208 million years ago, and the petrified prints were probably made around or in shallow freshwater lakes. The Prosauropod, an herbivore, probably came to this spot to graze on plants and get a little water. The Coelurosaur, a carnivore, was likely there to eat the Prosauropod. It's a bit of a drive to get to this site — a picnic lunch might be in order. From downtown St. George, take the Boulevard to River Road. After crossing the Virgin River make a quick left turn at 1450 South to Warner Valley Road. It's about 10 miles on a well-graded dirt road, but there are plenty of signs to guide you. You don't need a four-wheel drive vehicle, but you'll only want to make the trip in a car with a high center of gravity. Make sure there is no threat of rain.

"Whoop-de-do"
Utah Hwy. 9, Zion National Park, Springdale • 772-3256

An afternoon on the spillway or weir at Zion National Park is hard to describe in words. Just above the unnamed bridge on Utah 9 leading to Zion Visitors Center and Zion Lodge, the "whoop-de-do," as the locals have dubbed it for want of a better name, is nothing more than a wide spot in the Virgin River — a place where shallow water runs over and down a smooth manmade concrete diversion channel in the river. Its official purpose has to do with complicated things like irrigation and erosion control, but for kids, the whoop-de-do's only reason for being is for great fun on a hot summer day. Don't wear a new bathing suit for this experience. Frequent rides on the whoop-de-do will wear out a bathing suit in no time. Cutoff jeans are suggested. Kids of all ages love the adventure.

Zion Junior Ranger Program
Zion Nature Center (between south entrance and visitors center), Utah Hwy. 9 • 772-3256

Children ages 6 to 12 can earn a junior ranger patch by attending Zion National Park's Junior Ranger Program. In these morning and afternoon activities, park rangers lead children on nature hikes and teach them the flora, fauna and natural history of the canyon. There are two sessions daily from Memorial Day weekend to Labor Day weekend. Morning sessions run from 9 to 11:30 AM with registration beginning at 8:15 AM, and afternoon sessions are from 1:30 to 4 PM with registration starting at 1 PM. Cost is $2 per session, and children may attend either or both in a given day.

To become a full-fledged junior ranger and earn a certificate, badge and cougar patch, kids must attend one session of the program at the Zion Nature Center and two other National Park Service interpretive programs at Zion such as a guided walk, a patio talk or an evening event. Parents may leave children at the Nature Center for the 2½-hour programs but must be with their kids between sessions and prompt in picking them up. The age range is strictly enforced. Children should dress comfortably and wear sturdy shoes with closed toes — no sandals. Hats are good accessories on sunny days, and don't forget the rain gear if storm clouds are gathering.

Cedar City/Brian Head

Ashcroft Observatory
Southern Utah University, 351 W. Center, Cedar City • 586-7707

On Mondays, the Ashcroft Observatory, managed by faculty and students at Southern Utah University, opens for an evening of astronomical delight. The Southwestern Utah sky is crystal clear on most evenings, providing a panoramic view of the moon, stars and plan-

Kiddies pilot odd creatures at the Washington County Fair.

ets through the high-powered telescope. There are no set lectures at Ashcroft, but knowledgeable students from SUU will take all the time you want to answer your questions. Outside the observatory, plan to take a while to pick out constellations.

To get to the observatory, take 200 North about 4 miles west out of Cedar City, cross the railroad tracks, watch for the one and only observatory sign, then turn left. Continue another 1¼ miles or so to the fork in the road. Take the left fork and go up the hill. You can't miss it. Budget-minded stargazers will be delighted there is no charge to spend an hour or two at Ashcroft.

Brian Head Resort
259 S. Utah Hwy. 143, Brian Head • 677-2810

If they like the outdoors, year-round activities for kids offered through Brian Head Resort are plentiful. In winter, the resort has ski clinics to teach or build the prowess of young shushers or snowboarders (see our Outdoor Recreation chapter for a full listing of Brian Head offerings). During summer and fall seasons, the resort lifts shuttle people of any size to Brian Head Peak for an excellent view of the valley or for mountain biking and hiking. Horseback riding and nature walks to nearby Cedar Breaks National Monument are also recreation options.

Costs for most activities are limited to the rental of bikes, in-line skates or a horse.

Iron Mission State Park
585 N. Main St., Cedar City • 586-9290

At Iron Mission State Park, you won't find grass, trees or campgrounds. Iron Mission State Park is the official name for a wonderful museum administered by park rangers from the State of Utah's Division of Parks and Recreation. The museum is overflowing with an extensive collection of horse-drawn vehicles, including a bullet-scarred stagecoach from the time period that spawned Butch Cassidy and his Hole-in-the-Rock Gang. There are also more than 200 Native American relics — articles of clothing, hunting weapons and food processing tools — once used by Southern Paiutes in Southwestern Utah, southern Nevada and northern Arizona. There are other interesting displays about the Old West and life in the Iron Mission, now known as Cedar City. A picnic area is available, but there is no camping site.

Kids Pond
Wood's Ranch on Cedar Mountain, Utah Hwy. 14 • 586-5124

The Iron County Travel Council recommends Kids Pond, 12 miles east of Cedar City at Wood's Ranch, as a perfect place for kids to learn the art of fishing. Little anglers will get a kick out of baiting and casting and catching specially stocked trout. It's free, open only during the summer months and limited to kids younger than age 12 (although it's common knowledge that older fishermen enjoy Kids Pond too). Bring your own equipment. There are no rentals in the area. Wood's Ranch is beautifully situated among the trees and meadows in Dixie National Forest on Cedar Mountain, with the added attractions of a pavilion, horseshoes, fire pits and restrooms.

Mountain View Museum
10 S. 600 West, Parowan • 477-8100

The Mountain View Museum in Parowan is actually a working ranch where beautiful Belgian and the French Percheron draft horses are bred. These species go all the way back to King Arthur's days, when they were bred to carry knights in heavy armor. Mountain View Museum currently has a crop of 18 of these big guys, and new foals arrive every year. But in addition to the horses, the museum part of the ranch offers a collection of restored wagons, coaches and carriages. Mountain View Museum has a hearse dating back to the early 1800s, a romantic "vis-a-vis" used for weddings, a Studebaker wagon that originally carried all kinds of cargo, several covered wagons such as those used to transport early settlers to the Iron Mission, a doctor's buggy complete with black bag for house calls, an Amish wagon with battery-powered lights and a surrey with the fringe on top. Mountain View Museum also features an extensive gun collection — some are the real thing; others are reproductions of rifles and pistols. There is an authentic blacksmith shop with a forge and all the tools necessary to keep the horses shod. Farm implements such as mowers and plows dot the landscape. Mountain View Museum is open every day during daylight hours. There is no charge to wander around, though dona-

tions are welcome and appreciated. If you want to ride, the cost to hitch up a team is $70 for as many as can fit into the wagon of choice. The price includes a 45-minute tour of the property.

Utah Shakespearean Festival
240 W. College Ave., Cedar City
• 586-7878

Throughout the summer season, the Utah Shakespearean Festival offers a free grand showcase of Renaissance music and fun guaranteed to delight the young and young at heart. Prior to the stage production of the Bard's works, there is a greenshow, where three stages come alive in music, dance and song. The greenshow "puts the festive in festival" and is used to create general havoc and merriment among the patrons. Kids will be fascinated by the master falconer and his great birds of prey. Little people will also enjoy the comedy skits and puppet shows in the Shakespearean tradition. For complete details on one of the grandest yearly events in Southwestern Utah, see the June listings in our Annual Events chapter.

Bryce Canyon Area

There's no movie theater, no bowling alley, no skating rink and no high school football team in these parts. Here in the Bryce Canyon area kids create their own fun! "Close-knit" and "companionable" are adjectives used to describe the young people growing up in Panguitch, Tropic, Boulder and other Garfield County communities. They actively participate in organized activities such as homegrown marching groups, team sports at local schools, 4-H, Future Farmers of America and Little League baseball.

Future Farmers is particularly active in the community, with 53 students in grades 8 to 11 enrolled at Panguitch High School. The kids

---

INSIDERS' TIP

It should go without saying, but never, ever leave a child (or pets) alone in the car, even for a few minutes during summer, when temperatures inside a car can rise to 150 degrees in a matter of minutes.

study agricultural biology, animal sciences or horticulture and participate in state judging competitions. The FFA in Panguitch is unique in that one of its annual projects is the community's Fourth of July parade. It helps them learn to organize, recruit, advertise and keep accurate records.

Other options for Bryce Canyon area kids include ice skating or ice fishing at Panguitch Lake or in someone's backyard pond, hunting, fishing, canoeing, horseback riding and roping, hiking, tennis at the town park or swimming in the covered pool in downtown Panguitch. Family-oriented togetherness often involves all-terrain vehicles, and video parties are commonplace. It's simple: The family takes the ATV out somewhere, has a picnic lunch and just rides around for the day exploring or covering their favorite hills and valleys. Without a movie theater in town, the kids rent a video at the local grocery store and everyone brings something — chips, cold pop, candy, whatever — and they park themselves in one or the other's living room.

Rapelling on red rock cliff faces is growing in popularity around here, where the kids start climbing when they're 14 or 15, and Garfield County plans call for the creation in the next year or two of a bicycle path through Red Canyon State Park.

Paunsagaunt Wildlife Museum
250 E. Center St., Panguitch • 676-2500

The newest attraction in the Bryce Canyon area is the Paunsagaunt Wildlife Museum in Panguitch, open from May to November. On U.S. Highway 89, 24 miles from Bryce Canyon National Park, the wildlife museum exhibits more than 300 stuffed animals from North America in their natural habitat. In addition to western wildlife, the museum also houses a 50-foot display of exotic game animals from Africa, India and Europe including an African lion, baboon, lynx, monkey, deer and ante-

lope, impala, zebra, water buffalo, gnu, otters, owls, black bears, mountain lions and snakes. Kids and adults will also enjoy a spectacular display of rare birds of prey along with a unique collection of Native American artifacts, pottery, tools, weapons and fossils. Admission is $4 for adults and teens, $2.50 for children ages 6 to 12, and little ones younger than 6 are admitted free. Hours are 9 AM to 9 PM from late spring to late fall.

Kanab Area

Moqui Cave
5½ miles north of Kanab on U.S. Hwy. 89 • 644-2987

Kids and adults alike love this literal hole in the wall, where Lex Chamberlain carries on the legacy his father began 45 years ago. The huge opening in the sandstone, right alongside the highway, extends naturally 80 feet back into the bluff. As it was expanded to 200 feet deep by a silica sand mining operation decades ago, the Chamberlains found there was plenty of room to build a tavern and set up a dance hall. Lex and his wife, Lee Anne, have taken over the business and turned it into a museum with displays of artifacts, fossils and minerals. They've redone the exterior of the cave to give it an Anasazi cliff-dwelling look. The Chamberlains say that theirs is the largest display of fluorescent minerals in the country, and there's also an extensive exhibit of Native American artifacts, fossilized dinosaur tracks and a gift shop. The cave is open mid-February through mid-November, Monday through Saturday, from 8:30 AM to 7:30 PM. The cave remains cool during summer, but it's not so cold that you would need a jacket. Admission is $3.50 for adults, $3 for seniors, $2.50 for youngsters 13 through 17 and $1.50 for kids between 6 and 12. Kids younger than 6 get in free. (For more on Moqui Cave, see our Attractions chapter.)

INSIDERS' TIP

Tubing is no longer allowed in most areas of the river in Zion National Park, although you can still rent an inner tube from a vendor just outside the park and float from the south campground into town — a pleasant trek of about a mile.

Wednesday Night at the Gazebo
20 W. Center St., Kanab

This event, held weekly when it's warm enough, is about as close to the setting of a Norman Rockwell painting as you can get in today's society. Bring a picnic lunch, an old blanket and all the kids — things get started around twilight, when it starts to cool down. Enjoy live entertainment in front of the church on Center Street, where everyone just hangs out and enjoys being together.

Coral Pink Sand Dunes State Park
Sand Dunes Rd. off U.S. Hwy. 89, Kanab • 648-2800

It's the biggest sand box your kids will ever play in! Coral Pink Sand Dunes, with acres of dunes and trails, is a must for the youngsters. There is no age limit on running and rolling to your heart's content during the spring and summer or tubing the dunes in the winter. After a picnic lunch with the family, take the short trail to the pictographs. This ancient Native American "newspaper" is easy to find about 500 yards from the ranger station on a well-marked walkway. ATVs are welcomed among the dunes — either free-roaming or on designated trails. For more information on Coral Pink Sand Dunes, see our Parks and Other Natural Wonders chapter.

Frontier Movie Town
297 W. Center St., Kanab • 644-5337

Frontier Movie Town in Kanab is a great place for the little buckaroo or those of any age who love the genre of Hollywood westerns. Today's kids may not recognize all the black-and-white photos of stars who filmed here in Kanab's glory days as "Little Holly-wood," but they will still find it fun to wander the actual sets from *The Outlaw Josey Wales*, the Disney film *One Little Indian* and *Black Bart*, filmed in 1948. The windmill from *Fighting Gravity*, Keifer Sutherland's newest flick (not released as of this writing), the building backdrop from a Kenny Loggins video as well as assorted memorabilia from TV's *F Troop* and Sinatra's movie *Sergeants 3* are all on display. There's an acre of grass, trees and picnic tables in addition to the museum — all free to visitors. Trinkets are for sale in a small gift shop. For an extra treat, why not come for breakfast or lunch (prices range from $4.50 to $10 per person) or stay for dinner ($14.95 per person plus $3 each for the gunfight show)? On Wednesday night, you can enjoy Indian dancing for $3 per person.

Old Barn Playhouse at Parry Lodge
89 E. Center, Kanab • 644-2601

Kids of any age will enjoy the chance to cheer the hero or hiss and boo the villain of each delightful, locally written melodrama. Each summer, a different story of trials and travail, misery and mischief, runs six night a week from June 1 to Labor Day. The old barn where the performances are staged was part of the original purchase of the Parry Lodge in 1924. How long it had been there before that is anyone's guess, but it has new life as the Old Barn Playhouse. The cost for an evening of suffering and distress is $7 for adults, and kids are $3.50. There is no charge for the happy ending. To attract tourists, some motels offer their guests a "wooden nickel" — worth a $1 discount on each ticket. Groups of 10 or more will enjoy the Old Barn Night Dutch Oven Dinner, with spuds and a ticket to the performance.

Playing fields, courts and tracks are being put into place as quickly as resources will permit, but it never seems to happen fast enough to stay ahead of the demand.

Community Recreation

It's hard to imagine why anyone would want to be indoors in a region recognized worldwide for wonderful year-round weather and spectacular scenery. Well, maybe it isn't too hard to imagine it in July and August.

You may have already scanned the chapters on Golf, Outdoor Recreation, Parks and Other Natural Wonders and The Environment, so you get the picture as far as the outdoor stuff is concerned. License plates from everywhere attest to it: We've got some king-sized drawing cards.

This chapter is devoted to the retired or semi-retired, the tourists or the fully employed who just want a chance to play occasionally. Although the listings here are not completely comprehensive, they are presented as good starting points for finding activities to occupy a rare rainy afternoon or to satisfy an educational or social itch.

You will note there are not many individual listings for the Bryce Canyon and Kanab areas. In the communities in and around Bryce Canyon (such as Panguitch), the source for recreation is found at church or the high school. Neighbors and families will travel hundreds of miles to participate in or support drama, speech, music programs or sporting events. Elementary school boys and girls participate in Little League baseball or Junior Jazz basketball, and a fair share of teenagers are involved in rodeo.

In Kanab, a community known for "the greatest earth on show," there may not be as much of a need for organized activities. Who could ever grow weary of hikes or leisurely drives through some of the most spectacular scenery in the world? Community recreation options in the Kanab area are limited. The city pool is not currently in use, as it is being renovated. Little League and Junior Jazz is popular with the kids, but its viability from year to year depends a great deal on whether a parent is willing to accept the assignment as coach.

We start off our look at the community recreation options that are out there by providing listings for a couple of great clearinghouses for recreation information and activities. Next, we choose some popular participatory pursuits and offer individual listings throughout our Southwestern Utah coverage area.

Information and Programs

St. George/Zion

St. George Recreation and Leisure Services
285 S. 400 East, St. George • 634-5860

When does play become learning . . . learning turn into play? When it comes under the heading of St. George Community Education and Recreation, a cooperative program sponsored jointly by the City of St. George, Washington County School District and Dixie College. In this great agenda, which draws freely on the resources of the community's big three, it's easy to find something for everyone. Simply peruse the activities listed in the quarterly catalog that goes to every household in the county (contact the offices to have one mailed to you), sign up for the class, event, sport or adventure of your choice . . . then enjoy!

You can learn to make teddy bears, arrange silk or dried flowers, refinish furniture or do leaf painting. How about porcelain dollmaking, ceramics, basket weaving or lamp making? See the world through the lens of a camera, tackle the latest in line-dancing or express yourself in mysteriously beautiful Middle Eastern dance. Become proficient in CPR, first aid, karate, aerobics, fencing, yoga or massage. Develop skills in gardening, write your personal history or organize your memories into a scrapbook. Cut your teeth on investment fundamentals or the discovery of hand-dipping chocolates, Chinese cooking and automobile maintenance.

If sports is your interest, St. George Community Education and Recreation offers all levels of aerobics, men's basketball, co-ed volleyball and fast- or slow-pitch softball for men or women. Playing fields, courts and tracks are being put into place around the community as quickly as resources will permit, but it never seems to be quite fast enough to stay ahead of the demand.

Walking is very popular in the St. George area, as there are miles of beautiful, wide, city-maintained trails meandering from one end of town to the other. The Virgin River Parkway is 2.8 miles along the Virgin and Santa Clara rivers, between Bloomington Park and Hilton Drive. Fort Pierce Parkway is 1.8 miles, with a 188-foot pedestrian bridge spanning Fort Pierce Wash. The trail that runs between St. James Lane and Bloomington Hills North off Fort Pierce Drive provides access to a wide variety of wildlife and plants unique to Southwestern Utah. Additional trails are under construction. Hiking, in-line skating, skateboarding and bicycling can all be safely accommodated on these trails if everyone pays attention to the other guy. Water is unavailable along the trails, so always be sure to bring along an adequate supply, especially on very hot summer days.

The makeup of St. George Education and Recreation changes from season to season and from year to year. The diversity of offerings depends on community interests and resources, but if you don't find something to enjoy in any program year, your suggestions for improvement or new programs are encouraged. St. George Education and Recreation programs are ongoing at the St. George Recreation Center, open Monday through Friday from 7:30 AM to 9:30 PM and Saturday from 9 AM to 6 PM. The Art Center at 86 S. Main Street and Dixie College Continuing Education, 300 S. 800 East, are both open Monday through Friday from 8 AM to 5 PM.

FYI

Unless otherwise noted, the area code for all phone numbers listed in this chapter is 801 but will change to 435 in September 1997. Either area code may be used until March 22, 1998.

Cedar City/Brian Head

The Cedar City/Brian Head area is best known for Shakespeare and snow skiing. But as the population grows so does the demand for organized activities and things to do. The city's recreation department is doing a very impressive job of providing plenty of good choices. The listing is activities that follows is comprehensive but not meant to be all-inclusive.

Cedar City Recreation Department
110 N. Main St., Cedar City • 586-2950

The Cedar City Recreation Department has lots of creative, organized play time for kids and adults. Open Monday through Friday from 8 AM to 5 PM, the recreation director and staff spend their days planning activities for young

INSIDERS' TIP

The City of St. George, Dixie College and Washington County School District have combined their resources to create the Community Education and Recreation Program. Every resident of Washington County receives a catalog in their mailbox four times a year. In the St. George area, there is no such thing as "nothing to do!"

and old alike. In this family-oriented community — and depending on who is on the playing field — Mom, Dad or the offspring will make up the cheering section.

For the kids, organized sports include softball for girls (grades kindergarten through high school). This summer program currently has 300 kids enrolled with the numbers growing every year. American Youth Soccer Organization (AYSO) programs in Cedar City have 700 to 800 boys and girls, ages 4½ to 18, playing this popular sport from August through October. Flag football has 200-plus kids playing on 20 to 25 teams of 2nd- to 8th-graders. The numbers may vary slightly from year to year (they usually go up), but the schedule remains constant through September and October.

T-ball and machine-pitch baseball teams have been formed to give 250 little ones 5- to 8-years-old the chance to build their skills on the playing field before signing up for Little League. Junior Jazz programs (named for the Utah Jazz — the state's most notable professional sports team) has 900 2nd- to 12th-grade basketball enthusiasts matching up indoors during the cold winter months of November through January.

New programs created in 1996 include junior golf and a ski school at Brian Head. Junior golf saw more than 100 youngsters ages 8 through 17 working with pros at Cedar Ridge Golf Course (see our Golf chapter) to learn the difference between a wood and a wedge, a birdie and an eagle. This program gets under way as soon as school is out in June and goes until the bell rings in August. The ski school is a cooperative effort between Cedar City Recreation Department and Brian Head Resort. Two sessions of four Saturdays are held, beginning when there is enough snow. The $96 rate covers the cost of transportation, lift tickets and skis or snowboards for students ages 8 through 16.

Junior bowling is new in 1997, with an anticipated enrollment of more than 50 boys and girls ages 8 through 17. They will gather in the alley twice weekly throughout the summer months. And if that's not enough to keep the kids busy, the local Hershey Track Meet, which could potentially land Cedar City area kids in national competition in Hershey, Pennsylvania, is held in May at Parowan High School,

18 miles north of Cedar City. Regional competition scheduled in Milford in June, and the July state meet is held in Ogden, approximately 250 miles north.

Adults in the Cedar City area get together after work and on weekends to burn off calories and stress on the playing field, court or alley. Popular among the big kids are volleyball, running, basketball, softball and track. Forty teams with 10 to 12 players on each roster run up and down the basketball floor while the snow flies from November to mid-March. Summer softball teams number 50, divided into men's, women's and the very popular co-rec squads. These all play from April through August. The fall softball league has 20 adult teams with a dozen players on each. They play from the end of summer until the deer hunt in mid-October, when the weather cools and priorities change.

If running is your thing, Cedar City celebrates its birthday every year on November 11 with a 10K run beginning at the city park. The rec department can fill you in on the start time, which varies from year to year. Cedar City Recreation Department is also the place to call for more information about the Cedar City Municipal Park on the corner of Main and 200 North. For company parties, family reunions or impromptu fun and games, you'll find horseshoe pits, playground equipment, sand pit volleyball, covered pavilions, picnic tables and barbecues where you can make your own fun.

No Loafing Allowed: Area Recreation

Aerobics/Fitness Centers

St. George/Zion

Cardiax Fitness Center
145 N. 400 West, St. George • 628-9201
This "no gimmicks" club — one of three Cardiax in Utah — offers weight training and aerobics, yoga, T'ai Chi, massage therapy, Jujitsu, nutritional counseling, body-fat testing and group or personal fitness training. Opened in 1996, there is a friendly atmosphere

here, and the staff wants to help you get in shape and stay that way. Cardiax is open Monday through Friday from 5 AM to 10 PM, Saturday from 8 AM to 8 PM and Sunday from 10 AM to 4 PM. Club memberships are varied, designed for the already-toned bodybuilder or the squishy, 98-pound weakling! All contracts start with a $69 fee. Monthly charges range from $21 to $26.

Desert Palms Nautilus and Fitness Center
120 W. Hilton Dr., St. George • 628-4617, 628-4618

Desert Palms offers a positive, happy environment. This state-of-the-art fitness center opened in 1984 to bring neighbors, family members, seniors — everybody — together to work at staying in shape. Desert Palms features the standard machinery (treadmills and stair climbers) as well as free weights, an indoor pool, racquetball and basketball courts and aerobics instruction. There is a testing center, and personalized programs designed by experienced, certified trainers. There is also a full line of food supplements. Desert Palms is open Monday through Friday from 5:30 AM to 10 PM, Saturday from 8 AM to 8 PM and Sunday from 9 AM to 4 PM. A full facility membership for one month is $50. The annual equivalent is $45 per month, with tanning and/or massage extra. There are several creatively priced packages for students, seniors or those in between.

Eccles Fitness Center
425 S. 700 East, St. George • 652-7995

This attractive and well-designed fitness center and pool is open to the public . . . if the public is enrolled at Dixie College. Part of the college's "3 Credits or Less" program, the Eccles Fitness Center offers a semester's worth of workouts, swimming, basketball, and/or in-line skating. Classes are self-paced, only $57 (there is an extra $5 admission fee if this is the only class you are taking during the school year) and are

good for two college credits. The fitness center, which was remodeled in 1996, features top-of-the-line equipment for a good cardiovascular workout and two kinds of aerobics — step and water. The fitness center is open Monday through Thursday from 6 AM to 9 PM, Friday from 6 AM to 7 PM and Saturday from 7 AM to noon. Eccles is closed on Sunday. The outdoor pool is open mid-March to December.

Ballooning
St. George/Zion

Palledin Balloon Excursions
2414 E. 750 North Cir., St. George • 674-4602

"Up, up and awaaaaaay in this beautiful balloon . . ." A ride in a hot air balloon is a romantic, charming adventure. Flying high above the ground, carried by the wind, is something most people want to try at least once in a lifetime. There are a lot of variables here in pricing, time of day, weather conditions and distance traveled. Palledin Balloon Excursions offers a day package — two people for $125 each. This is popular for birthday surprises, anniversary gifts or marriage proposals! The owner of Palledin, who considers himself an ambassador for ballooning as a sport, also offers a reduced-rate excursion — generally $75 per person for about a half-hour. Rides, floating an average of 6 to 8 miles, are most frequently scheduled in the early morning hours when the air is stable and cool.

Bowling
St. George/Zion

Brentwood Fun Center
W. Utah Hwy. 9, Hurricane • 635-9560

This nice, clean combination 12-lane bowl-

Photo: Lyman Hafen

Youth soccer thrives in Southwestern Utah.

ing alley, video arcade and 18-hole miniature golf course is popular with residents of the Hurricane Valley as well as snowbirds wintering in nearby RV parks. Brentwood Fun Center is between the valley and I-15 on the road to Zion National Park. Open Sunday through Thursday from 11 AM to 11 PM and until midnight on Friday for Country Bowl and Saturday for Rockin' Bowl, Brentwood Fun Center is priced right at $1.75 per game for adults to age 55, $1.50 for bowlers younger than 16 and $1.25 for seniors. Shoe rental is 50¢ for everyone. Glow-in-the-dark pins, rock or country videos and a special rate of $5 for three games (plus shoes) make weekends at Brentwood Fun Center especially entertaining.

Dixie Bowl
146 City Center, St. George • 673-3272
Before there was golf, before there was a city pool . . . there was Dixie Bowl. It was 1959

when the doors opened to welcome residents of this then-tiny community to the concept of organized play. Today, Dixie Bowl is still a fun place to be. It's clean, friendly and the lanes are in excellent condition for the area's highest averages. There are automatic scorers, bumper lanes, billiards, a game room and a snack bar, all designed for family fun. Dixie Bowl has a junior league and popular men's and women's league play Monday through Thursday nights. Hours are 9 AM to 11:30 PM with a cost per game of $2.25 for adults and $1.75 for the kids. Shoes rent at a cost of 50¢.

Sunset West Bowling Center
1476 W. Sunset Blvd., St. George
• 674-4455
The area's newest bowling center is Sunset West, overlooking the very busy Sunset Boulevard between downtown St. George and downtown Santa Clara. Open since 1993, Sunset West has 20 lanes and lots of extras such

Photo: Jud Burkett

No matter which Southwestern Utah community you visit or live in, Little League baseball is a popular activity.

as automatic scoring, bumper pads, an arcade and pool table for the kids, lessons and classes, lockers, a pro shop and party rates. For the big kids, there's Doogles (a humorous blend of the names of the owners — Dewey and Gail), a combination bar and grill with darts, pool, daily lunch specials and a license to sell beer. The pro shop does an outstanding job of drilling and fitting balls and can order other equipment with next-day delivery. Leagues and group events such as family reunions and kids parties are quite popular. Parties start at an economical $4.25 per little person for a hot dog, drink and two games with shoes. Sunset West Bowling Center also offers a really great program that teaches kids bowling alley etiquette. This in-school program comes complete with a legal-size carpet "alley," plastic pins, rubber bowling balls and an instructional video. Bowling can become part of any classroom curriculum and at the same time builds on math, science and English skills. The regular cost for one game from 11 AM to 6 PM at Sunset West is $1.50 for kids and adults and $1.25 for those older than 55. After 6 PM and on weekends, the cost is $2.25 for bowlers older than 16, $1.50 for those 6 to 15. Shoes are an extra 50¢.

Cedar City/Brian Head

Alpine Lanes
421 E. Utah Hwy. 91, Cedar City • 586-1383

Alpine Lanes has all kinds of fun things to do, the most obvious of which takes place on the 20 bowling lanes that offer state-of-the-art computer scoring. When you get ready to step up to the line, just push "go" and modern technology will take care of the rest, though you can't expect it to keep you out of the gutter. League play, from September to April, is in place for men, women, mixed groups, seniors older than 55 and juniors ages 3 to 21. The cost for three games and shoe rental is $4 for the little guys and $10 for adult bowlers. If you want to try a whole different approach to this sport, you'll get a kick out of Country Bowl or Rockin' Bowl. Every Saturday night from 9 PM to midnight, they turn down the lights and turn up the music for a bowl-in-the-dark experience. Lighted pins are the target, but the aim is great fun set to music. Then rack 'em up for billiards, test your skills in the arcade and finish up the evening with a tasty burger or hot dog, french fries, popcorn and a tall, cold soda pop. It's more of a snack bar than a restaurant, but the food is good and the prices are right for a date or a family night out. Alpine Lanes is open

Monday through Thursday from 1 to 11 PM, Friday and Saturday 'til midnight and Sundays from 5 to 11 PM. Leagues bowl weekly and vary in the number of lanes used, so it's always a good idea to call ahead to see if there are open lanes.

Karate

St. George/Zion

Bobby Lawrence Karate Training Center
747 E. St. George Blvd., St. George • 674-0707

Bobby Lawrence Karate Training Center believes the family that kicks together, sticks together. Teaching and tournament competition is designed to give anyone, regardless of age, ability, confidence and a "yes, I can" attitude when faced with a situation requiring mental or physical self-defense. And, its fun! Bobby Lawrence Karate Training Center opened in 1993. The training center, with a martial arts supply store, is open Monday through Thursday from 4 to 8:30 PM.

Senkai/Japanese Karate and Amateur Boxing
955 N. 1300 West, No. 5, St. George • 673-9201, 673-1678

Karate, the ancient Japanese art of self-defense, trains the greatest fighters so they don't have to fight! This healthy alternative to violence helps young people focus on peace through physical training activities, builds self-confidence and leadership skills and diminishes prejudices. Senkai students of various ages have medaled in karate in the annual Utah Summer Games. This karate school also trains amateur boxers for a possible spot in regional, national or even Olympic competi-

tions. Karate classes are Tuesday and Thursday evening from 6 to 7:15 PM, Wednesday from 7:15 to 8:30 PM and on the second and fourth Saturday of the month from 10:15 to 11:30 AM.

Scuba Diving

St. George/Zion

Cetacean Scuba
945 N. 1300 West, St. George • 628-0418

Darrell Cashin, owner of Cetacean Scuba, says you'll understand the store name only after you've stopped in to meet him. Named for large, hairless underwater mammals with flipper-like forearms, Cetacean Scuba specializes in diving and snorkeling instruction in area lakes, rental of scuba diving gear, sales and repair. Cetacean Scuba also carries a full line of equipment including brand names like SeaQuest, Sherwood and Genesis, but their primary concern is safety. Diver certification comes after 20 hours of classroom and pool experience and a minimum of five dives in open water. Cetacean Scuba, open since 1992, also provides the only public safety search and recovery course in the area. Hours are Monday through Friday from noon to 6 PM and Saturdays by appointment.

Oasis Water Sports
439 N. Bluff St., St. George • 673-9755

Watersports in the desert? Sounds a little contradictory, but diving and related activities are pretty popular here in Southwestern Utah. Oasis Water Sports, certifying divers and their equipment since 1986, are also actively involved in community water cleanup and conservation projects each month. They provide special programs for local Boy Scout troops and serve as instructors at Dixie College. New owners offer service and equipment alteration Monday through Friday from 10 AM to 6 PM and Saturday from 10 AM to 3 PM.

Cedar City/Brian Head

Island Divers
1096 W. 200 North, Cedar City • 586-3469
Three-fourths of the earth's surface is under water. And Island Divers wants to introduce you to the rare and spectacular beauty below the surface of area lakes and distant oceans. Island Divers staffers teach scuba certification classes at Southern Utah University and sell, rent and repair a variety of scuba and snorkeling equipment including wet suits, watches, knives, travel bags and books. Open in Cedar City since 1993, Island Divers instills confidence in beginners and trains new instructors with the SSI system. As instructors at the university level, the folks at Island Divers are willing to work around class schedules to get students certified. Island Divers can also arrange trips to California, Mexico, Lake Mead (see our Daytrips and Weekend Getaways chapter) and other fun and interesting dive locations. The store is open Monday through Saturday from 10 AM to 6 PM.

Skating Rinks

St. George/Zion

Outer Limits Skate Center
1301 W. Sunset Blvd., St. George
• 628-2054
Outer Limits Skate Center does a great job entertaining the kids (see our Kidstuff chapter). With year-round classes in the area, a full 25 percent of elementary school students are off-track at any time during the year, causing parents to scramble for healthy activities. Outer

Limits offers skating and roller hockey, as well as racing and games like tag and dodge ball. Birthday, church or school parties and all-night skates bring youngsters back again and again. Many local schools take advantage of opportunities to reward students for good behavior or high grades with an afternoon of skating and arcade games. Outer Limits is closed Monday and Tuesday. On Wednesday and Thursday, skating takes place in two sessions: 6:30 to 9 PM and 9 to 11:30 PM for the night-owls. The cost including skates is $3.75 per person. On Friday and Saturday, hours are extended, and the price goes to $4.50. The kids will also enjoy Saturday afternoon skating from noon to 2:30 PM and from 3 to 5:30 PM.

Spanish Trails Roller Rink
21 S. Main St., Veyo • 574-2262
If you didn't know where to look, you'd miss this recreational opportunity altogether. Spanish Trails Roller Rink is upstairs over Spanish Trails Supply Company, a gas station and mercantile in Veyo, about 20 miles northwest of St. George. The roller rink has been around since 1977 and since it is one of the largest facilities in town, it's a popular spot for skating as well as family reunions, dancing and exercise classes. The rink is open from 8 to 10 PM on Saturday only or by appointment. The cost per person is $3.50 including skates or $15 for a family of up to six.

Swimming

St. George/Zion

St. George Municipal Pool and Hydrotube
250 E. 700 South, St. George • 634-5867
One of the most popular places to be on a

INSIDERS' TIP

The sesquicentennial of the arrival of the Mormon pioneers in the Salt Lake Valley is being celebrated throughout the state during 1997. Community events and activities are planned in every city and county to celebrate 150 years since Mormon pioneers arrived in the Valley of the Great Salt Lake on July 24, 1847.

hot summer day in Dixie is the city-owned and -managed municipal pool and hydrotube. This facility, between Dixie Middle School and the Dixie High School, opens Memorial Day and closes on Labor Day. The pool is 25 yards long and ranges in depth from 3½ to 11 feet. The complex includes 2-meter boards, a 250-foot hydrotube, a concession stand with all the usual cold drinks, candy, hot dogs and nachos, showers and a locker room. Three or four lifeguards keep watch over swimmers in the main pool, one is assigned to guard the fenced and parent-supervised kiddie pool and one is assigned to the hydrotube. The pool is open for lap swimming Monday through Friday from 6:30 to 9 AM and again from noon to 1 PM. "Open plunge" is scheduled from 1 to 9 PM on weekdays and noon to 9:30 PM on Saturday and holidays. Swimmers younger than 17 pay $1.25 each, and those older than 18 pay $1.75. A hydrotube pass is another $3 per person. The pool is available to rent after hours to large groups for $110 for 90 minutes of swim time, but reserve early. There's hardly a night all summer it isn't taken by a church group, club or business of some kind.

The city is about to break ground on a new, year-round pool complex adjacent to Snow Canyon Middle School. Actually, the middle school will have first rights to the use of two pools. A 25-yard-by-25-meter competitive pool will share the corner of Sunset Boulevard and Lava Flow Drive with a warmer, 150-foot leisure pool complete with slide and water play structures. The new complex will include locker room facilities and concessions. Plans are sketchy at this point, but the pool should be ready for use by New Years Day 1998.

Veyo Pool Resort
287 E. Veyo Resort Rd., Veyo • 574-2300

The perennial local favorite, THE swimming hole in Washington County for three generations changed ownership in 1995. The change brought with it a $200,000 facelift and the addition of some exciting amenities. The only thing about the Veyo Pool that has remained unchanged is the warm springs that generate 100 gallons a minute of crystal clear, pure mineral water. The 30 by 70-foot pool, with 5,000 square feet of decking, is new. Water falls 85

feet to the beautifully landscaped pool (it's a kick to sit underneath). The parking lot has been moved and paved. It was below the pool, but now you'll park on the ridge above and walk 250 feet or so down a pathway. The snack bar, with pool table available, still serves up tasty burgers, fries, cold drinks and ice cream.

An exciting addition is the largest rock-climbing park in Southwestern Utah — the second-largest privately owned one in the United States. The 120 routes (plans are for a total of 300 by the end of '98) range to suit everyone from beginner to expert. Although the pool will close after Labor Day, it plays host to the nation's largest rock-climbing demo day on the first Saturday in September. Overnight camping is available, but there are only two sites. There is also a climbers' camp requiring a 5-minute hike. The cost is $1 per person at the group campsite, with a minimum charge of $20. In other words, if one person shows up, the cost is $20; if 21 people show up, the cost is $21. Talk about bargains!

All day at Veyo Pool is only $2.25 per person. Rock climbing is also $2.25. The pool has in-and-out privileges for those who wish to swim and climb. Veyo Pool, a little past mile marker 19 on Utah 18 N. is 15 miles north of downtown St. George. The entire park is open noon to 9 PM from May 1 through Labor Day.

Cedar City/Brian Head

Iron County Swimming Pool
401 Harding Ave., Cedar City • 586-2869

Cedar City and the Iron County School District co-manage this busy public swimming pool adjacent to Cedar Middle School. The outdoor pool is 25 yards long and open to lap swimmers and the general public every evening from 6 to 10 PM during the warm months (usually mid-April until early September). The indoor pool is 25 meters, about half an Olympic-size pool, and open year round. Lap swimmers will have the place all to themselves from 5 to 7 AM, noon to 1 PM and 9 to 10 PM every evening except Sunday. The general public is invited to exercise or cool off any evening from 6:30 to 9:30 PM. Swim teams work out at scheduled times throughout the week. During the school year, 4th- through 8th-grade physical education classes are scheduled for lessons. Water aerobics are held 7 to 8 AM every weekday morning. On Sunday evenings, kayakers practice their rotations in the pool. And if there is ever any time when the pool is not in use, area Boy Scout troops are welcome to work on water-related merit badge requirements. For all pool use, the cost is $1.50 per swimmer. The hydrotube offers added fun for an extra $1.50 per person. To make it one of the least expensive family activities in the area, individual and family swim passes are available. For individual passes, the rate for is $50 for three months, $75 for six months and $100 for a year. Economical family rates for are $75 for three months, $110 for six months and $150 annually. (That's for a family of up to four members. Each additional family member would cost $7 for a three-month pass, $10 for a six-month pass and $15 for an annual pass.)

Parowan City Pool
89 S. 300 East, Parowan • 477-8066

The Parowan City Pool is one of the best things about summertime in the Iron County seat. Open June 1 through September, this 30-year-old landmark next door to Lions Club Park attracts kids from 1 to 6 PM every day except Sunday during the summer, and from 3 to 6 PM after school starts. Lessons are offered every second and fourth week in June, July and August. Three lifeguards keep a close watch on swimmers. There is also a baby pool, but parents are responsible for the safety of their own little ones since there is no lifeguard on duty there. Adults-only lap swimming is an option every morning from 7 to 8 AM during the week but not on Saturday. Families only are invited on Monday nights from 7 to 9 PM, and parents must be present. The cost for swimming is $1.50 for adults, $1 for kids

younger than 12. Season passes are available at a bargain-basement rate of $10 for 15 swims or $30 for the whole summer for kids, $50 for adults or $60 for a family of up to six. During off hours, the pool is available for parties of 25 or fewer guests at a rate of $15 per hour. Passes are for sale at Parowan city offices.

Southern Utah University Swimming Pool
300 S. 700 West, Cedar City • 586-7833

Part of the university's physical education department, this pool is designed to meet the needs of students matriculating at SUU. It is also available to the general public for open swimming or laps. The pool is open for public use from 7 to 10 PM on Monday and Wednesday through Friday, and noon to 5 PM on Saturday. Lap swimmers will have the place to themselves from 1 to 3 PM each Monday, Wednesday and Friday. The Olympic-size pool has a lifeguard but no diving board. Cost is $1 per person.

Bryce Canyon Area

Panguitch Community Pool
390 E. 100 South, Panguitch • 676-1325

This nice indoor pool doubles as a physical education option for students at Panguitch High School and as the community plunge. The pool is open year round, unless there is a home game — whichever home team is playing has first rights to use the shared locker room. In the summer, the pool is open Monday through Saturday from 1 to 4 PM and 6 to 8 PM. Winter hours are 6 to 8 PM on Monday, Wednesday, Friday and Saturday. There is also an open plunge on Friday and Saturday from 1 to 4 PM. Lap swimmers are welcome Mon-

---

INSIDERS' TIP

To get a good seat at the Dixie Roundup Rodeo (reserved seats sell out weeks in advance), take a blanket and go to a Sun Bowl ticket office promptly at 6 PM on the evening you wish to attend. Enter the arena, find a spot and lay your blanket over the seats you want. Then, feel free to go to dinner and return at about 7:45. The rodeo starts at 8, and there's an unwritten rule at the Sun Bowl that no one touches another visitor's blanket.

day, Wednesday and Friday from 6 to 7 PM, and water aerobics are taught Monday and Wednesday evening from 8 to 8:45 PM. Two lifeguards keep a close watch on swimmers. The cost to swim is only $1.35 per person. A six-month individual pass can be purchased for $30, and a family pass (only for those who share the same address) is available for $75. Annual passes are also available at a cost of $50 per person or $120 for a family.

Walking/Biking

St. George/Zion

The elaborate trail system, built and maintained by the St. George Parks and Recreation Department and volunteer trail rangers, is unique in Southwestern Utah. It is a labyrinth of paved trails through beautiful desert terrain, following the meandering of the nearby rivers.

The **Virgin River Parkway** connects the outlying residential neighborhood of Bloomington with downtown St. George, running 2.8 miles along the banks of the Virgin and Santa Clara rivers. It is picturesque and pristine, ideal for in-line skating, riding bikes or a brisk walk. The scenery is splendid in any direction. **Fort Pierce Parkway** is a nearly 2-mile walk around the St. George Golf Course from the Virgin River to the heart of the Bloomington Hills residential neighborhood. Fort Pierce Parkway features a 188-foot pedestrian bridge crossing the Fort Pierce Wash. There is access to a wide variety of wildlife such as lizards, birds and rabbits and plant life that thrives in this desert ecosystem.

For added enjoyment, take a short walk on a side trail built as eagle scout projects. **Hilton Drive Trail** connects the Virgin River Parkway at Hilton Drive to Snow Park extending the walk by another couple of miles. **Utah Highway 18 Trail** parallels the highway from Skyline Drive to the Snow Canyon turnoff. Other trails are being developed by the City of St. George. Walking has become one of the area's most popular community recreation options. There is no cost and no hours when the trails are closed. It's a healthy alternative to life on the couch, and you're more than likely to run into at least a few people you know along the way!

Peak golfing season in Utah's Dixie begins when the snow starts flying in the northern part of the state.

Golf

The idea of golf as a leisure-time activity in Southwestern Utah took more than 30 years to catch hold. In 1931, an editorial in the *Washington County News* suggested "a golf course is the first step toward making St. George a winter resort. If we had a course, and other like amusements, a large majority of people passing through would remain a few days and in some instances, as the town became better known, would establish winter homes here."

Prophetic as that statement now seems in a community where golf and religion run neck-and-neck for devotion among their followers, it was the mid-1960s before area business people overcame the majority opinion in the area that life was for working, not playing. Today the communities of Southwestern Utah and nearby Mesquite, Nevada, are home to 11 regulation golf courses and five nine-hole courses. Page, Arizona, approximately 150 miles from St. George and Cedar City, boasts another regulation layout, and several other courses in the region are in some stage or other of completion. The Southwestern Utah courses and the layout in Page are reviewed in this chapter. For an extensive rundown on the Mesquite courses and the Arnold Palmer Golf Academy at Si Redd's Oasis Resort Casino, see our Mesquite, Nevada, chapter.

Peak season begins in late October or early November, when the snow flies in northern Utah, driving the serious golfers south to get their fix. Note that all the courses in the region get really jammed between Christmas and Easter. Prices drop during the slow summer season, which is a great time to play unlimited golf at your leisure on any of the area courses — that is, of course, so long as you can take the dry desert heat. Most golfers want to tee off as close to dawn as possible, as daytime temperatures throughout the region regularly get into the low 100s between mid-June and early September.

Visitors from lower-elevation areas with more humid climates will be pleased to discover the ball will travel a little farther here and hook or slice a little less. Golfers from higher elevations along Utah's Wasatch Front or elsewhere may find they lose a little distance. Also remember many of our courses are laid out in sensitive desert areas. Exercise caution when hunting for golf balls in these areas, both for your own safety (rattlesnakes and other sometimes dangerous critters inhabit the desert) and the protection of the environment. Some golf courses prohibit walking in these areas entirely. Always abide by the rules at the course you are playing.

Many area hotels offer golf packages, which is a good way to get advance tee times. Local golfers can get a little frustrated with the difficulty in getting a mid-winter tee time, but with three new courses completed in the last couple of years, the pressure has been reduced. Nine additional holes that opened at Sunbrook in St. George in May 1997 will also help lower golf-related stress levels.

There is a wide variety of golf available in Southwestern Utah, from world-class desert layouts to more standard public links. St. George offers four municipal courses (Sunbrook, Southgate, Dixie Red Hills and St. George), and the courses in Hurricane (Sky Mountain), Washington (Green Spring), Cedar City (Cedar Ridge) and Page, Arizona (Lake Powell National), are municipals as well.

The only full-length course that closes in winter is Cedar Ridge in Cedar City, which is a couple of thousand feet higher in elevation than St. George and gets its share of snow. All three courses listed in Mesquite, about 35 miles southwest of St. George, are associated with casinos that offer golf and room packages. Non-guests may play as well, but tee times must be arranged directly through the golf course. If you want an experience to tell the folks about back home, plan a winter morning of skiing at Brian Head followed by an afternoon of golf in the St. George area — there aren't many places in the world where you can enjoy those two activities in the same day.

St. George/Zion

Bloomington Country Club
3174 W. Bloomington Dr. S., St. George • 673-2029

Since its completion in 1969, the venerable Bloomington Country Club is at least partially responsible for making St. George Utah's winter golf mecca. A private club, it does have reciprocal arrangements with most Utah clubs, and getting on as a member's guest, especially in the summer, is usually pretty simple.

This unpretentious, par 72 course looks like what it is — a fair golfing test designed for an older clientele. It measures 6948 yards from the tips. Built on a fairly level plot of land between the mesas southwest of St. George, Bloomington is probably the best golf course to walk in Southwestern Utah. Take some time on the practice green before playing because the greens may be a little faster than what you are accustomed to. This is not a difficult golf course, although three of the four par 3s can easily yield double bogeys.

Winter, peak season, prices for 18 holes run $50 to $100 per round. Summer prices are often as little as half that. No matter when you visit, add $15 for a cart. There is a snack bar, pro shop, driving range and practice green available.

FYI

Unless otherwise noted, the area code for all phone numbers listed in this chapter is 801 but will change to 435 in September 1997. Either area code may be used until March 22, 1998.

Dixie Red Hills
100 N. 700 West, St. George • 634-5852

Golfers wanting to experience all the St. George area has to offer won't have a complete visit without playing Dixie Red Hills. Treasured by local golfers, Dixie is the St. George area's oldest course, built in 1966. For golfers who can't get a tee time at one of the full-length courses during the busy winter season or who are just looking to hone their game for a pleasant couple of hours, Dixie Red Hills is not a disappointment.

A 2725-yard par 34 layout with three par 3s and only one par 5, the nine-hole course gets lots of play in winter and has a flavor all its own. A slicer's nightmare, five of the nine holes favor a right-to-left tee shot. Most of the greens are of the smallish, table-top variety requiring accuracy on the approach. The cost is $15 for nine holes, and carts are $5 per rider. Dixie has a driving range, practice green and snack bar, and lessons are available at the pro shop.

Entrada at Snow Canyon
2511 W. Entrada Tr., St. George • 674-7500

Breathtaking. Punishing. Spectacular. Demanding. Beautiful. Exasperating. Exhilarating.

Take your pick. They all describe this gorgeous, par 72 Johnny Miller design set against the red rocks of Snow Canyon. The highlight of the course, opened in the fall of 1996, is the stretch of three holes — 15, 16 and 17 — carved among the black lava. These visually stunning holes look like they could have come straight from Mauna Kea or Mauna Lani on the big island of Hawaii (minus the ocean, of course). No. 15 is bound to become a favorite — a very short par 4 where two 7-irons will

---

INSIDERS' TIP

Though rain is uncommon in the area, late summer lightning storms are not a time to try to finish those last few holes — get off the golf course. You will not get a siren ordering you off the course as you might in some Eastern and Midwestern states, but use common sense when the storms move in.

Jay Don Blake

Jay Don Blake, 38, is a PGA tour player with a top-20 ranking and more than $1 million in career earnings.

Blake joined the tour in 1987, five years after winning the NCAA Golf Championship while at Utah State University, where he was arguably one of the finest athletes in school history. He has played the Masters twice, walking the fairways and sharing the spotlight in 1991 and '92 at Augusta with some of the greatest golfers in history. He was a top-ten finisher six times in 1991 and won the '91 Shearson-Lehman Brothers Open in San Diego. Though he hasn't stood in the PGA winner's circle since, Blake has consistently finished in the money here in the States and has won tournaments on foreign soil. He placed second at the Bell South

Atlanta Classic in 1992 and the Motorola Western Open in 1996.

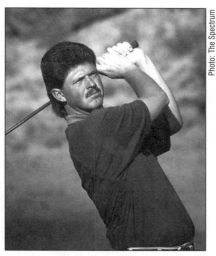

Photo: The Spectrum

Still, after the crowds have dissipated, Blake always comes back to his hometown of St. George, where golf history for himself and Southwestern Utah began. In a decade as a tour player, Blake has had numerous opportunities to move his home base, but he stays in Southwestern Utah because he like the small-town environment. Most important, Blake says, are his 14- and 18-year-old daughters, who live here. As far as his career goes, there are plenty of good courses to keep his game sharp here at home.

Blake has come a long way since the days his mother, Ilene, drove him the 750 miles round trip to junior tournaments in Salt Lake City. Often they slept in the car to save money. His dream of a professional career in the game began early. At age 10 he played the bright green fairways of Dixie Red Hills Municipal Golf Course and learned the game growing up in a family where everyone took to golf with a passion. By the

Southwestern Utah's Jay Don Blake hasn't won on the PGA Tour since 1991, but his 1995 earnings totaled nearly $350,000.

time he was 12, Blake was playing in junior tournaments, establishing himself as what some people consider the greatest homegrown golfer Utah has ever produced.

After playing the most famous, the most scenic and the most challenging golf courses in the world, Jay Don still enjoys the test and the familiar feel of Dixie Red Hills. "They did it right the first time," Blake says of Southwestern Utah's first course. "The place has stood the test of time. It's still as good a nine-hole course as you'll find anywhere."

As a college player, Blake always had to explain where St. George was when talking about his hometown. Nowadays no explanation is necessary. "The word is out about St. George," he says. "With 16 courses in the area, it has become a golfing hot spot."

The pro is also excited about the St. George attitude toward junior golf. "The courses are making time available to juniors and developing programs to help them improve," Blake says. And he points out other advantages for young players — good teachers, resources, facilities and weather for year-round practice.

reach the green in regulation. It is a beautiful hole but does not reward distance. (All the holes on the course have been named, and No. 15 is called "Mercy").

A punishing 7262 yards from the tips, Entrada at Snow Canyon is the longest course in the area but offers four tee lengths to suit higher handicaps. There is very little rough on this course — you go from fairway to desert or lava rock. Precise play is rewarded, while wayward shots are almost always punished with a penalty stroke. There is water on five holes, but that is not how you get in trouble on this golf course. There are hidden dangers on several holes (mostly sand traps and water), so first-time players would be wise to invest $5 for a yardage book available at the pro shop.

Given time to mature, Entrada should become one of the top-five golf courses in Utah. More difficult than Sunbrook, the course just down the road considered No. 1 in the state by many including *Golf Digest*, Entrada is not for someone who only plays a few times a year. Good golfers will find this a course designed to test every shot. The $60 peak season greens fees ($50 for Washington County residents) include a cart. Walking is not allowed, as the distance from tee to green is enormous, especially on the back nine. Fees go as low as $20 for local residents for twilight golf during the summer. Course amenities include a snack bar, pro shop and driving range. Lessons are available.

Green Spring Golf Course
588 N. Green Spring Dr., Washington • 673-7888

Green Spring, a memorable municipal golf course, can really chew up the weekend golfer. This 6717-yard, par 72 layout has become noted for a deep ravine running through two holes on the front nine. No. 5 is a short, downhill par 3 over the ravine requiring accurate club selection. No. 6 is undoubtedly the most difficult golf

hole in the state. Measuring 400 yards or more, depending on the tees, the narrow fairway runs parallel to the ravine for about 230 yards. The second shot requires a carry of nearly 200 yards to a fairly tight green with desert on two sides and the ravine on a third. Take a bogey on this hole as a fine score.

That's because any of a half-dozen holes at Green Spring can lead to triple bogeys or worse. It is one of those golf courses, however, where you can card a 94 and still say you had a great time. The par 3s are perhaps the most straightforward holes on the course but even they can be a problem if you miss the green. The trouble doesn't end there either. No. 11 demands a lay-out shot off the tee and an approach over water to a very narrow green. The par 4 No. 16 requires another approach over a ravine to a hilltop green.

Green Spring is evidence that you don't have to go to Palm Springs or Arizona to find superb desert golf. As you might suspect, walking this course is not recommended. Cost is $29.50 for 18 holes; $39 with a cart. Included at the facility are a driving range, practice green and snack bar. Lessons are also available.

Sky Mountain Golf Course
1030 N. 2600 West, Hurricane • 635-7888

The city of Hurricane has done itself proud with this golf course, which offers some of the most spectacular scenery in the state. The views from Nos. 17 and 18 are world-class, and the golf is pretty good as well on this par 72 layout that measures a modest 6313 yards from the tips.

There are some interesting holes that call for strategic shot-making, but average golfers can come away from Sky Mountain with a good score. The only glaring problem on the course is the No. 4 green, which is sloped so dramatically that putts from above the hole are virtually impossible to stop. No. 10 lacks imagination, but the rest of the golf course is very, very good.

INSIDERS' TIP

There is a single phone number to secure tee times for all St. George municipal golf courses (652-GOLF), but to use the computerized system, you must pre-register in person at St. George Leisure Services or call 634-5860 for more information.

Photo: The Spectrum

The 18th hole at Sunbrook presents a strong finish for Utah's top-rated golf course.

The par 5 18th is a fine finishing hole. If you are playing in the summer, mornings are your best bet — the afternoons can get pretty blustery. Winter golfers who haven't yet ventured to Hurricane are missing a treat.

Sky Mountain greens fees for local residents are $18.50 for nine holes and $33 for 18 including cart. For non-residents the cost is $20.50 for nine and $36 for 18, again, cart included. The course offers a driving range, practice green, snack bar and pro shop. Lessons are available.

Southgate Golf Course
1975 S. Tonaquint Dr., St. George
• 628-0000

One of St. George's four municipal courses, Southgate probably gets the most play and has the most active local men's and ladies' associations. The golf course features an excellent driving range to complement its golf school. Some recent renovations to the front nine have dramatically improved the course, which had suffered from mediocre conditions following flooding.

Southgate is similar to The Palms in Mesquite (see listing in our Mesquite chapter) in that it features two distinct styles — flat and traditional on the front nine with several holes running parallel to each other; hilly and imagi-

native in topography on the back side. A par 70 course with only one par 5 and three par 3s on the front, Southgate measures only 6400 yards from the tips. There are several challenging holes, but Southgate can yield low scores. Many holes are set up so that the average golfer can gun for par or better.

Southgate is the most convenient course to downtown St. George, which helps explain the difficulty in securing a tee time during peak season between Christmas and Easter. Rates are $9 for local seniors and $16 for other locals; $15 for non-resident seniors and $25 for other non-residents. Add $5 per rider for a cart. The course's pro shop includes a snack bar, and the golf school offers computer analysis of your swing.

St. George Golf Club
2190 S. 1400 East, St. George • 634-5854

The city has put a lot of effort into restoring this golf course in recent years, including the construction of an imaginative double green for Nos. 9 and 18, with approach shots for both over water. Despite the length here, the course is a favorite among local retirees. From the tips, it measures a whopping 7211 yards, making it one of the longest courses in the area and bringing trouble into play on many holes.

It's long and narrow, and a beast from the back tees, but you will find the course much more benign from any of the other four boxes. The front nine rises gradually uphill to No. 5, then slopes back to the clubhouse. Conditions were very rough a few years ago but have vastly improved. This is a good course to walk, but the trek back up to the clubhouse is a long one after the round is over. Average golfers can score well here if they stay off the tips and out of trouble on holes 3, 9, 13 and 15. Greens fees are $35, including cart, at St. George Golf Club.

Sunbrook Golf Course
2240 W. Sunbrook Dr., St. George
• 634-5866

With the opening of a new nine holes in the spring of 1997, Sunbrook no doubt has enhanced its position as Utah's No. 1-rated golf course, according to *Golf Digest*. The 27-hole complex features some of the best views and golf holes in southern Utah. Sunbrook has always attracted a lot of golfers in winter and has become a favorite for corporate and convention groups, even in the summer, when most southern Utah courses have very little play.

The course takes every advantage of the local terrain and requires equal parts brains and brawn. Each nine-hole portion has its own unique personality, and each comes with its own signature hole. The Pointe nine features a spectacular mesa-top par 4 that is reachable with a big tee shot and a little help from the prevailing wind. The Woodbridge nine is capped by a difficult par 3 island hole, followed by a long par 4 requiring a lay up off the tee and a long approach over water. The newest nine is Black Rock — highlighted by several holes through an old lava flow (hence the name) and accented with links-style heather bordering the rough. All 18-hole combinations are par 72.

Putting is particularly challenging, as many of the greens are multi-tiered and very large — finishing a round without a three-putt is an impressive feat. There are some truly lovely holes, highlighted by several running adjacent to the Santa Clara River on the Woodbridge and Black Rock nines. Perhaps Sunbrook's strongest asset is its consistency — the 27 holes hold up from start to finish and offer a complete golfing experience from links to striking desert layouts and everything in between.

The course has an irons-only driving range and a practice green with a great hilltop view of the layout and the surrounding area, including Pine Valley Mountain and Snow Canyon. Washington County residents play for $36 Monday through Thursday. Regular price is $46, and that includes a cart, which you are going to need. There's a snack bar and pro shop, and lessons are available.

Twin Lakes Golf Course
660 N. Twin Lakes Dr., St. George
• 673-4441

This is the golf course southbound drivers on Interstate 15 see as they enter St. George. Leave your bag in the car and bring a wedge, a 9-iron (maybe an 8-iron too) and your putter. All nine holes are par 3s, and the longest is the 152-yard No. 5, which plays downhill (but usually into the wind). Other holes range from 94 to 141 yards from the back tees. From the women's tees, the longest is 131 yards.

The only par 3 course in the area, Twin Lakes offers a chance to work exclusively on the short game. Most holes are pretty straightforward, and the greens are soft. The golf course is usually in good shape and is an easy walk. It's also tucked behind a ridge top, so if the wind is howling elsewhere, this might be a good alternative. Cost for nine holes is $6.50. Add $5.50 if you choose to use a cart. Note there is no pro shop or other amenities here.

Cedar City/Brian Head

Cedar Ridge Golf Course
200 E. 900 North, Cedar City • 586-2970

This pleasant, par 72 course in the Cedar City foothills offers an opportunity to get creative with your game. The course loses steam in the middle of the back nine, but the layout has enough overall imagination to compensate. The length from the back tees totals 6600 yards.

The No. 11 hole is a particularly interesting par 3 requiring accurate club selection from an elevated tee box. All the par 5s are fun to play. There is no water on the course, and many of the fairways connect to neighboring holes, so you won't need a lot of golf balls.

There's an excellent driving range and practice green at Cedar Ridge. The pro shop includes a snack bar, and lessons are available. Note the course is often closed in winter due to snow, the only course in the area at a high enough elevation to threaten winter play.

Thunderbird Golf Course
Junction of Utah Hwy. 9 and U.S. Hwy. 89, Mt. Carmel Junction • 648-2009

This unpretentious little nine-hole course sits on a hillside at the junction of U.S. Highway 89 and Utah Highway 9 just east of Zion National Park. The grass is very green and the course has a certain charm, but it is clearly intended for vacationing folks who need a quick golf fix between hikes. The course is in excellent shape, obviously getting a lot of attention from the management. Most golfers won't need a driver.

The short, par 31 layout measures 1934 yards from the back tees. Four of the nine holes are par 3s for men (one becomes a par 4 for women), and the longest hole is the 328-yard finishing hole, which plays downhill. The fairway grass is long, but there is little rough and little trouble on all but No. 8, which requires a short approach over a dry ditch. Most golfers consider the "pro shop" to be the adjacent convenience store. Cost is $8 for nine holes and $15 for 18. If you are itching to unpack the clubs while visiting Zion and/or Bryce Canyon parks but don't want to make the swing all the way to Hurricane or St. George, this will do just fine.

Kanab Area

Coral Hills Golf Course
700 E. Highway 89, Kanab • 644-5005

A deceptive course, Coral Hills is tucked up against Kanab's red hills, as the name im-

plies. The nine-hole layout favors a left-to-right game and includes some long, challenging holes. Total yardage is a beefy 3339 from the back tees on this par 36 course. The ball travels a long way in Kanab's light desert air, so adjust your club selection accordingly — about a half-club for those used to playing at mid-elevations; up to a full club for those accustomed to golfing at sea level.

The course is a fairly easy walk and offers some spectacular views of the Utah and Arizona landscape south of Kanab. It does occasionally snow in Kanab (the stuff rarely stays long), so call ahead if weather is a question. Nine holes at Coral Hill is $7.50, and carts are an additional $4 per rider.

Lake Powell National Golf Course
400 N. Clubhouse Dr., Page, Ariz.
• (520) 645-2023

Although Lake Powell National is a couple of hours from Kanab, it has proved very popular with Southwestern Utah golfers. This is a fun course, with breathtaking views of Lake Powell and the Glen Canyon Dam and an imaginative layout utilizing the topography nicely.

There are five tee lengths, and the par 72 course gets pretty long from the tips, where it totals 7064 yards. The fairways are generous and greens readable (putts will run toward the lake), which can result in good scoring. The back nine is a bit of hike, so check your pulse before rejecting a golf cart. Lessons are available, and there's a driving range and practice green. Greens fees for non-residents are $40 including a cart. Plans are in the works for a large pro shop and snack bar, but the course currently operates out of a small, temporary facility. As this course matures (Lake Powell National only opened in September 1995), it will be yet another reason to head to Lake Powell.

You won't need to travel far to find scenery, attractions, sights and sounds that differ greatly from red rock desert terrain.

Daytrips and Weekend Getaways

Once there was a tourist who, when asked how he enjoyed Bryce Canyon, responded, "It's nice, but once you've seen one red rock, you've seen them all."

Though most of us can't imagine such an attitude in an area so rich in scenic beauty — not to mention the arts and culture, history, golf and community events — we must admit that even here in paradise an occasional change "is as good as a rest."

In rare cases, a daytrip or a getaway weekend is a welcome break in the day-to-day monotony of perfection. You won't need to travel far to find scenery, attractions, sights and sounds that differ greatly from red rock desert terrain. Within a 300-mile radius from "downtown" Southwestern Utah (not considered that far in an area where it's common to go more than 50 miles between gas stations), you can find the bright lights of the big city, splash in the waters of the world's second-largest manmade reservoir, study ancient rock art and experience superior hiking, biking and kicking back. Though most of our recommendations are technically daytrips, it might be more realistic to classify at least a couple of our choices as weekend getaways. We'll let you decide for yourself which ones warrant an overnight stay to enjoy an extra day of exploration.

Viva Las Vegas

Let's dispense with the most obvious option first. This sparkling, storied, restless, exciting town is an easy drive from Southwestern Utah. About 125 miles south of St. George on Interstate 15, **Las Vegas** has so many monikers you can pick your favorite reputation: "the adult Disneyland," "the city that never sleeps," "Land of 1,000 Elvises" or "the entertainment capital of the world."

Everyone should see the **Las Vegas Strip** at least once in their lifetime. Whether its high noon, 4 in the afternoon or 4 in the morning, the place is guaranteed to be jumping.

But for all the adult entertainment, Las Vegas' promoters now recognize families are big business too. The new Las Vegas is family-friendly with such kid-favorite casinos as **Circus, Circus**, complete with high-wire acts, wild animals and clowns and **Treasure Island Casino**, where actors walk the plank and pirates fire cannonballs to sink ships hourly in the lagoon. Regular fireworks shows draw huge crowds. Visitors of any age will also enjoy a bite of the Big Apple at **New York, New York Casino**, just opened in January 1997. This long-awaited showplace is complete with skyscrapers and what seems like a mile-high roller coaster perched precariously above "the city."

In Las Vegas, there are dozens of casinos and approximately 100,000 hotel rooms with a 91 percent average, year-round occupancy. New projects are always under construction, promising to be bigger and better than the competition. New Year's Eve in Las Vegas was a major focus for the national celebration at the end of 1996. A dazzling fireworks show preceded the implosion of the **Hacienda Hotel and Casino**, with 500,000 cheering revelers in attendance. The event was so spectacular, it was scheduled for 9 PM Pacific time to usher in the new year for East Coast partiers along with the ball dropped in New York's Time Square at midnight.

But Las Vegas is not all glitz and glamour.

More than a million people with mortgages, kids, pets and jobs live in the greater Las Vegas area, which includes Henderson and Boulder. The nation's fastest-growing city saw more than 30,000 building permits issued in 1996. There is a healthy lifestyle and a healthy economy. The tax rate is low and medical facilities are high-tech and first-rate. The **University of Nevada at Las Vegas** has an outstanding reputation for turning out top-notch graduates. UNLV is also the home of the Runnin' Rebels, the famed (and infamous) college hoops team, and the school's Thomas and Mack Center hosts the **National Finals Rodeo** for 10 days beginning on the first Friday of each December.

McCarran International Airport moves travelers in and out of the area with professionalism. Many visitors bound for Southwestern Utah touch down on the McCarran tarmac.

There are dozens of museums, art galleries and cultural offerings along with exceptional shopping. Meals in Las Vegas casinos are priced ridiculously low, and restaurants try to outdo each other vying for hungry patrons. Churches are thriving (believe it or not), and people are employed. Bring a few rolls of quarters or a wad of bills . . . Include the kids or get away by yourself. Las Vegas must be seen to be believed. The **Las Vegas Chamber of Commerce**, 711 E. Desert Inn Road, Las Vegas, Nevada 89109, invites inquiries by mail, phone, (702) 735-1616, or fax, (702) 735-2011.

Lake Mead National Recreation Area

The **Lake Mead National Recreation Area**, about 100 miles south of downtown St. George, is 1.5 million acres of sparkling lakes and spectacular scenery. With more than 1,000 miles of shoreline in three states, Lake Mead was created by **Hoover Dam**, which was the largest dam ever built when it was completed in 1935. Today, it is classified as the highest concrete dam in the Western hemisphere.

Lake Mead NRA offers some of the country's best sport fishing, short desert hikes for the novice and demanding cross-country trails for the veteran hiker. With its dramatic changes in elevation, Lake Mead is also home to a surprising variety of rare plants and animals, including bighorn sheep, mule deer, coyotes, kit foxes, bobcats, ringtail cats, desert tortoise, lizards and snakes and a wealth of bird species.

Popular activities around Lake Mead include watersports, hiking, picnicking, scenic drives or just pitching a tent and relaxing. Largemouth and striped bass, rainbow trout, catfish, crappie and bluegill are plentiful in both Lake Mead and **Lake Mojave**. Boating, waterskiing, kayaking, canoeing, sailboating (and boarding) as well as swimming are major forms of water recreation. Because both lakes are clear and clean, snorkeling and scuba diving are gaining in popularity as well. There are six marinas at Lake Mead; three at Lake Mojave. Many of them can provide you with whatever watersports equipment you may want to rent. It's probably a good idea to call ahead to find out if they can take care of your specific needs.

Several paved roads — the most popular are Northshore Road and Lakeshore Road — wind through dramatic scenery where towering mountains, plateaus, desert basins with cacti and creosote bushes and vertical-walled canyons provide the backdrop to clear blue lakes. The big weekends — Memorial Day, Fourth of July and Labor Day — draw major crowds. Individual sites are available on a first-come, first-served basis. Reservations are required for groups of eight or more. The area around Lake Mead NRA also includes motels and RV campgrounds with hookups and concession-run stores. Closest to the Utah border, visitors at Lake Mead have two good accommodations options: **Overton Beach Resort**, (702) 394-4040, has full hookups for $16 a night; **Echo Bay Resort**, (702) 394-4000, offers motel rooms for $69 to $84 from April to November and as low as $45 during the off-season.

The best place to start your visit is at the **Alan Bible Visitor Center**, 4 miles northeast of Boulder, Nevada, on U.S. Highway 93. From 8:30 AM to 4:30 PM daily (until 5:30 PM from Memorial Day to Labor Day), the park staff will help you plan your stay and provide up-to-date information on activities and services. Exhibits, books, brochures, topographical maps and nautical charts are available. An outdoor botanical garden displays some of the area's interesting desert trees, shrubs and cacti. It gets plenty hot in the desert during the traditional tourist season, so plan accordingly.

For more information on the area, write Lake Mead National Recreation Area, 601 Nevada Highway, Boulder City, Nevada 89005, or call (702) 293-8907.

Valley of Fire State Park

Valley of Fire State Park, 90 miles south of St. George or 55 miles north of Las Vegas, is named for its brilliant red sandstone formations, created by erosion, wind and climate changes during millions of years. To get there, take I-15 south to Exit 75, then follow the signs on Nevada Highway 169. Entry into Nevada's first state park is $4 per vehicle.

The park covers more than 37,000 acres and is rich in the artifacts and petroglyphs of an ancient civilization believed to have inhabited the area around Valley of Fire nearly 11,000 years ago. Fall, winter and spring are the preferred seasons for visiting this beautifully scenic spot, as modern man may be uncomfortable in summer, when daytime temperatures soar to more than 100 degrees.

The park's **visitors center** has some interesting displays, live desert critters (mostly various snakes and lizards, safely secured behind glass), video presentations, souvenirs and printed information. Picnics are popular in shaded areas with water and restrooms located strategically throughout the park. **Two unnamed campgrounds** are easily found near the west end of Valley of Fire. Just follow the signs. A total of 51 sites in the two campgrounds are enhanced by shaded tables, available grills, water and restrooms. Each site is available for $11 per vehicle.

This beautiful state park is an ideal setting for dazzling photography or a great place to turn the kids loose to run and roam. Be sure to remind them not to pick wildflowers or other plants, or capture, feed or pester small critters. For more information, write Valley of Fire State Park, P.O. Box 515, Overton, Nevada 89040, or call (702) 397-2088.

While you're in the area, don't miss a more extensive exploration of Anasazi culture, as well as artifacts from the early residents of Moapa Valley, on display at the **Lost City Museum**, an actual Anasazi Indian site. In Overton, 14 miles north of Valley of Fire State Park, the museum at 721 S. Moapa Valley Boulevard is open daily from 8:30 AM to 4:30 PM. Admission is $2 for adults. Kids younger than 17 are admitted free. Note that the campgrounds mentioned are the only accommodations available in the Valley of Fire park. If you want to make your visit into a weekend, the nearest motels are in Overton.

Cove Fort

About midway through the state of Utah at the junction of I-15 and Interstate 70, you'll find historic **Cove Fort** halfway between the communities of Beaver and Fillmore. Take Exit 132 off I-15 if en route from Southwestern Utah, Exit 135 if you're coming from the Salt Lake City area or Exit 1 off I-70.

Built in 1867, Cove Fort served as a way station for pioneer travelers, miners, native or Spanish traders, mail carriers and others traversing the "Mormon Corridor" of settlements stretching from Idaho to California. While there is evidence the fort might have had a secondary purpose as protection against possible attack, the primary reason behind its creation by the LDS Church was to provide rest for weary travelers and food for their animals.

The fort was built in about seven months by Ira Hinckley and tradesmen from central Utah settlements. Construction materials consisted of black volcanic rock and dark limestone quarried from nearby hillsides. The walls are 100 feet long, 18 feet high and taper from

4 feet thick at the base to 2 feet thick at the top. The roof, 12 interior rooms and the massive doors at the east and west ends were constructed of lumber. The doors, originally filled with sand to protect those inside from errant bullets, have been emptied because of their extreme weight and awkwardness.

For many years the fort bustled with activity. Twice daily, stagecoaches arrived with a variety of roadworn travelers anxious for food and rest. Brigham Young, president of the LDS Church, was a frequent visitor during trips between Salt Lake City and St. George or other southern settlements. It was not unusual for 75 people each day to enjoy the hospitality of the fort's kitchen and dining room. Cowboys tended the church's tithing herds (the animals the early pioneers gave as their one-tenth offering to the church), and a blacksmith was kept busy reshoeing horses and oxen and repairing wagon wheels for travelers. A telegraph office in the fort, as well as regular news reports of the great and growing West from pony express riders, kept the little band of settlers from feeling completely shut off from the rest of the world.

The fort served an important function for nearly 20 years, but as times changed, the need for it diminished. In 1900, the church sold Cove Fort to a private owner. In 1989, the Hinckley family purchased and restored the fort, rebuilt some of the outbuildings and donated it back to the church as a historic site.

Today, Cove Fort is open daily for guided tours. In addition to the chance to explore the fort, modern visitors will get a close-up look at pioneer life in the outbuildings that include a blacksmith shop, the barn with a collection of wagons and farm implements on display, a bunkhouse and the restored Hinckley cabin, where a 14-minute informational video is regularly shown. There are always pioneer games for children that involve, now as a century ago, the creative use of household items or things found outside — buttons, tops, sticks and stones. An ice house is being restored, a large

garden produces a variety of vegetables in season and a hay derrick is still in use.

There are no concessions, but a picnic area with a dozen tables shaded by apple trees planted more than 100 years ago welcomes families who want to enjoy their own meal at the site. Restrooms are clean and plentiful. The fort opens daily at 8 AM, but because there is no interior lighting, it closes at sunset year round (including holidays). Tours of Cove Fort are free, but there are also no accommodations, gas stations or restaurants within 35 miles of the site. The nearest services are available in the central Utah community of Richfield, 38 miles east on I-70; in Fillmore, about 35 miles north; or in Beaver, approximately 35 miles south on I-15.

For more information, write Cove Fort, Utah 84713 (yep, that's all the address info you'll need), or call (801) 438-5547.

Fremont Indian State Park

Fremont Indian State Park is in **Clear Creek Canyon** at Exit 17 on Interstate 70, about 17 miles east of the junction with I-15, which is 120 miles north of St. George. The largest Fremont Indian site ever discovered in the state of Utah was unearthed during construction of I-70 and dedicated as a park in 1987.

Within the boundaries of the park there may have been 150 to 250 occupants of the **Five Fingers Ridge Village**, discovered in 1983 but dating back to 1000 A.D. For approximately 250 years, the Fremonts raised corn, beans and squash, supplementing their diet with the meat of deer, sheep, elk and bison hunted from the surrounding hillsides (see our History chapter). The park contains 40 pithouses, 20 storage areas, several different work sites, numerous examples of ancient rock art and a delightful museum filled with artifacts collected from Clear Creek Canyon.

Lake Powell offers boating amid red cliffs.

The 31-site **Castle Rock Campground** in the park has water, flush toilets, picnic tables and campfire grills but no electricity. The cost on weekends is $7 per vehicle. During the week, a campsite is only $5 a vehicle, which includes entry into the museum. Fremont Indian State Park is open daily from 9 AM to 6 PM between Memorial Day and Labor Day, 9 AM to 5 PM during the winter months and is closed on Thanksgiving, Christmas and New Year's Day. Admission is $5 per vehicle. Tours are self-guided, but park rangers are available to provide additional insight and are always willing to share legends and stories of the Fremonts.

For more information, contact Fremont Indian State Park, 11550 Clear Creek Canyon Road, Sevier, Utah 84766. Call (801) 527-4631 for information, or (800) 322-3770 for campground reservations. If you want to make a weekend of it, overnight accommodations including RV parks are plentiful in Richfield, about 21 miles northeast on I-70.

Canyonlands National Park

OK . . . We admit, it's more red rock! But Canyonlands National Park, designated by President Lyndon Johnson in 1964, is the largest of the five national parks in Utah. With its total of 337,258 acres, Canyonlands is wild America at its most untamed! Prehistoric Native Americans, cowboys, river explorers and uranium prospectors roamed this rugged southeastern corner of Utah, but few others dared.

To a large degree, Canyonlands is still pristine wilderness. The park is 50 miles south of Green River off I-70, about 400 miles east of St. George. You'll travel about midway through the state on I-15 before getting on I-70. Canyonlands' roads are mostly unpaved, its trails primitive, its rivers unrestrained. Native wildlife such as desert bighorn sheep, coyotes, mule deer and the occasional cougar roam freely. Time and the unrelenting Green and Colorado rivers have been the architects of the land, sculpting flat layers of sedimentary rock into hundreds of colorful canyons, mesas, buttes, fins, arches and spires.

There are many ways to explore Canyonlands — by trail or by river, on bicycle or on horseback, using a four-wheel drive vehicle to navigate a steep, rock road or traveling in the air-conditioned comfort of the family sedan. Paved and two-lane dirt roads lead to interesting natural features, overlooks, trailheads, picnic areas and developed campgrounds. More adventuresome four-wheel drivers may prefer one of several tortuous trails winding through the park — these trips can be as short as a day or longer than a week. One of the most popular is the 100-mile **White Rim Trail**, which can be driven in two days or leisurely explored over many days, taking advantage of primitive campgrounds along the way.

A backcountry permit is required for overnight trips. Always carry food, water and tools for emergencies. In remote areas, it is best to travel with two vehicles. By trail, short walks and long hikes lead to some of Canyonlands' most breathtaking scenery. Some short trails (a mile or less) to geologic features or Indian ruins have wayside exhibits or brochures that provide information about the area's scenery. Longer trails penetrate wilder regions, are generally primitive and may be strenuous. Never hike alone. Stay on trails and always carry a map and water.

By river, motorboats, rafts and canoes can navigate the quiet upper waters of both the Green and Colorado rivers that flow through the park. Rafting or special whitewater boats require a permit from park headquarters. Boat launch sites are north of the park. There are no services along the river. Cycling season begins in March and ends in November, though only the most daring will venture out on the trails in the heat of the summer. Four-wheel drive and mountain bike tours, hiking trips, horseback rides, and river float trips are operated by commercial tour guides. Tours vary greatly in territory covered, length, cost and amenities provided. Most operate year round out of nearby Moab or Green River, 50 miles to the north. A few options include **Rim Tours**, (800) 635-6622; **NAVTEC** (short for navigational technologies) **Expeditions**, (800) 833-1278; and **Kaibab Mountain Bike Tours**, (800) 451-1133.

Canyonlands has two modestly developed campgrounds open year round on a first-come,

The Hole-in-the-Rock

In 1880, a group consisting of 250 men, women and children, 80 wagons and 1,000 head of cattle found themselves facing insurmountable odds and impassable terrain. The settlers, on their way to land on the San Juan River in southeastern Utah, had searched two weeks to find a direct route between Southwestern and Southeastern Utah, only to find themselves 1,200 feet above the Colorado River gorge with winter rapidly approaching. For six weeks, the men labored to find a way down the sandstone cliffs. Ultimately, they chiseled and blasted a path through a steep crevice called Hole-in-the-Rock, their road a testimony to pioneer ingenuity and determination. Through

the opening, wagons and livestock were lowered one at a time, dangling precariously above the river as the party descended to the valley floor.

In all, the trek — expected to take six weeks — took six months. By April 1880, when they reached the sandy bottomland along the San Juan River, their food supplies were depleted, and the teams were worn to the point of exhaustion. Two babies were born along the way and, miraculously, no one died. Today the same trip takes six hours from the Southwestern side of the state, swinging a long way around Lake Powell.

first-served basis. Because both campgrounds are generally filled by noon, you may want to have an alternative plan in mind. Both **Squaw Flat** and **Willow Flat** campgrounds have picnic tables, grills and toilets. Squaw Flat has water only during the spring and summer months, but Willow Flat has no water. Entry fee into Canyonlands National Park is $4 for non-commercial vehicles. And be sure to ask someone in a park uniform before you set out on your adventures, since permits are required for many activities in the park. For more information, contact Canyonlands National Park, 2282 S. West Resource Boulevard, Moab, Utah 84532. Call for information at (801) 259-7164.

Arches National Park

Arches National Park, off I-70 at Utah's eastern boundary, boasts the world's largest concentration of natural arches. Carved by wind and sand over the course of eons of time, more than 2,100 arches have been catalogued within the boundaries of the park's 73,000 acres. Most major sights — including **Balanced Rock**, **Skyline Arch** and the **Fiery Furnace** — are easily accessible from an 18-mile paved road.

Reservations are required for ranger-guided walks into the Fiery Furnace and can be made at the **visitors center**, open daily from 8 AM to 4:30 PM from October to March and until 6 PM from April through September. Unpaved roads lead to several trailheads including the moderate 3-mile round-trip hike to **Delicate Arch**, the symbol of Utah's statehood centennial celebration in 1996. There are also some strikingly beautiful backpacking areas and unpaved four-wheel drive roads.

Devil's Garden Campground, the only campground in the park, is 18 miles from the entrance. There are no hookups or showers, but the campground does offer 52 sites, along with picnic tables and grills. No reservations are taken, so the campground fills on a first-come, first-served basis. Fees are $8 per site from March to October and $5 during the balance of the year. There are many camping opportunities outside the park with motel accommodations plentiful in nearby Moab.

Entrance to the park is just 5 miles north of Moab. Entry fees are $4 per vehicle or $2 per walker or cyclist. Golden Eagle, Golden Age or Golden Access passports, available at any national park, are also accepted. The 12-month Golden Eagle Passport is an unlimited access pass for federal parks and recreation areas, available at all park entrances for $25 per family. The Golden Access Passport provides free entrance for any U.S. citizen or resident with disabilities. For U.S. citizens and residents older than 62, the Golden Age Passport offers unlimited access for a one-time fee of $10. For more information, call (801) 259-8161, or write Arches National Park, North U.S. Highway 191, Moab, Utah 84532.

Moab

In fact, if sleeping outdoors on a rock isn't exactly your idea of a vacation, Moab, about 5 miles south of the entrance to Arches National Park or 40 miles from Canyonlands National Park, caters to the adventurer who also wants a good meal, a bed and a shower.

Despite its remote location, Moab is a well-developed town with plenty of choices for motels, nightlife, shopping and a surprisingly long list of good restaurants. Moab has been discovered, so don't take a chance on ambling into town and finding a motel room. No matter what time of the year you plan to visit the area, make reservations early.

The town is a magnet for outdoor enthusiasts. Whitewater rafters come to float the Colorado and Green rivers; hikers and four-wheelers explore the nearby national parks; backcountry skiers enjoy the challenge of skiing the LaSal Mountains in winter; and, last year more than 100,000 cyclists flocked to the area around Moab for world-class biking. For more information on Moab, contact the **Grand County Travel Council**, 210 N. 100 West, Moab, Utah 84532, or call (801) 259-8825 or (800) 635-MOAB.

Glen Canyon National Recreation Area

Before Maj. John Wesley Powell conducted the first scientific and geological survey of Glen Canyon in 1869, Lt. Joseph C. Ives led a party to the area in 1858. Ives' diary records his impression: "Ours has been a first and will undoubtedly be the last party to visit this profitless locality. It seems intended by nature that the Colorado River, along the greater portion of its lonely and majestic way, shall be forever unvisited and undisturbed."

In 1956, President Dwight Eisenhower pushed a button on his White House desk to set off a blast — the first of many during a period of nearly 10 years of construction of the **Glen Canyon Dam**, 6 miles south of the Utah-Arizona border. In this area, Lt. Ives thought would be forever undisturbed, 3 million tourists each year come to play in the lake created by the damming of waters from the Colorado and San Juan rivers. Adjectives such as spectacular, dramatic, thrilling or wondrous seem to fall short in describing **Lake Powell**. The second-largest reservoir in North America is a 186-mile-long manmade miracle, finally finished in 1964 by the completion of the dam. Including the numerous flooded canyons, Lake Powell has nearly 2,000 miles of shoreline, more than the entire West Coast of the United States.

The bright turquoise to deep blue water of the lake is surrounded by the colorful, surrealistic landscape of buttes, peaks and canyons. Hundreds of side canyons, inlets and coves sheltering Indian ruins and natural wonders make Lake Powell a paradise for photography, fishing, general exploring and houseboating, a great option for family vacations, reunions or other get-togethers. Concessionaires in the park offer this accommodation option. On the Utah side, call **Bullfrog Marina**, (800) 528-6154, for more information; on the Arizona shore at **Wahweap Marina**, call (520) 645-2433. Plan ahead to houseboat, as this is a very popular way to enjoy Lake Powell. If you're looking for last-minute reservations, persistence will sometimes pay off, but there aren't many cancellations. Houseboating can be expensive (up to $4,095 for a "Cadillac" week during the peak summer

season), so look at going in on the vacation with a large group. Other recreational opportunities include boating, water skiing, scuba diving, parasailing and swimming. Boat tours to **Rainbow Bridge National Monument** are conducted daily throughout the year from both Wahweap and Bullfrog marinas.

There are seven visitors centers or contact stations in the area, though only **Carl Hayden Visitor Center**, next to Glen Canyon Dam, is open year round. If you intend to rent a powerboat or houseboat or hope for a motel room or RV accommodations, again, plan ahead. At Bullfrog Marina, a comfortable overnight stay can be had at **Defiance House Lodge**, (801) 684-3032. **Ticaboo Lodge**, (801) 788-2110, is also an option. In the community of Page, Arizona, a few miles from Wahweap Marina, there are many motel choices. Some primitive camping options around the rim of the lake are accessible by car, but for the most part, those who enjoy Lake Powell also enjoy the chance to find an isolated cove along the shoreline where they can drop anchor and either snooze on the sandy beach or in a comfy houseboat.

Though the sheer size of Lake Powell and its close proximity to several national parks draws more than a million visitors a year to its shores, it is the undisputed magnificence of the landscape and the surprising serenity of the area that keeps them coming back. There are no noisy highways, condominium projects or resort villages to distract from the scenery and the stillness — nor are any planned. The nearest commercial enterprises are found in Page, Arizona, 15 minutes south.

The creation of Lake Powell was not without costs. Prehistoric, historic and religious sites revered by the Navajo nation and of value to Western historians are now under 500 feet of water. The Crossing of the Fathers, where Escalante and Dominguez passed over in 1776 (see our History chapter); the fording place

INSIDERS' TIP

The world's largest manmade excavation is the Kennecott Copper Mine, 25 miles southwest of Salt Lake City. An observation deck, accessible by U.S. Highway 48, is open April to October.

on the Hole-in-the-Rock Trail created by Mormon pioneers in 1880; gold-mining sites staked out in the 1880s, 1890s and early 1900s — all are gone due to Lake Powell, along with priceless rock art panels and villages of the Anasazi Indians. Even the glen from which John Wesley Powell surveyed the terrain in awe is lost.

But the reality of the dam came after years of careful negotiations between Native American tribes, historians, environmentalists and government officials. Today, visitors will find the lake bustling with activity as fun seekers explore the secrets of Lake Powell by boat, Jet Ski, other personal watercraft or underwater diving. Yet with thousands enjoying the area's bounty of scenic beauty, there will always be a deserted sandy cove or hidden canyon waiting just for you.

For more information, write the Glen Canyon National Recreation Area, P.O. Box 1507, Page, Arizona 86040. Call the recreation area offices at (801) 826-4315, Carl Hayden Visitor Center at (520) 608-6405 or Bullfrog Visitor Center at (801) 684-2243.

Great Basin National Park/ Lehman Caves

This 77,092-acre preserve is one of America's most recently established national parks. Established in 1986, the park is centered around 13,063-foot **Wheeler Peak**. Great Basin National Park/Lehman Caves captures bits and pieces of the western landscape characteristics of Nevada, Utah, California, Oregon, Idaho — even a little nibble off the southwestern tip of Wyoming. The park is about 150 miles northwest of Cedar City. From the I-15 exit for Beaver, it is a long drive over Utah Highway 21 to the Nevada border, but the road is well-marked.

The park is filled with streams, lakes, alpine plants, abundant wildlife and a variety of forest types including stands of ancient bristlecone pines. The park has developed facilities such as the **Great Basin National Park Visitor Center**, a scenic drive, four campgrounds and numerous hiking trails. One of the park's most important features is **Lehman Caves**, centerpiece of the former 640-acre Lehman Caves National Monument, one of Nevada's crown jewels absorbed by the newer park.

Lehman Caves, discovered about 1885 by rancher and miner Absalom Lehman, is one of the most richly decorated caves in the country — a small but sparkling gem where water has dripped for eons to create interesting and intricate formations in the interiors. It is a labyrinth of large rooms, corridors and small winding tunnels extending much deeper into the mountain than casual tour parties can safely proceed. Through a period of 2 to 5 million years, seemingly insignificant trickles of mineral-rich water have created a wonderful display of cave formations, scientifically referred to as speleothems. Lehman Caves also contains familiar structures with names we learned in junior high science classes. Stalactites, stalagmites, columns, draperies and flow stone are dramatic testimony of the forces of nature, but the cave's most delicate rarity are its shields. How shields were formed remains a marvelous mystery, but they are two roughly circular halves, almost like flattened clam shells.

The caves are in a fairly arid region. Moisture comes in the form of snow in the wintertime and infrequent thunderstorms during summer. But if you are planning to visit the cave, no matter the time of the year, bring a jacket and good walking shoes. Lehman Caves is consistently 50 degrees with 90 percent humidity! The cave tour takes about an hour and a half including a three-quarter mile walk on a paved trail with stairways and indirect lighting.

The entrance to Great Basin National Park is 5 miles west of Baker, Nevada, 15 miles west of the Utah-Nevada border and approximately 140 miles from Cedar City on Utah Highway 130. Great Basin is open daily (except Thanksgiving, Christmas and New Year's Day) from 7:30 AM to 6 PM from Memorial Day to Labor Day and from 8 AM to 5 PM during slower times. There is no fee to enter the park, but visitors who want to tour the cave can expect to pay $5 for adults and $4 for kids between the ages of 6 and 15. Children younger than 6 get in free. Golden Age and Access cardholders (see listing in this chapter for Arches National Park) get in for half price.

Other park facilities include a visitor center with exhibits and slide shows; trails and scenic drives open seasonally, as weather permits, through the mountain park; campfire programs; guided walks; junior ranger programs for the kids; and patio talks, presented on a covered courtyard immediately outside the visitor center's back door. All programs are offered from Memorial Day to Labor Day. The **Lehman Caves Cafe and Gift Shop** offers a limited menu. A few restaurants, a grocery store, a gas station and limited motel accommodations are options in nearby Baker. Otherwise, the nearest gas, goodies or hot shower can be found in Ely, Nevada, 70 miles to the west, or Delta, Utah, 100 miles to the east.

There are four developed campgrounds in Great Basin National Park. **Lower Lehman Creek Campground** has 11 sites open year round at 7,500 feet elevation via the park's Scenic Drive. The $5 daily fee provides water and pit toilets. **Upper Lehman Creek Campground** is only a half-mile farther and 300 feet higher on Scenic Drive, but it is open only from mid-May to mid-October. Twenty-four sites have water and pit toilets for $5 per day. **Wheeler Peak Campground** is at the end of the Scenic Drive at nearly 10,000 feet above sea level. There are 37 sites, water and pit toilets. Again, there is a $5 fee, but the campground is open only from mid-June to mid-October. **Baker Creek Campground** is found

at 8,000 feet. There are 32 streamside sites and pit toilets, but no water other than what runs in the stream (and it should be used with care or when treated).

There are some wonderful hikes and self-guided walks in Great Basin National Park. No permits are required to explore the backcountry, but for safety, backpackers are encouraged to complete a voluntary backcountry permit and ask for the latest trail information before setting out. For more information, contact the park at (702) 234-7331.

Salt Lake City

"This is the right place," Brigham Young said on July 24, 1847, as he gazed down into the Valley of the Great Salt Lake at the end of an arduous journey for the first company of Mormons. Others soon followed, and by 1869, when the transcontinental railroad was completed at Promontory Point, 60,000 early members of the LDS Church had reached the valley by way of wagons and handcarts.

Today, for many, it is still the right place. Selected as the site for the **2002 Winter Olympics**, Salt Lake City is the "Crossroads of the West," some 325 miles north of St. George and Southwestern Utah. It is home to three professional sports teams (most notably the NBA's **Utah Jazz**), the **University of Utah Medical Center**, where the first permanent artificial heart was created, and world-class cultural arts organizations including **Ballet West**, **Utah Symphony** and the **Utah Opera Company**. In the tops of the **Wasatch Mountains**, within a few miles of downtown Salt Lake City, skiers will find **Alta**, **Snowbird** and **Park City**, with some of the greatest skiing on earth.

Salt Lake City is headquarters of the 10 million member **Church of Jesus Christ of Latter-day Saints**. The **Mormon Tabernacle Choir** practices and performs in the **Tabernacle on Temple Square**, the state's top tour-

---

INSIDERS' TIP

Now in its 60th year, the Ute Stampede, held in Nephi (90 miles south of Salt Lake City on I-15) in July, is one of Utah's best-known and longest-running rodeos.

ist attraction. The **LDS Family History Library** contains the largest collection of genealogical records and resources on earth and is open to the public.

Members of other denominations and ethnic groups are also settling in the Salt Lake City area at an accelerated pace, and the character of the city is growing ever more worldly. The city is known for friendly, helpful people, wide, clean streets and attractive landscaping. The state's economy is the healthiest in the nation and unemployment is at a record low.

A weekend in Salt Lake — at least during your first visit — should certainly include a visit to Temple Square (particularly impressive during the Christmas season, when a million lights sparkle in the trees). Guides provide free tours, including a visit to the historic tabernacle (the famed choir rehearses on Thursday evenings). There is no charge. Across from Temple Square, visit the **Joseph Smith Memorial Building** where you can research your own family name on hundreds of computers available for public use. But beware! If you haven't already been bit by the genealogy bug, you're certain to be hooked on one of America's most popular hobbies after this experience.

Lagoon, about 15 miles north of downtown Salt Lake City off I-15, has long been Utah's favorite amusement park with wild and mild rides, entertainment, food and a Pioneer Village. It is open daily in the summer and weekends in the fall and spring. The adjacent **Lagoon A-Beach** is a water park with acres of water slides and swimming pools. **This is the Place State Park** at 2601 Sunnyside Avenue, is open for tours of the living history adventure of **Old Deseret Village**, accessible from I-15 at the 6th South Exit. The ongoing expansion and development of Old Deseret Village has been made possible by the Utah Statehood Centennial Commission and the generosity of many Utahns. You will experience daily pioneer life as you visit homes, stores, schools,

houses of worship and sites of cultural activities. This is the Place State Park is open daily from 11 AM to 5 PM (until 8 PM on Thursday).

Hogle Zoo, at 2600 Sunnyside Avenue, is across from This is the Place State Park. The zoo is open daily from 9 AM to 6 PM, providing children and adults the chance to see more than 1,200 strange and exotic animals, a petting zoo, a miniature railroad and hands-on exhibits.

The **Children's Museum of Utah** is at 840 N. 300 West in north Salt Lake City. This wonderful educational experience offers displays, programs and workshops for hands-on learning. On any given day, kids will have a great time enjoying cultural awareness activities, archeological digs, fantasy flights in a real cockpit of a jet or arts and crafts. The museum is open from 9:30 AM to 5 PM Monday through Thursday and Saturday. On Friday, hours are 9:30 AM to 8 PM. The cost is $3 for adults and children, but after 5 PM, children get in for $1.50 each. Kids younger than 2 are always admitted free. **Hansen Planetarium** at 15 S. State Street features star and science shows and laser shows in the dome-topped theater for a fun science experience. Open daily at varying hours, Hansen Planetarium also hosts classes, demonstrations and special events. Exhibits are free, and theater shows vary in price from $2 to $5.

The internationally acclaimed **Sundance Film Festival** is held each January in Park City, about 35 miles east of Salt Lake City by way of Interstate 80, while pianists prepare for years to compete in the **Gina Bachauer International Piano Competition**. All in all, Salt Lake City, about 325 miles north of St. George, is a diverse community with lots to offer tourists, industry and new residents. In the words of the SLC Olympic Organizing Committee, "The world is welcome here!"

For more information, contact the **Salt Lake City Travel Region**, 180 S. West Temple, Salt Lake City, Utah 84101, or call (801) 521-2822.

New residents of
Southwestern Utah will
find a variety of
locations, sizes, styles
and prices.

Neighborhoods and Real Estate

Southwestern Utah is a broad expanse of desert, sprinkled lightly with friendly communities where residents appreciate the area's physical attributes and take pride in their homes, property and growing neighborhoods. From the earliest days of settlement, in spite of facing daunting hardships and adversity, residents here have always worked hard to maintain the appearance of their communities.

Southwestern Utah is evolving. Almost every community — from the larger cities of St. George and Cedar City to the smaller towns and villages — is a pleasant mix of restored pioneer homes, condominiums, RV parks, an assortment of other single- and multifamily residences and some very impressive high-end custom addresses. Although rural communities such as Parowan, Enoch, Enterprise and Panguitch are feeling the pinch of progress — as steady growth from move-ins escaping the big city impact a generations-old lifestyle — they can still be described as small-town living at its best. Friendly neighbors, wide tree-lined streets, parks and museums and community events and activities all beckon to those interested in getting off the fast track.

The most popular building material available to the pioneers was adobe brick. In the first half of this century, commercially manufactured bricks were the building material of choice. About 1980, homebuilders began looking seriously, especially in the St. George area, at stucco. Lately, brick has made a resurgence, and even log homes are becoming more and more popular, particularly for recreational property such as mountain cabins.

But note that most of the homes referred to in this chapter as "pioneer-era" were made of native adobe. Depending on the color of the dirt at the site on which construction was taking place, the adobe bricks vary in color from a deep red to almost white. The homes were traditionally salt-box structures with chimneys on both ends of the house. Occasionally, as time, money and imagination would allow, homebuilders in the 1860s and '70s would get creative and build larger (even some two-story) homes with a little gingerbread trim along the roof line or front porch.

With the influx of new residents from all over the United States, in every age group and in all income brackets, the basics of life in Southwestern Utah have changed dramatically during the past three decades. But regardless of the impact these changes have on the area, there is still a home for everyone.

New residents of Southwestern Utah will find a variety of locations, sizes, styles and prices currently on the market, with the overall cost of housing ranking at about the national average of $120,000. Homes throughout the region range from as little as $30,000 for some mobile homes to $1.5 million for a luxury address. In this chapter, we'll detail what you can expect to pay for a home in a variety of different areas, and we will direct you to the real estate agencies that can help you find the perfect home.

St. George/Zion

St. George

The story is told of a farmer who calls his

family around to tell them of the demise of the family farm.

"It's all gone," he cries woefully. "The only thing we have left is the farmhouse and $2 million in the bank."

That about describes real estate conditions in St. George during the past two decades. St. George, in the heart of Utah's Dixie, is a city of straight, wide streets, enormous mulberry trees providing shade during the hot summer months and hundreds of busy, hard-working families. There are churches, schools, libraries, a central business district, a well-respected community college, Red Cliffs Mall (Southwestern Utah's first) and housing developments that show up seemingly overnight behind every ridge and on any hillside.

New building starts for all residential housing units, including single-family dwellings, townhomes, condominiums, apartment houses, mobile homes and RV parks reached their peak during the boom year of 1994 with 1,664 permits issued, but that has been generally regarded as an anomaly. Housing starts have since returned to a more manageable 977 in 1996, which city officials see as the result of a natural leveling off of the area's unprecedented growth during the past five years. The Southern Utah Homebuilders Association sponsors the annual Parade of Homes in St. George and surrounding communities (see our Annual Events chapter), and there is a comparable event in Cedar City hosted by the Iron County Homebuilders Association. Every year, local builders outdo themselves enticing prospective homeowners with exciting new and innovative ideas.

There are a few upper-six-figure price tags around, but an average, four-bedroom home in Washington County, taking into account all communities, sells for about $120,000. Community by community, the cost of a midrange home varies. In St. George, a homebuyer can expect to spend about $107,000 for a three-bedroom dwelling, while a townhome buyer in the same community would find an average price tag at about $103,000.

An interesting local trend in townhome construction involves finding a niche in the old neighborhoods of the downtown area. "Flag lots" (so named because the access, usually a long driveway from the main street, resembles a pole with the adjacent lot giving the appearance of a flag) are making good use of the inner recesses of the 1-acre city blocks of the Mormon village left over from pioneer times. A driveway to the interior of a city block generally provides access for the construction of two to six townhomes. St. George, because of its attraction to those wanting to spend a few months each year in the mild winter weather, has about cornered the Southwestern Utah market on condominiums and townhome projects. With names like The Mesas, Turtle Creek, Moon River, River Ridge, River Cove and new projects springing up in all four corners of town, the rumor that St. George is overbuilt frequently surfaces.

And from time to time that rumor may seem to have some basis in fact when large housing developments, office buildings and other structures spring up so quickly. But in 1996, 3,600 new residents moved into Washington County. With that kind of influx, housing and office space continue to be hot properties.

Until recently, St. George and the surrounding area had little to offer in the way of apartments and starter homes for young families. During the past decade, builders have noticed this missing piece in the housing market pie and have acted to create affordable housing for young families moving in to take jobs in the booming construction and service industry. In fact, the market has gone from virtually no available units to a current glut. At the moment, renters can take their pick of attractive, new apartment units with an average monthly payment of $550.

Bloomington

Before Bloomington was a golf course community, it was a pioneer settlement. In 1875, after a pattern of settlement and abandonment since 1867, Bloomington was officially listed as a community in the Washington

---

FYI

Unless otherwise noted, the area code for all phone numbers listed in this chapter is 801 but will change to 435 in September 1997. Either area code may be used until March 22, 1998.

County records. A few families found the location north of the Virgin River on the south side of St. George to be the perfect place to farm, raise their offspring and make brooms — one of Southwestern Utah's first cottage industries. The pioneer population dwindled away by about the turn of the century until only remnants of homes and the broom factory were left as signs of human habitation.

In 1968, Terracor, a major developer out of Salt Lake City, proposed the development of a planned luxury community they would call Bloomington, in this area that had again been abandoned since 1924. Their first plan centered around 10-acre estates complete with stables and gardens to attract those interested in horses. Second-home owners were their principle targets, and it didn't take long to see golf had a stronger pull than horseback riding. The idea of subdividing lots on the boundaries of a golf course became more appealing.

Terracor's developers nixed the traditional Mormon village layout with roads following a grid pattern, and instead opted for streets without sidewalks that would curve through the development to create a more tract-oriented, California feel with homes in similar styles and sizes. While half- and 1-acre ranchettes — nice family homes with adjacent horse property — were being subdivided and sold, plans for a golf course (St. George's second) were drawn up.

Today, Bloomington is a pleasant mix of approximately 2,000 condominiums, townhomes and moderate to high-end residential properties. Bloomington is home to approximately 3,500 residents and is about 5 miles south of the heart of St. George. The Bloomington Country Club is the unofficial center of the community, and the river separates "the gardens" from "the ranches." Bloomington streets are named after explorers, champion racehorses, famous golfers, Native American tribes, flowers or trees and America's most famous racetracks. Look for friends who live on Escalante, Hogan or Navajo north of the river. If you are looking for an address on Belmont, Swaps, Man-O-War or Pimlico, look to the south side of the river.

Bloomington has three LDS chapels (worship for other denominations would involve a trip to St. George), an elementary school and some limited commercial development (a gas station and one or two office buildings) along the frontage road adjacent to Interstate 15.

The residents are mostly families with teenagers, retired or second-home owners. The average three-bedroom, two-bath home on a ¼- to ½-acre lot in this clean, well-established community runs about $185,000.

Bloomington Hills

The success of Bloomington as a St. George neighborhood encouraged Terracor to design a second one over the low hills on the opposite side of I-15. In 1972, with the Bloomington Hills Golf Course (now St. George Golf Club) and 1,000 building lots as the components of their package, the developers called their new venture Bloomington Hills. The homes and properties started out less expensive than those in Bloomington to attract families, but the average cost of three-bedroom, 1,500 to 1,800-square-foot homes today in Bloomington Hills runs pretty much neck-and-neck with Bloomington in the $180,000 neighborhood. There is a wide range of options available from $120,000 to $450,000.

Residents of Bloomington Hills appreciate the convenience of neighborhood parks, numerous LDS churches (non-Mormon denominations are represented about 2 miles away in St. George) and an attractive new elementary school. There are no businesses in Bloomington Hills, although there is a new truck stop off I-15 Exit 4 and a gas and goodies mart on the northern boundary of Fort Pierce Road.

Washington City

This quiet little community north of St. George has begun to metamorphose since November 1989, when the Green Spring Golf Course became its neighbor west of I-15. Washington City has hinged its future on development in and around one of the state's most beautiful courses, but the whole plan nearly came apart when issues surrounding protection of the Mojave desert tortoise (see our chapter on The Environment) threatened the economic forecast. The terrain directly north and west of the course is habitat, and tortoises on the course are not uncommon during spring and fall. With the federally approved Habitat Conservation Plan now in place, developers may safely proceed with the construction of high-end custom homes around the course — average residence: three bedrooms at about $200,000.

Washington City had its beginning in pioneer times when the population grew up around the Cotton Mill (now the Historic Cotton Mill, see our Attractions chapter), where early settlers brought their cotton crops after 1865 for processing. Today, its wide streets carry residents to and from jobs in light industry, manufacturing, retailing and other employment in St. George and the nearby Millcreek Industrial Park.

On the south end of town, Redlands RV Park is one of the largest in the area. Redlands is home to many "snowbirds," who flee the cold winters in the north only to fly back to their nests with the return of warmer spring weather. Snowbirds at Redlands arrive in motor homes and camper trailers — many returning to the exact same site year after year.

On the north side of Washington City, mobile home parks and quiet neighborhoods of small homes offer a residential haven for seniors and families alike. The center of Washington City has seen a phoenix-like transformation since the Green Springs course opening. A new post office has been built, historic restoration of an old church building has taken place and the pioneer-era Cotton Mill now serves as a social center for the community. The average priced three-bedroom, post-World War II home in Washington City is about $96,000.

Santa Clara

The community known as Santa Clara — about 6 miles from downtown St. George — is actually made up of two neighborhoods: Santa Clara and "the Heights."

Tree-lined, old Utah Highway 91 runs through the town. Anyone who ever made the trip between Salt Lake City and Los Angeles "in the old days" will have fond memories of Frei's Fruit Stand, where a rest stop always included a slice of ice-cold watermelon, sweet,

juicy canteloupe, your choice of an apple, pear or peach and vegetables of every variety. After 40 years, Frei's still awaits a weary traveler (see our Shopping chapter). Many of the homes around Frei's are vintage pioneer, turn-of-the-century and war-year models. New construction appears from time to time, but the town of Santa Clara along the highway is clean, safe, well-established and comfortable. When homes do become available, the average three- or four-bedroom residence in this part of the area goes for about $144,000.

Santa Clara Heights, on the other hand, is a rapidly growing neighborhood on the plateau above Santa Clara. There are incredible views of fields of black lava rock and sandstone formations, particularly from homes along the ridge. Homes in Santa Clara Heights are mostly new — built within the last three to five years, as new construction moved out into the lava flow area along the edge of the ravine. Stucco is the preferred exterior building material, and tile roofs have been found to withstand the unrelenting desert sun well. The neighborhood features open space in the form of a city park, the Santa Clara Arboretum and Entrada, the new 18-hole golf course (see our Golf chapter).

A number of LDS church buildings (non-Mormon denominations are represented in nearby St. George), Santa Clara Elementary School and the addition in 1995 of Snow Canyon middle and high schools (which overlook the ravine created by ancient lava flow) round out the community. A few commercial properties are springing up on the highway through town, including the new Santa Clara city office building, a cactus nursery, a grocery store, a floral shop and, of course, Frei's Fruit Stand.

Kayenta

This unique residential community is at the base of Red Mountain approximately 7 miles west of St. George. Kayenta is 2,000 acres of some of the most beautiful desert landscape on earth. Homes are nestled into the hillocks created over the centuries by shifting blowing sands, and the entire subdivision of distinctly different, Southwestern-style homes is encircled by red rock. There is little grass, as the whole idea of living at Kayenta has to do with being at one with the natural terrain. It is bor-

Townhomes are popular second or winter homes for those seeking a break from the snow and cold in northern Utah, Wyoming, Montana or Idaho.

dered on the east and north by property owned and managed by the Bureau of Land Management and on the west by the Shivwits Indian reservation.

A diverse mix of residents — young and old, working and retired, couples and families — was attracted here from all over the globe. Folks have come to Kayenta from Hawaii, Iowa, Minnesota, Alaska and parts of Europe, but many of the locals find it too far out of town for serious consideration for a homesite. The common denominator between the neighbors is a love of the land. They hike, bike, photograph the landscape or simply enjoy the peace and quiet. Many are artists, and most are ecology-minded.

It's hard to pin down an average-priced home, because nothing is average about Kayenta. Homes range in size from 1,100 to 8,000 square feet on lots from 0.33 to 5 acres. All 150 homes already at Kayenta were custom-built to take full advantage of the characteristics of both the lot and the view. A single developer, Terry Marten, is responsible for Kayenta. Lots range from $40,000 for 0.33 to 0.5 acre tracts up to $100,000 for 3 acres. Cost of construction is currently in the $90- to $100-per-foot range, not including the lot.

This neighborhood is considered by some to be more than a little restrictive. Homes must be in the Southwestern style with earth tones only for exterior finishes. Outdoor lighting must be carefully planned to protect the view of the night sky. Only 25 percent of any lot can be used for the home and adjacent structures including driveways and courtyards — the remaining 75 percent is to remain in its natural state. Activities associated with construction may only impact the section of the landscape where the home will sit, with minimal damage to the surrounding terrain allowed.

Kayenta kids attend Santa Clara Elementary School, about 3 miles away, or Snow Canyon middle or high school, traveling to and from home on regularly routed school buses. Kayenta has a semi-commercial section that contains fully enclosed storage for RVs and boats (there is a restriction against storing such vehicles at the homesites), art studios and a community pool. These are amenities intended for use by Kayenta residents.

Leeds, Silver Reef

About 20 miles north of St. George is the community of Leeds, centrally located amid a cluster of recreational sites and points of interest. Leeds, and the adjacent neighborhood of

Silver Reef on the opposite side of I-15, are enjoying a modest boom, as those seeking peace and quiet are finding their way to these scenic, rural communities.

In Leeds, attractive new homes are interspersed among pioneer-era dwellings down the main thoroughfare. The business district consists of a few service stations, grocery stores with shelves full of camping gear, a cafe or two, a motel and a private RV park.

Silver Reef was once a thriving and boisterous community that grew — in less than 60 days — from no residents to a population of 1,500 following the discovery of silver in 1876 (see "Exceptions to the Village" in our History chapter). Then known as a rough-and-tumble mining town in stark contrast to the religious-based agricultural communities nearby, Silver Reef now attracts high-end custom home buyers who are retiring here or commuting to employment in the St. George area.

The community includes a few intact historic buildings, including the sturdy old Wells Fargo station. This stone building stood empty for many years, its heavy metal shutters squeaking in the wind. Today the old station has been nicely restored to house a small museum filled with Silver Reef memorabilia, an artist's studio and an art gallery (see our Arts and Culture chapter). The replicated Cosmopolitan Steakhouse, open Wednesday through Saturday, serves breakfast, lunch and dinner (see our Restaurants chapter). Homes in Silver Reef are nestled into the desert. At night, it's pitch black except for thousands of stars . . . during the day, it's quiet and peaceful.

Red Cliffs

Behind Red Cliffs Mall, between downtown St. George and Washington on the freeway frontage road, is a new development (actually several developments) that features comfortable, attractive starter homes for young families and downsized homes for seniors. The neighborhood is so new the trees are barely in the ground, but the potential for this area is bright. Its proximity to shopping, churches, schools and jobs is already enticing many to locate in the area.

More units were sold in the Red Cliffs area in 1996 than in any section of St. George. A new, medium range, three-bedroom home in the Red Cliffs area is priced at about $114,000.

Green Valley

It started as Green Valley Resort. The whole idea was to attract second-home buyers to this hilltop health resort 3 miles west of downtown St. George (see the Rentals section of our Accommodations chapter). Condominiums popped up and, starting in about 1980, the buyers came. But because the community proved so popular, many opted to sell their homes in other parts of the world to make the Green Valley area their permanent address.

Now, several developments of single-family custom homes have sprung up and established themselves below the resort. Some concerns with expansive soils (see The Environment chapter) slowed at least one hillside development, but growth in Green Valley has continued over the years. The neighborhood is a nice, homogenous blend of the older homes built in the early '80s, the spacious custom homes around nearby Sunbrook Golf Course (see our Golf chapter) and the condominiums and townhomes at the resort. Green Valley properties average about $137,000.

East of I-15

The east side of Washington County is rich with small towns with names like **Hurricane** (pronounced "HER-a-kin" by the locals) and nearby neighbors **LaVerkin**, **Toquerville**, **Springdale**, **Virgin** and **Rockville**, which is in Zion Canyon at the entrance to the national park. Most are home to quiet neighborhoods filled with community-minded citizens who mind their manners and their business.

Hurricane and LaVerkin are next door to one another on Utah 9, midway between I-15 and Zion National Park. The population of Hurricane is rapidly growing but at last count numbered about 5,000. LaVerkin, smaller but growing just as fast, has a population nearing 2,500. Toquerville, with about 1,200 residents, is just north of the sister cities, snuggled peacefully behind a hillside, hidden from the thousands of vehicles that run along the interstate every day. Twelve thousand cars a day run up and down Utah 9 in the area. The summer months offer orchards full of peaches, pears and apricots. The winter months find residents getting ready for the summer months.

The real estate market in Hurricane and LaVerkin is booming. The Hurricane-LaVerkin area was second countywide in property sales in 1996, according to statistics provided by the Washington County Board of Realtors. The average-priced home sells for $97,800 in Hurricane and slightly higher at $99,000 in LaVerkin, perhaps due to two new developments.

Springdale is just outside the gates of Zion, 59 miles from Cedar City and 43 miles from St. George. More than 3 million visitors travel through this little town, using the services provided by 400 full-time residents, give or take a couple dozen. Rockville has 250 residents and is referred to as one of Utah's most beautiful small communities. Right next door to Springdale in Zion Canyon, Rockville is picturesque in its resistance to big-city progress. The community of Virgin, a little south of Rockville and Springdale, has about 250 residents, most of whom think theirs is one of America's great small towns. Utah 9, one of the busiest roads in the state, runs right through town.

Realtors will tell you there are infrequent transactions in these smaller communities, where roots go down for generations, but the one or two sales each year average pricetags of about $105,000.

West of I-15

Thirty to 45 minutes away, these communities are a fair distance from downtown St. George, but for those who enjoy the wide open spaces or the peace and solitude of small-town living, these are good options.

Dammeron Valley, situated on Utah 18 about midway between St. George (17 miles to the north) and Pine Valley, attracts those who want a little elbow room between them and their neighbors. It is zoned for animals, so many residents enjoy an equestrian lifestyle. Dammeron is mostly a residential community, but limited commercial properties include the Dammeron Valley Steakhouse. Some of the properties are cabins for weekend getaways, some are year-round homes with a chunk of acreage. The most expensive to sell in 1996 went for $216,000.

Veyo is home to the Veyo Pool (see our Community Recreation chapter), a decorative lava rock company and a couple hundred really great folks who enjoy being out of the mainstream. Approximately 1,800 of them make their homes in this outlying community 18 miles north of St. George. Many are employed in the city but like to come home to a peaceful life in Veyo at the end of the day. **Central** is Veyo's sister community, another 10 miles north, and similar in most ways. The air here is crisp and clean, and many of the homeowners are full-time residents elsewhere who love the chance to slow down the pace by escaping to the cabin or the old family farm. Population in Central ranges from a few hundred in winter to nearly 800 in summertime. Gardening, horseback riding and exploring the mountains, meadows and apple orchards are enjoyable and common pastimes. For many years, these two communities even shared the same zip code, but growth and development have resulted in an expanding neighborhood and a post office for Central. There were only three real estate transactions in this area in 1996, but the average price was a moderate $148,000.

Enterprise, 35 miles north of St. George, is famous for its out-of-this-world sweet corn. The farming community has for years been relatively isolated except during the summertime Enterprise Corn Festival (see our Annual Events chapter), when hundreds of people arrive to enjoy the tasty crop or the Pioneer Day

INSIDERS' TIP

According to the Census Bureau, Utah has the 10th-highest rate of home ownership in the nation. In 1996, 72.7 percent of residents owned the home they lived in. Statisticians attribute the ranking to the high number of married couples, who are more likely to buy instead of rent.

rodeo and escape the Dixie heat — the higher elevation means it can be as much as 10 degrees cooler here. Enterprise has its own elementary and high school. As it grows, it is becoming more and more attractive to some residents of St. George who are finding explosive population growth not so much to their liking. Though there were only three sales in 1996, a medium-priced, two-bedroom home in Enterprise, built after World War II, will come with a price tag right at $100,000.

Cedar City/Brian Head

Cedar City

In terms of growth, Cedar City is where St. George was not too many years ago. It has been discovered. Since its 1993 designation as one of America's 10 best small towns (see our Area Overview chapter), Cedar City has experienced explosive growth.

Cedar City was originally named for an abundance of cedar trees that actually turned out to be junipers. Though the early settlers got the name wrong, the greenery adds a nice touch to this clean and attractive community with wide streets, parks and historic sites, a bustling business district, Southern Utah University, the world-renowned Utah Shakespearean Festival and Utah Summer Games (see listings for both in our Annual Events chapter), an impressive medical community and a fierce rivalry with neighboring St. George in all kinds of high school sports.

Utah Highway 91 runs north and south through the center of town. Serving as the primary state highway for many years before I-15 connected the state's north and south borders, Utah 91 is now known as Main Street. Downtown homes are a mixture of restored pioneer dwellings, early-20th century and pre- and post-war-era construction. These come on the market occasionally, starting from about $80,000 for a small, two- or three-bedroom, all-brick structure. Newer homes, built in the last 20 years, sell for about $140,000 downtown.

Cedar City development has only recently begun to move onto the hillside. Large, attractive homes are popping up on the ridge overlooking I-15 with fresh new communities taking shape. High-end developments such as Mesa Hills, Royal Hunte, Cross Hollows and Legacy Park offer custom construction and views, with homes ranging from $180,000 to $300,000. Starter homes west of town are attracting young families looking for something nice in the $80,000 to $100,000 range.

Enoch

The community of Enoch, 8 miles northwest of Cedar City, is home to about 3,000 family-oriented folks. This fast-growing community features minimum half-acre lots zoned by the city to allow homeowners to have farm animals such as horses or even a few cows (as long as they aren't an annoyance to the neighbors). Enoch Elementary School provides early education to 400 students. Then community kids are bused to middle and high schools in nearby Cedar City. You will find lots to like about this outlying community. It's quiet, with bargain prices for homes on oversized lots. Except for pigs or mink, you can have just about any kind of domestic animal on your property here. Prices average between $90,000 and $100,000.

Parowan

Parowan, the first Southwestern Utah community, is the Iron County seat and only about 15 miles from the Brian Head Ski Resort. It's beautiful here! Winters dust pioneer churches, schools and other buildings with a layer of snow, while summers find trees and flowers decorating yards and public building common areas. About 3,500 residents live within a few blocks of Main Street. The business district includes county and city offices, a library, small cafes and restaurants, automobile repair services, beauty shops, video places and a few grocery stores.

Great views, lots of history and peace and quiet are what Parowan is all about. The kids of Parowan attend their own elementary school, junior high and high school. It's a great place to live and the price is right with a large, medium-priced, four-bedroom home selling for about $90,000. New homes are beginning to come up for sale in Parowan, priced in the $100,000 range. This is small-town America. Parowan residents are usually families with a genealogy that

can be traced back for several generations. Some folks have spilled over into Parowan from the overflow moving into Cedar City.

Paragonah, Kanarraville, Summit

If you want rural living, take your choice of any of these three communities, each within a few miles of I-15 and none more than 15 miles from downtown Cedar City. These towns are picture-postcard perfect and very much in demand by would-be homebuyers. The properties are mostly older homes, but since the residents love the lifestyle in rural Southwestern Utah, they are rarely on the market. An average-priced, four-bedroom, two-bath home on a three-quarter-acre lot might sell for about $100,000 in 1997.

Brian Head

The resort community of Brian Head sits high atop Cedar Mountain in the Dixie National Forest. Clear and cool, the community is mostly made up of condominiums, cabin retreats, equipment rental and gift shops, cafes, ski lifts and bicycle trails. Year round, the population of Brian Head, 35 miles northeast of Cedar City, is a minuscule 102 residents.

The real estate market, however, is healthy, with strong sales of second homes for residents of other areas of Utah, Nevada and California. Brian Head also boasts a wide variety of vacation properties available. Summer-only or summer-access lots outside the city limits are not snow-plowed during the winter months but are priced right — as low as $5,000. A few back-country cabins are on the market in the $30,000 to $50,000 range, and large homes of up to 2,400 square feet range in price from $150,000 to $350,000.

Bryce Canyon Area

Some of the most topographically diverse terrain on the planet, the Bryce Canyon region is a study in contrasts. High mountain lakes and streams, twisted red rock geological formations, forests of green pines and blue spruce, two national parks (and a part of a third), three state parks, the nation's newest national monument, abundant wildlife, peaceful farms and eerie ghost towns, excellent tourist facilities and friendly locals all exist within the Garfield County borders.

Panguitch, the largest Garfield County community, is home to about 1,500 residents who make their living farming, in the tourist industry or as employees of the ever-present federal government. Panguitch has wide, typically Mormon streets, a healthy business district with a grocery store or two, tourist gift shops, a few restaurants, a number of motels and one all-night gas station.

According to real estate agents in the area, they sell more land than homes, but there is a nice selection of comfortable family homes or restored pioneer dwellings ranging in price from $25,000 to $98,000. As the world discovers the wonders of Garfield County, a few exceptional properties are springing up. These include a spectacular $250,000 cabin at Panguitch Lake and a $2 million property in Boulder, the county's smallest community.

Kanab Area

The town of **Kanab** is a central population encircled by such communities as **Orderville**, **Mt. Carmel**, **Big Water** and **Duck Creek Village**. Kanab's trademark "greatest earth on show" draws new residents in ever-increasing numbers and more than 3 million tourists annually who pass through on their way to Zion National Park or Glen Canyon Recreation Area in Nevada.

Kanab sits shoulder-to-shoulder with Fredonia on the Utah/Arizona border, sharing the lifestyle as well as the resources of the area. Although most residents of Kanab and Fredonia make regular trips into St. George, about 83 miles to the west, Kanab's downtown business district is beginning to develop to meet the needs of residents. A new, 38-bed hospital is under construction, scheduled for completion by the fall of 1997. The hospital will have nine acute care beds, three for obstetrical care and 26 for long-term care.

Kanab is a beautiful community that, like so many in Southwestern Utah, is suffering from some growing pains. But like so many other, similar settings, visitors and residents alike can be comfortable and safe walking to work or strolling under a night sky.

Real Estate Offices

St. George/Zion

The rapidly growing communities in and around St. George have attracted Realtors in much the same way miners flooded to Silver Reef in 1875 to search for silver in the sandstone. In the St. George area there are dozens of licensed brokers and sellers actively working.

The **Washington County Board of Realtors** — the local arm of the larger Utah Board of Realtors and, ultimately, the National Association of Realtors — is charged with protecting the welfare of the community. The board is responsible for the enforcement of the NAR Code of Ethics within its jurisdiction. It also organizes and maintains cooperative business practices such as the multiple-listing service and provides educational meetings and seminars for Realtors and the public.

Bill Potter Realty
75 S. 100 East, Ste. C2, St. George
• **673-8787, (888) 386-5525**

You know the story. Guy gets licensed, guy joins agency and makes it good . . . then does even better on his own. Bill Potter started his career in real estate in 1980 and now manages residential and commercial foreclosures for the state of Utah, in addition to matching people with property. Licensed to list and sell on both sides of the Utah-Nevada border, Bill Potter Realty specializes in homes, condos, investment properties and commercial real estate.

Century 21 Zion Realty
437 S. Bluff St., Ste. 102, St. George
• **673-9080**

Century 21 Zion Realty has been serving the needs of the homebuying public since 1973 and is dedicated to a superior level of customer satisfaction and quality service. The efforts of the 19 agents here were recognized in the spring of 1997: Century 21, the world's largest real estate system, presented the St. George office with the coveted Quality Service Pinnacle Award. Of 5,000 offices nationwide, only 200 were honored with this distinction. In a service-conscious society, will this award make a difference? According to the folks at Century 21 Zion Realty, it will only inspire them to work harder toward better service.

Certified Marketing
1086 S. Main St., No. 202, St. George
• **628-8058, (800) 574-8058**

Service is the top priority for the 20 agents of this locally owned agency, which has been in business since 1988. Specializing in property management and commercial and residential sales, Certified Marketing agents are among the best based on production figures.

Ence Realty
216 W. St. George Blvd., St. George
• 628-7700, (800) 424-3623

The Ence boys got their start as co-owners of a local feed store, but along the way they made the decision to build houses instead. Smart boys! Today Ence Homes, including their real estate division, is big — really big — in Southwestern Utah. Ence Realty's 25 agents have sold more than 3,000 properties in 40 years of business, many in 14 Ence Homes projects. For more information, the company has an Ence Information Center at 164 W. 700 South in St. George.

ERA Brokers Consolidated
201 E. St. George Blvd., St. George
• 628-1606, (800) ERA-BROKERS
1770 E. Red Cliff Dr., St. George
• 656-1965
10 N. 100 West, Hurricane • 635-4636
250 Mesquite Blvd, Mesquite, Nev.
• (702) 346-7200

You'll want to stop by this stylish new building even if you aren't shopping for a new home. ERA Brokers Consolidated has been first in service in the St. George market for more than 14 years, a distinction that has earned them a place on the Top 10 list of ERA offices nationwide. The 60 agents have more professional designations than any other agency in town. Note that ERA Brokers Consolidated has branches in St. George, Hurricane and Mesquite.

Holiday Resort Realty and Development
144 W. Brigham Rd., Ste. 4A, St. George
• 673-6172, (888) 673-6172

They weren't around when the pioneers settled Bloomington the first time, but these folks have sure been major players in the Bloomington real estate market for its second go-around. Holiday Resort Realty and Development has watched this St. George suburb grow up around them since 1983. The firm provides real estate sales, development and property management, backing up its claim of service with the exclusive "Holiday Resort Customer Service Card," which provides each cardholder with free copies, notary service, market analysis of your home, free incoming fax service, discounts on overnight condominium rentals and home warranty programs. Value is in full bloom at Holiday Resort Realty.

Mansell and Associates
1080 S. Main Plaza, Ste. 200, St. George
• 673-8282, (800) 573-4122

Mansell and Associates, with 14 offices in Utah, received the prestigious PHH Cup from PHH Home Equity Relocation Services, naming them No. 1 in relocation. They were also honored by the Better Business Bureau for ethics in business. So now when any of the 25 agents at the St. George office say Mansell is a trusted name in real estate, they can point to the award to back them up.

The Newspaper Rock

On the corner of Navajo and Geronimo streets in the St. George neighborhood of Bloomington, you'll find a large boulder covered in ancient rock art. The primitive notations on this community bulletin board for the Anasazi Indians who lived in the area 1,000 years ago might be announcements of a neighborhood block party, reminders of upcoming tribal meetings or advertisements for a sale of used family items. Today, the "newspaper rock," near the center of 2,000 homes, attracts scouting troops and families on outings.

The Property Shoppe
396 E. St. George Blvd., St. George • 628-2200

You can select from 20 buyer-friendly, experienced real estate agents at this locally owned agency. Standard residential and commercial sales are the strong suit here, but Property Shoppe agents are gaining a reputation for relocation and property exchanges, lots and acreage. As they like to say: "Real estate is what we know. Performance is what we sell."

Real Estate Professionals
161 W. 950 South, No. Q-4, St. George • 673-6752, (888) 673-6752

Kay Hancock is singlehandedly cutting a wide swath in the Southwestern Utah real estate market. Representing buyers exclusively, this owner/broker does not take listings from sellers, has no preference to any property but access to them all and works alone at her company. She knows the value of vacant land, improved residential and commercial properties in the area because she is also a certified general appraiser. Hancock has 23 years of experience in buying, selling and marketing real estate.

Realty Executives
590 E. St. George Blvd., St. George • 628-1677, (800) 652-1677

Jerry Jensen renamed his real estate company after his agents. He is proud of the residential and commercial sales, leasing and development business he began in 1976 on a downtown St. George corner. Today, he believes his productive professionals are the best realty executives in the local market.

RE/MAX First Realty
720 S. River Rd., Ste. E200, St. George • 674-0111

RE/MAX flashed onto the scene in 1991 and is now the top real estate office in sales volume in Washington County. In addition to being No. 1 locally, RE/MAX International awarded RE/MAX First Realty the title of No. 1 Small Market Office in the world. The foundation of success is built on the experience and knowledge of agents who recognize the individual needs of clients. Watch for the familiar RE/MAX hot-air balloon floating above the red desert whenever the sunshine and blue sky warrant a morning flight at the office.

RE/MAX Realty Resources
535 W. State St., Hurricane • 635-9414, (800) 690-9414

It's another high flying real estate agency. This one meets buyers' needs on the county's east side. A broker and six agents take prospective buyers from concept to completion, whether it's a starter home or a million-dollar address. RE/MAX Realty Resources has also built a reputation for relocation services and commercial development.

Sky Mountain Real Estate
687 N. 2600 West, Hurricane • 635-4653, (800) 905-7273

Sky Mountain Real Estate wants to sell you some of the most spectacular acreage in the world right on Sky Mountain Golf Course (see our Golf chapter), one of the most scenic courses in America. If you're into red rocks, clear blue skies and mind boggling, breathtaking, scenic splendor, then you've got to see this place.

Wardley Better Homes and Gardens
923 S. River Rd., Ste. 101, St. George • 674-4663

Talk about networking . . . Wardley Better Homes and Gardens is one of 22 offices in Utah with access to state-of-the-art technology to link agents and properties all over the country by way of the Internet. Through Wardley Better Homes and Gardens, sellers can have the benefit of superior marketing tools as well. Television advertising of properties, a full-service graphic design department, printing services for the creation of fliers and brochures that feature your property, full-color advertising in Better Homes and Gardens Guide to Homes magazine . . . this office has it all, along with the strength of other offices and sales executives throughout the state. This is a name you can trust.

Cedar City/Brian Head

Where there's rapid growth there's usually a gaggle of real estate agents looking to be the conduit between buyer and property. In the Cedar City area, the Iron County Board of Realtors serves as the governing body for doz-

A graded dirt road connects Utah 12 and U.S. Highway 89 through the Kodachrome Basin.

ens of agents. The board involves 13 directors including a multiple listing chairman and a professional service chair. The board provides individual agencies with current and pertinent information about real estate laws and regulations, and it gathers and maintains local data from multiple listing computers to track real estate trends in the area. The **Iron County Board of Realtors** offices are at 711 W. 200 North, Cedar City. Call them at 586-6944.

Following are listings of real estate agencies in the Cedar City area. Some are members of the Board of Realtors, others are not, but all are professional and anxious to help you find the home of your dreams.

Alpine Mountain Real Estate
69 Movie Ranch Rd., Duck Creek Village
• 682-2500

If you enjoy any combination of hunting, fishing, boating, biking, skiing, snowmobiling or other mountain sports, Alpine Mountain Real Estate can help you "escape to paradise in the pines." Their professional, friendly staff can help make your dream of owning your own piece of heaven a reality. Alpine Mountain's two agents specialize in listings and sales of

recreational properties, lots, cabins and mountain acreage.

Aspens Rental Agency and Realty
312 S. Utah Hwy. 143, Brian Head
• 677-2018

This family-owned and operated agency serves the community's real estate needs year round from the heart of this resort town. With 20 years of experience in the Brian Head marketplace, Aspens specializes in large condominium units and single-family residence sales and listings.

Brian Head Resort Properties
259 N. Utah Hwy. 143, Brian Head
• 677-2231

Brian Head Resort Properties is the oldest established brokerage in this resort community. Specializing in properties for sale in Brian Head since 1986, the agency's five real estate experts serve customers seven days a week from 9 AM to 5 PM. Centrally located in the mall between the ski shop, bike shop and mini market, Brian Head Resort Properties lists and sells condominiums, primary residences and second-home properties and lots.

Century 21 First Choice
464 N. Utah Hwy. 143, Brian Head
• 677-2100
961 S. Main St., Cedar City • 586-1221

This Century 21 office wants to be the first choice for all your real estate needs. More than 25 agents in two office locations are prepared to help you find just the right home, condominium or recreation property.

Coldwell Banker Corry Realty
86 E. Center St., Cedar City • 586-9411,
(800) 305-LIST
176 S. 100 East, Kanab • 644-2684

Offering "support you can count on," this agency has offices in Cedar City and Kanab. Specialists in residential, acreage and commercial properties, Coldwell Banker Corry Realty recently announced a new million-dollar seller to go with the eight members of its Multi-Million Dollar Sales Club. A total of 32 professional agents work here.

Color Country Real Estate
88 N. Main St., Parowan • 477-8970

A broker and 10 licensed agents at Color Country have a successful finger on the pulse of the Parowan real estate market. Color Country has been in business more than 26 years, offering listings and sales of residential homes, farms and acreage and recreational property.

Steve Corry Real Estate
337 S. Main St., Cedar City • 586-2525,
(800) 238-2526

Steve Corry Real Estate has been serving southern Utah since 1939. The family-owned agency with 10 professional agents has property management and insurance divisions, but has built a solid reputation for long-term stability on performance in real estate sales. For 1997, the company moves into an attractive new professional plaza.

ERA Realty Center
259 W. 200 North, Cedar City • 586-2777,
(800) 819-2771
45 E. Main St., Escalante • 826-4488
Duck Creek Village • 682-2387,
(800) 227-1550

With branch offices in Escalante and Duck Creek, ERA Realty Center has consistently controlled a good share of the Southwestern Utah real estate market since 1979. Presently marketing three new developments, ERA Realty Center has 36 agents — six have been honored three consecutive years at the ERA International Business Conference for achieving $7 million in sales or 50 sales in a year. That's not all six combined, that's each of them individually. And the icing on the cake? One member of the ERA Realty Center team was the top seller in the state of Utah and ranked 12th in the entire ERA nationwide network in terms of transactions — 120 during 1996.

High Country Realty
468 N. Utah Hwy. 143, Brian Head
• 677-3886, (800) 338-3886
24 N. Main St., Parowan • 477-8581

High Country Realty, with branch offices in Brian Head and Parowan, is best-known for friendly, efficient and straightforward agents. Since 1992, 10 licensed agents in the two offices have helped homebuyers find good buys on new or second homes and vacation or recreational property.

Priority One Real Estate
210 N. 300 West, No. 203, Cedar City
• 586-8181, (888) 586-8181

They've just opened their doors in the Cedar City area, but this full-service agency offers state-of-the-art technology designed to meet your real estate needs. Quality and service are priority one to 15 knowledgeable agents. Find the home of your dreams through a computer slide show, or surf the Priority One Internet web page for a preview of what's hot in residential homes or recreational property. Thinking about creating your own community? Priority One can also lend assistance to developers through their property development division.

United National/Adara Real Estate
491 S. Main St., Cedar City • 586-7202

If you're looking for an agency with a knowledge of the local terrain, United National/Adara Real Estate could be the company to deliver the best deal. For land sales, business opportunities, recreational properties, farms and ranches, this agency has covered the area for 12 years with a broker and two agents.

Bryce Canyon Area

In the Bryce Canyon area, most of the real estate is owned by the federal government. But you won't find any prettier land in all the world. Panguitch, the largest Garfield County community, has wide, typically Mormon streets and a healthy business district. According to real estate professionals in the area, they sell more land than homes, but there is a nice selection of comfortable family residences or restored pioneer dwellings on the market.

Kanab Area

There is no county board of Realtors in the Kanab area, but the following agencies do share information about listings. A multiple-listing service is in the works as well.

Adobe Realty
323 S. 100 East, Kanab • 644-2232

These new kids in town say they aren't trying to compete with the big companies. Their specialty is TLC and customer service. They've only been in the Kanab area for about a year, but Adobe offers 15 years of experience in residential, commercial and acreage listing and sales.

Century 21 Frontier Realty
7 W. Center St., Kanab • 644-2100, (888) 261-2100

A name you know from anywhere in the country, Century 21 is a company you can trust. Locally, Century 21 Frontier Realty has spent 10 years perfecting its craft. The agents are in the know when it comes to residential properties and acreage in the Kanab area.

ERA Utah Properties
30 E. Center St., Kanab • 644-2606

ERA Utah Properties specializes in "developing Kanab." In the 26 years this agency has been part of the growing Kanab area, it has made a name as a company with real estate experts who get the job done. The focus is residential, ranches and development. ERA Utah Properties was actively involved in building the Coral Hills Golf Course (see our Golf chapter).

Real Estate Publications

Comprehensive relocation guides, filled with lots of good information, demographics and other facts and figures, are available through the St. George Area Chamber of Commerce, 628-1658, and Cedar City Chamber of Commerce, 586-4484. Some real estate agencies have created their own publications as well.

The Spectrum, which serves the need to know in eight Southwestern Utah counties, has a weekly Homes and Real Estate section with up-to-the-minute information about the local housing market. Other real estate publications of note, available free at just about any realty office, grocery store and gas station include the following.

Advanced Showing Magazine
301 S. 1200 East, No. 10, St. George • 656-0099

This handsome, glossy publication is a newcomer to Southwestern Utah's real estate market. Two separate magazines promoting properties in Washington and Iron counties are published monthly with 9,000 copies distributed from various real estate offices and other sites in both counties.

Preview Real Estate Magazine
250 S. Donlee Dr., St. George • 673-1016

In their 15-year career, Jug and Jeanne Jones have successfully created Southwestern Utah's most-recognized real estate publication. Updated monthly, *Preview Real Estate Magazine* is available free of charge at more than 200 distribution points from Richfield, Utah, in the north to Mesquite, Nevada, in the south, and all points in between. Wherever you are in Southwestern Utah, you'll find this publication in most major stores, motels and real estate offices.

Elderhostel's "Discover Southern Utah" package provides seniors the opportunity to study college-level courses at Dixie College.

Retirement

A January 1997 front-page story in *The Spectrum* reported St. George had earned a spot in Ken Stern's *50 Fabulous Places to Retire in America*. The listing, one of many for the city and area in national rankings and publications, really came as no surprise to anyone who lives here.

For more than a decade now, St. George has been spotlighted, highlighted and focused on as a great place to spend those golden years. Often retirees are drawn here because they were impressed with the area while passing through at one time or another during their lifetime. Sometimes it is the result of fond memories of vacations in our grand circle of state and national parks or elsewhere among our natural wonders. Many have heard of the area from friends or read about this high desert country in national publications such as *Stern's*.

Whatever brings them here, St. George in particular and Southwestern Utah in general earn kudos from seniors for the wide array of landscapes and scenery, copious recreational opportunities and the area's small-town atmosphere. Other attractions for retirees, especially in St. George, are the weather, quality medical care (see our Healthcare chapter) and close proximity to the big-city worlds of Las Vegas and Salt Lake City (see our Daytrips and Weekend Getaways chapter).

Resources for seniors are often provided and/or managed through the Five County Association of Governments. Listings contained in this chapter are a reflection of the regional presence of this organization, headquartered in St. George. (The five counties of the group's name include the four in this guide's coverage area, plus Beaver County.) In this rural part of the state, some services and other resources are also provided through such national organizations as AARP, though they are administered from Salt Lake City and have more limited visibility in Southwestern Utah. The American Cancer Society, American Heart Association and other resource organizations do offer some support in each local community. The Daughters of the Utah Pioneers and Sons of the Utah Pioneers are active in most small towns and popular with seniors, preserving the state's history and heritage.

Interestingly, there is only one retirement community — really more of a senior apartment complex — and no other senior-specific housing developments in Southwestern Utah. Retirees blend in and harmonize with younger families. Seniors and students attend community events and church together, and a substantial number of older residents share the experiences of a lifetime in volunteer assignments at schools, libraries, food pantries, hospitals and dozens of other sites. Many residents have lived all their years in Southwestern Utah. Others are seasonal residents from northern Utah, Wyoming, Montana and Idaho — "snowbirds" attracted to the mild winter weather, particularly in St. George and across the state line in Mesquite, Nevada.

And Southwestern Utah welcomes them. With services and programs aplenty, the perfect climate and Dixie Regional Medical Center and the other facilities in the Intermountain Health Care group providing the above-mentioned state-of-the-art medical services (there's even a cancer treatment facility), Southwestern Utah is well-equipped and prepared to provide for the needs of a growing senior population.

Mix in events such as the Huntsman World Senior Games, the Utah Shakespearean Festival, Utah Winter Games and college sports, toss in a dash of great golf, terrific restaurants, shopping, and add the spice provided by a wide range of volunteer opportunities, and you come to see we have the necessary ingredients to make this one of the most fabulous places to retire in America.

Senior Information and Assistance

Five County Area Agency on Aging
906 N. 1400 West, St. George • 673-3548, 586-2975

The Five County Area Agency on Aging is based in St. George and provides community planning, training and services under the Older Americans Act, a federal law enacted in 1965. With a special emphasis on serving the socially and economically disadvantaged, Five County Area Agency on Aging programs are designed to assist older people in remaining independent and helping them live in their own homes for as long as possible.

Services available include general information and referral, transportation, legal assistance, case management, chore services, telephone reassurance, friendly visitation, recreation and socialization activities, respite care, letter writing and reading, shopping assistance, congregate meals, Meals on Wheels, community-based homemaker services and completion of Medicaid waivers.

Health Insurance Information Program
906 N. 1400 West St. George • 673-0700

What's the difference between Medicare Part A and Medicare Part B . . . and do I need them both? If I have both, am I covered for everything? How much is enough? Can I have too much? How do I know which plan is best for my circumstances?

If you're scratching your head over Medicare, Medigap, Medicaid or other insurance programs, there are trained volunteers throughout the five-county area anxious to help you find the answers. They are the counselors in the Health Insurance Information Program (HIIP), a state-funded program designed to lead seniors through the mysterious maze of paperwork associated with Medicare. The service is free. For more information or to find the name of a HIIP volunteer in your community, call the Five County HIIP Program at 673-0700.

Meals on Wheels
906 N. 1400 West, St. George • 673-3548, 586-2975

Homebound or unable to prepare your lunch or dinner? Meals on Wheels, a program administered by the Five County Area Agency on Aging, can help by delivering hot meals to your door up to five days a week. Individuals must be older than 60 and meet need qualifications. Call the Five County Area Agency on Aging or the senior center in your neighborhood to arrange an evaluation to access your need for this service. A donation of $2.25 for each meal is suggested but not required.

> ## FYI
> Unless otherwise noted, the area code for all phone numbers listed in this chapter is 801 but will change to 435 in September 1997. Either area code may be used until March 22, 1998.

SCORE
Dixie College Business Alliance Center, 225 S. 700 East, St. George • 652-7732

The local chapter of the Service Corps of Retired Executives is dedicated to helping all current and potential business owners achieve entrepreneurial success in Southwestern Utah. A half-dozen SCORE volunteers in the region mentor younger business owners, and they share their background and knowledge of business through individual counseling and leading or teaching workshops. Part of a national organization with more than 13,000 members, SCORE volunteers in Southwestern Utah help develop business plans, find financing and build management skills through the Business Alliance Center at Dixie College. Those interested in working for or with the SCORE program are invited to call for more information and times of weekly meetings.

Educational Opportunities

Elderhostel at Dixie College
123 E. 100 South, St. George • 673-3704

Elderhostel's "Discover Southern Utah" travel package provides seniors older than 55 the opportunity to study college-level courses at Dixie College, golf, brave the whitewater of the Colorado River, golf, explore Zion, Bryce Canyon and Duck Creek, examine history and heritage, golf, take part in the Utah Shakespearean Festival, play tennis and bridge . . . or golf!

Elderhostel is an independent, nonprofit organization offering short-term academic experiences for seniors. It started on a shoestring at the University of New Hampshire and has now blossomed into a worldwide network of dynamic programs for adult learners. Including those who participate through Dixie College, there are nearly a quarter-million older folks who travel and study in association with about 2,000 colleges and universities, museums, national parks and environmental education and conference centers in all 50 states, Canada and 49 foreign countries.

Most programs in the worldwide Elderhostel program last five or six days beginning on Sunday, and include 20 to 40 classmates with a variety of backgrounds and life experiences. Costs are kept low by reserving comfortable yet modest accommodations and eating in campus cafeterias and dining halls. Program fees range from $250 per person for local residents to as much as $650 per person for the Colorado River trip. Fees take care of meals, housing, field trips, lectures and activities. More information is available by writing Elderhostel at Dixie College.

Institute for Continued Learning
300 S. 800 East, St. George • 652-7670

More than 450 retired students are enrolled in the Institute for Continued Learning, a chartered club on the campus of Dixie College. Created in 1979 as the first group of its type in Utah, ICL is similar to many organizations now affiliated with colleges and universities throughout the country that offer various educational and social opportunities to retired and semi-retired men and women older than 50. Volunteer instructors share their knowledge and experience in such areas as geology, history, archeology, Spanish, French, "see and draw" art classes, line dancing and t'ai chi. Students examine the Constitution, explore the great classics, take Saturday-scheduled field trips two or three times each month to historic and scenic sites and socialize during the holidays or fair weather outdoor gatherings.

An annual registration fee of $30 covers the costs of postage and staff, but classes held weekly or biweekly during the school year are free for enrolled ICL members.

Employment and Volunteer Opportunities

Five County Retired and Senior Volunteer Program
906 N. 1400 West, St. George • 673-0700

"The only gift is a portion of thyself," said Ralph Waldo Emerson, and in his few words he captured the essence and state of mind of volunteerism in Southwestern Utah. More than 775 senior volunteers enrolled in the Five County Retired and Senior Volunteer Program (RSVP) regularly step outside the routine of daily living to provide for the needs of their neighbors. RSVP volunteers in and around St. George, Cedar City, Kanab and in the Bryce Canyon area are enthused about the program, contributing more than 80,000 volunteer hours in 1996 with a value to those communities in excess of $970,000.

Members of Five County RSVP are assigned, according to their interests or life experiences, to volunteer stations including but not limited to Dixie Regional Medical Center, Valley View Medical Center and other hospitals throughout the region, senior citizens centers, chambers of commerce, Dixie Center, Tuacahn Amphitheater and Center for the Arts, the Utah Shakespearean Festival, libraries and literacy programs, schools, food banks and dozens of other locations. Interested men and women older than 55 may sign up to teach children or adults to read, take non-driving residents to doctors' appointments, or craft, quilt, build or garden. Others can sing, dance, perform or usher at community events. Call for more information or to request an application and list of volunteer opportunities in your home town or relocation area.

Green Thumb
168 N. 100 East, St. George • 674-3820

Mature workers are in demand. For those

who haven't worked in a long time, never worked outside the home, receive Social Security or don't have a high school education, opportunities for developing competitive job skills are available through the Green Thumb program. It started in 1965, when Lady Bird Johnson's Beautification of America initiative hired 280 retired farmers to use their "green thumbs" to improve the nation's parks and highways.

Today, Green Thumb is a national nonprofit organization providing employment and training opportunities for older Americans, and giving low-income individuals age 55 or older a better chance to succeed. Through the Green Thumb program, Southwestern Utah benefits from essential services performed by program participants ranging from child and elder care to emergency assistance, crime prevention, health-care services and disaster relief. Most participants will be offered an average of 20 hours a week of community service work but are limited to not more than 1,300 hours a year. Participants are paid either the federal or state minimum wage, whichever is higher. The Green Thumb program proves experience works.

Job Service
40 S. 200 East, St. George • 673-3588

National chains such as Wal-Mart, Kmart and McDonald's use them liberally, and local businesses also see the value in hiring older workers. While most retirees moving to Southwestern Utah are ready to hang up their pinstripes and pick up their Pings, there are many employers who welcome the chance to hire a senior citizen. They say older workers bring experience, dependability, maturity, a strong work ethic, job commitment, stability and talent to the workplace. For the small percentage of seniors who still enjoy the challenge of full or part time employment, Job Service offices in most Southwestern Utah communities, have opportunities for willing workers up to age 90, whether they've lived here a short time or a lifetime.

Through Job Training Partnership Act (JTPA) programs, a Utah resident at least 55 years old may be eligible for no-cost employment and training options. JTPA offers job search assistance with a counselor who will teach older workers to appreciate their unique

abilities. Skills taught include resume writing, interviewing skills and job seeking techniques. Through JTPA on-the-job-training, a portion of the older worker's salary may be reimbursed to give employers an added incentive to hire.

JTPA skills training helps the older worker polish job skills at area schools and vocational centers. Training options provide assistance in adult basic education, office occupations, healthcare, manufacturing and more. There are Job Service offices in several Southwestern Utah communities including Kanab, Cedar City, Panguitch, Tropic and Orderville.

Entertainment and Athletic Opportunities

Huntsman World Senior Games
82 W. 700 South, St. George • 674-0550, (800) 562-1268

In 1996, the Huntsman World Senior Games played host to 3,500 senior athletes from all over the world. Men and women older than 50 from every state in the U.S. and 25 foreign countries gathered to play on the course, the court and on the track. For two weeks, these athletes run, jump, pedal, pitch and volley. They participate and medal in basketball, triathlon, bowling, cycling, golf, horseshoes, racquetball, road racing, softball, swimming, table tennis, tennis, basketball free throw and three-point shooting, bridge, soccer, volleyball and selected track and field events. The goal is "to foster health, friendship and world peace."

The city of St. George, Washington County, Dixie College, neighborhoods such as Green Valley and Bloomington, most local golf courses and more than 2,000 volunteers make the Huntsman World Senior Games possible through generous contributions of facilities and time. Donations of money, goods and services also come from many sources, in addition to the ongoing generosity of Jon M. Huntsman, chairman of the Huntsman Corporation, the games' major sponsor.

Opening and closing ceremonies have included world-class celebrity athletes such as Olympic track and field stars Jackie Joyner-Kersee, Florence "Flo-Jo" Griffith Joyner and

Retirees are attracted to Souhtwestern Utah by its climate and wide variety of activities.

her husband, Al Joyner, and baseball great Harmon Killibrew. Fireworks light up the sky, doves are released and dignitaries speak. But for many, the highlight of the event is the march of the athletes, where flags of 25 nations wave, the torch is lit and the games begin! Inquiries about the Huntsman World Senior Games are encouraged by mail or phone.

Panguitch Kitchen Band
151 E. 100 South, Panguitch • 676-2260

If you can hum or sing, even a little, the Panguitch Kitchen Band will move over and make you welcome! Back in 1947, when this unique musical group was formed, these ladies were known as the Bathing Beauty Band. But that was then, and this is now. The youngest of 16 kazoo players is 60 and the oldest will be 86 on her next birthday, but all have made their mark on the community by playing the famed toy musical instrument that produces a sound when the player hums into the mouthpiece.

The repertoire is admittedly dated, since they cling to the peppy numbers they knew in their youth. Dressed in pioneer dress and bonnets, they have more fun than anyone at community events where they are popular performers for any program.

Prime Time Performers
1461 E. Boulder Springs Rd., St. George • 673-2075

The world-traveling Prime Time Performers, under the direction of Ilene Hacker, is a senior ladies jazz dance team. This group of 35 active women older than 50 has strutted its stuff from St. George to New Zealand, from

Las Vegas to the Fiji islands and points in between since its creation in 1993. The dancers are mothers of 157 children, 332 grandchildren and 49 great-grandchildren.

Decked out in sequins and spangles, these gals from varying backgrounds have performed upbeat precision jazz and hip-hop routines at the famous Opera House in Sydney, Australia; in Auckland, New Zealand; in Nadi, Fiji; at the Polynesian Cultural Center in Laie, Hawaii; and in Branson, Missouri at the Jim Stafford Show and the Silver Dollar City Saloon. Locally, they are popular performers at Red Cliffs Mall events, Dixie College basketball halftime shows and drill team reviews, the opening ceremonies of the Huntsman World Senior Games, in various parades and at area health-care centers and civic club programs.

In 1997, the dancers are scheduled for events in Las Vegas, in and around the Salt Lake City area and in New York for the Big Apple Tour.

Senior Centers

St. George/Zion

In the St. George area, you'll find that a daily round of golf is the top priority for many retirees. Still, before and after taking to the links, many seniors enjoy spending time at the following centers.

Hafen Senior Citizens Center
235 N. 200 West, St. George • 634-5743

This center still draws a full house for lunch every Tuesday, Thursday and Friday. And why not, when in addition to a good meal and friendly conversation, the lunch crowd is entertained with music, dance, frequent speakers, seasonal fashions or talent shows? Transportation to and from the center is available for non-drivers, professional haircuts are provided for a nominal fee and basic health services such as checks for blood pressure, blood sugar and oxygen saturation levels are free.

Things to do at the Hafen Senior Citizens Center include instruction in oil and watercolor painting, dancing (social, line, square and tap), t'ai chi and yoga, bridge and bingo. Twice-monthly seminars are scheduled for those interested in more information on wills and trusts or health-care topics. Seniors can also get help with income taxes, meet together in a book club or take part in a Parkinson's disease support group.

Hurricane Senior Center
95 N. 300 West, Hurricane • 635-2089

This center is open daily from 9 AM to 3 PM with a whole lot of friendly interaction packed into those few hours. As in most other senior centers in the area, lunch is served at noon on Monday, Wednesday and Friday. Here in Hurricane, it costs $2.25 per meal. Bingo is scheduled after lunch on Mondays for 25¢ per card and craft activities are held on Tuesday for the cost of materials. For a small donation, seniors can get their ears lowered twice monthly by a barber on the premises, and free tests to monitor blood pressure and blood sugar levels are scheduled regularly. Bring your own popcorn for video movies shown on the second Tuesday of each month, don't forget a potluck dish for the Senior Social held the third Tuesday or trip the light fantastic at the Senior Dance held Thursday evenings.

Enterprise Senior Center
50 S. Center St., Enterprise • 878-2557

The senior center in Enterprise provides lunch three times a week on Monday, Wednesday and Friday. About 25 to 30 residents of the community usually show up for the meal, with an additional 25 or 30 receiving their hot meal from Meals on Wheels volunteers. The smallest senior center in the county does a yeoman's job of providing entertainment, fun and health-care resources to a growing senior population. Regularly scheduled entertainment from Enterprise or nearby communities such as St. George or Cedar City makes lunchtime lively and fun.

A home-health nurse shows up from time to time to check blood pressure and blood sugar levels. Field trips throughout the year include a ride to Cedar Mountain to see the autumn leaves, a summertime picnic at Pine Valley and shopping trips to Cedar City or St. George. A once-a-year fund-raiser for the senior center is held in conjunction with the annual Enterprise Corn Festival (see our Annual Events chapter), when seniors from other

Washington County centers "bus up" for a Dutch-oven dinner, fresh corn on the cob and a program.

Cedar City/Brian Head

Cedar City Senior Center
489 E. 200 South, Cedar City • 586-0832

Seniors get together for lunch each Tuesday, Thursday and Saturday at this center — the spread runs $2.25 for those over 60. In addition to the congregate meal, the Cedar City Senior Center has exercise equipment and a pool table, puzzles, bingo and lots of other reasons for seniors to gather. Regularly scheduled throughout the month, the Cedar City center offers blood pressure and blood sugar testing, hearing checks, shopping trips, movies and other opportunities for socializing.

Parowan Senior Center
68 S. 100 East, Parowan • 477-8925

The center in the Iron County seat provides lunch Monday, Wednesday and Friday at 12:15 PM for a suggested donation of $2.25 for those over age 60. If you bring any younger folks, it'll run them $4.75. In a regular month's time, seniors will enjoy a wide range of fun and educational activities such as quilting, exercise workouts, bingo, movies, blood pressure clinics, hearing aid checks, cancer clinics, a birthday celebration and lectures from local health-care professionals.

Bryce Canyon Area

With a large land mass and a small, scattered population, Bryce Canyon area retirees look to three senior centers as the gathering places for support, resources and socialization. Seniors in the Bryce County area find Five County Area Agency on Aging programs to fit their needs.

Panguitch Senior Center
55 S. Main Street, Panguitch • 676-2281

The programs of the Panguitch Senior Center, as well as the Escalante and Henrieville senior centers are administered by the Five County Area Agency on Aging. Panguitch seniors enjoy a wide variety of activities geared to their physical, emotional and social well-being. Lunch is served every Tuesday, Wednesday and Thursday for a $2.25 contribution. A van is available to provide transportation if needed. When the lunch dishes are done, seniors enjoy an afternoon quilting and catching up on the news of the neighborhood. A spirited game of bingo, viewing a new video release, a shopping trip or a van ride to a community event are other great ways these seniors interact with friends.

Escalante Senior Center
89 N. 100 West, Escalante • 826-4317

Bryce Canyon seniors enjoy life by remaining active and involved. Lunch is served every Tuesday, but unlike the other centers in the Bryce Canyon area, the other congregate meals are dinners on Wednesday and Thursday. The cost is $2.25 for those older than 60; $4.50 for younger guests. In the Escalante Senior Center, many activities and events are planned with a focus on socializing and fun. Escalante seniors gather for popcorn and videos, board games and lots of crafts such as beading projects, ceramics and quilting. When things get too quiet in Escalante, a couple dozen seniors climb into the community van and go shopping . . . in Richfield, about 100 miles northwest of Bryce Canyon, or Cedar City nearly 80 miles southwest. Escalante seniors attend all five plays performed each year at the Hale Center Theater in Teasdale, some 80 miles away. This lively band of travelers even has plans to take a trip this year to Colorado after a stopover to see the annual Castle Valley Pageant in Castle Dale, 100 miles north of their hometown.

Henrieville Senior Center
Utah Hwy. 12, Henrieville • 826-4317

In Henrieville (population 175) the best place to catch up on the news of the day is over lunch at the Henrieville Senior Center. For an economical donation of $2.25, the whole town can socialize over a home-cooked meal every Tuesday, Wednesday and Thursday. Transportation on the senior citizen van is available by calling the center. Shopping and sightseeing trips, crafts and games round out regularly scheduled activities. Blood pressure and blood-sugar testing is offered monthly by home care nurses.

Kanab Area

Kanab Senior Center
53 W. 450 North, Kanab • 644-5250

The senior center in Kanab has a lively schedule of activities throughout each month. There's an exercise class every morning, Monday through Friday, at 9 AM. Monday afternoons you'll find the women's chorus practicing for a performance, and later the Friendship Club gathers for a video party or friendly chitchat. Tuesday mornings everyone gets together for a ceramics class, then on Wednesday, the home health nurse is on hand to check blood pressure and blood sugar levels. Wednesday evening is Fun Night.

Hearing aid checks are scheduled periodically during the month, and from January through April 15, a tax counselor — part of AARP's Tax Counseling for the Elderly program (TCE) — will be on hand from time to time to help fill out forms for the IRS. Kanab Senior Center serves lunch Monday, Wednesday and Friday by reservation only, so call early to reserve your place at the table. If you're older than 60, the center suggests a donation of $2.25 for your meal. If you're younger than 60, it'll cost you $4.50.

Long Valley Senior Citizens Center
U.S. Hwy. 89 N., Orderville • 648-2504

The 55-and-older crowd in Orderville socializes at Long Valley on U.S. Highway 89. Lunch is served at noon on Monday, Wednesday and Friday. Tuesday is Fun Night, when Orderville seniors enjoy visiting and video viewing. The center also offers frequent opportunities to quilt and make ceramics, and the Old Time Band practices and performs often.

Assisted Care

Through local hospitals and home health agencies, seniors in Southwestern Utah have access to assistance that enables them to remain in their homes as long as possible. Services provided in the home range from skilled nursing to personal services such as help with showering or food preparation. Hospital-owned, county-owned or privately owned facilities and agencies range in size and scope but generally have services and professionals in all Southwestern Utah communities.

Five County Area Agency on Aging serves as a clearinghouse for information on assisted-care options. Call 673-3548 in the St. George or Kanab areas or 586-2975 for assistance in or around Cedar City or Panguitch. Dixie Regional Medical Center's Community Resource Center at 544 S. 400 East in St. George can also offer suggestions.

Adult Day Care

St. George/Zion

Extended Family
43 N. 800 East, St. George • 656-2273

Extended Family, Washington County's newest adult day-care service, provides respite services for elderly adults. Participants are those who need supervision or companionship but do not require skilled nursing assistance. Your loved ones will enjoy home-cooked meals, recreational activities with socialization and the opportunity to create their own circle of friends.

Extended Family is the safe, non-threatening environment of a social model rather than a medical model. Funded by the Five County Association of Governments, the Alzheimer's Association and other foundation grants, Extended Family also provides in-home respite care on a daily, weekly or monthly schedule. Call for more details.

Cedar City/Brian Head

Kindred Care
285 S. 200 East, Cedar City • 586-1128

Kindred Care, opened in the fall of 1994, provides adult day care for a maximum of 22 elderly seniors in the pleasant surroundings of large, attractively decorated rooms. Included at the facility are a large dining room, kitchen area and a fenced backyard. A subsidiary of the Iron Parke Corporation, a Utah nonprofit since 1984, Kindred Care is open from 9 AM to 5 PM Monday through Friday.

Activities are tailored to the interests of each

Photo: St. George Magazine

A high jumper soars over the bar at the Huntsman World Senior Games in St. George.

guest and include one-on-one time with staff members and volunteers, craft and art projects, games, physical exercise, gardening and outdoors and life skills development. Occasional activities include field trips to the library, bowling alley, local attractions and events. Clients take daytrips to local, state and national parks and participate in community service projects. An added benefit for seniors is an adjacent preschool that allows for inter-generational activities.

Nursing Homes and Long-term Care Facilities

When circumstances warrant the admission of an elderly loved one to a long-term care facility, it is comforting to know there are several excellent options available in communities throughout Southwestern Utah. Here are a handful of choices.

St. George/Zion

Color Country Care Center
233 S. 1000 East, St. George • 673-4310, 673-4038

This intermediate-care facility has been a regional leader in the industry for more than 25 years. Color Country Care Center is small, with only 25 beds, but provides a large measure of quality care to men and women in a congenial family atmosphere. Licensed in Utah and Nevada and Medicaid approved, Color Country provides 24-hour nursing, skilled nursing and dietician consultation, physical therapy, social services, personal grooming and homestyle meals — all at moderate prices. Roses bloom in a fenced yard with a canopy-covered patio, providing the opportunity for residents to enjoy the outdoors.

Comfort Cottage Residential Home
155 N. 300 West, Washington • 628-8329

In the comfort of a large luxury home, seniors in need of 24-hour care and attention find companionship in the friendly family atmosphere of Comfort Cottage. There is no institutional feel about this place — no long halls with numbered rooms. Each room says something about the individual who lives there, as clients can make their own spaces as homey as they choose. There are six rooms that serve a maximum of seven residents, and each room has cable TV and private phone lines. Comfort Cottage provides companionship, physical therapy, monitoring of medications, socializing and activities, homey Victorian decor, a heated pool and housekeeping services.

Residents enjoy three meals a day around the dinner table. Snacks are also provided, and residents, allowed free access to all areas of the facility, are welcome in the kitchen when the cookies come out of the oven. A sign hangs on the refrigerator reminding the staff: "Always use a soft voice. Give your senior friend the dignity of choice. Put their needs first." The folks at Comfort Cottage consider it an alternative to traditional nursing home care, and it was one of 11 residential-care facilities to receive a certificate of merit from the state of Utah in 1996.

The Meadows
950 S. 400 East, St. George • 628-0090

This is about as close to country-club living for seniors as you'll find anywhere. Beautifully appointed, The Meadows offers 117 apartments for residential care or independent living — there are studio apartments, one-, two- and three-bedroom options. Residents of The Meadows have the choice to use their own kitchen or take their meals together in the dining room. If guests are invited for dinner, there are even private dining rooms for entertaining.

The Meadows features activity areas, exercise equipment, physical therapy, meals, transportation, social activities, an on-site library, a common reception area, manicured grounds with a swimming pool and many opportunities for socialization with peers. If the time comes, apartments in the residential-care center include 24-hour skilled nursing care and health-care aides while allowing residents to maintain their valued friendships and familiar surroundings.

Red Cliffs Regional Rehabilitation and Convalescent Center
1745 E. 280 North, St. George • 628-7770

The staff at Red Cliffs Regional loves it when surprised visitors tell them "this sure doesn't look like a nursing home." Each semi-private room is large and beautifully decorated with a private bathroom and shower. The facility serves up to 150 residents and patients. It features an extra-large recreation room for activities and outdoor patio areas with benches and fountains. The front lobby — not unlike that of a posh, upscale hotel — has a fireplace and seating area ideal for quiet conversation with friends and visitors. All the trimmings — paint, wallpaper and furnishings — have been selected to enhance the setting.

The rehabilitation area is separate from the long-term care section, but Red Cliffs Regional does provide 24-hour skilled nursing services, long-term care and inpatient rehabilitation services including physical, occupational and speech therapies. In a separate, secured section, Red Cliffs also provides for the care of patients who have been diagnosed with Alzheimer's disease.

Rosecrest Manor
48 W. 700 South, St. George • 673-7398

Rosecrest Manor provides care for 13 elderly residents in an immaculately clean, homey atmosphere. The 4,000-square-foot residential-care facility has a large formal living room, a comfortable dining room and private bedrooms with cable TV and private telephone hookups. Staff cooks prepare delicious, aromatic meals. Socializing, games and group TV watching are ongoing in the garden room, which offers a view of a spacious backyard with grapevines, rose bushes, almond trees, flowers and a small vegetable garden.

Residents receive personal services such as manicures, and an activity director arranges regular musical programs and entertainment two or three times each week. The attractive facility has twice received a Certificate of Achievement from the State of Utah Licensing Division, and family members have noted marked improvement in the overall attitude and general well-being of their loved ones residing at Rosecrest Manor.

St. George Care and Rehabilitation Center
1032 E. 100 South, St. George • 628-0488

One of the largest long-term care centers in the area, St. George Care and Rehabilitation Center, with 159 beds, provides 24-hour care in private and semiprivate rooms with TV and phone services. In a smoke-free environment, residents receive physical, occupational, respiratory and speech therapies as needed. The two-year-old therapy center has an indoor pool and a large activity room with treadmills, stationary bicycles and equipment for strengthening muscles. Small private rooms allow for secluded workouts with therapists. A secured Alzheimer's unit provides for the care of patients with that diagnosis. Other services include complete laundry care, an on-site beauty and barber shop, religious programs and a rose garden in the center courtyard.

Zion Health Care Complex
416 N. State St., Hurricane • 635-9833

The Zion Health Care Complex serves the long-term care and rehabilitative needs of residents of the Hurricane Valley and adjacent communities. This facility opened for business in 1978 and provides skilled nursing care, nutritious meals and snacks, transportation, social aides, billing services and social activities for 62 residents in semiprivate rooms. The spectacular view of mountains and desert is best from the Zion Health Care Complex park and picnic pavilion, shaded by fruit trees planted when the facility first opened. Residents of the Zion Health Care Complex have presented prize-winning floats in the Washington County Fair Parade for three consecutive years.

Cedar City/Brian Head

Cedar Care Center
679 Sunset Dr., Cedar City • 586-6481

At Cedar Care Center, the emphasis is on living. An excellent recreation program includes a bulging calendar of events, frequent shopping trips and outings to community activities and sites, daily programming — even Sunday drives. The 44-bed intermediate and skilled nursing care center is Medicaid certified for 24-hour care. Professional services include rehabilitation therapy, social services, individualized personal care and regular consultations from a podiatrist, dietician, dentist, recreational therapist and others. The facility itself is light and airy with semiprivate and private rooms available.

Iron County Nursing Home
69 E. 100 South, Parowan • 477-3615

This small long-term care facility, in the Iron County seat, opened in 1953 to provide residents in-house therapy, social services, home-cooked meals, laundry and housekeep-

ing services as well as a busy schedule of activities. Thirty-one clients occupy two-bed rooms, and roommates are chosen carefully to assure they are compatible. Doors in each room open to the outside with a second door opening into a common hallway. Because the facility is smaller than most, staff and residents quickly become like family.

Bryce Canyon Area

Garfield Memorial Care Center
224 N. 400 East, Panguitch • 676-1265

Garfield Memorial Care Center is a 30-bed, long-term care, rehabilitation and skilled nursing facility. The two-year-old wing of the Garfield Memorial Hospital (see our Healthcare chapter) provides for patients following strokes, joint replacement surgery or other maladies. The facility provides a full-time physical therapist, recreational activities, regularly scheduled entertainment and a pleasant, homelike atmosphere. The center courtyard includes an atrium completed in 1996. Garfield Memorial Care Center is Medicare and Medicaid approved but also accepts private-pay residents.

Kanab Area

Kane County Hospital Nursing Home
220 W. 300 North, Kanab • 644-5811

In a separate wing of the Kane County Hospital (see our Healthcare chapter), patients in need of long-term care receive nursing care, nutritional assessment, individualized planned-care programs, social services and therapeutic restorative programs provided by qualified, licensed personnel. There are 13 residents who now share semiprivate rooms with a common dining area and recreational activities. This nursing home will double in size with the opening of the new Kane County Hospital, scheduled for fall of '97. A larger dining room will be used as an activity room. Bathrooms will be enlarged, a physical therapy pool is being worked into the plans and there will be an on-site beauty shop. The facility is Medicare and Medicaid certified.

Few hospitals its size
offer the diversity of
services and more than
90 physicians of Dixie
Regional Medical
Center.

Healthcare

Considering the fact that the population of our 10,000-square-mile area is less than 150,000, healthcare availability is more than adequate and the quality surprisingly high in Southwestern Utah.

Because we are less than a day's drive from the sprawling hospitals of urban centers such as Salt Lake City, Las Vegas and Los Angeles, the demand here for more specialized care didn't intensify until the population explosion of the last 10 years. Today, Cedar City and St. George have very well-equipped hospitals with physicians trained in most of the standard specialties. Smaller towns such as Kanab and Panguitch also have hospitals of their own with doctors on call.

Dixie Regional Medical Center, headquartered in St. George, has grown rapidly during the past two decades into one of the most respected rural regional medical centers in America. The hospital offers a wide range of care and several specialized departments including cancer treatment.

Finding the Right Doctor

Southwestern Utah is home to nearly 150 physicians, almost as many dentists and about two dozen chiropractors. In addition to general family dentists there are periodontists, oral and maxillofacial surgeons, orthodontists, pediatric dentists and endodontists.

Most of the doctors in a given community are well-known by the community at large. We suggest you ask a few friends or acquaintances for recommendations, realizing many of the doctors, especially physicians and dentists in general practice, usually don't have openings for two to six weeks. Most chiropractors are accessible on short notice. If you are new to the area, call the hospital nearest you for information on physicians. There are no official physician referral agencies in the region.

There has also been significant regional growth in home healthcare, rehabilitation clinics, eye care, dentistry and hearing services. This chapter is designed to give you an overview of the kinds of healthcare available in Southwestern Utah and some practical advice on how to find the care option that is right for you.

Dr. Higgins' Remedy

Dr. Silas G. Higgins came to St. George with the first Mormon pioneers in 1861. For 43 years he administered relief to the suffering settlers. Evidently he was also a psychologist. For those who would not be satisfied with an answer that nothing was wrong, he prescribed a harmless palatable compound made of dry orange peelings pounded to a powder and mixed with powdered magnesia. The powder was folded in paper and put in packages of a dozen. With subtle wit, he diagnosed one patient's complaint as a bad case of lethargy. Reports have it the patient, who did not know the definition of lethargy, worried considerably about his condition.

Hospitals

Zion/St. George

Dixie Regional Medical Center
544 S. 400 East, St. George • 634-4000

Because of its affiliation with Intermountain Health Care Corporation (a nonprofit corporation that owns 24 hospitals in five western states), Dixie Regional Medical Center has been able to bring the latest technologies in many specialties and departments to Southwestern Utah — services one might not expect to find in a market this size. DRMC's designation by Medicare as a Rural Referral Center and the contributions of a supportive community also have helped make possible the purchase of expensive technology. Few other hospitals this size (137 beds) have the diversity of services and the number of physicians that work at DRMC.

More than 90 doctors work at Dixie Regional. Their specialties cover a wide spectrum including orthopedics, OB/GYN, psychology, neurology, oncology, internal medicine, gastroenterology, oral surgery, podiatry, plastic surgery, urology, general surgery, pediatrics, radiation oncology and physical medicine.

DRMC has a 24-hour emergency care center and Life Flight is on call for transfer of trauma patients to larger urban hospitals by helicopter or airplane. Also on-site are a behavioral medicine and psychiatrics wing, blood bank, nutritional care and weight management services, intensive care, critical care, respiratory care, a same-day surgical center and a community resource center.

A cardiac catheterization lab allows cardiologists to be much more accurate in their decisions about sending patients home or referring them to a hospital specializing in heart surgery. Other diagnostic services include radiology and medical imaging, CAT scanning and MRI ability, angiography, mammography, endoscopy, nuclear medicine, sleep disorder diagnosis and pulmonary function testing.

Dixie's Cancer Center has treated more than 1,500 patients from throughout the tri-state area of Utah, Nevada and Arizona since it opened a decade ago. It was the first accredited cancer center in the state. Services include prevention education, early diagnosis, evaluation, treatment, rehabilitation and surveillance. Surgery, medical oncology, radiation oncology (DRMC has two linear accelerators), home healthcare, nutrition support, respiratory care and hospice aid are all part of the program. The Cancer Center is accredited by both the American College of Surgeons and the Joint Commission on Accreditation of Healthcare Organizations.

More than 400 in-service volunteers work at DRMC. There are opportunities for both adults and teens to be volunteers in such areas as information desks, hospice services, gift shops and even in the emergency room, admitting and helping transfer patients.

Cedar City/Brian Head

Valley View Medical Center
595 S. 75 East, Cedar City • 586-6587

Also part of Intermountain Health Care group of hospitals, the 48-bed Valley View Medical Center offers the services of more than 25 physicians. Specialties covered by the hospital staff include family practice, general surgery, internal medicine, OB/GYN, orthopedics, pediatrics, podiatry, radiology, urology and dermatology. Valley View has 24-hour emer-

> **FYI**
>
> Unless otherwise noted, the area code for all phone numbers listed in this chapter is 801 but will change to 435 in September 1997. Either area code may be used until March 22, 1998.

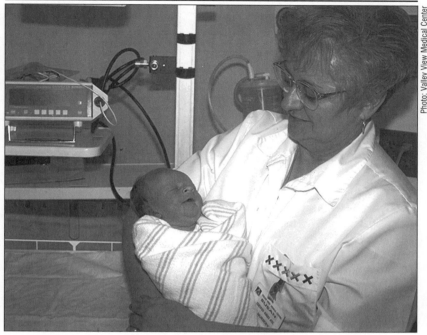

Photo: Valley View Medical Center

This newborn entered the world at Cedar City's Valley View Medical Center.

gency care, intensive care, same-day surgery options, hospice care and other services.

With a strong focus on prevention and support, Valley View offers prenatal and sibling classes, bereavement groups, CPR and first-aid instruction, support groups for victims of cancer, diabetes and Parkinson's disease, weight loss programs, a respiratory health club and a senior life club.

Nearly 100 men and women are members of the VVMC Auxiliary, a corps of volunteers who give special life to the hospital. They work at the reception desk, blood drives, the gift shop, snack bar and throughout the hospital. Many young people work as junior volunteers and a growing number of adults are working in the hospice program.

Bryce Canyon Area

Garfield Memorial Hospital
224 N. 400 East, Panguitch • 676-8811

This is a small-town facility with a huge heart. The hospital is organized to take care of the primary needs — from emergency to maternity — of Garfield County residents and visitors. It has 44 beds (30 of which are dedicated to long-term patients needing therapy, rehabilitation and geriatric services), and the staff includes three physicians (one is a surgeon), a nurse practitioner and a physician's assistant.

There's an adjacent walk-in clinic open from 9 AM to 5 PM weekdays that handles emergency needs, and a doctor is on call 24 hours a day at the hospital. As another Intermountain

INSIDERS' TIP

Dial 911 for emergency assistance throughout the entire Southwestern Utah area.

Health Care facility, the hospital handles routine surgeries and can effectively transfer patients to urban IHC hospitals (such as LDS Hospital in Salt Lake City) for the specialized care they need. Garfield County also offers limited clinical care in Circleville, Cannonville and Escalante.

Kanab Area

Kane County Hospital and Skilled Nursing Care
220 W. 300 North, Kanab • 644-5811

Many of the healthcare needs of Kanab area residents and visitors are taken care of at Kane County Hospital, which is owned by the county and managed by an elected board. This is a 33-bed facility with the majority of the beds used for elderly patients and others needing long-term nursing care. The hospital is served by two physicians. It offers 24-hour emergency care, radiology, routine surgeries, maternity care, home health, a lab and CAT scanning.

Currently, Kane County is in the process of building a new 38-bed facility with a clinic adjacent. An opening is scheduled for the fall of 1997. The new facility won't be much larger than the existing hospital but will be better equipped to meet the healthcare needs of the county.

Emergency Care

For emergency care, physicians are on call 24 hours a day at Dixie Regional Medical Center in St. George, Valley View Medical Center in Cedar City and at the smaller hospitals in Kanab and Panguitch (see our "Hospitals" section in this chapter).

Several ambulance services operate throughout the four-county area. Dialing 911 will put you in touch with help immediately.

Walk-in Clinics

Color Country Health Express
350 E. 600 South, St. George • 628-2445
595 S. Bluff St., St. George • 674-9933
429 W. 400 South, Cedar City • 586-2201

With two locations in St. George and one in Cedar City, these walk-in clinics are staffed by family nurse practitioners who offer a number of healthcare services. The available options include immunizations, treatment of acute illnesses, physical exams and cardiovascular screening and women's healthcare in the form of breast and pelvic exams and Pap and mammogram referrals.

Other Resources

Ask-a-Nurse
544 S. 400 East, St. George • 628-6200, ext. 2095

Dixie Regional Medical Center's Ask-a-Nurse phone line, 628-6200 ext. 2095, puts you in touch with a nurse immediately — someone who can answer your health question quickly or direct you to a better source. This service is available 24 hours a day.

Getting Down to Business

Dr. J.T. Affleck came to the mining town of Silver Reef, 17 miles northeast of St. George, during its boom in the 1880s. When the town faded, he moved to St. George and set up practice. Affleck was a skilled surgeon who never hesitated to cut someone open if he felt it was called for. On one occasion he removed a diseased kidney and its accompanying 4-pound tumor from a woman in Washington City — right in her own bedroom. He placed disinfected sheets over a large table and there performed his operation with what few instruments he carried in his bag. The woman recovered and lived 25 more years. In fact, she bore two sons after the operation and raised them to maturity.

A Home Away From Home

Larry and Mary Hogrefe of El Dorado, Arkansas, had planned to spend several days in St. George basking in the sunshine, enjoying the companionship of good friends and drinking in the scenery of Southwestern Utah. Instead, less than 24 hours after their arrival, Larry was admitted to Dixie Regional Medical Center in need of emergency surgery. This in a city more than a thousand miles from home and family.

While her husband underwent intestinal surgery, Mary drew strength from the kindness of the people around her. She was able to stay in the Jubilee Home, a home away from home just across the street from DRMC. It allowed her to spend hours on end at her  husband's bedside and still be able to relax, sleep and enjoy the comforts of home for a few hours a day. "They did all they could to make this unexpected ordeal as stress-free and as easy as possible for us," said Mary.

The Jubilee Home was built in 1991 through the efforts of the Dixie Health Care Foundation. Generous donations, both in cash and in kind, made it possible for the foundation to purchase prime property directly across the street from the medical center and build a beautiful house with a bright living area, kitchen and several bedrooms. Much of the actual construction was done as a donation by a local contractor.

People with loved ones at Dixie Regional Medical Center can stay for extended periods, or just for the night, across the street at the Jubilee Home.

Materials were contributed by local suppliers. Funds were raised through the annual Christmas-time Jubilee of Trees, and church and civic groups pitched in to do the landscaping and finishing touches. Nearly a thousand people have been able to stay in the Jubilee Home since it was built. It allows folks, especially from out of town, to be near and easily accessible to a loved one while in the hospital.

"While it wasn't the vacation we had envisioned," said Larry, "we feel very fortunate that when it became necessary for me to have emergency surgery, we had chosen the St. George area to visit. From the moment I entered the emergency room until my discharge eight days later, we were treated with a level of professionalism, courtesy and true concern never before encountered."

Those of us who live around here simply call it "The Dixie Spirit."

Dixie Regional Medical Center Resource Center

544 S. 400 East, St. George • 634-4000

Dixie Regional Medical Center has a Resource Center open Monday through Friday that is a clearinghouse for information on health services throughout the area. Located on the first floor of the hospital, the center also offers free printed and computer information on most any health concern you might have. Call DRMC for more information.

St. George Surgical Center

676 S. Bluff St., St. George • 673-8080

This is Southwestern Utah's only freestanding outpatient surgery center. It allows patients to have same-day surgery for certain procedures without having to check into a hospital. The center is staffed by many of the same surgeons affiliated with Dixie Regional Medical Center.

Southwest Center

354 E. 600 South, St. George • 628-0426
91 N. 1850 West, Cedar City • 586-8226
609 N. Main St., Panguitch • 676-8176
310 S. 100 East, Kanab • 644-8857

The Southwest Center, administered by the Southwest Center Authority Board, provides comprehensive mental health and substance abuse services to people in Southwestern Utah. Counseling for married couples, youth and abused children is provided along with assistance for alcohol and drug problems, depression, anxiety and stress, assertiveness, coping and parenting skills. No one is denied service because of an inability to pay. Each of the locations also offers outpatient services for youth and adults, day treatment programs, 24-hour residential support, supervised independent living services, social detoxification for substance abusers and a number of other services..

Southwest Utah Public Health Department

285 W. Tabernacle, St. George • 673-3528
88 E. Fiddlers Canyon Rd., Cedar City
• 586-2437
609 N. Main St., Panguitch • 676-8800
245 S. 200 East, Kanab • 644-2537

This government agency offers low-cost immunizations and various testings and screenings.

Franklin Quest Institute of Fitness

202 N. Snow Canyon Rd., St. George
• 673-4905

For more than a decade, the National Institute of Fitness has built a reputation at the foot of red sandstone towers near the entrance to Snow Canyon State Park. Two years ago, Franklin Quest Company purchased the institute from founders Marc and Vicki Sorenson and began to enhance the vision already established in this unique slickrock setting.

The expanded facility, now known as the Franklin Quest Institute of Fitness, includes lodging facilities, workout areas, indoor and outdoor pools, lecture halls, dining areas and trails leading to the hiking and climbing options of adjacent Snow Canyon State Park. The center is characterized by attractive Southwest-style stucco buildings, fountains and rock gardens.

"We see miracles happening here all the time," says FQIF marketing director Ron Johnson. "People visit Franklin Quest from every part of the country and from around the world. They come from all imaginable backgrounds and with varying physical goals. Some come because they want to lose weight, some because they want to change their lifestyle and some because they've tried everything else and still haven't found the answer."

The institute helps guests learn proper nu-

INSIDERS' TIP

If you're planning to move to Southwestern Utah, it's a good idea to establish contact or even appointments with a family physician well in advance of your arrival.

trition in lectures and classes on cooking, grocery shopping, mind-body attitudes, time management and disease prevention. They eat nutritious meals, work on state-of-the-art cardiovascular and weight-training equipment, swim in refreshing pools, attend water and step aerobics classes, participate in sessions of "spinning" on Schwinn equipment, play racquetball and tennis and relax in soothing whirlpools.

But for most, says Johnson, the true life change comes as they put on their walking shoes and venture up the road through Snow Canyon State Park. Among the vertical towers of rust-red sandstone guests "get out and move." They discover that their health and well-being are not attached to the numbers they read on the scale every morning but to their ability to walk from one point to another; their desire to climb to the top of a ridge; their joy in running a distance they've never reached before.

Guests can select accommodations ranging in price from $695 to about $1,500 a week. It is suggested you make reservations six months in advance.

Education and the arts
have always been a
priority in the small
communities of
Southwestern Utah.

Education

Upon arrival in the valleys of Southwestern Utah, the pioneer settlers immediately began to build schools. Education and the arts have always been a priority in the small communities of the region, and first-rate teachers are in abundant supply due to the desirability of living here. This chapter offers an overview of the public schools in the region and shares some of the private school options. You will note there are few private schools in the area, as there has traditionally been little demand for private education here. We also introduce you to the excellent higher education opportunities in our corner of the state.

Public Schools

About 98 percent of kindergarten through 12th-grade students in Southwestern Utah attend public schools. Historically, there has been a strong trust between citizens and their school districts in the region, hence, few private schools. Each of the four counties has a school district governed by a locally elected school board. They have excellent elementary, middle and high schools, but the growing population of the area, especially in Washington County, is stretching funds and resources to the limit. Some schools have gone to year-round operation with intermittent track-on and track-off periods (explained in more detail in the Washington County School District section below) in order to more efficiently use facilities. Yet the schools are well-maintained, the teachers are highly qualified and motivated and the results are competent kids prepared to enter college.

Washington County School District
189 West Tabernacle, St. George
• **673-3553**

This is one of the fastest growing school systems in the state, accounting for nearly one-third of the total student growth in the state of Utah. With more than 18,000 students in 1996, the district has grown by 31 percent since 1991. Such monumental change in a relatively short time has challenged the district to keep up with funding and space needs. Yet the schools in Washington County are among the best in the state, and students consistently score on par or higher than state and national averages on standardized tests. As one administrator puts it, "We've learned how to get better results with less money here."

The teacher pool is very deep in Washington County, so there has been no problem hiring a sufficient number of qualified teachers. The district has dealt with the system's explosive growth in part by instituting year-round school in most of its elementaries. On this track system, the school year is broken down into four "tracks" that determine the time frames students will spend in school. Students have the option of selecting their track or taking the track chosen for them by computer. School begins in late July for tracks A, B and C, and mid-August for track D. Throughout the school year, ending in early June for track A and early July for tracks B, C and D, students are "on track" (in school) for several weeks then "off track" (on break) for two to three weeks four times during the year. This system allows the district to get 25 percent more use from its buildings.

Along with its space-stretching efforts, the district continues a vigorous construction program with new schools popping up across the Southwestern Utah landscape. A bond issue recently approved by county voters will provide $70 million for new schools and additions during the next six years. This comes on the heels of a $33 million bond approved in 1994. Because of growth in the tax base, these large bonds have not raised residents' taxes. Among the construction projects planned are a new 6th grade center in St. George ($4.8 million), Diamond Valley Elementary ($3.2 million), a $2.5 million renovation at Enterprise Elementary School and a fourth high school for the St. George area projected for completion in the year 2001 at a cost of $26 million.

There are nine year-round elementary schools in Washington County including Woodward, which is exclusively for 6th graders in the greater St. George area. Seven non-year-round elementary schools serve the county. Secondary schools in the district include Dixie, Pine View, Snow Canyon and Hurricane middle schools and high schools, plus Enterprise High School. The district also has an alternative high school, Mill Creek, for students in grades 10-12 who, for whatever reason, don't fit the mold of a traditional high school. It is a school with a history of success stories.

Iron County School District
75 N. 300 West, Cedar City • 586-2804

With more than 6,500 students, the Iron County School District operates 11 schools. Iron County students are offered many opportunities to stretch their learning abilities. The elementary schools practice a philosophy of individualized education, encouraging students with particular gifts or talents to develop them under the guidance of the teacher in small groups called cooperative learning

FYI

Unless otherwise noted, the area code for all phone numbers listed in this chapter is 801 but will change to 435 in September 1997. Either area code may be used until March 22, 1998.

teams. Due to the area's rapid growth, the student-teacher ratio in Iron County public schools varies from 24-to-1 to 30-to-1. While class size remains a concern for officials and the ratio is admittedly higher than desirous, no significant impact on student performance has been shown.

High school students can earn university credit through a variety of Advanced Placement courses. Iron County also cooperates with Southern Utah University and Utah State University to provide secondary school students the opportunity to take college-level classes while in high school. Students in 5th, 8th and 11th grades throughout the district take the Stanford achievement test and traditionally score above national norms. Many specialized programs are available in the district including vocational education, special education, Youth In Custody, Students at Risk, Chapter One and adult education.

There are four elementary schools in Cedar City (East, South, North and Fiddlers), each with 400 to 600 students in grades K-5. The town of Enoch, just northwest of Cedar City, has Enoch Elementary (K-5) with 425 students. To the north, Parowan Elementary (K-6) has 400 kids, and Escalante Valley Elementary (K-6) has more than 100 students. Cross Hollows Intermediate School in Cedar City serves

Old Sorrel

The 1897 enabling legislation creating what is now Southern Utah University provided funding for the first year of instruction but appropriated nothing for construction of a building where that instruction could occur. In a Herculean effort, the

townspeople came together and built the building with their own hands and their own meager resources. In order to pull it off, they sent brave crews into the mountains east of town to obtain lumber. The first group set out with wagons during the winter and were forced back by deep snow drifts. They would have never made it out alive and the school might never have been built if it hadn't been for the legendary horse "Old Sorrel" who pushed and strained through the drifts, opening the way for their safe return. A majestic statue of the horse stands on the SUU campus today.

Photo: Courtesy Dixie College

Dixie College graduates march during commencement exercises.

nearly 900 of the area's 6th and 7th graders, and another 900 students in 8th and 9th grades attend Cedar Middle School.

Cedar High School has an enrollment of close to 1,300, and smaller Parowan High School (7-12) has about 450 students. Iron County Adult High School has a varying enrollment of about 30 students. This program allows working adults to finish their high school requirements at night to earn diplomas.

Kane County School District
746 S. Constitution Dr., Kanab • 644-2555

Just because a school district is small and remote doesn't mean it can't give its students a full and rewarding education. Kane County is an excellent example.

Physically, the schools in Kane County are isolated by canyons, mountains and deserts,

but technologically, they are connected with the world. The Kane County School District utilizes a combination of traditional classroom-teacher education and "Utah Link," which connects the schools with Ed Net through the University of Utah.

Through this Internet service, students in such remote places as Bullfrog and Big Water are offered the same educational resources as students in the larger cities. Consistent scores in the 70s on the Stanford Achievement Test point to the fact that Kane County students are getting an above-average education. With student-teacher ratios at about 21-to-1, Kane County puts a high priority on smaller class sizes.

The district serves about 1,500 students in a wide geographical area stretching from Bullfrog Marina on the northern end of Lake Powell to the town of Big Water at the southern end. District offices are in the county seat of Kanab. Kanab Elementary School, at 41 W. 100 North, has nearly 400 students, and 220 students attend Kanab Middle School at 190 East Center Street. Kanab High School, with a long tradition of athletic prowess, is at 59 E. Red Shadow Lane and has about 350 students.

North of Kanab, in the small town of Orderville, is Valley Elementary School with 180 students. Valley High School in Orderville has nearly 200 students. To the east of Kanab, near the shores of Lake Powell, Big Water School (K-12) serves about 75 students. Well to the north at Lake Powell, near the Bullfrog Marina, is Lake Powell School with about 50 students in grades K through 12.

Garfield County School District
145 East Center, Panguitch • 676-8821

What this school district might lack in size and fancy programs, it more than makes up for in personal attention and small class sizes. Student-teacher ratios in Garfield County run about 20-to-1.

Community support for the schools in Garfield County is high and is illustrated by strong volunteer involvement in classrooms on a daily basis. The curricula in these remote communities are not elaborate, but technology keeps Garfield County students in touch with the rest of the world through the Internet. Standardized test scores indicate that the old-fashioned, basic approach to reading, writing and math still produces excellent results.

Though it's one of the smallest school districts in the state, Garfield County's schools are found in some of the most beautiful settings in the world. From Boulder to Bryce Valley, from Escalante to Panguitch, you'd be hard-pressed to find more beautiful country per capita. This has always been a somewhat isolated area as far as permanent residency, yet the county annually plays host to millions of visitors during tourist season. Meanwhile, Garfield County's

small schools continue to educate the children of families who earn their livelihoods serving those tourists or operating farms and ranches that have existed here for six generations.

District offices are in the county seat of Panguitch where you'll find Panguitch Elementary School (K-6) with about 300 students, Panguitch Middle School with about 100 7th and 8th graders, and Panguitch High School with more than 200 students. Antimony Elementary School, in the beautiful mountain town of Antimony, has about 25 students in grades K-6. In the scenic town of Boulder is Boulder Elementary with about 30 students. Bryce Valley Elementary/High School, in full view of Bryce Canyon National Park in the little town of Tropic, serves about 250 students in grades K-12. Up in the farming and ranching town of Escalante are Escalante Elementary (K-6) with about 120 students, and Escalante High School with about 150 students.

Private Schools

Cedar Hills Christian School
81 N. 200 West, Cedar City • 586-0233

This multicultural school is housed in a beautifully restored historic home near the Southern Utah University campus in Cedar City. With about 40 students and four faculty members, the student-teacher ratio here is probably as low as you'll find anywhere in Southwestern Utah. The school offers instruction for children from preschool age to grade 12. Cedar Hills is non-denominational, prides itself on the variety of cultures represented by its students — they come from various ethnic and religious backgrounds. There's an emphasis here on classical education with a great deal of importance placed on the fine arts, humanities, history, and world literature, in addition to the standard subjects necessary to prepare students for college. This is the

---

INSIDERS' TIP

The Shakespearean Festival in Cedar City isn't all about entertainment. Every morning during the summer season, educational lectures and discussions are held beneath the trees on the festival grounds. You don't even need tickets.

only school in Southwestern Utah where uniforms are required and the only area private school that participates in the national Academic Decathlon. The school is funded entirely by tuition and private donations.

Montessori Elementary of St. George

1125 E. 700 South, St. George • 652-9200

St. George now has a complete Montessori elementary school with two trained and certified Montessori elementary teachers serving grades K-6, as well as a physical education and a sign language teacher. Currently, the school has reached capacity with 47 students. But there is an active waiting list, and the school will be expanding with more space and more certified teachers during the next few years. The school embraces the full Montessori curriculum, using tangible materials to introduce every aspect of study. The education of each child is self-directed and self-motivated. The school has grown in popularity in its short time here and should soon be in a better position to meet a growing demand.

Trinity Lutheran School

2260 E. Red Cliff Dr., St. George
• 628-1850

Serving grades 1-6, with a maximum student-teacher ratio of 20-to-1, Trinity Lutheran School is one of the few alternatives to public education in St. George. The school has certified teachers and is based on the curriculum guides for Lutheran elementary schools and the core curriculum guides for the state of Utah. There is a full-day kindergarten program. Subjects taught include religion, reading (a phonetic and whole language-based approach), printing and cursive writing, spelling, English grammar and composition, math, social studies, science and healthy lifestyles, music, art, physical education and computer education. Parents are asked to assist as volunteers in the classroom, and communication between home and school is a priority.

Tuacahn Center for the Arts

1100 Tuacahn Dr., Ivins • 652-3201

Beneath towering red sandstone cliffs about 12 miles from downtown St. George, Tuacahn Center for the Arts was established in 1994 to meet the growing need in Southwestern Utah for individual instruction in music, dance, drama and art. Students of any age can enroll for private instruction in violin, piano, guitar, brass, wind and other instruments. There are also classes in ballet, acting and voice. The school operates under a nonprofit foundation and employs some of the best-qualified teachers in Southwestern Utah. Kids in the St. George area can catch the Tuacahn shuttle after school for a ride to the school's remote setting, then they're returned to shuttle stops throughout the St. George area after their lessons.

Colleges and Universities

Southern Utah University
351 West Center St., Cedar City • 586-7741

In the middle of downtown Cedar City, Southern Utah University is the cornerstone of education in Southwestern Utah. Founded in 1897, the institution prides itself on the individual attention its students receive. With just 5,000 students, this is a comprehensive regional university with programs in more than 80 fields of study. In spite of its low student-faculty ratio, SUU is the most affordable university in the state for Utah residents.

SUU offers associate, pre-professional, bachelor and graduate degrees. Its education, science, business, theater arts and literature programs are highly regarded throughout the country, and it is home to the nationally famous Utah Shakespearean Festival, the American Folk Ballet and the Utah Summer Games. The school's new graduate program in education serves more than 300 students. Business students scored in the 99th percentile in the 1996 national field exam for business students, and SUU students have recently won national honors in theater, electronics, television production, dance, debate and law enforcement.

Set on a 112-acre campus of open lawns

FYI

Unless otherwise noted, the area code for all phone numbers listed in this chapter is 801 but will change to 435 in September 1997. Either area code may be used until March 22, 1998.

and pine trees, SUU's buildings range from the traditional, three-story, brick "Old Main" to the new, state-of-the-art, 80,000-square-foot library. At the center of campus is one of the most faithful reproductions of a Shakespearean Elizabethan theater found anywhere in the world. Because Cedar City is set at the base of the southern Wasatch Mountains, you enjoy four distinct seasons at SUU — colorful autumns, white winters (Brian Head Ski Resort is less than an hour away), bright green springtimes as the leaves return to the trees and warm summers just minutes away from national parks, monuments and forests.

There's an active life outside the classroom at SUU including more than 50 recognized clubs, a variety of planned excursions, student productions, a dynamic lecture series and a full range of intramural sports. The Thunderbirds of SUU have recently become affiliated with NCAA Division I-AA in varsity athletics. The school fields strong teams in most collegiate sports for men and women. Scholarships are offered for academics, athletics and leadership. There's financial assistance through Pell/SEOG and other grants, as well as student loans and work study.

Dixie College
225 S. 700 East, St. George • 652-7500

People who attend Dixie College invariably

Dixie Spirit

Dixie College alumni have a hard time explaining it, but they will swear to you it is real. They call it the "Dixie Spirit," and they claim the only way to truly understand it is to go to Dixie yourself. From its beginnings it is said the school has exuded an almost palpable pride and spirit. Maybe it started the night before the original Dixie Academy opened in September of 1911. On that night, legend has it a young man named Sam Brooks slept on the steps of the new institution of higher learning. He wasn't in line to buy tickets to a rock concert or a football game. He simply wanted to be the first student ever to register at Dixie College.

come away with something they call the "Dixie Spirit." It's a feeling of belonging engendered by this small community college and tied to its storied past, its loyal faculty, the temperate desert climate and the scenic surroundings. Whether you believe in the spirit or not, it's hard not to admire this two-year institution where 25 of the 75 full-time professors hold Ph.D.s, and many have extensive university teaching credentials.

With a history dating to 1911, Dixie College is one of St. George's most solid and important institutions. As a full-service, comprehensive community college, Dixie is not only the academic heart of Utah's Dixie region but also serves as the nucleus of area culture and entertainment. The school offers associate of arts, associate of science and associate of applied science degrees and certificates in vocational and technical fields.

More than 5,100 students attend Dixie, where a general education program is offered along with specialties in the sciences, pre-professional fields, fine arts, liberal arts and humanities, business and technology, family and consumer sciences and athletics. Bachelor's and master's degree programs are offered in association with Southern Utah University, Weber University and others. Vocational programs at the school include FAA-approved aviation programs, and automotive and graphic arts courses. Studies in music, theater arts and the humanities are taught by professors such as Ace Pilkington, an Oxford-educated and

Photo: Courtesy Southern Utah University

About 5,000 students attend Southern Utah University in Cedar City.

internationally recognized Shakespearean scholar.

In 1996, for the third year in a row, Dixie College led all other Utah institutions of higher education in growth. Once known as a laid-back school where students came to get a suntan and hike the slickrock, Dixie is now one of the top two-year institutions in America, based on consistent gold, silver and bronze medal awards bestowed at national junior college forensics, business and science competitions. Dixie grads qualify for universities and professional schools across the country.

Dixie is the clearinghouse for many of St. George's finest cultural and entertainment events, many of which are held on campus at the Dixie Center. The Celebrity Concert Series and the Southwest Symphony are produced by the school (see our Arts and Culture chapter). And the college is a perennial powerhouse in National Junior College Athletic Association sports. The men's basketball team won a national championship in 1985. The college provides a variety of programs for visitors to the area, and the campus runs one of the most active and sought-after Elderhostel programs in the country. It is also affiliated with the Sun Desert Golf Academy, the Discover Utah Travel Program and the Vic Braden Tennis College at Green Valley.

Mohave Community College - North Mohave Center

480 South Central, Colorado City, Ariz. • (520) 875-2799

About 40 miles southeast of St. George in Colorado City, Arizona, the North Mohave Center of Mohave Community College (headquartered in Kingman, Arizona, on the south side of the Grand Canyon) serves approximately 350 students in Southwestern Utah and Northern Arizona. While most of the college's enrollment is in Kingman, Lake Havasu City, and Bullhead City, Arizona, the North Mohave Center adds another educational option for Southwestern Utahns. Permanent facilities were constructed at Colorado City in 1992, including classrooms, a bookstore, a library, administrative offices, nursing lab and an instructional television center.

The school's largest program is in nursing, where students can earn both LPN and RN designations. Also popular is the basic liberal arts transfer degree, which students typically use to transfer to Southern Utah University or Northern Arizona University. Residents of Washington and Kane counties in Utah receive a "good neighbor" out-of-state tuition break.

Community and Continuing Education

Community Education

225 S. 700 East, St. George • 652-7671

Through the collaborative efforts of Dixie College, the City of St. George and the Washington County School District, community members have use of the public schools after school hours for a full range of educational opportunities. The community education program offers a variety of noncredit enrichment classes to all ages of the general public. Participants can select classes and activities including foreign languages, scouting merit badges, foods, dance, the arts and computers. The program is self-supporting through moderate tuition charges. Offerings are listed quarterly in the community education brochure.

Institute For Continued Learning

225 S. 700 East, St. George • 652-7670

Conceived, developed and directed by retirees in Southwestern Utah, the Institute for Continued Learning has functioned for nearly 20 years as a fully chartered club on the Dixie College campus. It provides a productive outlet for retirees and semi-retirees to continue their love for learning. There are study groups, socials and various activities in classes such as Spanish, geology, American government, dance, law, art, French, photography, music, Shakespeare, history, psychology, bridge, botany, T'ai Chi and many other subjects. Members also take educational field trips. Classes are offered in fall, winter and spring quarters, and the program is financed through annual membership dues.

In Utah, 63.5 percent of mothers are active in the work force — more than the national average of 58.8 percent.

Child Care

Beyond beautiful scenery, national parks and clear blue skies, Southwestern Utah is probably best-known for its explosive population growth. This has come about due to an unprecedented in-migration of new residents in recent years and a birth rate well above the national average.

In one of the nation's fastest-growing states, the Cedar City area had a growth rate of 20.6 percent between 1990 and 1994. In St. George the numbers totalled a staggering 26.1 percent growth in the same time period.

Compounding the issue is the fact that Utah owned the highest birth rate in the United States as of 1995. At 20.3 live births per 1,000 population, Utah was significantly above the national average of 14.8 and substantially ahead of the No. 2 state — California, at 17.8 births per 1,000. Texas (17.5), neighboring Arizona (17.2) and Alaska (17.0) rounded out the top five.

In terms of actual babies born, the statistic added up to the arrival of 39,556 new Utahns in 1995. Add to the mix the fact that 63.5 percent of Utah mothers are in the work force, a number higher than the national average of 58.8 percent. Statistics also show 30.5 percent of Utah men — traditionally the family breadwinner — earn below the poverty level for a family of four, making it virtually impossible for Utah moms to stay home with the kids.

The result is a child-care crisis in some areas. With both parents often working, parents in the more remote areas of Southwestern Utah may depend on family, friends and neighbors to ensure the safety and well-being of their kids. But in high growth areas such as St. George and Cedar City, there is also a good variety of child-care services. Choices include family child-care homes, licensed child-care centers and an assortment of recreational and educational programs.

Finding Quality Care

A good telephone interview can save you time, energy and worry in your search for child care. If you like what you hear on the phone with the provider, schedule an appointment during business hours and conduct your own on-site evaluation.

Ask some or all of the following questions: How many children are you licensed to care for? How many children will be in my child's class? How long have you been in business? What is your background and training? What recent continuing education classes have you taken? What is your daily schedule for the children? Do fees include lunches, snacks or field trips? Are parents free to make impromptu visits?

Remember, you can't be too cautious. Here are a few more inquiries: What is your policy for sick children? Do you hire a qualified substitute when you are on vacation? How much and what television programs are the children allowed to watch? What is the ratio of care providers to children? Do you have current CPR and first-aid certification? Will you provide me with a list of references?

The **Five County Childcare Resource Center** is available to assist parents in their search for quality child care in Southwestern Utah. The staff will refer parents to child-care agencies and provide tips and information about options, but does not make recommendations. This agency is housed in the Five County Association of Governments office and is funded by the Utah Office of Childcare, which has locations in St. George and Cedar City. For more information, call Five County Childcare Resource Center at 628-4843 in St. George or 586-8722 in Cedar City.

For an area as kid-friendly as Southwestern Utah, there are still surprisingly few officially organized alternatives to traditional child care. As of this writing there are no bonded babysitting services, sick-child options or church-affiliated child-care centers. The nearest nanny services are based in Salt Lake City. Five County Childcare Resource Center offers packets providing information on how to write a classified ad and conduct an interview for a nanny, but officials say they don't get many takers.

Child-Care Centers

There are several traditional, full-day child-care centers in the Southwestern Utah area caring for more than 12 children in a group. They are usually housed in community buildings or facilities designed and built for child care. They may serve infants and toddlers, preschool or school-age children. Most full-day programs are required to be licensed by the Utah Office of Licensing. Centers exempt from licensure are church-operated programs (again, there are currently none of those in our area) or those groups operated by the Utah Board of Education.

FYI

Unless otherwise noted, the area code for all phone numbers listed in this chapter is 801 but will change to 435 in September 1997. Either area code may be used until March 22, 1998.

St. George/Zion

The largest community in Southwestern Utah also has the broadest choice for child-care services. There are approximately 10 child-care centers in the St. George area that are licensed by the state. Contact Five County Childcare Resource Center for more information.

An option that, not surprisingly, has caught on here in neighborly Southwestern Utah has individual parents — usually stay-at-home moms — obtaining official licenses to care for children in their homes. Most everyone in this area knows someone willing to take in an extra child for a few hours a day, and the number of those licensed to do so in their homes around St. George now exceeds 75.

For the after-school crowd (8 and up) or "trackers" on year-round school schedules (see our Education chapter), **St. George Leisure Services** provides free play from early morning until after 9 PM every day except Sun-

day and major holidays. In the recreation center at 285 South 400 East in St. George, kids can play basketball, pinball or a choice of board games, do homework or watch television, all with limited supervision. St. George Leisure Services also offers an interesting curriculum of free or low-cost classes for summertime, after school and off-track times (see our Kidstuff chapter).

Cedar City/Brian Head

In the Cedar City area, there are only three licensed child-care centers, but about three dozen people have gone through the process to become licensed child-care providers and now offer that service in their homes. Again, Five County Childcare Resource Center will help you with information to find an option to meet your needs.

During the school year, home economics and education students at Southern Utah University in Cedar City participate as providers for children ages 6 weeks to 5 years in the university-sponsored child-care center. University students interact with the children under the supervision and tutelage of faculty instructors. The center at 43 South 200 West is used primarily by SUU faculty and students but offers services to the general public as well. The cost is $2 an hour for children younger than 2; $1.75 an hour for those older than 2.

From late June to early September, during the summer run of the Utah Shakespearean Festival, the same SUU center becomes a convenient child-care option for visitors in town to enjoy the plays. During all performances (but not during the Royal Feaste or other festival activities), the facility is professionally staffed by child-care providers. Cost is $7 for children up to age 10. Remember, no one younger than 5 is admitted to festival performances (see more information on the festival under June listings in our Annual Events chapter).

At Brian Head Ski Resort, the Children's Center (677-2036) is open during the regular ski season. From November through April the center accepts drop-in, non-skiing children

Photo: The Spectrum

In the '90s, Utah has led the nation in births per capita.

from 6 weeks to 8 years who are with families who want to spend a carefree day on the slopes. In addition to regular day care, the center also provides ski lessons. Ski school students range in age from 3 to 12. Reservations are recommended for the ski school.

Bryce Canyon, Kanab areas

In these remote areas, there are no state-licensed child-care centers currently operat-

ing. The best way to find stay-at-home people willing to take in an extra little person is simply to ask around. You will find most locals willing to help. Another option is to place a classified advertisement in either the *Garfield County News* or the *Southern Utah News* (see our Media chapter).

Southwestern Utah
is served by affiliates
of all the major
television networks.

Media

The media in Southwestern Utah consists mainly of one major daily newspaper, a number of community weeklies, a couple of locally published magazines, radio to meet nearly every musical preference and some brave attempts at hometown television.

Larger daily newspapers are available for home delivery and are particularly popular with people who have recently relocated from nearby metro areas. Salt Lake City's 62,000-circulation *Deseret News* and 130,000-circulation *Salt Lake Tribune*, and the 150,000-circulation *Las Vegas Review-Journal* are both available in Southwestern Utah with same-day delivery through local vendors.

Southwestern Utah is served by affiliates of all the major television networks including Fox and WB. In fact, in some parts of the region NBC programming can be received from Salt Lake City during one time period then seen again two hours later out of Las Vegas.

Newspapers

The Spectrum
275 E. St. George Blvd., St. George
• 674-6200

Perhaps the single strongest media presence in Southwestern Utah is *The Spectrum*. With editorial and advertising staffs in St. George and Cedar City, the region's only daily is distributed to 22,000 households in counties throughout Southwestern Utah and parts of Arizona and Nevada.

From its beginnings as a small, family-owned weekly shopper to today's status as a seven-day, full-color newspaper, *The Spectrum* has received recognition statewide and regionally for excellence in journalism. In 1996, the newspaper earned multiple honors from the Utah-Idaho-Spokane Associated Press Association including a first-place sports column, a first-place in feature photography and out-standing editorial achievement for non-deadline writing. The Utah Chapter of the American Planning Association also honored *The Spectrum* in 1996 for Outstanding Achievement in Journalism. *The Spectrum* also has been honored for outstanding achievement in photography and design by their parent company, Thomson Newspapers Inc., which owns more than 85 daily newspapers in North America.

The Spectrum reports daily on local, regional, statewide, national and international events. Covering a five-county area, the newspaper management is an active supporter of community activities and organizations. Their editorial position "to call them as we see them" has, at various times, endeared them to and infuriated the growing population they serve.

Senior Sampler
560 S. Valley View Dr., St. George
• 673-7604

Senior Sampler is distributed free from more than 50 pickup points in and around the St. George area, where seniors account for more than 15 percent of the general population. For those who prefer to get the paper in their mailbox, it is available for home delivery. *Senior Sampler* is published by St. George-based Merrick and Manstreet. Community news, topics of interest to seniors and advertising directed to this market are included in this weekly, which averages eight to 12 pages.

Garfield County News
120 N. Main St., Tropic • 679-8730

In the Bryce Canyon area, the *Garfield County News* has a total weekly distribution of 2,000 papers through mail subscription and over-the-counter sales. Its comprehensive coverage of county news includes happenings at Bryce Canyon National Park and updates on the newly created Grand Staircase-Escalante National Monument.

Iron County Bulletin
314 S. 100 West, Cedar City • 867-0304

The *Iron County Bulletin* is the newest entry into the race to provide up-to-the-minute information in this growing area. Published twice a month by the Vietnam Veterans Protection Association, a nonprofit corporation, the paper is distributed free from a variety of locations. The aim? Keeping up with what's going on in the various Iron County towns. The *Bulletin* currently has a circulation of about 5,000.

Southern Utah News
26 N. Main St., Kanab
• 644-2900

The weekly *Southern Utah News* is published each Wednesday for readers in the Kanab area. Delivered by mail to subscribers with additional distribution points around the Kanab area, the *Southern Utah News* has a total distribution of about 2,800. The paper covers the news from Lake Powell to Zion National Park.

Magazines

St. George Magazine
165 N. 100 East, St. George • 673-6333

St. George Magazine celebrates life in Utah's "color country" by reflecting the flavors, excitement and spirit of this unique region. The magazine's 14-year tradition of fresh, lively writing, coupled with bold, handsome and colorful graphics, has created a solid reputation for quality publishing not generally found in markets of comparable size. The magazine includes articles on people, homes, lifestyles, things to do, history, real estate, recreation, education, commerce and nostalgia. The magazine's goal is to chronicle the people who have lived here all their lives, to serve as a sounding board for those who have recently

moved here and to act as the area's ambassador to the world.

totalhealth
165 N. 100 East, St. George • 673-1789

For more than 18 years, *totalhealth* has been reporting on the world of natural health and alternative medicine — from the basics to the cutting edge. *totalhealth* examines the rudiments of nutrition, exercise, attitude and how the body, mind and spirit interact. It also chronicles the quantum leaps in information on how to live healthy and combat the problems of aging. Each issue offers a profile of the numerous atypical approaches to healthcare such as acupuncture, acupressure, homeopathy, Ayurveda, aromatherapy, herbal therapy, nutrition and fitness.

Mainstreet Business Journal
560 S. Valley View Dr., St. George
• 656-1525, (800) 409-7515

The *Mainstreet Business Journal* offers the small business owner an up-to-the-minute information edge. A weekly tabloid, the *Journal* addresses issues such as local economic development, the labor pool, area politics and government, banking and business, taxes, cash-flow management, sales techniques and computer applications. Like its sister publication *Senior Sampler*, the *Mainstreet Business Journal* is distributed free of charge at numerous pickup points throughout the area. Subscriptions are also available.

Television

In most Southwestern Utah communities, television reception is mediocre at best, with limited programming choices across the old-fashioned airways. Cable offers a nice clear picture and a variety of good program options,

---

FYI

Unless otherwise noted, the area code for all phone numbers listed in this chapter is 801 but will change to 435 in September 1997. Either area code may be used until March 22, 1998.

Photo: The Spectrum

Perhaps the single strongest media presence in Southwestern Utah, The Spectrum brings full-color local, regional, national and worldwide news into 22,000 households daily.

including reception of all the major networks (some from Salt Lake City and from Las Vegas), sports channels and superstations you would expect. Outside of those folks using direct-broadcast satellite systems, you'll find that most everyone is hooked up to cable.

The following listings are for the few broadcast options that originate from within our four-county area. Residents in the communities of Brian Head, Enoch, Panguitch and Parowan can arrange cable hookup by calling **Premiere Cable II Ltd.**, (800) 451-3029. Panguitch viewers have a second choice in **Southwest**

Cablevision, 676-2420. Cedar City's cable provider is **Insight Communications**, 586-7655. In the community of Enterprise, outside St. George, cable is provided by **Enterprise Cable TV**, 878-2455.

St. George and surrounding communities have several options including **Clear Vision Cable Services**, 674-2212, **Sky View Technologies**, 674-0320, or **Falcon Cable TV**, 628-3681. Kanab television watchers access their viewing options through **TCI Cablevision of Utah** at (800) 924-7662.

St. George/Zion

KSGI-TV
210 N. 1000 East, St. George • 628-1000

KSGI-TV is an independent "traditional family values" station broadcast on various channels of area cable systems. Viewers are assured family-oriented programming including local news, weather, syndicated shows and movies that are kid-friendly. KSGI, owned by Seagull Communications Corporation, is a strong supporter of local high school and college football, basketball and baseball. The station complements area sports coverage with regional and national games from the PAC-10 and Big West conferences and Colorado Rockies baseball.

MB Broadcasting
251 W. Hilton Dr., Ste. 200, St. George • 628-0484

MB Broadcasting provides local access for commercials and programs on KDLQ-Fox 13. It also offers advertising access on Clear Vision and Sky View cable systems. MB's nightly news provides five daily broadcasts of *Southern Utah News* on Clear Vision Cable Channel 19 along with *Dixie Commentary*, a 30-minute local talk show (also aired on Fox 13) featuring the area's most interesting people, places and events. The MB news updates are also aired five times daily on NBC3-LV.

Cedar City/Brian Head

CTV-12
86 W. Harding Ave., Cedar City • 586-5144

Cable channel CTV-12 is Southwestern Utah's local information source providing evening newscasts, weather updates and ski and road conditions. CTV-12 reaches 50,000 viewers through various cable companies. It is shown on Channel 10 in Parowan, Channel 23 in Enoch, Channel 12 in Cedar City and Channel 15 in St. George. Local programming includes "Talk of the Town" with in-studio interviews with area business leaders and personalities. "Showplace" gives businesses and events five-minute segments of on-location coverage. Area businesses can also contact CTV-12 for local advertising opportunities on CNN, TNT, ESPN and USA.

Kanab Area

K12ND-TV
325 N. 100 West, Kanab • 644-2561

K12ND provides community TV for residents of Kanab, Utah and Fredonia, Arizona — sister cities on opposite sides of the state line. Programming on the low-power, VHF transmission station includes local origination talk shows, city council meetings, high school sports and public service announcements, a weather display and an on-air bulletin board for business and events advertising.

Radio

In this high desert region, there are places along some interstates and highways where a clear FM radio signal from anywhere is nearly impossible to pick up. But on dark, clear nights, stations from as far away as Los Angeles to the south, Laramie, Wyoming, to the north and Denver to the east are windows on the world and voices in the darkness.

In and around St. George or Cedar City, there is a good mix of radio stations with a variety of format options. Several area stations combine styles and provide news and sports programming. Here's a rundown on what's out there, listed by format.

INSIDERS' TIP

More than 70 percent of the folks in Southwestern Utah are members of the Church of Jesus Christ of Latter-day Saints, more commonly known as the Mormon church or the LDS church. While the nickname "Mormon" was once considered derogatory, it is now widely used and acceptable.

Adult Contemporary

KCCA-107.1 FM • (520) 875-2222
KREC-98.1, 98.9 FM • 673-9812, 586-9893
KDXU-93.5 FM • 673-3579
KZEZ-99.7 FM • 628-1000

Country

KONY-FM 94.3, 103.1 • 628-3643
KSSD-FM: 102.3 in St. George and Panguitch, 92.1 in Kanab and 104.3 in the Bryce Canyon area.

News/Talk/Sports

KDXU-890 AM • 673-3579
KSGI-1450 AM • 628-1000
KSUB-590 AM • 674-0110, 586-5900

Oldies

KBRE-940 AM • 586-5273
KONY-1210 AM • 628-3643

Rock

KBRE-94.9 FM • 586-5273
KZHK-95.9 FM • 673-3579, 674-9959

For a place so steeped in one faith, Southwestern Utah has developed a healthy diversity of religious congregations.

Worship

It is no secret to anyone that when you come to Southwestern Utah, you come to Mormon country. In spite of the phenomenal influx of people from many religious backgrounds during the past 20 years, this corner of Utah is still predominantly Mormon. More than 70 percent of the population belongs to the Church of Jesus Christ of Latter-day Saints (LDS). The same holds true for the entire state, although the percentage is smaller in the Salt Lake City metropolitan area 325 miles to the north.

This is a reality visitors and new residents are going to face whether they're prepared for it or not. The culture and lifestyle of the Mormons are woven through the social fabric of Southwestern Utah. There is literally an LDS chapel in every neighborhood, and members of the church devote a significant portion of their time to religious worship and related social, recreational and service activities.

Yet for a place so steeped in one faith, Southwestern Utah has developed a healthy diversity of religious congregations. There was a time when it was difficult to live here and not be Mormon. While some feel it is still a challenge to be part of another denomination — especially for children, since Mormon kids are involved in so many social activities sponsored by their church — most non-Mormons we talk with say this isn't a major issue. Most say they've experienced a high degree of religious tolerance, and they can interact and enjoy close relationships with their Mormon neighbors regardless of differences in beliefs.

The Catholic Church has had a significant presence here since the days of mining at Silver Reef in the 1870s. The Presbyterian Church began missions and opened schools here as early as the 1880s. In recent years, the Episcopal Church has grown to the point that a beautiful new Southwest-style church has been built in St. George. Lutherans, Methodists, Baptists and non-denominational churches have established buildings and are drawing growing congregations throughout Southwestern Utah.

For those of us native to the area, it seems there have been great strides toward religious diversity in recent years, yet by most standards we still have a long way to go. There is no Jewish synagogue here, nor are any of the Middle Eastern or Oriental religions represented in Southwestern Utah.

As the area grows, more new churches and congregations will doubtlessly appear. At the same time, the LDS Church continues to grow, as a significant portion of those moving here are older Mormons who choose the area for retirement, or young Mormon families who see the area as an ideal place to raise children.

This chapter will give you an area-by-area overview of the many congregations and places of worship in Southwestern Utah. We start out, however, with a fairly detailed look at the LDS Church in general and its place in Southwestern Utah society. If you plan on visiting or moving here, understanding some of the church's theological linchpins and social functions will give you a good grounding as far as what to expect in your daily interaction with practicing Mormons. Bottom line — don't look for anything unusual.

More on Mormons

You will find few places in America where religion, history and culture are so inextricably entwined as in Utah. Nearly every community in the state, and certainly all those covered in this guide, was established as a result of colonization by the LDS Church.

Most of the communities began between 1847 and 1877, during Brigham Young's 30-year era as president of the church. Converts from the eastern seaboard, Canada, England and much of Europe and Scandinavia joined the church as a result of its early missionary efforts, then emigrated to the Valley of the Great Salt Lake. From there, many were selected to go on and settle more remote regions such as Southwestern Utah. People were often handpicked according to trade — butchers, bakers, coopers, musicians, cobblers, etc. — so each town had its needs covered (see our History chapter). Places of worship were built, and communities such as St. George, Cedar City, Kanab and Panguitch were governed by local clergy called by the church's "general authorities" in Salt Lake City.

Until the federal government established a non-Mormon governor in Utah in 1858, the highest tiers of the LDS hierarchy basically served as the territorial government. Needless to say, the Mormon Church pervaded every aspect of life in Utah during the state's formative years, and it was difficult for other churches to gain a toehold here.

But it wasn't long before Catholics, Episcopalians and Presbyterians had established missions in Utah. Non-Mormon immigrants began to flow into Utah with the opening of the transcontinental railroad in 1869. Southwestern Utah got its first influx of non-Mormons in the 1880s with the opening of the mines at Silver Reef. Historic Catholic and Protestant cemeteries in this area (considered a ghost town, though some beautiful homes have been built at Silver Reef in recent years) attest to the diversity of faiths the mines brought to the area.

But it took decades for separation of church and state to become a reality in Utah. Some would say the separation still has not occurred.

In Public Affairs

Some feel the church exerts undue influence in Utah's state and local political affairs. While the church technically does not endorse candidates for political office, it does come out strongly on issues it deems moral rather than political. The church's influence has obviously had an effect on the unusual liquor laws in the state (see a complete rundown of liquor laws in our Nightlife chapter), and during a campaign a few years ago to legalize pari-mutuel betting at Utah race tracks, the church played a major role in defeating the movement. When an adult store selling pornographic materials opened just across the state line in Mesquite in 1993, the LDS church mobilized with other denominations in the area — Baptists, Catholics, Episcopalians, Presbyterians — and staged a round-the-clock picket line on public property near the shop until the business was forced to close.

The fact that most present-day mayors and city council members are Mormons is simply a fact of demographics. The governor of Utah, Michael Leavitt, is a great-grandson of Dudley Leavitt, one of the legendary pioneers of Southwestern Utah. St. George's mayor, Dan McArthur, is a great-grandson of Daniel D. McArthur, another area pioneer.

The Church and Private Life

Though Mormons live in the mainstream today, they are still peculiar in the eyes of many. Devout Mormons adhere to a strict code called the Word of Wisdom that prohibits the use of alcohol, tobacco, coffee, tea and illegal drugs. This does not mean moderate or social use — it means no use whatsoever. Mormons do believe in the use of medicine and prescription drugs. And while they have faith in the healing power of the laying on of hands by

FYI

Unless otherwise noted, the area code for all phone numbers listed in this chapter is 801 but will change to 435 in September 1997. Either area code may be used until March 22, 1998.

INSIDERS' TIP

Conversation about a stake house is often confusing to new or non-Utahns, who may not know that in the vernacular of the LDS Church, a "stake" is the organization of several wards or congregations. In this instance, it is not a place to enjoy a medium-rare cut of meat.

priesthood holders, they also believe that illness and disease should be treated by trained medical professionals. In fact, a current member of the church's Council of the Twelve Apostles is Dr. Russell M. Nelson, one of the world's most highly regarded heart surgeons.

Mormons are expected to adhere strictly to the Ten Commandments in the Old Testament. Sexual abstinence before marriage and complete fidelity within marriage are not only taught intensely, but also are important factors in maintaining full fellowship in the church. Sunday worship is paramount. This is why much of the commercial, recreational, cultural and social activity in Southwestern Utah shuts down on Sundays, though the trend has changed significantly in the last 20 years.

Mormons generally have larger families than the national norm. This is not a requirement, but their theology and culture emphasize the sanctity and importance of the family. Monday nights are set aside for "Family Home Evening" in Mormon homes. There is no official sanction against birth control in the church. In fact, the only counsel given in that regard is that wives should be willing to bear children, although a mother's health and well-being are the most important factors in determining family size.

The church's missionary program has extended to every part of the globe. At the age of 19, worthy male members of the church are expected to fulfill a two-year mission that could take them anywhere from Russia to Las Vegas. Young women who desire to serve a mission may also do so at the age of 21. Women do not hold the priesthood in the church, but many teach classes and administer in church auxiliaries. The church, which has grown to a membership of nearly 10 million as a result of its missionary program, has approximately 50,000 missionaries in the field.

The church embraced the Boy Scout program early this century and has since become the largest sponsor of Boy Scout troops in the world. At age 8, most Mormon boys begin Cub Scouts and continue on through the Boy Scout program. The church does not sponsor Girl Scouts per se, but it does operate a similar program for young women ages 12 to 18.

Members in good standing, including those who might be serving in positions requiring multiple hours of church-related duties every week, pay one-tenth of their income to the church as a tithing. These funds, administered by the church leadership in Salt Lake City, are used to sustain the church and to build new chapels and temples all over the world.

Places of Worship

St. George/Zion

In recent years, the St. George area has become much more diverse in religious denominations. In addition to the churches mentioned below, you will find a number of other

Singing From the Same Page

The ecumenical spirit existing in Southwestern Utah today was first made manifest in the 1880s when Father Lawrence Scanlan established a Catholic mission, chapel,  hospital and school in the mining town of Silver Reef, 15 miles northeast of St. George. Near Christmas one year John Macfarlane, a U.S. surveyor in Silver Reef and the Mormon choir director in St. George, heard that Father Scanlan was looking for a place to hold a high Mass. Macfarlane arranged for the Catholics to use the newly built LDS tabernacle in St. George, which would hold 2,000 people. The Mormon choir learned the Latin words and sang the Mass. The tabernacle was filled with both Catholics and Mormons. Father Scanlan later became the first Catholic bishop of the Salt Lake City Diocese.

Baptist congregations, a Methodist church and various other Christian churches. The handiest way to access addresses and phone numbers for local houses of worship is to check the Yellow Pages.

Presbyterian and Catholic churches were established in Southwestern Utah in the 1880s to serve the non-Mormons lured to the area by the mines at Silver Reef, 17 miles northeast of St. George. Presbyterian minister Arthur Cort conducted services and Sunday school in St. George in a home at 259 W. 200 North, where a small chapel was later built in 1901.

Before the chapel was built, a bell donated by friends of the church from the eastern United States was rigged on a scaffold and rung each week before Sunday school. It rang along with the town's Mormon bells when Utah gained statehood in 1896. When the Presbyterians finally got their building up in 1913, the bell was hung in the belfry, where it rang for many years for the Presbyterians and later for the Catholics who bought the building.

In 1913, Sarah Louisa Conklin, who had served as a Presbyterian missionary in South America, came to St. George to teach kindergarten and Sunday school and to serve as a community worker. She taught in the little church for 35 years, endearing herself to St. George Mormons as well as people of other faiths. Many Mormon youngsters got their initial education at the feet of this beloved Presbyterian teacher. When she died at age 89 in 1949, her body was placed for viewing in the little Presbyterian Church on 200 North, but funeral services were conducted by a Mormon bishop and were held in the Mormon's West Ward Chapel — the only place large enough to accommodate the huge turnout.

After Miss Conklin's death, the old church was vacant until 1951 when it was purchased by the Salt Lake City Diocese of the Catholic Church. In 1979 it was enlarged, and in 1983, the **St. George Parish of the Catholic Church** received its first full-time priest. The Rev. Paul S. Kuzy became pastor in 1984 and served until his death in spring 1997. The old church was razed in 1990 and replaced on the same site by a much larger and very impressive white stucco Spanish-style church in 1991.

Mass is conducted in both English and Spanish at the church at 259 W. 200 North, 673-2604, as well as in Springdale at the Zion Park Lodge on Sundays at 7 AM.

In 1986, a Presbyterian task force conducted a thorough study of the St. George area to explore the need for another mainline protestant church in the growing community. The Utah Presbytery and the Shared Ministry (a state level coalition of six protestant denominations) determined the time was right to go forward. The Rev. John Mahon came to St. George from Oregon and established the

Brigham Gets His Way

Although he was greatly pleased to have the St. George Temple completed while he was still alive, Mormon President Brigham Young was blatantly disappointed with the original tower placed on the building. The aging and ailing leader had watched much of the temple construction from his winter home in St. George, but upon completion of

the structure in 1877, just months before he died, Young voiced his displeasure of the short and squatty tower.

Locals liked the tower the way it was, and Young went to his grave before he could convince them to build a taller one. But, as was the case in most matters, Brother Brigham still got his way. On October 16, 1878, a terrible electrical storm hit St. George, and a lightning bolt struck the temple tower and dome. It became necessary to rebuild the upper structure of the temple, and in the process, the design was changed and a taller, more attractive tower and dome were built.

Photo: The Spectrum

The St. George Catholic Church is one of a growing number of denominations with faithful members in Southwestern Utah's traditionally Mormon country.

Good Shepherd Presbyterian Church in April of 1988. Mahon and his family have been modern-day pioneers in bringing religious diversity to St. George and in helping a predominantly Mormon community realize that regardless of religious beliefs, all members of a community can work together for the common good. In 1991, the Presbyterians built a beautiful new earth tone, Southwest-style stucco building at 611 N. 2450 East, 628-9158.

About 15 years ago, a handful of Episcopalian families began gathering in each oth-ers' homes for prayer meetings in St. George. Later the Utah Diocese began to send a supply priest from time to time to celebrate the Eucharist with Episcopalians in St. George and Cedar City. By the late 1980s, a full-time priest was living in St. George and conducting services in an office building. Today, **Grace Episcopal Church**, 1072 E. 900 South, 628-1181, is one of the most handsome buildings in St. George. It is a large, brown mission-style church with a bell tower and a meeting area large enough to accommodate 400 people.

The Rev. Mary Allen is vicar and has a congregation of more than 250 people. In addition to the many youth, social, outreach and support programs offered at the church, the facility is also often used as a community gathering place for concerts and other activities.

The **Christian Science Society** holds Sunday services at 373 S. 100 East, 628-3454. They also have a reading room in the Gardener's Club Hall at 4 Ancestor Square, at the corner of Main and St. George Boulevard. The hall is the oldest public building still standing in St. George. Built in the mid-1860s, this was a meeting place for horticulturists in pioneer St. George.

Trinity Lutheran Church and School are established in a fine facility visible from I-15 between St. George and Washington at 2260 E. Red Cliff Drive, 628-1850. The Rev. Mark E. Sell is pastor, and the Christian day school serves students in grades K-7 (see our Education chapter). The **First Southern Baptist Church** has been established for more than 30 years at 326 S. 600 East, 673-4511.

The **Church of Jesus Christ of Latter-day Saints** has more than 120 wards in the St. George/Zion area. One particular chapel visitors enjoy attending is at 449 S. 300 East, 673-2011, just across the street from the giant white temple in the middle of the St. George Valley. In Hurricane there are several chapels, including one at 677 S. 700 West, 635-4725. The chapel in Springdale is in the middle of town on Zion Park Boulevard, 772-3911.

Cedar City/Brian Head

Growth in the Cedar City/Brian Head area has increased the diversity of places of worship. In addition to the churches mentioned below, you'll find several other denominations represented.

The congregation at **Community Pres-byterian Church** in Cedar City began with the Presbyterian mission schools in Parowan and Cedar City established in the 1880s. W. C. Cort, a brother to Arthur Cort, mentioned above, came out from the Presbyterian Theological Seminary in Chicago and opened a school in Parowan. He also opened a school in Cedar City, but the one in Parowan proved more successful since there was less opposition by the Mormons to the Presbyterians there.

The Rev. Claton S. Rice arrived in Cedar City in 1913 and gained the support of local Mormons as he preached in the city's court house. A newspaperman, a plumber and two Swedish families who were sheep herders joined together to form his congregation. When the county library became available it served as a meeting place for five years. Some students and faculty from the Branch Teachers College (the forerunner to Southern Utah University) began to attend worship services.

In 1925, the Reverend Elmer P. Geiser came to Cedar City and began plans to build a Presbyterian church. Funds were raised and the building where Cedar City's present-day congregation meets (64 E. 200 North, 586-8891) was built in 1926. Fifty-one people were in the congregation when the church opened. It was supported by missions until the 1980s, when the congregation became self-supporting. Today, the Rev. Charles Jeffrey Garrison and those who worship at the Presbyterian church in Cedar City are planning to build a new church in Fiddler's Canyon in the northeast sector of the city.

Cedar City's **St. Judes Episcopal Church** is at 354 S. 100 West, 586-3623. **Christ the King Catholic Church** is at 70 N. 200 West, 586-8298. There is also mass at the reservation center for Brian Head Ski Resort, 356 S. Utah Highway 143, on Saturdays at 8 PM from Christmas to Easter.

INSIDERS' TIP

The best way to acquaint yourself with the Mormon Church in Southwestern Utah is to spend an hour or so in the LDS Visitor Center on the St. George Temple grounds at the corner of 300 East and 500 South, 673-5181. See more on the center in our Attractions chapter.

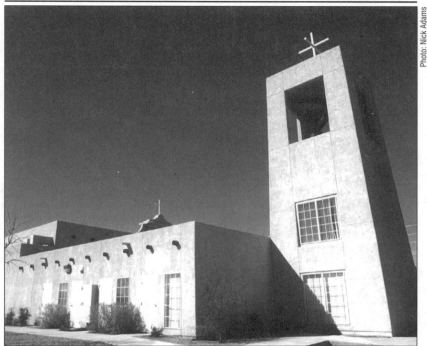

Photo: Nick Adams

The Grace Episcopal Church in St. George is one of 15 non-LDS congregations in Southwestern Utah's largest community.

Bryce Canyon Area

Other than the Church of Jesus Christ of Latter-day Saints, there are few churches or congregations in the Bryce Canyon area. The Mormons have been firmly ensconced in the small communities of Garfield County for five or six generations, and few non-Mormons had moved to the area until recently. The Panguitch Stake of the LDS church includes wards in each of the little towns of Tropic, Cannonville, Henrieville, Hatch, as well as the one in Panguitch, 550 S. 100 West, 676-8108. There is a Family History Center for genealogical research at 290 E. Center, 676-2201. The Panguitch LDS Seminary is in the same building.

Panguitch's **New Beginning Baptist Church** can be reached at 676-2157. The **St. Gertrude Mission of the Catholic Church** is at 955 S. Main, 586-8298.

Kanab Area

When the Mormons first settled Kanab they built a fort to protect themselves. Today the only thing remaining at the fort site is a monument near the south entrance to town. The Mormons survived threats from raiding Navajos to the east and eventually built a town that has grown into a thriving tourist center and popular retirement haven.

As is the case in all of Southwestern Utah, the Church of Jesus Christ of Latter-day Saints has remained dominant in Kanab. There are nearly 20 wards of the church in the greater Kanab area. Visitors wishing to attend the LDS church will find a chapel at 20 W. Center Street, 644-2961.

Kanab's **St. Christopher Catholic Church** is at 25 W. 200 South, 644-5652. The congregation of the **New Hope Bible Church** meets at 395 S. 200 East, 644-2994.

Mesquite has maintained a 30 percent growth rate during the past four years.

Mesquite, Nevada

It seems farther away than it really is.

Though you have to cross two state lines and cut through an awesome gash in the earth to get there, the city of Mesquite, Nevada, is just 37 miles southwest of St. George. Mesquite is right along Interstate 15, hugging the Arizona border so tightly you might wonder if it actually belongs in the storied state of Nevada it calls home.

In some ways this place, which has recently boomed into a full-fledged city, definitely does belong in Nevada. In other ways, it could just as easily be an adjunct to St. George. When you stop and seriously assess the place, it is really two towns — one sprinkled with the glitz of Las Vegas, another attached to the deep Mormon roots from which the community sprouted a century ago.

In this chapter we will look at Mesquite from the perspective of how it enhances the overall Southwestern Utah experience. We'll look at the community's history from its Mormon pioneer beginnings to today's resort and gaming industry boom. And we'll share information and tips regarding attractions and accommodations. Consider it a guide within a guide, directly focusing on this nifty little Nevada nugget.

Overview

Since 1992, Mesquite has been the fastest-growing city in Nevada. The community has sustained a 30 percent annual growth rate during the last several years, and there seems to be nothing standing in the way of that trend continuing into the next century. At the beginning of 1997, Mesquite's population was about 7,500, which may seem small to casual observers but is an amazing number to the city's oldtimers who marked the population at just 922 in 1980.

This "border boomer" of a town owes its phenomenal growth to a number of factors. The most obvious is the emergence of the resort and gaming industry. With four Las Vegas-style resort-casino complexes already established and two more on the way, Mesquite has become a destination for travelers from all over the world. But there's another factor behind the growth, and it has to do with the more traditional "hometown" qualities of Mesquite. Because Mesquite is still a small town, because of its relatively low taxes, warm climate, low crime rate, excellent schools and overall "liveability," people are moving here by the dozens to retire, to take advantage of jobs in the resort world or to set up a home base for a daily commute to jobs in Las Vegas, 80 miles to the southwest.

This once-sleepy agricultural community has come into its own in the last decade. Yet it still retains a feeling of small-town America. With the resort and gaming properties clustered on the east and west edges of the city, the heart of downtown Mesquite differs little from most any town in middle America.

Depending on your perspective, you might call this a slow, easygoing place to live or a fast-paced, action-filled destination. To some it's a hometown; to others, a boomtown. On either end of the city you'll find slot machines, blackjack tables, gourmet food and Jacuzzis. In between you'll rediscover the down-home memories of a good, thick malt on a patio table, the ping of a pinball machine or the peace of an evening walk along a quiet street. Each of the built-up bookends of the city has its own I-15 interchange.

Situated 1,600 feet above sea level, Mesquite is a bright patch of green (once hay fields, now golf courses) set along the Virgin River and the flanks of the 8,000-foot Virgin Mountains to the south. Summer temperatures often break the 110 mark, while most winter days hover in the 50s. In an average year you can count the total inches of rainfall on the fingers of one hand (4.34 inches annually).

Mesquite actually provides more jobs than its population can currently fill. About 20 percent of the city's work force commutes from St. George and other surrounding communities. The entertainment and recreation industry provides 52 percent of the employment in Mesquite. Si (rhymes with "eye") Redd's Oasis Resort has 1,200 employees, Casablanca (formerly Players Island) has nearly 1,000 and the Virgin River Resort employs nearly 800. The newly opened Rancho Mesquite Casino had a major challenge finding 200 new employees to operate the city's newest gaming facility.

Manufacturing is beginning to make some inroads, employing about 12 percent of the work force. Primex Plastics, a national company that produces such items as plastic truck-bed liners, has about 150 employees. Retail and personal services provide jobs for about 10 percent of the work force. Education and construction each make up 6 percent of the total employment picture. Clark County School District is fifth on the list of top-10 employers with 130 employees. Believe it or not, McDonald's is 10th with 35.

New homes are coming on the market all the time in Mesquite. The average cost of a 1,500-square-foot home in 1996 was $97,500. The average cost for a building lot was $40,000. Renting a two-bedroom apartment cost on the average about $550 a month, three-bedroom apartments were about $625 and a three-bedroom home went for about $900 per month. All these figures are basically on par with real estate prices in and around St. George.

The city has a municipal police department with 11 officers and eight staff members. Its volunteer fire department has five vehicles and 35 volunteers. The ambulance department has three vehicles. Mesquite's electrical power supply comes from the Overton Power District, and an average monthly residential power bill is about $60. The city's water is supplied through the Virgin Valley Water District and comes from several wells in the area. Current pumping capacity is 7.6 million gallons a day with peak daily demand at about 3.5 million gallons. An average monthly residential water bill is about $40.

Virgin Valley Elementary School, 150 N. Yucca Street, 346-5761, has 700 students in grades K-5. In spite of rapid growth, the school has been able to keep student-teacher ratios quite low by continually hiring new teachers. Nevada law requires a 15-to-1 student-teacher ratio for grades 1 and 2. In grades 3, 4 and 5, the school has been able to maintain a ratio of about 25-to-1. Because the elementary school took over the high school facilities when that school relocated a few years ago, the elementary has some excellent amenities you wouldn't expect at a grade school. They have a full-sized gym, large playing fields that include a baseball diamond, and they are located right next to the municipal swimming pool. The school takes pride in all areas but particularly boasts about its music, art and physical education programs.

Virgin Valley High School, 820 Valley View Drive, 346-2780, has more than 700 students in grades 6-12. Home of the Bulldogs, the school has a long history of sports prowess. The building is just a few years old and is a huge source of community pride. There are no institutions of higher learning in Mesquite.

FYI

Unless otherwise noted, the area code for all phone numbers listed in this chapter is 702.

Getting Here and Getting Around

Before Interstate 15 was completed through the Virgin River Gorge in 1973, old U.S. Highway 91 ran right through the heart of Mesquite. Today, the interstate runs along the north corridor of the city, but two exits, 120 at the west end and 122 at the east end, allow

easy access into town. At each of these exits you'll find the clusters of hotels and resort properties that have made Mesquite famous in the last decade. Between them, old U.S. Highway 91 (H-91 to the locals) is still Mesquite Boulevard. It runs through the middle of town on a 2-mile straight stretch.

Nearly everyone who comes to Mesquite arrives via ground transportation. Mesquite does have an airport, but air travel in and out of Mesquite Municipal Airport, 346-2841, is usually private or chartered. McCarran International Airport is 85 miles away in Las Vegas. Many visitors fly into Las Vegas and come to Mesquite by rental car (see our Getting Here, Getting Around chapter). There is no rail service to Mesquite and no public transportation system. There is one taxi cab service — Virgin Valley Cab, 250 W. Mesquite Boulevard, 346-7461. Each of the four major lodging properties offer courtesy shuttle service. They also provide tours of the area and transportation to St. George and Brian Head Ski Resort. It takes some logistical juggling, but using these shuttles between Mesquite and Southwestern Utah can be done.

History

For the Mormon pioneers who settled Mesquite more than a century ago, the third time was the charm. During the Mormon colonizing era in Utah, a settlement was established at Bunkerville along the south side of the Virgin River just downstream from present-day Mesquite. In a conference of church members at St. George in 1879, it was determined that another settlement should be established east of Bunkerville on the north side of the river.

By May 1882, 15 families and a total of 71 people were successfully farming the area known as Mesquite Flat. Members of the community had managed to dig long canals to irrigate their fields of alfalfa, wheat and cotton. Homes were built of adobe and rock. Later, lumber from mountains 50 miles away was transported in to build frame houses.

The Virgin River, which wends its way out

of the rugged Virgin Gorge to the northeast and meanders through the valley that bears its name, was and still is the lifeblood of the community. A heavy rainstorm at any time of the year could turn the serene Virgin into a nasty torrent. Just such a force gathered itself against the community of Mesquite Flat on a hot June day in 1882. Six miles of irrigation canals were destroyed by the flood brought on by the thunderstorm. Because the community was so dependent on the canal, the loss was nearly insurmountable. Work began immediately to repair the damage, but within a year, the capricious nature of the weather and the river had driven everyone out.

In 1887, Dudley Leavitt moved his large family to the flat and tried to make a go of it. Leavitt was a Mormon polygamist with five wives and 51 children. During the next four years, he and his industrious family would brave the heat, drought and flash floods of this desert valley, only to be forced at last to leave due to their inability to sustain themselves on the land.

Finally, in 1894, six Mormon pioneer families returned to Mesquite Flat to once more try and charm it into a settlement. They established themselves on the north bank of the Virgin River, rebuilt the canals and began farming 320 acres of irrigated land. This time it worked. The valley began to blossom as sage flats turned green with alfalfa and fields of wheat ripened in the searing summer sun. The third time truly was the charm and this time they stayed. Many of the descendents of those first six families still live in the Virgin Valley.

For most of this century Mesquite has been an agricultural community known for its dairies that supplied milk to the growing Las Vegas market. Farming and ranching were the center of the economy. But by virtue of its location on the main highway between Los Angeles and Salt Lake City, it also grew from the 1920s to the 1960s as a way station for travelers. There were a half-dozen motels and

as many cafes and restaurants along the highway through town.

Before I-15, Mesquite was known as the quiet bend in the road on the way to or from Las Vegas. Truckers pulled in at the west end of town for fuel, a chicken-fried steak and a couple of pulls at the slot machines that began showing up in town in the 1930s at the Western Village. Tourists stopped off for a cheeseburger and chocolate malt at the Polar Freeze or a hot beef sandwich at Fay's Cafe. Some might spend the night at one of the motels, but the next morning they were gone quick as a Southern Nevada cloudburst.

That was Mesquite before Si Redd came along. In 1981, a transformation began in what, until then, had been a very unassuming place. Redd, who made his fortune pioneering video poker in Nevada, bought the property where the old Western Village had stood, and the Peppermill Resort and Casino was built. In spite of the misgivings of many of the old-time Mormon residents, Mesquite's new era as a Vegas-style resort had begun.

The transformation was difficult for many of the deeply rooted Mormons to accept, but as time passed, they began to accept the inevitability of it all. And of course, as it turns out, some of the old Mormon families have profited significantly by selling their land to gaming developers.

Today the original Peppermill property has become Si Redd's Oasis Resort Hotel Casino. The Virgin River Hotel Casino was built a couple of years later on the east end of town. In the mid-1990s, Players Island Resort Casino Spa popped out of a large tract of farm ground on the west end of town. With the flood gates opened, the Rancho Mesquite Casino opened in January 1997. It is tied in with a new Holiday Inn on the east end of town. Developers of another major casino property called Mesquite Star hope to get that project off the ground sometime in 1997.

The town of Mesquite became an incorpo-

INSIDERS' TIP

Mesquite is in the Pacific time zone, an hour earlier than Mountain time in Utah. In other words, you can leave St. George at noon and arrive in Mesquite before noon.

rated city in 1985. Today, a drive through town reveals a city literally in the making. There's new construction on nearly every block as subdivisions, shopping centers and new businesses are being built. The city's residents — Mormons and non-Mormons, oldtimers and newcomers — have come to terms with the fact that the place is going to grow and change whether they want it to or not. The city council, made up of a healthy mix of old and new, seems committed to allowing new development while working hard to retain as much of the small-town atmosphere as it can. They seem to want the best of both worlds, allowing major resorts to flourish on the edges of town and holding onto the feel of small-town life within the 2-mile stretch in between. So far, with the enforcement of strong zoning laws that allow new gaming properties only on the outskirts of town, it seems to be working.

Hit the Jackpot: The Casino Resorts

Mesquite's main drawing card is geographic — it's tied to the fact that this small city sits on the Nevada side of the borders separating that state from Arizona and Southwestern Utah. A large portion of Mesquite's market comes from Southwestern Utah. It provides a major "best-of-both-worlds" scenario — the low-key, natural environment of Utah and the fast-paced action of Nevada just a half-hour away.

Nevada-style gaming and entertainment are found at four excellent resorts — two on each end of town — just off I-15. In fact, these 24-hour gaming attractions have become so popular, Mesquite is now the place many Las Vegas locals go to get away from the crowds and chaos of the Gaming Capitol of the World. In other words, Mesquite has become a resort's resort.

Bring on the Nightlife

They say the most exciting nightlife in Southwestern Utah is found in Mesquite, Nevada. If you're talking about the sort of nightlife that includes live music, bars, dancing and lounge acts, it's true. The proof is in the number of Utah license plates you'll see in Mesquite casino parking lots.

Mesquite's nightlife is contained, for the most part, in the casino properties at either end of town. In addition to the slot machines, blackjack tables and bingo parlors, they offer plenty of other nightly diversions, most of them with no cover charge and no drink minimums. It's that Nevada thing again — they plan on you dropping some coins in the slots or some cash on the tables on your way through the casino.

If you're taking advantage of the Nevadaesque entertainment offered such a short distance from St. George and plan on driving back to Southwestern Utah the same night, we again remind you that getting from one place to the other requires a drive through the narrow and treacherous Virgin River Gorge. It's a 15-mile stretch of winding, steep highway with a minimal median between northbound and southbound lanes and very little margin of error for drivers who might be negotiating it after an exciting night in Mesquite. Highway patrol troopers tell us there's as much concern about sleepy drivers in this canyon as there is about drivers who might have been drinking. If you are extra tired or have been drinking, turn the driving over to someone who is in complete control of his or her reflexes. This is one section of road requiring nothing less than a driver's full faculties. And remember, the legal drinking age in Nevada is 21, and the maximum allowable blood-alcohol level for drivers in the state is less than .10.

Low-priced Lodging in Mesquite

If you're staying over in Mesquite, you'll find lodging prices to be a strange, likeable animal. In December 1996, the Virgin River Resort advertised rooms for an unbelievable $6.99 per person, double occupancy. It is difficult to pin down average rates because they change constantly.

The only thing you can count on day in and day out is that rates here will probably be lower than in neighboring Southwestern Utah. Seldom will you pay more than $60 for a resort room in Mesquite. And if your timing is right, you might book a room at such a low rate you'll twinge with guilt — which seems to be the general idea in Nevada. . . . It'll make you feel better about dropping more coins into the slot machines or playing more chips at the blackjack tables. When making reservations ask for the best rates available, and check on upcoming seasonal offers and packages that include meals and golf or spa privileges.

As in our Accommodations chapter, each resort and motel listed in this chapter will have a price guide based on the price for a one-night, double-occupancy stay in the high season. Tax is not included, and remember: Rates in Mesquite can vary wildly, so it would always be wise to call the property directly for the best rates available and to check on seasonal discount offers. Unless otherwise noted, major credit cards are accepted at all these properties. If you have questions about what type of plastic to pack, call ahead. The accommodations will have from one to four dollar signs to denote prices as follows:

$	Less than $40
$$	$41 to $59
$$$	$60 to $89
$$$$	More than $90

Si Redd's Oasis Resort Casino
$$ • 897 Mesquite Blvd. • 346-5232, (800) 621-0187

This is where it all began for Mesquite. Located off the west I-15 interchange (Exit 120), the complex includes a 1,000-room hotel, four restaurants and a 50,000-square-foot casino.

It's the casino that sets this property apart from the others. The largest in Mesquite, it swirls with action 24 hours a day. There's blackjack, craps, roulette, poker, $100,000 keno, slot machines, video poker and video keno machines. The Oasis has a seven-story parking garage with free parking for guests. The garage, and the accompanying skywalk across the boulevard from garage to casino, can be a real lifesaver when temperatures outside start pushing 115 degrees. The staff is as friendly and accommodating to gambling novices as they are to wagering veterans. The four restaurants in the Oasis complex include the Paradise Buffet, the Redd Room Steak House, the Garden Room Coffee Shop and Peggy Sue's Diner (see our Restaurants listings in this chapter).

Rooms at the Oasis are nicely appointed with cable TV, double, queen and king beds and as much in-room coffee as you want. The resort has seven sparkling swimming pools lined with tall palm trees and complemented with waterfalls. There's also a complete health club and two tennis courts. Groups get together for old-fashioned hayrides and steak fries at the nearby Oasis Ranch. There's horseback riding, skeet and trap shooting and other outdoor activities. RVers will find complete facilities and 92 hookups for motor homes and trailers. Cost is $14 a night.

Entertainment options are plentiful at the Oasis. The dance floor at the Red Boot Saloon in the Oasis opens at 9 PM, and the action continues until 3 AM Thursday through Sunday nights. This is one of the most popular nightclubs around for dancing. Thursday is karaoke night. You can take the stage and try out your own vocal chords or dance to someone else's singing. Friday and Saturday nights feature live bands playing a variety of music. On Sunday nights there's always a fiesta with a Mexican band playing.

The Cascade Lounge also offers nightly live entertainment. The fun starts with a country-western band at 5 PM and continues with other acts until well after midnight.

Virgin River Hotel Casino
$$ • I-15 & N. Mesquite Blvd. • 346-7777, (800) 346-7721

Known for bingo and its race and sports book services, the Virgin River complex was established on a theme of old-fashioned hospitality. Daily I-15 Bingo sessions pay out as much as $10,000 to winners, and the Virgin River offers a full-service race and sports book. With this service, patrons of the casino get current odds on the day's football, baseball, basketball, hockey or other games and can also place bets on horse races at all the major tracks in the country. Many of these events are simulcast live on casino TV monitors.

The casino is open 24 hours a day and has more than 700 slot machines, video poker and live table games including blackjack, craps and roulette. The hotel has 723 rooms, all nicely appointed with cable TV and double or queen

Games People Play:
An Insiders' Wagering Primer

When it comes to gambling, Mesquite offers most everything its big brother does 85 miles down the road. But many people enjoy the gaming scene in Mesquite more than that of Las Vegas for a few simple reasons — there's virtually no traffic to fight, there's plenty of easily accessible parking near the casinos, the crowds inside are much smaller and the properties pride themselves on their friendly, accommodating reputations.

You do not have to be a guest at the hotel to enter and enjoy any of the amenities of the casinos. The doors of all four of the major casinos in Mesquite are open 24 hours a day to anyone of legal gambling age (that's 21) who wishes to come in and play. While minors may pass  through the casinos to enter restaurants, arcades or other amenities, they may not linger in the casino or stand by and watch while parents or others play the games. Such could constitute "minor loitering," an arrestable offense that carries a bail of $425.

If you're a gambling novice, don't hesitate to ask for instruction at the information desk. Each of the casinos offers gaming lessons on a regular basis. Slot managers, cocktail waitresses, people in the change booths and dealers in the pits are generally willing to answer your questions.

When you gamble, it's a good idea to stake yourself a certain amount of money to play with — an amount you can comfortably lose. Approach it as entertainment and decide how much you're willing to pay for that entertainment. No matter how good the odds may be, chances are that regardless of the intermittent wins and paybacks you garner, you may not leave the casino with more than you have wagered. If it was that easy, the casinos would not be in business. Still, the opportunity to win is there, and every day folks walk out with more money than they took in — in some cases much

The gaming boom has brought explosive growth to Mesquite.

more. All we're saying is don't put any more on the table or in the slots than you are prepared to lose there.

If entertainment and an exciting time are what you're looking for, you can stay and play in Mesquite on a pretty small budget. Some of the casinos even have penny **slots**, where you can play a dollar's worth of pennies for quite a while. There are nickel, dime, quarter, $1 and $5 slot machines as well as a variety of **video poker machines** that can

— continued on next page

entertain you for more than an hour on less than $20. Minimum bets on most table games are $2.

If you're playing for higher stakes, you already know a lot more about gaming than we can tell you, and you're well aware that Mesquite offers the same kind of opportunities to win or lose big as Las Vegas does.

If you're interested in wagering on **sports events and horse racing**, Mesquite has it all. Race and sports books get current odds on daily horse races, baseball, football, hockey and other events. You can make your bets and watch a simulcast of the contest as it unfolds on the casino's TV monitors.

Among the table games offered in Mesquite are **blackjack**, or **21**, a card game where the object is to be dealt cards having a higher count than those of the dealer up to but not exceeding 21. There's **craps**, a fast-paced, exciting game that offers a variety of bets on the layout. Each bet is dependent upon the point value of the upturned side of the two dice that have come to rest after being tossed by a patron called the "shooter."

Roulette is a game in which players bet on which numbered compartment of a revolving wheel a small ball will come to rest in. There are different variations of **poker** at each of the casinos. **Baccarat** is a card game where three hands are dealt and players may bet either or both hands against the dealer's.

Keno is a game you can play while involved in other games in the casino or even while you're eating in a casino restaurant. You mark the numbers you wish to play on a blank ticket — anywhere from one to 15 numbers. Then you mark the amount of numbers selected and the amount of your wager (usually a $1 minimum) in the space provided. A keno runner picks up your card and your wager. Then you can monitor the keno display board, usually visible throughout the casino, to see what 20 numbers are drawn at random and lighted as winning numbers. It's possible to win as much as $100,000.

Bingo is also big in Mesquite. Just step into the casino's bingo parlor and buy as many cards as you like for $3 apiece. The Virgin River Hotel Casino has a parlor seating 300 people with a progressive bingo pot that can pay out as much as $25,000.

---

bed options. The rooms are comfortable, but you're not expected to be spending much time in them. There's a full hookup, resort-affiliated RV park next door. The cost is $10 per night. The Virgin River features two large swimming pools, three Jacuzzis and a video arcade. The Chuckwagon Restaurant (see listing below) is open 24 hours a day offering crab, steak, ribs and the quarter-pound Border Burger.

At this resort, your nightlife options can be as sedate as dinner at the Chuckwagon and a first-run movie at the on-site Virgin River Cinemas or as all-out exciting as a night on the dance floor in the Virgin River Lounge. Four movie theaters, along with a great arcade, are part of the Virgin River complex. Live bands, mostly playing country-western music, do their thing in the lounge every night but Monday. There's a dance floor big enough for you to really get out and swing.

In between activities, which will no doubt include some time at the gaming tables or some arm exercise on the slot machines, there's bound to be a place waiting for you at the Virgin River's 100-foot Honduran mahogany bar.

CasaBlanca Resort and Casino (formerly Players Island)

$$ • 930 W. Mesquite Blvd. • 346-7529, (800) 896-4547

(Editors Note: As of July 1, 1997 the resort known as Players Island Resort Casino Spa changed ownership and became CasaBlanca Resort and Casino. Details of how the new ownership would change the resort were not available at press time for this book. Since CasaBlanca will offer much of what Players Island did, "only better and more — with a Moroccan theme," according to new management, we have chosen to share with you the information we had compiled for Players Island with the understanding that names, prices and other details will change as the new owners settle into this beautiful Mesquite property. Addresses will remain the same, and it is expected that the phone numbers will also be the same.)

On the far west edge of town off Exit 120, this is Mesquite's most physically alluring attraction. It's designed like a tropical island, surrounded by large pools, cascading waterfalls and tall palms. And it truly is the tropical retreat original owner Merv Griffin marketed it to be. Standing eight stories tall, the pink buildings, green lawns and blue water create an almost surreal contrast to the stark desert behind them.

The hotel has 500 rooms, 18 suites with Jacuzzi tubs and four three-bedroom, detached bungalows. The rooms are extra-large and designed with bright island colors and decor. You can choose between two queen beds or a single king, and there's cable TV. Unique in Mesquite is CasaBlanca's spa where you can indulge with a full-body message, facial, mud bath or just a long soak in a mineral water pool. Spa treatments range from $40 to $80. There are tennis courts, sand volleyball and the largest swimming pool in Mesquite — it looks more like a lagoon than a pool.

Gaming in the 24-hour casino includes slots, blackjack, craps, Caribbean stud poker, mini baccarat and roulette. For the kids (yes, Players Island caters to the whole family),

there's an incredible arcade with the latest in video game technology.

You can get a juicy steak or fresh seafood at the Plantation House Restaurant, have breakfast, lunch or dinner at the Reef Buffet or eat in the Tradewinds Cafe, which is open 24 hours (see our Restaurants listings below). Homemade cakes and pastries, espresso and cappuccino are available at the Island Bakery. There's also a complete RV park with full hookups at the south end of the property. Cost is $12 per night.

The nightlife at CasaBlanca is anchored by Toucans Night Club. Billed as the hottest nightclub north of Las Vegas, it's open from 10 PM to 3 AM on Friday and Saturday nights. There's a $5 cover charge for men, and ladies always get in free. The club features some live entertainment, a hot deejay playing a variety of dance music, huge video screens and a light show.

There's also live entertainment nightly beneath the illuminated, sky-art domed ceiling of the Cascade Lounge, located right in the center of the casino. There's no cover charge at the Cascades.

Rancho Mesquite and Holiday Inn
$$$ • 301 Mesa Blvd. • 346-4646, (800) 346-4611

Off eastbound I-15 at Exit 122, Mesquite's newest desert resort hotel casino, the Holiday Inn, opened in January 1997 with 215 oversized rooms and suites. Room options include two-bedroom suites, king beds with private

Pioneer Premonition

Mesquite's current mayor, Ken Carter, is a Mormon descendent of the community's original pioneers. He's not at all surprised by the growth of the town and the transformation of its landscape over the past decade. "When I was about 16," he recalls, "I vividly remember standing beside my great-grandfather on a hillside east of town. We were overlooking a barren stretch of sand, tumbleweeds, creosote bushes and sagebrush. He stretched his arm out and said, 'Someday you'll see this all green and beautiful.'" Carter says at the time it sounded like the most farfetched thing he'd ever heard. Today the mayor can stand in the same spot and see exactly what his great-grandfather had envisioned.

spas and beautiful poolside patio accommodations. There's a gift shop and exercise room in the hotel. Golf packages are available for all of Mesquite's courses as well as those in neighboring St. George.

The Rancho Mesquite Casino is Mesquite's newest, opening its doors in February 1997 with the motto: "The friendliest casino in the West." In addition to more than 500 slot machines and video poker games, the 45,000-square-foot casino offers table games including blackjack, craps and roulette along with a sports book.

Two bars allow guests to choose between live entertainment and dancing in the **Wild Cactus** or a more intimate and relaxed environment in the **Scorpion Bar**.

Other Accommodations

While most of the accommodations in Mesquite are tied to the major casino properties, there are other, more traditional places to stay if the gaming world is not the one you're looking for.

Hotels and Motels

Budget Inn Suites
$$ • 390 N. Sandhill Blvd. • 346-7444, (800) 463-6302

This brand-new, 67-room motel is just off Exit 122 on the east side of Mesquite. It's a quiet, traditional motel without a casino or any of the trappings associated with Mesquite's resort accommodations. There are king and double-queen rooms and luxury suites, and guests enjoy HBO, a swimming pool and a Jacuzzi. The surroundings are beautifully landscaped. Kids younger than 17 stay free, and nonsmoking rooms are available.

Stateline Motel Casino
$ • 490 W. Mesquite Blvd. • 346-5752

We've told you most of the gaming and accommodations options in Mesquite are at the east and west ends of town. Here's an exception to the rule. Right in the middle of Mesquite, 1 mile from either I-15 exit, this is a smaller, lower-key option to the larger, glitzy resorts. The Stateline has just 11 rooms, each with cable TV. The motel is tied to a small casino with 50 slot and poker machines. There's one blackjack table, keno, and a restaurant and bar that are open 24 hours a day. The bar has a big-screen TV.

Valley Inn Motel
$ • 791 W. Mesquite Blvd. • 346-5281

For years this little motel has flourished on Mesquite Boulevard in spite of the appearance of larger, fancier properties. The Valley Inn has 21 rooms with king or queen beds and cable TV with HBO. There's a swimming pool, and the motel is a short distance from restaurants and convenience stores. There are also six apartments at the Valley Inn that are rented on a weekly or monthly basis.

RV Parks

The Oasis, Virgin River and CasaBlanca resorts all have RV parks associated with the properties. Another excellent park we suggest you consider is just minutes from downtown Mesquite on the Arizona side of the state line.

Desert Skies RV Resort
99 Peppermill Palms Dr., Littlefield, Ariz. • (520) 347-4243

Little more than a mile from downtown Mesquite, just across the Arizona line and overlooking The Palms Golf Course, this is a great RV park with a long list of amenities. There are 165 sites as well as 175 park-model sites. The nightly rate for an RV hookup is $12.66. Weekly and monthly rates are also available. Desert Skies has a clubhouse with a swimming pool and spa. In addition, they have billiard tables, table-tennis tables, a craft room, shuffleboard courts, horseshoe pits, dog runs, a library, laundry facilities, restrooms, showers, mailboxes and a general store. There's also a 5,000-square-foot ballroom with a stage and

---

INSIDERS' TIP

December is an excellent month to get obscenely low lodging rates in Mesquite.

Photo: Jud Burkett

The Virgin River Casino is one of four major gaming resorts in Mesquite, Nevada, approximately 30 miles from the Utah border.

kitchen. The park management has planned activities going on year-round.

Restaurants

While gaming is Mesquite's most popular activity, next on the list would have to be eating. Following in the Las Vegas tradition of providing great dining options under the same roof as the casinos, Mesquite has a surprising number of excellent eating establishments for a town its size. Each casino has a buffet with all-you-can-eat breakfasts, lunches and dinners at almost unbelievably low prices. The resorts also have more upscale restaurants as well as cafes and coffee shops. But dining in Mesquite is not limited to the resorts. There are some freestanding restaurants we can recommend as well.

Just as you can find fairly inexpensive lodging in Mesquite, so can you eat well without spending much. We've included a price code to help you know what kind of tab to expect. The code denotes the cost of a reasonable dinner for two, without cocktails, wine, dessert or gratuity. Cash, travelers checks and most major credit cards are the norm for payment. Do not expect to use a personal check. If you're concerned about which credit cards are accepted, call ahead.

$	Less than $20
$$	$21 to $40
$$$	$41 to $60
$$$$	More than $60

Branding Iron Buffet
$ • Virgin River Resort Casino, I-15 and N. Mesquite Blvd. • 346-7721

A favorite among locals, this buffet is longer than a semi truck. It's all-you-can-eat, and there are plenty of choices — from beef, chicken and seafood to pasta, breads and all kinds of salads. For dessert, take your choice of pies, cakes, pastries and ice cream. Breakfast at the Branding Iron is $3.79, lunch $4.79, and dinner $6.99.

Carollo's
$$ • 561 Mesquite Blvd. • 346-2818

They claim to have the best ribs in Nevada at Carollo's, and we haven't found anyone to refute it. In fact, this restaurant in the Sun Valley Plaza, about midway through town on Mesquite Boulevard, is a favorite getaway for Southwestern Utahns. Open 24 hours a day, seven days a week, the specialty is barbecued baby-back ribs. Carollo's serves a variety of appetizers from chicken fingers to mozzarella sticks. The very affordable lunch menu has several sandwiches including the Carollo Italian Sausage sandwich. Dinner entrees include several variations on ribs as well as steaks, chicken, pasta and fish. There's a kids' menu with prices in the $3 to $4 range.

Chuckwagon Restaurant
$$ • Virgin River Resort Casino, I-15 and N. Mesquite Blvd. • 346-7721

Everything at the Virgin River Hotel Casino, including the Chuckwagon Restaurant, has been recently renovated. This establishment is known far and wide for great deals on excellent prime rib, not to mention crab, steak and ribs. Open 24 hours a day, the menu includes a variety of inexpensive choices for breakfast, lunch and dinner. Kids go for the quarter-pound Border Burger.

Garden Room Coffee Shop
$ • Si Redd's Oasis Resort Casino, 897 Mesquite Blvd. • 346-5232

Open 24 hours a day, the Garden Room has a laid back, relaxed atmosphere, where you can break away from the gaming tables for a snack, a drink, a $1.99 breakfast or a full prime rib or lobster dinner for less than $10.

Panda Garden
$$ • 10 Mesquite Blvd. • 346-3028

If you've got a hankering for Chinese food, this is an excellent choice. In the heart of "old Mesquite," just across the street from city hall, this restaurant is in the beautiful new One Mesquite Plaza. Though the architecture here is definitely Southwestern, the Panda Garden is all Chinese. The menu offers appetizers including egg rolls, fried won ton, teriyaki beef sticks and Chinese chicken salad. Soups include egg flower, hot and sour, and you can also sample tofu with fresh greens. Dinners include chef specialties such as House Pan Fried Noodle, Peony Blossom, Salmon Hwa-Suey, Five Flavors Shrimp and Mandarin Duck. There are also a number of poultry, beef and seafood entrees. Panda Garden is open for lunch and dinner.

Paradise Buffet
$ • Si Redd's Oasis Resort Casino, 897 Mesquite Blvd. • 346-5232

Take the escalator, which is just to your left as you enter the main or east entrance to the Oasis. At the top of the stairs you'll think you've walked into Hawaii. Among the greenery, waterfalls and Polynesian decor is a buffet where breakfast is served for $4.49, lunch for $5.49 and dinner for $7.49. It's all-you-can-eat all the time. On Wednesdays, Paradise Buffet features a Mexican theme, Thursdays it's Italian, Friday you can get two-for-one Chinese dinners, Saturdays feature Texas barbecue and Sunday brings a champagne dinner.

Peggy Sue's Fifties Diner
$ • Si Redd's Oasis Resort Casino, 897 Mesquite Blvd. • 346-5232

Here's a great place to step back in time and enjoy the kind of food many of us were raised on. The decor at Peggy Sue's hurtles you back in time with bright red, tuck-and-roll vinyl booth seats and jukeboxes playing '50s records. Sip on a cherry Coke while you dig the menu that includes Blueberry Hill pancakes, Yakety Yak curly fries, "Great Wings of Fire" spicy chicken wings, the Hound Dog hot dog and Twist and Shout spaghetti and meatballs. Peggy Sue's has thick shakes and a variety of burgers, and nothing on the menu is more than $8. A Baskin-Robbins ice cream and yogurt shop is just across the hall.

Plantation House
$$ • CasaBlanca's, 930 W. Mesquite Blvd. • 346-7529

This is Players Island's gourmet steak and seafood restaurant. Steak and lobster are the specialty here, and there's an excellent wine list. The restaurant has the look of a Mediterranean villa — it's small, quiet, romantic and intimate.

Redd Room Steakhouse
$$ • Si Redd's Oasis Resort Casino, 897 Mesquite Blvd. • 346-5232, (800) 621-0187

Inside Oasis Resort Casino, this is one of Mesquite's most elegant restaurants. The Redd Room is known for its fabulous steaks and seafood and is considered among locals the place to go when they want to celebrate some-

FYI

Unless otherwise noted, the area code for all phone numbers listed in this chapter is 702.

thing extra special. Though not absolutely necessary, reservations are suggested.

The Reef Buffet
$ • CasaBlanca's, 930 W. Mesquite Blvd.
• 346-7529

In the tradition of the great Las Vegas buffets, The Reef gives you all-you-can-eat breakfasts, lunches and dinners with a particular emphasis on seafood. The place is delightfully decorated with bright island colors of pink, purple and green. Breakfast is $5.50, lunch $6.50 and dinner $9.50. On Friday and Saturday there's a "Seafood Spectacular" buffet and Sunday brings a champagne brunch.

Tradewinds Cafe
$ • CasaBlanca's, 930 W. Mesquite Blvd.
• 346-7529

Open 24 hours a day, the Tradewinds is at the rear of the CasaBlanca. Its decor is consistent with the resort's bright island colors, and it's a great place to sit down for a quick breakfast, a satisfying sandwich or a nice dinner. Most everything here is less than $10.

Attractions

Desert Valley Museum
31 W. Mesquite Blvd. • 346-5705

This delightful little rock building in the middle of downtown Mesquite houses some fascinating artifacts and memorabilia of the community. Volunteer history buffs staff the museum, which is free to the public. Here you'll see the first five slot machines brought into the valley in 1936 and the state high school basketball trophies won by the great Virgin Valley teams of 1915 and 1916. There's a turn-of-the-century wedding dress on display, switchboards from the town's first telephone

system, old photographs, a whiskey still, quilts, a birthing table, farm machinery and even an old outhouse. The museum is open from 9 AM to 4 PM every day except Sunday.

Gold Butte Back Country Byway
Mesquite Chamber of Commerce,
850 W. Mesquite Blvd. • 346-2902

If you feel the need to get out into the hills surrounding Mesquite, stop in at the Mesquite Chamber of Commerce office and pick up *Nevada Back Country Byway: Gold Butte,* a flyer published by the Bureau of Land Management. This publication details a 62-mile scenic trip that starts south of Mesquite and will take you into the remote backcountry where names like Devil's Throat, Lime Ridge, Virgin Mountain and Whitney Pockets have been attached to the land for decades.

The first 24 miles are made along a narrow, paved road. The next 19 miles are on a relatively smooth, gravel road and the other 19 are on a lightly maintained dirt road that requires a high-clearance, four-wheel drive vehicle. If you're equipped to make the entire circle, great. If not, drive as far as you feel comfortable going, then turn back. Along the way, you'll see country where bighorn sheep, mountain lions and mule deer live. The desert tortoise also calls this country home. Virgin Peak, towering 8,000 feet above sea level, provides a beautiful contrast to the desert floor.

Follow the guidelines in the BLM flyer closely. Take plenty of water, make sure your vehicle has a full tank of gas and plenty of coolant in the radiator and plan your trek in accordance with the weather.

Oasis Ranch and Gun Club
Si Redd's Oasis Resort Casino,
897 Mesquite Blvd. • 346-5232

You'll make your arrangements at the Oa-

For an ideal view of Mesquite, take Exit 122 off I-15 and turn north on Mesquite Boulevard. Pass the Virgin River Resort and follow the signs north toward the Mesquite Airport. In two minutes you'll find yourself on the plateau above Mesquite where you can pull off the road and take in the view of the Oasis Golf Course and the entire expanse of the Virgin Valley to the south.

Great Views

CasaBlanca Resort and Casino is a pink paradise for gaming fans.

sis in downtown Mesquite, but the gun club and ranch are a couple of miles east of town near the Virgin River. The gun club is recognized as one of the best in the United States, featuring a fully automated 12-station course, sporting clays, traps and skeet. Open every day, the club offers a challenge for every level of shooter. It accommodates individual shooters as well as large corporate groups and tournaments, some of which have been televised on ESPN. The recent "Shooters Delight" special offered two nights at the Oasis and 200 rounds at the gun club for $129 on Sunday through Thursday and $149 on Friday and Saturday.

In addition to the gun club, the 1,200-acre ranch offers horseback riding and old-fashioned hayrides on horse-drawn wagons. You can make arrangements at the hotel for horseback rides ranging from $15 for one hour, $25 for two hours, $45 for a half-day and $85 for a full day. Overnight rides, which include meals and camping, are $145 per person and must be arranged at least 48 hours in advance. An evening hayride is $25 per person and includes a steak fry with beans, biscuits, coffee and cobbler.

Virgin River Gorge
I-15 Between St. George and Mesquite

One of the most incredible stretches of highway in the entire interstate system is the 15-mile section of road between Mesquite and St. George that cuts through the Virgin River Gorge. Here, the river cuts a winding gash through the limestone of the Virgin Mountains, creating a mini Grand Canyon.

Mountain man Jedediah Smith traversed this canyon in the 1820s on his way to California, but travelers later bypassed it for a century and a half. The original U.S. Highway 91 made a swing well to the north to avoid it. In the 1960s, highway engineers decided to route the new freeway through the gorge, much to the dismay of locals who knew just how unaccommodating the canyon was. The result was an engineering miracle. The road was blasted through the canyon, tacked to the ledges and finally completed in 1973. At the time it was finished, it had cost more than any other stretch of road in history, and even cost the life of this writer's scoutmaster who operated one of the giant earth-moving rigs in the canyon.

To see the Gorge, you simply drive through it. We suggest you pull off at the Cedar Pockets exit midway through the canyon to marvel for a moment at what it took to make it possible for you to be standing where you are. What you will see is, basically, a smaller version of the Grand Canyon. Limestone cliffs will tower around you, and the Virgin River flows below.

Golf

Mesquite has become as well-known for

its great golf courses in recent years as it is for its resort casinos.

The Palms and the Oasis golf clubs are both integral parts of Si Redd's Oasis Resort. The Palms has earned a reputation as "nine holes of beauty followed by nine holes of sheer terror." The Arnold Palmer-designed Oasis Golf Club is now Virgin Valley's flagship of golf, recognized by some as one of the best new layouts in the United States.

CasaBlanca Golf Club opened in the fall of 1996. It's a Cal Olson signature-designed, 18-hole championship course with stunning views of the Virgin Mountains on the horizon. The Beaver Dam Golf Resort, 8 miles east of Mesquite off I-15, is a beautiful little nine-hole course. Following is a closer look at what awaits you at Mesquite area courses.

Beaver Dam Golf Resort

I-15 Exit 8 (8 miles east of Mesquite on Ariz. Hwy. 91), Beaver Dam Resort, Ariz.
• (520) 347-5111, (800) 626-5006

This pleasant-looking, nine-hole course is tree-lined, unlike most in the area, since it is laid out in the flood plain of the Virgin River and not on desert or mountain terrain. It stretches 2668 yards from the back tees with a par of 34.

The conditions are uneven, and the quirky layout equally rewards good fortune and good golf. Still, many holes have merit, and the environment is laid back. The most interesting holes are 1 and 2, which run parallel to each other. No. 4 is another good one, a short par 5 with a modest right-to-left turn. The course

loses some steam toward the end. There is a driving range at the facility. Prices for area residents are $9 for nine holes and $15 for 18 (two trips around the nine). Non-residents pay $11 for nine and $16 for 18. Tack on $4.50 per rider for a cart. Beaver Dam is near the south entrance to the Virgin River Gorge on I-15 between St. George and Mesquite.

Oasis Golf Club

851 Oasis Blvd., off I-15 Exit 122
• 346-7820, (800) 910-2742

The Oasis is home to an Arnold Palmer golf school and is fashioned among the ravines and ridges of the Nevada desert. In addition to the 18-hole championship course, there is a nine-hole, par 37 executive course used mostly by the school.

If price is no object, the 7008-yard Oasis layout is a must-play course. Conditions are superb, and the holes are splendid. Arnie seems to have found a fondness for blind tee shots, as there are several, so some local knowledge helps. If the play is slow (it rarely is), take some time to admire the views. The course is pricey (and rumored to be going up), but packages are available through the Oasis Hotel and Casino in Mesquite. As of now, hotel guests play for $100, and other golfers will need to cough up $165 for 18. Cart usage is included. There is a driving range, a good practice green, a snack bar and pro shop. The Arnold Palmer Golf Academy (see listing below) is an excellent teaching facility. There is a lot of construction going on around

The Virgin Bloat

In the early days of the Virgin Valley, fresh drinking water was a premium. The water from the Virgin River was so unpalatable locals called it "Virgin Bloat." Roy Waite, who ran a store along the highway in Bunkerville, just down the river from Mesquite, had a reputation for storytelling. One time a tourist stopped in and commented about how old all the people looked around those parts. "Oh yes," Roy replied, "we've got people around here that are two or three hundred years old. They drink this Virgin water and they live forever." More than once Roy was able to talk visitors into trading their pure palatable water for equal amounts of Virgin Bloat from the local fountains of youth.

the course as a housing development rises from the desert, but the main distractions are the views, the rabbits and the demanding golf.

The Palms Golf Club
897 Mesquite Blvd., off I-15 Exit 122
• 346-5232 ext. 3777, (800) 621-0187

This is Mesquite's first golf course and sports a distinctly split personality. The front nine is flat and traditional with a lot of water and broad fairways. The back nine is the "mountain course," requiring uphill and downhill shots, tee shots over ravines and skill in reading greens. The par 72 layout plays to 6982 yards from the back tees, but be selective when hitting the driver and consider putting it away on many holes on the back nine — often accuracy is more important than distance.

The conditions are usually good, but winds can be hot and gusty on summer afternoons when the temperature is typically 100-plus. Golf packages are available through the Oasis Hotel and Casino. Current greens fees are $65 for hotel guests and locals, $95 for non-guests. Carts are included in the cost. The Palms is almost always in excellent condition and boasts some memorable holes, particularly on the mountainous back nine. Generally speaking, the course is quite playable. There is an excellent snack bar, plus a driving range, practice green and well-stocked pro shop. Lessons are available.

CasaBlanca Golf Club
930 Mesquite Blvd., off I-15 Exit 120
• 346-7529 ext. 6781, (888) 711-4653

Unlike the other two golf courses in Mesquite, both of which are owned and managed by the Oasis Hotel and Casino, CasaBlanca has a more traditional layout with only slight elevation changes. Generous fairways and five sets of tees make for a very playable golf course that can be testy from the tips while yielding low scores to average golfers playing the middle tees. The par 72 course measures 7011 from the back tees.

Conditions were very rough when the course first opened in the fall of 1996 but have improved considerably. The course generally follows the Virgin River channel and feels less like a desert course than many others in Southwestern Utah and southern Nevada. The holes tend to be less spectacular than those featured at other resort-style layouts in the area, but the golf course has a welcome, no-nonsense feel. The layout is straightforward, rewarding good golf and club selection without being punitive to the mid- to high-handicapper. Greens fees Monday through Thursday are $75 for hotel guests and locals and $85 for others. On Friday and Saturday, prices jump to $85 for hotel guests and area residents and $95 for others. Carts are included.

As the course matures and the waste areas grow in, CasaBlanca will be an attractive layout, particularly for guests of the CasaBlanca, who can get good package rates. One important note: CasaBlanca requires soft spikes — pack accordingly. There is a practice green and driving range and a snack bar at the pro shop.

Golf Instruction

Arnold Palmer Golf Academy
851 Oasis Blvd. • 346-7810

According to the instructors at the only Arnold Palmer Golf Academy west of the Mississippi, you can forget all the confusing talk you've heard about golf's mechanics and complexities. All these complications do is take away from your enjoyment of the game and prevent you from focusing on the fundamentals and attitude you need to play better and have more fun on the course.

"We don't believe in forcing an entirely new style of play on you," says academy director Brad Brewer. In small groups with a 4-to-1 student-teacher ratio, instructors work with players individually to improve specific areas of their game. Brewer says his staff works with students' natural skills instead of against them.

At the Oasis in Mesquite, Arnold Palmer and his associates have scratched out of the mesquite trees and rugged canyons some of the most breathtaking holes this side of Pebble Beach. The course itself is a masterpiece, but the addition of the Arnold Palmer Golf Academy truly sets it apart. Three on-site instructors, Doug Wherry, Randy Byers and Mike Smith, have been handpicked by Palmer. They offer programs such as "Mastering the Fundamentals," "The Scoring Zone," "Practice Like a Pro" and "Course Strategy."

Two-, three- and five-day academy packages, including lodging, are offered at the Oasis. Two-day single rates start at $850, and five-day single rates are $2,050. There's also à la carte instruction with half-day sessions for $175 per person, 90 minutes for $75 or one hour for $60. For $200, you can have an academy instructor join your group for an entertaining and challenging round of golf. Call ahead about special offers made from time to time. Recently the school ran a $39 introductory offer for a two-hour clinic on mastering the fundamentals.

Shopping

The shopping scene in Mesquite has not quite caught up with the resort scene. Just as St. George defers to Mesquite for high-octane nightlife, Mesquite residents often find their way to St. George for its many shopping options. Still, there are some interesting retail shops in such centers as Mesquite Plaza, midway through town on Mesquite Boulevard, the Riverside Commercial Center at 400 Riverside Drive, the Sun Valley Plaza at 561 Mesquite Boulevard and the two Desert Valley Plaza locations on north Mesquite Boulevard. Here are a couple of retail shops we're especially fond of.

Coyote Design
171 E. Mesquite Blvd. • 346-7330
This quaint stucco cottage with a red roof is a fun place to stop in the heart of Mesquite. The store itself is a tasteful lesson in Southwestern design. You'll discover an eclectic assortment of Southwestern gifts, baskets, art, pottery, accessories and furniture.

Southwest Spirit
561 Mesquite Blvd. • 346-6959
One retail store you definitely should visit while in Mesquite is Southwest Spirit. We suggest it mainly for its great boot and moccasin selection. It's an attraction in and of itself to walk in, get a whiff of new, fresh leather and browse through the beautiful boots and other footwear. Check out the great selection of gifts and souvenirs.

Healthcare

Mesquite is served by two health clinics. The nearest full-service hospital is Dixie Re-

gional Medical Center, 37 miles away in St. George, but here are two local centers to help serve your needs.

Mesquite Urgent Care and Medical Care Center
312 W. Mesquite Blvd. • 346-3030
This office has two physicians — one is a pediatrician and one a specialist in internal medicine. The doctors specialize in family practice and offer general healthcare. Walk-ins are accepted, but it's best to make an appointment if possible. Regular hours are 9 AM to 6 PM Monday through Friday and 9 AM to 2 PM on Saturdays, but a doctor is on call 24 hours a day.

Virgin Valley Medical Clinic
51 E. 100 South • 346-5771
This is a satellite facility of Dixie Regional Medical Center in St. George. It has one physician and seven staff members. Regular hours are 8 AM to 8 PM Monday through Friday and 8 AM to 4 PM on Saturday, but a doctor is on call 24 hours a day. If the clinic is closed, a phone call can get a doctor paged. In addition to emergency care, there are a number of outpatient services offered including physical therapy, speech and occupational therapy and audiology.

Media

Mesquite is served by the St. George based Spectrum daily newspaper and is the home of two successful weekly newspapers that can help you keep up with what's going on in the fast-paced little resort town. The Spectrum also publishes a weekly edition for Mesquite that is mailed to all households.

Desert Echo
225 Riverside Dr., Mesquite, NV • (702) 346-5151
In nearby Mesquite, Nevada, the *Desert Echo* publishes 20 to 32 pages weekly for distribution to 4,000 households in seven southern Nevada and western Arizona communities. Limited readership in Southwestern Utah includes several dozen subscribers and distribution points in and around St. George. The paper's specialty is its centerfold, which gives double-page coverage to special local activities and events.

Desert Valley Times
10 W. Mesquite Blvd., No. 114, Mesquite, Nev. • (702) 346-7495

The *Desert Valley Times* has seen tremendous growth commensurate with Nevada's fastest-growing small town. In just three years, the free, full-color tabloid has grown from a circulation of 1,200 to a weekly printing of 4,500. Issues include as many as 40 pages of local news and entertainment information including coverage of what's happening at Mesquite's four casino resorts. The paper is also available in the Virgin and Moapa valleys or by mail.

Index of Advertisers

Index

Going Somewhere?

Insiders' Publishing Inc. presents 40 current and upcoming titles to popular destinations all over the country (including the titles below) — and we're planning on adding many more. To order a title, go to your local bookstore or call (800) 765-2665 ext. 238 and we'll direct you to one.

Adirondacks

Atlanta, GA

Bermuda

Boca Raton and the Palm Beaches, FL

Boulder, CO, and Rocky Mountain National Park

Bradenton/Sarasota, FL

Branson, MO, and the Ozark Mountains

California's Wine Country

Cape Cod, Nantucket and Martha's Vineyard, MA

Charleston, SC

Cincinnati, OH

Civil War Sites in the Eastern Theater

Colorado's Mountains

Denver, CO

Florida Keys and Key West

Florida's Great Northwest

Golf in the Carolinas

Indianapolis, IN

The Lake Superior Region

Las Vegas

Lexington, KY

Louisville, KY

Madison, WI

Maine's Mid-Coast

Minneapolis/St. Paul, MN

Mississippi

Myrtle Beach, SC

Nashville, TN

New Hampshire

North Carolina's Central Coast and New Bern

North Carolina's Mountains

Outer Banks of North Carolina

The Pocono Mountains

Relocation

Richmond, VA

Salt Lake City

Santa Fe

Savannah

Southwestern Utah

Tampa/St. Petersburg, FL

Tuscon

Virginia's Blue Ridge

Virginia's Chesapeake Bay

Washington, D.C.

Wichita, KS

Williamsburg, VA

Wilmington, NC

Yellowstone

Insiders' Publishing Inc. • P.O. Box 2057 • Manteo, NC 27954
Phone (919) 473-6100 • Fax (919) 473-5869 • INTERNET address: *http://www.insiders.com*